# Public Rights: Copyright's Public Domains

Access to works in the public domain is an important source of human creativity and autonomy, whether in the arts, scientific research or online discourse. But what can users actually do with works without obtaining the permission of a copyright owner? Readers will be surprised to find how many different kinds of permitted usage exist around the world. This book offers a comprehensive international and comparative account of the copyright public domain. It identifies fifteen categories of public rights and gives a detailed legal explanation of each, showing how their implementation differs between jurisdictions. Through this analysis, the authors aim to restore balance to copyright policy debates, and to contribute to such debates by making practical law reform proposals. A major intervention in the field of intellectual property law and copyright, this book will appeal to lawyers, scholars and those involved in the administration of copyright law.

Graham Greenleaf is Professor of Law and Information Systems in the Faculty of Law, UNSW Sydney, Australia. His publications include *Asian Data Privacy Laws: Trade and Human Rights Perspectives* (2014). In 2010 he was awarded the Order of Australia (AM) for his work on free access to legal information and protection of privacy.

David Lindsay is Professor in the Faculty of Law, University of Technology Sydney, Australia. He is the General Editor of the *Australian Intellectual Property Journal* (AIPJ) and author of *International Domain Name Law: ICANN and the UDRP* (2007).

*Cambridge Intellectual Property and Information Law*

As its economic potential has rapidly expanded, intellectual property has become a subject of front-rank legal importance. *Cambridge Intellectual Property and Information Law* is a series of monograph studies of major current issues in intellectual property. Each volume contains a mix of international, European, comparative and national law, making this a highly significant series for practitioners, judges and academic researchers in many countries.

Series editors

Lionel Bently
*Herchel Smith Professor of Intellectual Property Law, University of Cambridge*

Graeme Dinwoodie
*Professor of Intellectual Property and Information Technology Law, University of Oxford*

Advisory editors

William R. Cornish, *Emeritus Herchel Smith Professor of Intellectual Property Law, University of Cambridge*

François Dessemontet, *Professor of Law, University of Lausanne*

Jane C. Ginsburg, *Morton L. Janklow Professor of Literary and Artistic Property Law, Columbia Law School*

Paul Goldstein, *Professor of Law, Stanford University*

The Rt Hon. Sir Robin Jacob, *Hugh Laddie Professor of Intellectual Property Law, University College, London*

Ansgar Ohly, *Professor of Intellectual Property Law, Ludwig Maximilian University of Munich, Germany*

A list of books in the series can be found at the end of this volume.

# Public rights

*Copyright's public domains*

Graham Greenleaf
*UNSW Australia*

David Lindsay
*University of Technology Sydney*

# CAMBRIDGE
UNIVERSITY PRESS

University Printing House, Cambridge CB2 8BS, United Kingdom

One Liberty Plaza, 20th Floor, New York, NY 10006, USA

477 Williamstown Road, Port Melbourne, VIC 3207, Australia

314–321, 3rd Floor, Plot 3, Splendor Forum, Jasola District Centre, New Delhi – 110025, India

79 Anson Road, #06-04/06, Singapore 079906

Cambridge University Press is part of the University of Cambridge.

It furthers the University's mission by disseminating knowledge in the pursuit of education, learning, and research at the highest international levels of excellence.

www.cambridge.org
Information on this title: www.cambridge.org/9781107134065
DOI: 10.1017/9781316460214

© Graham Greenleaf and David Lindsay 2018

This publication is in copyright. Subject to statutory exception and to the provisions of relevant collective licensing agreements, no reproduction of any part may take place without the written permission of Cambridge University Press.

First published 2018

Printed in the United Kingdom by Clays, St Ives plc

*A catalogue record for this publication is available from the British Library.*

*Library of Congress Cataloging-in-Publication Data*
Names: Greenleaf, G. W. (Graham William), author. | Lindsay, David, (Law teacher), author.
Title: Public rights : copyright's public domains / Graham Greenleaf, David Lindsay.
Description: New York : Cambridge University Press, 2018. | Series: Cambridge intellectual property and information law | Includes bibliographical references and index.
Identifiers: LCCN 2017061570 | ISBN 9781107134065 (hardback)
Subjects: LCSH: Fair use (Copyright). | Public lending rights (of authors).
Classification: LCC K1447.25 .G74 2018 | DDC 346.04/82–dc23
LC record available at https://lccn.loc.gov/2017061570

ISBN 978-1-107-13406-5 Hardback

Cambridge University Press has no responsibility for the persistence or accuracy of URLs for external or third-party internet websites referred to in this publication and does not guarantee that any content on such websites is, or will remain, accurate or appropriate.

# Contents

| | |
|---|---|
| *Foreword* | *page* vii |
| *Preface* | xi |
| *Acknowledgements* | xii |
| *Table of Cases* | xiv |
| *Table of Legislation* | xxvi |
| *Table of International Instruments* | xlv |

| | | |
|---|---|---|
| **Part I** | **What is the Copyright Public Domain?** | 1 |
| 1 | The Copyright Public Domain – A New Approach | 3 |
| 2 | A Definition of the Copyright Public Domain | 27 |
| 3 | Categories of Public Rights | 54 |
| **Part II** | **Constraints and Supports, Global and National** | 85 |
| 4 | The Global Public Domain – Limits Imposed by International Law | 87 |
| 5 | The Global Public Domain – Exceptions and Enforcement | 123 |
| 6 | National Public Domains – Supports and Constraints | 152 |
| **Part III** | **Public Domains: Categories of Public Rights** | 183 |
| 7 | Works Outside Copyright Protection – Part I | 185 |
| 8 | Works Outside Copyright Protection – Part II | 215 |
| 9 | Works Where Copyright Has Expired | 247 |
| 10 | Non-Infringing Uses of Protected Works | 279 |
| 11 | Copyright Exceptions and Limitations – Comparative Approaches | 325 |

| | | |
|---|---|---|
| 12 | Copyright Exceptions and Limitations – Categories | 350 |
| 13 | Compulsory Licensing – Variations | 392 |
| 14 | Compulsory Licensing – Subject Areas | 433 |
| 15 | Voluntary Licensing Creating Public Rights | 475 |
| 16 | The De Facto Public Domain – Internet-Enabled Public Rights | 518 |

**Part IV  Conclusions** — 541

| | | |
|---|---|---|
| 17 | Reform Agendas for the Copyright Public Domain | 543 |

*Bibliography* — 563
*Index* — 589

# Foreword

The term 'public domain' bears different meanings, according both to the time and context of use. The notion is hardly new. Victor Hugo, in his opening discourse at the International Literary Congress in 1878,[1] spoke in favour of protecting 'literary property', but also of the need to create a 'public domain'. More provocatively, he proposed that, after the death of an author, the law should give all publishers the right to publish any book, subject to the requirement of paying the direct heirs of the author a 'very low fee' of no more than 5 per cent or 10 per cent of the net profit. This 'simple system', he went on to ague, would combine 'the unquestionable property of the writer with the equally incontestable right of the public domain'. The book, 'as a book', belonged to the author, but as 'a thought, it *belongs* – the word is not too extreme – to the human race'. Indeed, if it came to a question of choosing between the two rights here, it would certainly be the right of the author that would be sacrificed, 'because the public interest is our only concern, and that must take precedence in anything that comes before us'. Such sacrifice, however, was unnecessary, because Hugo saw both subsisting alongside each other, in an equal and balanced complementary relationship.

Hugo's views may seem at variance with our knowledge of the subsequent developments after that initial literary congress of 1878, which led ultimately to the creation of the Berne Convention for the Protection of Literary and Artistic Works in 1886 and the gradual ratcheting up of authors' rights protection that occurred in successive revisions of that Convention and national laws. Nonetheless, he was speaking at a time

---

[1] Held concurrently with the Universal Exhibition in Paris of that year. The proceedings of the congress were published as Société des gens de lettres de France, *Congrès littéraire internationale de Paris 1878, Comptes rendus in extenso et documents* (Paris, 1878), but without the discourse of Victor Hugo on 8 June 1878 at the opening of the congress. This is reproduced in an article published online in 2009 at www.sens-public.org/article.php3?id_article=648 ('Ce discours d'inauguration fut prononcé par Victor Hugo lors de l'ouverture du Congrès littéraire international en 1878'). The English translation used in the text is at www.thepublicdomain.org/2014/07/18/victor-hugo-guardian-of-the-public-domain/

when authors' rights were protected in the most rudimentary and limited fashion in many countries, and where there were still vast open ranges where there was no protection at all for the works of foreign authors, even in as important an emerging economy as the United States of America. Accordingly, meaningful authors' rights protection still had to be established both internationally and nationally before it became necessary to speak of the need to balance these rights with those of the public, let alone to consider whether there was any need to sacrifice one in favour of the other.

Notwithstanding this, the notion of the public domain was recognised in the first iteration of the Berne Convention in relation to obligations of member countries to protect all works at the moment of its coming into force which had not yet 'fallen into the public domain in the country of origin'.[2] This notion of the public domain – as excluding works no longer protected in their country of origin – obviously differed from the way in which Victor Hugo had used the term to denote (a) the lack of protection for the 'thoughts' of the author as distinct from the form in which they were published and (b) the more radical notion that, following the death of the author, there should be no restriction on third-party republication, subject to the payment of a small royalty to direct descendants of the author. But it is clear that the concept of the public domain was a malleable one and there was nothing in the first Berne Act to suggest that any of these understandings of it was inconsistent with the Convention's newly adopted obligations to protect authors.[3]

In truth, the notion of a broader, albeit shifting, public domain has always been accommodated within the interstices of the Berne Convention and its associated agreements, whether this is to be found within its national treatment obligation which leaves much latitude to national laws as to what is protected (or not), its formulation of the exclusive rights specially to be granted to Berne claimants, or the array of limitations and exceptions to which such rights may be subjected. For the most part, Berne and WCT obligations set minimal levels rather than ceilings on what must be protected and allow considerable flexibility as to how this is to be done. For example, the obligation to protect reproduction rights hardly answers the questions of how close the reproduction must be to the original, the quantum taken or the form of the reproduction where this occurs only transiently. Again, the obligations with respect

---

[2] Berne Act 1886, Article 14.
[3] Indeed, while the concept of a paying public domain has only subsequently been recognised in a handful of Berne countries, it is notable that it was included in section 17 of the Tunis Model Law on Copyright for Developing Countries developed by WIPO in 1976 as a way of providing protection for works of 'folklore'.

to public communication rights provide no guidance as to the distinction between what is 'public' – and to be protected – and what is 'non-public' – and therefore unprotected. Similar flexibilities are to be found in relation to allowable limitations and exceptions as demonstrated by national implementations of the three-step test. Further examples could be given, but the overriding conclusion must be that what lies outside the scope of these obligations, even on the most rigid authors' rights interpretation, resides in what can be correctly called 'the public domain'. This position is affected only to a small degree by the adoption of later obligations, such as those under the TRIPS Agreement, while none of these international obligations affects the question of what national legislators may do, in the first place, with respect to their own authors and works.

The public domain, like air, is therefore all around us, but its scope and dimensions are only imperfectly perceived. While we have long framed debate in this area in terms of authors' rights, we have neglected, apart from rhetorical flourishes, to consider properly what is comprehended within the surrounding public domain and, indeed, what is meant by the word 'public'. There is a pressing need for identification and description of the scope and content of these concepts, and this is the monumental task that has been undertaken by the authors of the present work. Both Graham Greenleaf and David Lindsay are ideally suited for this mission and have executed it with an attention to detail and rigour of analysis that are truly impressive. They present a compelling argument for the recognition of 'public rights' in the public domain as the necessary complement to the protection of authors' rights and articulate a coherent and comprehensive taxonomy for analysing and understanding these rights. As readers will see, the terrain they sketch is far from simple, and the various public domains they uncover in their analysis emerge as a series of unevenly defined spaces that intersect at various points along the spectrum of authors' rights. In some instances, the lines of demarcation are clearly defined and readily justified; in others, they are blurred or overlap, meaning there may not be much satisfaction for those looking for 'bright line' solutions. The achievement of the authors, however, is to present these matters in an untarnished and readily understandable way, and to provide the starting points for further investigation. The range of issues with which they deal is extensive and covers the gamut of modern copyright scholarship and policy discussion, with the consequence that there is much here also for readers wishing to pursue particular issues such as orphan works, extended collective licences, user-generated content, to mention only a few. But the real joy of the work for the reader is to be found in the way the authors present a consistent and realist argument throughout about the role of the public domain and public rights. Of particular interest here is their penultimate chapter in which they analyse the de facto public domain that has emerged on the Internet – an issue which we all know about subconsciously but rarely address expressly.

This is a distinguished contribution to our understanding of the relation between authors' rights and the public domain, and I congratulate the authors on their achievement.

SAM RICKETSON
*Melbourne Law School,*
*University of Melbourne*
*March 2018*

# Preface

In this book we examine copyright law primarily from the perspective of the users of works (in aggregate, 'the public'), rather than from the usual perspective of authors or copyright owners. The central question we ask is 'what can users do with works, without obtaining the permission of a copyright owner?' By putting the rights and abilities of users in the foreground, rather than relegating them to what is left after the exclusive rights are exhausted, we provide a new account of copyright's public domain, and of the 'public rights' which comprise it. We regard the public domain as not just important, but essential: for intellectual development, for public discourse and (not least) for replenishing the sources which nourish creativity.

This book is a global examination, because copyright public domains are different in every country in ways which are both important and complex. Nevertheless, there are globally consistent elements arising from both the constraints of international copyright law (sometimes weaker than imagined) and from the more recent uniformities arising from the globalising force of the Internet and its primarily expansive effects on public domains. Without claiming to be comprehensive, we present both the global elements of the copyright public domain and the great extent of its national diversities.

We hope that this book will contribute to revitalising discussion of both the concept of the public domain in copyright law and what can practically be done to protect and enhance it. We have both contributed to all chapters, and are equally responsible for Chapters 1–3 and 17. DL had principal responsibility for Chapters 4 and 5 and 7–12, and GG for Chapters 6 and 13–16.

The topic has proven too large to confine within a reasonable allowance of printed pages, so we have provided a free Online Supplement on SSRN (https://papers.ssrn.com/abstract_id=3144310) which contains additional details relevant to each chapter, indicated in footnotes.

The law is stated as at 31 August 2017.

Graham Greenleaf and David Lindsay

# Acknowledgements

***Graham Greenleaf*** would like to thank the many people and institutions who have contributed to his work on the copyright public domain for over a decade. Work leading to this book commenced under an Australian Research Council Linkage Project, 'Unlocking IP', in which numerous Chief Investigators and Industry Partners participated (see www.cyberlawcentre.org/unlocking-ip/) from 2006 to 2009. Three Conferences (2004, 2006, 2009) were organised by the project, through the Cyberspace Law & Policy Centre at UNSW Australia Faculty of Law. Thanks to David Vaile, Philip Chung, Catherine Bond, Abi Paramaguru, Ben Bildstein and Sophia Christou for their valuable work on that project. I was also assisted by visiting fellowships at the AHRC/SCRIPT Research Centre for the Study of IP and Technology Law, University of Edinburgh (2007, 2010) and Kyung Hee University College of Law, Seoul (2008).

Early versions of some of the arguments in the book were published in the *Australian Intellectual Property Journal*, *SCRIPTed* (University of Edinburgh) and *Global KHU Business Law Review* (Kyung Hee University, Seoul). Opportunities for conference presentations were provided by the 'Copyright Futures' Conference, Canberra, 2009; the 'Blue Sky' Conference, Sydney, 2010; the SCuLE Lecture, Exeter University Faculty of Law, 2012; the Australian IP Academics Conference, Adelaide 2012 and Fremantle, 2016; CREATe Glasgow, 2013; European University, Florence, 2015; and Australian Digital Alliance Conference, Canberra, 2016. Thanks to Brian Fitzgerald, QUT, Creative Commons Australia and the Australian Digital Alliance for organising many of these events and keeping discussion of the public domain alive in Australia, and to Whon-il Park and to Charlotte Waelde for international invitations to do so. Philip Griffith and Adrian Sterling encouraged me to stay interested in copyright law. I would like to offer particular thanks to David Lindsay for his willingness to co-author the book, which has benefited a very great deal from his expertise on international and comparative copyright law, and from his collegiate and collaborative approach.

# Acknowledgements

**David Lindsay** would like to thank Monash Law School for supporting this project during a period of sabbatical in 2016–17, and my former colleagues at Monash, especially Ann Monotti and Sharon Rodrick, for their collegiality and support. I am indebted to Sam Ricketson, from Melbourne Law School, and David Brennan, from UTS Law School, for detailed feedback on draft chapters. In particular, I would like to thank Graham Greenleaf for his invitation to become a co-author. Completing the project has been stimulating and challenging in equal measure. We are both committed to the importance of protecting the interests of authors, of the public domain as an integral part of copyright law, and of civil debate on issues of improving copyright law. In addition, we are united in a belief that scholarship based on a sound analysis of the law as it is and drawing from the best of different legal cultures and traditions can assist with developing realistic proposals for improving copyright law.

As joint authors, we would both like to thank all of the following for generously reading and commenting on chapters of the book or earlier drafts (in alphabetical order): T. G. Agitha, Sara Bannerman, Judith Bannister, Catherine Bond, David Brennan, Roger Clarke, Robert Cunningham, Ronan Deazley, Peter Drahos, Kristofer Erickson, Sean Flynn, Michael Fraser, Andres Gaudamuz, Michael Geist, Anne Flahvin, Yahong Li, Lydia Loren, Jani McCutcheon, Ross McLean, Kylie Pappalardo, Sam Ricketson, James Scheibner and Nic Suzor. We would also like to thank Catherine Bond for being involved in this project for a long period of time, until other obligations prevented her continued involvement. Responsibility for the text, its errors and omissions, remains with us alone.

Our thanks to Cambridge University Press, and particularly to our editor, Kim Hughes, for her continuous patience, flexibility and warm support and to Emma Collison for her very effective production management.

Graham dedicates this book to Jill Matthews for her loving and patient support and encouragement, not to mention tedious proofreading, editing, critiquing and indexing, throughout a very difficult period.

David dedicates the book to his partner, Robyn Parker, who has been and remains a constant support.

# Table of Cases

### Australia

*Australasian Performing Rights Association Ltd* v. *Commonwealth Bank of Australia* (1992) 111 ALR 671, 292
*Australian Olympic Committee* v. *Big Fights* [1999] FCA 1042, 510
*Avel Pty Ltd* v. *Multicoin Amusements Pty Ltd* (1990) 18 IPR 443, 298, 537
*Collier Constructions Pty Ltd* v. *Foskett Pty Ltd* (1990) 19 IPR 44, 243
*Commonwealth of Australia* v. *John Fairfax & Sons Ltd* (1980) 147 CLR 39 ('Defence Papers case'), 220, 242
*Concrete Pty Ltd* v. *Parramatta Design & Developments Pty Ltd* (2006) 70 IPR 468, 524
*Cooper* v. *Universal Music Australia Pty Ltd* (2006) 71 IPR 1 (Full Federal Court), 293
*Copyright Agency Ltd* v. *Haines* (1982) 40 ALR 264, 344
*Copyright Agency Ltd* v. *New South Wales* (2008) 233 CLR 279, 524
*Cuisenaire* v. *Reed* [1962] VR 719, 284
*De Garis* v. *Neville Jeffress Pidler Pty Ltd* (1990) 95 ALR 625, 220, 341, 344, 373
*Desktop Marketing Systems Pty Ltd* v. *Telstra Corporation Ltd* (2002) 55 IPR 1, 189, 191, 317
*Elwood Clothing Pty Ltd* v. *Cotton On Clothing Pty Ltd* (2008) 80 IPR 566, 317
*Fairfax Media* v. *Reed International* (2010) 88 IPR 11, 197
*Golden Editions Pty Ltd* v. *Polygram Pty Ltd* (1996) 34 IPR 84, 166
*Grain Pool of Western Australia* v. *Commonwealth* (2000) 202 CLR 479, 234
*Greenfield Products Pty Ltd* v. *Scott Bonnar Ltd* (1990) 95 ALR 275, 210
*Haines* v. *Copyright Agency Limited* (1982) 42 ALR 549, 373
*Haupt* v. *Brewers Marketing Intelligence (Pty) Limited* [2006] SCA 39 (RSA), 191
*IceTV Pty Ltd* v. *Nine Network Australia Pty Ltd* (2009) 239 CLR 458 ('IceTV'), 189, 190, 200, 205, 307, 310, 317

*Lange* v. *Australian Broadcasting Corporation* (1997) 189 CLR 520, 234
*Maggbury Pty Ltd* v. *Hafele Australia Pty Ltd* [2001] HCA 70, 171
*Nine Network Australia Pty Ltd* v. *Australian Broadcasting Corporation* (1999) 48 IPR 333, 341
*Nintendo Co. Ltd* v. *Centronics Systems Pty Ltd* (1994) 181 CLR 134, 234
*Pacific Film Laboratories Pty Ltd* v. *Federal Commissioner of Taxation* (1970) 121 CLR 154, 280
*Pavey Whiting & Byrne* v. *Collector of Customs (Vic)* [1987] AIPC 90–409, 243
*Plix Products Ltd* v. *Frank M Winstone (Merchants) Ltd* (1984) 3 IPR 390, 284
*Polo/Lauren Company* v. *Ziliani Holdings Pty Ltd* (2008) 173 FCR 266, 537
*Roland Corporation* v. *Lorenzo & Sons Pty Ltd* (1991) 22 IPR 245, 200
*Smith Kline & French Laboratories (Australia) Ltd* v. *Secretary, Department of Community Services and Health* (1990) 17 IPR 545, 243
*Stevens* v. *Kabushiki Kaisha Sony Computer Entertainment* (2005) 221 ALR 448, 286
*TCN Channel Nine Pty Ltd* v. *Network Ten Ltd* (2002) 55 IPR 112, 220, 339, 341
*TCN Channel Nine Pty Ltd* v. *Network Ten Pty Ltd* (No 2) (2005) 216 ALR 631, 307
*Telstra Corporation Limited* v. *Phone Directories Company Limited* (2010) 194 FCR 142 ('PDC'), 190
*Telstra Corporation Ltd* v. *Australasian Performing Right Association Ltd* (1997) 191 CLR 140, 292
*Trumpet Software* v. *OzEmail Pty Ltd* [1996] FCA 560; (1996) 34 IPR 481, 492
*Universal Music Australia Pty Ltd* v. *Cooper* (2005) 65 IPR 409, 293
*Venus Adult Shops Pty Ltd* v. *Fraserside Holdings Ltd* (2006) 70 IPR 517, 237, 238
*Victoria Park Racing and Recreation Grounds Company Limited* v. *Taylor* (1937) 58 CLR 479, 317
*Zeccola* v. *Universal City Studios* (1982) 46 ALR 189, 317

### Belgium

*Lichôdmapwa* v. *L'asbl Festival de Théâtre de Spa, Le Tribunal de première instance de Nivelles, Belgium,* 28 October 2010, 502

## Canada

*Alberta (Education)* v. *Canadian Copyright Licensing Agency (Access Copyright)*, 2012 SCC 37, [2012] 2 SCR 345, 50, 342, 344, 345, 374

*Aldrich* v. *One Stop Video Ltd* (1987) 39 DLR (4th) 362, 238

*CCH Canadian Ltd* v. *Law Society of Upper Canada* (2004) 1 RCS 339; 236 DLR (4th) 395 ('CCH'), 14, 50, 189, 191, 234, 244, 342, 344, 345, 367

*Eastern Book Co.* v. *Modak* (2008) 1 SCC 1, 191

*Galerie d'Art du Petit Champlain Inc.* v. *Claude Théberge* [2002] 2 RCS 336, 343

*Pasikniack* v. *Dojacek* [1929] 2 DLR 454, 238

*Society of Composers, Authors and Music Publishers of Canada (SOCAN)* v. *Bell Canada*, 2012 SCC 36, [2012] 2 SCR 326, 50, 342, 344

*Society of Composers, Authors and Music Publishers of Canada (SOCAN)* v. *Canadian Association of Internet Providers* [2004] SCR 427, 356

*The Canadian Copyright Licensing Agency (Access Copyright)* v. *York University* (2017) FC 669, 375

*Théberge* v. *Galerie d'Art du Petit Champlain Inc.* [2002] 2 SCR 336, 285

*United Airlines Inc.* v. *Jeremy Cooperstock* (2017) FC 616, 367

## China

*Yang Luo-Shu* v. *China Pictures Press* (Shandong High Court, 2007), 346

## European Court of Human Rights

*Ashby Donald and Others* v. *France* [2013] ECHR 287, 233

## European Union

*ACI Adam BV* v. *Stichting de Thuiskopie* (Case 435/12), [2014] All ER (D) 83 (Apr), 402

*Art & Allposters International BV* v. *Stichting Pictoright* (Case C-419/13), [2015] All ER (EC) 337, 285, 296, 297

*Bezpeènostní softwarová asociace – Svaz softwarové ochrany* v. *Ministerstvo kultury* (Case C-393/09), [2010] ECR I-13971, 24, 195, 313

*British Horseracing Board Ltd* v. *William Hill Organization Ltd* (Case C-203/02), [2004] ECR I-10415, 192

*Butterfly* v. *Briciole de Baci* (Case C-60/98), [1999] ECR I-3969; [2001] 1 CMLR 587, 259

# Table of Cases

*Commission of the European Communities* v. *Ireland* (Case C-175/05), [2007] ECR I-3, 301

*Commission of the European Communities* v. *Kingdom of Spain* (Case C-36/05), [2006] ECR I-313, 301

*Commission of the European Communities* v. *Republic of Italy* (Case C-198/05), [2006] ECR I-107, 301

*Commission of the European Communities* v. *Republic of Portugal* (Case C-53/05), [2006] ECR I-6215, 301

*Deutsche Grammophon* v. *Metro* (Case 78/70), [1971] ECR 487, 295

*DR and TV2 Danmark A/S* v. *NCB – Nordisk Copyright Bureau* (Case C-510/10), [2012] 2 CMLR 1280, 331

*Eva-Maria Painer* v. *Standard Verlags GmbH* (Case C-145/10), [2011] ECR I-12533, 24, 195, 260, 331, 358

*Fixtures Marketing Ltd* v. *Organismos Prognostikon Agonon Podosfairou EG (OPAP)* (Case C-444/02), [2004] ECR I-10549, 192

*Fixtures Marketing Ltd* v. *Oy Veikkaus Ab* (Case C-46/02), [2004] ECR I-10365, 192

*Fixtures Marketing Ltd* v. *Svenska AB* (Case C-338/02), [2004] ECR I-10497, 192

*Football Association Premier League Ltd* v. *QC Leisure* (Joined Cases C-403/08 and C-429/08), [2011] ECR I-9083, 289, 331, 352

*Football Dataco Ltd* v. *Yahoo! UK Ltd* (Case C-604/10), [2012] 2 CMLR 703, 24, 193, 195

*GS Media BV* v. *Sanoma Media Netherlands BV* (Case C-160/15), [2017] 1 CMLR 921, 290, 291

*Hewlett-Packard Belgium SPRL* v. *Reprobel SCRL* (Case C-572/13), [2016] Bus LR 73, 402

*Infopaq International A/S* v. *Danske Dagblades Forening* (Case C-5/08), [2009] ECR I-6569 ('Infopaq I'), 24, 195, 196, 204, 206, 260, 306, 307, 331, 352, 407

*Infopaq International A/S* v. *Danske Dagblades Forening* (Case C-302/10), ECLI:EU:C:2012:16 ('Infopaq II'), 352

*ITV Broadcasting Ltd* v. *TV Catchup Ltd* (Case C-607/11), [2013] FSR 36, 290

*Johan Deckmyn* v. *Helena Vandersteen* (Case C-201/13), [2014] All ER (D) 30 ('Deckmyn'), 332, 364, 365, 366, 369

*Laserdisken* v. *Kulturministeriet* [2006] (Case C- 479/04), ECR I-8089, 295

*Metronome Musik GmbH* v. *Music Point Hokamp GmbH* (Case C-200/96), [1998] ECR I-1953; [1998] 3 CMLR 919, 301

*Musik-Vertrieb Membran* v. *GEMA* (Joined Cases C-55 and 57/80), [1981] ECR 147, 295

Opinion 3/15: Opinion of the Court (Grand Chamber) of
    14 February 2017 – European Commission, 470
*Padawan SL* v. *Sociedad General de Autores y Editores de España (SGAE)*
    (Case C-467/08), ECDR 1; [2011] FSR 17, 402
*Peek & Cloppenburg KG* v. *Cassina SpA* (Case C-456/06), [2008] ECR
    I-2751, 295
*Phil Collins* v. *Imtrat Handelsgesellchaft mbh* (Joined cases C-92/92 and
    C-326/92), [1993] ECR I-5145, 256, 258, 259
*Phonographic Performance (Ireland) Limited* v. *Ireland* (Case C-162/10),
    [2012] CMLR 29, 289
*Productores de Música de Espana (Promusicae)* v. *Telefónica de España SAU*
    (Case C-275/06), [2008] ECR I-271 ('Promusicae'), 231
*Public Relations Consultants Association Ltd* v. *Newspaper Licensing Agency
    Ltd* (Case C-360/13), [2014] 2 All ER (EC) 959 ('Meltwater'),
    353, 357
*SAS Institute Inc.* v. *World Programming Ltd* (Case C-406/10), [2012] 3
    CMLR 55, 313
*Scarlet Extended SA* v. *Société Belge des Auteurs, Compositeurs et éditeurs
    SCRL (SABAM)* (Case C-70/10), [2012] ECDR 4; [2011] ECR I-
    11959, 231, 232
*Sociedad General de Autores y Editores de España (SGAE)* v. *Rafael Hoteles
    SL* (Case C-306/05), [2006] ECR I-11519, 24, 289
*Soulier and Doke* v. *Prime Minister of France and French Minister for Culture
    and Communication* (Case C-301/15), [2017] 2 CMLR 267, 407, 426,
    440, 536
*Stichting Brein* v. *Jack Frederick Wullems* (Case C-527/15), [2017] 3
    CMLR 1027 ('Filmspeler'), 291, 353
*Stichting ter Exploitatie van Naburige Rechten (SENA)* v. *Nederlandse
    Omroep Stichting (NOS)* (Case C-245/00), ECLI:EU:C:2003:68,
    401
*Svensson* v. *Retriever Sverige AB* (Case C-466/12), [2014] All ER
    (EC), 290
*Technische Universität Darmstadt* v. *Eugen Ulmer* (Case C-117/13), [2015]
    1 WLR 2017, 381
*UPC Telekabel Wien GmbH* v. *Constantin Film Verleih GmbH and Wega
    Filmproduktionsgesellschaft mbH* (Case C-314/12), [2014] Bus LR 541
    ('UPC Telekabel'), 232
*UsedSoft Gmbh* v. *Oracle International Corporation* (Case C-128/11),
    [2012] 3 CMLR 1039, 296
*Verwertungsgesellschaft Wort (VG Wort)* v. *Kyocera* (Joined Cases C-457/
    11 and C-460/11), ECLI:EU:C:2013:426, 326

## France

*Bsiri-Barbir* v. *Haarman & Reimer* [2006] ECDR 28 (C Cass), 212
CA Paris, 13 March 1986, D, 1987, SC, p 150, C. Columbet obs. (wrapping of Pont-Neuf), 211
*L'Oréal* v. *Bellure* [2006] ECDR 16 (CA Paris), 212

## Germany

*Berlin Wall Pictures*, Federal Court of Justice (Bundesgerichtshof – BGH) 23 February 1995, (1995) GRUR 673; (1997) 28 IIC 282, 512
*Germania 3* Gespenster am toten Mann, Federal Constitutional Court (Bundesverfassungsgericht – BVerfG) 29 June 2000, Zeitschrift für Urheber-und Medienrecht (ZUM) 2000, p. 867; 2001 GRUR 149, 234, 359
Regional Court of Hamburg (Landgericht Hamburg) decision of 16 November 2016, 501
Vorlage des Bundesgerichtshofs an den Europäischen Gerichtshofs zur Zulässigkeit des Tonträger-Samplings, Federal Court of Justice (Bundesgerichtshof – BGH) 1 June 2017, 365

## India

*Mohini Jain* v. *State of Karnataka* [1992] SC 1858, 377
*Mullin* v. *The Administrator, Union Territory of Delhi* [1981] AIR 746, 377

## Ireland

*Gormley* v. *EMI Records (Ireland) Ltd* [2000] 1 IR 74, 200

## Korea

Seoul High Court Decision (2010) na35260, decided 13 October 2010, 361
Supreme Court Decision 2005Do7793, 9 February 2006, 361
Supreme Court Decision 2009Da4343, 11 March 2010, 361
Supreme Court Decision 2012Do10777, 26 August 2014, 361
Suwon District Court decision, (2016) GoJung 432, decided 18 August 2016, 347

## Netherlands

*Curry* v. *Audax, District Court of Amsterdam,* 9 March 2006, Case no. 334492/KG 06–176 SR, 501
Den Haag Court of Appeal (Gerechtshof 's-Gravenhage) judgment of 4 September 2003, LJN-no. AI5638, Zaaknr: 99/1040, 233
*Kecofa* v. *Lancôme* [2006] ECDR 26 (Supreme Court), 202, 212
*Nederlands Uitgeversverbond and Groep Algemene Uitgevers* v. *Tom Kabinet,* Case no. C/13/567567/KG ZA 14–795 SP/MV, District Court of Amsterdam, 21 July 2014, 297

## New Zealand

*Copyright Licence Ltd* v. *University of Auckland* (2002) 53 IPR 618, 344
*Green* v. *Broadcasting Corporation of New Zealand* [1989] RPC 700, 209
*Henkel KGAA* v. *Holdfast New Zealand Limited* [2006] NZSC 102; [2007] 1 NZLR 577, 190
*Plix Products* v. *Frank M. Winstone (Merchants)* [1986] FSR 63 (High Court), 510
*University of Waikato* v. *Benchmark Services Ltd* [2004] NZCA 90, 191
*Wham-O MFG Co.* v. *Lincoln Industries* [1984] 1 NZLR 641, 210

## Spain

*SGAE* v. *Fernandez,* Lower Court number six of Badajoz (Spain), 17 February 2006, 502

## United Kingdom

*A-G* v. *Guardian Newspapers (No 2)* [1990] 1 AC 109, 237
*Ashdown* v. *Telegraph Group Ltd* [2002] Ch 149, 218, 234, 242, 244, 340
*Baigent* v. *Random House Group* [2007] FSR 579, 309, 316
*Blair* v. *Osborne & Tomkins* [1971] 2 QB 78, 524
*British Leyland Motor Corporation* v. *Armstrong Patents Co. Ltd* [1982] FSR 481, 510
*Cary* v. *Kearsley* (1802) 170 ER 679, 311
*Creation Records* v. *News Group Newspapers* [1997] EMLR 444, 209
*Designers Guild* v. *Russell Williams* [2000] 1 WLR 2416, 307, 315
*Dicks* v. *Yates* (1881) 18 Ch D 76, 197
*Donoghue* v. *Allied Newspapers Ltd* [1938] 1 Ch 106, 314
*Ernest Turner Electrical Instruments Ltd* v. *Performing Rights Society Ltd* [1943] Ch 167, 292

Table of Cases                                               xxi

*Express Newspapers plc* v. *News (UK) Ltd* [1990] 1 WLR 1320, 218
*Exxon, Re* [1982] Ch 119, 197, 204
*Football Dataco Ltd* v. *Sportradar GMBH* [2013] 2 CMLR 932, 193
*Francis, Day & Hunter Ltd* v. *Twentieth Century Fox Corporation Ltd*
    [1940] AC, 197, 204
*Glyn* v. *Weston Feature Film Company* [1916] 1 Ch 261, 237
*Green* v. *Broadcasting Corporation of New Zealand* [1989] 2 All ER
    1056, 199
*Gyles* v. *Wilcox* (1741) 2 Atk 141, 311
*Hadley* v. *Kemp* [1999] EMLR 589, 200
*Harms (Inc) Ltd* v. *Martans Club Ltd* [1927] 1 Ch 526, 292
*Hawkes & Son Ltd* v. *Paramount Film Service Ltd* [1934] Ch 593, 307
*Hollinrake* v. *Truswell* (1894) 3 Ch 420, 197
*Hyde Park Residence Ltd* v. *Yelland* [2001] Ch 143, 218, 237
*Ibcos Computers Ltd* v. *Barclays Mercantile Highland Finance Ltd* [1994]
    FSR 275, 315
*Jefferys* v. *Boosey* (1854) 10 ER 681, 314
*Jennings* v. *Stephens* [1936] Ch 469, 292
*John Richardson Computers* v. *Flanders* [1993] FSR 497, 315
*Joy Music Ltd* v. *Sunday Pictorial Newspapers Ltd* [1960] 2 QB 60, 365
*Kelly* v. *Morris* (1886) LR 1 Eq 697, 187
*Kenrick* v. *Lawrence* (1890) 25 QBD 99, 315
*King Features Syndicate Inc.* v. *Kleeman Ltd* [1940] 3 All ER 484, 284
*Ladbroke (Football) Ltd* v. *William Hill (Football) Ltd* [1964] 1 WLR 273,
    187, 307, 309
*LB (Plastics) Ltd* v. *Swish Products* [1979] RPC 551, 312
*Lion Laboratories Ltd* v. *Evans* [1985] QB 526, 242
*Lucasfilm* v. *Ainsworth* [2010] Ch 503; [2012] 1 AC 208, 210
*Macmillan & Co. Ltd* v. *Cooper* (1924) 93 LJPC 113, 187
*Morris* v. *Ashbee* (1868) LR 7 Eq 34, 187
*Morris* v. *Wright* (1870) LR 5 Ch App 279, 187
*Newspaper Licensing Agency Ltd* v. *Meltwater Holding BV* [2011] RPC 209;
    [2012] RPC 1, 197, 198, 204, 206
*Nova Productions* v. *Mazooma Games* [2006] RPC 379; [2007] RPC
    589, 209
*Performing Right Society Ltd* v. *Harlequin Record Shops Ltd* [1979] 1 WLR
    851, 292
*Pro Sieben Media AG* v. *Carlton UK Television Ltd* [1999] 1 WLR 605,
    218, 340
*Public Relations Consultants Association Limited* v. *The Newspaper Licensing
    Agency Ltd* [2013] UKSC 18; [2013] 2 All ER 852, 353
*Rose* v. *Information Services Ltd* [1987] FSR 254, 197

xxii    Table of Cases

*SAS Institute Inc.* v. *World Programming Ltd* [2014] RPC 218, 307, 314
*Schweppes Ltd* v. *Wellingtons Ltd* [1984] FSR 210, 366
*Southey* v. *Sherwood* (1817) 2 Mer 435, 237
*Tate* v. *Fullbrook* [1908] 1 KB 821, 199
*Tate* v. *Thomas* [1921] 1 Ch 503, 199
*Total Information Processing Systems Ltd* v. *Daman Ltd* [1992] FSR 171, 315
*University of London Press, Ltd* v. *University Tutorial Press, Ltd* [1916] 2 Ch 601, 187
*Walter* v. *Steinkopff* [1892] 3 Ch 489, 218
*Williamson Music Ltd* v. *Pearson Partnership Ltd* [1987] FSR 97, 366

### United States

*A&M Records* v. *Napster, Inc.*, 239 F 3d 1004, 1014 (9th Cir 2001), 298
*Alberto-Culver Co.* v. *Andrea Dumon, Inc.*, 466 F 2d 705 (7th Cir 1972), 198
*Alexander* v. *Haley*, 460 F Supp 40 at 45 (SDNY 1978), 320
*American Broadcasting Companies, Inc.* v. *Aereo, Inc.*, 134 S Ct 2498 (2014), 294
*American Geophysical Union* v. *Texaco Inc.*, 60 F 3d 913 (2nd Cir 1994), 337
*Andrea Blanch* v. *Jeff Koons*, 467 F 3d 244 (2nd Cir 2006), 338
*Arnstein* v. *Porter*, 154 F 2d 464 at 468 (2nd Cir 1946), 308
*Artifex Software* v. *Hancom US District Court*, 2017 US Dist. LEXIS 62815 (ND Cal, Apr 25, 2017), 491
*Authors Guild, Inc.* v. *Google, Inc.*, 804 F 3d 202 (2nd Cir 2015), 457, 528, 536
*Authors Guild, Inc.* v. *HathiTrust*, 755 F 3d 87 (2nd Cir 2014), 376, 457
*Baker* v. *Selden*, 101 US 99 (1880), 318
*Banks* v. *Manchester*, 128 US 244 (1888), 223
*Bateman* v. *Mnemonics, Inc.*, 79 F 3d 1532, 1542 (11th Cir 1996), 50
*Bill Graham Archives* v. *Dorling Kindersley Ltd*, 448 F 3d 605 (2nd Cir 2006), 338
*Bleistein* v. *Donaldson Lithographing Co.*, 188 US 239 (1903), 210
*Bobbs-Merrill Co.* v. *Strauss*, 210 US 339 (1908), 298
*Campbell* v. *Acuff-Rose Music, Inc.*, 510 US 569 (1994), 335, 336, 337, 362, 367
*Capital Records, Inc.* v. *Thomas*, 579 F Supp 2d 1210 (D Minn 2008), 298
*Capitol Records, LLC* v. *ReDigi Inc.*, 934 F Supp 2d 640 (SDNY 2013), 285, 299

*CCC Information Services, Inc.* v. *Maclean Hunter Marketing Reports, Inc.*, 44 F 3d 61 (2nd Cir 1994), 321

*Chatauqua School of Nursing* v. *National School of Nursing*, 211 F 1014, 1015 (WDNY 1914), 309

*CMM Cable Rep., Inc.* v. *Ocean Coast Props., Inc.*, 97 F 3d 1504 (1st Cir 1996), 198

*Columbia Pictures Industries, Inc.* v. *Professional Real Estate Investors, Inc.*, 866 F 2d 278 (9th Cir 1989), 293

*Concrete Machinery Co., Inc.* v. *Classic Lawn Ornaments, Inc.*, 843 F 2d 600 (1st Cir 1988), 309

*Dellar* v. *Samuel Goldwyn, Inc.*, 104 F 2d 661 (CA2 1939), 334

*Devils Films, Inc.* v. *Nectar Video*, 29 F Supp 2d 174 (SDNY 1998), 239

*Dr Seuss Enterprises* v. *Penguin Books USA, Inc.*, 109 F 3d 1394 (9th Cir 1997), 368

*Drauglis* v. *Kappa Map Grp., LLC*, 128 F Supp 3d 46 (DDC 2015), 502

*Eldred* v. *Ashcroft*, 537 US 186 (2003), 229, 230, 235, 252, 253, 263, 264, 277

*Emerson* v. *Davies*, 8 F Cas 615 (Mass CC, 1845), 187

*Feist Publications, Inc.* v. *Rural Telephone Service Co.*, 499 US 340 (1991) ('Feist'), 188, 190, 191, 205, 224, 228, 230, 321

*Field* v. *Google Inc.*, 412 F Supp 2d 1106 (D Nev 2006), 355, 527

*Folsom* v. *Marsh*, 9 F Cas 342 (CCD Mass 1841), 334

*Golan* v. *Holder*, 132 S Ct 873 (2012), 98

*Goldstein* v. *California*, 412 US 546 (1973), 201

*Graham* v. *John Deere Co.*, 383 US 1 (1966), 228

*Great Minds* v. *Fedex Office and Print Services*, US DC E. Dist. NY (Hurley, Snr Dist J), Order on Motion to Dismiss, 24 February 2017, 502

*Harper & Row, Publishers, Inc.* v. *Nation Enterprises, Inc.*, 471 US 539 (1985), 221, 228, 336, 337, 362

*Hoepker* v. *Kruger*, 200 F Supp 2d 340 (SDNY 2002), 98

*Jacobsen* v. *Katzer*, 2007 US Dist. LEXIS 63568 (ND Cal 2007), 490

*Jacobsen* v. *Katzer*, 535 F.3d 1373 (Fed Cir 2008), 490

*Kelley* v. *Chicago Art District*, 635 F 3d 290 (7th Cir 2011), 201

*Kern River Gas Transmission Company* v. *Coastal Corporation*, 899 F 2d 1458 (5th Cir 1990), 320

*Kirtsaeng* v. *John Wiley & Sons, Inc.*, 133 S Ct 1351 (2013), 299, 304

*Lasercomb America, Inc.* v. *Reynolds*, 911 F 2d 970 (4th Cir 1990), 171

*Magic Marketing* v. *Mailing Services of Pittsburgh, Inc.*, 634 F Supp 769 (WD Pa. 1986), 198

*Matthew Bender & Co.* v. *West Publishing Co.*, 158 F 3d 674 (2nd Cir 1998), 224

*Matthew Bender & Co.* v. *West Publishing Co.*, 158 F 3d 693 (2nd Cir 1998), 224
*Mazer* v. *Stein*, 347 US 201 (1954), 212
*Mitchell Brothers Film Group* v. *Cinema Adult Theatre*, 604 F 2d 852 (5th Cir 1979), 238
*Morrisey* v. *Proctor & Gamble Co.*, 379 F 2d 675 (1st Cir 1967), 319
*National Comics Publications Inc.* v. *Fawcett Publications Inc.* 191 F 2d 594 (2nd Cir 1952), 511
*New Era Publications International ApS* v. *Henry Holt and Co., Inc.*, 873 F 2d 576 (2nd Cir 1989), 337
*Nichols* v. *Universal Pictures Corporation*, 45 F 2d 119 (2nd Cir 1930), 319
*Oasis Publishing Co.* v. *West Publishing Co.*, 924 F Supp 918 (D Minn 1996), 224
*On Command Video Corp.* v. *Columbia Pictures Industries*, 777 F Supp 787 (ND Cal 1991), 294
*Perfect 10, Inc.* v. *Amazon.com, Inc.*, 508 F 3d 1146 (9th Cir 2007), 355, 527
*Peter Letterese and Associates, Inc.* v. *World Institute of Scientology Enterprises, International*, 533 F 3d 1287 (11th Cir 2008), 337
*Peter Pan Fabrics, Inc.* v. *Martin Weiner Corp*, 274 F 2d 487 at 489 (2nd Cir 1960), 309
*ProCD, Inc.* v. *Zeidenberg*, 86 F 3d 1447 (7th Cir 1996), 170
*Quality King Distributors Inc.* v. *L'anza Research International*, 523 US 135 (1998), 299
*Ringgold* v. *Black Entertainment Television, Inc.*, 126 F 3d 70 (2nd Cir 1997), 309
*Salinger* v. *Random House, Inc.*, 811 F 2d 90 (2nd Cir 1987), 337
*Sandoval* v. *New Line Cinema Corp*, 147 F 3d 215 (2nd Cir 1998), 310
*Sega Enterprises Ltd* v. *Peak Computer, Inc.*, 977 F 2d 1510 (9th Cir 1992), 355
*Shaw* v. *Lindheim*, 919 F 2d 1353 (9th Cir 1990), 309
*Sid & Marty Krofft Productions, Inc.* v. *McDonald's Corp*, 562 F 2d 1157 (9th Cir 1977), 309
*Sony Corporation of America* v. *Universal City Studios, Inc.*, 464 US 417 (1984), 334, 336
*Southco, Inc.* v. *Kanebridge Corp.*, 390 F 3d 276 (3rd Cir 2004) ('Southco III'), 198
*Suntrust Bank* v. *Houghton Mifflin Co.*, 268 F 3d 1257 (11th Cir 2001), 341, 368
*Trandes Corp.* v. *Guy F Atkinson Co.*, 996 F 2d 655 (4th Cir 1993), 170
*UMG Recordings, Inc.* v. *Augusto*, 628 F 3d 1175 (9th Cir 2011), 299

*Universal City Studios Productions LLLP* v. *Bigwood*, 441 F Supp 2d 185 (D Me 2006), 298

*US* v. *American Society of Composers, Authors and Publishers*, 627 F 3d 64 (2nd Cir 2010), 293

*Vernor* v. *Autodesk, Inc.*, 621 F 3d 1102 (9th Cir 2010), 298

*Versata Software, Inc.* v. *Ameriprise Financial, Inc.*, (2014), US D. Ct, W. D. Texas, Austin Div., unreported WestLaw 950065, 491

*Walker* v. *Time Life Films, Inc.*, 784 F 2d 44 (2nd Cir 1986), 320

*Warner Brothers* v. *RDR Books*, 575 F Supp 2d 513 (SDNY 2008), 535

*West Publishing Co.* v. *Mead Data Central, Inc.*, 799 F 2d 1219 (8th Cir 1986), 224

*Wheaton* v. *Peters*, 33 US (8 Pet.) 591 (1834), 223

*White Smith Music Publishing Co.* v. *Apollo Co.*, 209 US 1 (1908), 280

## World Trade Organization (WTO)

China – Measures Affecting the Protection and Enforcement of Intellectual Property Rights, WTO Panel Report WT/DS-362/R (26 January 2009), 240

United States – Section 110(5) of the US Copyright Act, WTO Panel Report WT/DS160/R (15 June 2000), 130, 132

# Table of Legislation

### Australia

Constitution
  s. 51(xviii), 234
Copyright Act 1879 (NSW), 156
Copyright Act 1905 (Cth)
  s. 28, 466
  s. 30, 466
Copyright Act 1968 (Cth), 409, 511
  Pt. III, Div. 6, 410
  Pt. IVA, Div. 4, 409, 459
  Pt V, Div 2AA, 164
  Pt. VA and VB, 409, 459
  Pt. VI (ss. 154 to 159), 413
  Pt. VII, Div. 2 (ss. 182B to 183E), 471
  s. 10, 164, 517
  s. 10(1), 200, 210, 287, 293, 341
  s. 14(1)(a), 307
  s. 21, 281, 283
  s. 21(1), 283
  s. 21(1A), 285
  s. 21(3), 284
  s. 22(1), 200
  s. 22(3)(a), 200
  s. 22(4), 200
  s. 22(6), 293
  s. 27, 281
  s. 29(1), 298
  s. 29(1)(a), 200
  s. 29A, 268
  s. 31(1)(a) and (b), 283

s. 31(1)(a)(ii), 298
s. 31(1)(a)(iii) and (iv), 288
s. 31(1)(b)(ii), 298
s. 31(1)(iii) and (iv), 292
s. 32, 208
s. 32(1) and (2), 200
s. 33(2), 267, 268
s. 33(3), item 1, 268
s. 33(3), items 2 and 3, 268
s. 34(1), 267
s. 37, 537
s. 40, 341
ss. 40 to 43A, 173
s. 41, 341
s. 41A, 341, 366
s. 42, 341
s. 42(1), 219
s. 43A, 354
s. 43A(2), 354
s. 43B, 287, 354
s. 43B(2), 354
s. 43C, 45
ss. 44A to 44F, 538
s. 47B(3), 172
ss. 47C to 47F, 172
s. 47H, 172
s. 48A, 384
s. 49, 384
s. 49(5A), 384
s. 49(5AB), 384
s. 49(7A), 384
s. 51, 384
s. 51AA, 384
s. 52, 384
ss. 54 to 64, 409, 471
ss. 74 to 77A, 284
ss. 89 to 92, 208
s. 89(1), 200
s. 90(1), 200
s. 92, 200
s. 93, 268
s. 93(2), 268

s. 93(3), 269
s. 94(1), 268
s. 95(1), 269
s. 96, 269
s. 100A, 219
s. 102, 537
s. 103A, 173, 341
s. 103AA, 341, 366
s. 103B, 173, 219, 341
s. 103C, 173, 341
s. 104, 173
s. 108, 410
ss. 108 and 109, 409, 471
ss. 110A and 110B, 173
s. 111, 45
s. 111A, 173, 354
s. 111A(2), 354
s. 111B, 287, 354
s. 111B(2), 354
s. 112A, 538
s. 112C, 538
s. 112D, 538
s. 112DA, 538
s. 113E, 341
s. 113H(1), 383
s. 113H(2), 383
s. 113J(1), 383
s. 113J(2), 383
s. 113K, 383
s. 113L, 383
s. 113M, 383
s. 113P(1), 410, 460
s. 113P(1)(a), 410
s. 113P(1)(d), 460
s. 113P(1)(e), 460
s. 113P(2), 460
s. 113P(4), 460
s. 113Q(2), 461
s. 113S, 460
s. 113T, 461
s. 113V, 410
s. 113W, 411

s. 115(3), 166
s. 116(2), 166
s. 116A, 178
s. 116AB, 354
ss. 116AC to 116AF, 164
s. 116AD, 354
s. 116AG, 354
s. 116AH, 354
ss. 116AK to 116AQ, 178
s. 116AN, 178
s. 116AN(2) to (9), 44
s. 136, 413
s. 153F, 410
s. 180, 269
ss. 182E to 183E (Pt VII, div 2), 471
s. 195AM(1), 274, 281
s. 195AM(2) and (3), 274
s. 195AW, 511
ss. 195CA to 195CJ, 156
s. 195CC, 156
s. 195CD(1)(c)(i), 156
s. 195CE, 156
s. 195CF, 156
s. 200AAA, 354
s. 200AB, 384
s. 200AB(1), 342
s. 200AB(2) to (4), 342
s. 200AB(3), 374
s. 200AB(6), 342
s. 200AB(7), 342
s. 249(2), 178
Copyright Amendment Act 1980 (Cth), 341
Copyright Amendment (Disability Access and Other Measures) Act
    2017 (Cth), 267, 409, 459
  Sch. 1, item 56, 342
Copyright (International Protection) Regulations 1969 (Cth)
  reg. 4(1), 270
  reg. 5, 270
Copyright Legislation Amendment Act 2004 (Cth), 164
Copyright Regulations 1969 (Cth)
  reg 20Z, 178
  Sch. 10A, 178

Table of Legislation

Legal Deposit Act 2012 (WA), 156
Libraries Act 1982 (SA), 156
Libraries Act 1984 (Tas), 156
Libraries Act 1988 (Qld), 156
Libraries Act 1988 (Vic), 156
Publications (Legal Deposit) Act 2004 (NT), 156
Telecommunications Act 1997 (Cth), 164
United States Free Trade Implementation Act 2004 (Cth), 164

### Austria

Federal Law on Copyright in Works of Literature and Art and on Related Rights (*Urheberrechtsgesetz* – UrhG) (BGBl. No 111/1936 as amended)
Art. 44, 217
Art. 79(1), 217

### Bahamas

Copyright Act, 1998 (Ch 323)
ss. 58 to 60, 333

### Bangladesh

Copyright Act 2000 (No 28 of 2000)
s. 72, 333

### Belgium

Law on Copyright and Neighbouring Rights of 30 June 1994 (as amended)
Art. 22(1)(6), 366
Art. 22.1.4bis and 4ter, 371, 372

### Brazil

Law No. 9610 of February 19, 1998, on Copyright and Neighbouring Rights
Art. 41, 272

### Brunei

Copyright Order
reg. 148, 428

## Canada

Copyright Act 1985, RSC, 1985, c. C-42
- s. 3(1)(g), 289
- s. 6, 272
- s. 9(2), 272
- s. 12, 225
- ss. 29 to 32.2, 343
- s. 29, 343, 367, 374
- s. 29.1, 343
- s. 29.2, 343
- s. 30.04, 100
- s. 30.1, 385
- s. 30.2(1), 344, 384, 385
- s. 30.2(2), 385
- s. 53(2), 100
- s. 66, 375
- s. 77, 442

## Chile

Intellectual Property Law (Ley 17.336 *sobre la Propiedad Intelectual*)
- Art. 11(c), 513

## China

Computer Software Regulations
- Arts. 16 and 17, 345

Constitutional Law
- Art. 35, 235
- Art. 47, 235

Copyright Law 1990
- Art. 4, 243, 244
- Art. 5(1), 222
- Art. 5(2), 221
- Art. 9, 468
- Art. 21, 270, 271
- Art. 22, 345
- Art. 22(1), 345
- Art. 22(11), 466
- Art. 22(12), 466
- Art. 23, 462
- Art. 33(2), 220

xxxii    Table of Legislation

   Art. 39, 271
   Art. 40(3), 471
   Art. 42, 271
   Art. 44, 471
   Art. 45, 271
Copyright Law 2010, 418
   Art. 8(2), 418
   Art. 48, 243
Copyright Law Implementing Regulations
   Art. 22, 418
   Art. 30, 220
   Art. 31, 471
   Art. 32, 220
Implementing Regulations on the Copyright Administrative Punishment
   Art. 3(4), 419
Law for Advancement of Science and Technology 2007
   Art. 20, 419
Regulations on Collective Management of Copyright
   Arts. 3 and 5, 418
   Art. 6, 419
   Art. 7(4), 419
   Art. 9, 419
   Art. 41, 419
   Art. 44, 419
Regulations on Protection of the Right of Communication through Information Network ('Internet Regulations')
   Arts. 6 and 7, 345
   Art. 8, 462
   Art. 9, 345
   Art. 10, 462
   Art. 11, 462
Software Regulations, 419

**Colombia**

Copyright Law No. 23 of January 28, 1982 (*Sobre derechos de autor*)
   Art. 21, 272
   Art. 187.3, 513
   Art. 188, 513

## Côte d'Ivoire

Law No. 96–564 of July 25, 1996, on the Protection of Intellectual Works and the Rights of Authors, Performers and Phonogram and Video Producers
Art. 45, 272

## Denmark

Copyright Act, 422, 423
Art. 50(2), 423

## Fiji

Copyright Act
s. 159, 428, 429
s. 159(2), 429
s. 160, 429
s. 161, 429
s. 162, 429

## France

Intellectual Property Code (*Code de la propriété intellectuelle*)
Art. L112-1, 202
Art. L112-1.4, 202
Art. L112-2, 202, 211
Art. L112-5(4), 365
Art. L121-1, 274
Art. L121-2, 274
Art. L122-3, 282
Art. L122-5(3), 217
Art. L122–5(4), 358
Art. L122-5(9), 217
Art. L134-1, 407
Law on the digital exploitation of the out-of-print books of the twentieth century (*LOI n° 2012–287 du 1$^{er}$ mars 2012 relative l'exploitation numérique des livres indisponibles du xx$^e$ siècle*), 407

## Germany

Constitution (Basic Law – *Grundgestez*)
Art. 5(3), 233, 359

Law on the Administration of Copyright and Neighbouring Rights 1965
(*Urheberrechtsgesetz* – UrhG)
  Art. 2(1), 202
  Art. 2(2), 202
  Art. 5, 222
  Arts. 13d and 13e, 455
  Art. 15(2), 288
  Art. 16(1), 282
  Arts. 18 and 19, 289
  Art. 24, 359, 365
  Art. 48, 217
  Art. 49(1), 217
  Art. 49(2), 217
  Art. 51, 358, 359
  Art. 52(a), 371, 372
  Art. 64, 274
  Art. 95a(2), 179

### Guinea

Law Adopting Provisions on Copyright and Neighbouring Rights in the People's Republic of Guinea (No. 043/APN/CP, of 9 August 1980)
  Art. 42, 272

### India

Copyright Act 1956
  s. 65A(1), 179
Copyright Act 1957
  Ch. VI, 420
  s. 2(k), 225
  s. 11, 421
  s. 14(c)(i), 284
  s. 21, 512
  s. 21(1), 512
  s. 21(2A), 512
  s. 21(3), 512
  s. 22, 272
  s. 25, 272
  s. 31, 420, 472
  s. 31(1), 472
  s. 31(1)(a), 472
  s. 31(1)(b), 472

s. 31A, 420, 447
s. 31A(6), 420
s. 31B, 421, 470
s. 31C, 421, 471
s. 31D, 421, 471
s. 32, 377, 420, 466
s. 32(1), 421
s. 32(1A), 420, 421
s. 32A, 377, 420, 421, 462
s. 32A(4), 447
s. 32B, 420
s. 52(1)(b), 356
s. 52(1)(c), 356
s. 52(1)(zb), 470
s. 52(i), 377
s. 52(j), 377
s. 52(n), 387
s. 52(o), 387
s. 52(p), 387
s. 52(q), 225
Copyright (Amendment) Act 1983, 420
Copyright (Amendment) Act 2012, 420, 421
Copyright Rules 2013
   Ch. VI, 470
Information Technology Act 2000 ('ITA')
   s. 2(w), 165
   s. 79, 165
Information Technology (Amendment) Act, 2008, 165

### Israel

Copyright Act 2007
   s. 5(5), 221
   s. 19, 333
   s. 38, 272

### Italy

Law for the Protection of Copyright and Neighbouring Rights, Law No 633 of 22 April 1941, (as amended)
   Art. 12, 282
   Arts. 13 to 19, 282
   Art. 70(1), 372

### Japan

Copyright Act (Act No. 48 of 6 May, 1970, as amended)
Art. 13, 223
Art. 67, 442

### Kenya

Copyright Act, CAP 130, Rev. 2014
s. 45(1), 513
s. 45(3), 513

### Korea

Copyright Act
Art. 28, 361
Art. 35bis, 356
Art. 35ter, 333
Art. 35ter(1), 346
Art. 50, 442
Art. 50(1), 442

### Liberia

Copyright Law
s. 2.7, 333

### Malaysia

Copyright Act 1987
s. 3, 284
Copyright (Amendment) Act 2012
s. 13(2), 333

### Mexico

Federal Law on Copyright of 24 December 1996
Art. 29, 273

### Netherlands

Copyright Act 1912 (as amended)
Art. 18b, 366

### New Zealand

Copyright Act 1994
  s. 27(1), 225
  ss. 226 to 226E, 180

### Nigeria

Copyright Act (Chapter C.28, as codified 2004)
  Sch. 1, 272

### Philippines

Intellectual Property Code [Republic Act No. 8293]
  ss. 11 and 12, 333
  s. 175, 221

### Russian Federation

Civil Code of the Russian Federation, Pt IV No. 230-FZ of 18 December 2006
  Art. 1281, 272
Law No. 72 of 20 July 2004, 272

### Singapore

Copyright Act 1987 (Chapter 63)
  s. 15(1B), 285
  s. 26(1)(a)(iii) and (iv), 288
  s. 35, 333
  s. 197(3)(a), 62, 276

### Sri Lanka

Intellectual Property Act, No. 36 of 2003
  ss. 11 and 12, 333

### Sweden

Act on Copyright in Literary and Artistic Works (Law No. 729 of 30 December 1960, as amended)
  Art. 22, 358

## Switzerland

Federal Act on Copyright and Related Rights of 9 October 1992
  Art 29(2), 272

## Taiwan

Copyright Act 2007
  s. 65, 333

## Uganda

Copyright and Neighbouring Rights Act 2006
  s. 15, 333

## United Kingdom

Broadcasting Act 1996, 416
  s. 137, 172
Copyright Act 1775, 261
Copyright Act 1814, 54 Geo. III, c. 156, 250
Copyright Act 1842, 393
Copyright Act 1911, 51, 208, 224, 250, 284, 417
  s. 1(2), 306
  s. 2(1)(i), 339
Copyright Act 1956, 200
  s. 2(3), 263
  s. 3(4), 263
Copyright and Duration of Rights in Performances Regulations 2013 (SI 2013/1782)
  reg. 6, 261
  reg. 8, 261
  reg. 16(d), 262
Copyright and Related Rights Regulations 1996 (SI 1996/2967)
  regs. 16 and 17, 262
Copyright and Rights in Performances (Certain Permitted Uses of Orphan Works) Regulations 2014 (SI 2014/2861) ('Orphan Works Permitted Use Regulations'), 443
  reg. 2, 445
  reg. 3, 446
  reg. 3(5), 445
Copyright and Rights in Performances (Extended Collective Licensing) Regulations 2014 (SI 2014/2588) ('ECL Regulations'), 428
  reg. 4(2)(a) and (b), 428

Copyright and Rights in Performances (Licensing of Orphan Works)
    Regulations 2014 (SI 2014/2863) ('Orphan Works Licensing
    Regulations'), 443
  reg. 4(1), 443
  reg. 4(2) and (3), 443
  reg. 4(4), 443
  reg. 4(5), 444
  reg. 4(9), 443
  reg. 5, 444
  reg. 6(2), 444
  reg. 6(3), 444
  reg. 6(5), 444
  reg. 6(6), 444
  reg. 8, 444
  reg. 9, 444
  reg. 10(1), 444
  reg. 10(2), 444
  reg. 11, 445
  reg. 12, 445
  reg. 13, 444
  reg. 13(3), 445
Copyright and Rights in Performances (Quotation and Parody)
    Regulations 2014 (SI 2014/2356), 360, 366
Copyright and Rights in Performances (Research, Education, Libraries
    and Archives) Regulations 2014 (SI 2014/1372), 372, 382
Copyright, Design and Patents Act ('CDPA') 1988, 200, 201, 250, 260,
    261, 263, 269
  Chapter III (ss. 28 to 76), 172
  s. 1(1), 208
  s. 3(2) and (3), 199, 219
  s. 4, 200
  s. 4(1), 209, 210
  ss. 5A and 5B, 200
  s. 12(7), 260
  s. 13B, 261
  s. 15, 260
  s. 16(1)(b), 297
  s. 16(1)(ba), 302
  s. 16(1)(c), 292
  s. 16(1)(c) and (d), 288
  s. 16(1)(d), 291
  s. 16(3)(a), 306

## Table of Legislation

ss. 17 to 21, 281
s. 17(2), 282, 285
s. 17(3), 284
s. 17(6), 286
s. 18(2), 297
s. 18(3), 297
s. 18A, 302
s. 18A(1), 302
s. 18A(2), 302
s. 18A(3), 302
s. 19, 292
s. 20(1), 291
s. 20(2), 291
s. 21(3), 287
s. 28(1), 172
s. 28A, 286, 353
s. 29(1), 340
s. 30, 340
s. 30(1), 219
s. 301, 263
s. 30(1ZA), 360
s. 30(2), 218
s. 30A, 340, 366
s. 32, 372
s. 32(2), 372
s. 33, 373
s. 34, 373
s. 35, 373
s. 35(4), 373
s. 36, 372
s. 36(1), 372
s. 36(5), 372
s. 36(6), 373
s. 36A, 373
s. 40A(1), 302
s. 40A(2), 302
s. 40B, 382
s. 41, 382
s. 42, 382
s. 42A, 382
s. 43, 382
s. 44, 446

s. 50D, 172
s. 51, 284
s. 58(2), 219
s. 66, 302, 416, 468
s. 66(1), 468
s. 66(3), 468
s. 73(4), 416
s. 86, 274
ss. 116A to 116D, 427
s. 116A(4), 428
ss. 135A to H, 416
s. 137, 416, 429
s. 141, 417, 461
s. 143, 417
s. 170(2), 262
s. 171(2), 219, 242
s. 174, 372
s. 178, 218
s. 296A, 172
s. 296B, 172
s. 296ZE, 44, 178
s. 296ZE(10), 178
Sch. 1, cl. 12, 261
Sch. 6, 263
Sch. A1, 445
Sch. ZA1, 443, 445
Sch. ZA1, para. 1(1), 446
Sch. ZA1, para. 2(2), 445
Sch. ZA1, para. 2(4), 445
Sch. ZA1, para. 3, 446
Sch. ZA1, para. 4, 446
Sch. ZA1, para. 5, 446
Sch. ZA1, para. 5(3), 446
Sch. ZA1, para. 5(4), 446
Sch. ZA1, para. 5(9), 446
Sch. ZA1, para. 6, 446
Sch. ZA1, para. 7, 446
Duration of Copyright and Rights in Performances Regulations 1995 (SI 1995/3297) ('Duration Regulations'), 260
Electronic Commerce (EC Directive) Regulations 2002 (SI 2002/2013) regs. 17 to 19, 164

Enterprise and Regulatory Reform Act 2013
  s. 76, 262
  s. 77, 427
European Union (Notification of Withdrawal) Act 2017, 25
Human Rights Act 1998, 64, 218, 242, 340
Literary Copyright Act 1842 (5 & 6 Vict. C. 45), 248
  s. III, 250
Public Lending Right Act 1979, 302
Re-Use of Public Sector Information Regulations 2015 (SI 2015/1415) ('PSI Regulations'), 224, 507
Statute of Anne 1709, 8 Anne, c. 19, 247, 249, 250

## United States

Code of Federal Regulations, 37 CFR, Ch. II
  § 202.19, 155
Constitution
  1st Amendment, 50, 60, 235, 264
  Art. 1, s. 8, cl. 8 ('Intellectual Property Clause'), 200, 228, 235, 264
Copyright Act 1790, Cong. Ch. 1–15
  § 1, 250
Copyright Act 1831, Cong. Ch. 21–16
  § 1, 251
  § 2, 251
  § 16, 251
Copyright Act 1909, Cong. Ch. 60–320
  §§ 7 and 8, 251
  § 23, 251
Copyright Act 1976, Pub. L. No. 94–553 (17 USC), 50, 263, 503
  § 101, 201, 212, 223, 283, 287, 293
  § 102(a), 201, 212
  § 102(b), 318
  § 104A, 98, 105, 266
  § 104A(e), 266
  § 105, 223
  § 106(1), 283
  § 106(3), 298, 300
  § 106(4), 293
  § 106(5), 293
  § 107, 334
  §§ 108 to 118, 334
  § 108(a)(1), 386

Table of Legislation  xliii

§ 108(a)(2), 386
§ 108(a)(3), 386
§ 108(b), 385
§ 108(c), 385
§ 108(d), 385
§ 108(e), 385, 386
§ 108(f)(3), 386
§ 108(f)(4), 386
§ 108(g)(2), 385
§ 108(i), 386
§ 109(a), 298, 299, 300
§ 109(c), 294
§ 110(1), 375
§ 110(2), 375
§ 110(5), 130, 132, 138
§ 111, 418
§ 113(b), 284
§ 114(d)(1), 418
§ 114(d)(2), 418
§ 115, 417, 471
§ 117, 354
§ 118, 418
§ 119, 418
§ 301, 266
§ 301(a), 170
§ 301(b), 266
§ 302, 251
§ 302(a), 265
§ 302(b), 265
§ 302(c), 265
§ 303, 251
§ 303(a), 265
§ 304, 251
§ 407, 155
§ 411, 100
§ 602(a)(1), 299
§ 602(a)(3), 386
(Sonny Bono) Copyright Term Extension Act 1998, Pub L.
    No. 105–298, tit. I, 112 Stat. 2827 (17 USC) ('CTEA'), 6, 101, 252,
    253, 264, 265
§ 102(3)(a), 263
§ 102(3)(b), 264

§ 102(d), 264
§ 302, 229
Digital Millennium Copyright Act ('DMCA') (17 USC)
§ 512, 160, 161
§ 512(a) to (d), 162
§ 512(b)(1), 527
§ 512(e), 162
§ 512(i)(1)(B), 163
§ 512(i)(2), 163
§ 512(j)(1)(A), 163
§ 512(k)(1)(B), 162
§ 1201, 176
§ 1201(d) to (j), 176
Technology Education and Copyright Harmonization (TEACH) Act of 2002, Pub L. No 107–273, § 13301, 116 Stat 1758 (2002), 375
Visual Artists Rights Act of 1990, Pub L 101–650 (17 USC) ('VARA')
§ 106A, 274, 275
§ 113(d), 275
§ 301(f)(2)(C), 275
§ 302(a), 275

# Table of International Instruments

*(Instruments are indexed by their short titles)*

Beijing Treaty – Beijing Treaty on Audiovisual Performances, Adopted by the Diplomatic Conference on 24 June 2012, 91
   Art. 2(a), 112
   Art. 13(2), 133
Berne Convention – Berne Convention for the Protection of Literary and Artistic Works, Paris Act relating to the Berne Convention for the Protection of Literary and Artistic Works of 9 September 1886, completed at Paris on 4 May 1896, revised at Berlin on 13 November 1908, completed at Berne on 20 March 1914, revised at Rome on 2 June 1928, revised at Brussels on 26 June 1948, revised at Stockholm on 14 July 1967, and revised at Paris on 24 July 1971, 1161 UNTS 3, 10, 57, 58, 59, 61, 62, 63, 64, 65, 66, 67, 68, 69, 78, 90, 91, 92, 93, 95, 101, 106, 112, 114, 118, 119, 120, 123, 125, 128, 129, 131, 133, 138, 139, 140, 144, 149, 154, 158, 160, 175, 176, 185, 186, 207, 214, 250, 254, 255, 256, 258, 263, 267, 270, 282, 283, 294, 297, 300, 305, 313, 328, 369, 377, 401, 405, 425, 426, 457, 464, 476, 505, 509, 548, 549, 557
   Preamble, 90, 123
   Arts. 1 to 21, 94, 131
   Art. 1, 108
   Art. 2, 92, 107, 109, 113, 127
   Art. 2(1), 108, 109, 110, 196, 207
   Art. 2(2), 111, 199
   Art. 2(3), 109
   Art. 2(4), 127, 215, 221
   Art. 2(5), 108, 109, 195
   Art. 2(6), 107
   Art. 2(7), 96, 110, 256
   Art. 2(8), 126, 136, 195, 215

Art. 2(9), 216
Art. 2*bis*, 127
Art. 2*bis*(1), 127, 136, 215, 216, 226
Art. 2*bis*(2), 136
Art. 2*bis*(3), 128
Art. 5, 471
Art. 5(1), 96, 239
Art. 5(2), 99, 100, 121, 157, 239
Art. 5(3), 99, 105
Art. 5(3)(d), 358
Art. 6*bis*, 131
Art. 6*bis*(2), 104, 273
Art. 7, 103, 105, 259
Art. 7(1), 103, 254
Art. 7(2), 104
Art. 7(3), 103
Art. 7(4), 103, 271
Art. 7(6), 103, 104
Art. 7(8), 96, 105, 106, 266, 269, 271
Art. 7*bis*, 103
Art. 8, 116
Art. 9, 285
Art. 9(1), 115, 116
Art. 9(2), 129, 130, 131, 379, 396, 400, 403, 431, 433, 436, 437, 454, 459, 465, 466, 467, 472, 473, 558, 559
Art. 9(3), 115
Art. 10, 357, 363, 390
Art. 10(1), 134
Art. 10(2), 134, 369, 377, 458
Art. 10*bis*(1), 137, 216, 220
Art. 10*bis*(2), 137, 216, 400
Art. 11, 116
Art. 11*bis*, 400, 471
Art. 11*bis*(1), 142
Art. 11*bis*(2), 132, 142, 144, 400, 401, 425
Art. 11*bis*(3), 137, 139
Art. 11*ter*, 116, 288
Art. 12, 109, 116
Art. 13(1), 142, 143, 400, 401, 470
Art. 13(2), 472
Art. 14, 47, 97, 248
Art. 14(1), 118

Art. 14(1)(ii), 117
Art. 14ter(2), 96
Art. 17, 236, 240, 241, 245
Art. 18, 97, 99, 105, 147, 248
Art. 18(1), 97, 266
Art. 18(3), 97
Art. 20, 91, 131
Art. 33, 147
Appendix, 131, 142, 143, 144, 459, 462, 465, 473
  Art. 1, 143
  Art. II, 466
  Art. II(2)(a), 463
  Art. III, 472
Brussels Satellite Convention – Convention Relating to the Distribution of Programme-Carrying Signals Transmitted by Satellite, done at Brussels on 21 May 1974, 1144 UNTS 3, 91

CRM Directive (EU) – Directive 2014/26/EU of the European Parliament and of the Council of 26 February 2014 on collective management of copyright and related rights and multi-territorial licensing of rights in musical works for online use in the internal market, OJ L84/72, 20 March 2014, 23
Recital 12, 426

Database Directive (EU) – Directive 96/9/EC of the European Parliament and of the Council of 11 March 1996 on the legal protection of databases, OJ L77 of 27 March 1996, 22, 109, 192, 196, 206, 213, 294, 316, 329
Art. 1(2), 192
Art. 3(1), 192, 194
Art. 5(a), 286
Art. 5(c), 295
Art. 7(1), 192
Art. 10(1), 257

ECHR – Convention for the Protection of Human Rights and Fundamental Freedoms, 4 November 1950, ETS N0. 005, 213 UNTS 221, 60, 61, 231, 233, 235
Art. 10, 233, 235, 242, 553
Art. 10(2), 233
Enforcement Directive (EU) – Directive 2004/48/EC of the European Parliament and of the Council of 29 April 2004 on the

Enforcement of Intellectual Property Rights, OJ L157/
5 April 2004 (corrected version OJ L195/16, 2 June 2004), 24

EU Charter (EU) – Charter of Fundamental Rights of the European
Union, 2010, OJ C364, 61, 231
Art. 6, 231
Art. 7, 231
Art. 8, 231, 232
Art. 10, 232
Art. 11, 231, 232, 290
Art. 17(2), 24, 231, 427
Art. 51, 231
Art. 52(1), 24

Geneva Phonograms Convention – Convention for the Protection of
Producers of Phonograms Against Unauthorized Duplication of
their Phonograms, done at Geneva on 29 October 1971, 866
UNTS 67, 91

InfoSoc Directive (EU) – Directive 2001/29/EC of the European
Parliament and of the Council of 22 May 2001 on the harmonisation of certain aspects of copyright and related rights in the
information society, OJ L167/10, 22 June 2001, 22, 24, 25, 195,
255, 314, 329, 372, 389, 405, 528, 536
Recital (9), 24
Recital (18), 426, 427
Recital (21), 306
Recital (23), 289
Recital (28), 289, 295
Recital (29), 296
Recital (32), 330
Recital (35), 402
Recital (36), 371, 380, 402, 406, 461
Art. 2, 282, 286, 306, 352
Art. 2(a), 407
Art. 3, 289, 291
Art. 3(1), 289, 407
Art. 3(2), 289
Art. 3(3), 296
Art. 4(1), 294
Art. 4(2), 295
Art. 5, 67, 222, 242, 326, 329, 396, 402, 405, 407, 408, 427, 440, 454,
456, 466, 472

Art. 5(1), 286, 330, 352
Art. 5(2), 330, 394
Art. 5(2)(a), 177, 406, 461
Art. 5(2)(b), 406, 461
Art. 5(2)(c), 177, 371, 380
Art. 5(2)(d), 177
Art. 5(2)(e), 177, 406
Art. 5(3), 330, 471
Art. 5(3)(a), 177, 370
Art. 5(3)(b), 177, 470
Art. 5(3)(c), 216
Art. 5(3)(d), 358, 360
Art. 5(3)(e), 177
Art. 5(3)(f), 216
Art. 5(3)(k), 364, 366
Art. 5(3)(n), 371
Art. 5(4), 330
Art. 5(5), 330
Art. 6(3), 406
Art. 6(4), 177
Art. 8(3), 232

Marrakesh Treaty – Marrakesh Treaty to Facilitate Access to Published Works for Persons Who are Blind, Visually Impaired, or Otherwise Print Disabled, done at Marrakesh on 27 June 2013, 10, 23, 67, 92, 95, 120, 140, 146, 350, 351, 433, 469, 550
Art. 2(a), 140
Art. 2(c), 140
Art. 4(1), 140
Art. 4(4), 140, 470
Art. 4(5), 140, 469
Art. 10(3), 140
Art. 11, 133, 140
Art. 12, 140

Orphan Works Directive (EU) – Directive 2012/28/EU of the European Parliament and of the Council of 25 October 2012 on certain permitted uses of orphan works, OJ L299/5, 27 October 2012, 23, 160, 408, 427, 437, 439, 445, 446, 447, 453, 454, 455, 456
Art. 1(1), 438
Art. 2(1), 438
Art. 3, 438

Table of International Instruments

Art. 3(1) to (5), 438
Art. 3(6), 439
Art. 4, 438
Art. 5, 439, 440
Art. 6(1), 438
Art. 6(3), 439

Rental and Lending Rights Directive (RLRD) (EU) – Council Directive 92/100/EEC of 19 November 1992 on rental right and lending right and certain rights related to copyright in the field of intellectual property, OJ L346/61, 27 November 1992, 22, 302, 329, 407
Recital (10), 301, 302
Art. 1(2), 301
Art. 2(1), 301
Art. 3(1), 300
Art. 3(2), 300
Art. 6, 301, 302
Art. 6(3), 301, 302
Art. 8(2), 401

Resale Right Directive (EU) – Directive 2001/84/EC of the European Parliament and of the Council of 27 September 2001 on the resale right for the benefit of the author of an original work of art, OJ L272/32, 13 October 2001, 22

Rome Convention – International Convention for the Protection of Performers, Producers of Phonograms and Broadcasting Organizations, done at Rome on 26 October 1961, 496 UNTS 43, 90, 96, 133, 259, 328, 399, 400, 431, 458, 471, 558
Art. 1, 112
Art. 2(2), 96
Art. 3(a), 112
Art. 3(b), 112
Art. 3(c), 112
Art. 3(f), 113
Art. 7(2)(2), 144
Art. 9, 112
Art. 12, 144
Art. 13(d), 144
Art. 14, 106, 255
Art. 15(1), 139
Art. 15(1)(a), 138
Art. 15(1)(b), 138

Art. 15(1)(c), 139
Art. 15(2), 139, 143

Satellite and Cable Directive (EU) – Council Directive 93/83/EEC of 27 September 1993 on the Coordination of Certain Rules concerning Copyright and Rights Related to Copyright applicable to Satellite Broadcasting and Cable Retransmission, OJ L248/15, 6 October 1993, 22
Art. 9(2), 426

Software Directive (EU) – Council Directive of 14 May 1991 on the legal protection of computer programs (91/250/EEC), OJ L122/42, 17 May 1991, 22, 213, 296, 300, 314, 329
Art. 1(2), 313
Art. 1(3), 194
Art. 4, 300
Art. 4(2), 295, 296
Art. 4(c), 295
Art. 5(2), 171, 329
Art. 5(3), 171, 329
Art. 9, 171

Term Directive (EU) – Council Directive 93/98/EEC of 29 October 1993 harmonizing the term of protection of copyright and certain related rights, OJ L290/9, 24 November 1993, 22, 62, 106, 255, 257, 258, 259, 260, 263, 269, 270, 272, 276, 416, 510
Recital (5), 256
Recital (6), 256
Recital (10), 256
Recital (11), 256
Art. 1(1), 256
Art. 1(2), 257
Art. 1(3), 257
Art. 2(2), 257
Art. 3, 258, 261
Art. 4, 262
Art. 6, 194, 260
Art. 7, 258
Art. 7(1), 258
Art. 7(2), 258
Art. 9, 259
Art. 10(2), 259, 262
Art. 10(3), 262

Term Extension Directive (EU) – Directive 2011/77/EU of the European Parliament and of the Council of 27 September 2011 amending Directive 2006/116/EC on the term of protection of copyright and related rights [2011] OJ L265/1, 256, 258, 261, 269
- Art. 1(1), 258
- Art. 1(2), 258
- Art. 1(2)(b), 257

TEU (EU) – Consolidated Version of the Treaty on the European Union, 2010 O.J. C 83/01
- Art. 6, 231
- Art. 6(1), 231
- Art. 6(3), 231

TFEU (EU) – Consolidated Version of the Treaty on the Functioning of the European Union, Arts 34 and 35, 2008 O.J. C 115/47, 230, 256

TRIPs Agreement – Marrakesh Agreement establishing the World Trade Organization (with final act, annexes and protocol), concluded at Marrakesh on 15 April 1994, 1867 UNTS 3, Annex 1 C, Agreement on Trade-Related Aspects of Intellectual Property Rights, 58, 66, 90, 91, 92, 98, 104, 106, 115, 119, 120, 129, 131, 138, 140, 147, 149, 266, 549
- Art. 2(2), 129, 131, 132
- Art. 3(1), 96
- Art. 4, 92, 96, 105
- Art. 4(b), 105, 107, 255, 259
- Art. 9(1), 92, 94, 108, 120, 131, 132, 239
- Art. 9(2), 65, 110, 313
- Art. 10(1), 110
- Art. 10(2), 109, 187
- Art. 11, 118, 300
- Art. 12, 104, 254
- Art. 13, 129, 130, 131, 132, 133, 342, 403
- Art. 14(4), 118, 119, 300
- Art. 14(5), 106
- Art. 14(6), 97, 133
- Art. 41(1), 240
- Art. 63, 148

UCC – Universal Copyright Convention, Signed at Geneva on 6 September 1952, 216 UNTS 132, 90

Table of International Instruments

WCT – WIPO Copyright Treaty (with annex), Geneva, 20 December 1996, 2186 UNTS 121, 66, 91, 94, 108, 109, 110, 115, 119, 133, 140, 161, 285, 286, 351, 525
- Preamble, 124, 369
- Art. 1(4), 285
- Art. 2, 65, 110, 313
- Art. 4, 110
- Art. 5, 109, 110
- Art. 6, 294, 295
- Art. 6(1), 118
- Art. 6(2), 118, 294
- Art. 7, 300
- Art. 7(1), 119
- Art. 8, 288, 289
- Art. 9, 103, 254, 271
- Art. 10, 133
- Art. 11, 161, 175, 176
- Art. 12, 161
- Art. 16(2), 133

WPPT – WIPO Performances and Phonograms Treaty (with annex), Geneva, 20 December 1996, 2186 UNTS 203, 66, 91, 94, 96, 115, 119, 255, 328
- Preamble, 124
- Art. 2(a), 112
- Art. 2(b), 112
- Art. 2(f), 113
- Art. 4(1), 96
- Art. 5, 104
- Art. 5(2), 104
- Art. 8(1), 118
- Art. 10, 117
- Art. 12(1), 118
- Art. 14, 117
- Art. 16, 139
- Art. 16(1), 139
- Art. 16(2), 133, 139
- Art. 17, 106

Table of International Instruments    iii

WCT – WIPO Copyright Treaty (with annex), Geneva,
20 December 1996, 2186 UNTS 121, 60, 61, 94, 108, 109, 110,
115, 119, 133, 136, 161, 285, 286, 371, 555

Preamble, 124, 360
Art. 1(4), 285
Art. 2, 65, 110, 313
Art. 4, 110
Art. 5, 109, 110
Art. 6, 294, 298
Art. 6(1), 118
Art. 6(2), 118, 294
Art. 7, 300
Art. 7(1), 139
Art. 8, 285, 280
Art. 9, 103, 254, 271
Art. 10, 138
Art. 11, 101, 175, 176
Art. 12, 161
Art. 16(2), 143

WPPT – WIPO Performances and Phonograms Treaty (with annex),
Geneva, 20 December 1996, 2186 UNTS 203, 60, 61, 94, 96,
115, 119, 255, 328

Preamble, 124
Art. 2(a), 112
Art. 2(b), 112
Art. 2(f), 163
Art. 3(1), 96
Art. 5, 194
Art. 5(2), 104
Art. 8(1), 118
Art. 10, 117
Art. 12(1), 118
Art. 14, 117
Art. 16, 139
Art. 16(1), 139
Art. 16(2), 133, 139
Art. 17, 100

*Part I*

# What is the Copyright Public Domain?

# 1 The Copyright Public Domain – A New Approach

| | | |
|---|---|---|
| 1.1 | Introduction: Rethinking the Copyright Public Domain | 3 |
| 1.2 | Previous Approaches to the Public Domain | 4 |
| 1.3 | A New Approach to Copyright Public Domains | 6 |
| 1.4 | An Outline of the Book | 8 |
| 1.5 | A 'Realist' Perspective: Assumptions and Methodology | 10 |
| 1.6 | Copyright and the Public Domain: Theoretical Perspectives | 12 |
| 1.7 | Public Domain Values | 17 |
| 1.8 | A Role for Copyright: Not a Rejection | 20 |
| 1.9 | Jurisdictional Perspectives | 20 |
| 1.10 | Conclusion | 25 |

## 1.1 Introduction: Rethinking the Copyright Public Domain

Texts and articles on copyright law conventionally organise the law through the lens of the rights of the owners of works – both the creators of works and others, such as exclusive licensees, with commercial interests in them. Orthodox treatments therefore focus on copyright subsistence, exclusive rights, infringement, ownership and exploitation; the organising principle is the exclusive property rights in works or other protected material. For convenience, this book generally uses the term 'works' in a non-technical sense to refer to all forms of creative expression, including what are commonly referred to as neighbouring and related rights, and without regard to the extent of their protection (if at all) by copyright law, meaning that it also refers to unprotected material as 'works'.

This book takes a different approach, based on an alternative perspective, of how copyright law might be conceptualised if we put the 'user' (and, in aggregate, 'the public')[1] of works, and the 'rights' of users, in the

---

[1] This is not meant to imply that authors and owners are not also members of 'the public'. As we explain in Chapter 2, our analysis avoids drawing simplistic distinctions between private rights of owners and public rights of users.

foreground, rather than being relegated to what is left after the exclusive rights are exhausted. Our core question is 'what can users do with works, without obtaining the permission of a copyright owner?' This question derives from our fundamental understanding of the public domain as being essential to protect the negative liberty of users to use works for their own purposes: [1.6.3]. By focusing on this question, and on what we refer to as 'public rights', we aim to reinvigorate the notion of 'the public domain' in copyright law, while building on the extensive literature in this area. In the process, our analysis aims to render new insights into the nature of copyright, which can sometimes be obscured by automatic and unthinking foregrounding of exclusive rights. This chapter outlines our basic approach, while our conceptual framework and terminology are further explained in Chapter 2.

This chapter is structured as follows. We begin by reviewing previous scholarly work on the copyright public domain. Second, we explain how our approach builds on this work, and identify our original contributions. After that, we set out the four-part structure of our book, consisting of our conceptual framework, constraints on and supports for national public domains, detailed comparative analysis of national laws and our conclusions. Fourth, we describe our analytical approach, which we call a 'realist' perspective, and our main assumptions and methodology. This leads to an explanation of the relationship between our approach and copyright theory, and our justification for a conception of the public domain as the freedom or ability to use works without permission. Sixth, we summarise traditional values we regard as supporting the public domain, and explain how these relate to our conception of it as permission-free uses of works. Seventh, we qualify our critical analysis of copyright law by acknowledging the role of exclusive rights in promoting important values. As copyright law is essentially territorial, the chapter then reviews conceptual approaches to copyright in national laws, identifying the main jurisdictions covered in this book. Given the importance of the EU for our comparative analysis, we describe the main features of EU copyright law, as well as the relationship between EU and UK copyright law, including the implications of the UK decision to withdraw from the EU. We summarise our approach in the concluding section to the chapter.

## 1.2    Previous Approaches to the Public Domain

Despite continuing interest in the public domain, mainstream copyright law texts generally fail to recognise it as a fundamental concept, giving it only passing mention when discussing expiry of the copyright term, and

## 1.2 Previous Approaches to the Public Domain

sometimes the principle that copyright does not extend to ideas or facts (the 'idea/expression dichotomy'). The public domain, on this traditional view, is defined negatively by reference to those things that do not merit protection, being summed up as follows by Krasilovsky in 1967:

> Public domain in the fields of literature, drama, music and art is the other side of the coin of copyright. It is best defined in negative terms. It lacks the private property element granted under copyright in that there is no legal right to exclude others from enjoying it and is 'free as the air to common use'.[2]

Our approach to the public domain draws upon previous substantial contributions, many dating from the 2000s, which made important breakthroughs, but left many issues unresolved. While building on this work, we aim to take it further by grounding our analysis in an ambitious survey of international and national copyright laws. But, before doing so, it is important for us to review previous approaches.

The modern literature on the public domain can be traced to a 1981 article by David Lange, where he argued that recognition of new intellectual property rights (IPRs) should be offset by recognition of rights in the public domain.[3] The article cautioned against the tendency to over-expansion of IPRs by legislatures and courts, and argued for better recognition of rights in the public domain. It stimulated further interest, including Litman's seminal 1990 article which, as part of a critique of the view that authors create from thin air, argued for a positive justification for the public domain as the source of raw material for producing original works.[4] In 1991, Patterson and Lindberg first claimed that the public domain was the basis for a law of users' rights, arguing that copyright is 'a law for consumers as well as for creators and marketers'.[5]

The 1990s therefore marked a transition from an approach which sought to defend the public domain against encroachments from expanding IPRs to a focus on identifying and justifying positive values which underpin it. Impetus was given to attempts to build positive accounts of the public domain by developments in the United States, notably the

---

[2] M. Krasilovsky, 'Observations on the public domain' (1967) 14 *Bulletin of the Copyright Society* 205 at 205. The phrase 'free as the air to common use' comes from the Brandeis J dissent in *International News Service* v. *Associated Press* 248 US 215 at 250 (1918).
[3] D. Lange, 'Recognizing the public domain' (1981) 44(4) *Law and Contemporary Problems* 147; J. Boyle, 'The second enclosure movement and the construction of the public domain' (2003) 66 *Law and Contemporary Problems* 33 at 59; J. Cohen, 'Copyright, commodification, and culture', in L. Guibault and P. B. Hugenholtz (eds.), *The Future of the Public Domain: Identifying the Commons in Information Law* (Kluwer Law International, 2006), p. 132.
[4] J. Litman, 'The public domain' (1990) 39(4) *Emory Law Journal* 965.
[5] L. Ray Patterson and S. Lindberg, *The Nature of Copyright: A Law of Users' Rights* (University of Georgia Press, 1991), pp. 3–4.

twenty-year extension of the copyright term in 1998.[6] Concerns outside the United States were inspired by EU directives in 1993 concerning the copyright term and in 1996 protecting non-original databases, as well as proposals for an international database treaty.[7]

Scholarly attention to these issues culminated with the 2001 Duke Law School conference on the public domain, and papers resulting from it, which presented diverse analyses of positive values of the public domain.[8] Lange, for example, revisiting the issue, suggested that the public domain should be reimagined as a 'status' given to exercise of the creative imagination that could protect acts of creative appropriation against proprietary claims.[9] Boyle, on the other hand, advanced a complex affirmative argument for the public domain by analogy with arguments for protecting the natural environment, claiming that there are commonalities in various positive interests and values underpinning the public domain, which can clarify debates about creation, innovation and free speech.[10] The 2000s therefore saw the emergence of a rich literature addressing values supporting a positive view of the public domain.[11]

## 1.3  A New Approach to Copyright Public Domains

Building on this literature, this book endorses a positive account of the public domain, with implications for its definition being explained in Chapter 2. Although values supporting the public domain are introduced in this chapter, it is not the main intention of this book to engage with theoretical debates about public domain values; nor does it attempt to provide a particular theory of the public domain. Instead, the book develops a second theme arising from the public domain literature: that is, we agree with Samuelson that building a positive, descriptive account

---

[6] Sonny Bono Copyright Term Extension Act, Pub L. No. 105-298, tit. I, 112 Stat. 2827 ('CTEA').
[7] See P. Samuelson, 'Enriching discourse on public domains' (2006) 55 *Duke Law Journal* 783 at 787 n. 21.
[8] Papers presented at the conference were collected as articles published in (2003) 66 *Law and Contemporary Problems*.
[9] D. Lange, 'Reimagining the public domain' (2003) 66 *Law and Contemporary Problems* 463 at 474.
[10] Boyle, 'The second enclosure movement'.
[11] See, for example, L. Lessig, *The Future of Ideas: The Fate of the Commons in a Connected World* (Random House, 2001); Y. Benkler, 'Through the looking glass: Alice and the constitutional foundations of the public domain' (2003) 66 *Law and Contemporary Problems* 173; R. Coombe, 'Fear, hope, and longing for the future of authorship and a revitalized public domain in global regimes of intellectual property' (2002–3) 52 *DePaul Law Review* 1171; Cohen, 'Copyright, commodification, and culture'; V.-L. Benabou and S. Dusollier, 'Draw me a public domain', in P. Torremans (ed.), *Copyright Law: A Handbook of Contemporary Research* (Edward Elgar, 2007), pp. 161–84.

## 1.3 A New Approach to Copyright Public Domains

of what is in the public domain is essential to understanding its positive character.[12]

To do so, we go beyond previous attempts at mapping the public domain in two main ways. First, we provide an exhaustive account of the legal categories that we contend comprise the copyright public domain. This is based on our expansive definition of the public domain, which is explained and justified in Chapter 2, and which leads us to identify fifteen public domain categories, which we also call 'public rights'. Our approach is consistent with broad definitions of copyright's public domain proposed by some others, but we refine and extend the analysis, conceptualising the public domain as the complete and equal complement to the proprietary domain of copyright law. In sum, we conceive of 'copyright' not merely as the rights comprising owners' rights, but as a complex system of inter-related rights and interests, with users' 'rights' also being a positive bundle of rights: [2.4.2]. This reconceptualisation enables us to show that there are areas of copyright law and practice which are more significant to the public domain than often assumed, such as compulsory licences and some types of voluntary licensing. While traditional approaches disaggregate limits and exceptions to exclusive rights, treating different categories in isolation, our analysis enables common features of these rights and interests to stand out. The public domain that emerges is a collection of specific 'abilities' or 'rights', but with conceptual connections between the rights, just as the traditional approach sees copyright as a conceptually linked collection of related 'exclusive rights' of copyright owners.

Second, our approach is firmly anchored in detailed analysis of positive law in each of our fifteen public domain categories, an endeavour which is even more unusual for being conducted across numerous jurisdictions. Moreover, in focusing on international copyright law and on comparative analysis of the law in selected jurisdictions, we attempt to transcend previous jurisdiction-specific accounts of the public domain.[13] Throughout, our conviction is that it is impossible properly to understand the complexity of the public domain, let alone propose measures for supporting public domain values, in isolation from detailed knowledge of the law. That said, at a number of points in the book, and especially in our account of the de facto public domain in Chapter 16, we readily acknowledge that practices and norms are as important to the public domain as the strict legal position.

---

[12] P. Samuelson, 'Challenges in mapping the public domain', in Guibault and Hugenholtz (eds.), *The Future of the Public Domain*, pp. 7–8.
[13] Patterson and Lindberg's 1991 book is, for example, US-centric.

We therefore attempt to provide the first systematic and comprehensive analysis of the concept and legal constituents of the copyright public domain, going beyond previous schematic and jurisdiction-specific exercises. We have deliberately limited our analysis to the copyright public domain (and not in relation to all IPRs) partly to make the project achievable, but also to focus on building a better understanding of copyright law. While we acknowledge the significance of restrictions on the public domain arising from laws outside copyright, such as the EU database law or confidentiality law, these issues are primarily dealt with in Chapter 6, which addresses extra-copyright constraints on the copyright public domain.

While we adopt a user-centric approach to the public domain, we also stress there is no sharp dichotomy between creators and users of works. On the contrary, creators are also users of existing works, and their relationship to those works (and to the public domain) is an important part of their creativity. Neither do we deny the importance of conferring exclusive rights on authors: in market-based economies creativity depends, although not entirely, both on exclusive rights in works and rights of users, including users that are creators: [1.7]–[1.8]. The difficulties, of course, lie in determining the legal boundaries between proprietary exclusive rights and the public domain.

## 1.4 An Outline of the Book

The argument by which we develop our approach to the copyright public domain is reflected in the four-part structure of the book.

Part I, consisting of Chapters 1 to 3, sets the framework for our analysis. In the rest of Chapter 1 we set out our main assumptions, establishing the conceptual foundations for our expansive approach to the public domain based on permission-free uses of works. We also briefly identify traditional public domain values. Finally, as copyright law is inherently territorial, we introduce perspectives on copyright legal jurisdictions. Chapter 2 focuses on our definition of the public domain, which is based on permission-free uses. This approach recognises that the proprietary/public domain distinction is not merely a distinction between works that are or are not protected, but a distinction that exists within each work. The chapter expands upon and justifies the elements of our definition, as well as explaining our use of the terminology of 'public rights'.

Chapter 3 identifies the fifteen categories of the copyright public domain, which form the lynchpin of the book. Following from the territorial nature of copyright, the fifteen categories, which are more

## 1.4 An Outline of the Book

exhaustive than previous approaches, are drawn from our analysis of selected national laws. The categories are: (1) Works failing minimum requirements; (2) Works impliedly excluded; (3) Works expressly excluded; (4) Constitutional and related exclusions; (5) Works in which copyright has expired; (6) Public domain dedications; (7) Public policy refusals against enforcement; (8) Public interest exceptions to enforcement; (9) Insubstantial parts; (10) Ideas or facts; (11) Uses outside exclusive rights; (12) Statutory exceptions; (13) Neutral compulsory licensing; (14) Neutral voluntary licensing; and (15) De facto public domain of benign uses. The chapter comprehensively defines and describes each category.

Part II of the book, consisting of Chapters 4 to 6, turns to the law, introducing legal regimes outside of national copyright laws that condition national public domains. Chapters 4 and 5 introduce and explain international copyright law, concentrating on those elements of international law that have the most effect on national public domains. Chapter 4 explains the relevant essential elements of the international legal framework, while Chapter 5 deals with the framework for copyright limitations and exceptions and the international enforcement regime. As we explain, while international law generally acts as a constraint on national public domains, it does not completely determine the shape of public domains. Although our fifteen public domain categories are based on national copyright laws, the practical importance of a category for the public domain can depend upon laws that are external to the copyright category, and may be external to copyright law. We refer to these as laws that either support or constrain public domains, causing them to thrive or shrink. In Chapter 6, we identify the most important types of supports and constraints, and illustrate them through examples.

Part III, which is the bulk of the book, is a detailed comparative examination of each of the fifteen categories identified in Chapter 3, how they are implemented in national jurisdictions, and the implications of the category for the public domain. Chapters 7–17 therefore comprehensively describe and analyse: 'works' outside copyright protection (Chapters 7–8); works where copyright has expired (Chapter 9); permissible uses of works (Chapter 10); copyright exceptions and limitations (Chapters 11–12); compulsory licences (remunerated use exceptions) (Chapters 13–14); neutral voluntary licensing (Chapter 15); and a category we refer to as 'the de facto public domain' (Chapter 16). These last two chapters, in our view, present a partial corrective to the constraining effects of international copyright law, because they show that there has developed over recent decades an Internet-enabled global expansion of the public domain.

Part IV, which consists of Chapter 17, looks to the future of the public domain and proposes realistic reforms, which might be achievable under national laws, and which might protect and support copyright public domains.

Taken together, the book is a comprehensive attempt at defining and identifying the legal contents of the global public domain and national public domains, and analysing the implications for copyright law.

## 1.5 A 'Realist' Perspective: Assumptions and Methodology

We describe as 'realist' the perspective we have taken, and explain here its purpose and limitations. Although this book is a comprehensive overview of copyright from the perspective of the public domain, it is far from an exercise in reimagining copyright from first principles.[14] We are more concerned with determining the shape and scope of public domains under current copyright laws, taking a 'realist' approach to international copyright law, which can be summed up as 'what if we are stuck with copyright treaties as they are now, with little prospects of significant change?'[15] This approach is, we contend, soundly based in the history and development of international copyright law. As explained in Part II, the history of international copyright law has been characterised by progressive expansion of copyright protection and, with few exceptions – notably, the recent Marrakesh Treaty assisting visually impaired and print-disabled people – few express concessions to users' rights. Moreover, the Berne Convention, which remains the centrepiece of international copyright law, has not been amended for nearly half a century, illustrating the substantial difficulties in achieving multilateral agreement.

Existing international copyright law is therefore a constraint within which national laws must pragmatically work. Applying our realist perspective, from the analysis of constraints imposed by international law and the comparative analysis of national laws, we identify flexibilities which may assist in protecting or potentially expanding national public domains. To the extent

---

[14] R. Giblin and K. Weatherall (eds.), *What If We Could Reimagine Copyright?* (Australian National University Press, 2017).

[15] Our approach has affinities with, but is not identical to, the 'legal realist' school of international law: see, for example, G. Shaffer, 'The new realist approach to international law' (2015) 28(2) *Leiden Journal of International Law* 189. It is also similar to that taken by the Australian Productivity Commission in its report on intellectual property (IP) arrangements, which acknowledged that law reform occurs in a 'constrained environment', including constraints arising from international IP law: Productivity Commission (Aus.), 'Intellectual property arrangements', Report 78 (23 September 2016), pp. 5–6.

## 1.5 A 'Realist' Perspective: Assumptions and Methodology

this book has a reformist agenda, therefore, it arises from the fact we consider that there are flexibilities, and that many countries fail to take advantage of the full range of opportunities for protecting the public domain. In Chapter 17 we therefore seek to identify the most prominent opportunities, and to recommend measures for enhancing the public domain.

We have not developed a new normative theory of the public domain, nor do we attempt to identify an optimal balance of rights and interests of creators, owners and users. Our 'realist' objectives are far more modest. We start from some assumptions, which we elaborate below. First, we endorse the view that the public domain is not merely what is left over after the exclusive rights are exhausted, but has positive value as an integral part of the copyright system, and which is as important as the exclusive rights of owners. Second, we reject a property-centric, or 'proprietarian' view of copyright, which automatically privileges exclusive rights over other rights and interests. Third, following from this, we argue that copyright law's focus on exclusive rights can reinforce proprietarianism and, as a result, obscure the importance of the public domain. Fourth, we contend that copyright law can be improved by more explicit recognition of the importance of the public domain, including in how the fifteen public domain categories we identify in this book are doctrinally defined. Fifth, however, applying a 'realist' perspective, we accept that reforms that will be appropriate must depend on the country, and detailed assessments of the balance of rights between creators, owners and users as applied to particular legal issues. As is clear from Parts II and III of the book, copyright law is an extraordinarily complex collection of specific doctrines and rules, most of which are more the product of history than principle. While we acknowledge that each issue, such as the scope and duration of rights, or the nature and extent of copyright exceptions, should be assessed on its merits, we argue that explicitly taking the public domain into account in copyright doctrines can improve both the clarity and substance of copyright laws. In short, our public domain perspective is meant as a corrective to one-sided proprietarianism and, taking the public domain into account can not only cast light on copyright law but assist in identifying approaches to law reform which appropriately ensure that public domain values are not overlooked. Therefore, while we do not attempt to formulate an optimal balance of rights and interests, this does not prevent us from suggesting how the law might look if the public domain is properly factored into the analysis. Moreover, unsurprisingly, to the extent that copyright law has been based on unbalanced proprietarianism, our perspective suggests that existing laws may be wanting inasmuch as they have failed to take the public domain seriously.

## 1.5.1 Methodology

Following from our 'realist' perspective, and the assumptions identified above, in this section we explain our essential methodology. Much of our approach builds upon the fundamental assumption that the public domain has positive value, and is the equal and opposite complement to the copyright proprietary domain. Applying our 'realist' approach, taking the law as it is, we systematically identify the fifteen legal categories of the public domain. In Part II, we explain how international copyright law establishes constraints on the public domain, and identify structural features of international copyright law that explain and condition these constraints. In this, our focus is firmly on the positive law; we do not purport to provide a political economy which explains how these structures have evolved. Given our limited objectives, and our realist perspective, we explain the consequences of international copyright law, but generally refrain from proposing reforms to international law.[16]

We then turn, in Part III, to national copyright laws, and engage in detailed comparative doctrinal analysis of each of the fifteen public domain categories in national laws. As copyright law has developed predominantly from the perspective of exclusive rights, it is inevitable that our treatment of international and national copyright laws often reads like a traditional exposition of copyright law, although we approach this through the lens of the public domain. Building on our exposition we therefore inject a public domain perspective into the analysis of each of the categories, explaining how public domain considerations may be relevant to doctrinal analysis. From this, we identify practical steps that can be taken to expand or protect public domains. Our guiding assumption throughout is that a thorough grounding in doctrinal law must provide the basis for copyright law reform. That said, we acknowledge that any legal and policy analysis necessarily implies some theoretical assumptions, and we therefore explain our baseline theoretical perspective in the section immediately following.

## 1.6 Copyright and the Public Domain: Theoretical Perspectives

The conventional approach to understanding copyright is first to justify exclusive rights, by reference to one or more theoretical paradigms such as

---

[16] There is no shortage of scholarly work proposing reforms to copyright law, often from a national perspective, but sometimes addressing international copyright law. For recent examples, see D. Gervais *(Re)structuring Copyright: A Comprehensive Path to International Copyright Reform* (Edward Elgar, 2017); Giblin and Weatherall (eds.), *What If We Could Reimagine Copyright?*

natural rights or instrumentalist approaches; then, from within that paradigm, establish the case for limits or exceptions to those rights. We, however, challenge this approach by placing the public domain at the centre of our analysis, or at least on an equal footing with exclusive rights. In general, however, we are agnostic about justifications for copyright law, as we do not see that it is necessary to resolve complex theoretical issues for the purpose of emphasising and clarifying the importance of the public domain, in accordance with the assumptions we have set out above. There are, nevertheless, some important qualifications to our theoretical agnosticism.

First, as we have foreshadowed, we reject 'proprietarianism', by which we mean the automatic privileging of property rights over all other rights and interests: [1.6.1]. Second, following from our agnostic approach, we accept the merits of theoretical pluralism, acknowledging, for example, the respective claims of natural rights, instrumentalist and critical perspectives.[17] Third, despite our theoretical pluralism, we are comfortable applying instrumentalism, which is the dominant theoretical approach to copyright: [1.6.2]. Fourth, we accept that approaches such as ours, which are aimed at preserving and extending the public domain, do necessarily entail a critical perspective on copyright law, as a corrective to unbridled proprietarianism. In acknowledging this, however, we accept that public domain theory cannot on its own provide a complete normative foundation for IPRs.[18] Fifth, in this book we argue that the essence of the public domain is the freedom and autonomy of users to use works for their own purposes, which underlies the diverse values the public domain supports: [1.6.3].

### 1.6.1 Against Proprietarianism

This book embraces the importance of a positive view of the public domain, and the diverse values which support the public domain: [1.7]. The starting point for much of our analysis is the rejection of 'proprietarianism', which we take to mean an approach that 'assigns to property rights a fundamental and entrenched status', so that property rights are automatically accorded normative priority over other rights and

---

[17] Our pluralistic approach is consistent with that proposed by Resnik, who has argued that no single theoretical perspective is adequate, and that intellectual property justifications must take into account a number of fundamental values: D. Resnik, 'A pluralistic account of intellectual property' (2003) 46 *Journal of Business Ethics* 319.

[18] See R. P. Merges, *Justifying Intellectual Property* (Harvard University Press, 2011), pp. 6–7 explaining the importance of the public domain and the difficulties in it forming the foundation of a coherent justification for IPRs.

interests.[19] As Drahos has pointed out, proprietarianism can draw equally from both natural rights and instrumentalist arguments, but without necessarily taking into account nuances of complex theoretical perspectives, with the result that it is not a theory so much as 'a creed and an attitude which inclines its holders towards a property fundamentalism'.[20] Proprietarianism as an ideology can result in kneejerk copyright 'maximalism', where any extension of IPRs is regarded as a good in itself.

The ideologies of proprietarianism and maximalism influenced the expansion of IPRs in the late twentieth and the twenty-first centuries; but these developments have been complex and, at least at the level of judicial decision-making, subject to countervailing forces.[21] Our fundamental point is that, even within dominant theoretical perspectives (as opposed to critical perspectives), it is impossible to justify unbridled proprietarianism and maximalism; and it is very difficult to find any theorists who support these perspectives.[22] While rejecting proprietarianism, however, we are not 'public domain maximalists', in that we accept that automatic privileging of the public domain may also amount to an unthinking fundamentalist ideology. Therefore, even within the scope that international copyright law allows for national public domains, we do not suggest it should automatically be exercised to the full. As we argue in [1.8] our view of copyright involves accepting that protection of both authors and users may promote the public interest. On the other hand, our public domain perspective, which necessarily involves rejecting the proprietarianist ideology, also means we are critical of laws and theories which overlook the importance of the public domain, or do not sufficiently take it into account.

### 1.6.2 Qualified Instrumentalism

This book is not aimed at justifying copyright. However, theory has an undeniable role in both justifying and critiquing the copyright system. Especially in common law jurisdictions, the dominant theoretical justification for copyright has been instrumentalist, couched in utilitarian terms

---

[19] P. Drahos, *A Philosophy of Intellectual Property* (Aldershot, 1996), pp. 200–3.
[20] *Ibid.* 201.
[21] See, for example, the recognition of copyright exceptions as users' rights by the Canadian Supreme Court in *CCH Canadian Ltd* v. *Law Society of Upper Canada* (2004) 1 RCS 339; 236 DLR (4th) 395, as discussed at [2.4].
[22] See, for example, Drahos, *A Philosophy of Intellectual Property*, 202, making much the same point.

## 1.6 Copyright and the Public Domain: Theoretical Perspectives

of maximising net social benefit by creating incentives for producing works, while also maximising access to and use of those works.[23]

Debates concerning foundational justifications of IPRs, such as the controversy generated by Merges' rejection of instrumentalist justifications and Lemley's critique of Merges' project of establishing a rights-based foundation,[24] are important. That said, we agree with those who argue that no single philosophical perspective is adequate to capture the complexity of copyright law.[25] While inevitably messy, a degree of methodological pluralism is, in our view, inescapable if we are to capture the full complexity of the interplay of rights and interests, involving authors, owners and users, that together comprises the copyright system. For example, in justifying the public domain, sometimes instrumentalist arguments emphasising the inefficiencies of over-propertising resources might be appropriate,[26] while at other times limitations on property rights might be justified by an appeal to a Rawlsian conception of 'fairness' or distributional justice.[27]

While remaining agnostic on theory, our 'realist' approach leans towards instrumentalism, first of all, because it is the dominant perspective in contemporary intellectual property public policy debates. For example, in Australia, a 2016 Productivity Commission report into the intellectual property (IP) system adopted an exclusively instrumentalist approach, starting from the proposition that '[t]he goal of IP policy should be to achieve a balance between the incentive to create and the risk of damaging the productive use of new ideas through overprotection'.[28] In our experience, most official policy documents overwhelmingly adopt instrumentalism.

Second, although convincing arguments supporting the public domain can be made from a natural rights perspective,[29] naive conceptions of copyright as a natural right of authors can easily lead to overbroad

---

[23] See Merges, *Justifying Intellectual Property*, 2; J. Hughes and R. P. Merges, 'Copyright and distributive justice' (2016) 92 *Notre Dame Law Review* 513 at 514; Resnik, 'A pluralist account of intellectual property', 323.

[24] Merges, *Justifying Intellectual Property*, 3; M. Lemley, 'Faith-based intellectual property' (2015) 62 *UCLA Law Review* 1328.

[25] See Resnik, 'A pluralist account of intellectual property'; R. Giblin and K. Weatherall, 'If we redesigned copyright from scratch, what might it look like?', in Giblin and Weatherall (eds.), *What If We Could Reimagine Copyright?*, 18.

[26] See, for example, M. Heller and R. Eisenberg, 'Can patents deter innovation? The anticommons in biomedical research' (1998) 280 *Science* 698.

[27] See Drahos, *A Philosophy of Intellectual Property*, 171 ff.; Resnik, 'A pluralist account of intellectual property', 329–30.

[28] Productivity Commission (Aus.), 'Intellectual property arrangements', 5.

[29] A. Drassinower, 'A rights-based view of the idea/expression dichotomy in copyright law' (2003) 16 *Canadian Journal of Law and Jurisprudence* 1 at 21.

proprietarianism. As Deazley, for example, has put it, the 'language of intellectual property *as natural property right* has provided one of the key foundations for the rampant expansionism which is the story of copyright law throughout the twentieth and into the twenty-first century'.[30] As a general proposition, therefore, we argue that restrictions on the public domain, including proposals to expand copyright protection, should be assessed by reference to their overall social benefit. While there are sometimes benefits in applying a rights-based analysis in evaluating copyright and the public domain, in general we consider public domain values may be best supported by an instrumentalist approach.

### 1.6.3 *Copyright and Negative Liberty: A User Perspective*

Copyright law consists of negative rights in the sense that they impose obligations on people not to do things: in short, not to copy (or distribute) protected works without permission. It prevents people from doing certain things with works, unless they have the permission of the rights holder. By conditioning uses of works on permission, copyright interferes with people's freedom to do things with works, or with their 'negative liberty'.[31] Moreover, copyright establishes these negative rights over 'information', which, once created, is an inexhaustible resource in that use by one person does not reduce the amount of the resource available for others.[32] As Drahos argues, the negative form of rights comprised in the copyright over a non-exhaustible resource is particularly significant as 'the pattern of interference that intellectual property rights set up in the lives of others is far greater than in the case of other kinds of rights'.[33] As we explain, the freedom (or autonomy) to do things with works lies at the heart of many of the diverse values that are supported by the public domain: [1.7].

Proprietarianism (or copyright maximalism) fails to factor in the effect of exclusivity on the negative liberties of users, and so is inimical to the public domain. As Benkler has pointed out, from the perspective of freedom of expression, a restriction on the public domain redistributes freedom in that '[i]t reduces the negative liberty of all those previously privileged to use information in a particular way in order to enhance the positive liberty – the capacity to govern the use of one's utterances – of the

---

[30] R. Deazley, *Rethinking Copyright: History, Theory, Language* (Edward Elgar, 2006), p. 152.
[31] See I. Berlin, 'Two concepts of liberty', in *Four Essays on Liberty* (Oxford University Press, 1969).
[32] This is known as non-rivalry in consumption.
[33] Drahos, *A Philosophy of Intellectual Property*, 211.

newly declared owner'.[34] Our positive view of the public domain expands this to encompass not merely expressive freedoms, but other forms of negative liberty, including the freedom to participate in cultural activities.

The positive view of the public domain as essential to the liberty or autonomy of people to do things with works has important implications for our definition of the public domain, which we propose in Chapter 2. Nevertheless, we acknowledge that an exclusive focus on individual freedom or autonomy, as a constraint on proprietary rights and as an expression of the positive values of the public domain, has limitations. Chander and Sunder, for example, argue that such a focus overlooks equality and distributional concerns, in that even if a resource is freely available it may not be able to be accessed and used by all, and there may be circumstances where restrictions on the public domain promote social equality.[35] Against this, however, we point out that no single view of the public domain, no more than a single theory of copyright, can hope to capture the full complexity of the role of copyright in our societies and economies. As explained further in Chapter 2, our focus in this book is on promoting positive uses of works by users, and not addressing social inequality: [2.2.3].

## 1.7 Public Domain Values

Why the public domain is important is indicated by surveying the values we regard as supporting it. Just as copyright may be supported by a diversity of values, so too is the public domain. However, the values identified as supporting the public domain inevitably depend upon the perspective adopted.[36]

From the 1990s, one main theme in public domain scholarship has been the importance of recognising it as an essential resource and, in doing so, rejecting the ideology of the 'romantic author', namely that authors are geniuses that 'create out of nothing'.[37] As Litman memorably put it, 'the very act of authorship in *any* medium is more akin to translation and recombination than it is to creating Aphrodite from the foam of

---

[34] Y. Benkler, 'Free as the air to common use: First Amendment constraints on enclosure of the public domain' (1999) 74 *New York University Law Review* 354 at 393.
[35] By, for example, conferring protection on traditional knowledge See A. Chander and M. Sunder, 'The romance of the public domain' (2004) 92 *California Law Review* 1331. See also, from a different perspective, Hughes and Merges, 'Copyright and distributive justice'.
[36] Samuelson, 'Enriching discourse on public domains', 826.
[37] J. Boyle, *Shamans, Software, and Spleens: Law and the Construction of the Information Society* (Harvard University Press, 1996), p. 52; Litman, 'The public domain'; Chander and Sunder, 'The romance of the public domain'.

the sea'.[38] Without supporting any particular theory of creativity, we agree that creation is a complex social practice involving multiple interrelations between authors, users and culture.[39] Likewise, the relationship between a user and a work is complex, sometimes involving the creative use of the work, sometimes involving consumptive uses of the work and, especially with technologically rich uses, often involving gradations between what Cohen defines as the 'romantic user' and the 'economic user'. We therefore agree with Cohen that 'if creative practice arises out of the interactions between authors and cultural environments... failure to explore the place of the user in copyright law is a critical omission'.[40]

While there are well-known limitations to an approach based on a model of autonomous, self-determining individuals, as outlined above, our main argument for supporting the public domain is the need to protect and enhance the negative liberties involved with use of works. At the heart of our conception of the public domain is the impossibility of drawing hard and fast distinctions between authors and users, as authors invariably draw on the public domain to produce new works. If copyright is aimed at promoting creativity, however defined, then the role of the public domain as the source of raw materials for new creations is as central to the creative process as the exclusive economic rights designed to spur creativity.[41] At the core of the values supporting the public domain, therefore, is its role in supporting authorship and as a building block for new creation and, accordingly, supporting a creative society.[42] Quite apart from 'creative' uses, access to and use of public domain information, such as facts or data, is a key element in generating new knowledge.[43] As Birnhack suggests, the public domain is 'where knowledge is created and where it lies awaiting new interpretations, new applications and new meanings'.[44]

The public domain (or the exercise of what we call 'public rights') is also an important means by which these values are advanced. As Cohen argues, the public domain is central to cultural practices, so, at a minimum, access to cultural material, whether works of high or mass

---

[38] Litman, 'The public domain', 966.
[39] J. Cohen, *Configuring the Networked Self: Law, Code, and the Play of Everyday Practice* (Yale University Press, 2012), pp. 63 ff.
[40] *Ibid.* 66.   [41] Litman, 'The public domain', 967.
[42] See Samuelson, 'Enriching public domains', 826; Benabou and Dusollier, 'Draw me a public domain', 172 (referring to the 'core element of the freedom to create').
[43] Samuelson, 'Enriching public domains', 826; Samuelson, 'Challenges in mapping the public domain', 22. J. Reichman and P. Uhler, 'A contractually reconstructed research commons for scientific data in a highly protectionist intellectual property environment' (2003) 66 *Law & Contemporary Problems* 315.
[44] M. Birnhack, 'More or better? Shaping the public domain', in Guibault and Hugenholtz (eds.), *The Future of the Public Domain*, 60.

## 1.7 Public Domain Values

culture, is essential to cultural participation.[45] Moreover, the public domain is a cornerstone of the central negative liberty of freedom of expression; without it people would be 'under a legally enforceable obligation not to speak except with the permission of someone else'.[46] Associated with this, free access to information, and freedom to communicate information and opinion, at a minimum concerning political matters, is essential to democratic processes, including the collective self-determination necessary for deliberative democracy.[47] A particular aspect of this is permission-free use of and access to information, such as legal or administrative information, necessary for the functions of government.[48] Use of and access to information, and more broadly creative works, is obviously essential to education[49] and, also, in promoting other important social objectives, such as public health and safety.[50] Overall, permission-free use of and access to works can be seen as promoting and enriching individual freedom and self-determination in a Millian sense of 'freedom to flourish'.[51]

This necessarily brief survey of public domain values is subject to important qualifications. First, as Benabou and Dusollier have pointed out, the distinct values or functions of the public domain are commonly intertwined:

> The journalist using a piece of information in a newspaper article is both acting as an author – freedom to create – and as a messenger of content – freedom of expression, access to culture, etc.[52]

Second, and more importantly, most of these values, including the negative liberties of freedom of expression and self-determination, are

---

[45] See Cohen, 'Copyright, commodification, and culture', *ibid.* See also T. Ochoa, 'Origins and meanings of the public domain' (2003) 28(2) *University of Dayton Law Review* 215.

[46] Benkler, 'Free as the air to common use', 358; D. Zimmerman, 'Is there a right to have something to say? One view of the public domain' (2004) 73 *Fordham Law Review* 297. Although copyright prohibits the use of expression, not ideas or facts, there are occasions, such as with photographs, where there is no good substitute for using expression.

[47] Birnhack, 'More or better?', 69 ff.

[48] See E. Lee, 'The public's domain: the evolution of legal restraints on the Government's power to control public access through secrecy or intellectual property' (2003) 55 *Hastings Law Journal* 91.

[49] Samuelson, 'Enriching discourse on public domains', 827.

[50] Samuelson, 'Challenges in mapping the public domain', 22.

[51] See P. Drahos, 'Freedom and diversity – a defence of the intellectual commons', in P. Jayanthi Reddy (ed.), *Creative Commons: International Perspectives* (ICFAI University Press, 2008–9), pp. 50–7; also at [2006] *Australasian Intellectual Property Law Resources* www.austlii.edu.au/au/other. On Mill's concept of self-determination, see, for example, W. Donner, 'Mill's utilitarianism', in J. Skorupski (ed.), *The Cambridge Companion to Mill* (Cambridge University Press, 1998).

[52] Benabou and Dusollier, 'Draw me a public domain', 172.

supported by the proprietary domain just as much as the public domain, especially in so far as the proprietary domain promotes the creation of new works and supports the autonomy and self-determination of authors. This qualification, that neither domain should be regarded as absolute, is expanded on in the next section of the chapter.

## 1.8  A Role for Copyright: Not a Rejection

Placing the public domain at the forefront of our analysis of copyright implies a critical perspective on copyright laws but, on the other hand, our realist approach means we accept the constraints imposed by international copyright law. In addition to this, despite our theoretical agnosticism: [1.6.2], we are convinced there are very good arguments for supporting copyright from both instrumentalist and rights-based perspectives. Furthermore, as Drassinower has argued, rights-based accounts of copyright may not only support authors' rights, but also support the public domain as a 'matter of inherent dignity'.[53]

Consequently, we do not argue against the default position of copyright law that requires permission for uses of copyright works that fall within the exclusive rights of copyright owners. In short, while completely rejecting proprietarianism: [1.6.1], we accept the role played by exclusive economic rights in protecting and promoting the interests of authors and of the creative industries and, with necessary qualifications, promoting the public interest. Moreover, conferring exclusive rights on authors to prevent permission-free uses of works, within limits, can promote the values of freedom and autonomy that, as we explain above, underpin the importance of the public domain: [1.6.3].

## 1.9  Jurisdictional Perspectives

As copyright law is inherently territorial, our doctrinal analysis inevitably deals with national legal traditions. In this section of the chapter, we therefore explain the main national copyright law traditions, and identify the jurisdictions we focus on in this book. We then explain the essential features of EU copyright law, an important and unique territorial jurisdiction, and the implications of EU law for UK copyright law, including the legal position following the UK decision to withdraw from the EU.

In this book, the term 'copyright' refers to what is commonly encompassed by that term in common law jurisdictions, but also to authors' rights (*droit d'auteur* in France and *Urheberrecht* in Germany) in civil law

---

[53] Drassinower, 'A rights-based view of the idea/expression dichotomy', 21.

1.9 Jurisdictional Perspectives

jurisdictions. The common law and civil law are often contrasted, with the common law approach to copyright being characterised as predominantly instrumentalist and aimed at promoting the public interest or social utility defined largely in economic terms, and the authors' rights approach being aimed at protecting the natural rights (or dignity) of authors in works as expressions of the 'inalienable personality of the author'.[54] There remains some truth in this broad contrast, with common law systems being focused on the copyright work as the object of protection and civil law systems on protecting the rights of authors (as expressed in the work). The distinction is also apparent in approaches to the protection of subject matter such as phonograms and broadcasts, which are produced by legal persons and not created by authors. As explained in Chapter 4, although common law systems protect subject matter such as this under copyright law, under civil law systems it cannot, by definition, be protected by authors' rights and is therefore protected as 'neighbouring or related rights'. For much of its history international copyright law was the result of compromises between the authors' rights tradition which, based on natural rights, tends towards a high level of protection, and the more pragmatic common law tradition.[55]

In practice, however, differences between the perspectives must not be overstated. The laws in both copyright and authors' rights jurisdictions have always incorporated elements of both instrumentalist and natural rights justifications.[56] It is, moreover, misleading to assume there is anything like a uniform authors' rights tradition, as there are important differences between the major civil law systems.[57] Furthermore, although there are differences in the philosophical justifications for protection, both traditions endorse significant limitations

---

[54] T. Dreier, 'Balancing proprietary and public domain interests: inside or outside of proprietary rights?', in R. Dreyfus, D. Zimmerman and H. First (eds.), *Expanding the Boundaries of Intellectual Property: Innovation Policy for the Knowledge Society* (Oxford University Press, 2001), p. 298. See also S. Ladas, *The International Protection of Literary and Artistic Property* (The Macmillan Company, 1938), pp. 1–12; A. Strowel, '*Droit d'auteur* and copyright: between history and nature', in B. Sherman and A. Strowel (eds.), *Of Authors and Origins: Essays on Copyright Law* (Clarendon Press, 1994), pp. 235 ff.; J. C. Ginsburg, 'A tale of two copyrights: literary property in revolutionary France and America' (1990) 64(5) *Tulane Law Review* 991.

[55] S. Ricketson and J. C. Ginsburg, *International Copyright and Neighbouring Rights: The Berne Convention and Beyond* (2nd edn, Oxford University Press, 2005), [2.03]–[2.04], [2.49].

[56] Ginsburg, 'A tale of two copyrights', 994–5; M. Senftleben, *Copyright, Limitations and the Three-Step Test: An Analysis of the Three-Step Test in International and EC Copyright Law* (Kluwer Law International, 2004), p. 10; E. Samuels, 'The public domain revisited' (2002) 36 *Loyola of Los Angeles Law Review* 389 at 397.

[57] Ricketson and Ginsburg, *International Copyright and Neighbouring Rights*, [2.03]; Ladas, *The International Protection of Literary and Artistic Property*, chap. 1.

and exceptions to authors' rights, as a result of pragmatic as well as theoretical considerations.[58]

The comparative legal analysis of the public domain categories in Part III of the book makes no attempt to be comprehensive in the jurisdictions covered. There is an emphasis on the common law jurisdictions of the United Kingdom, United States, Australia, and, to an extent, Canada. The laws of civil law jurisdictions, especially France and Germany, are also taken into account, particularly where there are important differences in approach (as is EU law, discussed immediately below). In addition, the analysis refers to other national jurisdictions as relevant, especially the important jurisdictions of China and India.

### 1.9.1 EU Harmonisation, the UK and Brexit

As a result of significant harmonisation that has occurred since the 1990s, it is impossible to consider the law of EU Member States, including the UK, without taking into account EU copyright law. As Hugenholtz explains, there have been three stages in the harmonisation of EU copyright law: harmonisation by directives (1991 to 2001); consolidation and harmonisation by 'soft law' (2001 to 2009); and harmonisation by activist judicial interpretation by the ECJ (post-2009).[59]

During 1991–2001, seven directives were adopted, most of which dealt with discrete areas, such as computer programs, rental and lending rights, and database protection.[60] The most important, the 2001 InfoSoc Directive, was intended to deal with copyright challenges of the 'digital agenda', including by harmonising basic economic rights, and introducing obligations relating to technological protection measures and rights management information. However, it went beyond this objective, particularly by introducing detailed provisions relating to exceptions: Chapters 11–14. Its breadth provided the basis for subsequent judicial harmonisation of principles of EU copyright law by the ECJ. Following this initial period, there were fewer legislative initiatives, with two further

---

[58] See, for example, Ricketson and Ginsburg, *International Copyright and Neighbouring Rights*, [13.01].

[59] P. B. Hugenholtz, 'Is harmonization a good thing? The case of the copyright *acquis*', in A. Ohly and J. Pila (eds.), *The Europeanization of Intellectual Property Law* (Oxford University Press, 2013), pp. 58–73.

[60] The seven EU directives (full titles and citations for which are in the Table of International Instruments) were: the Software Directive of 1991; the Rental and Lending Rights Directive of 1992; the Satellite and Cable Directive of 1993; the Term Directive of 1993; the Database Directive of 1996; the InfoSoc Directive of 2001; and the Resale Right Directive of 2001.

## 1.9 Jurisdictional Perspectives

directives, dealing with orphan works[61] and collective management of copyright in musical works for online uses,[62] being introduced in 2012 and 2014 respectively.

The Digital Single Market Strategy has recently resulted in renewed focus on legislative activity. In 2016, the European Commission issued proposals for two new directives and three regulations in what is known as the 'copyright package'. The most important is for a Directive on copyright in the Digital Single Market, which is intended to enhance cross-border access to copyright works in the EU and facilitate new uses in research and education by introducing new mandatory exceptions and measures to improve EU cross-border licensing.[63] Two parts of the package, a proposed directive and a proposed regulation, relate to the 2013 Marrakesh Treaty to assist Visually Impaired Persons.[64] Two further parts of the package are proposed regulations to prohibit unjustified geo-blocking in the internal market and to promote cross-border provision of services ancillary to broadcasts and facilitate digital retransmission.[65] As some proposals are controversial, at the time of writing it was unclear how they might fare in the EU legislative process.

In addition to applying to EU Member States, the main copyright directives extend to members of the European Economic Area (EEA), namely Iceland, Liechtenstein, Norway and Switzerland.[66] For the sake of simplicity, when this book refers to directives, it assumes they apply to

---

[61] The EU Orphan Works Directive of 2012.    [62] The EU CRM Directive of 2014.
[63] European Commission, Proposal for a Directive of the European Parliament and of the Council on copyright in the Digital Single Market, COM (2016) 593 final, Brussels, 14 September 2016.
[64] European Commission, Proposal for a Directive of the European Parliament and of the Council on certain permitted uses of works and other subject-matter protected by copyright and related rights for the benefit of persons who are blind, visually impaired or otherwise print disabled, COM (2016) 596 final, 14 September 2016; European Commission, Proposal for a Regulation of the European Parliament and of the Council on the cross-border exchange between the Union and third countries of accessible format copies of certain work and other subject-matter protected by copyright and related rights for the benefit of persons who are blind, visually impaired or otherwise print disabled, COM (2016) 595 final, 14 September 2016.
[65] European Commission, Proposal for a Regulation of the European Parliament and of the Council on addressing geo-blocking and other forms of discrimination based on customers' nationality, place of residence or place of establishment within the internal market, COM (2016) 289 final, 25 May 2016; European Commission, Proposal for a Regulation of the European Parliament and of the Council laying down rules on the exercise of copyright and related rights applicable to certain online transmissions of broadcasting organisations and retransmissions of television and radio programmes, COM (2016) 594 final, 14 September 2016.
[66] See Annex XVII to the EEA Agreement, discussed in S. von Lewinski, 'Introduction', in M. M. Walter and S. von Lewinski (eds.), *European Copyright Law: A Commentary* (Oxford University Press, 2010), [1.0.71] ff.

EEA members without expressly mentioning this, and it refers to the directives throughout as EU directives, regardless of when they were adopted.

The period 2001–2009 was marked by little EU copyright legislative activity, with the exception of a 2004 directive dealing with the enforcement of IPRs.[67] In 2009, however, in the landmark *Infopaq I* ruling, the ECJ initiated a new phase of judicial harmonisation, by interpreting the InfoSoc Directive as imposing a harmonised originality standard and a harmonised infringement standard.[68] This judicial harmonisation, which has resulted in a relatively 'thick' *acquis communautaire*, has been applied in subsequent ECJ rulings,[69] and extended to a harmonised interpretation of what is meant by the exclusive right of public communication.[70]

The combination of EU legislation and judicial harmonisation by the ECJ limits the scope for EU Member States to adjust their copyright laws, and therefore define their own national public domains. This is especially important as, in general, harmonisation requires a 'high level' of protection with, for example, Recital (9) to the InfoSoc Directive providing that 'harmonisation of copyright and related rights must take as a basis a high level of protection, since such rights are crucial to intellectual creation'.[71] Moreover, judicial harmonisation, in the interpretation of EU directives, incorporates the EU human rights framework, with Article 17(2) of the Charter of Fundamental Rights of the European Union providing, without apparent qualification, that 'intellectual property shall be protected'.[72] Although the rights granted under the Charter are not absolute, any limitations on the rights must be proportionate, must be provided by law and must respect the essence of those rights.[73] Nevertheless, as harmonisation of EU copyright law is far from complete,

---

[67] The EU Enforcement Directive of 2004.
[68] Case C-5/08, *Infopaq International A/S* v. *Danske Dagblades Forening*, [2009] ECR I-6569 ('*Infopaq I*').
[69] See Case C-393/09, *Bezpecnostni Softwarova Asociace – Svaz Softwarove Ochrany* v. *Ministerstvo Kultury*, [2010] ECR I-13971; Case C-145/10, *Eva-Maria Painer* v. *Standard Verlags GmbH* [2011] ECR I-12533; Case C-604/10, *Football Dataco Ltd* v. *Yahoo! UK Ltd*, [2012] 2 CMLR 703.
[70] See Case C-30605, *Sociedad General de Autores y Editores de España (SGAE)* v. *Rafael Hoteles SL*, [2006] ECR I-11519 and subsequent cases, discussed at [10.2.6].
[71] In *Infopaq I*, the ECJ identified this as the main objective of the InfoSoc Directive: *Infopaq I* at [40].
[72] The EU Charter of 2010, Art. 17(2). See C. Geiger, 'Intellectual property shall be protected? – Article 17(2) of the Charter of Fundamental Rights of the European Union: a mysterious provision with an unclear scope' (2009) 31(3) *European Intellectual Property Review* 113.
[73] EU Charter, Art. 52(1); M. M. Walter, 'Fundamental rights', in Walter and von Lewinski (eds.), *European Copyright Law: A Commentary*, chap. 4.

there remain important variations in the laws of EU Member States, which are referred to in this book where relevant.

In June 2016, a majority of British voters in a referendum supported the UK leaving the EU. In March 2017, following passage of the European Union (Notification of Withdrawal) Act 2017 (UK), the UK formally invoked Article 50(2) of the Treaty on European Union, which initiated a two-year period of negotiating the conditions for withdrawing from the EU.[74] In March 2017, the UK published a White Paper, which explained that the status of EU law in the UK would be dealt with by the 'Great Repeal Bill', which would convert EU law into UK domestic law.[75] Amongst other things, the Bill proposes to preserve the rights conferred under EU treaties and provide that historical ECJ case law has the same precedential value as decisions of the UK Supreme Court. Furthermore, the Bill provides for delegated legislation to correct statutes to rectify problems arising from leaving the EU. The consequence of EU copyright law being converted into domestic law is that the supremacy of EU law over UK law will cease, and the UK Parliament will be able to repeal or amend EU law. For example, the UK could enact a copyright exception along the lines of the US fair use exception, which might not be permissible under the InfoSoc Directive.[76] In relation to the package of proposed EU law reforms referred to above, if EU regulations are introduced during the negotiation period, they will become part of UK law, and the UK might be required to implement directives during the two-year period. As much of EU copyright law seems likely to remain in place for a period following its proposed conversion into UK domestic law, this book adopts an approach of first explaining relevant EU copyright law before turning to how EU law has been implemented in the UK, which remains valid for the immediate future.

## 1.10 Conclusion

In this chapter, we have explained that we reject a purely negative view of the public domain as what is left over after the exclusive rights are exhausted and adopt a positive view, in which the public domain is the

---

[74] See Prime Minister's letter to European Council President Donald Tusk, 29 March 2017 www.gov.uk/government/uploads/system/uploads/attachment_data/file/604079/Prime_Ministers_letter_to_European_Council_President_Donald_Tusk.pdf.
[75] Department for Exiting the European Union, Legislating for the United Kingdom's withdrawal from the European Union, Cm 9446 (2017). The European Union (Withdrawal) Bill 2017 (UK) was introduced to the House of Commons on 13 July 2017.
[76] R. Arnold, L. A. F. Bently, E. Derclaye and G. B. Dinwoodie, 'The legal consequences of Brexit through the lens of IP law' (2017) 101(2) *Judicature*, available at https://papers.ssrn.com/sol3/papers.cfm?abstract_id=2917219.

equal and opposite complement of copyright's exclusive rights. In sum, we claim that the orthodox textbook approach of focusing on exclusive property rights can lead to an unbalanced view of copyright, and tend to overbroad proprietarianism. While we make no claim to advancing the theoretical foundations of copyright – accepting a pluralist perspective, but also qualifiedly supporting an instrumentalist approach – we argue that putting the public domain in the foreground allows us to elucidate issues and considerations that are neglected by the orthodox approach. Nevertheless, we reject the simplistic assumption of a sharp opposition between authors and users, agreeing with Drassinower that 'what matters is not that we take sides in the opposition of author and public but that we seek discursive possibilities that grasp the conditions of their co-existence as aspects of a single system'.[77] Accepting that both authors and users promote the public interest, and accepting the complexities involved in analysing the interactions between authors, owners and users, our main goal is to promote understanding of the copyright system as a whole. We therefore come not to bury copyright, but to praise the public domain as an essential part of the copyright system, and to promote discussion by systematic exploration of the legal implications of a public domain perspective, in a level of detail not previously attempted.

[77] A. Drassinower, 'Taking user rights seriously', in M. Geist (ed.), *In the Public Interest: The Future of Canadian Copyright Law* (Irwin Law, 2005), p. 479 n. 42.

# 2 A Definition of the Copyright Public Domain

2.1 Introduction: Towards a Definition of the Copyright
    Public Domain                                              27
2.2 Expanding the Definition's Scope                           33
2.3 A Proposed Definition                                      40
2.4 Further Terminological Issues                              47
2.5 Conclusion                                                 53

## 2.1 Introduction: Towards a Definition of the Copyright Public Domain

This chapter defines the copyright public domain, as a basis for identifying its categories. A great deal of effort is spent defending the public domain, or advocating its expansion, but with insufficient clarity about what is being defended or advocated, with participants in debates often at cross-purposes. A sound basis for determining what is within, and what is outside, the copyright public domain requires a definition that is based on the values which support it: [1.7]. This chapter proposes and justifies our definition, and the associated concept of 'public rights'.

It is then possible comprehensively to identify and define fifteen categories of the copyright public domain, based on our analysis of national public domains in the jurisdictions studied in this book: [1.9]. Our methodology in identifying public domain categories is grounded in doctrinal analysis of laws in selected jurisdictions: [1.5.1]. Our categories are therefore based upon a 'best endeavours' strategy, where there is always scope for refinement. But a definition must come first.

### 2.1.1 Early Approaches to Definition

Since David Lange stated in 1981 that 'the public domain tends to appear amorphous and vague, with little more of substance in it than is invested in patriotic or religious slogans on paper currency',[1] many supporters of the public domain have refrained from defining it, or not been precise about its contents.[2] Especially in the early literature, we find elusive statements such as: 'the public domain ... delineates an important sphere in which the people have equal rights, and ultimate power, over information, ideas and knowledge';[3] 'the public domain would be a place like home, where, when you go there, they have to take you in and let you dance'[4] and 'a sanctuary confirming affirmative protection against the forces of private appropriation'.[5] Often more attention has been paid to the rhetoric of the 'public domain' than to explaining what it means in both theory and practice.[6] Significantly more attention has, however, been given to definitional issues since the 2001 Duke Law School conference on the public domain: [1.2].

### 2.1.2  One Definition or Many

In 2001, Samuelson noted that the public domain had, until then, been almost completely 'uncharted'.[7] Based on a traditional negative definition of the public domain as 'a sphere in which contents are free from intellectual property rights',[8] she proposed a 'map' of its contents.[9] Responding to criticisms,[10] Samuelson subsequently proposed a non-US-centric map, while noting that significant differences between national laws 'makes international map-making of the public domain a significant challenge'.[11] We agree it is challenging, but are assisted by aspects of our approach differing from Samuelson's.

First, unlike Samuelson, we do not define the public domain as content that is free of any intellectual property right (IPR), but we confine ourselves to the copyright public domain. While the content we define as being in the public domain may remain protected by trade mark or patent law, this disadvantage is outweighed by a more precise focus on copyright law. We therefore agree with Deazley, who also confined his focus to copyright, concluding that a more accurate or precise picture of the public

---

[1] Lange, 'Recognizing the public domain', 177.   [2] Deazley, *Rethinking Copyright*, 103.
[3] Lee, 'The public domain', 119.   [4] Lange, 'Reimagining the public domain', 470.
[5] *Ibid.* 466, 470.
[6] This rhetorical basis is well argued in Boyle, 'The second enclosure movement', 68.
[7] Samuelson, 'Mapping the digital public domain', 148.   [8] *Ibid.* 149.   [9] *Ibid.* 151.
[10] Samuelson, 'Challenges in mapping the public domain'. In this refinement, she identified seven distinct definitions of the public domain, which could be matched to seven variations of her initial map, and which illustrated how her basic schema could be adapted to apply to different definitions.
[11] *Ibid.* 12.

## 2.1 Introduction

domain can be obtained from separately analysing what it means for distinct IPRs.[12] Since our objective is to analyse the implications of the public domain specifically for our understanding of copyright law, a broader focus on all IP law would render the analysis too diffuse. Instead, we take into account restrictions imposed under other areas of the law, including IP laws such as trade mark or confidentiality law, as constraints which may restrict the effectiveness of the copyright public domain: [6.3.4].

Second, Samuelson says her non-US-centric map may present the public domain at too high a level of generality.[13] While we propose a highly abstract general definition of the copyright public domain, we identify the detailed categories of the public domain in the next chapter. In Part III we examine the precise contents, under national laws, of each category. So our analysis does not remain at a level of generality.

While Samuelson initially supported a single definition, Boyle argued that there are many 'public domains', which reflect different theories of the public domain.[14] According to Boyle, '[t]he public domain will change its shape according to the hopes it embodies, the fears it tries to lay to rest, and the implicit vision of creativity on which it rests'.[15] Samuelson subsequently took up this challenge by identifying thirteen distinct conceptions of the public domain in the literature,[16] but with some overlaps between the conceptions.[17] While Samuelson's strategy of applying different terms to distinguish different public domain definitions has some value,[18] it does not resolve the problem of potential confusion engendered by different definitions. It also fails to deal with the need for an overarching definition that can unify different aspects or categories of the copyright public domain, and provide the basis for systematically investigating the legal contents of the categories.

We do, however, agree that the public domain can be seen as a cluster of related concepts (not necessarily one single concept) and accept there are significant challenges in proposing a single, all-purpose definition.

---

[12] Deazley, *Rethinking Copyright*, 105–6.
[13] Samuelson, 'Challenges in mapping the public domain', 11.
[14] Boyle, 'The second enclosure movement', 68–9.   [15] *Ibid.* 62.
[16] Samuelson, 'Enriching discourse on public domains'; Boyle, 'The second enclosure movement', 59–62.
[17] Samuelson, 'Enriching discourse on public domains', 816 ff. Noting overlaps between the definitions, Samuelson further identified three clusters or foci: the legal status of information resources (that is, whether the resource is free from intellectual property rights); freedoms to use information resources (that is, permissible uses of resources that are protected by intellectual property law); and the accessibility of information resources (which takes into account the extent to which, for example, unpublished information may be inaccessible).
[18] *Ibid.*

That said, we believe there is much to be gained, especially in analytical clarity, from a 'working' definition, which enables us to distinguish between what is and is not a part of the public domain. By 'working' definition, we mean no more than a definition that is adapted to the purpose of our analysis. Although we support the usefulness of a single definition, this does not mean we discount the advantages of pluralistic accounts, or multiple definitions, as suggested by both Samuelson and Boyle.

Our approach conceives the copyright public domain, in Wittgenstein-influenced terms, as a web of related concepts with 'family resemblances' between different aspects of the public domain.[19] In this chapter we propose a definition that unifies different concepts of the copyright public domain, with the 'family' of related concepts being identified in the next chapter as distinct public domain categories. Accordingly, on our approach, there is a single 'copyright public domain' which can be satisfactorily defined (for our purposes), but which consists of a network of related concepts, with somewhat 'fuzzy' boundaries between the copyright proprietary domain and each of these categories. The copyright public domain can only be completely understood by disaggregating it into its component legal categories. To clarify our terminology further, when we refer to 'copyright public domains' in this book we are not referring to different conceptions of the public domain, but to differences in national public domains: [1.3]–[1.4].

### 2.1.3 A Positive Definition

Traditional definitions of the public domain define it in negative terms as that which is not protected by IPRs or, more narrowly, copyright.[20] In a 2011 study of the public domain prepared for WIPO, for example, Dusollier adopted a negative definition, but also acknowledged that 'any attempts to assess the value of the public domain should go further and focus on what could positively define the public domain, i.e. the free use of the elements contained therein and the absence of an exclusivity in such elements'.[21] This book takes up this challenge by proposing a positive account of the public domain, regarding it as

---

[19] L. Wittgenstein, *Philosophical Investigations*, tr. G. Anscomb (3rd edn, Blackwell, 1973). For a similar approach to the concept of 'privacy', see D. Solove, 'Conceptualizing privacy' (2002) 90 *California Law Review* 1088.
[20] Deazley, *Rethinking Copyright*, 104.
[21] S. Dusollier, 'Scoping study on copyright and related rights and the public domain', WIPO, 30 April 2011 www.wipo.int/edocs/mdocs/mdocs/en/cdip_7/cdip_7_inf_2.pdf (p. 6).

2.1 Introduction 31

the complete and equal complement to the copyright proprietary domain: [1.3].

On our analysis, our positive account reflects the positive values which support the copyright public domain. Those values include, but are not limited to, the freedom to access and use works for the purposes of: creating new works, exercising freedom of expression, including freedom of political expression, and, more broadly, participating in cultural practices, and promoting autonomy and self-determination: [1.7].

The first part of our proposed definition therefore means rejecting negative definitions of the public domain, and defining it positively in terms of the freedom (or negative liberty) to use 'works' (as we use that term in this book, to refer to all content and/or information resources): [1.6.3].

### 2.1.4 Freedom to Use Works without Permission

If the public domain is defined by reference to the freedom of users to use works, this raises questions about exactly what is meant by 'freedom' in this context.[22] We answer this question by proposing that it is use that is not subject to permission from another. The second part of our definition of the copyright public domain, which is the touchstone of our working definition, is therefore that it includes works that are free to be used without permission.[23] This understanding of 'freedom' was well captured by Lessig, who expressed it as follows:

> [The] 'public domain' is free.... It is also, and distinctly, 'permission free'. I do not need the permission of Disney to copy the ideas in *Steamboat Willie*. Nor do I need its permission to make a 'fair use' of its foundational character. In this sense, a resource is 'permission free' if the right to use the resource does not depend upon anyone's subjective will.[24]

Applying a traditional, negative definition results in a focus on material that is not protected by copyright, namely works in which copyright has expired, or unprotectable ideas or facts, which together comprise what Samuelson refers to as 'the public domain of the ineligibles and the expireds'.[25] Defining the public domain by reference to whether use is

---

[22] Boyle, 'The second enclosure movement', 57–8.
[23] In this, we agree with Deazley: see Deazley, *Rethinking Copyright*, 107.
[24] L. Lessig, 'Re-crafting a public domain' (2006) 18 *Yale Journal of Law & the Humanities* 56 at 57.
[25] Samuelson, 'Enriching discourse on public domains', 790. Chander and Sunder refer to this as the 'crumbs theory' – that 'the public domain consists in the scraps left over after property rights have consumed their share': 'The romance of the public domain', 1337.

conditioned on permission, however, means that it includes more than just content not protected by copyright, but extends to all uses of copyright-protected works that do not require permission. As Benabou and Dusollier explained this point, 'the freedom to copy entailed by the public domain occurs at different places within the copyright regime, not only outside its scope of protection but also within the rules of protection itself'.[26]

Litman, in her influential 1990 article: [1.2], was one of the first to extend the concept of the public domain beyond unprotected works, defining it to mean a 'commons that includes those aspects of copyrighted works which copyright does not protect',[27] as a prerequisite for creative practices. This expansive definition followed from her understanding of the public domain as a source for creative appropriation meaning that, as Boyle later put it, 'the public domain includes the recyclable, unprotected elements in existing copyrighted works as well as those works that are not protected at all'.[28]

This formulation, however, begs questions about what is meant by the unprotected elements of copyright works including, importantly, whether or not this includes exceptions to exclusive rights. Benkler, for example, defined the copyright public domain more precisely than Litman as 'the range of uses of information that any person is privileged to make absent individualized facts that make a particular use by a particular person unprivileged'.[29] Applying this relatively broad definition, he was able to incorporate permission-free uses of copyright works, such as short quotations of texts or lending a book to a friend. But, where the law is unclear, how does a user know if they are free to use a resource? Benkler addressed this by confining his definition to permissible uses that are 'easy cases', meaning that he excludes uses that might fall within the US fair use exception, but whether or not they are permissible can only be ascertained after a detailed inquiry concerning individualised facts.[30] Subsequently, Deazley characterised this distinction as one between the public domain and the perceived public domain.[31]

On this issue, we agree with Deazley's criticism of Benkler's approach: if the public domain includes only uses that are 'easy cases', where it is clear that a use is permitted, then it must equally exclude material falling within traditional negative definitions as, for example, it is often notoriously difficult to distinguish ideas from expression. Moreover, as Deazley points out, users' perceptions do not alter the legal reality as to whether or

[26] Benabou and Dusollier, 'Draw me a public domain', 172.
[27] Litman, 'The public domain', 968.   [28] Boyle, 'The second enclosure movement', 61.
[29] Benkler, 'Free as the air to common use', 361–2.   [30] *Ibid.* 362.
[31] Deazley, *Rethinking Copyright*, 120.

not a use is permitted, and may depend on the level of public education of what is or is not permitted by copyright.[32]

## 2.2 Expanding the Definition's Scope

Building on the above elements, we define the copyright public domain to include all uses of works that do not require the permission of the copyright owner. At a minimum, this extends beyond works not protected by copyright to include permissible uses of copyright-protected works, including uses falling outside of the exclusive rights.[33] Accepting this general approach, however, we then need to ask more systematically, what is the full scope of the definition? The following analysis addresses four specific issues: exceptions to copyright protection; access as distinct from use; remunerated uses; and uses allowed under licences.

### 2.2.1 Inclusion of Exceptions in the Copyright Public Domain

Those, such as Samuels, who support a traditional, negative view of the public domain regard copyright exceptions as concessions to exclusive rights that recognise a public interest in particular uses, and not as part of the public domain.[34] For the study on the public domain prepared for WIPO, as indicated above, Dusollier adopted a traditional definition, and specifically rejected the inclusion of exceptions. She argued that this would create two separate copyright public domains involving, first, material clearly not protected by copyright and, second, material whose free use depends upon the circumstances, such as material falling within an exception.[35] Dusollier further identified three main differences between the public domain, as traditionally defined, and copyright exceptions which she claimed justified excluding exceptions while the public domain is free for anyone, exceptions are generally limited to certain classes of uses or contexts; while the traditional public domain consists of what is not protected by copyright, exceptions are permissible generally only where there is a public interest that outweighs exclusivity, such as where consistent with the application of the three-step test under international copyright law; and the traditional public domain is relatively settled, whereas copyright exceptions are based on policy decisions that are unsettled at an international level.[36]

---

[32] *Ibid.* 120–1.
[33] For a similar approach, see Benabou and Dusollier, 'Draw me a public domain', 173.
[34] E. Samuels, 'The public domain in copyright law' (1993) 41 *Journal of the Copyright Society of the USA* 137 at 166–7.
[35] Dusollier, 'Scoping study on the public domain', 8–9.   [36] *Ibid.* 9.

We disagree with each of these points. First, if, as we argue, the public domain is based upon freedom to use works, this objective can still be furthered by permission-free uses that are not available to everyone, provided that the use is available to a significant section of the public and there is no discrimination between users entitled to the use. On this, Dusollier herself agrees that the traditional public domain and copyright exceptions have similar objectives and justifications, as they both promote practices such as creative and cultural activities.[37]

Second, as with our rejection of Benkler's limitation of the public domain to exceptions that are 'easy cases', merely because some evaluation is required to determine whether or not a use is permitted should not exclude it from the public domain, as accepting this argument would also exclude elements traditionally accepted as part of the public domain, such as ideas or facts. Our central argument is that it is whether or not permission is required to use a work that is determinative; in this, a requirement that a use must also satisfy a public interest test, such as might be applied in determining if it is a fair use or fair dealing, is irrelevant.

Third, although there is admittedly limited harmonisation of copyright exceptions at the international level, we explain throughout this book that there are also significant national variations in most other elements of the copyright public domain. It is not at all clear why a working definition of the public domain should require universal agreement on exceptions, particularly when public domains are nationally based. Overall, on our view, Dusollier's justifications for excluding exceptions from the public domain do not withstand scrutiny.[38]

### 2.2.2 Permission-Free Access?

In our argument so far, we have not clearly distinguished between permission-free access and permission-free use.

Copyright consists of exclusive rights over the use of copyright works, and therefore does not include an access right.[39] As Deazley points out, however, a use may fall within the copyright public domain, in that permission is not required for the use, but it is impossible for the use to

---

[37] Ibid. 8.
[38] They also do not seem consistent with Dusollier's earlier co-authored work which specifically concluded that the public domain could include exceptions to exclusive rights: Benabou and Dusollier, 'Draw me a public domain', 173.
[39] Although laws prohibiting the circumvention of technological protection measures (TPMs) may come close to conferring a de facto access right: J. C. Ginsburg, 'From having copies to experiencing works: the development of an access right in US copyright law' (2003) 50 *Journal of the Copyright Society of the USA* 113.

## 2.2 Expanding the Definition's Scope

be exercised as the work is not publicly accessible.[40] For example, copyright may have expired in a work, such as a diary, but it may be impossible for the work to be used because it has not been published. Deazley therefore drew a conceptual distinction between the copyright public domain of works (published and unpublished) and the 'intellectual commons', which includes only works that have been made public.[41]

Issues relating to access to unpublished works are concerned more with areas of the law other than copyright, such as confidentiality law. As our analysis is confined to copyright law, we agree with Deazley that the copyright public domain should be limited to permission-free use and not extend to permission-free access. On our approach, however, issues concerning difficulties in accessing a work, making it impossible for the work to be used, are best taken into account in assessing elements outside of copyright law that support or constrain the public domain's effectiveness: Chapter 6.

### 2.2.3 Permitted Uses that Require Payment: Compulsory Licences

If, as we argue, the public domain is defined by reference to freedom to use works without permission, the question arises as to whether it extends to uses that do not need permission, but require payment. After all, a requirement for payment may, in practice, restrict the extent to which a particular user is able to use a work. This issue has divided public domain scholars.

In what is known as a liability rule, as opposed to a property rule, under copyright compulsory licences there is no need for permission to use works, but users must pay fair compensation for uses restricted by copyright.[42] According to Benkler, to form part of the public domain a use must be 'free' both in the sense that permission is not required, and in the sense that it involves no payment.[43] Similarly, arguing against the 'romantic' assumption of public domain supporters that merely because use of a resource is permitted it will be used equally by all, Chander and Sunder defined the public domain as:

> Resources for which legal rights to access and use for free (or for nominal sums) are held broadly.[44]

---

[40] Deazley, *Rethinking Copyright*, 107–9. For the importance of accessibility to information in the context of the public domain, see E. Lee, 'The public's domain'.
[41] Deazley, *Rethinking Copyright*, 110.
[42] G. Calabresi and A. Melamed, 'Property rules, liability rules, and inalienability: one view of the cathedral' (1972) 85 *Harvard Law Review* 1089.
[43] Boyle, 'The second enclosure movement', 61–2.
[44] Chander and Sunder, 'The romance of the public domain', 1338.

This definition reflected their analysis that differential access to resources, including resources in the public domain, can reinforce inequality.[45]

Lessig, on the other hand, defined the commons as a resource that is free, in the sense of being open to all and not in the sense of requiring no payment, explaining that:

> By a commons I mean a resource that is free. *Not necessarily zero cost, but if there is a cost, it is a neutrally imposed cost or equally imposed cost.* ... The point is not that no control is present; but rather that the kind of control is different from the control we grant to property.[46]

As Boyle has pointed out, the approach taken to this issue depends upon how freedom to use a work is understood: if it is viewed as a negative freedom from constraints imposed by others, then the objective of non-discriminatory use is not compromised by a requirement for payment, but if it is interpreted as a positive freedom, then payment is a constraint.[47] If multiple values support the public domain – including creative uses of public domain materials, freedom of expression, and freedom to engage in cultural practices: [1.7] – at least some of these values are promoted by a view of the public domain as freedom from constraints, regardless of whether or not payment is required. For example, as Boyle argues, liability rules may promote innovation or creativity by restricting control arising from monopoly power.[48] Furthermore, as Benabou and Dusollier point out, payment may support the public domain by creating an incentive to invest in providing access or preserving public domain works.[49]

We consider that the public domain should support the negative liberty to use works without permission: [1.6.3]. We have not addressed considerations of social inequality, not because these issues are unimportant but because our focus is on promoting positive uses, especially creative uses. Our definition therefore includes uses where permission is not required, even though payment may be required, provided that the terms of remunerated use, including price, are ultimately determined by a 'neutral party', not by the copyright owners or their representatives, and are on equal terms for all licensees. Furthermore, remunerated uses play

---

[45] Chander and Sunder argue that the focus of public domain advocates on liberty 'elides equality concerns, specifically the just distribution of wealth and cultural power': *ibid.* 1334.
[46] L. Lessig, 'The architecture of innovation' (2002) 51 *Duke Law Journal* 1783 at 1788 (emphasis in original).
[47] Boyle, 'The second enclosure movement', 63.   [48] *Ibid.* 64.
[49] Benabou and Dusollier, 'Draw me a public domain', 182–3. The public domain may also therefore include the *domaine public payant,* under which a fee is paid for use of material in the public domain, with the amounts being used for cultural purposes.

## 2.2 Expanding the Definition's Scope

a large role in practice alongside unremunerated exceptions to copyright, and it would therefore be artificial to exclude them from our treatment of exceptions: Chapters 13 and 14.

### 2.2.4 The Contractually Constructed Public Domain: Voluntary Neutral Licences

So far, our definition of the public domain has focused on works that are not protected by copyright and uses of works that do not require permission, as determined by the internal limits of copyright law. Since the 1990s, new models of use of information resources have emerged in the form of free or open source software (FOSS), Creative Commons, and similar licences: Chapter 15. Their emergence inspired much of the renewed interest in the public domain.[50] On these models, private ordering, in the form of contractually imposed restrictions which are based on copyright law, is used to promote use. For instance, the General Public License (GPL) gives any person permission to use software code, including to add to or modify it, provided that similar use conditions apply to (or 'run' with) any derivative works produced under the licence.[51] Similarly, Creative Commons licences effectively allow copyright owners contractually to 'waive' rights to control works conferred by copyright law, thereby promoting access and use.

The innovation behind these models was to use legal restrictions on freedom to promote freedom. Under these models, therefore, restraints imposed under contracts and copyright law are employed to promote freedom to use information resources. As Boyle explained, innovations such as open source software challenged the traditional dichotomy between intellectual property and the public domain:

> The old dividing line in the literature on the public domain had been between the realm of property and the realm of the free. The new dividing line, drawn on the palimpsest of the old, is between the realm of individual control and the realm of distributed creation, management, and enterprise.[52]

This paradigm shift derived from a fundamental rethinking of the management of resources held in common associated with Ostrom's work on the political economy of the commons.[53] In a critical distinction, Ostrom

---

[50] Boyle, 'The second enclosure movement', 64.
[51] R. P. Merges, 'A new dynamism in the public domain' (2004) 71 *University of Chicago Law Review* 183; Y. Benkler, 'Coase's penguin or, Linux and the nature of the firm' (2002) 112 *Yale Law Journal* 369.
[52] Boyle, 'The second enclosure movement', 66.
[53] E. Ostrom, *Governing the Commons: The Evolution of Institutions for Collective Action* (Cambridge University Press, 1990).

distinguished between public goods, such as lighthouses, in which it is difficult to exclude users of the light, but one person's use does not subtract from another's, from common pool resources, like irrigation systems or libraries, where it is also difficult to exclude users but one person's use does subtract from another's.[54] Ostrom further distinguished open access regimes, where no one has a legal right to exclude others from a resource, from common property regimes, where members of a defined group have a bundle of legal rights over a resource, including the right to exclude.[55] The central insight derived from this distinction is that, contrary to theories of the 'tragedy of the commons',[56] which posit that private property rights are the only solution to over-use or under-use of resources held in common, common pool resources can be managed by a common property regime that allows for collective control of shared resources.[57]

If the public domain is defined in purely negative terms as freedom from IPRs, uses permitted under contractual regimes, such as free and open source software (FOSS) licences, would not be part of the public domain as they depend upon works being protected by copyright.[58] Similarly, if the public domain is defined purely as a realm of absolute freedom, in opposition to the realm of control that is the private property regime, then regimes such as open source software do not fit easily within the public domain, as they depend upon the ongoing control of the resource that is conferred by copyright.[59] As opposed to this, contractually constructed access and use regimes, such as FOSS licences, can be regarded as forms of privately managed common resources. For this reason, theorists of open innovation, such as Lessig, have referred to these regimes as part of the 'commons' rather than using the term 'public domain'.[60] As explained further below, however, the legal literature on the 'commons' tended to use the term loosely, including as a synonym for the public domain, leading Hess and Ostrom to argue for greater 'clarity, shared meanings, and a common language to research this area better'.[61]

On our approach, which views the public domain from a user's perspective, it is the freedom to use a work without permission that is

---

[54] C. Hess and E. Ostrom, 'Ideas, artefacts, and facilities: information as a common pool resource' (2003) 66 *Law and Contemporary Problems* 111 at 120.
[55] *Ibid.* 121–2.   [56] G. Hardin, 'The tragedy of the commons' (1968) 162 *Science* 1243.
[57] C. Rose, 'The comedy of the commons: custom, commerce, and inherently public property' (1986) 53 *University of Chicago Law Review* 711.
[58] Samuelson, 'Enriching discourse on public domains', 799.
[59] Boyle, 'The second enclosure movement', 64–5.
[60] Lessig, 'The architecture of innovation'.
[61] Hess and Ostrom, 'Ideas, artefacts, and facilities', 114.

## 2.2 Expanding the Definition's Scope

important, and not whether the source of the freedom is a legal limitation on copyright law, such as a copyright exception, or private ordering by means of a copyright licence. Similarly, from the perspective of the copyright owner, once a regime such as a FOSS licence is in place, any ability to exclude users from the resource is lost. While it is true that use of the resource is subject to restrictions, in that users must agree not to privatise or (under some licences) commercialise the resource, this is not a condition that prevents use of the resource for purposes within the licence, which often includes creating new works. By analogy with compulsory licences, the agreement to comply with the licence condition may be interpreted as the price that is paid to use the work.

Deazley raised a significant issue about 'permission' when noting that materials covered by such licences 'only reside within the public domain as a result of a wide-ranging *a priori* permission – there is no need to ask for permission to use, as permission has already been granted'.[62] Unlike any other public domain category (except voluntary relinquishment of copyright), voluntary licensing involves a positive consensual act by a copyright owner to the use of their work, by making it available under the licence, and in that sense uses require permission. For Deazley, this element of permission led him to exclude works under such licences from the copyright public domain, while still including them in the 'de facto public domain'.[63] We disagree with his conclusion and argue that there are numerous factors that distinguish a particular class of voluntary licensing, which we call 'neutral' licences (including Creative Commons licences and some open source licences), from voluntary licences negotiated between individual parties or their representatives. These neutral licences remove the terms of use and identity of users of works under one of these licences so far from the influence of the copyright owner that the initial 'permission' involved by the owner's decision to use one of these licences is not a disqualifying factor. The factors supporting our analysis are as follows.

First, the licence terms must have been determined by a body which is independent of individual copyright owners (or their representatives) and can reasonably be considered to be acting in the 'public interest' in determining the terms. Examples of such 'neutral' bodies, in relation to particular types of licences, are discussed in Chapter 15. Second, the terms of the licence may impose some restrictions on uses which may be made of the work (for example, some will only allow 'non-commercial' uses, and some will not allow modifications of the work), but they do not allow the copyright owner to vary the terms. Third, the licence cannot be

---

[62] Deazley, *Rethinking Copyright*, 107 n. 26.   [63] *Ibid.*

revoked by the licensor in relation to any licensee already using the work under the licence, but it can be revoked in relation to future licensees. Fourth, the licence (and thus the permission-free use) is available to members of the public, or to a significant class of the public, on equal terms with other members of the public, so the owner cannot exercise any discretion as to who is eligible to become a licensee. There are also other less significant conditions: [3.3.14].

Such contractually based regimes differ from individually negotiated voluntary licences in that, once the licence is established, use of the resource by anyone who agrees to comply with the licence terms is no longer controlled by the copyright owner. If these conditions are satisfied, then it is irrelevant that the source of the freedom lies in restrictions derived from copyright law, as the regime promotes the objectives served by permission-free use of the work for purposes such as the creation of new works.

## 2.3 A Proposed Definition

We can now combine the elements of the definition of the public domain to propose a working definition. We adopt a positive definition of the public domain, as the freedom to use works, as opposed to traditional definitions, which regard the public domain purely negatively. The touchstone of our concept of the public domain is the freedom to use works without permission from the copyright owner, as this freedom supports the ability of users to make use of works for purposes such as creativity, freedom of expression or other cultural practices. While access to a work may be a precondition for free use, this does not affect our copyright-centric definition, but is taken into account in the analysis of extra-copyright measures needed to support the copyright public domain. Applying our core concept of the public domain, it is irrelevant that use may be conditioned on payment, because under compulsory licensing regimes use does not depend on permission from the copyright owner. Moreover, it is irrelevant whether the source of the ability to use a work is a legal limitation within copyright law or, as in FOSS licences, a contractually imposed constraint. What is important is that use is available on equal terms, and that it is impossible for the copyright owner to exert control by revoking permission.

Applying these elements, we define the copyright public domain as 'the ability of members of the public (including a significant class of the public, or intermediaries acting for their benefit) to use works, without seeking permission from a copyright owner, and to do so on equal terms

## 2.3 A Proposed Definition

including costs (if any) with other members of the public.' If a licence for such uses is necessary, it must be automatically available, on terms set by a neutral party, to the public (or to a relevant class or intermediary). This definition excludes licences where the terms are set (or changeable) solely by the copyright owner or their representative. More briefly, we describe the public domain in copyright as 'the public's ability to use works on equal terms without seeking permission'.

The definition is broadly consistent with other theorists who have adopted a positive approach to the public domain, such as Samuelson, Litman, Lessig and Deazley, but is more precise. It is broader than some other positive definitions, such as those proposed by Benkler or Benabou, in that it includes uses which, as a matter of law rather than perception, do not require permission, as well as permissible uses arising from contractual constraints, such as some voluntary licences. The definition deliberately refers to the 'ability' of users to use resources in order to avoid issues concerning whether the public domain is best regarded as protecting user 'rights', 'privileges',[64] or other possible terms: [2.4.2]. The corollary of our definition of the public domain is that the private or proprietary domain is 'the ability of the owners of copyright in works to refuse to allow other people to make certain uses of those works, except on terms set (and changeable) by them'.

The full significance of aspects of this definition will only become apparent when we discuss particular proposed categories of copyright public domains in later chapters. For example, the inclusion of 'a significant class of the public, or intermediaries acting for their benefit' is mainly relevant to some compulsory licences. The exclusion of licences obtained 'on terms set (or changeable) by a copyright owner', moreover, distinguishes between certain types of voluntary licences which are included in our definition (such as, Creative Commons licences) and the majority which are not. The requirement that terms and costs be non-discriminatory between those entitled to utilise a licence is particularly relevant to compulsory licensing. The requirement that any licence terms must be set by a neutral party excludes any licences which have their terms set (or changeable) by a copyright owner (which includes some open source licences), or other party such as a collecting society. Furthermore, the requirement that any licence be 'automatic' means that the user does not have to seek permission from anyone to avail themselves of the licence.

---

[64] Benkler, 'Free as the air to common use'.

### 2.3.1 Advantages of the Proposed Definition

We consider that our definition of the copyright public domain has significant advantages over other proposed definitions, which we summarise as follows.

*A User-Centred and Use-Centred Definition* If, as we argue, a definition of the copyright public domain should be based on freedom of users to use works, then it should capture the most important uses that members of the public can make of works. What is important to users is whether they can use the work for the specific use they wish to make of it, not whether they are able to make use of each and every one of the exclusive rights that comprise copyright in the work. The definition we propose achieves this purpose.

*The Origin of the Ability to Use is Irrelevant* On our view, it is the ability of users to use works that is important and not the source of that ability. It therefore should not matter whether the ability originates in exclusions from copyright law, from the internal limits on copyright law, from external limits on copyright (such as constitutional constraints) or from private ordering in the form of contractually imposed restrictions. It is also irrelevant that it may be difficult to determine whether or not a particular use falls within the public domain, because all sources of permissible uses have 'shifting boundaries'.[65] On our approach, moreover, the difficulties in determining whether a particular use falls within the public domain arise mainly in determining whether or not a use falls within a particular public domain category, and not in determining directly whether it falls within the general definition.

*Universal Availability is Not Determinative* Many permission-free uses that fall within our definition, especially those falling within copyright exceptions, allow uses for only some categories of user or some categories of use. What is important, from the perspective of the user, is whether or not permission-free use is available to support the purpose for which the user wishes to use the work, whatever that might be. As Deazley concludes, merely because 'the nature of the public domain may differ depending upon which interested party wishes to make use of any given work is not, in itself, problematic':[66] the key consideration is not the nature of the use, but whether or not the use is outside of the control of the copyright owner. Our definition therefore has the advantage of

---
[65] Dusollier, 'Scoping study on copyright and related rights and the public domain', 36.
[66] Deazley, *Rethinking Copyright*, 131.

## 2.3 A Proposed Definition

including all valuable permission-free uses, including those falling within copyright exceptions, within an expansive concept of the public domain that supports the freedom or autonomy of users to use works.

### 2.3.2 Relationship between Public and Private Domains

We contend that a significant advantage of our definition of the public domain is that it captures the complexity of the relationship between the public domain and the private, proprietary domain to an extent not achieved by other definitions; and its expansive scope allows for a greater appreciation of its importance, giving it equal prominence to the proprietary domain.

Traditional, negative definitions of the public domain tend to draw hard and fast distinctions between works that are protected by copyright and unprotected works, which are in the public domain. By focusing on the ability of users to use works, we include permissible uses of copyright-protected works within the public domain. In Boyle's terms, the issue concerns the 'granularity' of the definition, meaning whether the freedom to use works means only the freedom to use complete works, or whether it is more 'granular' in that it also includes freedom to use aspects of protected works, such as is permissible under a copyright exception.[67] By opting for a more granular approach, our view is that the dichotomy between the public and private domains does not occur between works that are or are not protected, but at the deeper level of the exclusive rights that comprise the copyright in the work. On our view, there are complementary proprietary and 'public' domains within the one work.

By adopting this more granular approach, we are able to regard the copyright system not as being divided between two halves, the proprietary and public domains, but as a continuum with many shadings between the 'purely private domain' and the 'purely public domain'.[68] Similarly, in Samuelson's analysis, she conceives of IP-protected resources and the public domain 'not as binary opposites, but rather as points along a continuum'.[69] The implications of the 'continuum' approach for the relationship between public and proprietary domains are examined immediately below.

---

[67] J. Boyle, 'Foreword: the opposite of property?' (2003) 66 *Law and Contemporary Problems* 1 at 30.
[68] G. Greenleaf, 'National and international dimensions of copyright's public domain (an Australian case study)' (2009) 6(2) *SCRIPTed* 259 www.law.ed.ac.uk/ahrc/script-ed/vo 16-2/greenleaf.asp [2.1].
[69] Samuelson, 'Enriching discourse on public domains', 785.

*A Continuum from Private to Public* On our view, all works fall somewhere on a continuum (or, more accurately, as explained below, 'on continua') between the purely 'private' and the purely 'public'. At the purely 'public' end of the continuum are, for example, the published works of Shakespeare or poems of Wordsworth, which are entirely open to the public. Even here, however, there are complexities. For instance, a historical script or musical score may be in a language or notation inaccessible to the public unless it is 'translated' into an accessible form. While the original script or score may be entirely 'public' in that copyright has expired, it is not accessible and able to be used without intervention which, if it results from an authorial contribution, may mean that the accessible form of the work is protected by copyright.

At the opposite purely 'private' or proprietary extreme, we consider this end of the continuum is empty in theory and for most practical purposes. For example, all works are subject to exceptions, such as general fair use or fair dealing exceptions in common law jurisdictions. As others, such as Samuelson and Deazley have pointed out, the extreme 'private' end of the continuum includes works subject to technological protection measures (TPMs) and/or contractual restrictions.[70] In relation to both TPMs and contractual restrictions, control over access and use of works may extend beyond the limited exclusive rights that comprise copyright. In both cases, however, there are limitations that mean that control over the work is less than absolute. In relation to TPMs, for example, all known forms of technological protection are subject to circumvention, and laws prohibiting circumvention of TPMs are subject to exceptions.[71] Furthermore, while uses of works may be restricted by contract, such as by contractual restrictions on access to online databases, such restrictions bind only contractual parties. On our analysis, the potential for TPMs and contracts to override legal limits to proprietary rights, such as copyright exceptions, are best considered as constraints on the public domain: Chapter 6.

Most works therefore exist somewhere on the continuum between purely 'private' and purely 'public' and, in so far as it is useful to continue to think in terms of a dichotomy between the public domain and the private domain, this exists within works more than between works. A significant advantage of this approach is that it enables a more nuanced

---

[70] *Ibid.* 821; Deazley, *Rethinking Copyright*, 125–7.
[71] See, for example, the exceptions relating to encryption research, computer security testing and law enforcement and national security in the Australian Copyright Act and the process under the UK Act for ensuring that users can, despite TPMs, take advantage of 'permitted acts': Copyright Act 1968 (Aus.), ss. 116AN(2)–(9); Copyright, Design and Patents Act 1988 (UK), s. 296ZE.

## 2.3 A Proposed Definition

and sophisticated analysis of the particular balance between proprietary rights and public uses in particular contexts than the alternative of distinguishing entire works that are purely 'private' from purely 'public domain' works.

*A Hierarchy of Public Domain Categories* Our definition of the public domain does not mean that all public domain categories are of uniform effect. The continuum of uses between the 'public' and 'private' poles, discussed above, makes this clear. Referring back to the fifteen categories identified in [1.3], and defined in Chapter 3, the first seven categories – which are roughly equivalent to the 'traditional' notion of the public domain – put every aspect of a work at the public pole, with no permission being required for any use made of a work (for example, works where the copyright term has expired). The next five categories affect the operation of some of the exclusive rights of the copyright owner under some circumstances, so some uses of a work require permission, but other uses do not (for example, free use exceptions to copyright). Two other public domain categories are contingent upon actions by copyright owners, whether by the positive act of voluntary neutral licensing, or acquiescence in de facto exercise of exclusive rights. Finally, and closest to the proprietary end of the spectrum because remuneration must be paid to the copyright owner, are compulsory licences. We therefore do not regard what we define as the public domain as uniform or homogeneous, but as a hierarchy of categories, from those closest to the purely public pole to those closest to 'private' uses.

*The Dichotomy at the Level of Each Exclusive Right* The above description of the relationship between the private and public domains is, however, still imprecise. If, as we argue, copyright exceptions are part of the public domain, then we need to take into account that some exceptions do not apply to all exclusive rights, but to some only. For example, while in common law jurisdictions fair dealing or fair use exceptions apply to all exclusive rights, some private use exceptions, such as for time-shifting of broadcasts or format-shifting of works, apply only to specific exclusive rights.[72]

From this, we infer that the dichotomy between the public and private domains occurs not only within works, but within each of the exclusive rights. Consequently, being more precise in charting the public domain requires plotting the public/private relationship on as many continua as there are exclusive rights for any category of work. This is complex enough

---

[72] See Copyright Act 1968 (Aus.), ss. 43C, 111.

in one jurisdiction but, given the considerable differences between national laws in the formulation of exclusive rights (Chapter 10) and in copyright exceptions (Chapters 11–12), cross-jurisdictional analysis is significantly more complex. The complexity is compounded by the extent to which some exceptions are available only for particular categories of works, or even subcategories, such as exceptions for computer programs. The location of a work on these continua can clearly change over time, most obviously at the points (if any) when it is published or made available, if the law concerning a particular exclusive right changes, when the work becomes subject to a voluntary licence, and when its term expires.

Therefore, our expansive approach to the public domain, which includes exceptions, compulsory licences and some voluntary licences, significantly complicates how the public domain is conceived. This complexity means that a series of continua, rather than a single continuum, best explains the relationship between private and public domains.

*The Shared Boundary of Public and Private Domains* Since, in our view, the traditional dichotomy between works protected by copyright and works in the public domain is simplistic, we argue it is more accurate to conceive of the copyright system as a complex patchwork of private and public uses. Nevertheless, it remains true that, as Deazley puts it, 'the private domain of copyright and copyright's public domain necessarily share the same boundary – that which is not copyright protected is public domain and vice versa'.[73] While our analysis makes the determination of the boundary more complex, it has not removed the need for determining the boundary. Furthermore, while on a negative definition of the public domain the boundary determines the limits to the proprietary domain, with everything not protected falling into the public domain, on our analysis, the boundary can be conceived as also defining the limits to the positive public domain.

According to Deazley, the complexities arising from an expansive, positive approach to the public domain mean that it is impossible to determine exactly what is in and what is not in the public domain at any given time.[74] While we agree this is challenging, and while the difficulties of determining the limits of copyright law are a major issue for this book, we do not think this is an insurmountable obstacle to defining the legal parameters of the public domain.

Our approach to the boundary of the public and private domains also assists better understanding of the dynamic, and mutually interdependent relationship between the two domains, as opposed to a static,

[73] Deazley, *Rethinking Copyright*, 131.   [74] *Ibid.*

simplistic approach. On our analysis copyright is not necessarily a zero-sum game, in that copyright protection does not necessarily diminish the public domain: the creation of a new copyright work increases the private domain but, as the work was not previously in existence, it also enriches the public domain of permission-free uses available, for example, by means of copyright exceptions. On the other hand, for authors and possibly copyright owners, sometimes 'less is more', in that they can benefit from permission-free use of works that are in the public domain. This 'win-win' result is seen in business models, such as open source software, that are based on forgoing some proprietary rights in return for the advantages arising from peer production. As explained further in Chapter 16, it is also apparent in the advantages arising from the de facto benign public domain created, for example, by search engines.

## 2.4  Further Terminological Issues

Before considering the categories that make up the copyright public domain, it is valuable to clarify some questions of terminology, including uses of the terms 'public domain', 'commons', 'public rights' and 'user rights'.

### 2.4.1  *Public Domain or Commons?*

The term 'public domain' originated in mid-nineteenth-century France and, from there, was adopted in Article 14 of the 1886 Berne Act: [9.1].[75] Regardless of debates over the precise definition of the term, the 'public domain' has always predominantly been a legal term, whereas 'commons', while widely used in the legal literature, is not a legal term of art. In the legal literature, the 'commons' has sometimes been used synonymously with the 'public domain', although there has been considerable terminological confusion, leading to calls for greater precision: [2.2.4].[76]

The 'commons' has been specifically used in debates about the justification for property rights arising from Hardin's analysis of the 'tragedy of the commons', and much of the literature on the commons has been concerned with refuting the proposition that property rights present the universal solution to over-use or under-use of resources held in

---

[75] J. C. Ginsburg, '"Une chose publique"? The author's domain and the public domain in early British, French and US copyright law', in P. Torremans (ed.), *Copyright Law: A Handbook of Contemporary Research* (Edward Elgar, 2007), p. 154; Ochoa, 'Origins and meanings of the public domain', 225.
[76] Hess and Ostrom, 'Ideas, artefacts, and facilities', 114.

common.[77] More precise analysis of common resources, by theorists such as Ostrom, revealed alternatives to private property that could, given certain conditions, address the problems of collective governance of resources, including institutional arrangements and social norms. While the terms 'public domain' and 'commons' are both used in opposition to 'property', theorists such as Boyle and Drahos have confined use of 'commons' to the collective management of shared resources, such as peer production through free and open source software (FOSS).[78]

The two terms have continued to be used inconsistently, however, such as by Deazley, in contrasting the copyright public domain, which consists of permission-free uses, from the 'intellectual commons', which consists of material that has been made public and which, accordingly, is publicly accessible.[79] While we do not propose to define the 'commons' or the 'intellectual commons', we agree with the generally accepted distinction that the public domain refers to uses of works (or resources) over which the copyright owner has no control, whereas the commons can encompass regimes where there may be a range of rights over shared resources. Following from this, it could be argued, consistent with Drahos, that the public domain 'does not respect the diversity of social arrangements in the way that the positive intellectual commons can do'.[80]

The distinction between the public domain and the commons is most relevant to our approach where a work is protected by copyright but, despite this, users are able to make permission-free use of the work. This is the case, for example, with uses permitted under compulsory licences, or where uses falling within our definition are permitted under neutral voluntary licences, such as some open source licences. While adopting an analysis based on the different regimes that can exist over shared resources, such as whether a resource is open to all or open only to a group, can result in more precise understanding of the advantages of the 'diversity of social arrangements' permitted by these regimes,[81] for the purposes of this book, what is significant is whether or not users can make permission-free use of a work. As we explain above, compliance with the conditions of an open source licence can be regarded as the price paid for 'free' use and not as a form of 'permission': [2.2.4]. Therefore, open source licences that are within our definition of the public domain may

---

[77] Chander and Sunder, 'The romance of the public domain', 1333.
[78] Boyle, 'The second enclosure movement', 66; P. Drahos, 'Freedom and diversity – a defence of the intellectual commons', in Jayanthi Reddy (ed.), *Creative Commons: International Perspectives*, 50–7; also at [2006] *Australasian Intellectual Property Law Resource* 1 www.austlii.edu.au/au/other/AIPLRes/2006/1.html.
[79] Deazley, *Rethinking Copyright*, 110–11.   [80] Drahos, 'Freedom and diversity'.
[81] *Ibid.*

also be regarded as forming part of a contractually constructed commons, but this is not central to our analysis.

That said, the 'commons' literature does have some implications for our analysis. First, as Hess and Ostrom have suggested, if we regard property as a 'bundle of rights', then a 'commons'-based analysis allows non-property regimes to be seen not just as an absence of rights, but as also consisting of a diversity of rights over shared resources.[82] We extend this type of analysis in the following section, explaining how permission-free uses may be regarded as 'public rights'. Second, one advantage of 'commons'-based analysis is the extent to which it may help in identifying the variety of circumstances in which resources may be 'appropriated' from the commons and become commoditised or privatised, in what is sometimes called the 'enclosure of the commons'.[83] On our analysis, the extent to which copyright owners may remove resources from the commons is limited by internal safeguards of copyright law, such as the principles that copyright does not protect ideas, or that usually only the taking of 'original' material amounts to infringement. Therefore, in copyright law, as potentially opposed to other IP regimes, the commons is usually only depleted by changes to the law, such as retrospective extensions to the copyright term or, in some cases, judicial decisions. Third, the focus of the 'commons' literature on management of shared resources draws attention to institutions (other than the legislature and courts) which have a significant effect on how effectively the commons operate, and whether they do so in the public interest. In copyright law, these institutions include collecting societies, organisations that produce neutral voluntary licences and complaint-handling bodies (for compulsory licences); their governance is therefore a significant normative issue in relation to those components of the public domain: [13.6].

### 2.4.2 'Public Rights'

So far, we have defined the public domain in terms of the *ability* of users to use works without permission, without further explaining how this ability might best be characterised. We now explain why, reflecting our conception of the public domain as the complete and equal complement of the private proprietary domain, the *ability* of users to use works can also be expressed as *public rights*.

---

[82] Hess and Ostrom, 'Ideas, artefacts, and facilities', 121 ff.
[83] Boyle, 'The second enclosure movement'.

In their 1991 book, Patterson and Lindberg first claimed that the public domain was the basis for a law of users' rights: [1.2].[84] This analysis, which was influenced by the US First Amendment, was taken up by some US courts in characterising the fair use exception. For example, in *Bateman* v. *Mnemonics*, Birch J stated that, following its codification in the 1976 United States Act, 'fair use should no longer be considered an infringement to be excused; instead, it is logical to view fair use as a right'.[85] Nevertheless, the characterisation of the fair use exception under US law remains unsettled, and the terminology of 'rights' has not been generally adopted by US courts: [11.3].

This differs from the position in Canada where, in *CCH*, the Canadian Supreme Court expressly adopted a 'users' rights' perspective on the Canadian fair dealing exception: [11.4.3]. In that case, McLachlin CJ stated that:

> The fair dealing exception, like other exceptions in the Copyright Act, is a user's right. In order to maintain the proper balance between the rights of a copyright owner and users' interests, it must not be interpreted restrictively.[86]

In doing so, the Court specifically endorsed the following statement from Vaver's text on *Copyright Law*:

> User rights are not just loopholes. Both owner rights and user rights should therefore be given the fair and balanced reading that befits remedial legislation.[87]

Following *CCH*, the language of users' rights has become entrenched in Canadian copyright law, being expressly applied by the Canadian Supreme Court in two of five landmark copyright decisions handed down in 2012.[88] While the *CCH* judgment is not trouble-free: [11.4.3],[89] by according users equal status with owners, it comes close to our balanced view of the relationship between the public and proprietary domains. As Vaver has explained, the use of the terminology of 'rights' in the context of exceptions such as fair dealing:

---

[84] L. Ray Patterson and S. Lindberg, *The Nature of Copyright: A Law of Users' Rights* (University of Georgia Press, 1991).
[85] *Bateman* v. *Mnemonics, Inc.*, 79 F 3d 1532, 1542 (11th Cir, 1996).
[86] *CCH Canadian Ltd* v. *Law Society of Upper Canada* (2004) 1 RCS 339; 236 DLR (4th) 395 at [48].
[87] D. Vaver, *Copyright Law* (Irwin, 2000), p. 171.
[88] *Society of Composers, Authors and Music Publishers of Canada (SOCAN)* v. *Bell Canada*, 2012 SCC 36, [2012] 2 SCR 326; *Alberta (Education)* v. *Canadian Copyright Licensing Agency (Access Copyright)*, 2012 SCC 37, [2012] 2 SCR 345.
[89] D. Gervais, 'Canadian copyright law post-*CCH*' (2004) 18 *Intellectual Property Journal* 131.

to balance rights is to balance similar entities, while balancing a right against an exception is either nonsensical or starts off with a linguistic bias against the exception.[90]

In supporting the terminology of 'rights', Vaver also pointed to the tradition of referring to fair use as a 'right' that pre-dated the introduction of statutory fair dealing exceptions in the 1911 UK Copyright Act.[91]

As the Canadian and US experiences indicate, debates over users' rights have focused on the status of copyright exceptions, especially fair use or fair dealing exceptions, and have occurred in jurisdictions where copyright jurisprudence has been influenced, expressly or otherwise, by a constitutional right to freedom of expression. Nevertheless, from the perspective of the public domain, we contend there is value in using the terminology of 'rights', rather than terms such as 'privilege', 'liberty', 'power' or 'immunity', as this best expresses the multifaceted relationship between creators and users, which fails to be captured by terminology that places users in a subservient position to authors or owners. Furthermore, we argue there is considerable value in extending the term beyond copyright exceptions, to include all permission-free uses of works. One advantage of the 'commons' literature, explained above, is that it allows for more precision in analysis of open or shared resources in ways that are not possible from a simple property/non-property dichotomy. Following this, if we characterise property as a 'bundle of rights', then there are analytical advantages in also characterising permission-free uses as a 'bundle of rights'.

However, to use 'rights' to refer to all permission-free uses does raises difficult jurisprudential issues, and the full implications of the terminology need to be explored in more detail than we do in this book. For example, as Benkler points out, to say that someone has a 'right' against someone else often means that the state can be enlisted to force others to respect that 'right', and not merely that the state is prohibited from interfering with a freedom or liberty.[92] Furthermore, our usage does not conform to a Hohfeldian analysis of rights as, for example, every permitted use falling within our definition of the public domain is not matched by a corresponding duty.[93] We acknowledge that, in most of the jurisdictions we consider, it is inaccurate, as a matter of positive law, to refer to exceptions, or other permitted uses, as 'rights'.[94] However, in

---

[90] D. Vaver, 'Copyright defenses as user rights' (2013) 60 *Journal of the Copyright Society of the USA* 561 at 669.
[91] *Ibid.* 669–70.   [92] Benkler, 'Free as the air to common use', 363.
[93] Vaver, 'Copyright defenses as user rights', 669.
[94] Burrell and Coleman are clearly correct in observing that 'we believe that although copyright law *ought* to recognise "users' rights", it is a mistake to describe the current

jurisdictions where copyright law is affected by a bill of rights, it could be argued that some permitted uses are derivative from rights such as freedom of expression, or the right to access and use information. Also, there are some permission-free uses that fall within our concept of the public domain, such as the de facto copyright public domain discussed in Chapter 16, which cannot be referred to as 'rights' on any analysis. Therefore, if readers prefer to keep the *de jure* and de facto public domains separate,[95] while recognising the existence of both, that is understandable. Our deliberate use of the term 'abilities' can always encompass both forms of permission-free uses.

We therefore do not apply the term 'rights' in any technical sense but, in much the same way as the Canadian Supreme Court has used the term, we believe it can be used to emphasise the importance of public domain uses in the copyright system, and the equivalence between such uses and proprietary rights. While our approach is not dissimilar to the Canadian 'users' rights' perspective, however, we prefer the term *'public* rights' for four reasons. First, in the non-technical sense in which we use 'rights' in this book, users may have rights that are not confined to permission-free use. For instance, where a use is permitted under a voluntary licence granted by the copyright owner, while this may be characterised as a permission or a 'privilege', the user can be regarded as having individual 'rights' against the copyright owner, and these might be termed 'user rights', not 'public rights'. Second, the term better reflects the extent to which the *'public* domain' protects permission-free uses. Third, on our definition, it is important that permission-free uses be open to the public, or to a section of the public, while the term 'user' tends to convey the impression that the focus is only on individual users or uses, thereby diluting the focus away from the public interest in the use. We therefore use the term 'public rights' in preference to 'user rights' or 'public domain rights', as this better indicates who can exercise the rights, or in whose interests they are exercised. Fourth, the term 'user' might imply that uses are predominantly consumptive in nature, as opposed to creative, and therefore less important than the creative activities of authors.

By adopting the terminology of 'public rights' we do not mean to imply that the rights of authors or creators are not also 'public', and we unequivocally accept there is a public interest in protecting authors' rights: [1.8]. We are simply saying that copyright law embodies a complex set of rights and interests, that there is no single 'correct' terminology, but that for the

provisions in these terms': R. Burrell and A. Coleman, *Copyright Exceptions: The Digital Impact* (Cambridge University Press, 2005), p. 10.
[95] Deazley, *Rethinking Copyright*, 116.

purpose of this book, which is focused on the public domain, the term 'public rights' has advantages. Furthermore, as we do not use 'rights' in any technical sense, we are comfortable with use of the more neutral term 'abilities'.

## 2.5 Conclusion

In this chapter, we have argued for a positive view of the copyright public domain, based on the freedom of users to use works without requiring permission. Building on this, the public domain includes uses permitted under copyright exceptions, compulsory licences and some voluntary licences, such as FOSS licences. This approach recognises the values which support the public domain, including freedom to use works for creating new works, freedom of expression, and user autonomy and self-determination. It is the ability to engage in permission-free uses that is important, and not whether payment is required (under a compulsory licence) or the legal source of the ability (under a neutral voluntary licence). The public domain can be summarised as 'the public's ability to use works on equal terms without seeking permission': [2.3]. We do not claim this is the only possible definition, but adopt it as a working definition [2.1.2].

The concept of the copyright public domain as consisting of a positive 'bundle of rights', that encompasses all permission-free uses, enables a more precise and nuanced identification and analysis of its components, and the complex relationships between public and private domains, than other approaches. The complex boundaries of the exclusive rights of copyright owners also set the limits on the positive uses that comprise the public domain, which we argue can usefully be termed 'public rights'.

In the next chapter we operationalise the definition by identifying and describing the constituent components of the copyright public domain, in the form of fifteen public domain categories derived from our 'best endeavours' analysis: [2.1]. Each category must satisfy the technical definition of the 'public domain' proposed in this chapter, but be legally and logically distinct from the other categories. This disaggregation of the public domain into distinct categories of 'public rights' enables the precise analysis required for a comprehensive and rigorous description of the copyright public domain, and for examination of the issues involved in balancing the proprietary and public domains in particular legal contexts.

# 3 Categories of Public Rights

3.1 Introduction: What Are the Public's Rights to Use Works without Permission?   54
3.2 Categories of Public Rights   55
3.3 Fifteen Categories: Definitions and Examples   57
3.4 The Public Domain as the Sum of Public Rights   72
3.5 A Positive Statement of Public Rights in Lay Person's Terms   74
3.6 Comparing Categorisations of the Copyright Public Domain   76
3.7 Conclusions and Hypothesis: Fifteen Categories of the Public Domain   82

## 3.1 Introduction: What Are the Public's Rights to Use Works without Permission?

In the previous chapter we defined the copyright public domain in two ways. The brief definition was 'the public's ability to use works on equal terms without seeking permission'. The more technical definition is that the copyright public domain is 'the ability of members of the public (including a significant class of the public, or intermediaries acting for their benefit) to use works, without obtaining the permission of a copyright owner, on the same terms including costs (if any), as other members of the public'. Furthermore, if a licence to make such uses is necessary, the licence must be automatically available, on terms set by a neutral party, to the public (or to a relevant class or intermediary).

Applying this definition, the elements that make up a public domain can best be explained by answering a simple question: 'What rights do the public have to use works without asking for permission?' Assuming the work in question is protected by copyright, this is the same as to ask: 'What rights do persons other than the copyright owner have to make use of the work without requesting permission from the copyright owner?' But we also have to ask which works are not protected by copyright at all, where there is no need at all to consider the rights of owners.

For convenience, we use 'works' to include all forms of creative expression, whether or not protected by copyright: [1.1].

In this chapter, we set out the legal categories (or 'public rights') that make up the copyright public domain. This book does not purport to be a comprehensive comparative study of all national copyright laws. Instead, we propose a set of categories that we consider satisfactorily explain the copyright public domains in the main jurisdictions referred to: [1.9]. On this basis, we propose fifteen public domain categories, which we identify and discuss in the rest of this chapter. Given the non-exhaustive nature of this study, it is best to regard these categories as a working hypothesis, as analysis of the laws of additional countries may reveal further categories: [2.1].

*The National Basis of Public Domains* A 'work', on our definition, does not have a uniform global status. This would make no sense as the public domain, or more accurately, public domains, have a territorial basis because copyright law is territorial. The principle of territoriality means that copyright is determined by the law of the jurisdiction in which copyright protection is claimed. The territorial basis of public domains is fundamental to international copyright law: [4.3]. This is so, even though some elements of the public domain may be near universal: [4.1], and some national public domains may have spillover effects on other national public domains: [16.3]. Consequently, when we discuss public domain categories, we are referring to national public domains, even though most categories may be relevant to most national jurisdictions.

## 3.2 Categories of Public Rights

Applying our framing question, analysis of national laws – initially based on UK and Australian laws,[1] then extended to other jurisdictions – results in the identification of fifteen categories where the public are able to use works without permission, which correspond to what we refer to as public rights: [2.4.2]. The categories are as follows:
1. Works failing minimum requirements
2. Works impliedly excluded
3. Works expressly excluded
4. Constitutional and related exclusions and exceptions
5. Works in which copyright has expired
6. Public domain dedications

---

[1] G. Greenleaf and C. Bond, '"Public rights" in copyright: what makes up Australia's public domain?' (2013) 23 *Australian Intellectual Property Journal* 111.

7. Public policy refusals against enforcement
8. Public interest defence to enforcement
9. Insubstantial parts
10. Ideas or facts
11. Uses outside exclusive rights
12. Free use exceptions and limitations
13. Neutral compulsory licensing
14. Neutral voluntary licensing
15. De facto public domain of benign uses.

The aggregate of these categories in any given jurisdiction is, in our view, the copyright public domain for that jurisdiction. We have ordered these categories so that the first seven encompass the position where a work as a whole is (with some qualifications) not protected by copyright law at all, meaning that the work is free to be used for any purpose by any person. Category 4, constitutional and related exclusions and exceptions, has a special status as extra-copyright limitations imposed by national constitutions or similar legal norms: [3.3.4], may exclude works from copyright protection but may also except uses of protected works, such as by extending existing exceptions. The remaining categories concern works that are protected by copyright, but identify uses not requiring permission of the copyright owner. Categories 9–11 are uses outside the exclusive rights of the copyright owner, whereas categories 8, and 12–13 are uses which would otherwise be within the owner's exclusive rights but which the law allows to the public or classes of the public under certain conditions as limitations or exceptions: [11.1]. Category 14 is where the copyright owner, not the law, voluntarily puts certain uses of her works beyond her continuing control. Category 15 is where, by forbearance rather than positive licensing, copyright owners do something similar. Categories 14 and 15 together comprise the 'Internet-enabled' copyright public domain.

The inclusion of a category does not necessarily imply that, in a particular country, the category has any content. For example, in Australian copyright law, there is no clear content in category 3, and it is debatable whether there is any content in categories 6, 7 and 8. However, these categories may have content in other jurisdictions; category 8, for example, has some importance in the UK.

Of the fifteen public domain categories, the last four (12–15) have expanded greatly in the quantity and significance of their content over the last forty years since development of the personal computer and the Internet. They are, in practice, important categories of the modern copyright public domain. The other eleven categories have either not changed so significantly, or in the case of categories 2, 5 and 11 have generally contracted in national public domains.

## 3.3 Fifteen Categories: Definitions and Examples

The rest of this chapter explains the fifteen categories and how they are consistent with our definition of the public domain. The relationship of each category to international copyright law is indicated as, applying our realist perspective: [1.4], we are concerned not with rewriting international copyright law, but with what is achievable under current laws. To illustrate each category, we give brief examples of how the category is reflected in selected national laws, with cross-references to the relevant sections of Part III. We then propose definitions of each category: [3.4], before explaining the relationships between the categories. The chapter concludes with an explanation of how our categories compare with approaches taken by others who have attempted to 'map' public domain categories, namely Samuelson, Dusollier and Deazley: [3.6].

### 3.3.1 Works Failing Minimum Requirements

The first category is works that fail to meet the minimum standards for copyright protection required by national laws, and is potentially the simplest category. Minimum standards include originality requirements and, depending on the national regime, may also include failure to meet *de minimis* requirements (such as titles or headlines), and requirements of fixation (embodiment in a tangible medium).

*Definition and International Law* The minimum requirements category consists of works that fail to meet the minimum standards required for copyright protection (originality, and in some countries a *de minimis* rule or fixation), and may therefore be used by any person without any permission.

The Berne Convention[2] implies a minimum threshold of authorial creation for Berne-protected literary and artistic works, but there is considerable flexibility in how this can be applied in national laws: [4.6.1]. Berne does not prohibit insubstantial works from being protected, and does not require fixation nor prevent fixation being required: [4.6.4]. Formalities for subsistence of copyright are, however, prohibited: [4.4].

*National Examples* There is considerable variation between countries in what are the 'minimum requirements' for protection, so the public domains of some countries are more expansive than those of

---

[2] Full titles and citations of conventions are in the Table of International Instruments.

others: [7.2]. For example, in most common law countries the standard of originality is relatively minimal, requiring little more than that the work originate from an author, although a minimum authorial contribution is also required. Works that have not been reduced to a material form ('fixation') are generally not protected in most common law jurisdictions, although the definition of 'material form' is liberal. In contrast, in general, civil law jurisdictions apply a higher creativity threshold, requiring that a work must bear the imprint of an author's personality, but commonly do not impose a fixation requirement. Despite these broad differences, detailed analysis of national laws indicates that differences between common law and civil law jurisdictions should not be overstated.

### 3.3.2 Works Impliedly Excluded (Statutory 'Gaps')

National copyright laws define the categories of subject matter that they protect, by either inclusive or exclusive definitions, and the courts continue the task of definition. As a result, there is always the likelihood of gaps, where some forms of expression do not fit into the protected subject matter under national laws. We refer to these as 'implied' statutory exclusions, largely for want of a better term. It is fundamental that copyright never has and still does not protect all forms of original creative expressions, and so there are forms of expression, or categories of 'works' which are not protected by copyright at all, and are therefore part of the public domain, free for others to copy and use.

*Definition and International Law*  The 'statutory gaps' category consists of works that do not fall within protected copyright subject matter, as defined in national legislation, and which may therefore be used by any person without permission.

The Berne Convention provides an inclusive definition of 'literary and artistic works' as 'every production in the literary, scientific and artistic domain, whatever may be the mode or form of its expression' and requires protection of such works: [4.6.1]. Berne, and the TRIPs Agreement, also require or allow certain other categories of works to be protected: [4.6.2]. But, as a minimum rights treaty, Berne does not prevent copyright laws protecting subject matter that falls outside its already broad definition.

*National Examples*  The practice of states varies in implementation of these Berne-required protections: [7.3]. Some countries' laws, such as in France and Germany, contain a broad statement of the 'works' protected, followed by a list of examples (a non-exhaustive or open-ended list). In contrast, legislation in most common law countries (apart from

3.3 Fifteen Categories: Definitions and Examples    59

the United States) has no overarching (inclusive) definition of protected subject matter, but an exclusive (closed) list of categories (for example, the eight categories specified in the UK and Australia). In general, open-ended definitions may result in fewer works being in the public domain, because new (or newly recognised) forms of expression, such as new forms of artistic works, are more likely to be protected.

### 3.3.3 Works Expressly Excluded

International copyright law provides that limited categories of works, which would otherwise be required to be protected, may be expressly excluded from protection; but there is very considerable variation in how this category is implemented in national laws.

*Definition and International Law* The category of 'works expressly excluded' comprises those types of otherwise copyrightable subject matter which national laws exclude completely from copyright protection, and which may therefore be used by any person without permission.

The Berne Convention provides for only three express exclusions from the works required to be protected: one mandatory ('news of the day') and two optional (official texts of a legislative, administrative and legal nature, plus official translations of them, and political and legal speeches): [5.3]. The optional exclusions allow national discretion concerning partial or conditional exclusions, as occurs in China with public speeches. As a minimum rights treaty, Berne does not allow complete exclusion from copyright protection of any forms of subject matter within its definition of 'literary and artistic works', other than those mentioned. The 'news of the day' exclusion may mean little more than that facts are not protectable: [5.3.1]. The optional 'official texts' exemption is an important subcategory, but its scope is uncertain: [5.3.2].

*National Examples* Because permissible exclusions under Berne are narrow, national laws have little scope for completely excluding protectable works from copyright. Moreover, as the scope of the mandatory exclusion is uncertain, and the other permissible exclusions are optional, national laws may not implement them to the extent possible. For example, Australian law does not expressly exclude 'news of the day' from protection, leaving implementation of the mandatory exclusion to interpretation of the idea/expression dichotomy by courts or fair dealing exceptions. As far as optional exclusions are concerned, Australian law does not expressly exclude any categories, protecting official government works, for example, under general copyright law and Crown copyright: [8.2.2].

Some countries explicitly exclude 'news of the day': [8.2.1],[3] but many others utilise exceptions rather than exclusions. Most jurisdictions exclude statutes, judicial opinions and other official texts from copyright; with many also applying a reduced level of protection to other official public documents, such as government reports: [8.2.2]. The US exclusion of 'any work of the United States Government' is an example of a broad implementation of this permissible exclusion.

### 3.3.4 Constitutional and Related Exclusions and Exceptions

National constitutions may protect the public domain by imposing limits on the extent to which the public domain may be restricted by legislation or the courts. These limits are usually based on the constitutional protection of human rights, especially the right to freedom of expression. By the inclusion of 'related exclusions' in this category, we are primarily referring to European treaty-based limits, including limits arising from the EU treaties and the European Convention on Human Rights (ECHR), or potentially to other treaties with similar effect: [8.3.2]. As these limitations arise from sources of law other than copyright law we refer to them as 'external' limitations.[4] The limitations may take the form of either exclusions of works from protection, or the exception of uses of protected works.

*Definition and International Law* This category includes those situations where a country's constitution (or treaty obligations) are such that otherwise copyrightable subject matter may be used without permission, because of either exclusions of works from protection, or the exception of uses of protected works. Such uses may be limited to particular purposes, or to particular classes of users. The 'treaty obligations' referred to here are those arising directly from non-copyright international agreements, not international copyright law.

---

[3] China, Costa Rica, Italy, Korea and Rwanda are examples of countries which expressly exclude 'news of the day': Dusollier, 'Scoping study on copyright and related rights and the public domain', 31.

[4] Drassinower refers to these external limitations as 'exceptions properly so-called', as they represent 'the nexus of an encounter between copyright and other juridical interests': A. Drassinower, 'Exceptions properly so-called', in Y. Gendreau and A. Drassinower (eds.), *Language and Copyright* (Carswell/Bruylent, 2009), p. 222.

*National Examples*   In the United States, there are constitutional limitations on copyright under the Intellectual Property Clause and, potentially, the First Amendment but, due to internal free speech safeguards in copyright law, their practical effect has been limited: [8.3.1]. These effects do, however, include the 'constitutionalisation' of the exclusion of non-original works. The position in Europe is complex as, apart from national constitutional protections, limitations may be based on the ECHR in addition to EU law, including the EU Charter of Fundamental Rights: [8.3.2]. To date, while EU copyright law has been 'constitutionalised' within the EU human rights framework,[5] the influence of these rights-based limitations has been confined to interpretation of EU directives and their implementations in national laws. In addition, EU treaties relating to non-discrimination and the internal market have resulted in limits on copyright holders engaging in territorial partitioning of markets in the EU. Furthermore, where rights are entrenched in national constitutions (as in Germany), or rights-based treaties are directly enforceable (as in the Netherlands), rights-based limitations may result in expansive interpretations of exceptions, or permission-free uses beyond copyright exceptions. In contrast, Australia is an example of a country where there are no likely significant constitutional limitations on copyright: [8.3.3].

## 3.3.5  Works in which Copyright Has Expired

Historically, the most common usage of 'public domain' was to refer to works in which copyright had expired. Because international copyright law does not set a ceiling on the copyright term, but sets minimum terms, variations in national laws may and do extend copyright terms longer than the Berne and other international copyright minima. In recent decades, public domains in many countries have contracted as a result of term extensions.

*Definition and International Law*   This is a category where a work may be used by any person without permission, because the term of copyright of the work has expired.

Since 1908, Berne has set the minimum term for literary and artistic works at 'the life of the author and fifty years after his death', but it is a minimum which Member States may exceed: [4.5.1]. In relation to

---

[5] See J. Griffiths, 'Constitutionalising or harmonising? – the Court of Justice, the right to property and European copyright law' (2013) 38 *European Law Review* 65; O. Afori, 'Proportionality – a new mega standard in European copyright law' (2015) *International Review of Intellectual Property and Competition Law (IIC)* 889.

neighbouring rights, international agreements generally set the minimum term at fifty years from first fixation or publication: [4.5.4]. The Berne principle of national treatment does not apply to copyright duration of foreign works, with the rule of comparison of terms, meaning the term must not exceed that in the country of origin, applying unless legislation in the country in which protection is claimed provides otherwise: [4.5.3].

*National Examples* An increasing number of countries have gone beyond the Berne minimum term, particularly since the EU Term Directive in 1993 establishing a general term for works of seventy years *post mortem auctoris* (or *pma*): [9.5]. The United States essentially matched the EU term in 1998: [9.7]. Most countries now protect works for either fifty years *pma* or seventy years *pma*, but there are more national variations than might be expected. Canada and China are examples of significant countries that have not extended terms beyond the Berne minimum: [9.10]. At the other extreme, Mexico has a term of 100 years *pma*. Historically, there have also been variations in the protection of unpublished works, with Australia until recently providing perpetual protection for unpublished works, and Singapore continuing to provide perpetual protection for unpublished governmental works.

## 3.3.6 Public Domain Dedications

Voluntary relinquishment of copyright, or 'public domain dedications' as they are sometimes called, are not prohibited by international copyright law, but their effectiveness varies between countries.

*Definition and International Law* This category is where a copyright owner, by an intentional act which is legally effective in the jurisdiction in question, relinquishes any claim to copyright in a work, so that the work may be used by any person without permission.

International copyright law has nothing directly to say on voluntary relinquishment: [15.6.1]. Relinquishment is essentially a question of ownership, which is left to national laws. Berne does not otherwise either require or prevent national laws allowing intentional voluntary abandonment.

*National Examples* The results of this national discretion are mixed: [15.6]. There are statutory provisions in some countries providing for such relinquishment, including in Chile, Kenya and India. In common law jurisdictions where there are no such statutory provisions, such as Australia, academic opinion is divided as to whether abandonment of copyright is possible. European civil law jurisdictions generally do not accept abandonment of copyright. In contrast, in the United States there is a judicially developed doctrine permitting abandonment: [15.6.2].

### 3.3.7 Public Policy Refusals against Enforcement

Laws may refuse enforcement of copyright because of the content of a work (such as obscene or offensive works), so others may make use of it without risk of copyright infringement. But this is a fragile public domain, because of shifting social norms and because users will otherwise usually have to comply with laws regulating use of works with such content.

*Definition and International Law* This category is where laws prevent copyright in a work being enforced because of its content, with the effect that any person may make use of the work without permission from the copyright owner but subject to other laws.

Berne explicitly allows (but does not require) national laws to permit, control or prohibit, the circulation, presentation or exhibition of any work or production, where a competent authority finds it necessary: [8.4]. According to a WTO Panel decision this cannot extend to complete denial of copyright protection. Refusal of enforcement is usually for content control or other purposes of public order, and any user would usually be subject to other laws relating to the work.

*National Examples* Countries vary greatly in whether they allow refusal of enforcement of copyright: [8.4.1]–[8.4.3]. In the UK, there is a long history of courts holding that the content of a work was so objectionable that enforcing copyright in the work was against public policy. Chinese legislation also supports refusal of enforcement where this would violate relevant laws.

### 3.3.8 Public Interest Defence to Enforcement

This aspect of the public domain varies from the previous category because it is a defence available to a particular defendant, not to all users of the work, due to there being a public interest in the use of the work (typically, to bring it to public attention).

*Definition and International Law* This category is where laws allow a defence to copyright infringement of a work because it would be against the public interest to prevent a particular use of the work by a particular user.

The Berne allowance of 'public order' restrictions on enforcement of copyright may be broad enough to also allow public interest defences, but this is contested, as is the possibility of such a defence being justified under the three-step test: [8.5].

*National Examples* This is a narrow category, with the defence having support in some common law countries, but being contested and of uncertain scope [8.5]. In the UK there is judicial support for the defence, as influenced by the Human Rights Act 1998 (UK). Chinese legislation supports refusal of enforcement where this would jeopardise public interests, but this principle is also of uncertain scope.

### 3.3.9 Insubstantial Parts

How much of a copyright work must be taken and used by someone else for it to be a 'substantial part' of the work is one of the most elusive aspects of copyright law. 'Insubstantial copying' (or something similarly described), which can occur without permission, is an important, but often unrecognised, part of the copyright public domain.

*Definition and International Law* This category is where the part of a work which is used is not sufficient to constitute an infringement, according to the standards set by national laws, so such uses by any person do not require permission.

International copyright law provides no guidance on the threshold for determining whether or not a use is an infringement, leaving this to national laws.

*National Examples* A *de minimis* threshold for infringement exists under all copyright laws, but there is no clear dividing line: [10.3]. In the UK, Australia and many other countries the law requires that a 'substantial part' of a work must be used before there is infringement. EU case law has altered the UK test of substantiality, but the extent of the change is uncertain. In the United States, a test of 'improper appropriation' requires a finding of 'substantial similarity' between the copyright work and the allegedly infringing copy; but US courts have applied a variety of tests, associated with different circuits.

## 3.3.10 Facts and Ideas

The 'idea/expression dichotomy' generally reflects the principle that uses of facts, information or ideas derived from a work are outside the scope of the exclusive rights of the copyright owner, and therefore are part of the public domain. The dichotomy performs a number of public domain functions, including that copyright does not protect: the 'meaning' or subject matter of a work; the 'building blocks' of works, such as mere facts; the functions of utilitarian works; or material that is not copyright subject matter, such as laws of nature or mathematical formulae. While sometimes the dichotomy operates to exclude ideas or facts from protected subject matter, most national laws apply the dichotomy in distinguishing permissible use of ideas or facts from impermissible use of protected expression.

*Definition and International Law* This category is where only facts, information or ideas derived from a work are used. Any person may use these aspects of the work without permission, because such uses are outside the scope of the exclusive rights of the copyright owner.

Berne does not include an express statement of the principle, but assumes it by requiring that a work be protected 'whatever may be the mode or form of its expression': [4.6.3]. The principle is expressly incorporated in Article 9(2) of the TRIPs Agreement, and in Article 2 of the WCT. Implementation, however, is left to national laws.

*National Examples* The relative indeterminacy of the idea/expression dichotomy, arising from difficulties in determining what are 'ideas' or 'facts', is seen in its treatment in national case law: [10.4]. In the United States, the dichotomy has been codified, and courts have developed subsidiary principles, the merger and *scènes à faire* doctrines, to refine its application: [10.4.4]. But all jurisdictions experience difficulties in consistently applying the dichotomy.

## 3.3.11 Uses Outside Exclusive Rights

Anyone can use a work in ways that do not fall within the exclusive rights of the copyright owner. There are two aspects to this category of the public domain: (i) uses of works which are generically different to the exclusive rights and which therefore would not be expected to be prevented by copyright; and (ii) uses of works that are not generically different from the exclusive rights but are not prohibited, even though we might expect they would, perhaps because of drafting deficiencies or technological change, as well as policy choices.

## Categories of Public Rights

*Definition and International Law*  Any person may make use of a work in ways which do not come within one of the exclusive rights of the copyright owner, without obtaining permission.

Berne and other international agreements have progressively extended the exclusive rights of copyright owners: [4.7]. Through complex and largely complementary provisions, Berne, TRIPs, the WCT and the WPPT require a substantially comprehensive set of exclusive rights including reproduction and adaptation, public performance and communication and, to some extent, distribution. TRIPs requires Member States to establish a commercial rental right for computer programs and cinematographic works, and the WCT does similarly in relation to a rental right for computer programs, cinematographic works and works embodied in phonograms: [4.7.4].

*National Examples*  The abstract and general nature of how minimum exclusive rights required by international law are expressed leaves flexibility for the interpretation and implementation of the rights in national laws. National copyright laws adopt three main approaches to defining the exclusive economic rights: some specify the restricted acts in detail; some laws broadly identify the set of specific exclusive rights without defining the rights in detail; and some laws generally provide that copyright confers the exclusive right to make economic use of a work, often accompanied by illustrative examples: [10.2.1].

Uses falling outside of the exclusive rights can be an important part of the public domain. Some common examples include that, under national laws, copyright owners have not been able to restrict tangible copies of works (for example, books or DVDs) being read or viewed, lent, or resold. Other examples are the 'public' limitations on the performance and communication rights, which leave private performances and communications as acts outside the exclusive rights of the copyright owner. Differences in when a performance or communication is 'public' can create differences in the scope of national public domains.

### 3.3.12  *'Free Use' Exceptions and Limitations*

International copyright law limits the extent to which countries may enact free use exceptions (or limitations) to exclusive rights. Nevertheless, these exceptions are potentially the most complex category of the copyright public domain, as they are the single most important mechanism for expressly balancing copyright and other public policy objectives. Given the lack of harmonisation in international law, this category is subject to very considerable national variations.

## 3.3 Fifteen Categories: Definitions and Examples

*Definition* The 'free use' category is where, because of a statutory provision, a person (the 'permitted user') is able to make use of a work in ways which would otherwise come within one of the exclusive rights of the copyright owner (the 'permitted use'), without obtaining permission, and without payment of any remuneration to any party.

The permitted use may be limited to particular permitted users (such as educational institutions, or libraries and archives) and may be limited to particular contexts or purposes.

*International Law* While the Berne Convention sets floors on protectable works and exclusive rights, it sets a ceiling on permissible exceptions. Berne includes specific free use exceptions to some of the minimum rights it guarantees, but also incorporates a general limitation on permissible exceptions under national laws, in the form of the 'three-step test': [5.2]. The three-step test allows national laws to permit the use of works 'in certain special cases, provided that such reproduction does not conflict with a normal exploitation of the work and does not unreasonably prejudice the legitimate interests of the author': [5.4.1]. While the Marrakesh Treaty for blind, visually impaired and print disabled persons is, to date, the sole international agreement to be principally concerned with copyright exceptions: [4.2.1], there are proposals for other 'exceptions' treaties, such as a treaty for exceptions for libraries and archives: [12.1].

*National Examples* National jurisdictions take three main approaches to exceptions: [11.1.3]. Most civil law jurisdictions have closed lists of specific permissible exceptions: [11.5]. This approach is also reflected in EU law, especially in the closed list of specific permissible exceptions in Article 5 of the InfoSoc Directive: [11.2]. However, these closed list exceptions are usually codified at a high level of abstraction and generality, leaving it to courts to interpret and apply them. In contrast, US copyright law's fair use doctrine is an open-ended exception which requires the courts to engage in case-by-case analysis of whether the use, taking into account its purpose, complies with identified 'fair use factors': [11.3]. In Commonwealth common law jurisdictions, the dominant approach has been to rely on 'fair dealing' exceptions, which are more flexible than the closed list approaches, but differ from fair use in that they are confined to uses for specified purposes. 'Fair dealing' exceptions have been interpreted expansively in some jurisdictions, such as Canada, and restrictively in other jurisdictions, such as Australia: [11.5]. In addition, in common law jurisdictions, national laws include many more specific exceptions, commonly more detailed and more specific than those in the codes of civil law jurisdictions. There is very considerable variation in the specific categories of 'free use' exceptions under national laws: see Chapter 12.

### 3.3.13 Neutral Compulsory Licensing

Compulsory licences are the only part of the public domain where the permitted uses are intended to result in revenue to the copyright owner. We use 'statutory licence' to distinguish between licences created and made mandatory by statutory provisions, as distinct from extended collective licences (ECLs) which only come into existence on the initiative of a collecting society (CS).

*Definition of Public Domain Category* The compulsory licence category is where rights holders are required by or under legislation to allow their works to be used by parties specified by the licence terms, on conditions and for a fee set by a neutral body on public interest grounds, and on equal terms for licensees: [13.1].

The following factors are, on our analysis, consistent with compulsory licensing being part of the public domain: [13.2]. Not all copyright owners, only some, may be subject to compulsion in relation to use of their works. Copyright owners may opt out from the licence scheme. Eligible licensees may be either any member of the public (by application to a licensing body), or a significant class of the public designated by status (particularly institutions, or occupational categories), or parties taking up a licence available to all parties in a category (usually from a CS). Payment of fees for uses of work may only be contingent, not automatic (for example, in some orphan works schemes). These result in at least four main forms of statutory licences, only some involving a CS: [13.2.2].

*International Law* The Berne Convention explicitly permits three kinds of remunerated use exceptions under national copyright laws: mechanical recording of musical works; rebroadcasting and cable retransmissions; and compulsory licensing allowing translation and reproduction in developing nations: [5.5]. Berne may also permit remuneration for some otherwise unremunerated exceptions, such as certain uses of works for 'reporting current events'. However, as with free use exceptions, the most significant Berne provision making compulsory licensing possible is the 'three-step test', which is the basis of most permissible exceptions under national laws, including remunerated exceptions: [5.5.5].

*National Examples* The structure of the two main types of compulsory licences used globally – statutory licences and extended collective licences (ECLs) – have many common features, with their main differentiating factor being that ECLs originate from voluntary proposals to license by copyright owners represented by a CS, even though subsequently created by legislation or a tribunal: [13.3]. Both ECLs and statutory licences allow use of works owned by copyright owners not represented by the CS.

There is considerable variation between countries in relation to the subject matter of statutory licences, which are used more extensively in some countries such as China, India and Australia. The Paris Appendix, the one Berne compulsory licensing provision which was ostensibly to assist developing countries, is over-restrictive and over-technical, and has failed to meet its objectives: [14.5].

*3.3.14 Neutral Voluntary Licensing*

An important expansion of public rights in copyright in the last two decades has been because of voluntary licensing to the public of copyright works by copyright owners, using pre-designed licences not written by the owner or their representatives. These voluntary licences are at no cost to licensees, and are usually to the public at large, but are subject to compliance with certain conditions set out in the particular licence. This category includes software licences (particularly 'free and open source software' (FOSS) licences) and open content licences (particularly Creative Commons licences).

Unlike other public domain categories (except voluntary relinquishment of copyright), voluntary licensing involves a positive consensual act by a copyright owner to the use of their work (the decision to utilise one of these licences), and in that sense involves their 'permission'. However, by specifying conditions on when voluntary licences are part of the public domain, so as to put the terms of use and identity of users of works under one of these licences beyond the influence of the owner, this initial 'permission' ceases to be a determining factor: [2.2.4], [15.1.2].

*Definition of Public Domain Category* This category applies where a copyright owner grants a licence allowing uses of the copyright owner's work, which would otherwise be within the exclusive rights of the copyright owner, subject to the following conditions:
(1) the terms of the licence have been determined by a neutral body (meaning a body that is independent of individual copyright owners or their representatives) that can reasonably be considered as not acting on behalf of any particular owner but neutrally on behalf of all;

70    Categories of Public Rights

(2) the terms may impose restrictions on the uses which may be made of the work (consistent with the following conditions);
(3) the terms allow reproductions of the work licensed to be distributed by the licensee;
(4) the terms do not allow any variation of terms by the copyright owner (they may only decide whether they will apply it to a work that they own);
(5) the licence cannot be revoked, in relation to any licensee already using the work under the licence (it can be denied in relation to future licensees);
(6) the licence is granted to the public, or to a significant class of the public, on equal terms, so that the copyright owner cannot exercise any discretion about which individuals are eligible to become licensees;
(7) copies of the licence are freely available, so anyone can be a licensor;
(8) the licence is not granted in response to the licensee expressing interest in using the work;
(9) the terms do not require remuneration to the copyright owner (a licence fee).

*International Laws* International copyright law does not have any significant effects on voluntary neutral licensing, either in limiting or facilitating it: [15.1.1].

*Global and National Examples* Most significant voluntary licensing to the public is via global, not national, licensing schemes, for two reasons: (i) global applicability of licence terms; and (ii) viral licensing propagating licence terms: [15.1.1]. The two main global types of licences are 'free and open source software' (FOSS) licences, and Creative Commons (CC) licences: [15.2–15.3]. National legislation does not usually address voluntary licensing agreements, and does not include any specific provisions assisting enforceability of voluntary public licences. Under most national laws there are similar issues concerning enforcement of voluntary licences to the public. However, in both Europe and the United States, case law consistently supports enforceability of FOSS and CC licences: [15.2.4] and [15.4].

### 3.3.15 *De facto Public Domain of Benign Uses*

We propose that a de facto public right exists when the vast majority of affected copyright owners in a jurisdiction (or, more often, globally) consider they should not attempt to prevent what would be an otherwise

## 3.3 Fifteen Categories: Definitions and Examples 71

infringing use of their work, because the use is sufficiently in their own interests (a 'benign use'). As a practical matter, for this category to be effective, there must also be sufficient disincentives (including 'opt-outs') for those copyright owners who do not hold this opinion, to dissuade them from litigating and thus potentially destroying the practice.

Alternatively, in particular cases (particularly with old content) there may be little likelihood of there being many copyright owners who are alive, locatable or likely to become aware of the uses made of the work. The age and nature of the works and the public benefit of the uses (such as in museums, archives or libraries) may also reduce the likelihood of any objections.

For inclusion in the public domain it is not sufficient that some significant uses of copyright works in breach of exclusive rights go undetected, or that copyright owners do not think enforcement action is worthwhile (sometimes called 'tolerated use').

*Definition of Public Domain Category* The category of the de facto public domain comprises those situations where the public (or a class of intermediaries) is able to make significant uses of works, which uses are (at least arguably) contained in the copyright owner's exclusive rights, but which, as a matter of practice or custom, go unchallenged because copyright owners recognise that not objecting to such uses is in their interests.

On the basis of limited but important examples, we suggest in [17.2] that a de facto public right is more likely to arise when all or most of ten factors are present: (1) The practice organises the content better through some technical or organisational innovation; (2) Obtaining prior consent from all copyright owners is not practicable; (3) The public benefits from the use being made of exclusive rights; (4) The copyright position of the works covered is unclear in relation to the use being made of exclusive rights, at least in relation to some works or under some common circumstances; (5) Few copyright owners are alive, locatable, or likely to become aware of the uses made of the work; (6) Most of the relevant class of copyright owners will benefit from the use being made; (7) Few if any copyright owners will suffer significantly from the use being made, including through direct competitive use of the content by the intermediary; (8) A reasonably effective opt-out mechanism is provided; (9) Opting out is unattractive so only a minority do so; and (10) There are few if any incentives toward litigation by those dissatisfied with the practice. The more of these factors apply, the more likely is a commons of benign uses to arise.

*International Law*  Because this is a de facto, rather than a *de jure*, part of the public domain, international copyright law does not have anything to say on the topic. There are no exceptions to copyright based simply on accepted (or long-standing) national practices, custom or the acquiescence of rights holders, and if they did exist they would convert de facto rights into *de jure* rights.

*Global and National Examples*  Key examples are of near-global application, such as the operation of Internet search engines to create a global commons of searchable content: [12.2.3]. Other examples may include a de facto public domain for private use machine translations, and some mass digitisations and other uses of collections by cultural institutions based on low risk-assessment: [12.2.5].

## 3.4  The Public Domain as the Sum of Public Rights

The fifteen categories of public rights that together comprise the copyright public domain are listed below, omitting clarifying factors, mentioned above, which are not determinative of whether the category applies.

(1) Where works fail to meet the minimum standards required for copyright protection (originality and, in some countries, *de minimis* requirements or fixation), they may be used by any person without permission.

(2) Where works do not fall within protected subject matter as defined in national legislation, they may be used by any person without permission.

(3) Where works which otherwise fall within one of the categories of protectable subject matter are excluded by national laws from copyright protection they may be used by any person without permission.

(4) Where a country's constitution, or related obligations (including obligations under treaties) so provide, otherwise copyrightable works may be used without any permission. Such uses may be limited to particular purposes or particular classes of users.

(5) Where a work may be used by any person without permission, because the copyright term has expired.

(6) Where a copyright owner, by an intentional act which is legally effective in the jurisdiction in question, relinquishes any claim to copyright in a work, the work may be used by any person without permission.

(7) Where laws prevent copyright in a work being enforced because of its content, any person may make use of the work without obtaining permission from the copyright owner.

## 3.4 The Public Domain as the Sum of Public Rights

(8) Where laws allow a defence to copyright infringement in a work because it would be against the public interest to prevent a particular use of the work by a particular user, that user may make that use of the work.

(9) Where the part of a work which is used is not sufficient (or too insubstantial) to constitute an infringement, such uses by any person do not require permission.

(10) Where only facts, information or ideas derived from a work are used, any person may use these aspects of the work without permission, because such uses are outside the scope of the exclusive rights of the copyright owner.

(11) Where a use of a work does not come within one of the exclusive rights of the copyright owner, any person may use the work in that way without permission.

(12) Where, because of a statutory exception, a person (the 'permitted user') is able to make use of a work in ways which would otherwise come within one of the exclusive rights (the permitted use), without obtaining permission, and without payment of any remuneration to any party, the permitted user may make the permitted use.

(13) Where copyright owners are required by or under legislation to allow their works to be used by parties specified by the licence terms, on conditions and for a fee set by a neutral body on public interest grounds, and on equal terms for licensees.

(14) Where a copyright owner has granted a licence to the public, or to a significant class of the public, allowing uses of the copyright owner's work, which would otherwise be within the exclusive rights of the owner, the public (or a significant class thereof) may make these uses of the work without obtaining permission. The licence terms: (i) must have been determined by a 'neutral' body; (ii) may impose restrictions on the uses which may be made of the work; (iii) must not allow any variation of terms by the copyright owner; and (iv) must not require a licence fee. The licence: (v) must not be able to be revoked, or altered, in relation to any licensee already of the work; (vi) must be freely available; and (vii) must not be granted in response to the licensee expressing interest in using the work.

(15) Where significant specific uses of works are contained in the copyright owner's exclusive rights (at least arguably), but as a matter of practice or custom, these uses go unchallenged because copyright owners recognise that this is in their interests (but have the ability to opt out of the practice), the public (or a class of intermediaries) is able to make these uses of the work without permission.

74    Categories of Public Rights

These fifteen categories together comprise the copyright public domain, despite their apparently disparate descriptions, because of the related (but not identical) ways in which the public has a right to use works without permission of a copyright owner. There is no other factor shared by all fifteen categories. They vary concerning the scope of 'the public' that may exercise the right, although nine of the categories require that any person may do so, but the others either require or allow limitation of the use to a class of the public.

## 3.5   A Positive Statement of Public Rights in Lay Person's Terms

Copyright legislation provides a positive statement of the exclusive rights of copyright owners, although there is complexity and fragmentation in the formulation of exclusive rights under national laws: [10.2]. The preceding technical definitions of the public domain categories, and the descriptions of how each of its categories are exemplified in various laws, give only an indirect sense of the positive nature of copyright public domains. As we argue, however, on our positive view of the public domain: [2.1.3], it is important for 'public rights' to be treated as equal and equivalent to proprietary rights.

A positive brief summary of these public rights, intended to be understandable by those who are not copyright law experts, follows. Because public rights differ between national jurisdictions, it is not possible to give generic global examples, so we have used illustrative Australian implementations of the categories. Following each 'plain English' description, the public domain categories to which it relates are noted. Some of the fifteen categories are probably empty in Australia (3, 4, 6, 7 and 8), so it is also possible to state in similar terms some of the limitations of Australia's copyright public domain, as shown in items 11–15 in Table 3.1.

The fifteen points in Table 3.1 do not map Australia's public domain directly onto the fifteen public domain categories, but they do account for all fifteen categories: some points encapsulate more than one category, and some categories require more than one point to summarise. For any other national jurisdiction, a similar summary of its public domain's content and omissions would be possible, and it would almost certainly be different from the summary of the Australian public domain.

As is clear from the comparative analysis of the public domain categories in Part III of this book, there are diverse reasons for the limits to copyright and the exclusive proprietary rights which correspond to the

## 3.5 A Positive Statement of Public Rights in Lay Person's Terms

Table 3.1 *A plain English summary of Australia's copyright public domain*

| | | |
|---|---|---|
| 1 | Anyone has a right to make any use of any work that does not originate from a human author, or does not have more than a minimal amount of expression, or has not been reduced to a material form. | 1 |
| 2 | Anyone has a right to make any use of insubstantial parts of a work, or use ideas, facts or information derived from it. | 9, 10 |
| 3 | Anyone has a right to make any use of a work which does not fit in the eight defined categories of copyright subject matter (literary, dramatic, musical or artistic works, or sound recordings, films, broadcasts or typographical arrangements). | 2 |
| 4 | Anyone has a right to make any use of a work in any way which falls outside the copyright owner's defined exclusive rights for that type of work. | 11 |
| 5 | Anyone has a right to make any use of any work in which copyright has expired. | 5 |
| 6 | Where a statutory exception applies to everyone, anyone has a right to make use of the works specified in the ways allowed. | 12 |
| 7 | Where a statutory exception applies to only some classes of persons, they have a right to make use of the works specified in the ways allowed. | 12 |
| 8 | Where a statutory licence applies to a class of works, a specified class of persons has a right to use the works according to the licence, but must pay fees to a collecting society. | 13 |
| 9 | Anyone has a right to make use of a work to which there applies a voluntary licence created by a neutral body (such as a FOSS or CC licence), according to the licence terms. | 14 |
| 10 | As a practical matter, anyone has a right to make use of works in circumstances where copyright owners routinely do not object (most often Internet-related uses) because they consider those uses benefit them. | 15 |
| 11 | No types of works are expressly exempt from copyright protection. | 3 |
| 12 | The Australian Constitution does not limit copyright protection. | 4 |
| 13 | It is not possible to relinquish copyright in works to the public. | 6 |
| 14 | No works are refused copyright protection because their content is against public policy. | 7 |
| 15 | There is no generally accepted defence to copyright infringement based on the public interest in use of a work. | 8 |

public rights identified above. For example, the right to use ideas or facts protects the freedom of expression of users and the freedom to use parts of works in order to create new works. Similarly, the rights to use non-original or insubstantial parts of works supports the ability to use material in new works, but may also reflect the excessive costs of establishing more extensive proprietary rights. The right to use works permitted by a statutory exception may reflect a variety of public interests, including rights to freedom of expression, access to information and education, or to use works to create new works. The categories of 'public rights' identified above, which are derived from doctrinal analysis of the positive law, therefore reflect a patchwork of overlapping or related concepts: [2.1.2], which are unified solely in so far as they are rights to permission-free use of works.

## 3.6 Comparing Categorisations of the Copyright Public Domain

This chapter has proposed a taxonomy of the copyright public domain by identifying the fifteen categories that comprise it, applicable at least to those countries on which we have focused. While defining the public domain has attracted considerable attention: [2.1], few have attempted systematically to identify the categories that make up the copyright public domain. In the following sections we identify the similarities and differences between our proposed categories and those proposed by those who have attempted a similar exercise, namely Samuelson, Dusollier and Deazley. The similarities and differences between these taxonomies and ours are summarised in Table 3.2.

### 3.6.1 Samuelson's 'Conceptions' of the Public Domain

In one of the earliest attempts to identify the positive constituents of the public domain, Samuelson proposed a 'map' of its contents: [2.1.2].[6] Samuelson's map was not confined to the copyright public domain, was US-centric and attempted to identify the 'contents' of the public domain but not the legal categories. Subsequent versions were less US-centric.[7] In further work, still grounded in US copyright law, Samuelson identified thirteen 'conceptions' of the public domain from the literature, which she clustered around three main foci: the legal status of information resources, freedoms to use information resources and the accessibility of information resources.[8] The first two foci are relevant to our approach, and, based on these, seven of Samuelson's conceptions can be seen as similar to our public domain categories, such that it is informative to attempt to map these conceptions onto our categories: see table in [3.6.4]. We find six of her conceptions are similar to our categories, and that this is arguably so in a further six.[9] However, such comparisons

---

[6] P. Samuelson, 'Mapping the digital public domain: threats and opportunities' (2003) 66 *Law and Contemporary Problems* 147.
[7] P. Samuelson, 'Challenges in mapping the public domain', in Guibault and Hugenholtz (eds.), *The Future of the Public Domain*, 7–25.
[8] Samuelson, 'Enriching discourse on public domains', 816.
[9] See the Online Supplement for our attempted comparison.

3.6 Comparing Categorisations of the Copyright Public Domain    77

remain somewhat speculative because our focus is limited to the copyright public domain, whereas hers is not, as well as being for a different purpose. We also differ from her project in that we argue that there is a unifying thread underlying all fifteen of our categories, namely that they each identify the ability or right to use works without permission. To the extent there are some similarities or overlaps, we identify these in our comparative Table 3.2: [3.6.4].

### 3.6.2  Dusollier's Narrow Categorisation

In her 2011 study for WIPO, Dusollier adopted a traditional, negative definition of the public domain: [2.1.1] as being 'composed of elements that are by themselves unprotected, whatever the circumstances of their use'.[10] Within this paradigm, Dusollier identified the following five public domain categories:[11]

1. *Ontological public domain*: Works not protected because they are not expressions according to the idea/expression dichotomy, consisting of 'ideas, facts, style, methods, intrigue, mere information, concepts'.[12]
2. *Subject matter public domain*: Works that do not meet the 'requirements for protection', namely: (a) originality; (b) fixation; and (c) nationality of the work.[13]
3. *Temporal public domain*: Works that have fallen into the public domain after the expiry of the copyright term.[14]
4. *Public policy domain*: Works that are 'explicitly excluded from the field of protection'.[15] In this category, Dusollier includes only three kinds of works: (a) the mandatory exclusion under Berne of 'news of the day'; (b) the optional exclusion under Berne of official texts of a state; and (c) other public policy exclusions under national laws. Dusollier does not, however, mention the optional exclusion under Berne for political or legal speeches and, unlike Deazley, she does not include restrictions on copyright on policy grounds arising from non-statutory sources.[16]
5. *Voluntary public domain*: Dusollier includes as her fifth category 'relinquishment of copyright', meaning the voluntary dedication of a protected work to the public domain through some intentional act of the copyright owner, such as 'abandonment'.[17] According to Dusollier, the voluntary public domain 'differs from open access or freeware licenses, to the extent that they aim at a complete

---

[10] Dusollier, 'Scoping study on copyright and related rights and the public domain', 20.
[11] *Ibid.* 35.     [12] *Ibid.* 22.     [13] *Ibid.* 23–5.     [14] *Ibid.* 25–9.     [15] *Ibid.* 29.     [16] *Ibid.* 31–2.
[17] *Ibid.* 32–4

renunciation of the protection of copyright, while the latter only grant freedom to use works but retain the existence and exercise of copyright'.[18]

While each of Dusollier's categories broadly corresponds with analogous categories in our taxonomy, her analysis of the components of the copyright public domain is limited by her narrow definition of the public domain.[19] This means that, under her approach, it is impossible to include permissible uses of works that are protected by copyright, such as uses falling outside of the exclusive rights or uses of insubstantial parts of a work. It also excludes uses that are specifically permitted by statutory exceptions, which, on our analysis, is a significant category. Dusollier's categories therefore seriously underestimate the scope and value of the copyright public domain.

Given the way in which Dusollier's categories map to ours, it might be suggested that our fifteen categories could be divided into two groups, one group of categories relating to the negative public domain of unprotected works and one relating to the positive public domain of permitted uses of copyright-protected works. We do not, however, think too much emphasis on this distinction is helpful as, applying our positive conception of the public domain: [1.2], we think it is important to understand the categories in their entirety as comprising positive rights to use 'works', regardless of whether or not the work is protected by copyright.

### 3.6.3 Deazley's Expansive Categorisation

Of those who have attempted to map or categorise the public domain, Deazley's approach comes closest to ours. As we agree with Deazley that the copyright public domain extends to permission-free uses, we also agree that the public domain must 'incorporate those aspects or features of a copyright protected work that nevertheless do not require permission prior to such use'.[20] Applying these principles, Deazley summarises the elements of the UK copyright public domain as follows:[21]

> copyright's public domain incorporates those works which do not qualify for copyright protection, those works which do but are out of the copyright term, as well as such use of those works which fall on the right side of the idea-expression line, which are allowed for within the statutory framework (use of an insubstantial part, the permitted acts), or which are permissible as a result of judicial intervention with that regime at common law (on public policy grounds, or as being in the public interest).

---

[18] *Ibid.* 32.
[19] For our rejection of Dusollier's reasons for adopting a narrow definition of the public domain see [2.2.1].
[20] Deazley, *Rethinking Copyright*, 111.   [21] *Ibid.* 118.

## 3.6 Comparing Categorisations of the Copyright Public Domain 79

From this, we interpret Deazley as proposing the following eight categories:

1. 'those works which fail to meet whatever threshold requirements have been stipulated before protection will be attributed to them' ('non-original' works);[22]
2. 'works whose periods of protection have expired';[23]
3. 'ideas, generic plots, themes and so on, as well as certain unoriginal materials';[24]
4. 'use of an insubstantial part of a work';[25]
5. uses of a copyright work outside the 'acts restricted by copyright' (or 'private domain of what is copyright protected');[26]
6. 'any use which falls within the statutorily defined "acts permitted in relation to copyright works"';[27]
7. 'use of works which the courts refuse to protect on the grounds of public policy';[28] and
8. uses of a work which would otherwise amount to copyright infringement which are authorised by the courts because they are in the public interest (which can be considered 'within the common law public interest defence').[29]

While we agree with Deazley's overall approach, we consider that he applies the touchstone of 'use without the need for permission'[30] too narrowly. In short, we differ from Deazley in two main respects. First, although we include all of his categories in our own, we consider there are other categories of the public domain that his analysis does not capture, or which he rejects. Second, in our view, some of his categories combine elements which we consider are valuable to disaggregate.

Deazley excludes from his definition of the public domain uses of a work made under voluntary licences, such as Creative Commons or open source licences, on the basis that such uses still require a priori permission from the copyright owner, and he therefore describes works subject to such licences as part of the 'de facto public domain' as distinct from the 'legal public domain': [2.2.4]. We, however, reject this distinction, mainly on the basis that once what we refer to as a 'neutral' licence is in place, the work is able to be used by members of the public (or a class of the public) without permission. We therefore include neutral voluntary licensing as a distinct category. Furthermore, Deazley does not discuss

---

[22] *Ibid.* 110–11.   [23] *Ibid.* 111.   [24] *Ibid.* 113.   [25] *Ibid.*
[26] *Ibid.* 106. While Deazley does not explicitly list this as one of his categories of the public domain, he does include the permitted acts as part of his summing-up, so we read him as meaning to include this category: *Ibid.* 118.
[27] *Ibid.* 113.   [28] *Ibid.* 115.   [29] *Ibid.* 117.   [30] *Ibid.* 107.

80    Categories of Public Rights

works that are expressly or impliedly excluded from copyright protection, so the status of these categories is uncertain under his analysis. Deazley also does not expressly refer to compulsory licences but, on the other hand, neither does he expressly suggest that uses of works must always be free of cost to be part of the public domain, so they may well form part of his sixth category. Given the distinctive features of compulsory licences, however, we consider that works subject to compulsory licences should be a distinct public domain category: [2.2.3]. Finally, Deazley acknowledges the distinction between the 'perceived public domain' where 'in practice the manner in which it functions is bound up in individual perceptions',[31] and the 'legal public domain'. While Deazley does little more than acknowledge this distinction, we incorporate it into our analysis in two ways. First, it is relevant to our category of the de facto public domain, in which permission-free uses of works are possible as a matter of practice or custom, rather than law: Chapter 16. Second, we deal with perceptions of copyright and the public domain as being relevant to both supports and constraints on the public domain: Chapter 6.

### 3.6.4   Comparison with Our Categories

The comparison between our fifteen categories and the categorisations by Samuelson, Dusollier and Deazley, is summarised in Table 3.2. Our categorisation is the broadest in the number of categories, but it is notable that each of the fifteen categories is shared with at least one of the other three taxonomies. The main reasons for the differences have already been stated: Samuelson has different objectives; Dusollier applies a traditional, narrow approach to the public domain so that many of our categories are excluded; and Deazley has not considered some categories that, on our analysis, should be included, or sufficiently differentiated from others.

In comparison with Deazley's eight categories, which is clearly most relevant to the UK, we have added the following: (2) and (3), works expressly or impliedly excluded from copyright protection; (4) constitutional limitations; (6) public domain dedications; (14) voluntary licensing; and (15) our extension to de facto public rights. We have also separated free from paid statutorily allowed uses, thus adding (13) neutral compulsory licences as a separate category.

The differences between our categories and those we have attributed to Samuelson are less marked (although we assume she would

[31] *Ibid.* 118.

3.6 Comparing Categorisations of the Copyright Public Domain 81

Table 3.2 *Comparison of copyright public domain taxonomies*

|   | Our categories | Samuelson (US) | Deazley (UK) | Dusollier (generic) |
|---|---|---|---|---|
| 1 | Fails minimum requirements | √ (1) | √ (1) | √ Subject matter public domain |
| 2 | Works impliedly excluded | * (4), (12) | ? | ? |
| 3 | Works expressly excluded | * (1) | ? | √ Public policy public domain |
| 4 | Constitutional and related exclusions | √ (3) | ? | ? |
| 5 | Copyright has expired | √ (1), (12) | √ (2) | √ Temporal public domain |
| 6 | Public domain dedications | * (6) | ? | √ Voluntary public domain |
| 7 | Public policy refusals | ? | √ (7) | ? |
| 8 | Public interest exceptions | ? | √ (8) | ? |
| 9 | Insubstantial parts | * (1) | √ (4) | ? |
| 10 | Mere facts, ideas etc. | √ (2) | √ (3) | √ Ontological public domain |
| 11 | Uses outside exclusive rights | * (4) | √ (5) | *Excludes* |
| 12 | Statutory exceptions | √ (5) | √ (6) | *Excludes* |
| 13 | Neutral compulsory licensing | ? | * Part of (6) | *Excludes* |
| 14 | Neutral voluntary licensing | √ (6) | 'de facto' public domain | *Excludes* |
| 15 | De facto public domain of benign uses | * (5) | ? | ? |

* The author is not explicit on the points marked * but it can be implied that they are included.
? The author does not discuss, or exclude, points marked ?, so it is uncertain if they are included.

include some categories she does not explicitly mention). The most significant differences are that she does not include the de facto public domain, nor the public domain created by compulsory licensing. We have proposed a public domain wider than that proposed by either Deazley or Samuelson, but note that some of the differences may be explained by the jurisdictions that are the main focus of their analyses, namely the United States for Samuelson and the United Kingdom for Deazley.

## 3.7  Conclusions and Hypothesis: Fifteen Categories of the Public Domain

Drawing on our core notion of the copyright public domain as the right to use works without permission, and on the territorial nature of copyright law, this chapter has proposed fifteen categories of public rights, which we claim are necessary and sufficient to describe public domains in those legal jurisdictions we have examined. In this chapter we have defined each of those categories, and have hypothesised that the copyright public domain is the sum of the fifteen identified public rights. In other words, if we are right, there are no elements of the copyright public domain that do not fit within one of the fifteen categories, so that the question of whether a work or use falls within the public domain can be determined by asking whether it falls within one of the fifteen categories.

The categories are legal categories, most having their source in copyright law, although some are based on sources external to copyright, namely constitutional exclusions or limitations (category 4) or voluntary licences based on contract law (category 14). What we term the de facto public domain (category 15) is, however, based on practice or custom. As we have mapped legal categories, and not the 'contents' of the public domain, our categories are mutually exclusive. On the other hand, given the nature of copyright law, there are often uncertainties or ambiguities in whether a work or use is within a public domain category or the copyright owner's proprietary domain. We take up this issue in our conclusions in Chapter 17.

While the first seven of our categories encompass circumstances where a work as a whole is not protected by copyright (bearing in mind complexities associated with category 4, constitutional exclusions and limitations: [8.3]), the remaining nine categories (including some instances of category 4) are concerned with uses of works that are protected by copyright but do not require permission from the copyright owner, which can be referred to as 'public domain uses'. While the first seven categories reflect more traditional concepts of the public domain, such as Dusollier's, we agree with those such as Samuelson and Deazley who claim that the public domain cannot properly be understood without taking into account the extent to which users are free to use copyright works, meaning that the distinction between the public and proprietary domains does not occur solely between works but also within works at the level of the exclusive rights: [2.3.2]. Our analysis goes beyond Samuelson's and Deazley's, however, in that we are more comprehensive and rigorous in pursuing the implications of our technical definition of the copyright

## 3.7 Conclusions

public domain, which can be summarised as 'the public's ability to use works on equal terms without seeking permission'.

The fifteen categories each define a distinct 'ability' or 'public right' to use works without permission. As argued above, these abilities or rights (except 15) are legally defined, although most are defined in negative terms by copyright law. It is, nevertheless, important not to fall into the trap of conceptualising the categories in negative terms, as merely those uses not protected by copyright, but to see them as positive abilities or rights, and we have provided a brief positive statement of the public rights, based on Australian copyright law: [3.5]. While we have argued that our fifteen categories are mutually exclusive, we also claim that the categories of public rights reflect a patchwork of overlapping or related concepts, which are related to the diverse reasons for the limits to copyright or justifications for the public domain. It is in this sense that we argue that the public domain can be conceptualised as a web of related concepts, with 'family resemblances' between the concepts, but which are unified by our working definition: [2.1.2]. In our view, there is much interesting work to be done in teasing out the relationships between conceptions of the public domain that underpin our fifteen categories. Although we do return to this issue in Chapter 17, that is not the main project that we have undertaken. This book is directed primarily at the detailed exposition and analysis of the contents of each of the fifteen categories, from the point of view of international copyright law and comparative national laws (undertaken in Parts II and III) and in drawing practical conclusions from that analysis (set out in Part IV).

*Part II*

# Constraints and Supports, Global and National

# 4 The Global Public Domain – Limits Imposed by International Law

| | | |
|---|---|---|
| 4.1 | The Global Public Domain | 87 |
| 4.2 | International Copyright Law | 89 |
| 4.3 | The Twin Pillars: National Treatment and Minimum Rights | 95 |
| 4.4 | Prohibition of Formalities | 99 |
| 4.5 | Term of Protection | 102 |
| 4.6 | Protectable Subject Matter | 107 |
| 4.7 | Exclusive Rights | 114 |
| 4.8 | Conclusions: International Copyright and the Public Domain | 120 |

## 4.1 The Global Public Domain

As copyright law is territorial, in that copyright does not exist independently of national laws, copyright public domains are jurisdictional or national, and therefore distinct. Nevertheless, given a degree of commonality between national copyright laws,[1] we can ask if it makes sense to talk about a global public domain. We conclude that it is sensible as a result of two factors. The first, international copyright law, is historical and legal, while the second, the effect of global Internet practices, is more recent, technological and, in part, conventional.

This chapter and the next introduce the global public domain created by the 'patchwork' of international copyright agreements that constitute international copyright law.[2] This chapter explains the framework of protection established by international copyright law, while the next chapter introduces the framework for exceptions and limitations, and the international enforcement regime.

---

[1] P. Goldstein and P. B. Hugenholtz, *International Copyright: Principles, Law, and Practice* (Oxford University Press, 2010), p. 4.

[2] P. Geller, 'From patchwork to network: strategies for international intellectual property in flux' (1998) 31 *Vanderbilt Journal of Transnational Law* 553.

Before analysing categories of national public domains, it is essential to understand international copyright law, as this imposes significant constraints on national laws. As this chapter explains, however, the legal constraints must be analysed against the broader background of shifting international strategies of major actors, including state parties and non-state stakeholders. Moreover, as explained in Chapters 15 and 16, to conceptualise the global public domain, it is also necessary to take into account the normative and practical implications of contemporary Internet practices, particularly 'neutral' voluntary licensing, the de facto public domain and the 'Internet spillover' of national public domains.

The global public domain, as we conceive it, therefore has historical, legal, technological and practical dimensions; it cannot be properly mapped without taking each of these into account.

### 4.1.1 What is the Global Public Domain?

A number of approaches could be taken to delineating the global public domain. For example, given similarities between national copyright laws, it might be possible to analyse national laws to determine a baseline degree of conformity in what, at a minimum, falls within the public domain. On this approach, the global public domain is the lowest common denominator of overlap between national public domains. Another approach was proposed by Taubman, who suggested that:

> Perhaps the international public domain could be construed as a congeries of national public domains.[3]

On this approach, the global public domain would be the aggregation of all national public domains.

But there are both practical and theoretical objections to these approaches. First, it is not feasible to examine all dimensions of the public domain for each and every national copyright law. Second, this approach would be contrary to both the history and principles of international copyright law. The development of international copyright law may be explained in terms of a struggle between universalists, who have favoured a universally applicable law based on first principles, and pragmatists, who have been prepared to sacrifice principles for the sake of reaching agreement.[4] Given the traditionally different assumptions of national

---

[3] A. Taubman, 'The public domain and international intellectual property treaties', in C. Waelde and H. McQueen (eds.), *Intellectual Property: The Many Faces of the Public Domain* (Edward Elgar, 2007), p. 68.
[4] Ricketson and Ginsburg, *International Copyright and Neighbouring Rights*, [2.03]–[2.04]; Goldstein and Hugenholtz, *International Copyright*, [3.1.2].

legal systems concerning copyright and authors' rights: [1.9], it is unsurprising that, in the negotiation of international agreements, pragmatism has prevailed. This means that international copyright law is based on the principle of national treatment and there is no universal copyright code: [4.3]. The failure of universalism means there is considerable diversity in national laws and, accordingly, national public domains.

Nevertheless, due to the universalist tendency as well as some convergence in national approaches, over time there has been an increase in substantive elements of international copyright law.[5] The international agreements dealt with in this book can therefore be regarded as an international copyright law, although still of a qualified kind. It should also be acknowledged that, by their nature, international agreements are expressed at a higher degree of generality than national laws, leaving scope for differences in interpretation and implementation.[6] Moreover, there is, in practice, a tolerance of diversity in national laws that goes beyond the strict letter of international copyright law: [5.7].

As this chapter explains, international copyright agreements, while far from requiring strong uniformity in national public domains, do nevertheless impose significant constraints on national public domains. The global public domain, as a matter of law, is therefore defined primarily negatively by the legal constraints imposed by the complex system of treaties which, as this and the next chapter explain, consists of minimum levels of protection and ceilings on permissible exclusions and exceptions.

## 4.2 International Copyright Law

International copyright law consists of a complex series of nested international agreements, which are multilateral, regional and bilateral. This chapter focuses on the multilateral agreements, which are the main source of the global public domain.

This section of the chapter identifies the main multilateral agreements that constitute international copyright law. Following this, we put the agreements in context, by explaining the historical trajectory of international copyright law and identifying the main structural features of the international framework which constrain the global public domain and, by extension, national public domains.

---

[5] Ricketson and Ginsburg, *International Copyright and Neighbouring Rights*, [2.04]; J. C. Ginsburg, 'International copyright: from a "bundle" of national copyright laws to a supranational code' (2000) 47 *Journal of the Copyright Society of the USA* 265.

[6] S. Ricketson, 'WIPO study on limitations and exceptions of copyright and related rights in the digital environment', WIPO SCCR, Ninth Session, Geneva, 23–27 June 2003, p. 5.

### 4.2.1 The Principal Multilateral Agreements

**Berne Convention**  The lynchpin of international copyright law is the Berne Convention,[7] which, although substantially unchanged since 1971,[8] remains the principal copyright treaty, and sets the template for all other copyright conventions.[9] The Berne Convention was introduced in 1886, with revisions in 1908 (Berlin), 1928 (Rome), 1948 (Brussels), 1967 (Stockholm) and, finally, the Paris Act of 1971. As most of the current 172 Berne member countries have adhered to the Paris Act,[10] and as the TRIPs Agreement imposes the Paris text's minimum standards, this book concentrates on the Paris text.

According to its Preamble, Berne is intended to 'protect, in as effective and uniform a manner as possible, the rights of authors in their literary and artistic works'. This, however, has never meant that public interest limitations on copyright have been overlooked: [4.2.2]. Berne is solely concerned with ensuring protection of works in Member States other than the work's country of origin. In furthering this objective, Berne introduced the fundamental principle of national treatment: [4.3]. The principle is supplemented by minimum standards of protection, which impose minimum terms and minimum rights. Berne is confined to literary and artistic works, resulting in separate treaties that apply to other subject matter.

**Universal Copyright Convention**  For much of its history, significant countries, including the United States, the former Soviet Union, China and several Latin American, African and Asian countries, were not members of the Berne Union. This led to efforts to establish a bridge between Berne and non-Berne countries, which culminated in the 1952 Universal Copyright Convention (UCC). Given its diminished importance, we do not deal with the UCC in detail.

**Rome and Neighbouring Rights Agreements**  According to the authors' rights tradition, copyright works originate from natural authors: [1.8]. This tradition was challenged by mechanical processes for

---

[7] The full titles and citations of all conventions are in the Table of International Instruments.
[8] Very minor amendments were made in 1979: 'General report of the Governing Bodies of WIPO and the unions administered by WIPO', Tenth series of meetings, Geneva, 24 September to 2 October 1979, AB/X/32 (Geneva: WIPO, 1979).
[9] J. C. Ginsburg and E. Treppoz, *International Copyright: US and EU Perspectives* (Edward Elgar, 2015), p. 1.
[10] US Copyright Office, *International Copyright Relations of the United States*, February 2017 www.copyright.gov/circs/circ38a.pdf. A small number of countries are not Berne members, including Iran, Iraq and North Korea.

producing works, such as photography, film, phonograms (sound recordings) and broadcasts. While photographs and films were assimilated to authors' rights, a line was drawn at protecting sound recordings, broadcasts and performances, which were termed 'neighbouring rights'.[11] This resulted, in 1961, in a separate treaty, known as the Rome Convention. Rome establishes minimum protection for neighbouring rights, but imposes minimum standards that are lower than those set by Berne.

There are three additional multilateral neighbouring rights treaties. The Phonograms Convention, which came into force in 1973, protects producers of phonograms against record piracy, but has been largely superseded by the TRIPs Agreement. The Satellite Convention, which entered into force in 1979, protects broadcasting organisations by preventing unauthorised distribution of programme-carrying signals transmitted by satellite. The Beijing Treaty, adopted in 2012 but not yet in force, grants performers rights in fixed audiovisual performances, addressing a gap in other neighbouring rights treaties.

*WIPO Treaties: The 'Digital Agenda'* The challenges of digital technologies and the Internet led to a diplomatic conference in Geneva in 1996 which resulted in two treaties: the WIPO Copyright Treaty (WCT) and the WIPO Performances and Phonograms Treaty (WPPT). The WCT, which is a 'special agreement' within Article 20 of the Berne Convention, in what is known as the 'digital agenda', expanded on Berne to establish a right of communication to the public and rules collateral to traditional copyright, in the form of protections against the circumvention of technological measures and against the removal of rights management information.[12] The WPPT supplements and expands on neighbouring rights protected under Rome, and extends the 'digital agenda' reforms to sound recordings and performances.

*The TRIPs Agreement* From the 1980s, international copyright protection became enmeshed in negotiations over free trade. This reflected the increased economic significance of trade in intellectual property products and gridlock in established multilateral processes, arising from fundamental differences between economically developed countries and emerging and lesser developed economies.[13] Intellectual property

---

[11] Goldstein and Hugenholtz, *International Copyright*, [2.2.2].
[12] M. Ficsor, *The Law of Copyright and the Internet: The 1996 WIPO Treaties, their Interpretation and Implementation* (Oxford University Press, 2002).
[13] Goldstein and Hugenholtz, *International Copyright*, 71–3; L. Helfer, 'Regime shifting: the TRIPs Agreement and the new dynamics of international intellectual property making' (2004) 29 *Yale Journal of International Law* 1.

rights were integrated into the Uruguay Round of the GATT trade negotiations, resulting in 1994 in the Agreement on Trade-Related Aspects of Intellectual Property Rights (the TRIPs Agreement), as an annexed agreement to membership of the World Trade Organization (WTO). Article 9(1) of TRIPs incorporates the substantive standards of Berne, apart from the protection of moral rights, as a baseline minimum of copyright protection. By linking the Berne minima to the international free trade system, TRIPs was the impetus for additional countries to adhere to the Berne Convention. The TRIPs Agreement also clarified and extended the Berne standards, especially in relation to computer programs, compilations of data and a rental right.

More importantly, TRIPs superimposed the international trade paradigm on the Berne template.[14] In particular, TRIPs established standards for enforcing intellectual property rights, and enabled Member States to invoke the WTO dispute-settlement procedures. By establishing an enforcement regime, TRIPs reinforced the mandatory nature of international copyright norms and reduced discretion for national policy-making, with implications for national public domains: [5.7].[15]

*Post-TRIPs Free Trade Agreements*   Since the TRIPs Agreement there have been a range of regional and bilateral free trade agreements incorporating intellectual property obligations and, in general, expanding the substantive protections under TRIPs, implementing what is known as the 'TRIPs-plus' agenda.[16] This book refers to TRIPs-plus agreements, commonly initiated by the United States, mainly where they illustrate new norms. This process is reinforced by Article 4 of TRIPs, which implements the most-favoured-nation (MFN) principle, which prohibits Member States from treating nationals of another Member State less favourably than the nationals of any other country: [4.3].

*The Marrakesh Treaty*   The Marrakesh Treaty was adopted in 2013 and entered into force in September 2016. It requires contracting states to establish a standard set of limitations and exceptions to permit reproduction, distribution and making available published works in formats accessible to blind, visually impaired and print disabled people, and to permit exchange of such works across borders. Marrakesh is significant as it is the first copyright treaty aimed at enhancing accessibility of copyright works, and therefore supporting the public domain. It is, moreover,

---

[14] Ginsburg and Treppoz, *International Copyright Law*, 1–2.   [15] *Ibid.* 272.
[16] R. Burrell and K. Weatherall, 'Exporting controversy? Reactions to the copyright provisions of the US–Australia Free Trade Agreement: lessons for US trade policy' (2008) 2 *University of Illinois Journal of Law, Technology & Policy* 259.

the first international agreement to require substantive changes to national laws relating to domestic claimants rather than simply with respect to foreign rights holders.

### 4.2.2 Historical Trajectory and Structural Effects of International Agreements

Just as copyright and the public domain were arguably 'born together',[17] so the global public domain was constructed by the birth and development of international copyright law. Berne was designed to protect authors in the context of international trade in copyright material, and the imperfect protection of foreign authors under national laws and under the complex bilateral treaties in place in the nineteenth century. While the express object of Berne is 'to protect, in as effective and uniform a manner as possible, the rights of authors': [4.2.1], in practice the Berne template resulted from messy compromises between European juristic traditions that differed on the nature of copyright and authors' rights.[18]

The difficult task of reaching multilateral agreement, and the influence of the authors' rights tradition, rooted in the view that authors have a natural property right in their work, meant that rights and interests other than those of authors and publishers were not at the forefront of negotiations leading to Berne. It would be a mistake, however, to conclude that public domain values and considerations were entirely absent. For example, in debates leading to the Convention, attention was given to the desirability of allowing reproductions of articles of newspapers and periodicals, as well as works intended for instruction, works of a scientific nature and chrestomathies.[19] As Bannerman has argued, for the period from the 1880s through to the 1920s, it is incorrect to assume an exclusive focus on authors' rights, as there was general agreement on the importance of principles supporting 'access to knowledge', at least in relation to the reproduction of scientific articles, copying for educational purposes, the free flow of news and translation between languages.[20]

International copyright law, and especially the Berne template, is often seen as a complex system of rigid, immutable rules that establish inflexible limits on national laws. This is reinforced by there being no substantive revision of Berne since 1971. This view, however, tends to reify a particular, ahistorical conception of international copyright law which overlooks the

---

[17] M. Rose, 'Nine-tenths of the law: the English copyright debates and the rhetoric of the public domain' (2003) 66 *Law and Contemporary Problems* 75 at 76.
[18] Ladas, *The International Protection of Literary and Artistic Property*, 82–6.   [19] *Ibid.* 85.
[20] S. Bannerman, *International Copyright and Access to Knowledge* (Cambridge University Press, 2016), p. 16.

complexity of the negotiations in revisions of Berne, not to mention other copyright treaties. Furthermore, it ignores the flexibilities available to state parties that result from the generality and complexity of international copyright law. While we should recognise that there is nothing inevitable about the current international framework, however, we must understand its essential elements in order to know precisely what legal flexibilities are available. In addition, we should appreciate that the dense thicket of nested agreements dealt with in this chapter incorporate structural biases.

The structural features of international copyright law, which condition global and national public domains, and which should be borne in mind in our explanation of international law, are as follows. First, in accordance with both history and the text of Berne, international protection is aimed expressly at protecting the rights of authors, meaning that public interest considerations are dealt with mainly by exclusions, limitations and exceptions to those rights. Second, the Berne system is based on the twin pillars of national treatment, meaning that Berne members must give foreign members the same treatment as their own nationals, and minimum levels of protection. The minimum protections mandated by Berne, and other international agreements, relate to protectable subject matter, the term of protection and exclusive rights. Significantly, the Berne system sets a floor of minimum levels of protection and does not set ceilings. Third, Berne is based on the fundamental principle that protection must be given without formalities, so there is effectively a presumption in favour of protection. Fourth, given the breadth of protectable subject matter and exclusive rights, the main public domain safeguards are exclusions, limitations and exceptions. Nevertheless, the Berne system imposes ceilings on permissible exclusions, limitations and exceptions, with most being optional and not mandatory. Fifth, Article 9(1) of TRIPs, which superimposes the international free trade paradigm on the Berne system, incorporates Articles 1–21 of Berne, and therefore incorporates the Berne model of minimum levels of protection and limited exceptions. Sixth, post-Berne treaties, including TRIPs, the WCT and WPPT, build on Berne by generally expanding protection by, for example, introducing rental rights and a generalised public communication right. Seventh, TRIPs introduced a mechanism for enforcing international copyright law and, in doing so, reduced the practical discretion of nation states to craft their own approaches to the public domain.

Although international copyright law is the result of complex shifting agendas, in which the balance between authors' rights and the public domain was never immutable,[21] the structural features identified above reflect an inexorable historical trajectory. That trajectory has seen

[21] *Ibid.* 119–22.

a levelling up of protections under national laws to minimum Berne thresholds, then the augmentation of protection in post-Berne treaties, including multilateral treaties and TRIPs-plus agreements. As explained in the first point, on this model, public domain values have been taken into account in exclusions, limitations or exceptions, but not generally in the formulation of the minimum protections. This process has resulted in a dense thicket of international copyright law, with a complex structure of protectable rights matched by complex exclusions and exceptions.

The rest of this chapter maps the elements of international copyright law which together establish the boundaries of the global public domain, in the form of minimum levels of protection. The four elements of international copyright law which establish these minimum protections are: the prohibition on formalities; minimum terms of protection; breadth of the protected subject matter; and minimum exclusive rights.

Before turning to the four elements, it is necessary first to introduce the twin pillars of international copyright law: the principles of national treatment and minimum rights.

*4.2.3 International Copyright Law as a Given*

International copyright law bears the marks of its contested history, with a relative neglect of the public domain. Given its history and structure, there is scope for reforming the international system.[22] In reality, however, the Berne Convention, substantially unchanged since 1971, is unlikely to be reformed; and post-Berne treaties have yet to bolster the public domain, with the limited exception of the Marrakesh Treaty.[23] Given these circumstances, this book asks what can be done to protect and enhance the public domain within the constraints of existing treaties. Therefore, while we do not discount the importance of debating treaty reform proposals, detailed analysis of their merits is not our purpose.

## 4.3 The Twin Pillars: National Treatment and Minimum Rights

The 'twin pillars' of international copyright law are the principle of national treatment and the obligation to confer minimum levels of protection.[24]

---

[22] Gervais, *(Re)structuring Copyright*; Giblin and Weatherall (eds.), *What if We Could Reimagine Copyright?*
[23] As we point out in Chapter 12, there are current proposals for introducing treaties dealing with exceptions, especially exceptions for libraries and archives, and educational uses.
[24] Ricketson and Ginsburg, *International Copyright and Neighbouring Rights*, [6.90]; Ginsburg and Treppoz, *International Copyright Law*, 261.

The national treatment principle, set out in Article 5(1) of Berne, is a principle of non-discrimination (as opposed to reciprocity) which requires Berne members to give the same level of protection to foreign authors as to their own nationals. As such, the principle both acknowledges and entrenches differences in protection under national laws. In addition to the principle of national treatment, Article 5(1) sets a minimum level of protection by requiring Berne members to protect the 'rights specially granted by this Convention'. While the obligation to provide minimum protection does not apply to works produced by authors in the country of origin, as countries usually give the same protection to their own nationals as to foreign authors, it is only where greater protection is given than the Berne minima that there are differences.[25] Article 5(1) therefore results in differences in national public domains, but limits the scope for national laws to vary the level of protection.

Under Berne, there are few exceptions to the principle of national treatment, these being confined to the copyright term,[26] protection of applied art and industrial design,[27] and the resale royalty right.[28] Apart from Berne, the principle of national treatment underpins other international copyright and neighbouring rights treaties, but with different formulations. The neighbouring rights treaties (Rome and the WPPT), for example, require national treatment only in relation to the specific rights guaranteed by the respective conventions.[29] The principle of national treatment in Article 3(1) of TRIPs applies to 'the protection of intellectual property' and encompasses a broader range of rights than the Berne principle.[30] In addition, in Article 4, TRIPs adopts a most-favoured-nation (MFN) principle, which prohibits Member States from treating nationals of another Member State less favourably than the nationals of other countries. This means that where a TRIPs member enters a bilateral or multilateral agreement, or TRIPs-plus agreement, that confers greater protection than the TRIPs minimum on nationals of treaty parties, it must also confer the same level of protection on nationals of all TRIPs member countries. The across-the-board increase in protection that results from the MFN principle results in a corresponding reduction of the public domain.

---

[25] Ricketson and Ginsburg, *International Copyright and Neighbouring Rights*, [6.90].
[26] Berne Convention, Art. 7(8).   [27] Berne Convention, Art. 2(7).
[28] Berne Convention, Art. 14*ter* (2).   [29] Rome Convention, Art. 2(2); WPPT, Art. 4(1).
[30] Ricketson and Ginsburg, *International Copyright and Neighbouring Rights*, [4.35]; Goldstein and Hugenholtz, *International Copyright*, [4.2.3.2].

## 4.3.1 National Treatment and Retroactive Protection

The principle of national treatment has created problems where a work, required to be protected under Berne, is not protected in a non-Berne country, and therefore is part of the national public domain, but the country subsequently joins Berne. The problem arises because, by adhering to Berne, the Member State must protect Berne works regardless of whether they are in the public domain.[31] The problem is therefore that these works may cease to be in the public domain after accession to Berne. The issue of the extent to which 'retroactive protection'[32] may be required for such works is addressed by Article 18, the only Berne article to refer to the 'public domain'.[33]

Article 18(1) states that:

> This Convention shall apply to all works which, at the moment of its coming into force, have not yet fallen into the public domain in the country of origin through the expiry of the term of protection.

This Article establishes the rule that copyright protection must be applied to works required to be protected under Berne, including works that are in the public domain in the country where protection is claimed, unless the work has fallen into the public domain through expiry of the term of protection. Therefore, if a foreign work was not protected in a new Berne member for a reason other than term expiry – such as, due to failure to comply with formalities – Article 18(1) would require retroactive protection (or reviving protection where it had expired), removing the work from the public domain.

If unmodified, this retrospectivity would result in hardship for those acting in reliance on access to public domain works (known as 'reliance parties'). To deal with this, Article 18(3) confers flexibility by providing that, in the absence of any special conventions such as bilateral treaties, Member States must determine 'the conditions of application' of the retrospectivity principle. Although the term is not used, any conditions in favour of reliance parties must be 'transitional', and while the

---

[31] Ricketson and Ginsburg, *International Copyright and Neighbouring Rights*, [6.112].
[32] As the WIPO Guide to copyright treaties points out, strictly speaking 'retroactivity' is a misnomer, as Article 18 requires only that obligations under Berne be respected from the time of entry into force of the Convention, and not be given retrospective effect: M. Ficsor and WIPO, 'Guide to the copyright and related rights treaties administered by WIPO and glossary of copyright and related rights terms', WIPO, 2003 www.wipo.int/edocs/pubdocs/en/copyright/891/wipo_pub_891.pdf, [BC-18.1].
[33] The term 'public domain', which appeared in Article 14 of the 1836 Berne Convention (the antecedent provision to Article 18), was taken from French copyright law: T. Ochoa, 'Origins and meanings of the public domain'. Article 18 is incorporated by reference into TRIPs: TRIPs Agreement, Art. 14(6).

conditions may regulate retrospectivity, they must not completely deny retrospective protection.[34]

Issues relating to retroactive protection of public domain works arose when the United States joined Berne in 1989. In its initial implementation legislation, the United States gave no protection to works that had fallen into the public domain in violation of Article 18.[35] Subsequently, on adhering to TRIPs, in 1994, US Congress modified the position, providing for restoration of public domain works (such as those failing to comply with formalities) under certain conditions, which allow infringement actions to be commenced against reliance parties only after the owner gives notice of intent to enforce copyright, and only for acts of infringement that commence or continue twelve months or more after the notice.[36] In addition, anyone who created a derivative work based on a restored work is entitled to continue to exploit the work subject to paying reasonable compensation to the copyright holder.

The 1994 amendments removed the need to resolve difficult questions involving the interpretation of Article 18, including whether loss of protection under pre-1989 US law due to a failure to renew copyright following an initial term arose from expiration of the term (in which case Article 18(3) would prohibit retrospective protection) or a failure to comply with formalities (in which case some form of restrospectivity would be required).[37] The combination of retrospective protection conferred by the amendments, and the failure of a challenge under US constitutional law in *Golan v. Holder*,[38] meant that works such as Prokofiev's *Peter and the Wolf* and Shostakovich's *Preludes and Fugues Op. 87* were removed from the public domain in the United States.[39]

### 4.3.2  National Treatment and the Global Public Domain

The result of the twin pillars is that multilateral agreements 'set a floor, but no ceiling, for the scope of copyright protection'.[40] The application of

---

[34] Ricketson and Ginsburg, *International Copyright and Neighbouring Rights*, [6.123]. See also I. Karp, 'Final report, Berne Article 18 study on retroactive United States copyright protection for Berne and other works' (1996) 20 *Columbia-VLA Journal of Law & the Arts* 157; A. Bogsch, 'WIPO views of Article 18' (1995) 43 *Journal of the Copyright Society of the USA* 181.

[35] D. Gervais, '*Golan v. Holder*: a look at the constraints imposed by the Berne Convention' (2011) 64 *Vanderbilt Law Review En Banc* 147.

[36] 17 USC §104A. For discussion, see *Hoepker v. Kruger*, 200 F Supp 2d 340 (SDNY 2002); E. Townsend Gard, 'In the trenches with §104A: an evaluation of the parties' arguments in *Golan v. Holder* as it heads to the Supreme Court' (2011) 64 *Vanderbilt Law Review En Banc* 199.

[37] Goldstein and Hugenholtz, *International Copyright*, [8.4].    [38] 132 S Ct 873 (2012).

[39] 132 S Ct 873, 893, 904 (2012).    [40] Ginsburg, 'International Copyright', 278.

national treatment therefore results in a 'levelling up', where any flexibility is in increasing protection relative to baseline standards, with the ability to reduce protection constrained. This is reinforced by the operation of the TRIPs MFN principle, which requires WTO members to confer any higher levels of protection provided under post-TRIPs agreements equally to the nationals of all WTO members. As a matter of international copyright law, there is therefore little resistance to increasing protection, but it is difficult or impossible to expand the public domain by adjusting the level of copyright protection downwards. Furthermore, bilateral agreements that increase protection have effects beyond the parties to the agreements.

Given that most countries are members of Berne, Article 18 has limited practical effect. Nevertheless, the rule of retroactive protection throws light on the biases of international copyright law. By requiring restoration of copyright to some works previously in the public domain, Article 18 entrenches the primacy of the twin pillars over other considerations such as the importance of public domain works as raw materials for derivative works.

## 4.4 Prohibition of Formalities

The Berne rule prohibiting formalities is one of the most significant constraints on the global public domain. Article 5(2) of Berne establishes the principle that the 'enjoyment and the exercise' of copyright protection under the Convention must not be subject to formalities. The rule against formalities applies only to foreign works, leaving Berne members free to impose formalities on domestic works. This is made clear by Article 5(3), which provides that '[p]rotection in the country of origin is governed by domestic law'.

The prohibition on formalities was introduced by the Berlin revision in 1908. Prior to this, protection was conditioned on compliance with formalities in the country of origin. Difficulties of proving compliance with formalities in foreign jurisdictions, the denial of protection of works for trivial failings and the ineffectiveness of international attempts to simplify evidence of formalities, effectively made the case for their abolition.[41]

---

[41] J. C. Ginsburg, '"With untired spirits and formal constancy": Berne compatibility of formal declaratory measures to enhance copyright title-searching' (2013) 28 *Berkeley Technology Law Journal* 1583, 1589; Ricketson and Ginsburg, *International Copyright and Neighbouring Rights*, [6.86]–[6.87]; [6.101].

## 4.4.1 What are 'Formalities'?

To understand the rule against formalities, it is important to acknowledge some complexity in determining whether particular arrangements are prohibited by Article 5(2). A good example of the difficulties is section 30.04 of the Canadian Copyright Act, which creates an exception from infringement for works available through the Internet in favour of educational institutions unless a clearly visible notice prohibiting the infringing act is posted at the Internet site from which the work is available.[42] As this provision denies copyright protection in the absence of notice in the correct form, it is arguable that it contravenes the rule against formalities.[43] On the other hand, as the notice requirement is one of a number of exclusions from an exception, and not a prerequisite for subsistence of copyright or for bringing enforcement proceedings, it may not be interpreted as a prerequisite for the 'enjoyment' or 'exercise' of copyright.

Article 5(2) does not prohibit all formalities, but merely prohibits laws that make the 'enjoyment' or 'exercise' of copyright in foreign works subject to formalities. Formalities may therefore be applied to domestic works, and voluntary systems of formalities may be applied to all works. The best-known example of formalities that apply exclusively to domestic works is the US law that requires registration as a condition for instituting infringement proceedings in relation to any 'United States work'.[44] While making copyright in domestic works conditional on formalities is permissible, however, countries are unlikely to impose requirements that disadvantage domestic authors.[45]

More importantly, Berne does not prohibit measures other than those for which copyright protection or enforcement is conditioned on formalities, including voluntary registration systems or notification of matters such as authorship.[46] If registration or notification is entirely voluntary, however, there are questions about the incentives for complying. There is nothing in Article 5(2) that prevents Berne members from conferring advantages, such as evidentiary presumptions or additional remedies, in return for compliance with formalities. For example, under the Canadian Act a certificate of registration creates a presumption of subsistence and ownership of copyright.[47] Caution is, however, required in crafting

---

[42] Copyright Act 1985 (Can), RSC 1985, c. C-42, s. 30.04.
[43] Ginsburg, '"With untired spirits and formal constancy"', 1608 n. 92.
[44] 17 USC §411 (1976).
[45] Ricketson and Ginsburg, *International Copyright and Neighbouring Rights*, [6.92].
[46] For a survey of voluntary registration systems, see WIPO SCCR, *Survey of national legislation on voluntary registration systems for copyright and related rights*, SCCR/13/2, Geneva, 9 November 2005.
[47] Copyright Act 1985 (Can), RSC 1985, c. C-42, s. 53(2).

4.4 Prohibition of Formalities    101

incentives, especially if they confer additional remedies, as there may be difficulties in distinguishing offering enhanced remedies (which is permissible) from denying effective remedies (which is impermissible).[48]

Formalities are not generally imposed as a condition for protecting neighbouring rights, it apparently being assumed that protection will be free of formalities.[49]

### 4.4.2 Formalities and the Public Domain

The introduction of the Berne rule against formalities should be seen as part of a broader shift from a paradigm of copyright as a grant by the state, conditioned on a public act such as registration, to one of copyright as arising solely from the author's act of creation.[50] This shift effectively endorsed the *droit d'auteur* approach to copyright, in which protection arises as of right, as distinct from more instrumentalist approaches.[51]

Conditioning copyright on formalities creates a default that copyright will not subsist unless the claimant takes positive action to 'opt in' to protection.[52] On the other hand, a rule against formalities protects works by default, requiring a positive act by a claimant to 'opt out' of protection. As many more works will be protected in regimes with a rule against formalities than where formalities are mandated, Article 5(2) is a significant constraint on the public domain. For example, for much of its history US law required owners to re-register in order for protection to be renewed following an initial term, yet from 1883 to 1964 fewer than 11 per cent of owners exercised the right to re-register.[53] The US entry into Berne therefore caused a contraction of the US public domain.

While the rule against formalities ensures that authors are not deprived of protection, including for trivial omissions, requiring formalities operates as a filter that may prevent protection of unmeritorious works.

---

[48] Ricketson and Ginsburg, *International Copyright and Neighbouring Rights*, [6.108].
[49] *Ibid.* [19.09].
[50] J. C. Ginsburg, 'A tale of two copyrights: literary property in revolutionary France and America', in Sherman and Strowel (eds.), *Of Authors and Origins*, 131–58; Ricketson and Ginsburg, *International Copyright and Neighbouring Rights*, [6.101]; R. A. Epstein, 'The dubious constitutionality of the Copyright Term Extension Act' (2002) 36 *Loyola of Los Angeles Law Review* 123 at 124; D. Gervais and D. Renaud, 'The future of United States copyright formalities: why we should prioritize recordation, and how to do it' (2013) 28 *Berkeley Technology Law Journal* 1459 at 1463.
[51] The prohibition on formalities was, however, one of the reasons for Latin American countries initially to spurn Berne in favour of the Montevideo Convention: J. Belido, 'Latin American and Spanish copyright relations (1880–1904)' (2009) 12(1) *Journal of World Intellectual Property* 1.
[52] C. Sprigman, 'Reform(alizing) copyright' (2004) 57 *Stanford Law Review* 485.
[53] W. Landes and R. Posner, 'Indefinitely renewable copyright' (2003) 70 *University of Chicago Law Review* 471 at 473.

Concerns that copyright is overbroad in scope or excessive in duration, have led to calls for the reintroduction of formalities.[54] According to advocates, an advantage of reformalisation would be that it would enrich the 'formality-fed public domain' by removing works that would otherwise be automatically protected.[55]

The analysis of rules imposing formalities is, however, more complex than suggested by the argument that filtering out works beneficially expands the public domain. One problem is that mandatory formalities disadvantages individual authors relative to corporate copyright owners, who are more likely to take affirmative steps, such as registration, to ensure protection.[56] Moreover, it is important to disentangle the various arguments that might justify formalities. In addition to their role in filtering out material, some of which may not deserve protection, formalities, such as the creation of public registers, perform important information roles, including: signalling that works are protected by copyright and thereby increasing certainty, especially for those who wish to use material to create new works; and notifying third parties of the identity and contact details of copyright owners, thereby reducing transaction costs for those wishing to license works.[57] Even within the parameters set by the rule against formalities, the flexibilities available, such as the potential for voluntary systems of registration, provide scope for creative mechanisms for improving access to works for purposes such as the creation of derivative works: [6.2.2]. In addition, statutory deposit systems can also play a valuable role: [6.2.1].

## 4.5 Term of Protection

Historically, the core meaning of the 'public domain' referred to works in which the copyright term had expired: [9.1], the fifth of our public domain categories. Despite the harmonising effect of international copyright law, there are considerable variations in copyright terms under national laws, creating major differences between national public

---

[54] Sprigman, 'Reform(alizing) copyright'; J. Gibson, 'Once and future copyright' (2005) 81 *Notre Dame Law Review* 167; Lessig, 'Re-crafting a public domain'; S. van Gompel, 'Formalities in the digital era: an obstacle or opportunity?', in L. Bently et al. (eds.), *Global Copyright: Three Hundred Years Since the Statute of Anne, From 1709 to Cyberspace* (Edward Elgar, 2010), pp. 395–423; P. Samuelson, 'Preliminary thoughts on copyright reform' (2007) *Utah Law Review* 551.
[55] Ginsburg, '"With untired spirits and formal constancy"', 1585.
[56] *Ibid.*; N. Elkin-Koren, 'Can formalities save the public domain? Reconsidering formalities for the 2010s' (2013) 28 *Berkeley Technology Law* 1537 at 1543.
[57] Elkin-Koren, 'Can formalities save the public domain?', 1541–5; D. Gangjee, 'Copyright formalities: A return to registration?', in Giblin and Weatherall (eds.), *What If We Could Reimagine Copyright?*, 234–46.

### 4.5 Term of Protection

domains: Chapter 9. Regardless of these differences, there has been an inexorable tendency to longer copyright terms under multilateral, regional and bilateral agreements.

#### 4.5.1 General Minimum Duration Rule under Berne

In the early years of Berne, it proved difficult to reach agreement on the duration of protection.[58] Since the 1908 Berlin revision, however, the minimum term for works, now set out in Article 7(1), has been 'the life of the author and fifty years after his death'. Berne therefore establishes a floor on duration of protection, but not a ceiling. This is confirmed by Article 7(6), which provides that '[t]he countries of the Union may grant a term of protection in excess of those provided by the preceding paragraphs'.

#### 4.5.2 Special Duration Rules under Berne

*Anonymous and Pseudonymous Works* As it is impossible to calculate a term set by reference to the life of an author for works where an author cannot be identified, Berne establishes a special rule for anonymous and pseudonymous works. Under Article 7(3), the minimum term for such works is set at fifty years 'after the work has been lawfully made available to the public'. Berne creates another special rule for works of joint authorship, where two or more authors collaborate on a work. In such cases, Article 7*bis* provides for the term to be calculated by reference to the death of the last surviving author.

*Photographs, Applied Art and Films* Under Article 7 of Berne, the general rule on duration is subject to exceptions for three categories of works: photographic works, works of applied art and cinematographic works. Article 7(4) sets a minimum term for photographic works of twenty-five years from the making of the work, but otherwise leaves the duration of protection to national laws. Article 9 of the WCT, however, provides that, in relation to photographic works, contracting parties are prohibited from applying Article 7(4) of Berne, which effectively entrenches the general Berne standard of life plus fifty years, removing the 'durational discrimination against photographs'.[59]

Article 7(4) also provides a minimum term for works of applied art that are protected as artistic works of twenty-five years from the making of the

---
[58] Ricketson and Ginsburg, *International Copyright and Neighbouring Rights*, [9.14] ff.
[59] Ibid. [9.64].

work, but otherwise leaves the term to national laws. As Berne members are not required to protect works of applied art as artistic works, the main consideration is whether or not these works are protected in the first place. Where works of applied art are protected as artistic works, most Berne members apply a term of life plus either fifty or seventy years.[60]

Article 7(2) provides for two possible terms for cinematographic works: 'fifty years after the work has been made available to the public with the consent of the author' or, 'failing such an event within fifty years from the making of such a work, fifty years after the making'. In accordance with Article 7(6), it is possible for Berne members to adopt the general term for works of life plus fifty years, or some other longer term.

*Moral Rights*  Fundamental disagreements between Member States concerning the conceptual and juridical basis of moral rights has led to much controversy concerning the duration of moral rights. Intractable differences between Berne members resulted in a compromise being reached at the 1967 Stockholm revision, now set out in Article 6*bis*(2). This provision establishes the basic rule that moral rights, after the death of the author, are to last for at least the duration of the economic rights.

Apart from moral rights in works, Article 5 of the WPPT provides for performers' rights of attribution and integrity in live and recorded aural performances. The duration of performers' moral rights, set out in Article 5(2), mirrors Article 6*bis*(2) of Berne, establishing the basic rule of protection of at least until the expiry of the economic rights.

While protection of moral rights after expiry of economic rights arguably does not affect the copyright public domain as, following our definition, it does not affect the permission-free use of works, we argue that persistence of moral rights means that works cannot be regarded as fully falling into the public domain until moral rights expire: [9.11].

*TRIPs Minimum Requirements*  In certain circumstances, such as cinematographic works, Berne provides for the copyright term to be set on a basis other than life of the author. Article 12 of TRIPs provides that where a term of protection of a work (other than a photographic work or work of applied art) is set by reference to a basis other than the life of a natural person, the term must be no less than fifty years after the end of the year of authorised publication, or, for unpublished works, fifty years from the end of the year of the making of the work. For cinematographic works, there is a potential inconsistency between Article 7(2) of Berne, which refers to the time at which the work is 'made available', and

---

[60] *Ibid.* [9.49].

## 4.5 Term of Protection

Article 12 of TRIPs, which refers to 'authorised publication', with some disagreement on the implications of the differences in wording.[61]

### 4.5.3 Rule of Comparison of Terms

The rules on copyright duration established under Article 7 of Berne are the most important exception to the principle of national treatment. In place of national treatment, Article 7(8) adopts a principle known alternatively as the rule of comparison of terms or the rule of the shorter term.[62] Under this rule, which is based on reciprocity and not non-discrimination, the term of protection must not exceed the term set in the country of origin of the work, unless legislation in the country where protection is claimed provides otherwise. Therefore, where the term of protection in the country of origin is less than the term in the protecting country, the lesser term must be applied, unless legislation in the protecting country provides otherwise. The proviso to the rule means that national jurisdictions are free to apply the principle of national treatment in place of the rule of the shorter term.[63]

In the unlikely event that the term in the country of origin does not comply with the Article 7 minima, it seems that the minimum terms required by Berne must be applied.[64] In any case, in accordance with Article 5(3), it is open for Berne members to provide less protection to their own nationals than they must provide foreign authors under Article 7. While rare, the United States has taken advantage of this flexibility by refusing to restore copyright to domestic works which had entered the public domain by failure to comply with formalities, protection for which would otherwise be required by Article 18 of Berne: [4.3.1].[65]

*Exemption from the MFN Principle* Article 4 of the TRIPs Agreement adopts the MFN principle: [4.3]. If this principle applied to minimum terms of protection, it could affect the application of the Berne rule of comparison of terms, as greater protection for nationals of some WTO members would need to be extended to all WTO members. This result is, however, prevented by Article 4(b) of TRIPs, which provides that 'any advantage, favour, privilege or immunity' granted in accordance

---

[61] For different interpretations of this potential inconsistency, see *ibid.* [9.62] (arguing that the provisions may be interpreted consistently) and D. Gervais, *The TRIPs Agreement: Drafting History and Analysis* (2nd edn, Sweet & Maxwell, 2003), p. 142 (arguing that the provisions may result in different terms).
[62] Goldstein and Hugenholtz, *International Copyright*, [8.31].
[63] Ricketson and Ginsburg, *International Copyright and Neighbouring Rights*, [9.55]. The US and Canada, for example, do not apply the rule of comparison of terms.
[64] *Ibid.* [9.55].   [65] 17 USC §104A.

with Berne is exempted from the MFN principle. This provision effectively extends the exemption from the MFN principle to the rule of comparison of terms established by Article 7(8) of Berne.[66]

### 4.5.4 Neighbouring Rights

In relation to neighbouring rights, as they may be produced by juridical persons, a term based on the life of an author makes no sense. Article 14 of Rome establishes a minimum term of protection of twenty years, with the following different starting points for different categories of subject matter: for phonograms, and performances fixed in phonograms, from the date of fixation; for non-fixed performances, from the time of performance; and for broadcasts, from the time of broadcast.[67] The minimum terms for performances and phonograms were extended by TRIPs to fifty years from the end of the year in which the fixation was made or the performance took place.[68] The WPPT sets the minimum term for performances fixed in phonograms at fifty years from the end of the year of fixation; and for phonograms, at fifty years from the end of the year of publication, or for unpublished phonograms at fifty years from the end of the year of fixation.[69]

### 4.5.5 TRIPs-plus Term Extensions

Since TRIPs, the term of protection has been extended by regional and bilateral copyright treaties, such as the EU Term Directive and the Australia–US Free Trade Agreement: Chapter 9. This has resulted in two main international standards for the duration of copyright: the Berne minimum of life plus fifty years and a TRIPs-plus standard of life plus seventy years: [9.10], [9.12].

### 4.5.6 Copyright Term and the Public Domain

A limited copyright term is a fundamental safeguard for the copyright public domain: [9.1]. In accordance with the Berne model, international copyright law establishes uniform rules for the minimum terms of protection. Despite this, there are considerable variations in the copyright terms set by national laws: Chapter 9. The national variations are reinforced by the application of the rule of comparison of terms, and the exemption of

---

[66] Ricketson and Ginsburg, *International Copyright and Neighbouring Rights*, [9.61].
[67] In each case, the twenty-year duration runs from the end of the calendar year in which the relevant event occurs.
[68] TRIPs Agreement, Art. 14(5).   [69] WPPT, Art. 17.

### 4.6 Protectable Subject Matter

term duration from the MFN principle under Article 4(b) of TRIPs. Nevertheless, as international copyright law does not establish any ceilings on the copyright term, variations in national laws invariably relate to terms longer than the Berne minima. Moreover, the absence of an international ceiling means that national laws could theoretically provide an unlimited term.

For example, until recently, Australia had a perpetual term for unpublished works: [9.8], and Singapore provides perpetual protection for unpublished government works: [3.3.5], [9.12]. The structure of international copyright law therefore means that the protection of the public domain by means of a ceiling on duration depends entirely on limits set by national laws.

The lack of ceilings on the copyright term reflects the structural biases of international copyright law: [4.2.2]. Furthermore, the application of a rigid minimum term to all Berne works, which applies a 'one-size-fits-all' model, creates problems for categories of works, such as computer programs, which do not seem to require the incentive of a lengthy term: [9.12].

### 4.6 Protectable Subject Matter

The third element of international copyright law with a significant effect on national public domains is the broad scope of works and subject matter required to be protected. To begin, it is important to appreciate that, in accordance with the general model, international copyright treaties set floors for protected subject matter, and not ceilings.[70] This means that national laws are free to extend protection to subject matter beyond that required by international law, but they cannot narrow the categories of protected works. Works that are outside of the scope of protectable subject matter fall into a number of our public domain categories: Category 1 ('works failing minimum requirements'), Category 2 ('works impliedly excluded') and Category 10 ('facts and ideas').

The works protected under Berne are identified in Article 2, which, in Article 2(6), requires those works to 'enjoy protection in all countries of the Union'. Accordingly, if a work falls within a category identified in Article 2, there are obligations to apply the principle of national treatment and the substantive minimum levels of protection.

#### 4.6.1 *Authorial Works*

Berne members and TRIPs signatories are obliged to protect the works identified in Article 2 of Berne as falling within the category of 'literary

---

[70] Goldstein and Hugenholtz, *International Copyright*, [6.1].

and artistic works'.[71] The protected works under Berne are clarified and extended by provisions of TRIPs and the WCT.

Article 2(1) of Berne defines 'literary and artistic works' expansively to mean 'every production in the literary, scientific and artistic domain, whatever may be the mode or form of its expression'. The definition then provides a long, non-exhaustive list of illustrative works. There are two main components of the definition: an implied minimum qualitative standard and a requirement that a work falls within a protected category.[72]

It is accepted that the Article 2(1) definition implies a minimum threshold of authorial creation. This is implicit from Article 2(5), which mandates protection of collections of works, such as encyclopaedias and anthologies, 'which, by reason of the selection and arrangement of their contents, constitute intellectual creations'.[73] This interpretation is also implied by Article 1, which refers to 'protection of the rights of authors'.[74] Among national laws, there is agreement that the standard of intellectual creation or originality means that a work must be the product of an author's intellectual efforts and not be copied. There are, however, significant differences between national laws in the formulation and content of the minimum threshold: [7.2].

The list of works set out in Article 2(1) is extensive, covering those categories traditionally regarded as literary, dramatic, musical and artistic works, and extending to works such as choreographic works and works of architecture. If a category is included in the list, it must be protected by Berne countries.[75] As the list is illustrative only, however, Berne members are free to add new categories; but, if they do, applying the principle of national treatment they must confer the same protection on works produced by nationals of other Berne countries. Moreover, as Berne does not attempt to define the works in the enumerated categories, it is a matter for national laws to determine if, for example, a work is a 'sculpture' or a 'drawing'; and this exercise of categorising works is often far from straightforward. With the exception of works of applied art, referred to below, the greatest variation in protection under national laws occurs with photographic works, with significant variations in the originality threshold and duration of protection.[76]

---

[71] Article 9(1) of TRIPs incorporates the Berne Paris text by reference.
[72] Goldstein and Hugenholtz, *International Copyright*, [6.1].
[73] Ricketson and Ginsburg, *International Copyright and Neighbouring Rights*, [8.03].
[74] Goldstein and Hugenholtz, *International Copyright*, [6.1]. [75] *Ibid.* [8.08].
[76] Y. Gendreau, A. Nordemann and R. Oesch (eds.), *Copyright and Photographs: An International Survey* (Kluwer Law International, 1999).

## 4.6.2 Other Works Specifically Protected

In addition to the works enumerated in Article 2(1), other paragraphs of Article 2 extend protection to further specific kinds of works. As previously mentioned, Article 2(5) requires the protection of collections of works, such as encyclopaedias and anthologies, which 'by reason of the selection and arrangement of their contents, constitute intellectual creations'. The main issue in determining whether works falling within this category are protected under national laws is the level of intellectual creativity required for protection: [7.2].

Uncertainty concerning whether such compilations of non-copyright material are protected under Article 2(1) of Berne seems to be resolved by provisions of TRIPs and the WCT. Article 10(2) of TRIPs requires protection of compilations of data or other material 'which by reason of the selection or arrangement of their contents constitute intellectual creations', and Article 5 of the WCT is almost identical. Although these provisions do not require protection of compilations which fail to satisfy an originality threshold, this does not prevent jurisdictions from protecting such compilations under *sui generis* laws, such as the EU Database Directive.[77]

Article 2(3) of Berne provides for protection of derivative works, namely '[t]ranslations, adaptations, arrangements of music and other alterations of a literary or artistic work'. This provision must be read with Article 12, which provides for authors to 'enjoy the exclusive right of authorizing adaptations, arrangements and other alterations of their works'. The production of a derivative work, referred to in Article 2(3), may therefore amount to an infringement of the original work on which the derivative work is based. It is unclear whether the protection of derivative works, which is expressed to be 'without prejudice to the copyright in the original work', extends to works produced without permission of the owner of copyright in the original work, or is confined to works produced with permission or works derived from works in the public domain.[78]

For some time, there was uncertainty about whether computer programs were protected as literary works under Berne.[79] However, regardless of arguments about the appropriateness of their protection as copyright works, the position was put beyond doubt by TRIPs and the

---

[77] Database Directive (EU). The full titles and citations of all Directives are in the Table of International Instruments.
[78] Goldstein and Hugenholtz, *International Copyright*, [6.1.2.6].
[79] WIPO, 'Model provisions for the protection of computer software' [1977] *Industrial Property* 265.

WCT. Article 10(1) of TRIPs provides for computer programs 'whether in source or in object code' to be protected as literary works under Berne, with a substantially identical provision in Article 4 of the WCT.

Article 2(7) of Berne leaves it to legislation in Berne countries to determine the extent of protection of works of applied art and industrial designs and models, and the conditions of protection. The special treatment given to this category of works arises mainly because they may be entitled to separate protection under industrial designs laws, but also because of very different national approaches to the potential overlap between copyright and industrial designs protection.[80]

### 4.6.3 Exclusion of Protection for Ideas

In addition to determining the works falling within the definition of 'literary and artistic works', the scope of protected works under Berne depends upon express and implied exclusions: Chapter 5. There is, however, one general exclusion from protection that is so central to determining protectable subject matter that it is best dealt with in defining the scope of protection: the principle that copyright does not extend to ideas or facts. Although a fundamental principle of copyright law is that expression is protected, and not ideas or facts, Berne does not include an express statement of this principle. Nevertheless, Article 2(1) effectively requires protection of a work 'whatever may be the mode or form of its expression'; and it is accepted that this wording confirms the principle (or underlying assumption) that protection does not extend to ideas and facts.[81]

The idea/expression dichotomy was first expressly incorporated into international copyright law by Article 9(2) of TRIPs, which states that:

> Copyright protection shall extend to expressions and not to ideas, procedures, methods of operation or mathematical concepts as such.

Article 2 of the WCT incorporates the principle in almost identical terms. The related principles that copyright does not extend to ideas or facts are especially important in determining the scope of protection of computer programs and compilations of data. In recognition of this, both Article 4 of the WCT, which requires protection of computer programs, and Article 5, which requires protection of original compilations of data,

---

[80] Goldstein and Hugenholtz, *International Copyright*, [6.1.2.10].
[81] *Ibid.* [8.06]–[8.07]. The principle may also be implied from the requirement for a literary or artistic work to be a 'production': Ficsor and WIPO, 'Guide to copyright', [BC-2.10].

include Agreed Statements which require the scope of protection of the relevant works to be read with the principle established by Article 2. In relation to computer programs, this means that copyright does not extend to the 'method of operation' or functions performed by a program,[32] while in relation to compilations of data Article 5 means that copyright in the compilation must be independent of any copyright in the data.[83]

As the principle that copyright does not protect ideas or facts most commonly arises in the context of whether parts of a protected work are free to be used as unprotected ideas or facts, the considerable national differences in applying the principle are dealt with in Chapter 10 of this book, which deals with permission-free uses of protected works: [10.4].

### 4.6.4 The Requirement of Fixation

A further area of significant differences between national laws is whether a work must be fixed in a tangible form to be protected. The current Berne provision, Article 2(2), arose from controversy concerning choreographic works which had been required to be 'fixed in writing or otherwise', giving rise to the implication that all other works were to be protected regardless of fixation.[34] This Article leaves the issue of fixation to be determined by the laws of Berne members, by providing that it is 'a matter for legislation in the countries of the Union to prescribe that works in general or any specified categories of works shall not be protected unless they have been fixed in some material form'.

As a general proposition, common law jurisdictions require fixation as a condition of protection, whereas civil law jurisdictions do not.[85] At the 1967 Stockholm revision conference, several Berne members claimed that requiring fixation was in breach of the then text of Berne, as fixation might be relevant as an evidential requirement but could not precondition copyright subsistence.[86] The variations in national laws, which are permitted by Berne's 'flexible fixation standard',[87] are explained at [7.2.14]. Where fixation is a condition for protection it can bolster the public domain as unfixed works, such as purely oral works, will not be protected: [7.2.15].

---

[82] Ricketson and Ginsburg, *International Copyright and Neighbouring Rights*, [8.124].
[83] *Ibid.* [8.131].  [84] *Ibid.* [8.18].
[85] Goldstein and Hugenholtz, *International Copyright*, [6.1.5].
[86] E. Adeney, 'Authorship and fixation in copyright law: a comparative comment' (2011) 35 *Melbourne University Law Review* 677 at 682.
[87] E. White, 'The Berne Convention's flexible fixation requirement: a problematic provision for user-generated content' (2013) 13(2) *Chicago Journal of International Law* 685.

### 4.6.5 Neighbouring Rights Protection

Neighbouring rights treaties require the protection of performances, phonograms and broadcasts. Article 1 of Rome establishes that the protection of neighbouring rights is independent from copyright protection.

Rome does not define performances, but in Article 3(a) defines 'performers' to mean 'actors, singers, musicians, dancers, and other persons who act, sing, deliver, declaim, play in, or otherwise perform literary or artistic works'. There are two elements to this definition: those who qualify as performers and the subject matter of their performances. The definition appears broad enough for conductors to be performers.[88] The WPPT seems to confirm this by including those who 'interpret' works within the definition.[89] Under Rome, the performer must perform only a 'literary or artistic work', which, although confined to the scope of works protected under Berne, does not require that the works are protected by copyright, but may extend to public domain works.[90] The WPPT extends the protection of performers beyond literary and artistic works to include 'expressions of folklore'.[91] The Beijing Treaty, which extends the protection of performers to fixations in audiovisual works, defines 'performers' in identical terms to the WPPT.[92] In addition, Article 9 of Rome allows national laws to extend protection to 'artists who do not perform literary or artistic works', which includes variety and circus artists.[93]

A 'phonogram' is defined by Article 3(b) of Rome to mean 'any exclusively aural fixation of sounds of a performance or of other sounds'. The Convention protects the rights of producers of phonograms, with a 'producer of phonograms' being defined to mean the person or legal entity that first fixes the sounds.[94] While the definition of 'phonogram' is linked to the fixation of performances it is not confined to performances, but extends to fixations of 'other sounds', such as bird songs and other nature sounds.[95] As the definition is limited to 'exclusively aural fixations', this excludes fixations in audiovisual works, including films. This is made more explicit by the definition of 'phonogram' in Article 2(b) of the WPPT, which expressly excludes fixations of sounds 'incorporated into a cinematographic or other audiovisual work'. An Agreed Statement to the Article 2(b) definition provides that rights in a phonogram are not to

---

[88] Ficsor and WIPO, 'Guide to copyright', [RC-3.4].   [89] WPPT, Art. 2(a).
[90] Goldstein and Hugenholtz, *International Copyright*, [6.2.1].   [91] WPPT, Art. 2(a).
[92] Beijing Treaty, Art. 2(a).
[93] Goldstein and Hugenholtz, *International Copyright*, 234.
[94] Rome Convention, Art. 3(c).
[95] Ricketson and Ginsburg, *International Copyright and Neighbouring Rights*, [19.09]; Ficsor and WIPO, 'Guide to copyright', [RC-3.11].

### 4.6 Protectable Subject Matter

be affected by its incorporation in a film or audiovisual work, meaning that the use of a phonogram as part of a soundtrack is to be protected.[96]

Rome also protects the rights of broadcasting organisations and defines 'broadcasting', in Article 3(f), to mean 'the transmission by wireless means for public reception of sounds or of images and sounds'. The protection therefore applies to broadcast signals and does not extend to the contents of the broadcast, such as films or television programmes. The definition does not extend to transmissions over wires, such as cable television or Internet streaming. While the WPPT does not deal with the rights of broadcasting organisations, it includes a definition of broadcasting which addresses some of the uncertainties in the Rome definition by expressly incorporating transmissions by satellite and transmission of encrypted signals.[97]

The protection of neighbouring rights, while part of the international framework, creates complexity in relation to protectable subject matter. Much complexity arises from the extent to which subject matter such as phonograms and broadcasts include other works, such as literary, dramatic or musical works. Those seeking to use this subject matter to, for example, produce derivative works, may face a thicket of ownership rights and interests. The complexity of overlapping rights and interests, not to mention difficulties that can arise in determining if content falls within protected categories, has an adverse effect on the public domain in that it exacerbates uncertainties about what is or is not protected, and complicates the process of clearing relevant rights.

#### 4.6.6 Protectable Subject Matter and the Public Domain

International copyright law mandates, or allows for, the protection of an extraordinarily broad range of subject matter. Over time, the scope of protectable subject matter has extended from text-based literary works, to encompass all kinds of dramatic, musical and artistic works, then extending to photographs, architectural works, computer programs and databases, not to mention subject matter protected by neighbouring rights. Applying the general Berne model, Article 2 of Berne requires the protection of core categories of works, but enables Member States to protect works not falling within categories expressly listed.

Determining what is and what is not protected subject matter is fundamental to defining the public domain, as material that does not fall within a protected category is, by definition, in the copyright public domain. Yet, under international copyright law, this is an area that is replete with

---

[96] Ficsor and WIPO, 'Guide to copyright', [PPT-2.8].    [97] WPPT, Art. 2(f).

uncertainties, ambiguities and national variations: [7.3]. For example, not only are Berne members free to extend the categories of protected works, there is also scope for determining what falls within protected categories, such as 'sculptures' or 'drawings'. There are, for example, considerable variations between national laws in the protection of works of applied art and photographs. Moreover, within broad parameters, there is scope for applying different originality thresholds, differing requirements for fixation, and diverse interpretations of the principle that copyright does not extend to ideas or facts.

All of this means that delineating protectable subject matter is one of the most complex areas of copyright law, but also an area marked by significant national variations in public domains. In addition, the complexity associated with determining protectable subject matter, including the potential thicket of ownership rights and interests in complex subject matter, can have adverse effects on the public domain by creating difficulties in determining whether material is protected and, if so, identifying relevant rights holders. One effect of the complexities in defining protectable subject matter (and identifying owners) is to exacerbate difficulties in negotiating licences to use works. In some circumstances these costs and difficulties have been dealt with by establishing either free use or remunerated use exceptions: Chapter 5.

## 4.7 Exclusive Rights

The fourth element of international copyright law that defines and constrains the global public domain consists of the minimum rights required to be protected. According to our approach, merely because a work is protected by copyright does not mean that it falls outside the public domain, as uses of works that are not restricted by exclusive rights are part of the copyright public domain: [2.1.4]. For example, it has always been the case that copyright law does not prevent uses such as reading or viewing texts, or sharing single tangible copies of works, such as books or DVDs: [10.2.1]. Defining the scope of the minimum exclusive rights mandated by international copyright law therefore sets the parameters for what we call public domain uses, with uses falling outside of exclusive rights being the eleventh of our public domain categories.

National copyright laws take quite different approaches to defining exclusive rights: [10.2.2]. Differences in national approaches resulted in compromises in defining the minimum core of rights required by international copyright law. For example, Berne initially contained only exclusive rights for making translations and publicly performing translations

4.7 Exclusive Rights                                                    115

although, at that time, national laws contained many more rights.[98] Since then, there has been a piecemeal accretion of exclusive rights.[99] Furthermore, as explained below, gaps in the rights established by Berne have been clarified and expanded by subsequent agreements, especially the WCT, WPPT and TRIPs. The expansion of exclusive rights has, however, been accompanied by some expansion of exceptions to the exclusive rights: [5.6].[100]

This book does not try to be comprehensive about exclusive rights, but describes the main rights in works as the basis for mapping the most important public domain uses. This section of the chapter, and the comparative analysis in Chapter 10, address the following categories of exclusive rights: reproduction and adaptation; public communication and performance; distribution; and rental and lending rights.

### 4.7.1 Reproduction and Adaptation Rights

The reproduction right is the oldest, and most fundamental, of the exclusive rights, but was not expressly incorporated into Berne until the 1967 Stockholm revision. Article 9(1) of Berne provides that:

> Authors of literary and artistic works protected by this Convention shall have the exclusive right of authorizing the reproduction of these works in any manner or form.

While the reproduction right was implicit in earlier texts of Berne, and included in the national laws of all Berne members, it was not expressly introduced earlier due to failure to agree on the scope of the right.[101] For example, technological innovations such as pianola rolls and gramophone records, and later films, raised questions about whether the right encompassed mechanical reproductions such as these.[102] When an express reproduction right was finally introduced, it was therefore considered necessary to address its application to such reproductions, with Article 9(3) providing that:

---

[98] Ricketson and Ginsburg, *International Copyright and Neighbouring Rights*, [9A.06]; Goldstein and Hugenholtz, *International Copyright*, 298.
[99] Ricketson and Ginsburg, *International Copyright and Neighbouring Rights*, [9A.06].
[100] Goldstein and Hugenholtz, *International Copyright*, 298.
[101] Ricketson and Ginsburg, *International Copyright and Neighbouring Rights*, [11.04].
[102] *Ibid.* [11.07]. In the US, the Supreme Court in *White-Smith* v. *Apollo* 209 US 1 (1909) held that piano rolls were not infringing copies of musical works, leading to the introduction of a compulsory licence for mechanical reproduction of musical works in the 1909 Act: J. Litman, 'The exclusive right to read' (1994) 13 *Cardozo Arts & Entertainment Law Journal* 29 at 46; J. Lui, 'Regulatory copyright' (2004) 83 *North Carolina Law Review* 87 at 97.

> Any sound or visual recording shall be considered as a reproduction for the purposes of this Convention.

As Ricketson and Ginsburg observe, a 'fundamental question on which both article 9(1) and (3) fail to offer clear guidance is the meaning of the term "reproduction"'.[103] This has led to significant practical issues in determining the scope of the right: [10.2.3].

Changes in the form of a work that are not reproductions may infringe the allied exclusive rights of translation or adaptation. As explained above, the translation right was the first exclusive right included in Berne,[104] with Article 8 of the Paris text providing that authors of literary and artistic works 'shall enjoy the exclusive right of making and of authorizing the translation of their works'. The main issue in determining the scope of the translation right is whether it extends to the translation of one computer language to another; the consensus being that it does.[105]

A separate adaptation right was not incorporated in Berne until the 1948 Brussels revision, as prior to this adaptations were regarded as reproductions.[106] Article 12 of Berne provides that authors of literary and artistic works have 'the exclusive rights of authorizing adaptations, arrangements and other alterations of their works'. It seems that 'adaptation' refers to versions of a work in another form, such as dramatisations of a novel, while 'arrangement' refers to versions within the same form, such as arrangements of a musical work for another musical instrument.[107] 'Other alterations' is a catch-all category, which may include parodies and burlesque.[108] There are considerable variations in the way in which national laws implement the adaptation right, with some regarding it as separate from the reproduction right and others regarding it as a species of reproduction: [10.2.5]. Nevertheless, the scope of the adaptation right is critical in determining the extent to which making derivative versions of a work is permissible, and therefore amount to public domain uses.

### 4.7.2 Communication and Performance Rights

Works may be communicated to the public through non-material means by performances (whether live or recorded) or by electronic means, such as broadcasting or Internet communications. Articles 11 and 11*ter* of Berne provide that authors of dramatic, dramatico-musical, musical

---

[103] Ricketson and Ginsburg, *International Copyright and Neighbouring Rights*, [11.26].
[104] *Ibid.* [11.15].   [105] Goldstein and Hugenholtz, *International Copyright*, [9.1.3].
[106] Ricketson and Ginsburg, *International Copyright and Neighbouring Rights*, [11.28].
[107] *Ibid.* [11.34]; Goldstein and Hugenholtz, *International Copyright*, [9.1.3].
[108] Ricketson and Ginsburg, *International Copyright and Neighbouring Rights*, [11.34].

## 4.7 Exclusive Rights

and literary works have exclusive public performance rights in their works. As the right extends to performances 'by any means or process', the right includes performances by recorded media, such as sound recordings or films.

It is important to distinguish a performance, which occurs in the presence of an audience, from a communication, which occurs by means of electronic communications. The rights to public communication in Berne are scattered throughout the Convention, which essentially establishes two categories of communication rights. First, Articles 11, 11*ter* and 14(1)(ii) provide for a general communication right for performances of dramatic, dramatico-musical and musical works, recitations of literary works and adapted cinematographic works. Second, Article 11*bis*(1) provides that authors of literary and artistic works have exclusive rights to broadcast their works to the public, communicate them to the public by wireless diffusion, or to rebroadcast the work. As Berne does not confer a single, uniform communications right, there are gaps in its coverage.[109] For example, public exhibitions of artistic works are not covered; and on-demand or interactive transmissions may not be covered.

To address some of these gaps, Article 8 of the WCT provides that:

> authors of literary and artistic works shall enjoy the exclusive right of authorizing any communication to the public of their works, by wire or wireless means, including the making available to the public of their works in such a way that members of the public may access these works from a place and at a time individually chosen by them.

While Article 8 is expressed in technologically neutral terms, it is clear that the 'making available' right was intended to apply to access to works by means of the Internet, such as downloading from websites. In what is known as the 'umbrella solution', it was decided that the Article 8 right can be implemented in any exclusive right under national laws, at the discretion of Member States.[110] The 'making available' component of the right is extended to fixed performances and producers of phonograms by Articles 10 and 14 of the WPPT.

The boundary between uses within the exclusive rights and public domain uses is essentially set by whether or not a performance or communication is 'public'. There are many differences in national approaches to the distinction between 'public' and 'non-public' and

---

[109] *Ibid.* [12.43] ff.; P. B. Hugenholtz and S. van Velze, 'Communication to a new public? Three reasons why EU copyright law can do without a "new public"' (2016) 47(7) *International Review of Intellectual Property and Competition Law (IIC)* 797.
[110] Ficsor, *The Law of Copyright and the Internet*, 204–9, 496–509.

limited guidance is provided on this point by international copyright law: [10.2.6].[111]

### 4.7.3 Distribution Right

The distribution right is a right to control the sale and circulation of copies of a work which, in some jurisdictions, is dealt with as part of a 'right of destination'.[112] Berne does not include a general right of distribution but, in Article 14(1), includes a distribution right for cinematographic reproductions or adaptations. Article 6(1) of the WCT, however, creates an exclusive right to make works and copies of works available to the public 'through sale or other transfer of ownership'. The distribution right in the WCT is subject to Article 6(2), which ensures that the right may be confined to the initial sale of a work by national laws providing for exhaustion after the first sale or other transfer of ownership. An Agreed Statement to Article 6 provides that the distribution right is confined to 'fixed copies that can be put into circulation as tangible objects'. The WPPT also incorporates distribution rights in relation to fixed performances and phonograms.[113]

Limits to the distribution right, such as the EU 'exhaustion' and the US 'first sale' doctrines, establish the balance between intangible rights in a work and the property rights in a tangible embodiment, such as a physical copy. Limits on the right therefore set the permissible scope for public domain uses of a work after first sale, such as sale of second-hand books or lending of copies. Considerable difficulties have arisen in applying the distribution right to the sale or electronic distribution of digital works that are not embodied in physical forms: [10.2.7].

### 4.7.4 Rental and Lending Rights

Rental and lending rights were never part of Berne, and first appeared as part of international copyright law in Articles 11 and 14(4) of TRIPs. The introduction of a rental right was intended to deal with the threat, raised by cheap copying technologies, of the reproduction right being

---

[111] Ricketson and Ginsburg, *International Copyright and Neighbouring Rights*, [12.02].
[112] A. Ohly, 'Economic rights', in A. Ohly and E. Derclaye (eds.), *Research Handbook on the Future of EU Copyright* (Edward Elgar, 2009), p. 219. On the 'destination right', see F. Gotzen, 'The right of destination in Europe' (1989) 25 *Copyright* 218. The 'destination right' under French law differs from a distribution right in that it is regarded as an emanation from the reproduction right and not a distinct right, and it incorporates a rental right.
[113] WPPT, Arts 8(1) and 12(1).

undermined by the potential for those renting products, such as software and films, to make multiple copies.[114]

Article 11 of TRIPs requires WTO members to establish an exclusive commercial rental right for computer programs and cinematographic works. The limitation to 'commercial' rental excludes non-commercial activities, such as those of non-profit libraries, from the scope of the right. In relation to cinematographic works, the obligation does not arise 'unless such rental has led to widespread copying of such works which is materially impairing the exclusive right of reproduction'. Article 14(4) of TRIPs extends the rental right to producers of phonograms and, subject to national laws, any other rights holders in phonograms, such as performers.

Article 7(1) of the WCT, which mirrors the rights in TRIPs, requires signatories to establish a commercial rental right for computer programs, cinematographic works and works embodied in phonograms. Article 7 differs from Article 14(4) of TRIPs in that it provides that the right applies to authors of works embodied in phonograms, not the producers of phonograms.

Under national copyright laws, the rental right is exempted from limits on the distribution right, such as the EU 'exhaustion' and the US 'first sale' doctrines. While international copyright law does not provide for lending rights, a controversial public lending right, with implications for public domain uses, has been introduced in the EU: [10.2.8].

### 4.7.5 Exclusive Rights and the Public Domain

Once material is protected by copyright, international copyright law mandates a core of exclusive economic rights. There is, however, no single international statement of minimum rights; they are scattered throughout Berne and in subsequent treaties, namely the WCT, WPPT and TRIPs. This illustrates the relatively haphazard way in which economic rights have been extended in response to changed circumstances, particularly new distribution technologies. While the extension of exclusive rights has tended to be at the expense of public domain uses, it has also led to the expansion of exceptions, which have become the focus of debates about public domain uses.

Exclusive rights are fundamental to defining the public domain, as copyright does not prevent uses outside the scope of the rights. As this section of the chapter has explained, however, the minimum rights required by international law are expressed at an abstract and general

---

[114] Goldstein and Hugenholtz, *International Copyright*, [9.1.2.2].

level, leaving much flexibility for the interpretation and implementation of the rights in national laws. Public domain uses therefore depend principally upon delineating the scope of exclusive rights under national laws, with considerable national variations: Chapter 10.

## 4.8 Conclusions: International Copyright and the Public Domain

In this chapter we have mapped, in significant detail, the main elements of international copyright law (apart from copyright exceptions) that condition national public domains. While, on our approach, the detail is essential, in this concluding section we draw some high-level generalisations about the practical implications of international copyright law for global and national public domains.

International copyright law is a dense thicket of interlocking or nested agreements with complex rules that, on our analysis, create a global public domain, but also impose serious constraints on national public domains. The effects of the international regime on public domains are conditioned by structural features of the international framework, which cumulatively result in a levelling up of national protection to certain minimum standards, with scope for ratcheting up protection over and above those minima: [4.2.2]. There is, moreover, an ossification of international standards resulting from the main treaty, Berne, being last revised in 1971, and the incorporation of the Berne template into international trade law by Article 9(1) of TRIPs. While international copyright law should not be regarded as immutable, and while there are interesting proposals for treaties aimed at protecting the public domain by expanding exceptions: [12.1], it is impossible to deny the historical trajectory towards greater protection, with contrary developments, such as Marrakesh, being rare and having limited scope. It is difficult to be optimistic about future developments in multilateral copyright law, given the gridlock experienced since 1971, associated as it has been with apparently irreconcilable national interests.

The twin pillars of Berne, the principles of national treatment and minimum rights, set the framework for international copyright law, by establishing minimum levels of protection for foreign authors, and requiring that foreign authors be given the same protection as domestic claimants. This results in a 'levelling up' of protection under national laws, with the international framework setting floors, but no ceilings. This paradigm has been reinforced by the combination of post-TRIPs agreements, which have ratcheted up protection, and the TRIPs MFN principle, which requires signatories to confer any higher levels of

## 4.8 Conclusions: International Copyright and the Public Domain

protection under such agreements to the nationals of all TRIPs members.

The rule against formalities, in Article 5(2) of Berne, embodied a paradigm shift in international protection in favour of the view that copyright arises from the creative acts of authors, and is not a conditional grant from the state. While there were good historical reasons for addressing the problems of national systems requiring formalities, the rule is one of the most significant constraints on the global public domain, as it effectively creates a presumption in favour of protection. That said, even within the parameters set by Berne, there is scope for national mechanisms for addressing potential imbalances arising from the rule by, for example, voluntary systems of recordation or registration.

While a limited term of protection should be one of the main safeguards for public domains, the terms set by the international framework, starting with the minimum terms required by Berne, and extended by post-TRIPs agreements, are very long. Moreover, as the international framework sets only floors it is possible, under international copyright law, for national laws to establish very lengthy or even perpetual protection. While there are more variations in copyright terms under national laws than often thought, and flexibility in the duration of protection of domestic works, the lengthy terms required by international copyright law are a major constraint on public domains.

International copyright law establishes broad minimum categories of protectable subject matter, but with substantial uncertainties about the boundaries between what is and is not protected. The uncertainties arise from both the open-ended definition of protectable categories of works under Berne and flexibilities in defining what falls within specific categories. Furthermore, there is much scope for national differences in applying general copyright principles for determining whether or not works are protected, including the originality threshold and the idea/expression dichotomy. While the categories of protectable subject matter have significantly expanded over time, with implications for public domains, the scope for variations in national laws is considerable.

Just as subject matter required to be protected under international copyright law expanded, the minimum exclusive rights have also expanded, but in relatively unsystematised and haphazard ways. National differences in approaches have resulted in harmonisation of exclusive rights at only a very general level. There is therefore much scope for national variations, and it is only through detailed analysis of national laws that a clear picture can emerge of this element of the copyright public domain.

122   The Global Public Domain – Limits Imposed by International Law

The stated objective of Berne is effectively and uniformly to protect the rights of authors. In sum, this, together with the expansive approach taken by international copyright law to protectable subject matter and exclusive rights, has meant that copyright exceptions have assumed potentially the most important role in safeguarding public domains. The international framework for limitations and exceptions is dealt with in the next chapter. As the international legal framework is only effective if it is implemented, the next chapter also addresses the implications of arrangements for enforcing international copyright law for the copyright public domain.

# 5 The Global Public Domain – Exceptions and Enforcement

| | | |
|---|---|---|
| 5.1 | Introduction | 123 |
| 5.2 | Exclusions, Limitations and Exceptions | 124 |
| 5.3 | Works Expressly Excluded | 125 |
| 5.4 | Free Use Exceptions | 128 |
| 5.5 | Remunerated Use Exceptions | 141 |
| 5.6 | Exclusions, Exceptions and the Public Domain | 145 |
| 5.7 | Enforcement of International Copyright Law | 147 |
| 5.8 | Conclusion: Exceptions, Enforcement and the Public Domain | 150 |

## 5.1 Introduction

The combination of the stated objective of Berne – to protect the rights of authors 'in as effective ... a manner as possible': [4.2.1] – and the breadth of minimum levels of protection means that, in international copyright law, public interest considerations have figured mostly in setting limitations and exceptions to copyright. Despite the express aim of Berne, which seems to require a high level of protection, it is important to understand that public interest considerations have always played a role in limiting copyright. As Ficsor points out, the Berne preamble's statement that protection be as effective 'as possible' assumes, first, that conditions in some countries may prevent conferring the highest possible protection and, second, that protecting authors must be balanced against other public interests.[1]

The importance of public interest limitations was recognised from the beginnings of the international system; when Numa Droz, Chairman of the 1884 Berne Conference, made his closing speech, he referred to the need for attending 'to the fact that limitations on absolute protection are dictated, rightly in my opinion, by the public interest'.[2] That copyright is

---

[1] Ficsor and WIPO, 'Guide to copyright', [BC-Pr.5].
[2] See *Actes de la Conférence internationale pour la protection des œuvres littéraires et artistiques réunie à Berne du 8 au 19 septembre 1884*, International Office, Berne, 1884, p. 68 (closing speech to the 1884 Conference).

124     The Global Public Domain – Exceptions and Enforcement

a balance between the rights of authors and public interest considerations is further confirmed by explicit statements in the Preambles to the WCT and WPPT, which specifically recognise:

> the need to maintain a balance between the rights of authors and the larger public interest, particularly education, research and access to information, as reflected in the Berne Convention.[3]

As explained more fully in Chapter 12, the contemporary importance of exceptions at the international level is illustrated by the attention that has been given, since 2004, to exceptions by WIPO's Standing Committee on Copyright and Related Rights (SCRR), and especially to exceptions for educational activities, and libraries and archives: [12.1].

This chapter describes and analyses exclusions, limitations and exceptions to copyright under international copyright law. First, the chapter introduces the terminology we use to refer to legal limitations on copyright. Second, it explains how international law provides for three categories of limitations, namely exclusions, free use exceptions and remunerated use exceptions. Following an exposition of the law in each category, the implications for the global public domain are explained.

Although the complex thicket of international copyright law conditions national public domains, the extent to which it does so ultimately depends upon enforcement, or the threat of enforcement. This chapter therefore concludes with an explanation and analysis of the regime for enforcing international copyright law, focusing on the WTO dispute resolution mechanism. As we suggest, enforcement is a complex part of international copyright law, with a degree of implied tolerance of national variations, and a selective approach to initiating enforcement proceedings. The generality with which international rules are expressed, and the complexities of the enforcement regime, mean there is more flexibility in implementing international agreements than commonly supposed.

## 5.2     Exclusions, Limitations and Exceptions

The final element of international copyright law that conditions national public domains, and the element in which public interest considerations are most explicitly taken into account, are exclusions, limitations and exceptions. The terminology in this area is, however, highly contested. In this book, we distinguish 'limitations', which define the scope of exclusive rights, from 'exceptions', meaning uses that would otherwise fall within an exclusive right, but operate as 'divergences' or derogations

---

[3] *WCT*, Preamble; *WPPT*, Preamble. The full titles and citations of all treaties and conventions are in the Table of International Instruments.

from the right: [11.1.1]. For the sake of convenience, however, we generally use the term 'exceptions'. The exclusions and exceptions dealt with in this chapter encompass material in categories 3 ('works expressly excluded'), 12 ('free use exceptions') and 13 ('neutral compulsory licensing') of our public domain categories.

In addition to exceptions, this chapter deals with 'exclusions' from protection, meaning subject matter completely outside of the scope of copyright, as opposed to uses falling outside the exclusive rights. While, strictly speaking, exclusions might belong with the treatment of protectable subject matter in Chapter 4, they are dealt with in this chapter, as the three categories – exclusions, limitations and exceptions – are the main internal copyright mechanisms for protecting public rights.[4] In addition, permissible exclusions are often implemented in national laws as exceptions from exclusive rights. While the comparative analysis of national laws relating to express exclusions is dealt with at [8.2], limitations and exceptions under national laws are addressed in Chapters 11 and 12.

Under international copyright law, it is possible to distinguish three broad categories of exclusions, limitations and exceptions.[5] The first category – exclusions – mandates or permits express exclusions from protectable subject matter. The second category – free use exceptions – allows for national jurisdictions to permit uses of protected works, such as uses for educational purposes or reporting news, without the need for compensation to be paid to copyright owners. Finally, the third category – remunerated use exceptions – provides for uses to be made of protected works subject to payment of owners.

## 5.3  Works Expressly Excluded

Berne provides for three express exclusions of works required to be protected: one mandatory and two optional. Unlike Berne, neighbouring rights treaties do not include express exclusions from the scope of protected subject matter, but deal with these issues by means of exceptions. The Berne exclusions relate to news of the day, laws and other official texts, and political and legal speeches.

---

[4] On the values underpinning limitations and exceptions, see P. Samuelson, 'Unbundling fair uses' (2009) 77 *Fordham Law Review* 2537; J. C. Ginsburg, 'Exceptional authorship: the role of copyright authorship in promoting creativity', in S. Frankel and D. Gervais (eds.), *Evolution and Equilibrium: Copyright this Century* (Cambridge University Press, 2013), pp. 15–28.

[5] Ricketson and Ginsburg, *International Copyright and Neighbouring Rights*, [13.01]–[13.02].

## 5.3.1 News Items or Facts

The sole mandatory exclusion from protectable subject matter, set out in Article 2(8) of Berne, provides that:

> The protection of this Convention shall not apply to news of the day or to miscellaneous facts having the character of mere items of press information.

Berne does not expressly prohibit the protection of ideas or facts; although this exclusion is implied: [4.6.3]. Article 2(8) is therefore the closest that Berne comes to an express recognition of the principle.[6] This provision, however, has a complex history, with much uncertainty concerning its purpose and scope.[7] In particular, it is unclear whether the exclusion applies to works that would otherwise be protected under Berne or merely confirms the principle, already implicit in the Convention, that facts are not protected.

Given difficulties in distinguishing 'news of the day' or 'press information' from other content, the second more limited interpretation seems preferable. Moreover, the extrinsic material relating to the provision supports this interpretation. For example, documents prepared for the Stockholm revision conference suggest that the provision is a specific application of the principle that copyright does not protect facts, while emphasising that it applies *a fortiori* to news items.[8] Following from this, Article 2(8) appears to refer to individual news items or facts, meaning that copyright may still subsist in original selections or arrangements of facts.[9]

While Article 2(8) is couched in mandatory terms, it does not prevent Berne members from protecting factual news material under another area of law, such as unfair competition law, or even under copyright law. This arises from its wording, which simply prevents the 'protection of this Convention' from applying to such material. Therefore, while a jurisdiction may protect this material, if it does so the Berne principle of national treatment does not apply, so there is no obligation to extend protection to nationals from other Berne countries.

The exclusion of news of the day is complemented by permissible exceptions for the press and media: [5.4.2]. There are considerable variations in how national laws implement exclusions and exceptions for the press and media, with many national laws relying on exceptions, such as fair dealing exceptions, and not exclusions: [8.2.1].

---

[6] Goldstein and Hugenholtz, *International Copyright*, [6.1.3.1].
[7] Ricketson and Ginsburg, *International Copyright and Neighbouring Rights*, [8.105].
[8] *Ibid.* [8.106]. [9] Ficsor and WIPO, 'Guide to copyright', [BC-2.75].

## 5.3 Works Expressly Excluded

### 5.3.2 Laws and other Official Texts

The first optional exclusion in Berne, which applies to laws and other official texts, is set out in Article 2(4), which provides that:

> It shall be a matter for legislation in the countries of the Union to determine the protection to be granted to official texts of a legislative, administrative and legal nature, and to official translations of such texts.

This provision, inserted by the Stockholm revision, was a compromise between different approaches to the protection of laws and official texts, which, although denied protection in most Berne members, are protected under the doctrines of Crown and Parliamentary copyright in the UK and Commonwealth jurisdictions.[10] From its context it is clear that Article 2(4) applies to material that would otherwise be protected by copyright. The effect of Article 2(4) is to confer significant flexibility on Berne members, which are free to implement regimes ranging from no protection whatsoever to full copyright protection, and a wide variety of national approaches has in fact occurred: [8.2.2]. There is also considerable uncertainty about the scope of material, other than official legislative texts and court decisions, that may fall within Article 2(4).

### 5.3.3 Political and Legal Speeches

The second optional exclusion in Berne, which enables national laws to exclude protection for political speeches, is recognised by Article 2bis(1), which provides that:

> It shall be a matter for legislation in the countries of the Union to exclude, wholly or in part, from the protection provided by ... [the Convention] ... political speeches and speeches delivered in the course of legal proceedings.

This exclusion can be traced to a compromise reached at the Rome revision between countries, especially France, supporting the extension of protection to non-fixed, oral works and those, such as the UK, committed to confining protection to works fixed in a material form.[11] The compromise led to the express inclusion of 'lectures, addresses, sermons and other works of the same nature' in the protected works listed in Article 2, but did not mandate the protection of non-fixed works: [4.6.4].[12] As part of the compromise, Article 2bis, which confers flexibility on the extent of protection of some of these works, was also included.

---

[10] Goldstein and Hugenholtz, *International Copyright*, [1.3.2].
[11] Ricketson and Ginsburg, *International Copyright and Neighbouring Rights*, [8.16]–[8.17].
[12] Subsequently, the Paris Act incorporated an express provision reserving the ability of Berne member states to make protection conditional on fixation: Article 2(2).

The Article 2*bis*(1) optional exclusion expressly recognises the public interest in access to political and legal information. While there is scope for debate about what may be a 'political speech', the provision is broad enough to permit national laws to exclude the protection of this subject matter in whatever form the speech takes.[13] The exclusion is, however, limited by Article 2*bis*(3), which requires Berne members to reserve the rights of authors of lectures, addresses and similar works – including political speeches – to make collections of these works (and prevent others from publishing collections of such speeches).

### 5.3.4 *The Public Domain and Works Expressly Excluded*

Few categories of works are expressly excluded from copyright by Berne, and two of the three categories are permissible and not mandatory. Complete exclusion of categories of otherwise copyrightable subject matter therefore plays a relatively minor role in constituting the global public domain. The sole mandatory exclusion, for news items and facts, is subject to significant national differences in how it is implemented: [8.2.1]. For the two optional exclusions, countries may choose whether to exclude them partly or not at all, and may apply conditions on the exemption. However, the majority of countries have utilised the exemption to exclude documents constituting the law, although with varying practices in relation to other official texts: [8.2.2], indicating the importance of this optional exclusion.

The exclusion of particular subject matter from protection, whether mandatory or permissive, is based on the assumption there is a public interest in unfettered access to, and use of, these works. From the nature of the excluded subject matter, it is clear that the public interests safeguarded by exclusions concern the public domain values of freedom of expression, access to information and the free and transparent flow of information necessary for democratic processes and the rule of law: [1.7].

## 5.4 Free Use Exceptions

Free use exceptions permit unremunerated uses of copyright works that would otherwise amount to infringements, and therefore are vitally important to the public domain. Unlike exclusions, exceptions concede that copyright exists in the relevant works, but then carve out permitted uses where there is a public interest in the uses not being controlled by

---

[13] Ricketson and Ginsburg, *International Copyright and Neighbouring Rights*, [8.20].

## 5.4 Free Use Exceptions

copyright owners.[14] Berne includes specific free use exceptions to some of the minimum rights guaranteed by the Convention, but also incorporates an important general limitation on permissible exceptions under national laws, in the form of the 'three-step test'.

### 5.4.1 Berne Article 9(2) and the 'Three-Step Test'

The three-step test establishes an international standard or norm that is applied in determining whether exceptions under national laws are acceptable and, by establishing a ceiling on exceptions, is the single most important provision of international copyright law relating to exceptions. As set out in Article 9(2) of Berne, the test provides that:

> It shall be a matter for legislation in the countries of the Union to permit the reproduction of such ... [protected works] ... in certain special cases, provided that such reproduction does not conflict with a normal exploitation of the work and does not unreasonably prejudice the legitimate interests of the author.

The test can be traced to the introduction of an express general right of reproduction in the 1967 Stockholm revision: [4.7.1].[15] This gave rise to a need to consider what permissible exceptions to the reproduction right might be, involving a balance between the economic interests of copyright owners and the public interests that were recognised in exceptions under national laws.[16] The wording of Article 9(2) is therefore confined to exceptions to the reproduction right.

Subsequently, Article 13 of TRIPs extended the test, in a slightly modified form, to all exclusive rights under copyright, not just the reproduction right. While there is potential for a more liberal interpretation of the three-step test under TRIPs than the Berne test, Article 2(2) of TRIPs, which provides that it is not to be interpreted as derogating from the obligations of members under Berne, prevents this.[17]

*The TRIPs Panel 'Homestyle' Decision* Much ink has been spilt on the meaning of the three cumulative elements of the test, with Ricketson and Ginsburg concluding that 'there is still considerable uncertainty and even ambiguity over its scope'.[18] The most comprehensive legal interpretation of the elements of the test is the 2000 decision of the

---

[14] *Ibid.* [13.02].   [15] *Ibid.* [11.19].   [16] *Ibid.* [13.04]–[13.05].
[17] Ricketson and Ginsburg, *International Copyright and Neighbouring Rights*, [13.102]–[13.103]. One potential difference in application arises from the fact that the Berne test refers to the 'legitimate interests of the author' while the TRIPs formulation refers to the 'legitimate interests of the right holder', as authors and rights holders may be different persons.
[18] *Ibid.* [13.10].

WTO Panel which considered whether the US 'homestyle' and business exemptions for public performances of musical works complied with Article 13 of TRIPs.[19] In reaching its conclusion that the business exemption – which allowed non-dramatic musical works to be played in business establishments, such as bars, restaurants and stores – violated Article 13, the Panel gave extended consideration to each of the cumulative elements of the test.

As a general point, the Panel noted that the TRIPs test was to be interpreted consistently with Article 9(2) of Berne and, as such, was intended to provide for only limited or narrow exceptions.[20] Consistently with this, the Panel interpreted the first step, 'certain special cases', as being confined to clearly defined circumstances that were, in effect, exceptional, meaning that an exception 'should be narrow in a quantitative as well as a qualitative sense'.[21] On the other hand, the Panel concluded that the requirement that an exception be confined to 'certain special cases' should not be equated with the need for a 'special purpose', and should not involve a normative evaluation of the public policy purpose of a national exception.[22]

In relation to the second step, of not conflicting with the normal exploitation of a work, the Panel adopted a predominantly economic analysis. The Panel therefore interpreted 'exploitation' to mean extracting economic value from the relevant rights, and conflicting with 'normal exploitation' to mean depriving a rights holder of 'significant or tangible commercial gains'.[23] That said, the Panel observed that the second step cannot be interpreted as ruling out every use of a work that involves some commercial gain by those entitled to an exception, as this would rule out almost all conceivable exceptions.[24]

Finally, in relation to the third step – not unreasonably prejudice the legitimate interests of the rights holder – the Panel again emphasised the

---

[19] WTO Panel, WT/DS160/R – 15 June 2000 United States – Section 110(5) of the US Copyright Act, *Report of the Panel*. For commentary on the Panel decision, see J. C. Ginsburg, 'Toward supranational copyright law? The WTO Panel decision and the "three-step test" for copyright exceptions' (2001) 187 *Revue internationale du droit d'auteur* 3; J. Oliver, 'Copyright in the WTO: the panel decision on the three-step test' (2002) 25 *Columbia Journal of Law & the Arts* 119; M. Ficsor, 'How much of what? The three-step test and its application in two recent WTO dispute settlement cases' (2002) 192 *Revue internationale du droit d'auteur* 111; D. Brennan, 'The three-step test frenzy – why the TRIPS panel decision might be considered *per incuriam*' [2002] 2 *Intellectual Property Quarterly* 212; D. Gervais, 'Towards a new core international norm: the reverse three-step test' (2005) 9(1) *Marquette Intellectual Property Law Review* 1.
[20] WTO Panel, WT/DS160/R – 15 June 2000 United States – Section 110(5) of the US Copyright Act, *Report of the Panel*, [6.97].
[21] *Ibid.* [6.109].   [22] *Ibid.* [6.111]–[6.112].   [23] *Ibid.* [6.165]; [6.183].
[24] *Ibid.* [6.182].

## 5.4 Free Use Exceptions

economic interests of the copyright holder, concluding that 'prejudice to the legitimate interests of rights holders reaches an unreasonable level if an exception or limitation causes or has the potential to cause an unreasonable loss of income to the copyright owner.'[25] In applying this step, there may be a difference between the Berne and TRIPs tests: as TRIPs excludes the moral rights of authors, and as the third step under TRIPs refers to the interests of the 'right holder' and not the 'author', it is natural that economic interests should predominate in the context of TRIPs, whereas 'legitimate interests' under Berne should include all interests of an author, both economic and non-economic.[26] In any case, as the step requires both that the interests be 'legitimate' and that any prejudice be 'unreasonable', this implies a normative analysis in which the proportionality of the harm to the copyright owner must be balanced against other public policy objectives.[27]

> *Relationship between Three-Step Test and other Berne Exceptions* Berne includes both express specific free use exceptions and implied minor exceptions. While Article 9(2) makes no reference to the specific exceptions, it has always been assumed that the specific exceptions are excluded from the scope of the general test.[28] Moreover, as Article 9(1) of TRIPs incorporates Articles 1–21 and the Appendix to Berne (with the exception of Article 6*bis*), it also incorporates the express exceptions established under Berne.

The relationship between Article 13 of TRIPs and the Berne express exceptions is, however, complex, especially as Article 13 is expressed generally and does not refer to permissible exceptions under Berne.[29] In understanding the relationship between Berne and TRIPs, it is important to bear in mind, first, that Article 2(2) of TRIPs provides that the agreement is not to derogate from existing obligations under Berne and, second, that as a 'special agreement' under Article 20 of Berne, TRIPs must either grant more extensive rights than under Berne or otherwise be consistent with Berne.

The result seems to be as follows. Where the requirements of an express exception under Berne and Article 13 are consistent, the express exception and the TRIPs three-step test can be applied cumulatively, therefore requiring express exceptions to also conform to the TRIPs three-step

---

[25] *Ibid.* [6.229].
[26] Ricketson and Ginsburg, *International Copyright and Neighbouring Rights*, [13.24].
[27] *Ibid.* [13.26]. It is arguable that this form of balancing is also permissible under the second step.
[28] *Ibid.* [13.10].   [29] Senftleben, *Copyright, Limitations and the Three-step Test*, 89.

test.[30] Where, however, a Berne exception is not consistent with Article 13 of TRIPs, such as where an exception under a national law might comply with the three-step test but not with the requirements for an express exception under Berne,[31] applying the Article 2(2) non-derogation principle, and possibly the maxim *lex specialis legi generali derogate*, the requirements for the Berne exception should be applied to the exclusion of the TRIPs three-step test.[32] The TRIPs three-step test therefore cannot be relied upon to extend the scope of the express exceptions under Berne, such as by allowing an unremunerated exception where Berne provides for a remunerated exception.

An additional complexity concerns whether the incorporation of the Berne provisions by Article 9(1) of TRIPs also incorporates the implied minor exceptions (see below). The issue was addressed by the WTO Panel in its decision on the US 'homestyle' and business exceptions, which concluded that, as Article 9(1) of TRIPs incorporates not only the express provisions of Berne but also the Berne *acquis*, it also incorporates the minor exceptions doctrine.[33] On this view, the minor exceptions must comply with the TRIPs three-step test although, as *de minimis* uses, this should not be an issue.[34] More importantly, applying the Article 2(2) non-derogation principle, Article 13 cannot be used to extend exceptions beyond those allowable under the minor exceptions doctrine.[35]

The end result, in practical terms, is that the TRIPs three-step test cannot be used to extend the specific Berne exceptions, whether express or implied.

---

[30] Ricketson and Ginsburg, *International Copyright and Neighbouring Rights*, [13.110]–[13.112]. Commentators agree that the Article 13 three-step test is to be applied as an additional safeguard to the express specific exceptions under Berne, but not as an alternative basis for extending those exceptions: Senftleben, *Copyright Limitations and the Three-step Test*, 121–2; J. Reinbothe and S. von Lewinski, *The WIPO Treaties 1996* (Butterworths/LexisNexis, 2002), pp. 130–2; Ficsor, *The Law of Copyright and the Internet*, 302–3.

[31] This may be the case with the exception allowing for a compulsory licence for broadcasting works under Article 11*bis*(2) of Berne, which conceivably could be justified as an unremunerated exception under the three-step test.

[32] Ricketson and Ginsburg, *International Copyright and Neighbouring Rights*, [13.112].

[33] WTO Panel, WT/DS160/R – 15 June 2000 United States – Section 110(5) of the US Copyright Act, *Report of the Panel*, [6.63]. For criticisms of the WTO Panel decision on this and related points, see Brennan, 'The three-step test frenzy'; Ricketson and Ginsburg, *International Copyright and Neighbouring Rights*, [13.113] ff.

[34] The WTO Panel equated 'minor exceptions' with exceptions permitted by the three-step test, but on this we agree with commentators who conclude it was almost certainly wrong: Ricketson and Ginsburg, *International Copyright and Neighbouring Rights*, [13.114]; Brennan, 'The three-step test frenzy', 223–4.

[35] Ricketson and Ginsburg, *International Copyright and Neighbouring Rights*, [13.114].

## 5.4 Free Use Exceptions

*The Three-Step Test and Compulsory Licences* The consensus is that the three-step test can be complied with by either free use exceptions or remunerated use exceptions: [14.2.3]. It is, nevertheless, important for compulsory licences to comply with the third step, that they do not 'unreasonably prejudice the legitimate interests of authors'. While payment of remuneration means that more extensive uses may be permissible under a compulsory licence than under a free use exception, payment alone does not necessarily ensure compliance: there must still be no 'unreasonable prejudice'.

*The Three-Step Test: Neighbouring Rights, the WCT and Disability Exceptions* Although Article 13 of TRIPs extended the three-step test to all exclusive rights in copyright works, it did not extend it to neighbouring rights. Under Article 14.6 of TRIPs, in relation to neighbouring rights, exceptions under national laws are limited to 'the extent permitted by the Rome Convention', which is explained below.

In addition to Article 13 of TRIPs, however, the three-step test has been adopted and applied to minimum rights established under the WCT, the WPPT and the Beijing Treaty.[36] Article 10 of the WCT, which incorporates the three-step test, includes an Agreed Statement which indicates that exceptions under national laws that have been considered acceptable under Berne may be carried forward and 'appropriately extended into the digital environment', including by devising new exceptions. Article 16(2) of the WPPT effectively extends the application of the three-step test by providing for the test to be applied to exceptions to the rights of performers and producers of phonograms.[37]

Finally, Article 11 of Marrakesh provides that exceptions introduced to facilitate access to relevant works by visually impaired persons and persons with print disabilities must comply with the three-step tests under Berne, TRIPs and the WCT.

### 5.4.2 Express Mandatory and Permissible Exceptions

Berne includes one mandatory and four specific permissible free use exceptions. The exceptions are as follows.

---

[36] WCT, Art. 10; WPPT, Art. 16(2); Beijing Treaty, Art. 13(2).
[37] Ficsor and WIPO, 'Guide to copyright', [PPT-16.4].

*Quotations* The mandatory exception, set out in Article 10(1), requires Member States to permit 'quotations from a work which has already been lawfully made available to the public, provided that their making is compatible with fair practice, and their extent does not exceed that justified by the purpose'. The exception for quotations is the only mandatory exception in international copyright law, and therefore comes closest to being an express public right.

For the exception to apply, three conditions must be satisfied. First, the work must have been 'lawfully made available to the public', which means making the work available in any form, including public performance or broadcasts.[38] Second, making the quotation must be 'compatible with fair practice', which commentators agree incorporates considerations similar to the three-step tests, namely whether the quotation conflicts with the normal exploitation of the work and unreasonably prejudices the legitimate interests of the author.[39] Third, the quotation must not 'exceed that justified by the purpose', which, although no purposes are specified, may be confined to particular accepted purposes, such as criticism, political or scholarly debate, or illustration.[40]

While the length of a quotation is an important consideration, there is no rule that the quotation of a whole work can never be justified.[41] Apart from the three conditions, Article 10(1) refers to a particular kind of quotation, namely 'quotations from newspaper articles and periodicals in the form of press summaries', which obviously refers to summaries that are, or include, verbatim quotations.

The very considerable variations in the national approaches to the quotation exception are dealt with at [12.3].

The remaining four kinds of express free use exceptions under Berne are not mandatory, their implementation being left to national legislation.

*Educational Exceptions* The first of the permissible exceptions, in Article 10(2), allows exceptions for the use of literary and artistic works 'to the extent justified by the purpose ... by way of illustration in publications, broadcasts or sound or visual recordings for teaching, provided that such utilization is compatible with fair practice'. Copyright exceptions for education and teaching have a long history, with the main effect of Article 10(2) being to set limits for permissible exceptions. Unlike Article 10(1), the purpose of the exception is spelt out, being confined

---

[38] Ricketson and Ginsburg, *International Copyright and Neighbouring Rights*, [13.41].
[39] *Ibid.*; Ficsor and WIPO, 'Guide to copyright', [BC 10.6].
[40] Ficsor and WIPO, 'Guide to copyright', [BC 10.9].
[41] E. Adeney, 'Appropriation in the name of art? Is a quotation exception the answer?' (2013) 23 *Australian Intellectual Property Journal* 142.

## 5.4 Free Use Exceptions

to teaching, which is accepted as including teaching at all levels, but not necessarily adult education.[42] In addition, the exception is confined to use 'by way of illustration', which essentially means by example for the purpose of teaching,[43] but does not necessarily exclude use of the whole work.[44]

The original 1886 Berne text contained a broader exemption, covering both educational and scientific purposes, not only 'for teaching', and applied to the use of 'portions', not merely 'by way of illustration'. These provisions were, however, challenged and narrowed by writers' groups and others over the course of successive revisions.[45]

National exceptions for educational uses are extraordinarily varied, with, in general, different approaches being adopted by common law and civil law jurisdictions: [12.5].

*Press and Media Uses* The second set of permissible exceptions concerns uses by the press and media, and includes use of articles in newspapers and periodicals and use of works for the purpose of reporting and informing the public. The specific non-mandatory news and press exceptions complement the mandatory exclusion for news of the day in Article 2(8).

Article 10*bis*(1) makes it a matter for national legislation 'to permit the reproduction by the press, the broadcasting or the communication to the public by wire of articles published in newspapers or periodicals on current economic, political or religious topics, and of broadcast works of the same character, in cases in which the reproduction, broadcasting or such communication thereof is not expressly reserved'. The limitations on the exceptions permitted under this provision are as follows. First, it applies only to newspaper and periodical articles on current economic, political or religious topics, and to analogous broadcast works. The content of the excepted articles is limited to particular topics, and does not extend to articles on other topics, such as sports reports, or literary or artistic reviews.[46] Moreover, by being confined to analogous 'broadcast works', questions may be raised about whether or not it is permissible to extend exceptions to other online content. While there seems no obstacle preventing national laws from interpreting 'newspapers' and 'periodicals' as including online versions,[47] this may not be the

---

[42] Ficsor and WIPO, 'Guide to copyright', [BC 10.16]–[BC 10.17].
[43] *Ibid.* [BC 10.1].
[44] Ricketson and Ginsburg, *International Copyright and Neighbouring Rights*, [13.45].
[45] Bannerman, *International Copyright and Access to Knowledge*, 57–67.
[46] Ricketson and Ginsburg, *International Copyright and Neighbouring Rights*, [13.53].
[47] *Ibid.*

case with online videos or streaming services. Second, while exceptions are limited to reproductions by the press, and to broadcasting or other public communications, this seems to encompass dissemination of translations, as well as public receptions of communications.[48] Third, the exception cannot be applied in the event of an express reservation by the copyright owner.[49] Finally, it is a condition for the exception to apply for the source of the work to 'always be clearly indicated'.

The development of film raised issues of whether or not works included in films of current events – such as musical works performed as part of the event or artistic works filmed in the background – should be excluded from copyright protection.[50] Article 10*bis*(2) provides that it is a matter for national legislation 'to determine the conditions under which, for the purpose of reporting current events by means of photography, cinematography, broadcasting or communication to the public by wire, literary or artistic works seen or heard in the course of the event may, to the extent justified by the informatory purpose, be reproduced and made available to the public'. The important limitation on this exception is that the permissible use of the work must be confined 'to the extent justified by the informatory purpose', generally meaning that it must not be otherwise practicable to make the report without including the relevant work.[51] As the provision leaves it to national legislation to determine the 'conditions' for exercise of the exception, this implies that it may be made subject to payment under a compulsory licence.[52]

As the specific optional exceptions for press and media uses can be seen as complementing the Article 2(8) exclusion for news of the day, national variations in the implementation of the exceptions are dealt with as express exclusions in Chapter 8: [8.2.1].

*Press and Media Uses of Lectures and Addresses* Article 2*bis*(1) of Berne allows for national legislation to exclude political speeches entirely from copyright protection: [5.3.3]. A third category of permissible exceptions, in Article 2*bis*(2), makes it a matter for national legislation 'to determine the conditions under which lectures, addresses and other works of the same nature which are delivered in public may be reproduced by the press, broadcast, communicated to the public by wire and made the subject of public communication ... when such use is justified by the informatory purpose'.

---

[48] *Ibid.*   [49] Ficsor and WIPO, 'Guide to copyright', [BC 10*bis*. 3].
[50] See, for example, *Hawkes & Son (London) Ltd* v. *Paramount Film Service Ltd* [1934] 1 Ch 593.
[51] Ricketson and Ginsburg, *International Copyright and Neighbouring Rights*, [13.55].
[52] *Ibid.*

## 5.4 Free Use Exceptions

The limits on the permissible exception for lectures and addresses may be usefully compared with the limits on exceptions permitted under Article 10*bis*. First, Article 2*bis*(2) applies to all lectures, addresses and like works that are delivered in public, and is not confined to works on current topics or reporting of current events. Second, the exception allows for reproduction by the press, broadcasting and public communications, but does not extend to making a film of the lectures or addresses.[53] Third, like Article 10*bis*(2), the use must be justified by its 'informatory purpose'; but while the purpose of that provision is 'reporting current events', the purpose of exceptions permitted by Article 2*bis*(2) is the more general one of informing the public.[54] Like Article 10*bis*(2), the exception for addresses and lectures provides for national legislation to determine the 'conditions' for exercising the exception, which presumably could include making it subject to the payment of remuneration. As with the optional exclusion in Article 2*bis*(1), any exception must preserve the rights of authors to make collections of lectures, addresses and like works.

*Ephemeral Recordings by Broadcasting Organisations* The fourth optional Berne exception relates to recordings of works made by a broadcasting organisation for use in its own broadcasting. After clarifying that permission to broadcast a work does not imply permission to record the work, Article 11*bis*(3) provides for it to be a matter for national legislation to 'determine the regulations for ephemeral recordings made by a broadcasting organization by means of its own facilities and used for its own broadcasts'. The wording of this provision allows for national laws to introduce unremunerated exceptions for ephemeral recordings, but is broad enough to require remuneration under a compulsory licensing regime.[55]

The following limits apply to exceptions under national laws. First, such laws must authorise only 'ephemeral' recordings, and clearly cannot authorise permanent recordings.[56] Second, the recordings must be made by the broadcasting organisation's own facilities. Third, the recording must be used for the organisation's own broadcasts, and not for any other purpose, although it can be made in advance of a broadcast.

In addition to the exception for ephemeral recordings, Article 11*bis*(3) allows for national legislation to permit the preservation of such recordings in official archives 'on the ground of their exceptional documentary character'. This exception is limited, in that preservation can only be in

---

[53] *Ibid.* [13.53].   [54] *Ibid.*   [55] Ficsor and WIPO, 'Guide to copyright', [BC-11*bis*. 27].
[56] Ricketson and Ginsburg, *International Copyright and Neighbouring Rights*, [13.76].

'official archives' and cannot be of all works, but only those justified by 'their exceptional documentary character'.

*Minor Exceptions or Reservations* Apart from express exceptions, it is accepted that Berne includes implied minor exceptions, or 'minor reservations'. The issue of implied exceptions first arose in the context of the introduction of a public performance right in the 1948 Brussels revision, when questions were raised about the status of existing exceptions under national laws.[57] While the Brussels conference raised the possibility of including an express provision dealing with these exceptions, it was decided against this, in the process confirming that the exception must be minor or genuinely *de minimis*.[58]

An Agreed Statement to the Brussels conference specifically mentioned minor implied exceptions for 'religious ceremonies, military bands and the needs of child and adult education'.[59] These examples are not exhaustive, but clearly illustrative only. In accordance with their source in the *de minimis* principle, implied exceptions cannot generally include acts carried out for commercial purposes and, moreover, cannot extend to all not-for-profit activities.[60] On this point, however, the WTO Panel decision on the US 'homestyle' exception, which confirmed the existence of the doctrine under both Berne and TRIPs, concluded that 'we are not in a position to determine that the minor exceptions doctrine justifies only exclusively non-commercial uses of works and that it may under no circumstances justify exceptions to uses with a more than negligible impact on copyright holders'.[61]

The implied minor exceptions doctrine, however, extends only to exceptions to the public performance and communications rights.[62]

### 5.4.3 Free Use Exceptions to Neighbouring Rights

In relation to neighbouring rights, Rome does not include mandatory exceptions, but Article 15(1) enables Member States to introduce four kinds of exceptions. First, Article 15(1)(a) allows Member States to introduce exceptions for private use which, although raising difficult definitional issues, clearly cannot extend to professional or commercial uses.[63] Second, Article 15(1)(b) allows exceptions for the 'use of short

---

[57] *Ibid.* [13.79]; Ficsor and WIPO, 'Guide to copyright', [BC-11.12].
[58] Ricketson and Ginsburg, *International Copyright and Neighbouring Rights*, [13.82].
[59] Ficsor and WIPO, 'Guide to copyright', [BC-11.12].   [60] *Ibid.* [BC-11.26].
[61] WTO Panel, WT/DS160/R – 15 June 2000 United States – Section 110(5) of the US Copyright Act, *Report of the Panel*, [6.58].
[62] Ficsor and WIPO, 'Guide to copyright', [BC-11.13].   [63] *Ibid.* [19.12].

excerpts in connexion with the reporting of current events', which is comparable to the exception for newspaper and periodical articles allowed under Berne. Unlike the Berne exception, however, the Rome exception can permit only the use of 'short excerpts', not entire articles. Third, Article 15(1)(c) allows exceptions for 'ephemeral fixation by a broadcasting organisation by means of its own facilities and for its own broadcasts', which parallels Article 11bis(3) of Berne, although slightly differently worded. In particular, the Rome provision seems to allow only for an exception for ephemeral recordings, which would not extend to a remunerated compulsory licensing regime. Fourth, Article 15(1)(d) allows for an exception for 'use solely for the purposes of teaching or scientific research', which, by referring to 'scientific research', goes beyond the use of works for the purpose of teaching under Berne.[64]

Article 15(2) of Rome extends beyond the specific exceptions allowed under Article 15(1) to allow national laws to 'provide for the same kinds of limitations with regard to the protection of performers, producers of phonograms and broadcasting organisations, as it provides for, in its domestic laws and regulations, in connexion with the protection of copyright in literary and artistic works'. As most countries are Berne members, this provision effectively allows for exceptions under national laws that are Berne compatible. Article 15(2) is, however, limited to free use exceptions, as it specifically provides that compulsory licences are permissible only to the extent they are compatible with Rome, and not with Berne. This means that compulsory licences expressly permitted under Berne are not permitted under the Rome Convention.

As Rome preceded the Berne three-step test, it does not include a version of that general test. Article 16 of the WPPT, however, includes both a version of Article 15(2) of Rome and of the three-step test. Under Article 16(1) of the WPPT, contracting parties may provide for the same kind of exceptions to the protection of performers and producers of phonograms as is provided under their national laws 'in connection with the protection of copyright in literary and artistic works'. As with Article 15(2) of Rome, this allows for national laws to include exceptions that are Berne compliant. Furthermore, Article 16(2) extends the three-step test to national exceptions to the rights of performers and producers of phonograms. As Article 16(1) does not include a provision, such as that in Article 15(2), limiting compulsory licences to those compatible with Rome, national laws could provide compulsory licences in relation to WPPT rights provided they are both permissible under Berne and comply with the three-step test in Article 16(2).[65]

[64] *Ibid.* [19.15].  [65] *Ibid.* [19.69].

### 5.4.4 Free Use Exceptions under the Marrakesh Treaty

Article 4(1) of the Marrakesh Treaty makes it mandatory for contracting parties to introduce free use exceptions to the rights of reproduction, distribution, making available to the public and public performance, to facilitate the availability of works in accessible format copies by visually impaired persons and persons with print disabilities (known as 'beneficiary persons'). The works covered by Marrakesh are confined to literary and artistic works under Berne 'in the form of text, notation and/or related illustrations, whether published or otherwise made publicly available in any media', but includes audiobooks.[66] Moreover, the exception is confined to the exercise of the relevant exclusive rights by an 'authorized entity', which is defined to mean 'an entity that is authorized or recognized by the government to provide education, instructional training, adaptive reading or information access to beneficiary persons on a non-profit basis', and includes government institutions and non-profit organisations.[67]

Under Article 4(2), national exceptions must be made subject to the following conditions: the 'authorized entity' must have lawful access to the work or a copy of the work; the work must be converted to an 'accessible format copy', but cannot introduce changes other than those needed to make the work accessible to beneficiary persons; such accessible format copies must be supplied exclusively to be used by beneficiary persons; and the activity must be undertaken on a non-profit basis. The national laws implementing Marrakesh may confine the exceptions to works in which the particular accessible format is not available commercially under 'reasonable terms'.[68] Although Marrakesh allows for free use exceptions to facilitate the availability of works in accessible format copies, it also provides for national laws to comply by a remunerated use exception, such as a compulsory licence.[69] While contracting parties have considerable flexibility in how they comply with their obligations under Marrakesh,[70] with greater flexibility being given to least-developed countries,[71] any exceptions must also comply with the three-step tests under Berne, TRIPs and the WCT.[72]

### 5.4.5 Free Use Exceptions and the Public Domain

The international framework for free use exceptions includes: a general test, the three-step test, which sets a limit on permissible exceptions under

---

[66] Marrakesh Treaty, Art. 2(a); Agreed Statement concerning Article 2(a).
[67] Marrakesh Treaty, Art. 2(c).   [68] Marrakesh Treaty, Art. 4(4).
[69] Marrakesh Treaty, Art. 4(5).   [70] Marrakesh Treaty, Art. 10(3).
[71] Marrakesh Treaty, Art. 12.   [72] Marrakesh Treaty, Art. 11.

national laws; one mandatory exception, for quotations; and four permissible exceptions, as well as implied minor exceptions. As explained above, the general three-step test cannot be used to extend the scope of the specific exceptions. While the three-step test establishes some flexibility, it is based on the presumption that exceptions must satisfy each of the three steps to be justified. Moreover, persistent uncertainties with the interpretation and the application of the test can, on the one hand, inhibit the extent to which the test can be used to justify exceptions under national laws, but on the other hand give scope for variation unless and until challenged: [5.6].

That said, as is clear from the comparative analysis of exceptions in Chapters 11 and 12, there is considerable scope for national laws to take greater advantage of the flexibilities provided by international copyright law than is currently the case. The specific exceptions recognise a range of public interests in the use of works protected by copyright for the purposes of public domain values such as creating new works (the quotation exception), freedom of expression (quotation, and press and media exceptions), education and democratic processes (press and media exceptions). They also recognise that there are circumstances where there is little harm to the copyright owner from the use, or where it would be more costly to require payment for the use than to allow it,[73] such as ephemeral recording of works by broadcasters and minor implied exceptions.

It remains the case, however, that most free use exceptions are permissive, not mandatory, with the recent example of the mandatory exception to facilitate access to works by visually impaired persons being notable mainly as a departure from the general rule. As is clear from Chapters 11–14, countries often face a choice about implementing exceptions as free use or remunerated use exceptions.

## 5.5 Remunerated Use Exceptions

International copyright law provides for certain exceptions to infringement that are available only upon payment to the copyright owner, which are also known as compulsory licences. The comparative analysis of remunerated use exceptions under national laws is undertaken in Chapters 13 and 14.

As such licences come within our definition of the public domain, provided certain conditions are met: [2.2.3], we argue they are an

---

[73] W. Gordon, 'Fair use as market failure: a structural and economic analysis of the *Betamax case* and its predecessors' (1982) 82(8) *Columbia Law Review* 1600.

essential part of the global public domain. Berne permits the following three kinds of remunerated use exceptions: mechanical recording of musical works; rebroadcasting and cable retransmissions; and compulsory licensing allowing translation and reproduction in developing nations under the Paris Appendix. As discussed above, Berne may also permit remuneration for otherwise unremunerated exceptions, such as certain uses of works for 'reporting current events'.

### 5.5.1   Mechanical Recording of Musical Works

Article 13(1) of Berne provides for Member States to permit 'reservations and conditions on the exclusive right granted to the author of a musical work and to the author of any words ... to authorize the sound recording of that musical work, together with such words, if any'. The second part of Article 13(1) goes on to provide that countries may only apply reservations and conditions where it is not 'prejudicial to the rights of these authors to obtain equitable remuneration which, in the absence of agreement, shall be fixed by competent authority'. This means that the 'reservations and conditions' cannot allow for free use of musical works, or for compensation less than 'equitable remuneration'.[74]

The provision allows for Berne members to introduce an exception to the reproduction right consisting of a compulsory licence confined to making sound recordings of musical works (and words accompanying such works). The establishment of a permissible remunerated use exception for making sound recordings of musical works essentially recognised a practice that developed in the early stage of the recording industry; and, as such, it has operated to protect the economic interests of the recording industry.[75]

### 5.5.2   Broadcasting, Rebroadcasting and Cable Retransmissions

Article 11bis(1) of Berne confers exclusive rights of broadcasting and retransmission via rebroadcasting or via wired retransmission, on authors of literary and artistic works: [4.7.2]. Article 11bis(2) provides for it to be a matter for legislation in Berne members to determine the conditions for exercising these rights provided they 'shall not in any circumstances be prejudicial to the moral rights of the author, nor to his right to obtain equitable remuneration which, in the absence of agreement, shall be fixed by competent authority'.

---

[74] For the meaning of 'equitable remuneration', see [13.3.2].
[75] Ricketson and Ginsburg, *International Copyright and Neighbouring Rights*, [13.59].

## 5.5 Remunerated Use Exceptions

The remunerated use exception under Article 11*bis*(2), first introduced in the 1928 Rome Act, was clearly modelled on Article 13(1). The exception allows for compulsory licences for all or any of the exclusive rights in Article 11*bis*(1), but cannot apply to wired transmissions (such as Internet streaming) or to retransmissions of works originally transmitted via wire.[76] The broadcasting compulsory licence in Article 11*bis*(2) was a compromise between those who argued that dissemination by broadcasting should be completely assimilated to the exclusive rights of authors, on the one hand, and those favouring state intervention to protect cultural and social interests in broadcasting, on the other.[77]

### 5.5.3 Compulsory Licensing in Developing Nations: Translations and Reproductions

From the 1960s, developing countries were more assertive in pursuing their interests in international copyright forums, leading to tensions with developed countries.[78] There were two main issues: the ability of developing countries to translate foreign works into their own languages; and the ability of developing countries to republish books published overseas, when no local publication had occurred. These demands eventually resulted in a compromise at the Paris revision conference which added a detailed appendix to Berne, known as the Paris Appendix. The Paris Appendix allows for developing countries to subject the translation and reproduction rights to compulsory licences. To take advantage of the Appendix, a developing country must deposit a notification with WIPO declaring it will take advantage of either or both of the compulsory licences for translations and reproductions, and the declaration must be renewed each ten years.[79]

The Paris Appendix requires legislation that includes complex conditions for compliance with either of the compulsory licences it permits, and its strict terms have had very limited direct effect, although compulsory licences for educational purposes have often been introduced: [14.3].

### 5.5.4 Remunerated Exceptions and Neighbouring Rights

In relation to neighbouring rights, Article 15(2) of Rome provides that compulsory licences are permissible only to the extent they are compatible with that Convention: [5.4.3]. This means that, outside of

---

[76] *Ibid.* [13.71].     [77] Ficsor and WIPO, 'Guide to copyright', [BC-11*bis*. 20].
[78] Ricketson and Ginsburg, *International Copyright and Neighbouring Rights*, [14.01] ff.; Bannerman, *International Copyright and Access to Knowledge*, 133.
[79] *Berne Convention*, Appendix, Art. I.

compulsory licences expressly permitted by Rome, the compulsory licences permitted under Berne, such as the broadcasting licence under Article 11*bis*(2), cannot be justified in relation to the rights protected under Rome.[80] Three broadcasting-related compulsory licences are permitted under Rome, in relation to: fixations of performances for broadcasting purposes (Article 7(2)(2)); broadcasting and public communications of phonograms (Article 12); and communication to the public of certain broadcasts (Article 13(d)).

### 5.5.5  Remunerated Exceptions and the Public Domain

Two of the remunerated use exceptions expressly permitted by Berne (mechanical recording of musical works; rebroadcasting and cable retransmissions) are of continuing importance, but the compulsory licences allowing translation and reproduction in developing nations under the Paris Appendix have proven to be ill-considered and of less importance. Berne may also permit remuneration for some of the otherwise unremunerated exceptions, especially as remunerated exceptions are capable of satisfying the three-step test: [5.4]. In Chapters 13 and 14, illustrating the importance of the flexibility in allowing choice between free use and remunerated exceptions, remunerated exceptions not expressly provided for in Berne are shown to be of considerable and growing significance in national laws.

The justifications for remunerated exceptions, which are a 'halfway house' between full copyright protection and free use, may differ from justifications for free use exceptions. Remunerated uses, like those permitted by the Paris Appendix, may still be justified by public interest considerations, such as the public interest in access to works. Historically, however, as with the exception allowing for broadcasting compulsory licences under Berne, some exceptions have arisen from failure to agree on whether or not a new use should be subject to control by the copyright owner.

Furthermore, remunerated use exceptions may be justified where the costs of negotiating individual licences outweigh the benefits of those licences, so it is more efficient for payments to be made by collective management under a compulsory licence.[81] This may be the case, for example, where there are uncertainties concerning the definition of the relevant rights and/or in identifying the rights holders. Especially in

---

[80] Ricketson and Ginsburg, *International Copyright and Neighbouring Rights*, [19.16].

[81] Gordon, 'Fair use as market failure'; R. P. Merges, 'Contracting into liability rules: intellectual property rights and collective rights organizations' (1996) 84(5) *California Law Review* 1293.

circumstances where there is a public interest in access to copyright works, difficult decisions may need to be made about whether a use should be remunerated or unremunerated, with significant differences in national laws as to which uses fall within which kind of exception: Chapters 12–14.

## 5.6 Exclusions, Exceptions and the Public Domain

Given the breadth of minimum protectable subject matter and the scope of minimum exclusive rights under international copyright law, exclusions and exceptions to copyright have become the main safeguards for copyright public domains. As the complexity and scope of protectable subject matter and exclusive rights expanded over time, so exclusions and exceptions have also become more complex. The importance of exceptions to the protection of what we call public rights (and public domain values) is illustrated by the extent to which debates over the scope of exceptions and limitations, such as the merits of a fair use exception or the potential for new 'exceptions' treaties, have moved to the centre of debates about copyright policy.

The specific exclusions and exceptions under international law were introduced to: protect freedom of expression, especially by the press and media; promote access to public information, such as laws and official documents, and support democratic processes; and support educational uses. The ability of authors to use copyright material in new creations is protected by the mandatory exception for quotation, but also by the three-step test. Overall, however, the mandatory and permissible exclusions and exceptions have the appearance of haphazard and ad hoc development, with most being subject to detailed limitations, and with little in the way of coherent justifications, such as by reference to positive public domain values. Moreover, as Bannerman has argued, the history of international copyright law was characterised by a change in the status of exceptions from the early period, from the 1880s to 1920s, where they were initially regarded as essential safeguards for access to information, but with access-oriented exceptions being progressively restricted or eliminated.[82] For example, by the 1920s, exceptions for scientific publications had been removed, exceptions for educational use and news were narrowed, and authors had acquired exclusive rights over translations, with no new relevant exceptions until the largely ineffective provisions of the Paris Appendix.[83]

---

[82] Bannerman, *International Copyright and Access to Knowledge*, 16. For a summary of the categories of restrictions on copyright under national laws prior to the Berne Convention, see Ladas, *The International Protection of Literary and Artistic Property*, 40–4.

[83] Bannerman, *International Copyright and Access to Knowledge*, 32–122.

The place of exclusions and exceptions within international copyright law is indicative of the preference given to authors' rights over other rights and interests which support the public domain. While Berne and other treaties set floors on protectable subject matter, duration of protection and exclusive rights, the same treaties set ceilings, especially in the form of the three-step test, on permissible exceptions. Furthermore, most exclusions and exceptions are permissive, with only the exclusion for news of the day and the quotation exception being mandated. The effects of the mandatory exclusion and exception are, however, limited: the exclusion for news of the day is no more than an instance of the principle that copyright does not protect facts, while the quotation exception is subject to limitations, such as compliance with 'fair practice', and is implemented in very different ways in national laws: [12.3].

Considerable problems arise from the most important restriction on permissible exceptions, the three-step test. Partly due to the test resulting from compromises struck at the 1967 Stockholm revision, the test is marred by ambiguities and indeterminacy. The application of the test has not been assisted by the narrow interpretation applied by the WTO Panel in the 'homestyle' decision. Potentially more significantly, the test operates entirely as a ceiling on exceptions, so that national exceptions are subject to scrutiny as to whether they comply. To address the structural asymmetry arising from the need for justifying exceptions, Gervais has suggested that the test should be 'reversed', meaning that the third step, the effect of a use on the rights holder, becomes the most important consideration, such that uses are effectively permitted unless they have an adverse effect on the economic interests of the rights holder.[84] Another suggestion, perhaps unlikely to be followed, has been to interpret the three steps as discretionary or permissive, so that each of the steps operates simply as a factor to be taken into account in determining whether a use is permissible rather than the steps being exhaustive, mandatory criteria.[85] In any case, the indeterminacy of the test together with the presumption that exceptions are unjustified unless they satisfy each of the three steps function as significant constraints on the protection of public domains by means of exceptions.

The Marrakesh Treaty is a limited, but potentially significant, shift in the international paradigm relating to copyright exceptions. Although Marrakesh allows considerable flexibility in how obligations are implemented, it establishes a new mandatory exception to enhance accessibility

---

[84] Gervais, 'A new core international copyright norm'.
[85] K. Koelman, 'Fixing the three-step test' (2006) 28 *European Intellectual Property Review* 407.

to works by visually impaired persons. Moreover, for the first time, an international copyright treaty has mandated the application of an exception to domestic rights holders. While there is scope for new multilateral instruments to harmonise and consolidate exceptions, particularly exceptions for educational uses or libraries and archives: [12.1], there are no indications at present that such proposals are likely to be adopted.

## 5.7 Enforcement of International Copyright Law

As explained in Chapter 4, international copyright law conditions national public domains by rules setting minimum levels for protectable subject matter, copyright duration and exclusive rights. As is usual with international agreements, the rules are expressed at a high level of generality, meaning that the precise scope of public domains depends upon detailed implementation in national laws, but also that national jurisdictions retain much 'wriggle room'. While understanding the implications of the international legal framework is essential to analysis of national public domains, the international framework may not mean much unless it is accurately reflected in national laws, and this depends in part upon the effectiveness of mechanisms for ensuring compliance. The importance of enforcement is illustrated by the United States effectively ignoring its obligations to provide retroactive protection under Article 18 of Berne until the coming into effect of the WTO dispute resolution mechanism: [4.3.1].[86]

In the last part of the twentieth century, there was an increased emphasis on enforcement of international intellectual property agreements. This emphasis was associated with the increased centrality of intellectual property in international trade and, with TRIPs, the superimposition of the international trade paradigm on the Berne template.[87] While TRIPs incorporates the substantive Berne minima, it built on these by adding significant elements from international trade law, especially the MFN principle and a dispute resolution mechanism.

Under Berne, from the 1948 Brussels revision, it was possible for Berne members to bring disputes concerning the interpretation or application of the Convention before the International Court of Justice (ICJ).[88]

---

[86] A. Chander, M. Sunder and U. Le, '*Golan v. Holder*' (2012) 106 *American Journal of International Law* 637.
[87] J. C. Ginsburg, 'International copyright: from a "bundle" of national copyright laws to a supranational code', 271.
[88] Berne Convention, Art. 33. See also Rome Convention, Art. 30.

This mechanism was, however, never invoked, with important developing countries making permissible reservations opting out of the ICJ jurisdiction.[89] Moreover, as Ricketson and Ginsburg argue in relation to the potential application of customary international law, there has been a considerable degree of toleration of potential non-compliance with the Convention due, mainly, to the overarching objective of preserving the Berne Union.[90]

TRIPs, however, introduced dispute prevention and settlement mechanisms which, to some extent, replaced the previous implicit toleration of diversity with a more adversarial model. First, Article 63 of TRIPs mandates transparency of relevant intellectual property laws, by requiring members to publicise laws, regulations, judicial decisions and administrative rulings, and to notify the Council for TRIPs of laws and regulations. This effectively provides access to national laws so that members can assess their implications, and the degree of compliance with the international framework. Second, Article 64 of TRIPs incorporates the detailed dispute resolution mechanism for international trade disputes established by Articles XXII and XXIII of the GATT, as elaborated by the Dispute Settlement Understanding. The procedures, which begin with mandatory consultations, may result in a binding ruling by a WTO Panel, with the possibility of an appeal on points of law. Non-compliance by a Member State is dealt with by a 'subtle calibration of suspensions',[91] which can result in trade sanctions.

Since the entry into force of TRIPs, the dispute settlement mechanism has been invoked just ten times in relation to copyright and neighbouring rights issues, with the United States initiating eight complaints and the European Communities initiating two.[92] Of these, eight disputes were settled and just two – the complaint of the European Communities concerning the US 'homestyle' and business exceptions for public performance of musical works[93] and the US complaint against China concerning criminal enforcement for copyright infringement on a commercial scale[94] – progressed to WTO Panel resolutions. The limited number of

[89] Ricketson and Ginsburg, *International Copyright and Neighbouring Rights*, [17.88].
[90] *Ibid.*   [91] *Ibid.* [4.38].
[92] See World Trade Organization, 'Index of disputes issues' www.wto.org/english/tratop_e/dispu_e/dispu_subjects_index_e.htm#selected_subject, which lists the following disputes: DS28 (9 February 1996); DS42 (28 May 1996); DS82 (14 May 1997); DS83 (14 May 1997); DS86 (28 May 1997); DS115 (6 January 1998); DS124 (30 April 1998); DS125 (4 May 1998); DS160 (26 January 1999); DS362 (10 April 2007).
[93] WTO Panel, WT/DS160/R – 15 June 2000 United States – Section 110(5) of the US Copyright Act, Report of the Panel.
[94] WTO Panel, WT/DS362/R – 10 April 2007 China – Measures Affecting the Protection and Enforcement of Intellectual Property Rights, Report of the Panel.

## 5.7 Enforcement of International Copyright Law

disputes, the identity of the complainants and the very small number of WTO Panel decisions, all illustrate the importance of understanding the wider international political context behind inter-state enforcement of international copyright law.

The selective nature of use of the WTO dispute settlement process indicates how this is part of a broader range of strategies pursued by copyright producing countries and private stakeholders. The wider context includes the use of informal suasion by producer countries, but also strategies of forum shifting or regime shifting.[95] For example, the gridlock in negotiating revisions to Berne since the 1970s was a factor influencing producer countries to shift their attention to the international trade paradigm, whereas the difficulties encountered with multilateral negotiations led to a shift to promoting nested, post-TRIPs bilateral agreements. As Helfer points out, however, it is not only powerful states that engage in regime shifting to promote their interests, but weaker states do so as well, in a shifting chessboard of complex negotiations across multiple regimes.[96]

The complexity of international copyright law, including the strategic use of regime shifting, has implications for national public domains. First, the complexity of the international regimes makes it difficult definitively to claim that a national regime is in breach of international obligations.[97] This is reinforced by the generality with which international rules are expressed, which creates flexibility. Second, the strategic use of formal enforcement, such as WTO dispute settlement, suggests that there remains a degree of implied tolerance of divergences in national laws, even where it may be doubtful that the laws are in strict compliance with the minimum standards mandated by the Berne model. Third, the detailed international rules explained in this and the previous chapter should not be taken entirely at face value, as they have complex effects. To an extent, they operate in a symbolic way, when they are invoked to support the agendas of powerful state or non-state actors. On the other hand, the flexibility of international rules, and the limited recourse to formal enforcement in the context of national divergences from the rules, suggests there is more leeway – both practical and legal – than is commonly assumed for nation states to develop creative solutions to support national public domains.

---

[95] L. Helfer, 'Regime shifting: the TRIPs Agreement and the new dynamics of international intellectual property making' (2004) 29 *Yale Journal of International Law* 1.
[96] L. Helfer, 'Regime shifting in the international intellectual property system' (2009) 7(1) *Perspectives on Politics* 39.
[97] *Ibid.* 42.

## 5.8 Conclusion: Exceptions, Enforcement and the Public Domain

The expansive approach taken by international copyright law to protectable subject matter and exclusive rights has meant that exclusions and exceptions assume a central role, possibly the most important role, in safeguarding public domains. As a consequence, as explored further in Chapters 11–14, many contemporary controversies concerning law reform focus on the character and scope of limitations and exceptions. Despite the importance of exceptions in protecting the public domain, and the extent to which a balance between copyright and the public interest has always been integral to the international framework, international copyright law structurally preferences authors' rights over exceptions: significantly, while the international framework sets floors on subject matter, duration and exclusive rights, it sets ceilings on exclusions and exceptions. In addition, the very limited mandatory exclusions and exceptions under international law effectively leave most significant decisions relating to exceptions to national laws. Particular difficulties arise from the general ceiling imposed on exceptions by the three-step test, as this leads to the presumption that exceptions are not justified unless each of the three conditions are satisfied, and creates indeterminacy in how the test might apply to national exceptions, especially potentially broad or open-ended national exceptions. These difficulties can limit the extent to which countries take advantage of the potential flexibilities available for crafting exceptions under international copyright law.

With the introduction of a mechanism for enforcing international copyright law, in the form of the WTO dispute resolution procedure, there has been a decrease in the discretion available for national laws to apply international standards flexibly, as states with an interest in maximising protection may threaten to invoke the mechanism, which may eventually result in sanctions. The selective use of the dispute resolution procedure to date, however, suggests that there is a degree of implied tolerance of diversity in national laws, which in fact always seems to have been the case, even where such laws may strictly be in breach of international standards. In any event, the dense complexity of international copyright law and the generality with which the rules are expressed mean that, in our view, there is much more flexibility in how national laws may be adjusted to protect public domains than commonly assumed.[98]

While this and the preceding chapter have made the case for there being a global public domain, it is clear that international copyright law leaves

---

[98] Samuelson, 'Preliminary thoughts on copyright reform'.

## 5.8 Conclusion: Exceptions, Enforcement and the Public Domain

enormous scope for national variations. It is only through an appreciation of the variations in national regimes, explored in Part III of this book, that it is possible to arrive at a satisfactory understanding of copyright public domains. Moreover, to understand fully the global public domain identified in this chapter, it will be necessary to examine the impact on it of contemporary Internet practices, which are dealt with in Chapters 15 (on voluntary licensing practices) and 16 (on the de facto public domain, and on 'Internet spillovers' of public domains).

# 6 National Public Domains – Supports and Constraints

6.1 The Copyright Public Domain's Supports and Constraints 152
6.2 Supports for Public Rights 153
6.3 Constraints on Public Rights 168
6.4 Conclusions: Essentials for an Effective Copyright Public Domain 182

## 6.1 The Copyright Public Domain's Supports and Constraints

For a richer, more realistic and more useful description of a country's copyright public domain it is necessary to consider not only the categories of public rights comprising a country's public domain, but also the penumbra of institutions and practices ('environmental factors') influencing the effective exercise of otherwise formal property rights. This chapter addresses these broader institutional and practical considerations, which either support or constrain particular public rights (but are not in themselves additional 'public rights'). Here we aim to identify which of the fifteen public rights are supported or constrained, and to give illustrative national examples of approaches that have expanded or protected the public domain. These supports and constraints vary a great deal among countries, and are often where much of the controversy in relation to the public domain arises.

On the positive side are 'supports for' public rights such as statutory deposit systems for copyright works, author location or registration systems, statutory immunities for 'benign' third parties, limited remedies and requirements to provide copyright content for free access, or as open content.

On the negative side are 'constraints on' public rights which detract from or defeat the effectiveness of public rights, including contractual provisions excluding public rights, technological protection measures (TPMs) and surveillance of uses (and users).

### 6.1.1 *Supports and Constraints in Public Domain Theory*

Other public domain theorists have recognised the significance of such factors, at least in part. Deazley discusses only what we call constraints, which he refers to as 'external considerations'.[1] He says the public domain (and its effective boundary with the private domain) 'can also be profoundly affected by various external considerations', particularly physical and technological barriers to meaningful access and use, and use of the law of contract to require individuals to 'contract out' of freedoms that they otherwise have, to use works. Lessig refers to what we call supports, when referring to 'crafting an "effective" public domain – meaning a free space that functions as a public domain, even though the resources that constitute it are not properly within the public domain', in order to 'map a strategy for [the public domain's] defense'.[2] Here he is referring to both what we call neutral private licensing, such as Creative Commons licences, and also the types of support factors to which we refer.

## 6.2 Supports for Public Rights

This section discusses the supports mentioned above. This list is not exhaustive. Other supports are discussed in later chapters, such as the supports given to neutral voluntary licensing (Chapter 15) by government purchasing preference policies for open source software, and open content publishing policies for official documents.

### 6.2.1 *Statutory Deposit Systems for Copyright Works*

One requirement for the effective operation of the public domain at the expiry of copyright in a work is that there is at least one copy of the work available to the public, which can then be reproduced (or other exclusive rights utilised) in accordance with applicable public rights. Such requirements are often called 'statutory deposit' systems, and also called 'legal deposit'.

Statutory deposit systems underpin the effectiveness of many aspects of the public domain, because exercise of public rights in relation to such works is otherwise subject to the chance availability of books in libraries, or their availability for purchase, contingencies that diminish over time. As well as being necessary for post-term exercise of rights, they may assist

---

[1] Deazley, *Rethinking Copyright*, 122–9; he also uses the term 'externalities', but this technical term does not seem appropriate in this context.
[2] Lessig, 'Re-crafting a public domain'.

in the location of rights holders for purposes of diligent searchers required by orphan works provisions. They can also help ensure against works being protected by TPMs after term expiry, or protected by TPMs during the copyright term against exercise of statutory exceptions: [6.3.3].

Statutory deposit systems are found in many countries. WIPO's 2010 survey[3] obtained responses from 88/189 WIPO Member States[4] and found that fifty-six respondents (73 per cent)[5] had mandatory legal deposit requirements.[6] These include many economically significant countries. Deposit requirements were usually supported by fines for noncompliance. In most countries, 'there are no different rules for works published online and off-line', and the rules 'for hard copy works are also applicable to electronic formats' although there are likely to be different procedures prescribed. Legal deposit authorities sometimes collect online materials themselves rather than requiring them to be submitted.[7] Depository institutions are typically the country's national library. Members of the public are usually allowed to access the deposited materials via such institutions, free of charge, and with search assistance for location of works.[8] A minority of countries (for example, the United States) provide linkages to ISBN numbers, some even to ISSN numbers.[9] Although, in accordance with Berne, a formality such as legal deposit cannot be a requirement for subsistence of copyright, in about half the responding states deposit may serve prima facie evidentiary purposes of date of creation and ownership.[10] In most countries the requirements apply to all materials published or printed in the country concerned, and also to print and electronic materials (in tangible formats) of foreign origin which are imported and intended for distribution within

---

[3] WIPO, 'Second survey on voluntary registration and deposit systems' www.wipo.int/copy right/en/registration/registration_and_deposit_system_03_10.html. The WIPO Committee on Development and Intellectual Property approved a thematic project on copyright and the public domain in 2010.
[4] WIPO Member States www.wipo.int/members/en.
[5] WIPO, 'Summary of the responses to the questionnaire for survey on copyright registration and deposit systems', B. Legal Deposit, 2010, WIPO *Summary B. Legal Deposit*, para. 29:; Mandatory legal deposit states include Albania, Algeria, Argentina, Austria, Bahrain, Belize, Brazil, Bhutan, Chile, China, Colombia, Costa Rica, Croatia, Czech Republic, Denmark, Finland, Greece, Guatemala, Hungary, Kenya, Republic of Korea, Ireland, Italy, Jamaica, Japan, Latvia, Liechtenstein, Lithuania, Luxembourg, Madagascar, Mexico, Republic of Moldova, Monaco, Montenegro, Namibia, New Zealand, Norway, Pakistan, Peru, Romania, Russian Federation, Saudi Arabia, Serbia, Singapore, South Africa, Spain, Sri Lanka, Sweden, Thailand, Trinidad & Tobago, Ukraine, United Kingdom and United States.
[6] WIPO, 'Summary', B. Legal Deposit.
[7] WIPO, 'Summary', B. Legal Deposit, para. 36.
[8] WIPO, 'Summary', B. Legal Deposit, paras. 41–43.
[9] WIPO, 'Summary', B. Legal Deposit, para. 44.
[10] WIPO, 'Summary', B. Legal Deposit, para. 31.

## 6.2 Supports for Public Rights

the country.[11] While deposit of literary and artistic works is usually required, coverage of the subject matter of related rights is more variable, as are the exceptions to what must be lodged.[12] No general information was given about the extent to which contact information was available concerning authors or publishers, or updates thereto.

In summary, it is common for statutory deposit systems to apply to both non-digital and digital subject matter, and to make it available for free access to the public via national libraries. Deposit of works published or printed within a country and imported work distributed within a county is typically required. This availability of content helps make the public domain viable. Systems may also assist location of rights holders.

*National Examples: The United States and Australia*  The United States and Australia are two examples of countries with the types of comprehensive statutory deposit systems that we consider essential for the long-term protection of the public domain. The United States has one of the most sophisticated systems,[13] even allowing registration of holograms. Statutory deposit is with the Library of Congress, but in most cases registration of a work with the US Copyright Office can also serve the purpose of statutory deposit, provided it is applied for at the same time: [6.2.2]. Statutory deposit may be required even though the author has no desire to register copyright in the work. The Library of Congress will only accept lodgement of published works: an author who wishes to register an unpublished work may have to lodge it with the Copyright Office. Deposit is mandatory for works published in the United States, and for works published outside the United States once the work is distributed in the United States. The works required to be deposited cover those in all forms including digital and online. There is a list of exemptions,[14] which includes musical works published only as sound recordings, and databases only available online in the United States. Two copies of works must usually be lodged, including two copies of CD-ROMs where that is the medium of publication. Where works published on CD-ROM are copy protected, a licence allowing up to five simultaneous users on a local area network must be provided. Instructions for displaying holograms, and a photo displaying the image must be lodged.

---

[11] WIPO, 'Summary', B. Legal Deposit, para. 34.
[12] WIPO, 'Summary', B. Legal Deposit, para. 33.
[13] 17 US Code §407; see W. Strong, *The Copyright Book: A Practical Guide* (6th edn, MIT Press, 2014), pp. 140–55 for a detailed explanation, from which the details in the following paragraph are taken.
[14] 37 CFR Ch II §202.19.

Australia does not have a registration system, and was not included in the WIPO survey. It has recently revised its requirements for deposit of digital materials. The federal Copyright Acts have for over a century required legal deposit of print works with the National Library of Australia (NLA). There are also inconsistent legal deposit requirements under state and territory laws.[15] In 2016, these legal deposit requirements under the Copyright Act were extended to include electronic and online materials in order to establish 'an effective scheme to preserve digital material'.[16] The federal deposit requirements apply to a website, web page, web file, book, periodical, newspaper, pamphlet, sheet of music, map, plan, chart or table, but do not apply to certain material, especially audiovisual works that are primarily gaming material or works shared exclusively by means of a private network.[17] A distinction is drawn between material 'available online', which is material communicated on the Internet, and material 'not available online', which includes offline electronic material, such as CDs of maps.[18] Publishers of relevant offline material are required to deposit a physical copy of the material with the NLA within one month after publication. Publishers of online material, on the other hand, are required to deposit material only when this is requested by the Director-General of the NLA or a delegate.[19] Where online material is freely available on a website, the process for collecting the material is automated, via a robot harvester, and the publisher simply must not do anything to prevent the collection.[20] If the online material is not freely available, or not available via a website, the publisher must deliver the material through the NLA's e-deposit service or some other agreed means.[21] Furthermore, if electronic material required to be deposited is protected by a technological protection measure, such as encryption, the publisher must provide the NLA with a version of the material that does not include the TPM.[22]

---

[15] Copyright Act 1879 (NSW); Publications (Legal Deposit) Act 2004 (NT); Libraries Act 1988 (Qld); Libraries Act 1982 (SA); Libraries Act 1984 (Tas); Libraries Act 1988 (Vic); Legal Deposit Act 2012 (WA). There is no legislation in the ACT, but legal deposit is encouraged by the ACT Heritage Library.
[16] Attorney-General's Department (Australia), *Extending the Legal Deposit Scheme to Digital Material: Regulation Impact Statement* (2014), p. 5; Copyright Act 1968 (Australia) ss. 195CA–195CJ.
[17] Copyright Act 1968 (Aus.), s. 195CE (meaning of 'National Library material').
[18] Copyright Act 1968 (Aus.), s. 195CF (meaning of 'available online').
[19] Copyright Act 1968 (Aus.), s. 195CC.
[20] National Library of Australia (NLA), 'Deposit of electronic publications with the National Library of Australia: guide to requirements for publishers (June 2016), pp. 7–8.
[21] *Ibid.* 8.    [22] Copyright Act 1968 (Aus.), s. 195CD(1)(c)(i).

## 6.2 Supports for Public Rights

*Conclusions: An Essential Support* Some form of statutory deposit scheme is essential for an effective public domain. These public domain functions of statutory deposit are usually overlooked.[23] Such a scheme must have provisions for deposit and preservation of digital materials. The requirement in both the United States and Australia to deposit a version of a work to which access is not restricted or otherwise defeated by a TPM is of particular importance.

We also recommend that a good statutory deposit system should enable any person who provides evidence of term expiry to obtain a professional standard digital copy of the work, at the marginal cost of producing such a digital copy. This will then enable both the free access provision of such works via the Internet, and the commercial reproduction of such works as have a market. Further recommendations to maximise the effectiveness of statutory deposit are given following the next section.[24]

### 6.2.2 Registration, Recordation and Location Systems

Berne[25] Article 5(2) prevents countries requiring formalities such as registration for enjoyment or exercise of copyright: [4.4]. However, systems for voluntary registration of works are permitted. Systems by which authors may be located (if alive), or the date of their death ascertained, are essential for the effective operation of various public rights. Author location systems may be instrumental in: determining if the copyright term has expired; determining if relevant 'orphan works' exemptions apply; the application of compulsory licensing regimes through collecting societies; and the effective operation of commercial licensing where works are still protected by copyright. Whether such systems are operated by government, or by private organisations representing rights holders, they can both improve the public domain, and assist authors to find licensees for their works or obtain remuneration for use of their works.

*Official Registration Systems* Many national jurisdictions have official voluntary registration systems. WIPO's 2010 survey[26] found that

---

[23] They are not mentioned in the WIPO, 'Summary', B. Legal Deposit, nor by D. Gangjee 'Copyright formalities: a return to registration', in Giblin and Weatherall (eds.), *What If We Could Reimagine Copyright?*, 222.

[24] G. Greenleaf, A. Paramaguru, C. Bond and S. Christou, 'Legal deposit's role in the public domain', UNSW Law Research Paper No. 2008-38 https://ssrn.com/abstract=1397463.

[25] Full titles and citations of all Conventions are in the Table of International Instruments.

[26] WIPO, 'Summary of the responses to the questionnaire for survey on copyright registration and deposit systems', A. Copyright Registration and Recordation, 2010 www.wipo.int/export/sites/www/copyright/en/registration/pdf/registration_summary_responses.pdf.

forty-six of eighty responding countries had voluntary registration schemes,[27] usually operated by executive agencies, typically copyright or IP offices. Mandatory registration as a condition of subsistence of copyright is prohibited by the Berne principle of formality-free protection: [4.4], and WIPO found no breaches of that, except perhaps by Mauritius.[28] All types of copyright works can be registered.[29] Usually copies of the works registered must be lodged with the registration details; however, these copies are less frequently available to the public than they are under statutory deposit systems.[30] Such access is usually not free of charge, and may be hampered by administrative requirements and delays. Consequently, voluntary registration systems are generally much less useful for providing access to works for purposes of exercising public rights.

*Recordation Systems* 'Recordation' refers to those aspects of official registration systems that have some effect on property rights.[31] The WIPO survey found most official copyright registers function in a limited way as property registers;[32] nine require that transfers or licences of copyright be registered; twenty-five allow voluntary registration of such transfers or licences; but only thirteen countries allow the registration of security interests; and occasionally registration can give priority over other interests. The 'personal information of the author' must be recorded, presumably including location or contact information at the time, and in twenty-eight instances (the majority) it could be updated after registration.[33] The value of recordation systems is primarily to proprietary copyright interests, but they may in some cases support the public domain by assisting third parties who wish to make use of works to

---

[27] Albania, Algeria, Argentina, Austria, Bahrain, Belarus, Belize, Bhutan, Brazil, Colombia, Costa Rica, Ecuador, Germany, Ghana, Guatemala, Guinea, Hungary, Indonesia, Italy, Jamaica, Japan, Kenya, Korea, Kyrgyz Republic, Madagascar, Mauritius, Mexico, Mali, Moldova, Mongolia, Montenegro, Namibia, Nepal, Oman, Pakistan, Peru, Romania, Russia, Serbia, Slovenia, South Africa, Spain, Thailand, Tunisia, Ukraine, United States of America. WIPO, 'Summary', A. Copyright Registration and Recordation, para. 1.

[28] WIPO, 'Summary', A. Copyright Registration and Recordation, para. 11(a).

[29] WIPO, 'Summary', A. Copyright Registration and Recordation, paras. 6, 7. Some exceptional states that only allow registration of anonymous or pseudonymously published works (Austria and Germany), computer programs (Belarus and Russia) or films (South Africa), and there is great variety in relation to the subject matter of neighbouring rights

[30] WIPO, 'Summary', A. Copyright Registration and Recordation, paras. 13(c) and 18–19.

[31] 'Recordation or recordal requires that information about transfers or the creation of related property interests (such as charges) be made publicly available': Gangjee, 'Copyright formalities: a return to registration', 221.

[32] WIPO, 'Summary', A. Copyright Registration and Recordation, paras. 8–16.

[33] WIPO, 'Summary', A. Copyright Registration and Recordation, paras. 13(a) and 16.

## 6.2 Supports for Public Rights

work out if the term of a work has expired, to locate those who have an interest in it and to help satisfy diligent search requirements for orphan works.[34]

*Benefits of Official and Private Systems* The United States has one of the most well-established registration and recordation systems, with very strong incentives for voluntary registration, at least in relation to registrations by institutions or by professional authors.[35] Its advantages are primarily to rights owners' interests, and only modest for the public domain as an author location system.

The private sector, including collecting societies (CSs), hold very large stores of information about rights holders and works, probably 'the largest pool of information concerning copyright and related rights'.[36] A WIPO study indicates that the advantages of official systems are unlikely to be supplanted by these systems, and that their advantages for the public domain as location systems are limited (including evidence of diligent searches for missing rights holders), so we do not provide details here.[37]

*Finding Works under Public Domain Licences: Registers, Icons and Search Engines* The preceding discussions mainly concern the problems of determining whether the copyright term of a work has expired. However, from a public domain perspective, it is also important to be able to find content which is licensed under neutral voluntary licences (including FOSS software licences or Creative Commons (CC) licences): see Chapter 15. This can both assist wider use of such public domain works and provide subsequent users with more certainty that the original author did in fact license the content under such a licence. At present there are no effective registration facilities (public or private) for such works, although their location on particular sites may provide assurance. It is also possible to use search engines to search for content accompanied by one of the CC standardised set of icons and metadata, or similar metadata for particular FOSS licences.[38]

*Conclusions* Official voluntary copyright registration systems, most with recordation elements, are found in many countries. Such

---

[34] See the Online Supplement for further details.
[35] See the Online Supplement for a summary of the US system and its incentives.
[36] M. Ricoli, F. Morando, C. Rubiano, S. Hsu, M. Ouma and J. C. de Martin, 'Survey of private copyright documentation systems and practices', WIPO, 2011, p. 4.
[37] See the Online Supplement for a summary of some of the advantages of these private sector systems.
[38] For more details of all these location mechanisms, see the Online Supplement.

systems will usually be far more useful than statutory deposit systems both for locating authors and for identifying and locating other rights holders. However, neither system will usually assist in determining whether an author is deceased, enabling calculation of the copyright term (see Chapter 9).

Registration systems, both official and private sector, can support the public domain by facilitating identification and location of rights holders and calculation of copyright terms, but at present few countries make any systemic connections between their various public systems (legal deposit, registration of works or national identification systems) or between these systems and any private systems.[39] The EU-wide registry of orphan works established pursuant to the EU Orphan Works Directive is a notable exception: [14.2.4].

We consider that there are advantages for both proprietary rights and public rights if an official registration and recordation system is offered for voluntary registration, provided it has an efficient e-filing system, and online search facilities. Instead of compulsion, incentives to register are needed. Deposit of works may be able to be combined in the same system, but works deposited (including if in physical form) need to be provided to the national library so as to maximise long-term access. Cross-identification of both works and authors, between public and private systems (provided they are open to public access) should be a major goal. Some of our above conclusions are similar to those of Gangjee's concerning benefits of compulsory registration.[40] In our view they are valuable even though registration cannot be compulsory because of Berne.

### 6.2.3  Occasionally Safe Harbours: Statutory Immunities for 'Benign' Parties

Statutory immunities for some types of 'benign' parties, usually through notice-based schemes and variously called 'safe harbour' or 'take down' schemes[41] can be important practical supports for public rights. These

---

[39] WIPO, 'Summary of the responses to the questionnaire for survey on copyright registration and deposit systems', A. Copyright Registration and Recordation, 2010, para. 4.
[40] Gangjee, 'Copyright formalities: a return to registration', 247–8.
[41] Discussed at length in T. Wu, 'Tolerated use' (2007–8) *Columbia Journal of Law & the Arts* 617 n. 149: 'The first and perhaps most important example is the usage covered by s. 512 of the *Copyright Act* – the DMCA "safe harbor". Relevant to our purposes, s. 512 immunizes search engines (like Yahoo) and hosts of user-directed content (like a web-hosting site) from copyright liability until they are sent explicit notice of the infringing use (notice) and until the entity fails to take down the content subject to notice. For this reason, s. 512 is referred to as a "notice and takedown" system.'

## 6.2 Supports for Public Rights

schemes usually retain formal liability but limit the availability of remedies (in effect, to injunctions) provided the protected parties act in accordance with statutory standards. Intermediary immunities or safe harbours are the flip side of the increased demands from rights holders over the past forty years for various categories of intermediaries to be liable for copyright infringement even though they are not the direct infringer. Both intermediary liabilities and immunities have generated large bodies of scholarship, but our focus here is limited to immunities relevant to the copyright public domain.

To be of maximum value to the public domain, these safe harbour schemes must apply to institutional web hosts such as universities and museums, and not only to 'Internet intermediaries' like ISPs and search engines. Such immunities may be especially relevant where the material accessed or hosted by an intermediary consists, for example, of material where the copyright term is believed to have expired (but potentially might contain some orphan works), or open scholarship publishing projects (which potentially might contain items where licences are inadequate). If 'safe harbour' provisions did apply to cultural and educational institutions (and not only to ISPs and search engines), they would give them a limited 'buffer zone' for reasonable behaviour which may occasionally be in error but can be corrected. In effect they allow such institutions to provide access despite some risks of infringement. As with implied licences, we do not think that statutory immunities are in themselves a distinct category of the public domain, as the immunity is conditional upon a copyright owner not giving notice, and responses to it.

Some forms of safe harbour provisions are becoming a common feature of copyright laws globally. The United States implemented provisions of the 1996 WIPO Copyright Treaty (WCT),[42] including its obligations concerning enforcement of technological protection measures (TPMs) and rights management information (RMI),[43] in the Digital Millennium Copyright Act 1998 (DMCA):[44] [6.3.2]. As a compromise between different industry interests in the United States, Internet intermediaries obtained 'safe harbour' provisions in the United States as part of that Act. Since then, similar provisions to some of the 'safe harbour' provisions contained in that Act have been included in free trade agreements (FTAs) between the United States and twelve other countries.[45] Safe harbours

---

[42] WIPO Copyright Treaty (WCT), 828 UNTS 221, adopted in Geneva on 20 December 1996.
[43] WCT, Arts. 11 and 12, respectively.   [44] 17 USC §512.
[45] As detailed in Seng's extensive survey, these include Australia; Bahrain; Central America-Dominican Republic states; Chile; Columbia; Republic of Korea; Morocco; Oman; Panama; Peru; and Singapore: D. Seng, 'Comparative analysis of the national

have also been required by EU law and enacted in the UK and other EU Member States. They have been enacted in other countries including India, China, Japan and New Zealand, but often differing from the US or EU models. Two WIPO studies[46] analyse the position in thirty countries. Therefore, because of their wide global adoption, even if some of these existing safe harbour provisions are too limited to give major support to the copyright public domain, amendments to extend them may be easier to achieve than completely new provisions.

Below we mention only those aspects of the safe harbour schemes in the United States, the EU, and elsewhere which are of particular relevance to support for the public domain. A more detailed analysis is available online.[47]

*US DMCA Safe Harbor*  The provisions of the DMCA, in general terms, protect Internet intermediaries ('service providers') from monetary remedies and limit the injunctive or other equitable relief against them, for infringements of copyright where the primary infringer is a user of their services, if the service provider comes within one of four defined 'safe harbours'.[48] These are: (a) 'transitory digital network *communications*' (or 'mere conduit'); (b) *caching* of content made avaliable online by others; (c) *hosting* services ('storage at the direction of a user'); and (d) 'information location tools' ('referring or *linking* users to an online location containing infringing material or infringing activity'). The italicised terms are used for later comparisons.

The scope of safe harbours (b)–(d) extends to 'service providers' which means 'a provider of online services or network access, or the operator of facilities therefor',[49] which covers numerous providers of Internet-related services, including search engines. In addition, some safe harbour provisions may apply to non-profit institutions of higher education in relation to actions by their staff or graduate students.[50]

Some of the common elements of the four safe harbours include: that transmission or provision of content was by someone other than the service provider; the relevant action in relation to the material is by automated technical means by the service provider, and without selection by them; the service provider does not have actual knowledge that material or activities are infringing; nor are they aware of facts or circumstances

---

approaches to the liability of internet intermediaries' (preliminary version) (WIPO, 2010).
[46] *Ibid.* and I. Fernández-Diez, 'Comparative analysis on national approaches to the liability of internet intermediaries for infringement of copyright and related rights', WIPO, 2010.
[47] See the Online Supplement.   [48] 17 USC §512(a)–(d).   [49] 17 USC §512(k)(1)(B).
[50] 17 USC §512(e).

## 6.2 Supports for Public Rights

from which such knowledge is apparent; and they do not receive a financial benefit directly attributable to the infringing activity. In various ways, they must also act expeditiously to remedy the situation once they obtain such knowledge or awareness. There are also two general conditions for eligibility for protection with which all service providers must comply: (i) they must adopt and reasonably implement a policy for termination of repeat infringers, and inform their subscribers and account holders of it;[51] and (ii) they must accommodate and not interfere with 'standard technical measures' 'used by copyright owners to identify or protect copyrighted works'.[52]

The relevance here is that there can be many situations where the activities involved which come within safe harbours may involve information which is apparently within the public domain. If and when it turns out this is not so, service providers are able to remedy the problem by its removal. Such safe harbours are likely to encourage service providers to allow the provision of facilities via their services which include public domain information, but may occasionally (and usually inadvertently) include information to which public rights do not apply.

Although clearly of broad scope, there is still judicial and academic controversy around specific issues that affect the breadth of the safe harbours, including aspects affecting the public domain.[53]

*EU Directive and UK Implementation* The European Union's 2000 E-Commerce Directive[54] establishes three safe harbours in Articles 12–14, entitled 'Mere conduit', 'Caching' and 'Hosting' respectively, and the conditions for satisfaction of each are similar to (but simpler than) the scheme established in the United States. Notably there is no fourth safe harbour ('linking'). The Directive requires that, where the safe harbours apply, service providers are to be exempted from damages or criminal sanctions, but 'may be subject to injunctive relief, in accordance with member states' legal systems'.[55]

In so far as the public domain is concerned, an important difference from the United States is the scope of 'service provider' to which the Directive applies. It applies to any party providing an 'information society service',[56] but that term is in turn defined by other Directives,[57] such that

---

[51] 17 USC §512(j)(1)(A).   [52] 17 USC §512(i)(1)(B) and §512(i)(2).
[53] See Seng, 'Comparative analysis', para. 160; and see the Online Supplement for further details.
[54] Directive 2000/31/EC of the European Parliament and of the Council of 8 June 2000 on certain legal aspects of information society services, in particular electronic commerce, in the Internal Market (Directive on electronic commerce) ('E-Commerce Directive').
[55] C. Seville, *EU Intellectual Property Law and Policy* (Edward Elgar, 2009), p. 49.
[56] E-Commerce Directive (EU), Art. 2(b).   [57] E-Commerce Directive (EU), Art. 2(a).

'this definition covers any service normally provided for remuneration, at a distance, by means of electronic equipment for the processing ... and storage of data, and at the individual request of a recipient of a service.'[58] While other recitals clarify that 'provided for remuneration' does not limit 'service provider' to situations where the recipient of the information provides the remuneration directly, it is difficult to see that the scope of 'service provider' would include the types of non-profit institutions covered by the DMCA, including those in higher education.

The UK enacted the Electronic Commerce (EC Directive) Regulations 2002 in order to implement the EC E-Commerce Directive 2000. They provide three safe harbour defences (conduit, caching and hosting,[59] but not linking). The defences may apply to service providers of any 'information society service', and therefore have a broader application than to ISPs only, but probably a narrower scope than the DMCA.

*Other Countries: Australia and India* Australia has implemented a version of the US safe harbour provisions in such a narrow way as to make them largely useless. Safe harbour provisions[60] were introduced into Australia's Copyright Act to implement the Australia–US Free Trade Agreement.[61] As with the DMCA, the Australian provisions set up four types of safe harbours.[62] The principal problem with the provisions is that they apply only to a 'carriage service provider' (CSP), which is defined[63] as having the same meaning as in the Telecommunications Act 1997; that is, as a provider of 'a service for carrying communications by means of guided and/or unguided electromagnetic energy'. This definition applies to entities normally considered to be ISPs, but it is unlikely to apply to service providers such as YouTube and Facebook, universities or some search engines. The extension of these existing safe harbours to all service providers, as well as clarifying its application to all ISPs, has been recommended by multiple government reviews, including the Productivity Commission in 2016,[64] but met strong objections from rights holders. Draft provisions extending the safe harbour provisions to all service providers were dropped from 2017 copyright legislation.

---

[58] E-Commerce Directive (EU), Recital 17.
[59] Electronic Commerce (EC Directive) Regulations 2002 (UK), Regulations 17–19.
[60] See, for example, Copyright Act 1968 (Australia), Pt V Div 2AA, 'Limitation on remedies available against carriage service providers'.
[61] United States Free Trade Implementation Act 2004 (Aus.); Copyright Legislation Amendment Act 2004 (Aus.).
[62] Copyright Act 1968 (Aus.), ss. 116AC–116AF, respectively.
[63] Copyright Act 1968 (Aus.), s. 10, definition 'carriage service provider'.
[64] Productivity Commission, (Aus.) *Intellectual Property Arrangements*, Report 78, 2016, Recommendation 19.1.

## 6.2 Supports for Public Rights

It seems that Australia's safe harbours will continue to give very limited support to the public domain.

India's protections for intermediaries stem from s. 79(1) of the Information Technology Act 2000 (ITA), as amended in 2008,[65] which provides in sweeping fashion that 'an intermediary shall not be liable for any third party information, data, or communication link made available or hasted [*sic*] by him'. The ITA defines an intermediary in broad terms, and with a list of services that is only inclusive.[66] The safe harbour protection then applies to intermediaries who fit within one of three apparently disjunctive conditions, which if correct would result in extremely broad protection. However, as Seng points out, s. 79 is riddled with inconsistencies and ambiguities.[67]

*Conclusions* Safe harbour provisions such as are found in the countries discussed in this section are an essential support for the public domain, providing a 'buffer zone' for service providers in the event that their users who are involved with projects related to the public domain inadvertently include information which is outside its boundaries. However, to be effective, the scope of safe harbours must be broad enough to cover all types of Internet service providers, and must not be limited by the narrow definitions found in Australia or in EU Member States.

### 6.2.4 Limited Remedies

Safe harbour provisions are an example of a more general class of supports for the public domain. Where courts considering infringements are able to take into account mitigating factors relating to good faith attempts to exercise public rights in assessing remedies, this should encourage organisations to undertake an appropriate risk assessment approach to providing public access to content where there are low but unascertainable risks of copyright infringement.

For example, legislation may establish a defence which prevents the award of damages for copyright infringement where, at the time of

---

[65] Information Technology Act 2000 (India), as amended by the Information Technology (Amendment) Act, 2008.
[66] ITA (India), s. 2(w): '"intermediary," with respect to any particular electronic records, means any person who on behalf of another person receives, stores or transmits that record or provides any service with respect to that record and includes telecom service providers, network service providers, internet service providers, web-hosting service providers, search engines, online payment sites, online-auction sites, online-market places and cyber cafes.'
[67] Seng, 'Comparative analysis', paras. 61–3.

infringement, the defendant was unaware and had no reasonable grounds for suspecting that the act constituting an infringement was an infringement of copyright.[68] Account of profits is still allowed. Such a provision may be relevant, for example, if a party digitised and published a large body of documents reasonably believing that copyright in all such documents had expired, but this was not so for some of them. Another situation could be where a person obtained and used text believing it was subject to a Creative Commons licence, or used software believing it was subject to an open source licence, but this was not so. In the United States, it has been argued that 'the defence of innocent infringement may be available where a published work lacks a copyright notice'.[69] Such limited remedies have been proposed as part of the solution to orphan works problems in the United States and Australia [14.2.1], but are potentially of broader relevance.

Without attempting a comprehensive survey of the variety of such provisions we conclude that some provision for an innocent infringement defence should be included in any copyright law where the public domain is intended to contribute to national creativity.

### 6.2.5 Requirements to Provide Free Access / Open Content

Official requirements concerning documents can strengthen the public domain in two ways: by requiring pro-active distribution of free access or open content versions of documents which are otherwise copyright; and by allowing individuals to require provision to them of copies of documents otherwise protected by copyright.

*Open Content and Free Access Distribution* It is important to distinguish between 'free access' and 'open content', and to recognise that official requirements (or official supporting policies falling short of requirements) for distribution of otherwise copyright documents, by either of these approaches, are important supports for the copyright public domain.

'Open content' refers to otherwise copyright content which is made accessible with no copyright restrictions on its re-use, or at least fewer restrictions than copyright law provides. This is usually because the

---

[68] This example is from s. 115(3) of the Copyright Act 1968 (Aus.); see *Golden Editions Pty Ltd* v. *Polygram Pty Ltd* (1996) 34 IPR 84; see also s. 116(2), which creates a defence in relation to pecuniary remedies available to copyright owners in relation to actions for conversion or detention for infringing copies.

[69] Gangjee, 'Copyright formalities: a return to registration', 222, citing A. Reid, 'Claiming the copyright' (2016) 34 *Yale Law and Policy Review* 425.

## 6.2 Supports for Public Rights

content has been made available by the copyright owner under a 'neutral voluntary licence' (including Creative Commons licences, and Free and Open Source (FOSS) licences for software), and is therefore part of the public domain (see Chapter 15). Important examples concern government documents and data [15.5]. From the perspective of the 'open access' (OA) movement, Suber refers to open content as 'libre OA'.[70]

'Free access' falls short of open content, because the works concerned remain subject to copyright (and so, for example, republication remains prohibited), although access to them is provided free of charge and reproduction for private use is implied. Suber refers to this as 'gratis OA' and says it 'removes price barriers alone'.[71] However, where free access availability is required to be provided by copyright owners, or given significant and effective official encouragement, much of the practical benefit of the works being in the public domain may be achieved even though that technically is not the case. This is particularly so where the free access is provided online, thus maximising accessibility.

For example, in many common law jurisdictions, legislation and case law, and official reports, remain subject to Crown copyright: [8.2.2], but government legislation offices, courts, tribunals and law reform bodies routinely provide their documents to free access legal information institutes[72] for republication, as well as publishing some of them for free access on official websites. Another example is that free access publication of research outputs may be imposed on academic grant recipients as a condition of public funding.[73] For example, the Australian Research Council's (ARC's) Open Access Policy requires the outputs of ARC-funded research to be placed in free-access academic repositories within six months of publication, subject to copyright and licensing arrangements which may be in place between authors, institutions and publishers.[74]

*Freedom of Information / Right to Information and Similar Laws* Laws variously called freedom of information (FOI) or right to information (RTI) laws are the most general laws requiring that persons must be given access to, and usually copies of, documents held by government bodies,

---

[70] P. Suber, 'Open access overview' (2013, updated periodically) http://legacy.earlham.edu/~peters/fos/overview.htm; see also S. Harnad, 'The green road to open access: a leveraged transition' (2004) http://users.ecs.soton.ac.uk/harnad/Temp/greenroad.html.
[71] Suber, 'Open access overview'.
[72] Examples are BAILII, CanLII, AustLII, NZLII, PacLII and HKLII; see Free Access to Law Movement (FALM) www.falm.info/.
[73] Further details are in the Online Supplement.
[74] See Australian Research Council, *Open Access Policy*, v. 2015.1 (ARC, 2015) www.arc.gov.au/arc-open-access-policy.

which documents will often be copyright, depending on the jurisdiction and the source of the document. The right of access does not change the copyright status of the document disclosed, but in many cases will be the most valuable aspect of the document which would otherwise have been protected by copyright. There are also many examples of legislation which require that individuals be given on request, or that public access be provided without need for individual request, to documents of companies and other private sector bodies, which are otherwise protected by copyright and remain so protected after access is provided. These FOI/RTI laws will often require not only access to works to be provided, but also reproductions of them.

### 6.2.6  *Requirements of other National Laws Supporting Public Rights*

There are many examples of national laws, outside copyright laws, which require or allow uses to be made of works which would otherwise be in breach of copyright exclusive rights, or which require actions which support the public domain. They are too numerous to mention here, or to give national examples. Most typical in the first category are laws (other than FOI/RTI laws) which require public or private bodies to make and provide reproductions of otherwise copyright documents, particularly but not exclusively in countries where government works are protected by copyright. These include laws controlling public registers at all levels of government, required disclosures of processes including planning, patent and other IP registrations, and company disclosure requirements.

In the second category are archives laws, which preserve copies of documents which might otherwise be destroyed, often for long enough for the copyright term to expire, and otherwise (at least once they require access to be made available) often allow other public rights arising from statutory exceptions to be exercised.

## 6.3  Constraints on Public Rights

This section considers some of the factors which detract from or constrain the effective exercise of public rights: contractual exclusions; technological protection measures; and surveillance of uses (and users). Parallel import restrictions are considered in Chapter 16.

### 6.3.1  *Contractual Provisions Excluding Public Rights*

The extent to which contractual agreements may override statutory copyright exceptions is controversial, as a matter of both law and policy.[75] Contractual overrides may be seen as supporting party autonomy and freedom of contracting, but also as undermining the public interest objectives of copyright exceptions, with the capacity to narrow the public domain significantly. These effects are particularly likely where digital versions of works are used and have broadest impact where an intermediary such as a library is required by its contract with a publisher to require all its clients to agree to restrictive conditions in order to access the works in question.

In the absence of national legislative prohibitions, such 'contracting out' can be used to reduce the following public rights: to override completely all free use statutory exceptions to exclusive rights; to limit or prevent uses of the work which are outside the exclusive rights of the copyright owner; to prevent the use of insubstantial parts of a work; to restrict uses of subject matter which are outside copyright protection (impliedly or expressly excluded from copyright); to limit uses of works which are in fact under neutral voluntary licences; and to limit uses of works in which copyright has expired. It would be unusual, but with some licences may be possible, for 'contracting out' to override remunerated compulsory licences. When used in combination with technological protection measures, all of the above types of restrictions can be made more effective: [6.3.2]. In theory, therefore, there is not much of the public domain that contracts cannot reduce.

To what extent contracts are being used in practice to reduce the public domain is a separate question. Studies are needed of contracts for the provision of digital content, whether in the form of e-books, online databases, streaming services or otherwise, both with individual licensees/subscribers, and with institutions like libraries.

*US Pre-emption and Copyright Misuse Doctrines* Under US law, there are potentially significant restraints on the freedom of parties to contract around the limits of copyright protection,[76] but they are particular

---

[75] See L. Guibault, *Copyright Limitations and Contracts: An Analysis of the Contractual Overridability of Limitations on Copyright* (Kluwer Law International, 2002); L. Guibault, 'Wrapping information in contract: how does it affect the public domain?', in Guibault and Hugenholtz (eds.), *The Future of the Public Domain*, pp. 87–104; D. Lindsay, *The Law and Economics of Copyright, Contract and Mass Market Licences* (Centre for Copyright Studies Ltd, 2002); J. Carter, E. Peden and K. Stammer, 'Contractual restrictions and rights under copyright legislation' (2007) 23 *Journal of Contract Law* 32; M. Kretschmer, E. Derclaye, F. Favale and R. Watt, 'The relationship between copyright and contract law', Research commissioned by the Strategic Advisory Board for Intellectual Property Policy (UK) (2010) http://eprints.bournemouth.ac.uk/16091/1/_contractlaw-report.pdf.

[76] This section is based on Lindsay, *The Law and Economics of Copyright, Contract and Mass Market Licences*, 41–3.

to US law and dealt with only in summary here. First, if a contract entered into under state contract law is inconsistent with federal copyright law, the contract may be found to contravene the US pre-emption doctrine, of which there are two forms relevant to copyright. The first form arises under the Copyright Act provision that 'all legal or equitable rights that are equivalent to any of the exclusive rights within the general scope of copyright ... are governed exclusively by this title'.[77] In applying this provision, the US courts must determine whether a state law creates rights 'equivalent' to copyright, which has been interpreted to mean that rights created under state laws will not be pre-empted if they contain an 'extra element' over and above the rights comprised in the copyright[78] and they have usually found this 'extra element' in factors such as the agreement of the parties.[79] For example, in *ProCD, Inc.* v. *Zeidenberg*,[80] the Court of Appeals found[81] that rights created by contract were 'not "equivalent" to the exclusive rights comprised in the copyright because contractual rights bind only the parties to the contract' and are not 'a right against the world'. Restrictions on reproduction in an agreement relating to a database were therefore enforceable, and effective to protect the non-copyrightable content of a telephone directory database.

The second form of copyright pre-emption arises directly under the Supremacy Clause,[82] so that a contract may be pre-empted if there is a conflict between state enforcement of a contract and federal copyright law or policy.[83] However, US courts (including in *ProCD*) have failed to develop consistent criteria for determining whether contract terms are 'constitutionally' pre-empted by federal copyright law or policy.[84] So the extent to which this is likely to limit copyright pre-emption is quite uncertain.[85]

---

[77] 17 USC s. 301(a) (1994).
[78] See, for example, *Trandes Corp.* v. *Guy F Atkinson Co.* 996 F 2d 655 (4th Cir 1993).
[79] See M. Lemley, 'Beyond preemption: the law and policy of intellectual property licensing' (1999) 87 *California Law Review* 111 at 140.
[80] 86 F 3d 1447 (7th Cir 1996). [81] 86 F 3d 1447 (7th Cir 1996) at 1454.
[82] See W. Gordon, 'On owning information: intellectual property and the restitutionary impulse' (1992) 78 *Virginia Law Review* 149 at 155 n. 22; M. O'Rourke, 'Copyright preemption after the ProCD case: a market-based approach' (1997) 12 *Berkeley Technology Law Journal* 53 at 73 n. 108; Lemley, 'Beyond preemption', 141–4. See also *Goldstein* v. *California* 412 US 546 (1973).
[83] See Lemley, 'Beyond preemption', 141. As Lemley explains: 'Strictly speaking, federal law preempts state law, not particular private contracts. However, because private contracts are enforced through state law, federal law can and does preempt the enforcement of contracts in appropriate circumstances': 137 n. 108.
[84] Lemley, 'Beyond preemption', 143.
[85] Lemley has stated that 'What one can discern ... is that there are several different approaches to federal intellectual property preemption, and that the law of preemption is a mess': *ibid.* 115. The uncertainty concerning the law relating to copyright preemption explains, in large measure, the extensive academic literature on this topic.

## 6.3 Constraints on Public Rights

The other potentially significant copyright-specific restriction under US law arises under the doctrine of copyright misuse, which appears to be unique to the United States. Under this doctrine, developed since 1990,[86] some US courts have refused to enforce agreements that attempt to extend protection of copyright material beyond the limits set by copyright law, including limits on the duration of copyright protection.[87] In *Lasercomb America, Inc.* v. *Reynolds*,[88] the court refused to enforce a licence agreement that purported to prohibit the licensee from developing competing software for a period of ninety-nine years, a de facto extension of the copyright term.

These two US copyright doctrines therefore provide potential limitations on the extent to which it is possible to contract out from public rights, and in *Lasercomb* did so, but it is uncertain how effective these doctrines will prove to be. The US public domain depends a great deal on the fair use exception, and there is no specific statutory provision preventing contracting out from that exception. This is an important issue not only for the United States, but also for other countries, because of the extent to which copyright goods are licensed under copyright agreements of US origin.

*The UK and Australia: Specific Exceptions, General Uncertainty* In contrast with the United States, the law in the UK and Australia and similar common law jurisdictions has no equivalent to the US preemption doctrine. There is no doctrine of copyright misuse other than some very limited doctrines concerning public policy and public interest [8.4], but it is possible that some licences that attempt to impose restrictions on licensees over and above the restrictions established in copyright legislation might be found to contravene common law doctrines of unreasonable restraint of trade.[89]

Neither UK nor EU law prohibits contracting out of exceptions to copyright.[90] In the UK, McQueen et al. refer to an 'un-argued assumption ... that fair dealing prevails over contract [which] on closer

---

[86] The defence of copyright misuse appears generally to have been denied prior to the decision in *Lasercomb America, Inc.* v. *Reynolds* 911 F 2d 970 (4th Cir 1990): see Lemley, 'Beyond preemption', 151–8.

[87] See, for example, R. P. Merges, 'The end of friction? Property rights and contract in the "Newtonian" world of online commerce' (1997) 12 *Berkeley Technology Law Journal* 115 at 124–5.

[88] 911 F 2d 970 (1990).

[89] See Copyright Law Review Committee (CLRC), *Copyright and Contract* (CLRC, 2002), p. 20. The Australian High Court has considered contractual restrictions in restraint of trade in the context of a confidentiality agreement: *Maggbury Pty Ltd* v. *Hafele Australia Pty Ltd* [2001] HCA 70.

[90] However, Article 9 of the EU Software Directive of 1991 provides that '[a]ny contractual provisions contrary to Article 6 [decompilation] or to the exceptions provided for in

examination ... appears to be ill-founded, at least as a generalization'.[91] Burrell and Coleman point out that the UK legislation states that the provisions of the chapter dealing with 'permitted acts' (exceptions) 'relate only to the question of infringement of copyright and do not affect any other right or obligation restricting the doing of any of the specified acts'.[92] They conclude that it is 'therefore generally possible to contract out of the permitted Acts'.[93] They consider that the UK's 'piecemeal approach' to specifying when there cannot be contracting out is preferable, and note that this applies to 'a growing list of circumstances' including fair dealing by inclusion of an extract from a broadcast in another broadcast;[94] rights of lawful users of databases to do things necessary for accessing and using its contents;[95] and rights to make a back-up copy of a program, or to decompile, observe, study or test it.[96] However, these prohibitions on contracting out represent only a tiny sliver of the permitted acts provided for in Chapter III.[97] The prohibition is more 'non-existent' than 'piecemeal'. Burrell and Coleman give examples of deficiencies of a 'blanket prohibition' on contracting out, particularly where there are relationships between commercial parties, where it would be inequitable for one party to rely on statutory exceptions when that party had obtained the other party's content.[98] They do not support the status quo, recommending that there needs to be some means 'to ensure that new prohibitions on contracting out can be added quickly if evidence of inappropriate contracting out practices surface'.[99]

Australia's Copyright Act has no provision similar to s. 28(1) in the UK, and there is only one restriction on contracting out of copyright exceptions (concerning computer programs),[100] despite repeated calls for broader reform. Whether one statutory restriction implies, as a matter of statutory

Article 5(2) [back-up copying] and (3) [observation and study] shall be null and void'. Full titles and citations of all Directives are in the Table of International Instruments.
[91] H. McQueen, C. Waelde, G. Laurie and A. Brown, *Contemporary Intellectual Property: Law and Policy* (2nd edn, Oxford, 2011), p. 208.
[92] CDPA 1988 (UK), s. 28(1).    [93] Burrell and Coleman, *Copyright Exceptions*, 69.
[94] Broadcasting Act 1996 (UK), s. 137.    [95] CDPA 1988 (UK), ss. 50D and 296B.
[96] CDPA 1988 (UK), s. 296A.
[97] CDPA Chapter III (ss. 28–76) includes very large subject areas such as all the fair dealing exceptions, disability, educations, libraries and archives and so on.
[98] Burrell and Coleman, *Copyright Exceptions*, 70.    [99] *Ibid.*
[100] Section 47H prohibits agreements that have the effect of excluding or limiting some exceptions to copyright infringement that allow for the reproduction of computer programs for particular purposes (decompilation for studying the program; for making a back-up copy; for making interoperable products; for error correction; or for security testing): see Copyright Act 1968 (Aus.), ss. 47B(3), 47C, 47D, 47E, 47F. For further discussion, see Lindsay, *The Law and Economics of Copyright, Contract and Mass Market Licences*, 40–1.

## 6.3 Constraints on Public Rights

interpretation, that contracting out is permitted in relation to other exceptions, is uncertain.[101] The Copyright Law Review Committee (CLRC) concluded in 2002[102] that agreements were being used to exclude or modify the copyright exceptions, that existing contract law remedies were inadequate and that contractual overrides distorted the 'copyright balance'.[103] It recommended that provisions in agreements 'that exclude or modify the operation of certain copyright exceptions should have no effect',[104] applying to the fair dealing exceptions, library and archive exceptions and certain technology-related exceptions.[105] The Australian Law Reform Commission (ALRC) in 2013 agreed that 'contracting out puts at risk the public benefit that copyright exceptions are intended to provide and, therefore, some express limitations should be considered'.[106] However, it distinguished between exceptions that perform an important public purpose, which should be mandated, and other exceptions, which should be free to be contracted around (including a broad fair use exception, if adopted). However, if fair use were not adopted, limitations should be imposed on contracting out of purpose-specific fair dealing exceptions, including proposed exceptions for quotation, private use, educational use or library or archive use.[107] In 2016, Australia's Productivity Commission took a stronger approach than either the CLRC or the ALRC and recommended that the Copyright Act should make unenforceable any part of an agreement restricting or preventing a use of copyright material that is permitted by any copyright exception.[108] The Australian Government 'supports in principle' this recommendation but intends to consult in 2018 on how best to implement it.[109]

*Conclusions* International copyright law is silent on the topic of contractual overrides, so it is possible for national legislation to protect the public domain. Contractual overrides of public rights may operate as

---

[101] See discussion in Online Supplement. [102] CLRC, *Copyright and Contract*.
[103] As the CLRC put it: 'As the copyright interest is constituted by the exclusive rights of copyright, as defined within the framework of the exceptions to the rights set out in the Copyright Act, then any attempt to exclude or modify the exceptions by contract brings about a fundamental imbalance of these rights': *ibid.* 262.
[104] Ibid. 7.49 (p. 274).
[105] Copyright Act 1968 (Aus.) ss. 40, 41, 42, 43, 43A, 48A, 49, 50, 51, 51AA, 51A, 52, 103A, 103B, 103C, 104, 110A, 110B, and 111A.
[106] Australian Law Reform Commission, *Copyright and the Digital Economy*, ALRC Report 122 (November 2013), p. 450.
[107] *Ibid.* Recommendation 20-2 (p. 456).
[108] Productivity Commission (Aus.), 'Intellectual property arrangements', Recommendation 5.1.
[109] Australian Government, 'Response to the Productivity Commission Inquiry into intellectual property arrangements', Commonwealth of Australia, August 2017, p. 4.

significant constraints on the exercise of various public rights (not only statutory exceptions), although the extent of harm is unlikely to be as extensive as is theoretically possible. What happens in the United States affects the exercise of rights of purchasers of copyright goods in other countries, but the possible limitations on contracting out in US law depend on very US-specific doctrines, of little relevance elsewhere.

In other jurisdictions there is a choice between three policy options: no restrictions on contracting out of public rights (almost the current Australian position); a blanket prohibition on contracting out of any exceptions to copyright (Australia's Productivity Commission); or a legislative differentiation between those exceptions where contracting out should be allowed, and those where it should not, preferably based on some principled approach to the purposes of copyright and the public domain. UK law makes such a differentiation, and Australia's CLRC and ALRC recommend it. We recommend this last approach, but with the caveat that the purposes and benefits of the public domain must be taken fully into account, and that the default position should be that contracting out should not be allowed unless there is a demonstrable need in relation to specific exceptions.[110]

### 6.3.2 Technological Protection Measures (TPMs)

Technological protection measures (TPMs) and the legislation protecting them are clearly potential major constraints on the copyright public domain, as many have realised since proposals for such legislation arose in the mid-1990s.[111] In general terms, 'TPM' refers to the use of technologies to control or prevent access to, copying, modification, retention or deletion of content, primarily in relation to digital content. There are many TPM technologies including encryption, region coding and password systems.

TPMs and their legal protection have multiple adverse affects on the copyright public domain. If access to works can only be obtained within the technical limitations imposed by TPMs, many public rights may never be able to be exercised. First, TPMs may prevent access to works, effectively inhibiting uses permitted by copyright exceptions. Secondly,

---

[110] See also Lindsay, *The Law and Economics of Copyright, Contract and Mass Market Licences*, 110.
[111] Early criticisms include: J. Cohen, 'A right to read anonymously: a closer look at "copyright management" in cyberspace' (1996) 28 *Connecticut Law Review* 981; G. Greenleaf, 'IP, phone home: privacy as part of copyright's digital commons in Hong Kong and Australian law', in L. Lessig (ed.), *Hochelaga Lectures 2002: The Innovation Commons* (Sweet & Maxwell Asia, 2003).

## 6.3 Constraints on Public Rights

TPMs can prevent reproduction of content from a work, thereby preventing quotations, fair dealings or other public rights (including exercise of compulsory licences) which require some extent of reproduction to be effective. Thirdly, unless they can legitimately be circumvented, TPMs can also defeat the expiry of copyright in a work, by preventing it from ever being able to be accessed or used without restriction. Similar policy considerations apply to constraints and limitations imposed by TPMs as to those imposed by contractual overrides.[112]

The main legal and policy issue with TPMs is whether anti-circumvention laws should be confined to preventing circumvention of TPMS for the purpose of preventing copyright infringement, or whether they should also protect the use of TPMs to prevent uses which do not constitute infringements of copyright, including preventing non-infringing access to works, or uses which do not require permission.

*WIPO Copyright Treaty* Although there were some prior national provisions,[113] legal protection of TPMs first appeared in international copyright law in the WIPO Copyright Treaty (WCT). Article 11 of the WCT provides:

> Contracting Parties shall provide adequate legal protection and effective legal remedies against the circumvention of effective technological measures that are used by authors in connection with the exercise of their rights under this Treaty or the Berne Convention and that restricts acts, in respect of their works, which are not authorised by the authors concerned or permitted by law.

Two aspects of Article 11 could indicate that its scope is limited, in relation to copyright exceptions and other aspects of the public domain. First, the reference to 'in connection with the exercise of their rights under this Treaty or the Berne Convention' could imply that states are not required to protect measures such as access controls that limit the number of times a work may be viewed. Ricketson and Ginsburg conclude that such measures are used 'in connection' as required, because access controls underpin the exercise of the exclusive rights of reproduction, communication and distribution.[114] Second, the reference to 'or permitted by law' can be read as implying that legal remedies against circumvention are not required in relation to circumvention devices that can be used to enable acts permitted by exceptions and limitations allowed by Berne. Ricketson and Ginsburg argue that if national laws allowed free

---

[112] M. de Zwart, 'Technological enclosure of copyright: the end of fair dealing?' (2007) 18 *Australian Intellectual Property Journal* 7.
[113] Ricketson and Ginsburg, *International Copyright and Neighbouring Rights*, [15.02].
[114] *Ibid.* [15.13]–[15.16].

distribution of devices that could be used for such purposes, the prohibition would be meaningless, essentially because all circumvention devices are 'dual use' and can also be used to allow acts not permitted by authors, and that the requirement that protections be 'adequate ... and effective' reinforces this interpretation.[115] On this view, WCT Article 11 therefore gives little basis for arguments that circumvention devices to facilitate exercise of public rights must be allowed by national laws.

The WCT said nothing in addition to Article 11 to guide national legislators,[116] including about how, if at all, this requirement to provide legal remedies was to be balanced with any or all of the public rights in copyright allowed or required by international copyright law. As described above, TPMs have a great capacity to erode these rights, and, as Ricketson and Ginsburg put it, 'neither Berne nor the WCT contain mandatory limitations'[117] on such erosion.

However, Geist argues that, although it cannot be said that WCT Article 11 is unequivocally referring only to protection against acts infringing copyright, it is a provision which leaves a great deal of flexibility to national implementation, both in relation to whether prohibitions on circumvention technologies are required and on whether the exercise of exceptions to copyright may be protected.[118] His argument is based on the brevity of the language in the article and ambiguity in many of its terms, reinforced by the inconclusive and contested nature of its legislative history,[119] the considerable body of scholarly opinion favouring flexible interpretation[120] and the subsequent history of national implementations demonstrating such flexibility.[121]

We will only consider how TPMs prevent exercise of copyright exceptions and other public rights.

*United States* The Digital Millennium Copyright Act (DMCA) incorporated the anti-circumvention provisions into US law[122] and included prohibitions on trafficking in circumvention devices. It also included a series of exceptions allowing circumvention, which in summary are for:[123] acquisition decisions by non-profit libraries, archives and educational institutions; law enforcement, intelligence and related government activities; encryption research; preventing Internet access by

---

[115] *Ibid.* [15.18]–[15.20].    [116] *Ibid.* [15.20].    [117] *Ibid.* [15.23].
[118] M. Geist, 'The case for flexibility in implementing the WIPO internet treaties: an examination of the anti-circumvention requirements', in M. Geist (ed.), *From 'Radical Extremism' to 'Balanced Copyright': Canadian Copyright and the Digital Agenda* (Irwin Law Inc., 2010), 204–46.
[119] *Ibid.* 211–21.    [120] *Ibid.* 236–44.    [121] *Ibid.* 222–36.
[122] Now 17 US Code §1201 – Circumvention of copyright protection systems.
[123] 17 US Code §1201 (d)–(j).

## 6.3 Constraints on Public Rights

minors; protection of privacy (identification and disabling surveillance capabilities); and security testing. These exceptions do not address most exceptions under US copyright law, in particular access to works under the fair use exception. Only the privacy protection exception is related strongly, but indirectly, to the public domain.

*EU Directive and UK Implementation* The European Union's InfoSoc Directive[124] of 2001 may, according to Ricketson and Ginsburg, 'portend a grim future in this regard'.[125] The requirements of Article 6(4) appear at first glance as though Member States are intended to protect at least some public rights:

> Member States shall take appropriate measures to ensure that right holders make available to the beneficiary of an exception or limitation provided for in national law in accordance with [specific exceptions[126] allowed under Article 5 concerning: some remunerated compulsory licences; non-profit uses by libraries, museums etc.; some uses of ephemeral recordings; some uses in social institutions; teaching or research; assisting people with disabilities; and public security and proper reporting of official matters] the means of benefiting from that exception or limitation, to the extent necessary to benefit from that exception or limitation and where that beneficiary has legal access to the protected work or subject matter concerned.

The next paragraph says that Member States may also provide such measures in relation to private copying exceptions allowed under the Directive, under specified circumstances. So it seems that (subject to what follows), although there is no requirement to allow any uses of circumvention devices, rights holders will at least have obligations to respect and effectuate some public rights. However, Article 6(4) then says that all of these provisions

> shall not apply to works or other subject-matter made available to the public on agreed contractual terms in such a way that members of the public may access them from a place and at a time individually chosen by them.

Ricketson and Ginsburg describe the result as follows:

> This would mean that if the work is available to the public online on an on-demand basis, the copyright owner may impose conditions incompatible with the exceptions otherwise explicitly preserved by the Directive, and the member states, when implementing the Directive, must similarly honour those contractual overrides.[127]

The first paragraph of Article 6(4) will still apply to content available on tangible media such as CD-ROM, to which the 'contractual overrides'

---

[124] Full titles and citations of all Directives are in the Table of International Instruments.
[125] Ricketson and Ginsburg, *International Copyright and Neighbouring Rights*, [15.23].
[126] InfoSoc Directive (EU), Art. 5(2)(a) (2)(c) (2)(d) (2)(e) (3)(a) (3)(b) or (3)(e).
[127] Ricketson and Ginsburg, *International Copyright and Neighbouring Rights*, [15.23].

will not apply. But how long will this means of distribution survive now that both digital downloads and online subscription access are commonplace?

The UK has implemented Article 6(4) by a provision[128] which does not allow for any use of circumvention devices in order to exercise any of the specified exceptions ('permitted acts' in the UK). Instead, if a program prevents a person from carrying out a permitted act, they can complain to the Secretary of State, who can then issue directions to the copyright owner to comply,[129] and if they do not then the complainant will have a civil right of action. The contractual override paragraph of the InfoSoc Directive is reproduced in s. 296ZE(10). Ricketson and Ginsburg's pessimism about Article 6(4) is borne out by the conclusion of McQueen et al. that any protection of exceptions in the UK provisions can be nullified by contract.[130] Thus it appears that in a digital network environment the exceptions and limitations to copyright may be overridden by contract, or at the least that the procedure described above will not be available where *contract* limits the availability or use of the exceptions.

*Australia*  Australia was one of the earlier countries to introduce legislation protecting TPMs,[131] and amended its legislation following the US–Australia Free Trade Agreement.[132] Copyright owners may take an action against a person who knowingly circumvents an access control technological protection used to protect a work or other subject matter.[133] The seven exceptions set out in the Act do not allow any circumventing steps taken for the purpose of exercising public rights,[134] other than for the indirect relevance of the privacy exception. The eighth exception is for other acts prescribed in regulations,[135] based on submissions concerning need. Some of these regulations[136] do allow circumventions in order to exercise specific exceptions, including compulsory licences for education, assistance to people with disabilities, and some free use exceptions for research. However, most exceptions (including all fair dealing) are outside these provisions.

---

[128] CDPA 1988 (UK), s. 296ZE.
[129] McQueen et al., *Contemporary Intellectual Property*, 211 note lack of exercise of powers up to 2009.
[130] *Ibid.*   [131] Copyright Act 1968 (Aus.), s. 116A.
[132] Copyright Act 1968 (Aus.), ss. 116AK – 116AQ.
[133] Copyright Act 1968 (Aus.), s. 116AN(1).
[134] Copyright Act 1968 (Aus.), s. 116AN(2)–(9), respectively.
[135] Copyright Act 1968 (Aus.), s. 249(2) states the conditions under which regulations may be made.
[136] Copyright Regulations 1969 (Aus.), reg. 20Z and Schedule 10A.

## 6.3 Constraints on Public Rights

The government intended to review in 2017 whether these regulations should include new TPM exceptions to protect 'legitimate uses of copyright material'.[137]

In Australia, therefore, both contracts and technologies are independent and largely unrestricted means of excluding public rights. In the EU, the technological means of exclusion must in some cases be supported by contract. Law reform proposals on this point have achieved nothing in Australia.[138] Australian law, with a few more liberal minor exceptions, remains much the same as in the United States, exported via a free trade agreement. Other details are omitted here.[139]

*Other National Implementations Favouring Public Rights* It is incorrect to think that all national implementations of anti-circumvention protections are as hostile to protection of public rights as either the US/Australian approach or the UK interpretation of EU law. Geist provides a lengthy set of counter-examples, summarised in the following.[140]

Within the EU,[141] Germany limits anti-circumvention protection to works that are subject to copyright protection only, thus excluding non-copyrightable subject matter or works in the public domain.[142] Denmark only protects TPMs used to prevent copying, not those used to prevent access. Italy includes the right to make one private copy despite a TPM. Swiss law limits circumvention restrictions to where copyright infringements occur.

Outside Europe, implementations protecting public rights are also common. In Japan, circumvention restrictions only apply to copy controls, not access controls, and circumvention is allowed for all statutory exceptions. India's 2012 amendments to its law inserted s. 65, which limited its application to a person who circumvents an effective technological measure 'applied for the purpose of protecting any of the rights conferred by this Act, with the intention of infringing such rights',[143] and so does not apply to TPMs used for the purpose of protecting non-copyright aspects of works. It also requires an intention to infringe copyright. India also provides various exceptions found in other jurisdictions, and a more general one of 'doing anything [otherwise constituting

---

[137] Australian Government, Response to the Productivity Commission Inquiry, p. 4.
[138] Details are in the Online Supplement.
[139] See the Online Supplement for further details.
[140] Geist, 'The case for flexibility in implementing the WIPO internet treaties', 230–6.
[141] Geist cites for these examples, U. Gasser and M. Girsberger, 'Transposing the Copyright Directive: legal protection of technological measures in EU Member States: a genie stuck in the bottle?', Berkman Publication Series No. 2004-10 (2004).
[142] Copyright Act (Germany), para. 95a(2). [143] Copyright Act 1956 (India), s. 65A(1).

circumvention] for a purpose not expressly prohibited by this Act', including (provided records are kept) of assisting others to circumvent. New Zealand is similar, expressly permitting persons to circumvent in order to carry out permitted acts, and to enlist the assistance of a 'qualified circumventer' in order to assist them to do so.[144]

*Conclusions: 'A Grim Future'?* Fears of 'digital lock-up' have not yet been realised to the extent many feared, due largely to the need for owners to accommodate the demands of users, but there is no doubt that technological limitations on access and use have the capacity to be major extra-legal constraints on the exercise of most public rights. None of the alternative national approaches give much assistance to the public domain. On the one hand, the approach taken in the United States and Australia, of attempting to define the circumstances in which circumvention should be allowed, is desirable but only if it is extended to include at least those of the statutory exceptions (free or remunerated), which, as a matter of public policy, should not be able to be excluded by contract. On the other hand, the EU and UK approach does make an assessment that at least some of the exceptions should be respected by those using TPMs, but then allows this to be destroyed by a contractual override. To avoid Ricketson and Ginsburg's 'grim future' for the public domain, it is necessary to find a future somewhere between these 'dismal alternatives'.[145] Fortunately there is no shortage of better alternatives to consider, both within and outside the EU.[146]

### 6.3.3 Surveillance of Uses (and Users)

The public domain provides individuals with abilities to access and use creative works in order to support a range of public benefits. Two of the most important, the development of informed opinions and support of creativity, are less likely to occur if required to be carried out under observation or any form of surveillance, whether public or private. Any procedures which compulsorily record a person's activities, such as borrowing, browsing or reading, particularly if the data is available to third parties, will probably create a 'chilling effect' and therefore significantly affect the exercise of any public domain rights.[147] Neal Richards refers to

---

[144] Copyright Act 1994 (New Zealand), ss. 226–226E.
[145] Ricketson and Ginsburg, *International Copyright and Neighbouring Rights*, [15.25].
[146] InfoJustice.org, 'What are the best examples of laws on technological protection measures with exceptions for lawful uses?', 10 July 2013 http://infojustice.org/archives/30139.
[147] See Cohen, 'A right to read anonymously', 981.

## 6.3 Constraints on Public Rights

freedom from surveillance of intellectual activities as 'intellectual privacy', observing that:

> Intellectual privacy is the ability, whether protected by law or social circumstances, to develop ideas or beliefs away from the unwanted gaze or interference of others. Surveillance or interference can warp the integrity of our freedom of thought and can skew the way we think, with clear repercussions for the content of our subsequent speech or writing. The ability to freely make up our minds and to develop new ideas thus depends upon a substantial measure of intellectual privacy.[148]

Where surveillance is built into any system delivering intellectual property content, the public domain uses of that content are thereby threatened or inhibited.[149] While some forms of reporting or, loosely speaking, 'surveillance' may well be necessary to deter copyright breaches, such measures must always be proportionate to the potential inhibiting effects on the exercise of public rights and to infringements of the fundamental right to privacy. Since at least 2001, the growth of behavioural marketing as integral to Internet-based economies has made the surveillance of uses and users of all types of digital copyright works (news, social media content, music, movies etc.) vastly more extensive, complex and significant. Its effect on the public domain is only one small thread of what has been called 'surveillance capitalism',[150] the analysis of which is beyond the reach of this book. Nevertheless, the effects of user and usage surveillance on the exercise of public rights in relation to works is profound, because it is now so pervasive.

### 6.3.4 Requirements of other National Laws Constraining Public Rights

Many other national laws constrain what would otherwise be public rights. For example, confidential information laws will be effective to prevent both the exercise of statutory exceptions to copyright and the use of works in relation to which the copyright term has expired, provided the confidentiality is retained. Numerous other statutory secrecy requirements may have the same effect. Exceptions in archives laws and laws relating to public registers may nullify, for some categories of documents or proposed uses, the support that those laws otherwise give to public rights.

---

[148] N. Richards, 'Intellectual privacy' (2008) 87 *Texas Law Review* 387, 389.
[149] Greenleaf, 'IP, phone home: privacy as part of copyright's digital commons in Hong Kong and Australian law'.
[150] Shoshana Zuboff, 'Big other: surveillance capitalism and the prospects of an information civilization' (2015) 30 *Journal of Information Technology* 75–89.

## 6.4 Conclusions: Essentials for an Effective Copyright Public Domain

This chapter has demonstrated, without being comprehensive, why the categories of the copyright public domain cannot be considered in isolation when assessing a country's national copyright public domain. Other aspects of national laws, institutions and practices have a major impact on the effectiveness of the copyright public domain. For those who place a high value on the public domain, it may be as important, or more important, to attempt to maximise those aspects that support the copyright public domain, and to minimise the harm of those aspects that constrain it, as it is to reform the formal categories of the public domain. Also, these issues are largely outside the scope of international copyright law (TPMs partially excepted), so national initiatives are possible.

However, if we compare the overall effect of supports for the public domain with the constraints on it that we have discussed, the unfortunate conclusion must be that the constraints are far more powerful. Under current laws in most countries, the combination of contractual exclusions and TPMs has the potential to eliminate almost all aspects of the public domain, although it is a potential which is far from being realised as yet. Pervasive surveillance of users and uses of works in an increasingly digital use environment is, however, actuality not mere potential. Compared with these threats, the supports for the public domain provided by statutory deposit and voluntary registration systems, and narrow safe harbour provisions, is puny indeed. Among the most valuable national responses that can protect the public domain must be included the severe restriction of the capacity of contracts to override copyright exceptions and other public domain protections, the provision of exceptions to anti-circumvention measures for actions justified by those same exceptions and protections, and data privacy laws that limit data surveillance by transparency, proportionality and other means to protect intellectual privacy.

*Part III*

Public Domains: Categories of Public Rights

# 7 Works Outside Copyright Protection – Part I

7.1 Introduction 185
7.2 Works Failing Minimum Requirements 185
7.3 Works Impliedly Excluded from Copyright (Statutory 'Gaps') 207
7.4 Conclusion 214

## 7.1 Introduction

Our simplified definition of the public domain as 'the public's ability to use works without seeking permission' encompasses all 'works' (on our use of that term) that are not protected at all by copyright. This chapter and the next explain and analyse those parts of national public domains that fall completely outside of copyright protection, namely categories 1–4 and 7 of our fifteen public domain categories. This chapter deals with **Categories 1 and 2**: works that fail the minimum requirements for protection and works that are 'impliedly' excluded from protection as they fall outside the scope of protected works.

Under international copyright law, there are two main elements that set the scope of works falling within Berne: an implied minimum threshold for protection and a requirement that a work falls within a protected category: [4.6]. Categories 1 and 2 of our public domain categories are dealt with together in this chapter as they are free from copyright because they do not satisfy the minimum requirements for protection due to insufficient authorial contribution or because they are not protectable works.

## 7.2 Works Failing Minimum Requirements

It is fundamental to copyright law that not all 'creative works' are protected, as some works fail to meet the minimum requirements for protection. The first section of this chapter identifies and explains works that form part of national public domains because: they do not satisfy a minimum authorial contribution (originality); they fall within a *de minimis* rule that renders insubstantial works unprotectable; or because they fail to satisfy a requirement, imposed under some national laws, that works be fixed in a tangible form.

Works that fail minimum requirements for protection encompass a diversity of material, ranging from valuable ideas, facts or 'laws of nature', that may form the building blocks for creative works or new knowledge,[1] to relatively valueless material, such as shopping lists or doodles.[2] The core public domain value promoted by category 1 is the promotion of authorship to produce new works or new knowledge: 'unprotected' works are often the building blocks used to create new works. Permission-free use of these building blocks promotes creativity, as requiring permission to use 'simple' works would impose excessive transaction costs on authors.[3] This reflects the central function of the originality threshold, which is to promote or reward authorial creativity. The lack of protection for unoriginal content also furthers other important values, especially freedom of expression: for example, requiring permission to use short works – such as titles or short phrases – would lock up the building blocks of language.

The same, or similar, considerations underpin the principles that copyright does not protect ideas: [10.4] or insubstantial parts of works: [10.3].

### 7.2.1  Authorship and Originality: The International Framework

Berne implies a minimum threshold of authorial creation for Berne-protected works: [4.6.1]. While there are commonalities across jurisdictions in the principles that apply in determining the minimum authorial contribution, there are significant variations. At a general level, reflecting the distinction between copyright and authors' rights traditions: [1.9], common law jurisdictions apply a test of originality, meaning that a work must originate from an author, while civil law jurisdictions have applied a higher 'creativity' threshold, meaning that a work must bear the imprint of an author's personality.

The originality threshold is closely related to the 'idea/expression dichotomy': what is protected is original expression, meaning that once material is classified as 'idea' or 'fact' it is not protected, no matter how original. Idea/expression is dealt with in Chapter 10 as, in most national laws covered in this book, it arises in determining whether a use is

---

[1] Samuelson, 'Enriching discourse on public domains', 790.
[2] P. Samuelson, 'Challenges in mapping the public domain', in Guibault and Hugenholtz (eds.), *The Future of the Public Domain*, 23.
[3] See J. Hughes, 'Size matters (or should) in copyright law' (2005) 74 *Fordham Law Review* 575 at 614 ff.

infringing copyright, not in determining whether copyright subsists. While there are inevitable crossovers between the allied principles that copyright protects only original works and that copyright protects only expression, given that in most jurisdictions idea/expression is relevant to infringement, it makes sense for the latter principle to be dealt with as a permissible use and not in determining whether a work is protectable.

### 7.2.2  Authorship and Originality: The Common Law Background

This section of the chapter explains the traditional common law concept of originality, as a basis for understanding the current law.

The originality threshold under English law historically consisted of two related principles, the 'originating from the author' principle and a minimum authorial contribution.[4] The 'originating from the author' principle simply means that the work must originate from the author, in that it has not been copied, and does not require the work to be 'original' or novel.[5] The second principle was commonly reduced to the statement that a minimum quantum of labour, skill or judgement is required.[6]

Common law jurisdictions have had difficulties in applying the principle of minimal authorial contribution to 'low authorship' works, such as directories or databases, in which it is difficult to detect an authorial presence but which may require significant investment.[7] Traditionally, English law recognised that originality could arise from mere labour, applying the doctrine of 'industrious collection' or 'sweat of the brow' ('sweat').[8] This would lead to protection of works, such as directories, which result from collection of data, but in which the selection or arrangement of data might be limited.

Under international copyright law, considerable flexibility is established by the wording of Article 10(2) of the TRIPs Agreement:[9] [4.6.2], which provides that:

---

[4] See M. Birnhack, 'The Dead Sea Scrolls case: who is an author?' (2001) 23 *European Intellectual Property Review* 128; D. Lindsay, 'Protection of compilations and databases after *IceTV*: authorship, originality and the transformation of Australian copyright law' (2012) 38(1) *Monash University Law Review* 17.
[5] *University of London Press, Ltd* v. *University Tutorial Press, Ltd* [1916] 2 Ch 601 at 608–9 (per Peterson J). See also *Emerson* v. *Davies*, 8 F Cas 615 (Mass CC, 1845).
[6] See, for example, *Macmillan & Co. Ltd* v. *Cooper* (1924) 93 LJPC 113 at 121 (per Atkinson LJ); *Ladbroke (Football) Ltd* v. *William Hill (Football) Ltd* [1964] 1 WLR 273 (per Hodson LJ (at 285) and Devlin LJ (at 289)).
[7] J. C. Ginsburg, 'Creation and commercial value: copyright protection of works of information' (1990) 90 *Columbia Law Review* 1865.
[8] See, for example, *Kelly* v. *Morris* (1886) LR 1 Eq 697; *Morris* v. *Ashbee* (1868) LR 7 Eq 34; *Morris* v. *Wright* (1870) LR 5 Ch App 279.
[9] Full titles and citations are given in the Table of International Instruments.

> Compilations of data or other material, whether in machine readable or other form, which by reason of the selection or arrangement of their contents constitute intellectual creations shall be protected as such. Such protection, which shall not extend to the data or material itself, shall be without prejudice to any copyright subsisting in the data or material itself.

Many, but not all, common law jurisdictions have abandoned 'sweat'. Among those that have, however, there are differences in the formulation of the originality threshold. The sections immediately following explain the thresholds under US, Canadian and Australian law, as well as jurisdictions that continue to apply 'sweat of the brow'.

### 7.2.3  United States – Minimum 'Creative Spark'

In the United States, the 'sweat' doctrine, which had been accepted by some circuits,[10] was rejected by the Supreme Court in the landmark *Feist* decision.[11] After holding that originality was constitutionally mandated, the Court reiterated the 'originating from the author' principle, stating that originality 'means only that the work was independently created by the author (as opposed to copied from other works)'.[12] In relation to the 'minimum authorial contribution', however, the Court held that, to be original, a work must possess 'at least some minimal degree of creativity'.[13] It added, however, that 'the requisite level of creativity is extremely low ... The vast majority of works will make the grade quite easily, as they possess some creative spark ...'.[14]

Given there was insufficient creativity in the selection and arrangement of a 'White Pages' telephone directory, copyright does not subsist in works such as directories, which are the result of 'industrious collection', and which do not embody minimal 'creative spark' in their arrangement or selection.

US courts have, in practice, struggled to apply the ambiguous *Feist* 'creativity' threshold.[15] The *Feist* court's reasoning on originality was, moreover, related to its application of the fact/expression dichotomy, as the Court concluded that there can be no copyright in facts as they do not originate from an author (which is discussed further at [10.4.4]).

---

[10] M. Bitton, 'Trends in protection for informational works under copyright law during the 19th and 20th centuries' (2006) 13 *Michigan Telecommunications and Technology Law Review* 115.
[11] *Feist Publications, Inc.* v. *Rural Telephone Service Co.*, 499 US 340 (1991) ('*Feist*').
[12] *Ibid*. 345.    [13] *Ibid*.    [14] *Ibid*.
[15] D. Beldiman, 'Utilitarian information works – is originality the proper lens?' (2010) 14(1) *Marquette Intellectual Property Law Review* 1 at 12; D. Zimmerman, 'It's an original! (?): In pursuit of copyright's elusive essence' (2005) 28 *Columbia Journal of Law & the Arts* 187 at 188.

### 7.2.4 Canada – 'Skill and Judgement'

In its *CCH* decision,[16] which endorsed the language of 'users' rights': [2.4.2], the Canadian Supreme Court adopted a 'middle path' by rejecting both 'sweat' and the *Feist* 'minimal creativity' standard. In that case, McLachlin CJ held that an original work must be the 'product of an author's exercise of skill and judgment', but could not result from mere industrious labour, before adding that the 'exercise of skill and judgment required to produce the work must not be so trivial that it could be characterized as a purely mechanical exercise'.[17]

By avoiding 'industrious labour' and 'creativity', the Canadian court was concerned, first, to ensure that 'facts' are not protected and, second, to avoid complexities and ambiguities arising from the use of a 'creativity' standard: [7.2.7].

### 7.2.5 Australia – Minimum Human Authorship

Historically, Australia applied the 'sweat' doctrine to, for example, protect 'White Pages' directories.[18] In *IceTV*,[19] however, a case dealing with whether copying time and title information infringed copyright in a television guide, the Australian High Court effectively rejected 'sweat'. While the two judgments delivered in the case recast Australian law, they have generated uncertainty.

Concerning the minimum authorial contribution, the judgment of French CJ, Crennan and Kiefel JJ dismissed the dichotomy between 'sweat' and 'minimal creativity', stating that:

> 'Industrious collection' or 'sweat of the brow', on the one hand, and 'creativity', on the other, have been treated as antinomies in some sort of mutually exclusive relationship in the mental processes of an author or joint authors. They are ... kindred aspects of a mental process which produces an object, a literary work, a particular form of expression which copyright protects.[20]

Avoiding the 'labour, skill or judgement' test, the judgment said that all that is required is 'that the work originates from an author or joint authors from some independent intellectual effort'.[21]

Gummow, Hayne and Heydon JJ, concurring in the outcome but not the reasoning, emphasised the importance of a work originating from an author, being 'the person who brings the copyright work into existence, in

---

[16] *CCH Canadian Ltd v. Law Society of Upper Canada* (2004) 236 DLR (4th) 395 ('*CCH*').
[17] *Ibid.* 412.
[18] *Desktop Marketing Systems Pty Ltd v. Telstra Corporation Ltd* (2002) 55 IPR 1.
[19] *IceTV Pty Ltd v. Nine Network Australia Pty Ltd* (2009) 239 CLR 458 ('*IceTV*').
[20] *Ibid.* 478.  [21] *Ibid.* 479.

its material form'.[22] The judgment also avoided the 'labour, skill or judgement' test, stating that there must be 'sufficient effort of a literary nature'.[23] In the context of compilations, moreover, the judgment held that 'the author or authors will be those who gather or organise the collection of material and who select, order or arrange its fixation in material form'.[24] As the case was concerned with infringement, however, the comments on originality in the context of subsistence were *obiter*, and the judgment did not decide whether or not the *Feist* 'creative spark' or *CCH* minimal 'skill and judgement' standards should be adopted.

Subsequently, in *PDC*,[25] the Full Federal Court applied the *dicta* from *IceTV* in determining whether or not copyright subsisted in 'White Pages' directories. The Court held that copyright did not subsist as, due to the automated database production system, any protectable expression was generated by a computer program, and did not originate from human authors. The judgments confirmed the rejection of 'sweat' in Australia, mainly on the basis that *IceTV* held that copyright does not protect labour that is not directed to the form of expression of a work.

In relation to minimum authorial contribution, the *PDC* judgments adopted the test that authors of a compilation are those 'who gather or organise the collection of material *and* who select, order or arrange its fixation in material form'.[26] While there are considerable remaining uncertainties,[27] under Australian law, purely informational works such as some telephone directories are not protected as, following *IceTV*, 'sweat' alone is insufficient.

### 7.2.6 Common Law: Continuing Vitality of 'Industrious Collection'?

While 'sweat' has been rejected in the United States, Canada and Australia, it remains part of the common law in jurisdictions that continue to apply the traditional 'labour, skill or judgement' test, including New Zealand, South Africa and Singapore.[28]

In New Zealand, for example, in 2006 the Supreme Court, referring to English authorities, in *dicta* endorsed the low threshold of 'more than minimal skill and labour'.[29] In the principal New Zealand case, *University*

---

[22] *Ibid.* 494.  [23] *Ibid.*  [24] *Ibid.* 494–5.
[25] *Telstra Corporation Limited* v. *Phone Directories Company Limited* (2010) 194 FCR 142 ('*PDC*').
[26] *Ibid.* [71] (per Keane CJ); [107] (per Perram J); [164] (per Yates J) (emphasis added).
[27] J. McCutcheon, 'The vanishing author in computer-generated works: a critical analysis of recent Australian case law' (2013) 36 *Melbourne University Law Review* 915.
[28] E. Judge and D. Gervais, 'Of silos and constellations: comparing notions of originality in copyright law' (2009) 27 *Cardozo Arts & Entertainment Law Journal* 375.
[29] *Henkel KGAA* v. *Holdfast New Zealand Limited* [2006] NZSC 102; [2007] 1 NZLR 577 at [37].

*of Waikato*, the Court of Appeal held that copyright subsisted in a compilation of financial data, on the basis that sufficient 'time, skill, labour, or judgment' had been expended in producing the work.[30] The Court, however, also pointed out that copyright would not exist in the raw data, and that 'significant creative effort' had been expended on the compilation, including on the headings and format.[31] In South Africa, in 2006, the Supreme Court of Appeal applied the test of 'substantial skill, judgement and labour' in finding that a computer program was original, but expressly reserved the question of whether it should follow *CCH*.[32] In both jurisdictions, however, the highest courts have not been called upon to rule on the originality threshold. In India, on the other hand, the Indian Supreme Court, in a 2008 case involving copyright in headnotes to law reports, endorsed the *CCH* standard, but also applied the *Feist* 'minimum degree of creativity' test.[33]

### 7.2.7 Common Law Originality and the Public Domain

While the common law has historically protected 'low authorship' works, such as directories, there have been difficulties in applying the originality threshold to these works. In recognising 'sweat' as sufficient, common law courts effectively protected the 'fruits of labour' against misappropriation.[34] The inevitable logic was to protect facts or information where resources were invested in mere collection or compilation.[35]

Underlying the rejection of 'sweat' were concerns that facts should be free to be built upon. As McLachlin CJ said in *CCH*:

> When courts adopt a standard of originality requiring only that something be more than a mere copy or that someone simply show industriousness to ground copyright in a work, they tip the scale in favour of the author or creator's rights, at the loss of society's interest in maintaining a robust public domain that would help foster future creative innovation.[36]

Similarly, in *Feist*, O'Connor J held that, 'copyright assures authors the right to their original expression, but encourages others to build freely upon the ideas and information conveyed by a work'.[37]

---

[30] *The University of Waikato* v. *Benchmark Services Ltd* [2004] NZCA 90 at [27].
[31] *Ibid.* [42].
[32] *Haupt* v. *Brewers Marketing Intelligence (Pty) Limited* [2006] SCA 39 (RSA) at [36] n. 9.
[33] *Eastern Book Co.* v. *Modak* (2008) 1 SCC 1.
[34] S. Ricketson, 'Reaping without sowing: unfair competition and intellectual property rights in Anglo-Australian law' (1984) 7 *UNSW Law Journal* 1.
[35] See *Desktop Marketing Systems Pty Ltd* v. *Telstra Corporation Ltd* (2002) 55 IPR 1.
[36] *CCH* at [23]–[24]. [37] *Feist* at 349.

While rejecting 'sweat', however, the courts in the United States, Canada and Australia have applied different thresholds: in the United States, a minimum level of 'creativity'; in Canada, a minimum amount of 'skill and judgement'; and in Australia, a standard that at least rules out pure 'sweat'. At the heart of the problem, as suggested by Zimmerman, may be the tendency of courts to rely on formulaic standards, but more precision about the threshold would demand analysis of what is meant by 'originality' or 'creativity', ultimately referable to a theory of why some works merit protection but others do not.[38] This would doubtless impose high demands on courts but, as we argue, a public domain perspective can assist with this: [7.2.16].

The dilemma of the originality threshold is most apparent in the problem of how to encourage investment in factual compilations and databases while also promoting access. The EU specifically addressed the issue in a 1996 Directive, which had a major effect on 'originality' in the EU and the UK, and which is dealt with immediately below.

### 7.2.8  The EU Database Directive

The EU Database Directive,[39] adopted in 1996, established a *sui generis* regime for protecting databases.[40] The regime distinguishes databases protected by copyright, which must satisfy an originality threshold, from databases which do not meet that threshold, and which are entitled to *sui generis* rights to prevent extraction or reutilisation of a substantial part of their contents.

In drawing this distinction, the Directive harmonised the originality threshold for databases entitled to copyright, conferring protection on 'databases which, by reason of the selection and arrangement of their contents, constitute the author's *own intellectual creation*'.[41] Databases entitled to the *sui generis* regime, however, require only that there has been 'a substantial investment in either the obtaining, verification or presentation of the contents'.[42] In relation to the latter test, the ECJ has ruled that resources expended in creating data, such as resources used in producing football fixtures, must be disregarded.[43] According to English

---

[38] Zimmerman, 'It's an original! (?)'.
[39] Database Directive (EU). Full titles and citations of Directives are in the Table of International Instruments.
[40] Database Directive, Art. 1(2).   [41] Database Directive, Art. 3(1) (emphasis added).
[42] Database Directive, Art. 7(1).
[43] Case C-338/02, *Fixtures Marketing Ltd* v. *Svenska AB*, [2004] ECR I-10497; Case C-444/02, *Fixtures Marketing Ltd* v. *Organismos Prognostikon Agonon Podosfairou EG (OPAP)*, [2004] ECR I-10549; Case C-46/02, *Fixtures Marketing Ltd* v. *Oy Veikkaus Ab*, [2004] ECR I-10365; Case C-203/02, *British Horseracing Board Ltd* v. *William Hill*

## 7.2 Works Failing Minimum Requirements

case law, however, the purpose of the regime, which is to encourage investment in collection, must be taken into account and, on this basis, financial and human resources invested in producing live football data has been held to be sufficient.[44]

In relation to the originality required for copyright protection, in *Football Dataco*,[45] the ECJ ruled that creation of data cannot be taken into account in determining whether the selection or arrangement is the author's 'own intellectual creation'. Consequently, the effort put into scheduling football fixtures is irrelevant. Applying the harmonised standard, the Court held that, through the selection and arrangement of data, the author must express 'his creative ability in an original manner by making free and creative choices ... and thus stamp(s) his "personal touch"'.[46]

The result of the Directive is that, for copyright protection, the standardisation of the originality threshold has been raised in countries, notably the UK and Ireland, which traditionally applied 'sweat', so that selection or arrangement of data requiring 'intellectual creation' is required. In 2005, problems with the *sui generis* regime were identified in a Commission working paper; the problems included the failure to achieve the objective of stimulating the production of databases in Europe, but also that the regime had the potential to lock up information, including public domain information.[47]

### 7.2.9 'Originality' in Civil Law Jurisdictions

Historically, the *droit d'auteur* tradition applied a different and higher 'creativity' threshold than common law 'originality': [7.2.1]. This required that a work bear the imprint of an author's personality; in France known as *l'empreinte du talent créateur personnel*,[48] and in Germany 'the author's own intellectual creations' (*persönliche geistige Schöpfungen*).[49] As Rahmatian puts this:

---

*Organization Ltd*, [2004] ECR I-10415. For analysis of the cases, see T. Aplin, 'The ECJ elucidates the database right' (2005) 2 *Intellectual Property Quarterly* 204.

[44] *Football Dataco Ltd* v. *Sportradar GmbH* [2013] 2 CMLR 932.
[45] Case C-604/10, *Football Dataco Ltd* v. *Yahoo! UK Ltd*, [2012] 2 CMLR 703.
[46] *Ibid*. [38].
[47] Directorate General for the Internal Market and Services Working Paper, First evaluation of Directive 96/9/EC on the legal protection of databases, 12 December 2005.
[48] C. Cass. Civ. 1re, 13 novembre 1973.
[49] Law on Copyright and Neighbouring Rights (Urheberrechtsgesetz – UrhG) (Germany), Art. 2(2).

Not only must the work originate from the author, it must have been shaped by the author's individual distinct personality; it must not just be commonplace, a work that could be attributed to anyone.[50]

This does not, however, mean that works of low authorship were denied protection in authors' rights jurisdictions. Under German law, different standards of individuality were applied to different categories of work, with a high standard applied to some utilitarian works, such as instruction manuals, and a lower standard to informational works, such as directories and recipe books.[51] The flexible lower standard, embodied in the doctrine of 'small change' (*kleine Münze*), allowed copyright to extend to works such as directories, catalogues and price lists.[52] A similar doctrine, known as *petite monnaie*, extended protection to low authorship works, such as statistical studies and some telephone directories, under French law.[53] In determining whether to confer protection, however, mere labour was always insufficient, as the creative choices made by the author was the determinative consideration.

As explained immediately below, however, EU Member States must now apply a harmonised originality standard that may differ from the traditional threshold.

### 7.2.10 EU 'Harmonisation' of Originality and UK Law

In the EU, difficulties in applying traditional concepts of originality to software, databases and photographs led to harmonisation of the threshold for protection for those products in specific directives.[54] The harmonised threshold in these three areas requires a work to be 'the author's own intellectual creation'.[55] The precise content of this standard is not clear, but it seems to differ from both the English originality threshold and the authors' rights threshold.[56] While the EU Directives confined

---

[50] A. Rahmatian, 'Originality in UK copyright law: the old "skill and labour" doctrine under pressure' (2013) 44 *International Review of Intellectual Property and Competition Law (IIC)* 4 at 17.
[51] *Ibid.* 19; Beldiman, 'Utilitarian information works', 13–15; A. Rahmatian, *Copyright and Creativity. The Making of Property Rights in Creative Works* (Edward Elgar, 2011).
[52] Beldiman, 'Utilitarian information works', 14.
[53] Rahmatian, 'Originality in UK copyright law', 19. See, further, D. Gervais, '*Feist* goes global: a comparative analysis of the notion of originality in copyright law' (2002) 49 *Journal of the Copyright Society of the USA* 949 at 968
[54] Database Directive, Art. 3(1); Term Directive, Art. 6; Software Directive, Art. 1(3).
[55] Database Directive, Art. 3(1); Software Directive, Art. 1(3); Term Directive, Art. 6.
[56] Rahmatian characterises the standard as follows: 'Between the dog of the "skill and labour" originality of copyright and the cat of the "personal intellectual creation" originality of the author's rights systems, the "own intellectual creation" originality of the EU Directives is something like a hyena, which zoologically belongs to the order of the

## 7.2 Works Failing Minimum Requirements

harmonisation to specific subject matter, in a process described as 'harmonisation by stealth',[57] in the landmark *Infopaq I* ruling,[58] the ECJ has introduced a uniform originality threshold as part of the *acquis communautaire*.[59]

In *Infopaq I*, the ECJ interpreted the concept of 'reproduction' in the InfoSoc Directive, which applies to all works, as requiring the identification of 'works' and, on this basis, fully harmonised the originality threshold as part of EU law. In reaching this conclusion, the Court first ruled that Articles 2(5) and 2(8) of Berne presupposed that artistic or literary works must be 'intellectual creations', then generalised the thresholds under the specific Directives to require all works under the InfoSoc Directive to be 'the author's own intellectual creation'.[60] Expanding on this in the context of whether a series of eleven words might be original, the Court stated that it is 'through the choice, sequence and combination of those words that the author may express his creativity in an original manner and achieve a result that is an intellectual creation'.[61] While the ECJ has yet to make a definitive ruling on the meaning of 'own intellectual creation', it has subsequently endorsed the harmonised threshold.[62]

To date, the application of the harmonised standard by UK courts has been unclear and inconsistent, so that the threshold in the UK is best characterised as 'unsettled'.[63] Nevertheless, it is arguable, on the basis of

---

cat-like carnivore but has rather dog-like features': Rahmatian, 'Originality in UK copyright law', 22. See also A. Lucas-Schloetter, 'Is there a concept of European copyright law? History, evolution, policies and politics and the *Acquis Communautaire*', in I. Stamatoudi and P. Torremans (eds.), *EU Copyright Law: A Commentary* (Edward Elgar, 2016), pp. 7–22.

[57] L. Bently, 'Harmonisation by stealth: copyright and the ECJ', unpublished paper presented at the Fordham IP Conference, 8 April 2012 http://fordhamipconference.com/wp-content/uploads/2010/08/Bently_Harmonization.pdf.

[58] Case C-5/08, *Infopaq International A/S v. Danske Dagblades Forening*, [2009] ECR I-6569 ('*Infopaq I*'). For commentary, see S. Vousden, '*Infopaq* and the Europeanisation of copyright law' (2010) 1(2) *WIPO Journal* 197; E. Derclaye, '*Infopaq International A/S v. Danske Dagblades Forening* (C-5/08): wonderful or worrisome? The impact of the ECJ ruling in *Infopaq* on UK copyright law' (2010) 32(5) *European Intellectual Property Review* 247; E. Rosati, 'Originality in a work, or a work of originality: the effects of the *Infopaq* decision' (2011) 33(12) *European Intellectual Property Review* 746; Rahmatian, 'Originality in UK copyright law'.

[59] See Hugenholtz, 'Is harmonization a good thing?, 57–73.

[60] Case C-5/08, *Infopaq International A/S v. Danske Dagblades Forening*, [2009] ECR I-6569 at [37].

[61] *Ibid*. [45].

[62] Case C-393/09, *Bezpecnostni Softwarova Asociace – Svaz Softwarove Ochrany v. Ministerstvo Kultury*, [2010] ECR I-13971; Case C-145/10, *Eva-Maria Painer v. Standard Verlags GmbH* [2011] ECR I-12533; Case C-604/10, *Football Dataco Ltd v. Yahoo! UK Ltd*, [2012] 2 CMLR 703.

[63] E. Derclaye, 'Assessing the impact and reception of the Court of Justice of the European Union case law on UK copyright law: what does the future hold?' [2014] 240 *Revue internationale du droit d'auteur* 5 at 18.

ECJ rulings, that the harmonised standard requires that an author 'expresses his creative ability in an original manner by making free and creative choices' and, in doing so, stamps his or her 'personal touch' on the work.[64] This inevitably means that 'sweat' is no longer part of UK copyright law. Furthermore, as the harmonised standard is higher than the traditional English threshold: [7.2.2], it casts doubt on the continued authority of cases which depended on the low 'labour, skill and judgement' threshold.[65]

### 7.2.11 EU and UK 'Originality', and the Public Domain

In the EU, protection of databases created difficulties for authors' rights jurisdictions, and was a factor leading to the introduction of a database law. The Database Directive established *sui generis* rights for non-original databases, reserving copyright for databases that satisfied the threshold of the author's 'own intellectual creation'. The protection of non-original databases gave rise to international interest in protecting the public domain: [1.2]. Subsequently, in *Infopaq I*, the ECJ harmonised the EU threshold, applying the 'author's own intellectual creation' standard to all works. While there is uncertainty as to the meaning of the threshold, on the basis of ECJ rulings, it seems to require that a work expresses the 'free and creative choices' of an author. The harmonised threshold therefore casts doubt on traditional English 'low authorship' cases.

In so far as the harmonised threshold is higher than the traditional 'labour, skill or judgement' threshold, it results in more works falling below the threshold, and therefore forming part of the copyright public domain. The differences between the harmonised and traditional thresholds, however, continue to be uncertain; and, in any case, in the EU are offset by protection of non-original databases under the *sui generis* law.

### 7.2.12 Insubstantial 'Works'

Apart from 'originality', works may fail to be protected on the grounds that they are too insubstantial to meet a *de minimis* threshold. Under international copyright law, there is no express mention of short works, such as titles, in the definition of 'literary and artistic works' in Article 2(1) of Berne. As there is no requirement for insubstantial works (or

---

[64] Case C-604/10, *Football Dataco Ltd* v. *Yahoo! UK Ltd*, [2012] 2 CMLR 703 at [38].
[65] Most commentators conclude that the standards are inconsistent; see Rosati, 'Originality in a work', 754; Rahmatian, 'Originality in UK copyright law', 32.

## 7.2 Works Failing Minimum Requirements

'microworks')[66] to be protected, there are considerable differences in their protection under national laws.[67]

Under English law, copyright has been denied to insubstantial literary works, such as titles, slogans and headlines; but the legal bases for denying protection has been unclear. Copyright has sometimes been denied because the work lacks the labour, skill or judgement necessary to confer originality.[68]

Difficulties arise, however, where a short work, such as a title, results from skill, labour or judgement. In *Exxon*,[69] for example, the word 'Exxon', which was clearly the result of considerable effort and research, was held not to be a literary work at all as it was not 'intended to afford instruction, or information, or pleasure in the form of literary enjoyment'.[70]

At times, refusal to protect short works has been expressly linked to public domain concerns. For instance, in *Rose*,[71] Hoffman J held that the words 'The Lawyer's Diary 1986' involved too little skill and labour to be original, before adding that, '[i]n effect the plaintiff would have acquired a monopoly of part of the English language'.[72] A subtext in some of the judgments is that titles or slogans are better protected as trade marks or under the law of passing off.

Differences have arisen between Australian and UK courts in the treatment of newspaper headlines. In *Fairfax* v. *Reed*,[73] Bennett J in the Australian Federal Court held that, even if skill and labour were expended in their creation, newspaper headlines are too short and insubstantial to be literary works, or to be 'works' at all. This conclusion was influenced by public policy considerations that headlines, like titles of articles or books, are necessary to identify works; and that to confer protection would detrimentally affect bibliographic and reference systems.[74]

In *Meltwater*,[75] however, the English Court of Appeal applied the harmonised *Infopaq I* threshold to conclude that copyright could subsist in headlines. In that case, Meltwater conducted an online media monitoring service, which depended upon references to newspaper headlines. At first instance, Proudman J held that headlines could satisfy the

---

[66] See Hughes, 'Size matters', 576.
[67] Ricketson and Ginsburg, *International Copyright and Neighbouring Rights*, [8.115].
[68] See *Dicks* v. *Yates* (1881) 18 Ch D 76; *Francis, Day & Hunter Ltd* v. *Twentieth Century Fox Corporation Ltd* [1940] AC.
[69] [1982] Ch 119.
[70] [1982] Ch 119 at 139 (per Stephenson LJ, citing *Hollinrake* v. *Truswell* (1894) 3 Ch 420 at 428).
[71] *Rose* v. *Information Services Ltd* [1987] FSR 254.   [72] [1987] FSR 254 at 255.
[73] *Fairfax Media* v. *Reed International* (2010) 88 IPR 11.   [74] (2010) 88 IPR 11 at 25.
[75] *Newspaper Licensing Agency Ltd* v. *Meltwater Holding BV* [2012] RPC 1.

harmonised test of being 'the author's own intellectual creation' as there was 'considerable skill' in devising the headlines and, accordingly, they were capable of being 'independent literary works'.[76] The Court of Appeal agreed and, in the process, held that the *Infopaq I* test of 'intellectual creation' had not altered the traditional English 'originating from the author' test.[77]

In concluding that headlines could satisfy the EU originality threshold, the UK courts failed to consider the alternative basis for finding that copyright does not subsist in short works, namely that the works are too insubstantial to be literary works. Moreover, as Bently has pointed out, conferring copyright on titles and headlines will have a negative effect on businesses that depend upon headlines for citing, referencing and locating works.[78]

Under US law, 'short phrases', such as names and titles are not protected. According to a US Copyright Office circular, which has been cited and applied by the courts, '[b]rand names, trade names, slogans, and other short phrases or expressions cannot be copyrighted, even if they are distinctively arranged or printed'.[79] Copyright in short works, such as headlines or titles, is also commonly denied on the basis that they fail to satisfy the US originality threshold.[80] For example, in *Southco III*,[81] the Third Circuit denied copyright in nine-digit numbers used to denote fastener models, on the basis both that the numbers were not original and that they were short works analogous to phrases or titles. Even if a work such as a headline is original, it will probably be denied protection under the 'merger' doctrine: [10.4.4], as protection of 'short phrases' would prevent others from expressing the same idea.[82] Finally, assuming

---

[76] [2011] RPC 209 at [70]–[71].
[77] [2012] RPC 1 at [19]–[20]. This interpretation is contestable, as it seems clear from the ECJ ruling in *Football Dataco* that the two standards are different: see Derclaye, 'Assessing the impact and reception of the Court of Justice of the European Union case law', 19.
[78] L. Bently, 'Bently slams "very disappointing" ruling in *Meltwater*', 27 July 2011, The IPKat http://ipkitten.blogspot.com/2011/07/bently-slams-very-disappointing-ruling.html. See also D. Liu, '*Meltwater* melts not water but principle! The danger of the court adjudicating an issue without the ambit of referral' (2013) 35(6) *European Intellectual Property Review* 327.
[79] United States Copyright Office, 'Copyright protection not available for names, titles or short phrases', Circular No. 34 www.copyright.gov/circs/circ34.pdf.
[80] See *Alberto-Culver Co.* v. *Andrea Dumon, Inc*, 466 F 2d 705 (7th Cir 1972); *CMM Cable Rep., Inc.* v. *Ocean Coast Props., Inc*, 97 F 3d 1504 (1st Cir 1996). The classic case seems to have been *Magic Marketing*, in which copyright was denied in short phrases such as 'telegram', 'priority mail' and 'contents require immediate attention': *Magic Marketing* v. *Mailing Services of Pittsburgh, Inc.*, 634 F Supp 769 (WD Pa. 1986).
[81] *Southco, Inc.* v. *Kanebridge Corp.*, 390 F 3d 276 (3rd Cir 2004) ('*Southco III*').
[82] A. Yen, 'A preliminary First Amendment analysis of legislation treating news aggregation as copyright infringement' (2010) 12(4) *Vanderbilt Journal of Entertainment and Technology Law* 947 at 955–6.

copyright subsists, potentially infringing uses of short works may be excused under the fair use doctrine: [11.3]. The precise legal basis for denying protection to short works under US law is therefore as uncertain as it is in the other jurisdictions studied in this book.

### 7.2.13 Insubstantial Works and the Public Domain

International copyright law neither requires nor excludes insubstantial works, such as titles and headlines, from copyright protection. There are, nevertheless, compelling reasons for excluding insubstantial works from protection. Conferring copyright on short works, however original, may have the effect of locking up the building blocks for other works. Moreover, protection of titles or headlines can prevent uses, such as indexing services, which are essential for identifying and locating works, and therefore important for obtaining access. In any case, it is unlikely there is a need for an incentive to produce such works.[83]

In common law systems, copyright has commonly been refused for insubstantial literary works, but there has been no consistent approach. While some English cases have held that titles are insufficiently original, Australian law may deny protection on the basis that titles or headlines are not 'works'. Under US law, copyright has been denied in short phrases or exceptions on a number of bases, including the Copyright Office circular, lack of originality and the 'merger' doctrine.

In *Meltwater*, on the other hand, UK courts held that newspaper headlines could be protected as they are capable of satisfying the *Infopaq I* threshold, of being an author's 'own intellectual creation'. Furthermore, in *Infopaq I*, the ECJ ruled that part of a work, such as the eleven-word extracts in that case, could be protected if sufficiently original, in the sense of being the author's 'own intellectual creation': [10.3.1]. On this basis, it has been suggested that cases such as *Francis, Day & Hunter* and *Exxon*, in which UK courts have denied copyright to insubstantial works, are no longer good law.[84] Paradoxically, therefore, the harmonised EU originality threshold, which appears higher than the traditional English standard, has ensured that some short works, such as headlines, that might otherwise have been part of the public domain, are protected by copyright.

In his review of US law, Hughes supported the introduction of a general *de minimis* threshold, arguing that:

> If our goal is to create incentives for the building of houses, we do not necessarily need special incentives for the making of bricks or the mixing of mortar.[85]

---

[83] Hughes, 'Size matters', 610–13.
[84] Rosati, 'Originality in a work, or a work of originality, 755.
[85] Hughes, 'Size matters', 613.

Accordingly, he supports a multi-factor 'minimum size' test for determining whether or not a short work is protectable,[86] which would, to an extent, be consistent with the alternative bases the courts have found for denying protection.

While it is no doubt impossible to implement a single bright-line rule, we believe that public domain values could be supported by introducing a specific rule for distinguishing unprotectable short works from protectable works. As size alone is an imprecise and unworkable criterion, it seems to us that, as Hughes suggests, there are advantages in courts applying a multi-factor test.

### 7.2.14 Fixation

The principle that copyright does not subsist in a work unless it takes a material form is known as the principle of fixation. A fundamental distinction exists, broadly speaking, between common law jurisdictions, which impose fixation as a condition for copyright, and civil law jurisdictions, which do not. As Goldstein and Hugenholtz suggest, '[t]he division may have as much to do with differences in approach to pleadings and proof between the two traditions as it does with differences in the underlying philosophies of copyright and author's right.'[87]

Fixation has been justified in that it provides certainty for copyright subject matter, both as to whether a work exists and what the work is.[88] It has also been justified on the basis that copyright does not protect 'ideas' separate from form of expression, although it has been suggested that this conflates two conceptually distinct principles: fixation and idea/expression.[89] Furthermore, if fixation is connected with authorship, the requirement of fixation can determine the time at which a work comes into existence;[90] and if it is not connected with authorship, the time at which copyright arises.

Article 2(2) of Berne addresses irreconcilable differences in approaches to fixation by leaving this to national laws: [4.6.4]. This section of the chapter explains differences in approaches to fixation under national laws.

---

[86] *Ibid.* 634.   [87] Goldstein and Hugenholtz, *International Copyright*, [6.1.5].
[88] *Tate* v. *Fullbrook* [1908] 1 KB 821 at 832–3; *Tate* v. *Thomas* [1921] 1 Ch 503; *Green* v. *Broadcasting Corporation of New Zealand* [1989] 2 All ER 1056 at 1058.
[89] D. Brennan and A. Christie, 'Spoken words and copyright subsistence in Anglo-American law' (2000) 4 *Intellectual Property Quarterly* 4.
[90] A. Stewart, P. Griffith, J. Bannister and A. Liberman, *Intellectual Property in Australia* (5th edn, LexisNexis Butterworths, 2014), [6.7].

## 7.2 Works Failing Minimum Requirements

*UK Law* In the UK, the CDPA provides that copyright does not subsist in a literary, dramatic or musical work 'unless and until it is recorded, in writing or otherwise'.[91] Furthermore, the CDPA makes it clear that fixation can be satisfied by the work being recorded by someone other than the author, and regardless of whether the author consents to the recording.[92] For example, a speech or lecture is capable of being protected provided it is recorded, and irrespective of who records it. As the CDPA does not define 'recording', any form of fixation, such as computer memory or mobile phone, is sufficient. As there is no necessary connection between the author and the recording, the principles of authorship and fixation are distinct,[93] suggesting that a work can come into existence prior to fixation, but is only protected once fixed.[94]

Under the CDPA, there is no requirement of fixation for artistic works, but this seems implicit from the subcategories of artistic works.[95] In relation to other subject matter, the nature and statutory definitions of sound recordings, films and typographical arrangements mean that they must have a material form.[96]

*Australian Law* In Australia, the requirement of fixation arises from interlocking provisions of the Copyright Act. For both unpublished and published works the statutory conditions for subsistence require (like the 1956 UK Act) that a work be 'made',[97] which is defined to mean 'first reduced to writing or some other material form'.[98] The Act defines 'material form', in relation to a work or an adaptation, to include:

> any form (whether visible or not) of storage of the work or adaptation, or a substantial part of the work or adaptation.[99]

The definition of 'material form' is deliberately broad, extending, for example, to works stored in computer memory.[100] Like the CDPA, the definitions of sound recordings, films and published editions (typographical arrangements) impose a requirement of fixation.[101]

The requirement that a work be 'made', suggests a work does not exist until it is fixed. An interpretation of the Australian Act as equating fixation with authorship might be reinforced by the absence of an express

---

[91] CDPA, s. 3(2).   [92] CDPA, s. 3(3).
[93] Adeney, 'Authorship and fixation in copyright law'.
[94] *Hadley* v. *Kemp* [1999] EMLR 589. See also the decision of the Irish Supreme Court in *Gormley* v. *EMI Records (Ireland) Ltd* [2000] 1 IR 74.
[95] CDPA, s. 4.   [96] See definitions of 'sound recording' and 'film': CDPA, ss. 5A, 5B.
[97] Copyright Act 1968 (Aus.), ss. 32(1) (2); 29(1)(a) ('publication').
[98] Copyright Act 1968 (Aus.), s. 22(1).   [99] Copyright Act 1968 (Aus ), s. 10(1).
[100] *Roland Corporation* v. *Lorenzo & Sons Pty Ltd* (1991) 22 IPR 245 at 252.
[101] Copyright Act 1968 (Aus.), ss. 89(1), 90(1), 92, 22(3)(a), 22(4).

provision that fixation can be performed by someone other than the author. Moreover, this interpretation is supported by *dicta* in *IceTV*, stating that an author is 'the person who brings the copyright work into existence in a material form'.[102] As Adeney has argued, however, there is nothing in the Act that necessarily leads to the conclusion that an author must be the person who makes a work, and therefore fixes it.[103] The preferred position in Australia may therefore be that, like the CDPA, a work can be fixed by someone other than the author.

*US Law* In the United States, fixation is a constitutional requirement, with the Intellectual Property Clause specifically referring to the right of authors to their 'writings'.[104] The US Act specifically provides for copyright works to be 'fixed in any tangible medium of expression',[105] and further provides that a work is fixed when:

> its embodiment in a copy ... by or under the authority of the author is sufficiently permanent or stable to permit it to be perceived, reproduced, or otherwise communicated for a period of more than transitory duration.[106]

The US Act also provides that a work is 'created' when it is fixed for the first time.[107]

The requirement that fixation take place 'by or with the authority of the author' means that, unlike UK law, a work cannot be fixed by someone who is not the author, or not otherwise acting under the authority of the author. Moreover, the equation of creation with fixation suggests that a copyright work cannot exist prior to fixation.[108] The more restrictive requirement of fixation under US law means that, if a work is fixed by a third party, without the authority of the owner, copyright will not subsist, and the 'work' is therefore part of the public domain. For example, in the United States, an oral work, such as an *ex tempore* speech that is not fixed under the authority of the author, is not protected by copyright.

The US equation of authorship with fixation, and the requirement for fixation to be 'of more than transitory duration', are illustrated by cases

---

[102] (2009) 239 CLR 458 at 494 (per Gummow, Hayne and Heydon JJ), quoting H. Laddie, P. Prescott and M. Vitoria, *The Modern Law of Copyright and Designs* (Butterworths, 1980), [6.6].
[103] Adeney, 'Authorship and fixation in copyright law'.
[104] US Constitution, Art. I, §8, cl 8. In *Goldstein* v. *California* the Supreme Court stated that fixation 'may be interpreted to include any physical rendering of the fruits of creative intellectual or aesthetic labor': 412 US 546 at 561 (1973). For a history of fixation under US law, see M. Carpenter and S. Hetcher, 'Function over form: bringing the fixation requirement into the modern era' (2014) 82 *Fordham Law Review* 2221.
[105] 17 USC §102(a) (2012).  [106] 17 USC §101.  [107] *Ibid*.
[108] L. Loren, 'Fixation as notice in copyright' (2016) 96 *Boston University Law Review* 939 at 947.

## 7.2 Works Failing Minimum Requirements

involving works of art. In *Kelley*,[109] for example, an artist designed an elaborate garden. In that case, the Seventh Circuit held that even though the work could be 'perceived for more than transitory duration', as the garden's appearance depended upon the forces of nature, it lacked 'the kind of authorship and stable fixation required to support copyright'.[110]

*Civil Law: France, Germany, China* While US law applies a restrictive approach, in civil law jurisdictions fixation is generally not a condition for copyright protection. But there are important variations in the way these jurisdictions deal with fixation. In France, for example, fixation was once a requirement but was later abandoned,[111] with Article L112-1 of the Intellectual Property Code protecting 'the rights of authors in all works of the mind (*œuvres de l'esprit*), whatever their kind, form of expression, merit or purpose'.[112] This means that oral works, such as *ex tempore* speeches, are perfectly capable of being protected.[113] The position is, however, more complex than the absence of an express condition of fixation suggests. First, Article L112-2 of the Code provides that, to be protected, 'choreographic works, circus acts and feats and dumb-show works' must be fixed 'in writing or in other manner'.[114] Second, while copyright is not conditioned on fixation, there remains a need for evidence of a work which, in practice, may require fixation.[115]

Under German law, protection is also specifically given to works such as speeches, as well as works of pantomime, including choreographic works.[116] However, while fixation is not a precondition for protection, with copyright arising from the creation,[117] a work must be in a form that is perceptible to humans (*wahrnehmbare Formgestaltung*).[118] An extreme example of a low threshold for the requirement of 'perceptible form' is the

---

[109] *Kelley v. Chicago Art District*, 635 F 3d 290 (7th Cir 2011).    [110] *Ibid.* 303, 305
[111] Y. Gendreau, 'The criterion of fixation in copyright law' (1994) 159 *Revue internationale du droit d'auteur* 110 at 126.
[112] Code de la propriété intellectuelle (France), Art. L112-1.
[113] J.-L. Poitraut, 'An authors' rights-based copyright law: the fairness and morality of French and American law compared' (2006) 24 *Cardozo Arts & Entertainment Law Journal* 549 at 572. Article L112-2.2 of the *Code* specifically refers to 'lectures, addresses, sermons, pleadings and other works of such nature'.
[114] Code de la propriété intellectuelle (France), Art. L112-1.4.
[115] Poitraut, 'An authors' rights-based copyright', 573.
[116] Law on Copyright and Neighbouring Rights (Urheberrechtsgesetz – UrhG) (Germany), Art. 2(1).
[117] Law on Copyright and Neighbouring Rights (Urheberrechtsgesetz – UrhG) (Germany), Art. 2(2). A. White, 'The copyright tree: using German moral rights as the roots for enhanced authorship protection in the United States' (2010) 9(1) *Loyola Law and Technology Annual* 30 at 42 n. 66.
[118] E. Adeney, *The Moral Rights of Authors and Performers: An International and Comparative Analysis* (Oxford University Press, 2006), [9.29].

decision of the Dutch Supreme Court in *Kecofa* v. *Lancôme*,[119] holding that copyright could subsist in the scent of perfume as it was perceptible to humans.[120] That said, as in France, as a matter of practice, fixation may be required to establish infringement.[121]

The less than uniform approach to fixation in civil law systems is further illustrated by the law in China, where there is ambiguity.[122] As in France and Germany, there is no express requirement of fixation and the law expressly protects oral works, defined broadly as 'works created via spoken words, such as impromptu speeches, lectures and court debates'.[123] The law also specifically protects a form of unfixed works known as *quyi*, which are narrative and singing performances that have developed from indigenous folklore.[124] Nevertheless, Chinese law provides that works are only protected if they are capable of being reproduced in a tangible form.[125] This essentially means that non-fixed works, such as oral speeches, can be protected provided they are capable of fixation.

### 7.2.15 Fixation and the Public Domain

There is a conceptual distinction between civil law jurisdictions, which generally do not impose fixation as a condition of protection, and common law jurisdictions, which do. The authors' rights tradition regards copyright as arising from creation and, therefore, as not depending upon further steps, such as fixation. The copyright tradition, on the other hand, is more instrumentalist, regarding copyright as a reward for the effort in producing a work in material form. Purely as a matter of law, jurisdictions requiring fixation have richer public domains than those that protect unfixed works.

That said, there are complexities that undercut this apparent dichotomy. Bringing an action in civil law systems requires evidence of the work, which commonly means a form of fixation. Furthermore, in jurisdictions such as Germany, protection depends upon a work being in a perceptible form, which, while not the same as fixation, may still be a hurdle.

Within common law jurisdictions, there is a distinction between jurisdictions, such as the UK, where authorship is separate from fixation,

---

[119] [2006] ECDR 26.
[120] See C. Seville, 'Copyright in perfumes: smelling a rat' [2007] *Cambridge Law Journal* 49 at 51.
[121] Adeney, *The Moral Rights of Authors and Performers*, [9.29].
[122] See Y. Li and G. Greenleaf, 'China's copyright public domain: a comparison with Australia' (2017) 27 *Australian Intellectual Property Journal* 147 at 152.
[123] Implementing Regulations to the 2010 Copyright Law (China), Art. 4(2).
[124] See Baike Baidu https://baike.baidu.com/item/%E6%9B%B2%E8%89%BA/4062.
[125] Implementing Regulations to the 2010 Copyright Law (China), Art. 2.

and the United States, where authorship and fixation are correlated. Where fixation is separate from authorship, copyright can subsist even though the work is fixed by someone other than the author. Under US law, however, there is no copyright in works fixed by someone other than the author, and without the author's authority. The more restrictive approach to fixation in the United States means that some works that are in a material form may be in the public domain. The restrictive US approach to fixation is, however, partially offset by a more flexible approach to protectable subject matter: [7.3.2].

### 7.2.16 *Works Failing Minimum Requirements: A Public Domain Perspective*

Under national laws, works may fail to satisfy the minimum requirements for protection because: they do not meet the originality threshold; they are insufficiently substantial; or, in some jurisdictions, they are not fixed. For each subcategory, the courts ask whether the works should be protected, but sometimes whether they should not be protected. From our positive public domain perspective, we argue that greater clarity is possible by a more precise focus on when works should not be protected.

Concerning originality, the focus has been on whether the work should be protected, with different jurisdictions applying different tests. Moreover, in both common law and authors' rights jurisdictions, the reasoning is author-centric. For example, in common law jurisdictions, the 'originating from the author' test assumes that works will be protected unless they have been copied. The 'minimum authorial contribution' test qualifies this, but often tends to resolve to the question of whether the author's contribution is such as should be rewarded. To an extent, courts rejecting the 'sweat' doctrine reversed some of this reasoning by taking into account the importance of 'facts' remaining free for others to build upon; although, even here, in judgments such as *Feist* and *IceTV*, courts resort to questionable assertions, such as that 'facts' do not originate from authors.[126] In the EU, the 'author's own intellectual creation' test, influenced by the authors' rights tradition, is even more author-centric, apparently requiring that a work must reflect the 'free and creative choices' of an author. While this appears to have raised the threshold for protection in the UK, and overruled the 'sweat' cases, it has created uncertainty.

The law in every jurisdiction dealt with in this book has experienced difficulties in distinguishing unprotected from protected works, especially

---

[126] See J. Hughes, 'Created facts and the flawed ontology of copyright law' (2007) 83 *Notre Dame Law Review* 43.

in relation to 'low authorship' works such as factual databases. While part of the problem is that full copyright protection may not be the best means for protecting factual works, such as directories and databases, the only attempt at alternative protection, the EU Database Directive, has been problematic. Meanwhile, tests applied in jurisdictions such as the United States, Canada and Australia have been incapable of drawing clear lines, and have resulted in inconsistent decisions. Particular difficulties arise where 'factual' material is not collected or discovered, but originates from an author, such as compilations of price valuations, programme schedules and timetables. This is further complicated by difficulties in distinguishing 'ideas' or 'facts' from expression: [10.4].

Applying our 'realist' and public domain perspectives, we contend that an exclusively author-centric focus can obscure significant considerations relevant to the distinction between protected and unprotected works, and especially the value of permission-free uses. In this, we consider that uncertainties associated with author-centric tests cause problems for both creators and users. In this, we are by no means claiming that the inquiry should be user-centric, or that users' rights should prevail, but merely that, in borderline cases, this perspective should more explicitly be taken into account. While this already occurs, to an extent, through the application of idea/expression and fact/expression, we claim that more precision concerning underlying rights and interests may assist legal reasoning, as opposed to formulaic approaches to threshold tests. In short, while we acknowledge that an exhaustive analysis of the costs and benefits of conferring protection is too demanding for courts, there is scope for improving analytical precision beyond the existing tests.

In most jurisdictions, insubstantial works, such as titles or headlines, are not protected by copyright. But there is no consistency in the principles for denying protection, with courts variously finding that short works are not sufficiently original, consist of unprotectable ideas, or are not 'works'. Meanwhile, in *Meltwater*, UK courts have held that newspaper headlines are protectable as an author's 'own intellectual creation', with the *Infopaq I* ruling casting some doubt on previous UK cases denying copyright in insubstantial works. Courts denying protection to insubstantial works often take into account whether or not this material should be protected. We argue that there is merit in adopting an express *de minimis* rule that applies a multi-factor test, and takes into account the value of permission-free uses: [7.2.13].

International copyright law leaves it to national laws to determine whether to impose fixation as a condition for protection. While common law jurisdictions require that works be fixed to be protected, civil law jurisdictions generally do not. Therefore, non-fixed works, such as impromptu lectures or performances, are part of the public domain in jurisdictions requiring fixation, but may be protected where this is not a requirement. Where fixation is a prerequisite, there is a distinction between jurisdictions, notably the United States, that require a work to be fixed by or under the authority of an author, and jurisdictions such as the UK, where a work can be fixed by third parties. Where fixation is equated with authorship, works that are fixed otherwise than under the authority of the author, are part of the public domain.

The differences in national laws reflect different conceptual approaches, with authors' rights jurisdictions regarding protection as arising from creation, but common law jurisdictions regarding copyright as a reward for producing works in material form. From our instrumentalist perspective, we consider there is value in regarding copyright as a means for producing usable works. That said, the distinction between the two traditions should not be overstated: in civil law jurisdictions, fixation is often essential evidence in infringement cases and, in common law jurisdictions, performers' rights and the contemporary ubiquity of recording devices reduce the practical implications of the different approaches.

## 7.3 Works Impliedly Excluded from Copyright (Statutory 'Gaps')

Under international copyright law, the second element that sets the scope of works within Berne is the requirement that a work falls within a protected category: [4.6]. This section of the chapter explains how the second element is dealt with under national laws. While copyright laws define protectable subject matter, by doing so they also impliedly exclude certain 'works' from protection. This section of the chapter deals with category 2 of our fifteen categories by explaining how national laws impliedly exclude works from the scope of protected works.

Under Berne, Member States have considerable flexibility in determining the works to be protected; if a work falls within the enumerated list in Article 2(1) it must be protected, but members are free to add categories of works, creating much scope for national variations: [4.6]. Moreover, it is a matter for national laws to define the works that fall within protected categories and, by doing so, draw the line between protected and unprotected works. Overarching the entire area is the extent to which the history of copyright is, in part, a history of extending protection to new subject matter, especially in response to technological change, either by extending boundaries of existing categories of works or adding new categories.[127]

---

[127] See R. P. Merges, 'One hundred years of solicitude: intellectual property law 1900–2000' (2000) 88 *California Law Review* 2187.

A major distinction can be drawn between countries, such as the UK and Australia, which have a 'closed list' of protected categories, and civil law jurisdictions, which have a more flexible, 'open list' approach.[128]

### 7.3.1 'Closed List' Jurisdictions

The approach adopted to protected subject matter in most common law jurisdictions can be traced to the 1911 UK Act. The 1911 Act repealed previous subject specific Acts, bringing copyright protection for all works under one umbrella statute and, in doing so, introduced specific categories of protected works.

*UK and Australian Law* The UK Act, the CDPA, protects the following eight categories of works:
(a) original literary, dramatic, musical or artistic works;
(b) sound recordings, films or broadcasts; and
(c) the typographical arrangement of published editions.[129]
The Australian Act protects similar categories, but divides the categories into 'works', with original literary, dramatic, musical or artistic works being protected under Part III, and 'subject matter other than works', with sound recordings, films, broadcasts and published editions protected under Part IV.[130] This division broadly corresponds to that drawn between authors' rights and neighbouring or related rights in civil law systems: [4.2.1].

In countries such as the UK and Australia that adopt a 'closed list' approach, the classification or 'pigeonholing' exercise is of prime importance. If a work cannot be slotted into a category it is not protected. Moreover, in these jurisdictions, identifying the category in which a work belongs conditions much of the reasoning in copyright cases, including the analysis of infringement. This often leads to a formalistic focus on definitions, with some categories exhaustively defined in legislation, while others being left to the courts to flesh out.

In 'closed list' countries there are two main ways in which works slip through the 'gaps' and are therefore not protected. First, a work may clearly not match any of the listed categories, as might be the case, for example, with flower arrangements or 'living' sculptures.[131] Second,

---

[128] See T. Aplin, 'Subject matter', in E. Derclaye (ed.), *Research Handbook on the Future of EU Copyright* (Edward Elgar, 2009), pp. 49–76; J. Pila, 'Copyright and its categories of original works' (2010) 30(2) *Oxford Journal of Legal Studies* 229.
[129] CDPA, s. 1(1). [130] Copyright Act 1968 (Aus.), ss. 32, 89–92.
[131] S. Ricketson and C. Creswell, *The Law of Intellectual Property: Copyright, Designs and Confidential Information* (2nd rev. edn, Thomson Legal & Regulatory, 1999, ongoing electronic resource), [5.79].

a work may potentially be of a kind that could fall within one of the categories but, through a process of applying a 'closed' definition, is held to fall outside the categories; as might be the case, for example, with some utilitarian, mass-produced articles.

*'Works' Outside Defined Categories*  How 'works' escape protection by falling outside protected categories can be illustrated by two UK cases: *Creation Records*[132] and *Nova Productions*.[133] *Creation Records* concerned a collection of *'objets trouvés'* that had been assembled in and around a hotel swimming pool for the purpose of photographing an Oasis album cover. The problem facing the claimants was that the assemblage did not clearly fit within any of the 'closed list' categories; so they were forced to argue for expansive definitions, especially of the category of artistic works. As the CDPA exhaustively defines an 'artistic work',[134] the case focused on subcategories of artistic works. On this, arguments that the objects were a 'sculpture', 'collage' or 'work of artistic craftsmanship' were each dismissed. In reaching these conclusions, the Court applied a variety of techniques, including the use of dictionary definitions and reasoning by analogy with 'works' previously held to fall within a subcategory. The Court also had no difficulty in rejecting a claim that the scene was a dramatic work, as it was 'inherently static, having no movement, story or action'.[135]

*Nova Productions* concerned claims to copyright in an arcade video game. The claimants argued that the game was protected variously as an artistic work, literary works (design notes and a computer program), dramatic works and films. At first instance, Kitchin J held that the game was not a dramatic work because, like a television programme format,[136] it lacked 'sufficient unity to be capable of performance'.[137] The Court of Appeal held that copyright subsisted in each frame as an artistic work and the computer program as a literary work, but in neither case was there infringement. According to the Court, copyright could not subsist in an artistic work consisting of a series of frames (as opposed to an individual frame), as moving images are protected exclusively, if at all, as films.[138]

*Artistic Works*  Particular problems have arisen in determining the boundaries of an 'artistic work'. Under UK and Australian statutes, subcategories of artistic works (except for works of architecture and works

---

[132] *Creation Records* v. *News Group Newspapers* [1997] EMLR 444.
[133] *Nova Productions* v. *Mazooma Games* [2006] RPC 379; [2007] RPC 589.
[134] CDPA, s. 4(1).   [135] [1997] EMLR 444 at 448.
[136] See *Green* v. *Broadcasting Corporation of New Zealand* [1989] RPC 700.
[137] [2006] EWHC 24 at [116].   [138] [2007] EWCA Civ 290 at [17].

of artistic craftsmanship in the UK, and except for works of artistic craftsmanship in Australia) are protected whether 'of artistic quality or not'.[139] This reflects the principle known as the 'doctrine of avoidance',[140] which is that courts should refrain from making aesthetic judgements. As Justice Holmes put it in *Bleistein*:

> It would be a dangerous undertaking for persons trained only to the law to constitute themselves final judges of the worth of pictorial illustrations, outside the narrowest and most obvious limits.[141]

A difficulty arising from this principle is that it can result in courts protecting works outside the 'artistic' domain, such as utilitarian articles, on the basis they fall within a subcategory. The danger was realised in *Wham-O*,[142] where the New Zealand Court of Appeal held that the moulds for producing frisbees, and finished plastic frisbees, were protected as 'engravings'; and that wooden models of the frisbees were protected as 'sculptures'. In *Greenfield Products*,[143] however, Pincus J of the Australia Federal Court stepped back from this approach to conclude that moulds used to produce a drive mechanism for lawn mowers were not 'engravings'.[144] In that case, it was also claimed that the mechanism was a 'sculpture'. In rejecting this, Pincus J acknowledged that modern sculptures could include machine parts, but applied the 'ordinary meaning' of the word to conclude that the machine parts were not sculptures. The question remains, however, as to how a court can determine whether or not a work is an 'artistic work' without ruling on if it is 'artistic'?

These issues came before the UK Supreme Court in *Lucasfilm*,[145] which concerned a claim that the Stormtrooper helmet from the *Star Wars* film was a 'sculpture'. The Court held that the helmets were not sculptures, as each was 'utilitarian in the sense that it was an element in the process of production of the film'.[146] The Court, however, also approved judgments in the lower courts, which had rejected a comprehensive definition and, instead, applied a multi-factor test, emphasising the objective purpose of the object, namely its 'intrinsic quality of being intended to be enjoyed as a visual thing'.[147] Underlying these exercises in line drawing are concerns that copyright not protect purely functional articles, more appropriately protected under patent or industrial designs laws. But, in drawing lines, and despite the 'doctrine of

---

[139] CDPA, s. 4(1); Copyright Act 1968 (Aus) s. 10(1) (definition of 'artistic work').
[140] C. Farley, 'Judging art' (2005) 79 *Tulane Law Review* 805 at 814.
[141] *Bleistein* v. *Donaldson Lithographing Co.*, 188 US 239, 251 (1903).
[142] *Wham-O MFG Co.* v. *Lincoln Industries* [1984] 1 NZLR 641.
[143] *Greenfield Products Pty Ltd* v. *Scott Bonnar Ltd* (1990) 95 ALR 275.   [144] *Ibid.* 285.
[145] *Lucasfilm Ltd* v. *Ainsworth* [2012] 1 AC 208.   [146] *Ibid.* [44].
[147] *Lucasfilm Ltd* v. *Ainsworth* [2010] Ch 503 [75] (per Jacob LJ).

avoidance', it seems that the courts are invariably drawn to criteria involving aesthetic considerations.[148]

### 7.3.2 'Open List' Jurisdictions

The 'closed list' approach has been criticised for lacking flexibility and discriminating against creative works that fall in gaps between protected categories.[149] On the other hand, the 'open list' approach may lead to uncertainty and a lack of restraint in defining copyright subject matter.[150]

*French Law* As is clear from French law, a good example of the 'open list' approach, there remains a need for courts to determine what is and is not protectable, and therefore to 'impliedly' exclude works. While Article L112-1 of the Intellectual Property Code protects 'the rights of authors in all works of the mind (*œuvres de l'esprit*), whatever their kind, form of expression, merit or purpose',[151] Article L112-2 gives a non-exhaustive, illustrative list of protected categories, generally reflecting Article 2 of Berne, but with no further attempt to define the categories. A notable addition to the Article 2 Berne list in the French illustrative list is 'creations of the seasonal industries of dress and articles of fashion' (*les créations des industries saisonnières de l'habillement et de la parure*), which are not protected to the same extent in most other jurisdictions.

In contrast to the 'closed list' approach, French law can extend protection to new forms of creative expression, such as Christo's wrapped landscapes.[152] The difficulties in drawing lines between protected and unprotected subject matter in 'open list' jurisdictions can be seen in controversial cases dealing with copyright in the fragrance of perfumes. In 2006, the Cour d'Appel de Paris held that the 'original' scent of a perfume was protected as a 'work of the mind', especially as French law protects such works 'whatever their kind, form of expression, merit or purpose'.[153] Subsequently, the Dutch Supreme Court upheld a finding

---

[148] For a similar argument on the inevitability of aesthetic judgements under US copyright law, see R. Walker and B. Depoorter, 'Unavoidable aesthetic judgments in copyright law: a community of practice standard' (2015) 109(2) *Northwestern University Law Review* 343.

[149] A. Christie. 'A proposal for simplifying United Kingdom copyright law' [2001] *European Intellectual Property Review* 26.

[150] See especially the discussion in Aplin, 'Subject matter'.

[151] Code de la propriété intellectuelle (France), Art. L112-1.

[152] CA Paris, 13 March 1986, D, 1987, SC, p. 150, C. Columbet obs. (wrapping of Pont-Neuf).

[153] *L'Oréal* v. *Bellure* [2006] ECDR 16.

that the scent of perfume was protected, as the work was 'perceptible to humans, possessed an original character, and bore the personal stamp of its creator'.[154] Meanwhile, however, the French Cour de Cassation ruled that perfume fragrance was not a creative form of expression that was proper copyright subject matter.[155] While the decisions conferring copyright on perfumes were subject to much criticism,[156] the cases illustrate the problems encountered in applying an open-ended approach.

*US Law* Unlike other common law jurisdictions, the United States applies an 'open list' approach, protecting all original 'works of authorship' that are fixed, while providing an inclusive list of the following eight categories: literary works; musical works; dramatic works; pantomimes and choreographic works; pictorial, graphic and sculptural works; motion pictures and other audiovisual works; sound recordings; and architectural works.[157] Of these categories, four – literary works; pictorial, graphic and sculptural works; audiovisual works; and sound recordings – are further defined.[158] For example, 'pictorial, graphic and sculptural works' are defined, in part, to include 'works of artistic craftsmanship in so far as their form but not their mechanical or utilitarian aspects are concerned', thereby addressing fundamental difficulties in distinguishing artistic form from utilitarian function.[159] US courts have, however, been divided in their interpretation of the requirement that, to be protected, artistic features must be separable from an article's utilitarian aspects,[160] which presents difficulties for all copyright laws.

While the US Act applies an 'open list' approach, the history of protected works in the United States has been that new forms of subject matter, such as computer programs (literary works) and video games (audiovisual works), have been protected as falling within the listed categories rather than relying on the open-ended definition.[161] As in other common law jurisdictions, therefore, US courts tend to determine whether doubtful subject matter is protected by reasoning from analogy with existing works. Moreover, despite the application of an 'open list'

---

[154] *Kecofa* v. *Lancôme* [2006] ECDR 26; Seville, 'Copyright in perfumes: smelling a rat', 51.
[155] *Bsiri-Barbir* v. *Haarman & Reimer* [2006] ECDR 28.
[156] H. Jehoram, 'The Dutch Supreme Court recognises copyright in the scent of a perfume. The Flying Dutchman: all sails, no anchor' (2006) 28 *European Intellectual Property Review* 629; Seville, 'Copyright in perfumes: smelling a rat'.
[157] 17 USC §102(a) (2012).    [158] 17 USC §101 (2012).
[159] The definition applies the approach to works of applied art endorsed by the Supreme Court in *Mazer* v. *Stein*, 347 US 201 (1954).
[160] Goldstein and Hugenholtz, *International Copyright*, [6.1.2.10].
[161] See Aplin, 'Subject matter', 75.

7.3 Works Impliedly Excluded from Copyright (Statutory 'Gaps') 213

approach, protection of works in the United States is limited by the restrictive approach taken to the requirement of fixation [7.2.14].

### 7.3.3 Works Impliedly Excluded and the Public Domain

The scope of 'works' protected under national copyright laws is broad, ranging from software and databases to buildings, sound recordings and broadcasts, and in some jurisdictions extending to conceptual art or even perfumes. The history of copyright has seen ongoing expansion of the categories of protected works, especially in response to technological change. In this, there often appears to have been an implicit presumption favouring protection, with uncertainties sometimes being clarified by the legislature. For example, in the EU there is limited harmonisation of copyright subject matter but, to address uncertainties, the protection of computer programs and databases was harmonised in directives.[162]

Regardless of whether a 'closed list' or 'open list' approach is taken, outside of conventional subject matter there are considerable difficulties in distinguishing protectable from non-protectable creations. A major source of difficulty lies in the limitations of courts in distinguishing 'creative' from 'non-creative' productions, especially where, applying the 'doctrine of avoidance', they avoid aesthetic judgements. Nevertheless, particularly in distinguishing artistic works from three-dimensional functional articles, it seems that the courts are invariably drawn to implicit aesthetic considerations. A continuing source of difficulty arises, in the context of artistic works, from the challenges facing courts dealing with changes in the social understanding of creative practices.

While a 'closed list' approach has the advantages of certainty and greater potential restraint over the scope of copyright subject matter, in the case of borderline or novel subject matter, such as 'video games', closed definitions can lead to the courts applying strained reasoning or 'interpretative gymnastics'.[163] While the 'open list' approach gives courts more flexibility, it creates the risk of overprotection; although, in practice, courts in 'open list' jurisdictions also often engage in classification-like exercises.[164]

Overall, given the significant scope of existing copyright subject matter, we argue there are advantages, especially from the perspective of the public domain, in a 'closed list' approach, with decisions about protecting

---

[162] See Database Directive; Software Directive. The Software Directive does not, however, define a 'computer program'.
[163] Aplin, 'Subject matter', 70.   [164] *Ibid.* 74.

'new' subject matter being left to legislatures. That alone would not, however, remove the problems identified above, and in most jurisdictions there is scope for refining definitions of protected categories of works. In addition, it seems to us that there is potential for improvements in the criteria, whether explicit or implicit, applied by courts in determining whether 'creations' fall within protected categories, and particularly in distinguishing between 'artistic' and purely functional works. In general, therefore, we conclude that the public domain could be supported by more certainty in the boundary between protected works and works 'impliedly' excluded.

## 7.4 Conclusion

This chapter has focused on how the two main elements that set the scope of works falling within Berne – the minimum threshold for protection and the requirement that a work falls within a protected category – are dealt with under national laws. In doing so, it has explained the considerable complexities in how these elements are dealt with by national copyright laws, and the variations in the laws, leading to variations in national public domains. The chapter has suggested ways in which our approach, in providing a public domain perspective on these aspects of copyright law, has the potential to assist in addressing fundamental problems in distinguishing protected and non-protected works, and potentially dealing with significant differences between national laws.

# 8 Works Outside Copyright Protection – Part II

| | | |
|---|---|---|
| 8.1 | Introduction | 215 |
| 8.2 | Works Expressly Excluded | 215 |
| 8.3 | Constitutional and 'Human Rights' Limitations | 227 |
| 8.4 | Public Policy and *Ordre public* Exclusions | 236 |
| 8.5 | Public Interest Exceptions | 241 |
| 8.6 | Conclusion | 244 |

## 8.1 Introduction

The previous chapter addressed works that are not protected because they fail to meet minimum requirements for copyright protection or they fall outside the scope of protectable works. Works that satisfy these requirements may, nevertheless, still fall outside of copyright because they are excluded from protection. This chapter examines works that are not protected by copyright because: they are expressly excluded from protection (**category 3**); they are excluded by national constitutional law (**category 4**); or they are excluded (or otherwise limited) on the grounds of public policy or public interest considerations (**categories 7 and 8**). As the chapter explains, the main justifications for excluding copyright, or limiting the exercise of copyright, in these categories are to protect freedom of expression or freedom of the media, which are essential public domain values: [1.7].

## 8.2 Works Expressly Excluded

Berne includes express exclusions from protected works, with one mandatory exclusion and two optional exclusions: [5.3]. The mandatory exclusion, in Article 2(8), excludes 'news of the day', while the optional provisions allow for the exclusion of laws and other official texts (Article 2(4)) and political speeches (Article 2*bis*(1)). This section gives examples of the variety of implementations of these exclusions in national laws. These diverse approaches sometimes mean that a mandatory or permissible exclusion is implemented as an exception to infringement rather than an exclusion. The difference is that with an exclusion there is no copyright in the work but, with an exception, copyright subsists but uses of the work are excused from infringement. This chapter deals with these national implementations, regardless of whether they are implemented as exclusions or exceptions. Other exceptions are covered in Chapters 11 and 12.

### 8.2.1 'News of the Day' and Related Exceptions

The preferred interpretation of the mandatory exclusion of 'news of the day' by Article 2(8) of Berne is that it implements the principle that copyright does not protect facts, and not that it applies to exclude works that would otherwise be protected: [5.3.1]. Article 2(8) is supplemented by four other provisions. Article 10*bis*(1) makes it a matter for national legislation to permit reproduction and public communication of newspaper and periodical articles on current economic, political or religious topics: [5.3.1]. Article 10*bis*(2) makes it a matter for national legislation to allow use of works in reporting current events by film or broadcast: [5.4.2]. Article 2*bis*(1) allows for national legislation to exclude political speeches, which obviously assists news media: [5.3.3], and Article 2*bis*(2) makes it a matter for national legislation to determine the conditions under which public lectures and the like may be reproduced by media organisations 'when such use is justified by the informatory purpose': [5.4.2].

There are considerable variations in how national laws deal with these mandatory and permissible media-related exceptions.

*EU Law, Germany and France* Under EU law, optional exceptions (as opposed to an exclusion) for the press and media are provided for under Articles 5(3)(c) and 5(3)(f) of the InfoSoc Directive,[1] which partially harmonises copyright exceptions: [11.2]. Article 5(3)(c) first provides for exceptions for reproduction by the press, or the public communication, of published articles on current economic, political or religious topics. Second, it allows for exceptions for 'use of works or other subject-matter in connection with the reporting of current events, to the extent justified by the informatory purpose'. The two parts of Article 5(3)(c) closely reflect Articles 10*bis*(1) and 10*bis*(2) of Berne. Article 5(3)(f) of the InfoSoc Directive, which is based on Article 2*bis*(1) of Berne, allows for exceptions for the 'use of political speeches as well as

---

[1] Full titles and citations of all Directives are in the Table of International Instruments.

## 8.2 Works Expressly Excluded

extracts of public lectures or similar works or subject-matter to the extent justified by the informatory purpose'.

The differences in the implementation of Articles 5(3)(c) and 5(3)(f) in EU Member States illustrate the extent of national variations in media exceptions. Use of works for reporting news is generally permitted in EU Member States, but the details vary considerably. For example, Article 44(1) of the Austrian law allows for articles in a newspaper or periodical concerning 'current economic, political or religious issues' to be 'reproduced and distributed in other newspapers and periodicals', except where such reproduction is expressly prohibited; and Article 44(2) provides that such articles may also be publicly delivered and broadcast.[2] Article 44(3), however, specifically provides that press reports containing 'simple communications', which refers to 'news of the day', are not protected by copyright; but, under Article 79(1), press reports may not be reproduced in newspapers or periodicals until at least twelve hours has elapsed from their initial publication.

Article 49(1) of the German law provides that it is permissible to reproduce and distribute broadcast commentaries and individual articles from newspapers if they concern 'political, economic or religious issues of the day'; but unless the material consists of short extracts in the form of an overview, equitable remuneration must be paid to the author.[3] Distinguishing articles from facts, however, Article 49(2) provides that it is permissible to reproduce, distribute and publicly communicate 'miscellaneous information relating to facts or news of the day' which has already been publicly disseminated by the press or by broadcasting. Moreover, Article 48 makes it permissible to reproduce in newspapers or like journals, or communicate to the public, public speeches on issues of the day; but this does not extend to reproduction of speeches published in a collection of speeches by the author.

The French Intellectual Property Code, in Article L122-5(3), provides that, so long as the author and source are attributed, it is permissible to use works in press reviews or to disseminate public speeches made to political, administrative, judicial or academic gatherings, even in their entirety.[4] In addition, Article L122-5(9) allows for the reproduction, for information purposes, of a work of graphical, plastic or architectural art by means of the written press, audiovisual media or the online press, provided the author is attributed.

---

[2] Federal Law on Copyright in Works of Literature and Art and on Related Rights (Urheberrechtsgesetz – UrhG) (BGB1. No. 111/1936 as amended) (Austria), Art. 44.
[3] Law on Copyright and Neighbouring Rights (Urheberrechtsgesetz – UrhG) (Germany), Art. 49.
[4] Code de la propriété intellectuelle (France), Art. L122-5.

*UK Law* In the UK, where there are no general exceptions for 'news of the day', the media exceptions are dealt with mainly by the principle that there is no copyright in facts and by fair dealing exceptions. The approach is illustrated by *Walter* v. *Steinkopff*,[5] where the proprietors of *The Times* brought an action for copyright infringement against a rival newspaper for reproduction of extracts from a newspaper article by Kipling. Holding that the use was infringing, North J stated:

> It is said that there is no copyright in news. But there is or may be copyright in the particular forms of language or modes of expression by which information is conveyed, and not the less so because the information may be with respect to the current events of the day.[6]

The Court went on to find that the infringement could not be justified by a general custom of newspapers copying from one another without permission. In *Express Newspapers*,[7] however, Browne-Wilkinson VC observed that the courts would not find that a newspaper had a monopoly on news 'as opposed to the actual words used by its reporter' and suggested that a monopoly could be avoided by either the fair dealing defences or finding an implied licence.[8]

Section 30(2) of the UK CDPA[9] provides that copyright is not infringed by a fair dealing with a work (other than a photograph) for the purpose of reporting current events, provided sufficient acknowledgement of the work and author is made.[10] UK courts have taken a liberal approach in determining what amounts to a 'current' event[11] with, for example, the Court of Appeal holding it arguable that the death of Princess Diana was current a year afterwards.[12] In *Ashdown*, the Court of Appeal held that a liberal interpretation was justified as s. 30(2) is 'intended to protect the role of the media in informing the public about matters of current concern to the public'.[13]

The exception is not a blanket exemption, as it applies only where the dealing is 'fair'. In *Ashdown*, the Court of Appeal further held that, while in most circumstances freedom of expression would be adequately protected by the fact/expression dichotomy and fair dealing exceptions, there could be rare occasions where, pursuant to the Human Rights Act 1998 (UK), the right to freedom of expression

---

[5] [1892] 3 Ch 489.   [6] [1892] 3 Ch 489 at 495.
[7] *Express Newspapers plc* v. *News (UK) Ltd* [1990] 1 WLR 1320.
[8] [1990] 1 WLR 1320 at 1325.
[9] Copyright, Designs and Patents Act 1988 (UK) ('CDPA'), s. 30(2).
[10] CDPA, ss. 30(2), 178.
[11] *Pro Sieben A.G.* v. *Carlton Television Ltd* [1999] 1 WLR 605 at 614.
[12] *Hyde Park Residence Ltd* v. *Yelland* [2001] Ch 143.
[13] *Ashdown* v. *Telegraph Group Ltd* [2002] Ch 149 at [64].

### 8.2 Works Expressly Excluded

requires verbatim use of a work, even where this would not be a fair dealing.[14]

Apart from fair dealing for reporting news, uses of copyright works by the media may be protected by the fair dealing exception for the purposes of criticism or review or by the common law public interest defence.[15] In *Ashdown*, the Court rejected an argument that the public interest defence should be narrowly confined: [8.5.1].

Under the CDPA, the speaker is the author of the literary work constituting the speech once it is recorded.[16] A specific defence applies to protect media reports against claims for infringement of speeches for the purposes of reporting the speech to the public. The defence protects the use of a record of the literary work constituting the speech for the purpose of reporting current events or communicating the work to the public. It applies where the following conditions are satisfied: the record is a direct record of the speech and not taken from another recording; the speaker must not have prohibited the recording; the speaker or any other copyright owner must not have prohibited the use; and the use of the recording must be permitted by the person in lawful possession of the record.[17] Even without this defence, the author of a speech given in public, such as a politician, is likely to be found to have impliedly licensed reports of the speech.[18]

*Australian Law*  Australian law is similar to UK law in that there is no general exemption for 'news of the day', leaving the media to be protected by fact/expression and the fair dealing defences. The Australian fair dealing defences are, however, worded differently from the UK defences: [11.4.2]. Section 42(1) of the Australian Act provides that copyright in a work is not infringed by a fair dealing for the purpose of reporting news in a newspaper, magazine or similar periodical, or by reporting of news by means of a communication or in a film;[19] and s. 103B establishes an equivalent defence for sound recordings, films and broadcasts.[20]

As Australia has no equivalent to the UK Human Rights Act, there is no human rights foundation for holding that uses outside of the fair dealing exceptions may be excepted, such as under a broad public interest

---

[14] *Ibid.* [79].
[15] CDPA, ss. 30(1), 171(3). On the application of the fair dealing exception for criticism or review to the media, see Cornish, Llewelyn and Aplin, *Intellectual Property*, [14.04]–[14.05].
[16] CDPA, ss. 3(2), 3(3).   [17] CDPA, s. 58(2).
[18] Cornish, Llewelyn and Aplin, *Intellectual Property*, [14.07].
[19] Copyright Act 1968 (Aus.), s. 42(1).
[20] Copyright Act 1968 (Aus.), ss. 103B, 100A (definition of 'audio-visual item').

exception. There is limited authority on the Australian exception, but the 1980 *Defence Papers* case[21] is a good example of some difficulties. That case concerned an application to restrain unauthorised publication by the press of extracts from official defence documents. In opposing the application, the newspapers claimed that publication fell within the fair dealing or the public interest exceptions. Although Mason J took a liberal approach to interpreting 'news', he granted an interlocutory injunction, mainly on the basis of the difficulties in finding that a dealing with unpublished works could be 'fair'.

In another case, *De Garis*,[22] a press clipping service, which provided subscribers with hard copies of news articles, claimed that this was fair dealing for the purposes of research or study, criticism or review, or reporting news: [11.4.2]. In deciding that the exceptions did not apply, Beaumont J adopted a broad definition of what might amount to 'news', but also held that the exception could have no application in these circumstances as there was no report in a 'newspaper, magazine or similar periodical'. The difficulties in applying the exception are also illustrated by judgments of the Full Federal Court in *TCN Channel Nine*,[23] which concerned the use of 'clips' from television programmes by a light entertainment programme featuring a panel of discussants. While the Court agreed that 'news' might be entertaining, the judges differed on whether the appearance of the Australian Prime Minister on a light entertainment programme was, in itself, newsworthy or whether it was purely entertainment.[24]

*Chinese Law* In China, reprinting or abstracting of works published in newspapers or periodicals by other newspapers or periodicals is allowed, unless the author has opted out,[25] in accordance with Berne Article 10*bis*(1). The 2014 proposed reforms retain these provisions.[26] However, a newspaper or periodical can opt out from such republication 'where they have made an indication that they prohibit reprinting or republishing in a clear position in newspapers or periodicals they publish'.[27] It seems that the opt out must be placed in the text of a newspaper or periodical; it will not be sufficient for it to be indicated

---

[21] *The Commonwealth of Australia* v. *John Fairfax & Sons Ltd* (1980) 147 CLR 39.
[22] *De Garis* v. *Neville Jeffress Pidler* (1990) 95 ALR 625.
[23] *TCN Channel Nine Pty Ltd* v. *Network Ten Ltd* (2002) 55 IPR 112.
[24] Sundberg and Hely JJ held that the Prime Minister singing did not amount to 'news', while Finkelstein J concluded that the bringing of the Prime Minister's behaviour to the attention of viewers constituted news reporting.
[25] Copyright Law (China), Art. 33(2); Implementing Regulations (China), Arts. 30, 32.
[26] 2014 Draft Copyright Law (China), Art. 48.
[27] 2014 Draft Copyright Law (China), Art. 48, para 2.

by some technological measure such as a robot exclusion clause in the metadata of a website of a newspaper or periodical.[28]

*Other Jurisdictions* Common law jurisdictions, such as the UK and Australia, differ from most civil law jurisdictions in not providing broad exemptions for 'news'. Apart from the EU jurisdictions dealt with above, most other non-Commonwealth jurisdictions have variations of an express exclusion for 'news of the day', including, for example, China,[29] the Philippines,[30] Israel[31] and jurisdictions such as Russia, Kazakhstan, the Ukraine and Belarus.[32]

In the United States, there are no express exemptions for 'news of the day' or related exceptions. In *Harper & Row*,[33] moreover, the Supreme Court rejected an argument that the First Amendment required expansive interpretation of the fair use exception to encompass dissemination of news of public importance: [8.3.1]. Like other common law jurisdictions, 'news of the day' and related permissible exceptions are therefore dealt with under US law by means of internal copyright doctrines, especially fact/expression and the fair use exception.

### 8.2.2 Legal and Official Texts

Article 2(4) of Berne makes it a matter for national legislation to determine the protection granted to 'official texts of a legislative, administrative and legal nature, and to official translations of such texts'. This provision was a compromise reflecting differences in approach to protecting these texts between, on the one hand, most Berne countries and, on the other, British Commonwealth jurisdictions.

While the optional exclusion clearly applies to official texts of statutes and judgments delivered by courts, there is uncertainty about the scope of other material that may fall within it, arising from difficulties in determining what may or may not amount to an 'official text' that is of a 'legal nature'. For example, does an 'official text' encompass legal texts prepared by private parties, such as codes of practice, or submissions to legal

---

[28] This was left unresolved by the Supreme Peoples' Court, Explanations of Application of Law in Trials of Computer Network Copyright Disputes, November 2000, particularly Art. 3: see Xue Hong and Zheng Chengsi, *Chinese Intellectual Property Law in the 21st Century* (Sweet & Maxwell Asia, 2002), pp. 69–71.
[29] Copyright Law of the People's Republic of China, Art. 5(2).
[30] Intellectual Property Code of the Philippines [Republic Act No. 8293], s. 175.
[31] Copyright Act 2007 (Israel), s. 5(5).
[32] See J. Pilch, 'Fair use and beyond: the status of copyright limitations and exceptions in the Commonwealth of Independent States' (2004) 65(6) *College & Research Libraries* 468.
[33] *Harper & Row, Publishers Inc. v. Nation Enterprises Inc.*, 471 US 539 (1985).

committees such as commissions of inquiry?[34] While Article 2(4) implies that an unsolicited translation by a private party is outside the scope of the exclusion, its application to a translation of a legal text prepared by a private party at the request of an official body, or adopted by it, is open to question.[35] Berne members retain considerable flexibility in interpreting the scope of the exclusion.

While a majority of jurisdictions exclude statutes, judicial opinions and other official texts from copyright, in the UK and most Commonwealth countries these documents remain protected by the doctrines of Crown and Parliamentary copyright. That said, access to government and official material in these jurisdictions is now usually available either through open content licences allowing its reproduction, or simply by free access publication (without any express licence for republication), either by government bodies or by third parties such as legal information institutes.

*Countries with Express Exclusions* Most national laws exclude statutes, judicial opinions and other official texts from copyright; with many also applying a reduced level of protection to other official public documents, such as government reports.[36]

Official texts, and translations of them, are not mentioned in the EU InfoSoc Directive, Article 5 because the article deals with 'exceptions and limitations' and not exclusions from copyright. Laws of most EU Member States utilise this exclusion. For example, Article 5(1) of the German law expressly excludes '[l]aws, ordinances, official decrees and notices', as well as 'decisions and official grounds of decisions' from copyright protection.[37] In addition, Article 5(2) excludes 'other official texts published in the official interest for general information purposes' subject to requirements that, in using these works, the texts must not be altered and the sources must be acknowledged.

Outside of the EU, China's copyright law expressly excludes certain governmental documents ('laws and regulations, resolutions, decisions and orders of State organs, other documents of a legislative, administrative or judicial nature and their official translations').[38] Similarly,

---

[34] Ricketson and Ginsburg, *International Copyright and Neighbouring Rights*, [8.108].
[35] Goldstein and Hugenholtz, *International Copyright*, [6.1.3.2] consider this a 'vexed question'.
[36] *Ibid.*
[37] Law on Copyright and Neighbouring Rights (Urheberrechtsgesetz – UrhG) (Germany), Art. 5.
[38] Copyright Law of the People's Republic of China, Art. 5(1) provides that copyright does not protect the following: laws; regulations; resolutions; decisions or orders of state organs; other documents of a legislative, administrative, or judicial nature; and official translations of such works.

## 8.2 Works Expressly Excluded

Article 13 of the Japanese Copyright Act exempts a broad range of government documents from copyright, including: the Constitution, laws and regulations; government notices; judgments, decisions, decrees and orders of the courts; and translations and compilations of these documents.[39] Some Commonwealth jurisdictions like New Zealand and India (discussed below), also have either exclusions or exceptions.

*The United States* Of the common law jurisdictions, the United States has long exempted judicial decisions and statutes from copyright protection. The distinctive US approach can be traced to the landmark 1834 Supreme Court decision in *Wheaton* v. *Peters*,[40] where the Court held that 'no reporter has or can have any copyright in the written opinions delivered by this court; and that the judges thereof cannot confer on any reporter any such right.'[41] Subsequently, in *Banks* v. *Manchester*, the Supreme Court offered the following rationale for exempting law reports:

> The whole work done by the judges constitutes the authentic exposition and interpretation of the law, which, binding every citizen, is free for publication to all, whether it is a declaration of unwritten law, or an interpretation of a constitution or statute.[42]

This tradition is embodied in section 105 of the US Act, which provides that copyright 'is not available for any work of the United States Government', with such works being defined by section 101 as 'a work prepared by an officer or employee of the United States Government as part of that person's official duties'.[43] Significantly, the exemption applies only to federal government works, and does not extend to the works of state and local governments; and while legal precedent suggests that at least the text of state statutes and judicial opinions cannot be subject to copyright, there is inconsistency in state practices. Moreover, the exemption does not extend to works prepared by those who are not government officers or employees, such as private contractors. Given that copyright may subsist in such works, the US government may obtain copyright in privately prepared works.

The exclusion of US government works from copyright protection does not necessarily ensure access. For example, West Publishing was for some time able to assert a de facto monopoly in law reports by successfully claiming compilation copyright and copyright in its 'star pagination'

---

[39] Copyright Act (Act No. 48 of 6 May, 1970, as amended) (Japan), Art. 13.
[40] 33 US (8 Pet.) 591 (1834).   [41] 33 US (8 Pet.) 591 at 668 (1834).
[42] 128 US 244 at 253 (1888).   [43] 17 USC §§101, 105.

citation system.[44] In *Matthew Bender*, however, the Second Circuit applied the *Feist* originality standard: [7.2.3], to hold that West's arrangements and its insertion of citations indicating page locations lacked the requisite 'creativity' for copyright protection.[45] Nevertheless, and despite freedom of information laws, the US government remains able to restrict access to documents in which there is no copyright on grounds such as national security and export control.

*Commonwealth Jurisdictions* In the UK and most Commonwealth jurisdictions, as influenced by the 1911 UK Act,[46] official government texts are protected under the doctrines of Crown and Parliamentary copyright. The position is not, however, uniform across the Commonwealth.

As there is no exclusion of government documents in the UK, the Crown would have been entitled to copyright under usual principles of copyright law, but there are also special protections under doctrines of Crown privilege, statutory Crown copyright and statutory Parliamentary copyright.[47] Most Crown copyright material is available for re-use through the Open Government Licence and the UK Government Licensing Framework: [15.5]. The Re-use of Public Sector Information Regulations 2015 (the 'PSI Regulations') establish principles and rules for public sector bodies responding to requests for re-use of public sector information, making re-use (at marginal cost) mandatory in most cases. Use of material covered by Parliamentary copyright is governed by the Open Parliament Licence,[48] which is intended to allow such material to be used freely and flexibly, and consistently with the Open Government Licence.

Under Australian law, there is similar protection as in the UK, and government works are protected by general copyright law, the Crown prerogative rights and statutory Crown copyright, with many complexities remaining unresolved.[49] In Australia, government materials are most

---

[44] See *West Publishing Co.* v. *Mead Data Central, Inc.*, 799 F 2d 1219 (8th Cir 1986); *Oasis Publishing Co.* v. *West Publishing Co.*, 924 F Supp 918 (D Minn 1996).
[45] *Matthew Bender & Co.* v. *West Publishing Co.*, 158 F 3d 674 (2nd Cir 1998); *Matthew Bender & Co.* v. *West Publishing Co.*, 158 F 3d 693 (2nd Cir 1998). See E. Jarrah, 'Victory for the public: West Publishing loses its copyright battle over star pagination and compilation elements' (2000) 25 *University of Dayton Law Review* 163.
[46] U. Suthersanen, 'The first global Copyright Act', in U. Suthersanen and Y. Gendreau (eds.), *A Shifting Empire: 100 Years of the Copyright Act 1911* (Edward Elgar, 2013).
[47] See the Online Supplement for details.
[48] See www.parliament.uk/site-information/copyright-parliament/open-parliament-licence/.
[49] See the Online Supplement for details.

## 8.2 Works Expressly Excluded

often available for re-use through the official adoption by Australian governments of Creative Commons licences: [15.5].

There are important differences in approaches taken to Crown copyright in other Commonwealth jurisdictions. For example, the New Zealand Act provides that there is no copyright in legislation and judgments, and also excludes Parliamentary debates and reports from copyright protection.[50] In contrast, under Canadian law, government documents are protected by general copyright law, the royal prerogative and statutory Crown copyright, with section 12 of the Canadian Act preserving prerogative rights in judicial decisions and legislation.[51] In 2014, the Canadian federal government adopted the Directive on Open Government, which is designed to maximise the release of government information and data, as part of its Action Plan on Government 2.0.[52] In accordance with this Directive, free access to government information is provided by the Open Government Licence – Canada,[53] which, like the UK Open Government Licence, is not a Creative Commons Licence, but is compatible with Creative Commons.[54]

India adopts yet another approach. The Indian Act, like other Commonwealth jurisdictions, starts from the position that the government owns copyright in any 'Government work',[55] including any works made or published by or under the direction or control of any Indian government, department, legislature, court or tribunal.[56] However, it then excepts from infringement any reproduction of legislation, case law, law reform reports or similar official reports (in broad terms),[57] with limited exceptions.[58] Copyright law is therefore not an impediment to legal publications, whether online or paper-based.

Despite continuing legal complexities arising from Crown and Parliamentary copyright, the reality in most Commonwealth countries is that the online reproduction of legislation and case law is – one way or

---

[50] Copyright Act 1994 (NZ), s. 27(1).
[51] Copyright Act, RSC 1985, c. C-42 (Canada), s. 12. See E. Judge, 'Crown Copyright and copyright reform in Canada', in Geist (ed.), *In the Public Interest*, 550–94.
[52] Government of Canada, Directive on Open Government, 9 October 2014, www.tbs-sct.gc.ca/pol/dcc-eng.aspx?id=28108.
[53] Government of Canada, Open Government Licence – Canada (OGL- C 2.0), http://open.canada.ca/en/open-government-licence-canada.
[54] K. Mewhort, 'Creative Commons Licenses: options for Canadian open data providers', Canadian Internet Policy and Public Interest Clinic (CIPPIC), 1 June 2012.
[55] For details, see R. Singh et al., *Iyengar's Commentary on The Copyright Act* (7th edn, Universal Law Publishing Company, 2010), pp. 62–3.
[56] Copyright Act 1957 (India), s.2(k). [57] Copyright Act 1957 (India), s.52(q).
[58] Legislation must be accompanied by commentary 'or any other original matter' (which might include hypertext links), and publication of cases must not be prohibited by judicial order.

another – permitted and often assisted by government and judicial bodies, especially under open access policies, and at least where it is carried out on websites dedicated to legal content.

### 8.2.3 Works Expressly Excluded and the Public Domain

Within the framework established by international copyright law, the main express exclusions from copyright protection under national laws are for 'news of the day', political speeches and government information, including laws and other official texts. These exclusions recognise the importance of uses of this material for freedom of expression, freedom of the media, and the public right to access this information.[59] In particular, exclusions are important where the use of expression, and not merely facts or ideas, is necessary, such as accurately to report news or information, or properly to criticise or evaluate news or information. Moreover, freedom of expression and access to information that is in the copyright public domain are central to democratic processes and an informed citizenry: [1.7].[60]

Our analysis of exclusions for 'news of the day', and other permissible exclusions for the media, indicates that most national jurisdictions fail to take full advantage of the scope for exclusions permitted under international copyright law. While the mandatory exclusion in Article 2*bis*(1) of Berne is best interpreted as embodying the fact/expression dichotomy, which is implemented in some form in all national laws, there is much scope for the permissible media exclusions to be implemented in broader national exclusions or exceptions. This seems particularly so in most common law jurisdictions, where permission-free uses of 'news' and political information depend mainly on the application of the fact/expression dichotomy and fair dealing or fair use exceptions.

That said, especially given the low costs of copying and making available content online, there is a difficult balance between encouraging dissemination of news and related content while not undermining incentives for producing news, especially given the substantial challenges facing traditional media.[61] After all, copyright protection can advance the objectives of freedom of expression and freedom of the media by ensuring financial

---

[59] See, generally, P. B. Hugenholtz (ed.), *The Future of Copyright in a Digital Environment* (Kluwer Law International, 1996); N. Netanel, 'Locating copyright within the First Amendment skein' (2001) 54 *Stanford Law Review* 1.

[60] See M. Birnhack, 'More or better? Shaping the public domain', in Guibault and Hugenholtz (eds.), *The Future of the Public Domain*.

[61] See M. Stanganelli, 'Spreading the news online: a fine balance of copyright and freedom of expression in news aggregation' (2012) 34(11) *European Intellectual Property Review* 745.

returns for the creation of content. This consideration might suggest that, in this context, rather than blanket exclusions, it may be preferable to use exceptions as a means to promote the public domain values of freedom of communication and access to information. In any case, from our public domain perspective, we believe there is a good case for common law jurisdictions to implement clearer or more precise exceptions than the general fair dealing or fair use exceptions as, especially due to their uncertain application, general exceptions may not always be effective against practices such as attempts to use copyright to censor content.

From our perspective, analysis of exclusions for official texts, such as statutes and legal judgments, is more straightforward. As there is no need for incentives for the production of these works, there is a strong case for them to be made available free of copyright. The only possible case for some form of protection is as a means for asserting some control over the integrity and quality of government information. As there are other means to achieve this objective, such as the incentive for republishers to maintain their reputation,[62] we believe there is a good case for abolition of Crown and Parliamentary copyright in jurisdictions such as the UK and Australia. While the worst effects of government control of copyright in jurisdictions without express exclusions are being addressed by open licensing policies, unnecessary uncertainties and complexities can be addressed by clear express exclusions, which would benefit both government processes and public access to government information.

## 8.3 Constitutional and 'Human Rights' Limitations

It might be thought that international copyright law, which generally establishes floors on protection but no ceiling, might prevent further limitations on copyright protection. National copyright laws, however, are not enclosed systems, but operate in the broader context of national legal systems, including legal norms that may conflict with copyright.[63] Therefore, in addition to works not protected as a result of 'internal' copyright limits, such as express exclusions or exceptions, it is necessary to take into account 'external' legal limits, particularly those imposed by national constitutional laws.

This section of the chapter identifies and examines constitutional (and like) limits that support the public domain in the United States and Europe. These two jurisdictions are used as case studies for the influence

---

[62] Copyright Law Review Committee (CLRC), *Crown Copyright*, Copyright Law Review Committee, Barton, ACT (2005), 53 ff.
[63] Goldstein and Hugenholtz, *International Copyright*, [11.6].

of constitutional law, especially limitations based on protecting fundamental rights, on copyright laws. As explained below, the position in Europe is complex as a result of rights-based limitations imposed under EU law, but also those imposed on members of the Council of Europe. The section also refers to rights-based limitations under particular national laws, before explaining the position in Australia, which exceptionally does not protect rights in its Constitution.

### 8.3.1 The US Constitution

The most important constitutional limitations on copyright under US law arise from the Intellectual Property (IP) Clause of the Constitution, which grants Congress the power:

> To promote the Progress of Science and the Useful Arts, by securing for limited Times to Authors and Inventors the exclusive Right to their respective Writings and Discoveries.[64]

As the Supreme Court put it in a patent case, *Graham* v. *John Deere*, the IP Clause is 'both a grant of power and a limitation'.[65] In *Feist*, the Supreme Court held that the 'minimal creativity' threshold of originality was constitutionally mandated: [7.2.3].[66] The Court reasoned that the IP Clause prevented the protection of facts as 'they do not owe their origin to an act of authorship'.[67] The *Feist* threshold is therefore a clear constitutional limit on copyright.

In addition to limitations under the IP Clause, much attention has been given to potential limitations arising from the First Amendment.[68] The Supreme Court was first called upon expressly to address First Amendment limits on copyright in 1985 in *Harper & Row*.[69] In that case, it was claimed that copyright in the unpublished memoirs of former

---

[64] US Constitution, Art. I, §8, cl 8.
[65] *Graham* v. *John Deere Co.*, 383 US 1 at 5 (1966).
[66] *Feist Publications, Inc.* v. *Rural Telephone Service Co.*, 499 US 340 at 347 (1991), citing L. Ray Patterson and C. Joyce, 'Monopolizing the law: the scope of copyright protection for law reports and statutory compilations' (1989) 36 *UCLA Law Review* 719 at 763 n. 155.
[67] 499 US 340 at 347 (1991).
[68] The literature is extensive. See M. Nimmer, 'Does copyright abridge the First Amendment guarantees of free speech and press?' (1970) 17 *UCLA Law Review* 1180; R. Denicola, 'Copyright and free speech: constitutional limitations on the protection of expression' (1979) 67 *California Law Review* 283; N. Netanel, 'Locating copyright within the First Amendment skein'; E. Baker, 'First Amendment limits on copyright' (2002) 55 *Vanderbilt Law Review* 891; M. Birnhack, 'The copyright law and free speech: making-up and breaking-up' (2003) 43 *IDEA* 233; P. Samuelson, 'Copyright and freedom of expression in historical perspective' (2002) 10 *Journal of Intellectual Property Law* 319.
[69] *Harper & Row, Publishers Inc.* v. *Nation Enterprises Inc.*, 471 US 539 (1985).

## 8.5 Constitutional and 'Human Rights' Limitations

President Ford had been infringed by the unauthorised publication of a news article, which included between 300 and 400 words copied verbatim from a leaked manuscript. The key issue was whether the First Amendment required expansive interpretation of the fair use exception to encompass dissemination of news of public importance, and therefore excuse infringement. In rejecting the argument, the majority held, first, that the idea/expression dichotomy adequately protects free speech, and, second, that copyright itself embodies First Amendment values other than dissemination. In particular, the majority maintained that by providing an incentive for the creation of works, copyright is an 'engine of free expression';[70] and that freedom of expression includes the value of protecting an author's right to refrain from publication (although not to the extent of using copyright as 'an instrument to suppress facts').[71] Therefore, according to the Supreme Court, internal limits on copyright, especially idea/expression and the fair use exception, were generally sufficient to protect First Amendment values without the need for additional external constraints.

The main Supreme Court decision on constitutional limitations is *Eldred*,[72] which involved a challenge to the Copyright Term Extension Act,[73] which extended duration of copyright from life of the author plus fifty years to life plus seventy years: [9.7]. The constitutional challenge claimed that the extension for existing works contravened both the 'limited Times' prescription in the IP Clause and the First Amendment. Referring to past legislative practice of extending the term for existing works, the majority effectively concluded that so long as protection was not perpetual, the copyright term was within the competence of the legislature and not the court. The majority further held that it was generally a matter for the legislature to determine if a measure, such as term extension, advanced the IP Clause's objective, to 'promote the Progress of Science'. In relation to the First Amendment, the majority essentially endorsed the *Harper & Row* approach. Applying a similar analysis, the Court concluded that the speech-promoting incentives provided by copyright, and the internal 'built-in First Amendment accommodations',[74] namely idea/expression and fair use, generally meant that copyright and the First Amendment were complementary. That said, the majority acknowledged that copyright could be subject to a First Amendment challenge, but not where there is no alteration to 'the traditional contours of copyright protection'.[75]

---

[70] 471 US 539 at 558 (1985).   [71] 471 US 539 at 559 (1985).
[72] *Eldred* v. *Ashcroft*, 537 US 186 (2003).   [73] 17 USC §§302 at 304.
[74] 537 US 186 at 219 (2003).   [75] 537 US 186 at 221 (2003).

In the United States, there are therefore constitutional limitations on copyright under both the IP Clause and First Amendment. The IP Clause, in particular, denies protection to facts and material falling beneath the *Feist* threshold. In general, however, US courts have shown considerable deference to the legislature in determining constitutional limits. In relation to the IP Clause, it is largely a matter for the legislature to determine how best to 'promote the Progress of Science'. In relation to First Amendment challenges, internal free speech safeguards, especially idea/expression and fair use, have generally been regarded as sufficient to ensure consistency between copyright and the First Amendment. There are, however, some areas of uncertainty. For example, although, following *Eldred*, First Amendment challenges to copyright laws are possible if they change 'the traditional contours of copyright protection',[76] there is uncertainty about what this qualification means. Moreover, strong dissenting judgments in *Harper & Row* (Brennan J) and *Eldred* (Breyer J), both suggesting that internal limits on copyright are not sufficient to satisfy First Amendment concerns, provide considerable scope for future arguments about constitutional limitations.[77]

### 8.3.2 European Human Rights Law – EU and Council of Europe

In the EU, external limitations on copyright are established through general EU law. For our purposes, there are two relevant sources of EU law.[78] First, there are the rules of the Treaty on the Functioning of the European Union (TFEU)[79] establishing the economic freedoms, including the principle of non-discrimination, removing obstacles to the Internal Market, and prohibiting anti-competitive practices. These rules are significant to copyright law, but will only incidentally affect the public domain, so are not discussed here.[80]

Second, there are general principles of EU law based on fundamental rights, which require copyright to be balanced against other rights, such as freedom of expression or privacy. In addition to EU law, this section of the chapter identifies potential limitations imposed on copyright in Council of Europe jurisdictions by virtue of the European Convention

---

[76] For an argument that *Eldred* enhances the ability of courts to apply First Amendment limitations of copyright, see A. Yen, '*Eldred*, the First Amendment, and aggressive copyright claims' (2003) 40(3) *Houston Law Review* 673.
[77] For analysis, see D. Lindsay, 'Copyright and freedom of expression'.
[78] See A. Strowel and H. E. Kim, 'The balancing impact of general EU Law on European intellectual property jurisprudence', in Ohly and Pila, *The Europeanization of Intellectual Property Law*, 121–42.
[79] Full titles and citations of treaties are in the Table of International Instruments.
[80] See the Online Supplement for a discussion.

## 8.3 Constitutional and 'Human Rights' Limitations

on Human Rights (ECHR) and decisions of the European Court of Human Rights (ECtHR).

Under Article 6 of the Treaty on the European Union (TEU), the protection of human rights in the EU rests on three pillars: the EU Charter of Fundamental Rights;[81] the ECHR; and the common constitutional traditions of EU Member States.[82] Under Article 6(1) of the TEU, the Charter has 'the same legal value as the Treaties'. Furthermore, under Article 6(3), the fundamental rights guaranteed by the ECHR and the common constitutional traditions of Member States are 'general principles of EU law'. Although Article 17(2) of the Charter specifically provides that 'intellectual property shall be protected', it is clear that it is not an absolute right: [1.9.1].[83] Since the Charter came into effect, in a process referred to as 'constitutionalisation of IP law',[84] the EU rights-based framework has become increasingly important in establishing limits on exercise of copyright for the purpose of protecting other human rights, including freedom of expression (guaranteed by Article 11), and privacy and data privacy (guaranteed by Articles 7 and 8). Following from Article 51 of the Charter, EU legislation must be interpreted consistently with Charter rights; and the CJEU has set rights-based limits on copyright by interpreting EU copyright directives, and their implementation in the laws of Member States, to ensure consistency with the Charter. In establishing the balance between copyright and other rights, proportionality, which is a general principle of EU law, is emerging as an EU meta-principle establishing constitutional limits on copyright.[85]

The ECJ first referred to proportionality in the copyright context in its ruling in *Promusicae*.[86] In that case, Promusicae, a copyright society representing rights holders, applied to compel an ISP to disclose names and addresses of subscribers allegedly infringing copyright by means of a P2P service. The ECJ ruled that relevant directives did not require Member States to introduce an obligation on ISPs to disclose personal

---

[81] EU Charter, Art. 6.
[82] See, for example, A. Ohly, 'European fundamental rights and intellectual property', in Ohly and Pila, *The Europeanization of Intellectual Property Law*, 145–63.
[83] See Case C-70/10, *Scarlet Extended SA* v. *Société belge des auteurs, compositeurs et éditeurs SCRL (SABAM)* [2012] ECDR 4 at [43]; [2011] ECR I-11959.
[84] See J. Griffiths, 'Constitutionalising or harmonising? – the Court of Justice, the right to property and European copyright law' (2013) 38 *European Law Review* 65; C. Geiger, '"Constitutionalising" intellectual property law? The influence of fundamental rights on intellectual property in the European Union' [2006] *International Review of Intellectual Property and Competition Law (IIC)* 371.
[85] Afori, 'Proportionality – a new mega standard', 889.
[86] Case C-275/06, *Productores de Música de España (Promusicae)* v. *Telefónica de España SAU* [2008] ECR I-271 ('*Promusicae*'). The Charter was not yet binding.

data to protect copyright. In so ruling, the Court held that in transposing directives into national law, they must be interpreted consistently with the protection of fundamental rights and general principles of EU law, such as proportionality, requiring that a 'fair balance' be struck between the fundamental rights, such as between an IPR and privacy rights.[87]

The role of proportionality in balancing copyright and other rights has been important in dealing with legislation providing for no fault injunctions against intermediaries, such as ISPs, to deter or inhibit third party infringements.[88] In *Scarlet Extended*,[89] an injunction was sought against an ISP to compel it to filter all electronic communications passing its servers to prevent infringing downloads by means of P2P services. The ECJ applied the proportionality principle to conclude that requiring an ISP to install filtering software would not strike a 'fair balance' between copyright and an ISP's freedom to conduct business, which is guaranteed by Article 16 of the Charter.[90] In addition, the Court ruled that such a broad injunction would be a disproportionate interference with the right to personal data (of the ISP's subscribers), safeguarded by Article 8 of the Charter, and the right of freedom to receive or impart information, safeguarded by Article 10.[91]

Subsequently, in *UPC Telekabel*,[92] the owners of copyright in films applied for an injunction requiring an ISP to block access to a specific website from which users could unlawfully download or stream the films. The ECJ ruled that an injunction which did not specify the measures for blocking access could be consistent with EU law provided that, first, the measures do not 'unnecessarily deprive internet users of the possibility of lawfully accessing the information available' and, second, that they have the effect of preventing or making it difficult for internet users to access the offending material.[93] The Court, however, emphasised that the measures adopted by the ISP must be narrowly targeted in order to protect 'the fundamental right of internet users to freedom of information' under Article 11.[94]

While EU copyright law has been constitutionalised within the EU human rights framework, the ECJ's role is limited to applying the framework in making authoritative interpretations of EU law, particularly copyright directives. Nevertheless, the ECJ rulings applying the proportionality

---

[87] [2008] ECR I-271 at [68].   [88] See InfoSoc Directive, Art. 8(3).
[89] Case C-70/10, *Scarlet Extended SA* v. *Société belge des auteurs, compositeurs et éditeurs SCRL (SABAM)* [2012] ECDR 4 [2011] ECR I-11959.
[90] [2012] ECDR 4 at [49].   [91] [2012] ECDR 4 at [50]–[52].
[92] Case C-314/12 *UPC Telekabel Wien GmbH* v. *Constantin Film Verleih GmbH and Wega Filmproduktionsgesellschaft mbH* [2014] Bus LR 541 ('*UPC Telekabel*').
[93] [2014] Bus LR 541 at [64].   [94] [2014] Bus LR 541 at [55].

8.3 Constitutional and 'Human Rights' Limitations 233

principle to ensure that copyright is consistent with fundamental rights, clearly recognise the legitimacy of imposing rights-based limits on copyright. Moreover, by imposing limits on the extent to which intermediaries, such as ISPs, may be required to control access to information on the Internet, the ECJ rulings effectively support the de facto Internet public domain: Chapter 16.

Apart from EU jurisprudence, the ECtHR, which is responsible for interpreting the ECHR, acknowledged the scope for rights-based limits on copyright in *Ashby Donald*.[95] In that case, three fashion photographers, found to have infringed copyright under French law by posting photographs of clothes to a website, argued that this was a disproportionate interference with freedom of expression within Article 10 of the ECHR. While deciding there was an interference with the Article 10 right, the Court took into account the fact that the information did not relate to a debate of 'general public interest' and the commercial nature of the website to conclude that the restriction was justified as necessary in a democratic society under Article 10(2). The judgment, nevertheless, is a significant acknowledgement that the ECtHR may engage in rights-based review of the limits of copyright.[96]

### 8.3.3 Rights-Based Limits in National Laws

Rights-based limits on copyright are recognised in European jurisdictions where the ECHR has direct effect, or where rights are entrenched in national constitutions.

For example, in 2003, a Dutch court held that posting the full text of internal documents of the Scientology sect to a criticism website was protected under Article 10 of the ECHR, even though the documents did not fall within the Dutch quotation exception.[97] Similarly, in *Germania 3*, the German Constitutional Court reasoned that the quotation exception under German law: [12.3.2], should be interpreted expansively in the light of the right to artistic freedom guaranteed by Article 5(3) of the German Constitution to permit extensive extracts from two plays

---

[95] *Ashby Donald and Others v. France* [2013] ECHR 287. See C. Geiger and E. Izyumenko, 'Copyright on the human rights trial: redefining the boundaries of exclusivity through freedom of expression' (2014) 45 *International Review of Intellectual Property and Competition Law (IIC)* 316.
[96] Geiger and Izyumenko, 'Copyright on the human rights trial', 339.
[97] Gerechtshof 's-Gravenhage, Uitspraak: 4 September 2003, LJN-nummer. AI5638 Zaaknr: 99/1040 (Judgment of the Den Haag Court of Appeal of 4 September 2003, LJN-no. AI5638). See C. Geiger, 'Copyright's fundamental rights dimension at EU level', in E. Derclaye (ed.), *Research Handbook on the Future of EU Copyright* (Edward Elgar, 2009), pp. 27–48 at 47.

by Brecht in a work by the author, Heiner Müller.[98] Moreover, in *Ashdown*,[99] the English Court of Appeal relied on the Article 10 ECHR right expansively to interpret both the fair dealing exception for reporting news and the common law public interest defence which it found might, in certain circumstances, allow for verbatim use of a copyright work even where this is not otherwise a fair dealing: [8.2.1]. Finally, outside of Europe, a rights-based approach was applied by the Canadian Supreme Court in *CCH*,[100] to give an expansive interpretation to the fair dealing exception: [11.4.3].

### 8.3.4 Countries with No Constitutional Limitations: Australia

The external limits on copyright in jurisdictions with rights-based constitutions may be compared with the position under the Australian Constitution, which has very limited scope for imposing limits on copyright.

The IP clause in s. 51(xviii) of the Constitution has been expansively interpreted, for example, to confer power to legislate for rights not specifically mentioned.[101] It is sometimes claimed that extending IPRs may be prohibited as an acquisition of property without 'just terms' contrary to s. 51(xxxi) of the Constitution; but these claims have been rejected by the courts.

Some have argued that the implied constitutional protection of freedom of political communication recognised by the High Court[102] might limit IPRs, such as by reinforcing a public interest exception.[103] While the implied freedom may operate to limit laws that restrict freedom of political discussion, it has yet to be applied in the context of IPRs, and a role in limiting copyright, if any, appears likely to be narrowly circumscribed.

Even in jurisdictions with rights-based constitutions, there is obviously no effect on the public domain unless the rights are enforceable. For example, the Chinese Constitution protects rights to freedom of speech

---

[98] German Federal Constitutional Court, 29 June 2000, *Germania 3*, 2001 GRUR 149. For a translation of the decision, see E. Adeney and C. Antons, 'The *Germania 3* decision translated: the quotation exception before the German Constitutional Court' (2013) 35(11) *European Intellectual Property Review* 646.

[99] [2002] Ch 149.

[100] *CCH Canadian Ltd* v. *Law Society of Upper Canada* (2004) 1 RCS 339; 236 DLR (4th) 395.

[101] *Nintendo Co. Ltd* v. *Centronics Systems Pty Ltd* (1994) 181 CLR 134 at 160. See also *Grain Pool of Western Australia* v. *Commonwealth* (2000) 202 CLR 479.

[102] *Lange* v. *Australian Broadcasting Corporation* (1997) 189 CLR 520.

[103] M. Richardson, 'Freedom of political discussion and intellectual property law in Australia' (1997) 11 *European Intellectual Property Review* 631.

## 8.3 Constitutional and 'Human Rights' Limitations

and press,[104] and 'encourages and assists creative endeavours conducive to the interests of people that are made by citizens engaged in education, science, technology, literature, art and other cultural work';[105] but, in practice, these provisions are not directly enforceable.[106]

### 8.3.5 Constitutional Limitations and the Public Domain

National constitutions, or European-level treaties, may impose 'external' limits on copyright which may have the effect that some 'works' are not protected or otherwise limit the exercise of copyright.

In relation to works that are not protected, the IP Clause of the US Constitution has been interpreted as imposing a constitutionally mandated 'creativity' threshold for protection, effectively meaning that the Constitution prohibits protection of 'works' failing to meet the threshold. While, in general, internal copyright safeguards, such as idea/expression, are regarded as sufficient to ensure consistency with the US First Amendment, the *Eldred* court acknowledged the possibility of a First Amendment challenge where there is an alteration to 'the traditional contours of copyright protection'. That said, there is scope for future arguments about the extent to which the First Amendment may limit copyright law.

In the EU, limits on the exercise of copyright are established by treaty obligations to protect economic freedoms and the Internal Market, and the EU human rights framework. For example, EU law mandates the principle of Community-wide exhaustion, which makes it impermissible to use copyright territorially to partition markets in the EU.[107] The EU human rights framework can establish effective limits on copyright by means of ECJ interpretations of EU directives and supervision of implementation of directives in national laws. Directives and their implementation must be proportionate, in that they must establish a 'fair balance' between copyright and other fundamental rights, especially freedom of expression and privacy. For example, a national law implementing an obligation on an ISP to block Internet access is proportionate only if it is narrowly targeted and minimally effective. Moreover, under the ECHR, there is potential for the exercise of copyright to be limited where it might be found to be disproportionate to a fundamental right, such as freedom of expression. Under national laws, treaty obligations to protect rights, such as under Article 10 of the ECHR, create the potential for courts

---
[104] Constitutional Law of People's Republic of China, Art. 35
[105] Constitutional Law of People's Republic of China, Art. 47.
[106] See Li and Greenleaf, 'China's copyright public domain', 155.
[107] See the Online Supplement.

finding that uses falling outside of established exceptions, such as the quotation or fair dealing exceptions, should be permissible. Apart from this, rights-based considerations may be taken into account by the courts in giving expansive interpretations to existing exceptions, such as the quotation exception under German law, or the public interest exception in the UK.

In all, this section has explained that 'constitutional' law (broadly speaking), and especially constitutionally protected rights, can play a role in protecting the public domain, and especially in ensuring that national laws balance copyright against other rights, particularly freedom of expression and privacy. For the most part, however, courts have refused to apply rights-based constitutional principles to limit copyright, except in the clearest of cases. In general, then, this public domain category is of more potential importance than of current practical importance. There is, nevertheless, a growing awareness of conflicts between copyright and constitutional rights, notably freedom of expression and privacy, and especially in the online context.[108] We therefore suspect that as conflicts between copyright and other rights become more apparent, this public domain category, and principles such as proportionality which support these public rights, will become more significant.

## 8.4 Public Policy and *Ordre public* Exclusions

This section of the chapter identifies and explains the exclusion of copyright protection on public policy grounds, mainly on the basis that the content is 'offensive'. If a copyright owner cannot take steps to enforce their copyright because of such restrictions, the use may fall within our formal definition of the copyright public domain, regardless of whether or not the possession or use of such a work is prohibited by other laws, such as obscenity laws. We examine the paradoxical nature of this public domain category following an explanation of the law in selected jurisdictions, namely the UK, Australia, Canada, the United States and China.

In international copyright law, Article 17 of Berne provides that the Convention is not to affect the right of members of the Union 'to permit, to control, or to prohibit, by legislation or regulation, the circulation, presentation, or exhibition of any work or production in regard to which the competent authority may find it necessary to exercise that right'. This provision recognises the authority of sovereign states to limit private

---

[108] Afori, 'Proportionality – a new mega standard', 892.

8.4 Public Policy and *Ordre public* Exclusions

rights in the interests of maintaining 'public order' and, in particular, as part of the exercise of censorship powers.[109]

### 8.4.1 UK and Commonwealth Jurisdictions

There is a long history of English courts denying protection to works on the basis that the content is objectionable and, as such, it was against public policy to allow copyright to be enforced. The effect of denying protection is to place such works in the copyright public domain in that anyone is free to copy or publish the works, subject to compliance with other laws, such as defamation or obscenity laws. In the past, copyright has been denied on the basis that a work is obscene, immoral, defamatory, blasphemous or intended to deceive the public.[110]

In the UK, the legal effect and juridical basis of such exclusions is uncertain.[111] Lord Eldon was particularly active in refusing to protect works offending public morals, but prior to the Judicature Act this involved the equity court refusing to grant an injunction rather than outright denial of copyright.[112] In *Glyn* v. *Weston*,[113] however, Younger J denied copyright in Eleanor Glyn's novel, *Three Weeks*, on the basis that copyright could not subsist in 'a work of a tendency so grossly immoral'.[114] In *A-G* v. *Guardian Newspapers (No. 2)*,[115] the House of Lords cited *Glyn*, together with a case involving a work calculated to deceive the public, as examples of the court refusing equitable relief. Subsequently, in *Yelland*,[116] the Court of Appeal held that a court could be entitled to refuse to enforce copyright where a work is: '(i) immoral, scandalous or contrary to family life; (ii) injurious to public life, public health and safety or the administration of justice; (or) (iii) incites or encourages others to act in a way referred to in (ii)'.[117] It therefore appears that the current law is that rather than denying copyright, in such cases the English courts apply their inherent jurisdiction to refuse to enforce the copyright.

*Australia* While the English cases refusing relief have not been overruled, contemporary common law courts are reluctant to refuse to

---

[109] See Ricketson and Ginsburg, *International Copyright and Neighbouring Rights*, [13.88].
[110] Cornish, Llewelyn and Aplin, *Intellectual Property*, [12.58].
[111] See *Venus Adult Shops Pty Ltd* v. *Fraserside Holdings Ltd* (2006) 70 IPR 517 at [13] (per Finkelstein J).
[112] H. Laddie, P. Prescott, M. Vitoria, A. Speck and L. Lane, *The Modern Law of Copyright and Designs* (3rd edn, Butterworths, 2000), [20.3]. See, for example, *Southey* v. *Sherwood* (1817) 2 Mer 435 (concerning Robert Southey's *Wat Tyler*).
[113] *Glyn* v. *Weston Feature Film Company* [1916] 1 Ch 261.
[114] [1916] 1 Ch 261 at 270.   [115] [1990] 1 AC 109 at 294.
[116] *Hyde Park Residence Ltd* v. *Yelland* [2001] Ch 143.   [117] [2001] Ch 143 at 168.

enforce copyright on the basis of policies such as protection of public morals. In Australia, this is apparent from the decision of the Full Federal Court in *Venus Adult Shops*,[118] where the Court expressed concern about applying a legal test that was 'no more than a value-judgment based upon a variety of psychological apprehensions which we are unable to comprehend'.[119] In that case, the Court held there was no statutory basis under Australian law for finding that copyright does not subsist in material that offends against community standards and, furthermore, while such considerations might be taken into account in awarding discretionary remedies, the discretion was 'narrow'.[120]

*Canada* The position accepted by the Australian court is broadly consistent with Canadian law. In *Pasikniack* v. *Dojacek*,[121] Fullarton JA held that, unless the sale of a book was an offence, there was a right to restrain copyright infringement of an allegedly obscene book.[122] In a concurring judgment, Dennistoun JA acknowledged that copyright might be denied in a work that was intended to deceive the public, but could see no reason for refusing an injunction where 'it is honest work and not a fraud on the public'.[123] Both Fullarton and Dennistoun JJA held that if selling a book was an offence, damages would be unavailable. In *Aldrich*,[124] Davies J reviewed the law on copyright in obscene works before concluding that the Canadian Act did not deny copyright in obscene materials, but that a court would not award damages where there was no compensable act due to the work being illegal. On the other hand, the Court held that an injunction could be available to restrain infringements of even obscene works.

### 8.4.2 United States

Although prior to 1909 US copyright law included an express denial of copyright in obscene materials, the 1909 US Act did not retain this and allowed for registration of all works of an author. In the principal US authority, *Mitchell Brothers*,[125] Godbold J held that the omission of the obscenity exception in the 1909 Act reflected an intentional policy of according copyright protection, regardless of content. As the Court put it:

---

[118] *Venus Adult Shops Pty Ltd* v. *Fraserside Holdings Ltd* (2006) 70 IPR 517.
[119] (2006) 70 IPR 517 at [82] (per French and Kiefel JJ) quoting from J. Phillips, 'Copyright in obscene works: some British and American problems' (1977) 6 *Anglo-American Law Review* 138 at 168.
[120] (2006) 70 IPR 517 at [84].   [121] [1929] 2 DLR 454.
[122] [1929] 2 DLR 454 at [18].   [123] [1929] 2 DLR 454 at [62].
[124] *Aldrich* v. *One Stop Video Ltd* (1987) 39 DLR (4th) 362.
[125] *Mitchell Brothers Film Group* v. *Cinema Adult Theatre*, 604 F 2d 852 (5th Cir 1979).

## 8.4 Public Policy and *Ordre public* Exclusions

the absence of content restrictions on copyrightability indicates that Congress has decided that the constitutional goal of encouraging creativity would not be best served if an author had to concern himself not only with the marketability of his work but also with the judgment of government officials regarding the worth of the work.[126]

Moreover, Godbold J pointed out that providing for the protection of all works, both obscene and non-obscene, avoided practical difficulties in determining what is obscene as well as First Amendment issues. While *Mitchell Brothers* suggests that relief for infringement will not be denied to obscene works, in *Devils Films*,[127] a New York court refused to grant an injunction to restrain publication of infringing copies of pornographic videos on the basis of the public policy against distributing unlawfully obscene materials. In that case, the Court also rejected precedent suggesting that it lacked discretion to refuse remedies in such cases.

### 8.4.3 Civil Law Jurisdictions: Ordre public Exclusions

In civil law systems the equivalent to public policy exclusions is dealt with as part of the doctrine of *ordre public*. The doctrine derives from the sovereign police power of the state and entails the consequence that unlawful conduct is either prohibited or rendered void.[128] The best-known example of an exercise of the doctrine to deny copyright was Article 4 of China's 1990 Copyright Law which, in relevant part, provided:

> Works the publication and/or dissemination of which are prohibited by law shall not be protected by this Law.

The works denied protection included works that failed 'content review' by Chinese authorities on the grounds, for example, of unconstitutionality or immorality, as well as deleted portions of works edited to satisfy content review. In 2007, Article 4 was subject to a US complaint to the WTO, alleging that it was inconsistent with Articles 5(1) and 5(2) of Berne (as incorporated by reference in Article 9.1 of TRIPs). Articles 5(1) and 5(2) of Berne impose minimum obligations to protect copyright works, including foreign works, without formalities: [4.4]. In 2009, the WTO Panel ruled that, as Article 4 of the Chinese Law denied copyright to works or portions of works failing content review entirely, it was

---

[126] *Ibid.* [17].   [127] *Devils Films, Inc.* v. *Nectar Video*, 29 F Supp 2d 174 (SDNY 1998).
[128] K. Qingjiang, 'The doctrine of *Ordre public* and the Sino–US copyright dispute', Society of International Economic Law, Online Proceedings Working Paper No. 07/08 (on SSRN) (17 June 2008) https://papers.ssrn.com/sol3/papers.cfm?abstract_id=1147137.

inconsistent with Article 5(1) of Berne.[129] In addition, the Panel concluded that the denial of protection deprived judicial authorities of the 'effective' enforcement remedies required under Article 41.1 of TRIPs.[130] While China argued that Article 4 did not remove copyright from the works, but simply denied protection, the Panel held that denial of protection meant that the right was 'no more than a phantom right'.[131]

In relation to Article 17 of Berne, which gives Berne members the power to limit rights to maintain public order, the Panel ruled that, while this conferred power to control circulation, presentation or exhibition of works, this does not extend to 'eliminate ... [copyright] ... entirely with respect to a particular work'.[132] Given these findings, the Panel refrained from ruling on whether or not 'content review' was inconsistent with the rule against formalities. The practical result of the Panel ruling is that China remains able to maintain its censorship regime as 'copyright and government censorship address different rights and interests',[133] so long as it does not completely eliminate copyright.

In 2010, China amended Article 4 of the Copyright Law to remove the denial of copyright and replace it with a provision stating that:

> Copyright holders shall not violate the Constitution or laws or jeopardize public interests when exercising their copyright. The State shall supervise and administer the publication and dissemination of works in accordance with the law.[134]

Given the WTO Panel decision, the requirement that copyright holders 'shall not violate the Constitution or laws' cannot be interpreted to mean that copyright in the works can be completely denied.

### 8.4.4 Public Policy Exclusions and the Public Domain

As this chapter has explained, the importance of freedom of expression is central to the denial of copyright in works that are expressly excluded from protection, or where 'external' rights-based limitations are imposed

---

[129] WTO Panel Report, China – Measures Affecting the Protection and Enforcement of Intellectual Property Rights, WT/DS-362/R (26 January 2009), [7.117]–[7.119].
[130] Ibid. [7.179]. [131] Ibid. [7.67]. [132] Ibid. [7.132].
[133] Ibid. [7.135]. See D. Gervais, 'China – measures affecting the protection and enforcement of intellectual property rights' (2009) 103(3) American Journal of International Law 549; P. Yu, 'The US–China dispute over TRIPS enforcement', in C. Antons (ed.), The Enforcement of Intellectual Property Rights: Comparative Perspectives from the Asia-Pacific Region (Kluwer Law International, 2011).
[134] See Order of the President of the People's Republic of China No. 26, 26 February 2010; Decision of the Standing Committee of the National People's Congress on Amending the Copyright Law of the People's Republic of China (adopted at the 13th Meeting of the Standing Committee of the Eleventh National People's Congress on February 26th 2010).

on exercise of copyright. The relationship between freedom of expression and public policy exclusions from copyright protection is, however, complex. Historically, copyright was denied in works, such as 'obscene' works, not to enrich the public domain but because the content was disfavoured and held to be against public policy; the denial of copyright was to penalise the rights holder not to support use. This public domain category is therefore paradoxical.

Historically, this category included more works than is now the case, as courts are increasingly reluctant to deny copyright due to a work's content. Moreover, the WTO Panel decision referred to above makes it clear that, while content control or 'censorship' is permissible, Article 17 of Berne cannot be relied upon to deny copyright entirely. Nevertheless, where copyright is limited due to public policy considerations, such as by limits on remedies, this could ironically have the effect of encouraging the circulation of disfavoured content, just as official censorship can encourage clandestine dissemination of censored content. The historical denial of copyright may, in this sense, have supported a 'clandestine' or de facto public domain.[135] Even then, however, the practical effect of this unusual public domain category was limited by extra-copyright legal restrictions, such as obscenity laws; which remains the case in jurisdictions with strong censorship laws. In short, in most countries this category is now of more theoretical interest than practical importance.

## 8.5 Public Interest Exceptions

In the common law tradition, 'public policy exclusions' arose from 'negative' decisions by courts exercising their inherent jurisdiction to deny or limit copyright in a disfavoured work on public policy grounds, thereby de facto putting the work in the public domain. In another line of authority, common law courts have exercised their inherent jurisdiction to permit uses that would otherwise infringe copyright on the grounds that there is a positive public interest justifying the use.[136] Although, strictly speaking, this public domain category could fall within permitted uses of works protected by copyright (Chapter 10), or copyright exceptions (Chapters 11 and 12), it is examined here as it arises from the exercise of a potentially broad judicial discretion based on balancing copyright against other values, especially freedom of expression. This category differs from 'public policy exclusions' in that it operates as a defence for a particular user, and is not a general exclusion or limitation of copyright in the work: [3.3.8].

---

[135] Deazley, *Rethinking Copyright*, 115–16.
[136] *Ibid.* 116–17; Greenleaf and Bond, '"Public rights" in copyright', 136.

## 8.5.1 UK Law

In the UK, s. 171(3) of the CDPA provides that nothing in the Act 'affects any rule of law preventing or restricting the enforcement of copyright, on grounds of public interest or otherwise'. This recognises the common law public interest defence, which, in the UK, had been held to authorise uses amounting to disclosures of impropriety, but also extending to disclosures otherwise in the public interest.[137]

The principal UK authority is *Ashdown*,[138] in which the Court of Appeal rejected a narrow interpretation of the public interest defence: [8.2.1]. As the Court pointed out, where there is a conflict between copyright and freedom of expression, this can usually be accommodated by either idea/expression or the Court exercising its jurisdiction to refuse an injunction.[139] Taking into account the protection of freedom of expression under Article 10 of the ECHR and the UK Human Rights Act, however, the Court held that there were 'rare circumstances' where the public interest in disclosing or using a work prevailed over the copyright owner's rights, such as where verbatim reproduction is necessary to establish a document's authenticity.[140] In such circumstances, on our analysis, the use is within the public domain. That said, questions have been raised as to whether even this limited common law defence is compatible with EU law which, in the InfoSoc Directive, establishes an exhaustive list of copyright exceptions and requires that exceptions meet the three-step test.[141]

## 8.5.2 Australia

In contrast to the UK, in Australia, which has no bill of rights, the public interest defence has been narrowly construed or rejected. While a narrow public interest defence had been accepted in the *Defence Papers case*,[142] [8.2.1], the existence of the defence has been doubted in subsequent

---

[137] *Lion Laboratories Ltd* v. *Evans* [1985] QB 526.
[138] *Ashdown* v. *Telegraph Group Ltd* [2002] Ch 149.   [139] *Ibid.* [45]–[47]; [59].
[140] *Ibid.* [47].
[141] InfoSoc Directive, Art. 5. See J. Griffiths, 'The United Kingdom's public interest "defence" and European Union copyright law', in N. Lee, G. Westkamp, A. Kurr and A. Ohly (eds.), *Intellectual Property, Unfair Competition and Publicity* (Edward Elgar, 2014), pp. 289–308.
[142] *The Commonwealth of Australia* v. *John Fairfax & Sons Ltd* (1980) 147 CLR 39.

cases.[143] For example, in *Collier*,[144] in strong *dicta*, Gummow J stated that 'in my view, there is no legislative or other warrant for the introduction of such a concept into the law of this country'.[145] While the defence was not argued on appeal, the Full Federal Court cautiously avoided expressing a view.[146] Moreover, while there have been suggestions that a public interest defence may be based on an implied constitutional protection of political communication: [8.3.4], there are no indications of this being judicially accepted. In Australia, therefore, the balance between copyright and freedom of expression is likely to be struck by the courts in exercising their discretion to refuse remedies, rather than authorising uses on grounds of public interest.

### 8.5.3 China

A broad concept of 'public interest' is a more explicit part of China's copyright law than is the case in common law jurisdictions.[147] Tang, for example, has claimed that:

> The public interest, in the Chinese copyright regime, is not only a fundamental principle emphasised by the law and a recognised legal defence for copyright exemption, but is also a justification in its own right that regulates works free from copyright. Furthermore, it provides the legal basis for administrative copyright enforcement in China.[148]

While 'public rights and interests' are expressly referred to in Article 48 of the 2010 Copyright Law,[149] in the context of administrative enforcement of copyright, the most important provision, from the perspective of the public domain, is the second sentence of Article 4. This now provides that: 'Copyright holders shall not ... jeopardize public interests when exercising their copyright': [8.4.3]. It seems possible that Article 4 may be interpreted as establishing a limitation or exception to copyright infringement, although one that is currently of uncertain scope.[150]

Despite the express reference to 'public interest' or 'public interests' in China's law, the role of this concept is 'enigmatic',[151] and any potential

---

[143] *Pavey Whiting & Byrne v. Collector of Customs (Vic)* [1987] AIPC 90-409; *Smith Kline & French Laboratories (Australia) Ltd v. Secretary, Department of Community Services and Health* (1990) 17 IPR 545.
[144] *Collier Constructions Pty Ltd v. Foskett Pty Ltd* (1990) 19 IPR 44.   [145] *Ibid.* 57.
[146] *Collier Constructions Pty Ltd v. Foskett Pty Ltd* (1991) 20 IPR 666.
[147] Li and Greenleaf, 'China's copyright public domain'.
[148] G. Tang, *Copyright and the Public Interest in China* (Edward Elgar, 2011), p. 2.
[149] Copyright Law of the People's Republic of China, Art. 48.
[150] Li and Greenleaf, 'China's copyright public domain', 161.   [151] *Ibid.*

for it to operate as a general defence, as opposed to justifying administrative action by the state, remains inchoate.

### 8.5.4 Public Interest Exceptions and the Public Domain

The 'public interest' in copyright is highly contested,[152] but in the context in which it is used in this public domain category it refers particularly to the discretionary jurisdiction of UK courts to allow free use of copyright works where the right to freedom of expression outweighs the copyright interest. The UK public interest exception is dealt with in this chapter as, like rights-based limits, it entails balancing copyright against competing rights (especially freedom of expression) and, like public policy exclusions, the discretion arises from the court's inherent jurisdiction.

That said, as the Court of Appeal made clear in *Ashdown*, it is only in rare cases that, outside of internal limits such as idea/expression or fair dealing exceptions, the public interest in disclosure or use will outweigh the copyright owner's rights. In other common law jurisdictions, this balance is more likely to be struck by courts applying existing exceptions, such as the post-*CCH* expansive interpretation of the fair dealing exception in Canada, or the fair use exception in the United States. In Australia, on the other hand, there is some doubt as to whether even a narrow public interest defence, confined to exposure of iniquity, exists. In all common law jurisdictions, however, the courts can take the public interest into account in refusing discretionary remedies, such as injunctions.

In civil law jurisdictions, it is likely that these issues would be dealt with either through constitutional rights-balancing or the application of exceptions, such as the broad German exception for quotations: [12.3.2]. In China, however, there is scope for arguing that the 'public interest' can operate as a legal defence, pursuant to Article 4 of the Copyright Law, although there is much uncertainty on this point.

In sum, of jurisdictions reviewed for this chapter, it is only in the UK that the public interest exception is significant for the public domain and, even there, its operation is relatively narrow.

## 8.6 Conclusion

This chapter has dealt with public domain categories involving works that are not protected by copyright because they are expressly excluded, are

---

[152] R. Giblin and K. Weatherall, 'If we redesigned copyright from scratch, what might it look like?', in Giblin and Weatherall (eds.), *What If We Could Reimagine Copyright?*; I. Alexander, *Copyright Law and the Public Interest in the Nineteenth Century* (Hart Publishing, 2010).

## 8.6 Conclusion

subject to constitutional and rights-based limitations, are excluded due to public policy considerations, or subject to public interest exceptions. In addition to excluded works, the chapter has dealt with related exceptions that allow for permission-free uses without copyright being denied in relevant works.

The main theme arising from elements of national copyright laws examined in this chapter is the importance of the 'permission-free' public domain for promoting and protecting freedom of expression, access to information and freedom of the media, and for promoting democratic values and processes. In relation to express exclusions (Category 3), we have concluded that most jurisdictions have not taken full advantage of flexibilities allowed by mandatory and permitted exclusions under international law. We therefore consider that there is scope for clearer express exceptions under national laws for 'news' and political information. We also conclude that there is a strong case for exclusion of government information, including legislation and legal judgments, from copyright to the full extent permitted by international law, such as by abolishing Crown and Parliamentary copyright in relevant common law jurisdictions.

In relation to constitutional and rights-based limits on copyright (Category 4), courts in the United States and EU have been cautious in applying limitations on copyright where there are potential conflicts between copyright and competing rights. There is, however, some willingness to acknowledge that there are circumstances where, applying a proportionality or 'rights-balancing' analysis, rights to freedom of expression may outweigh the property rights of copyright owners. We consider there is considerable scope for further development of the jurisprudence in this area, whether in applying 'rights-based' analysis in interpreting existing exceptions, or in the analysis of the circumstances in which rights, such as the right to freedom of expression, might require permission-free uses beyond established exceptions.

Public policy and *ordre public* exclusions (Category 7), and public interest exceptions (Category 8), are further examples of where the rights of copyright owners may be subordinated to broader 'public interests'; in the first case, a public interest in protecting against 'offensive' works and, in the second case, the public interest in freedom of expression in particular contexts. Public policy exceptions are, in most jurisdictions, of marginal practical relevance to the public domain, given the reluctance of courts to deny copyright on the basis of the nature of the content. The more important 'public domain' issue relating to this category is the scope permitted under Article 17 of Berne, for state censorship to coexist with copyright. As far as public policy exceptions are concerned, as a result of expansive interpretation of the common law public interest exception, this has significance in the UK, but even there its practical effect is limited. In other jurisdictions, the public interest in freedom of expression is more likely to be addressed by the courts in refraining from awarding remedies, such as injunctions, or by other internal limits on copyright. On this, we conclude that the protection of the public domain value of freedom of expression is more likely to be advanced by rights-based jurisprudence and, even more so, the further development of copyright exceptions: Chapters 11 and 12.

# 9 Works Where Copyright Has Expired

| | | |
|---|---|---|
| 9.1 | Introduction | 247 |
| 9.2 | Extension of the Copyright Term: United Kingdom and United States | 249 |
| 9.3 | Term of Protection and the Public Domain | 251 |
| 9.4 | Copyright Term: The International Framework | 254 |
| 9.5 | EU Term Directive | 255 |
| 9.6 | UK Law | 260 |
| 9.7 | Copyright Terms: US Law | 263 |
| 9.8 | Copyright Terms: Australian Law | 267 |
| 9.9 | Copyright Terms: China | 270 |
| 9.10 | Term of Protection: Other Jurisdictions | 272 |
| 9.11 | Moral Rights | 273 |
| 9.12 | Conclusion: A Realist Perspective on Duration | 275 |

## 9.1 Introduction

**Category 5** of our fifteen public domain categories consists of works in which the copyright term has expired. The copyright term has been at the centre of historical struggles over the copyright public domain,[1] with conventional understandings confining the phrase 'works falling into the public domain' to works in which the term has expired.[2]

Even before the Statute of Anne, the importance of limits on duration of protection was recognised. For example, in his 1694 Memorandum opposing renewal of the Licensing Act, John Locke, objecting to perpetual rights, proposed that where a publisher purchases rights from an author:

---

[1] S. Martin, 'The mythology of the public domain: exploring the myths behind attacks on the duration of copyright protection' 36 *Loyola of Los Angeles Law Review* 253 at 253–4; Ricketson and Creswell, *The Law of Intellectual Property*, 2nd edn, 1999, ongoing electronic resource, [6.1].

[2] See Benabou and Dusollier, 'Draw me a public domain', 165, citing S. Choisy, *La domaine public et droit d'auteur* (Litec, 2002).

it may be reasonable to limit their property to a certain number of years after the death of the author, or the first printing of the book, as, suppose, fifty or seventy years.[3]

The copyright term was at the heart of the eighteenth-century dispute over whether perpetual common law copyright survived the Statute of Anne, known as the 'battle of the booksellers'.[4] In the nineteenth century, duration was again at the centre of debates about English copyright reform, with Talfourd and Wordsworth campaigning for an extension of the term to life of the author plus sixty years but, in the face of strong opposition, famously from Macaulay, eventually resulting in a new term, in the 1842 UK Act, of forty-two years from publication or life of the author plus seven years.[5]

Under international copyright law, the 1886 Berne Act originally provided, in Article 14, that the Convention applied to 'all works which at the moment of its coming into force have not yet fallen into the public domain in the country of origin', ensuring that protection would not be required to be restored to public domain works. The term 'public domain' in the Article was taken from French law,[6] with the phrase 'fall into the public domain' seeming to have originated in mid-nineteenth-century France to apply to expiry of the copyright term.[7] Article 18 of the Paris Act of Berne is more specific than the original provision, requiring restrospectivity for all works except for those that have fallen into the public domain solely 'through the expiry of the term of protection': [4.3.1]; thereby emphasising the importance of retaining works in the public domain on term expiry.

Duration of protection under national laws is one of the most complex and technical areas of copyright law. The complexities arise because of different terms that apply to different categories of works, different ways of calculating the terms for different works (and especially different starting points for calculating the terms), and changes in the copyright term over time which mean different terms for the same categories of

---

[3] See J. Hughes, 'Locke's 1694 Memorandum (and more incomplete copyright historiographies)' (2010) 27 *Cardozo Arts & Entertainment Law Journal* 555. See also M. Rose, 'Nine-tenths of the law: the English copyright debates and the rhetoric of the public domain' (2003) 66 *Law and Contemporary Problems* 75.

[4] A. Birrell, *Seven Lectures on the Law and History of Copyright in Books* (Cassell & Co., 1899); Deazley, *Rethinking Copyright*, 5, 14.

[5] See J. Feather, 'Publishers and politicians: the remaking of the law of copyright in Britain 1775–1842. Part II: the rights of authors' (1989) 25 *Publishing History* 45.

[6] T. Ochoa, 'Origins and meanings of the public domain' (2003) 28(2) *University of Dayton Law Review* 215 at 225.

[7] J. C. Ginsburg, '"Une chose publique"? The author's domain and the public domain in early British, French and US copyright law', in P. Torremans (ed.), *Copyright Law: A Handbook of Contemporary Research* (Edward Elgar, 2007), p. 154.

## 9.2 Extension of the Copyright Term

work at different times.[8] In particular, there can be byzantine difficulties in applying transitional provisions to determine the terms of works created under previous copyright laws. In the interests of simplicity, this chapter does not attempt to deal with transitional rules. Moreover, while it is customary to use comparative tables to summarise the terms for different works in different jurisdictions, we do not do this as we are attempting to explain the main rules, not to provide a calculator. The chapter does, however, attempt to convey some of the complexity by including detail on both the general legal framework and selected legal issues in our chosen jurisdictions.

As Patry points out, applying an instrumentalist view: [1.6], '[f]ixing the term of protection involves balancing the need to provide an adequate incentive to create while still ensuring that there will be a robust public domain from which new works may be developed.'[9] This chapter returns to the relationship between the copyright term and the public domain after first outlining the history of extension to the term under UK and US law. Following this, the chapter reviews constraints on countries setting their own terms under international copyright law. The chapter then explains the terms in selected jurisdictions, namely the EU, UK, United States, Australia and China, before surveying the terms in other jurisdictions, especially those that differ from international norms. Next, the chapter explains the relationship between terms of protection for economic rights and for non-economic, moral rights. The chapter concludes with analysis of the copyright term under national regimes and, applying our realist perspective, suggestions and recommendations arising from our analysis.

### 9.2 Extension of the Copyright Term: United Kingdom and United States

The history of duration of copyright protection is, in part, a history of ever-increasing terms. This can be illustrated by the history of copyright terms in the UK and the United States.

The Statute of Anne initially set the term for protection at twenty-one years for books in print, and fourteen years for new books, with an option of renewal for a further fourteen years if the author was living at the end of

---

[8] R. Deazley, 'Copyright and digital copyright heritage: duration of copyright', *Copyright 101*, *Copyright Codex* https://copyrightcortex.org/copyright-101/chapter-6, May 2017, p. 5.
[9] W. Patry, 'Choice of law and international copyright' (2000) 48 *American Journal of Comparative Law* 383 at 438.

the first term (when the rights reverted to the author).[10] Even then, the London booksellers continued to treat books falling outside of these terms as their perpetual property, obtaining injunctions in Chancery until, in *Donaldson* v. *Becket*,[11] the House of Lords held that copyright in published books was confined to the terms set by the Statute.[12] In 1814, the term for published books was extended to a fixed term of twenty-eight years or for the life of the author, whichever was longer.[13] As explained above, after a vigorous debate over the copyright term, the 1842 Act introduced a term for published books of life of the author plus seven years or forty-two years from publication, whichever was longer.[14]

In the eighteenth and nineteenth centuries there was a proliferation of UK Acts dealing with different categories of works, especially artistic works, with terms ranging from twenty-eight years from first publication to life plus seven years for works of fine art.[15] Meanwhile, by the early twentieth century, the majority of Berne members had adopted terms of protection of life of the author plus fifty years or more,[16] with the 1908 Berlin revision adopting a minimum non-obligatory term of life plus fifty years (also known as fifty years *post mortem auctoris* or *pma*).[17] In 1909, the Gorell Committee, established to consider the Berlin revision, recommended adopting the fifty year *pma* term for works, which was implemented in the 1911 UK Act.[18] This remained the term, with the 1988 CDPA applying it to all works including unpublished works (which formerly had perpetual protection), until 1995, when the current term of seventy years *pma* was adopted to implement a 1993 EU Directive: [9.5]. Due to complex transitional provisions, however, the '2039 rule': [9.6], means that copyright in certain categories of unpublished works will not expire until 2039.

In the United States, on the model of the Statute of Anne, the 1790 Copyright Act provided a minimum term for published books of fourteen years, with the possibility of renewal for an additional fourteen

---

[10] Statute of Anne, 1709, 8 Anne, c. 19 (Eng.); J. Feather, 'The book trade in politics: the making of the Copyright Act of 1710' (1980) 8 *Publishing History* 39.
[11] 1 ER 837 (HL 1774).   [12] Rose, 'Nine-tenths of the law', 77.
[13] Copyright Act of 1814, 54 Geo. III, c. 156 (Eng.), s. 4; Feather, 'Publishers and politicians'.
[14] Literary Copyright Act 1842 (5 & 6 Vict. C. 45), s. III.
[15] S. Ricketson, *The Law of Intellectual Property* (The Law Book Company Limited, 1984), [4.43] ff.
[16] Ricketson and Ginsburg, *International Copyright and Neighbouring Rights*, [9.16].
[17] *Ibid.* [9.17].
[18] *Report of the Committee on the Law of Copyright*, Cd 4976 (1909), p. 16; Ricketson and Creswell, *The Law of Intellectual Property*, [6.55].

years.[19] The term was extended by the 1831 Act to twenty-eight years, with a renewal period of an additional fourteen years, creating a maximum term of forty-two years.[20] Subsequently, the 1909 Act increased the renewal period from fourteen to twenty-eight years, establishing a maximum term of fifty-six years from first publication.[21] The 1909 Act used the term 'public domain' for the first time, specifically providing that the increased term would not apply to any works that were in the public domain and that, while copyright might subsist in a derivative work, this would not remove original works on which the derivative work was based from the public domain.[22]

The term of protection remained essentially as set by the 1909 Act until the 1976 Act, except for nine interim extensions for one or two year periods between 1962 and 1974.[23] The 1976 Act introduced a standard term for both published and unpublished works created on or after 1 January 1978 of fifty years *pma*, while increasing the term for existing works to seventy-five years from first publication.[24] Moreover, the 1976 Act established a term of seventy-five years from publication or 100 years from creation (whichever expired first) for works-for-hire, and anonymous or pseudonymous works.[25] Finally, in 1998, the term of protection for works was extended, essentially to match the EU term, to seventy years *pma*: [9.5]; with the term for works-for-hire and anonymous and pseudonymous works extended to ninety-five years from first publication or 120 years from creation.

## 9.3 Term of Protection and the Public Domain

Whenever the term has been extended, it has provoked controversy, especially as it prevents works, commonly including existing works, from entering the public domain for the extended period. Although in 1992 Ricketson claimed that the copyright term under international copyright law had been characterised by 'an almost complete absence of debate of the policy and theoretical issues involved',[26] term extensions,

---

[19] Copyright Act of 1790 (US), Cong. Ch. 1-15, §1 (1790); Ochoa, 'Origins and meanings', 224.
[20] Copyright Act of 1831 (US), Cong. Ch. 21-16, §§1, 2, 16 (1831); E. Samuels, 'The public domain revisited' (2002) 36 *Loyola of Los Angeles Law Review* 389 at 411–12.
[21] Copyright Act of 1909 (US), Cong. Ch. 60-320, §23 (1909); Samuels, 'The public domain revisited', 412.
[22] Copyright Act of 1909 (US), §§7, 8; Ochoa, 'Origins and meanings', 226–7.
[23] Samuels, 'The public domain revisited', 424.
[24] Pub. L. No. 94-553, §§302, 304; Ochoa, 'Origins and meanings', 229–30.
[25] Pub. L. No. 94-553, §§303; Samuels, 'The public domain revisited', 412 n. 107.
[26] S. Ricketson, 'The copyright term' (1992) 23 *International Review of Intellectual Property and Competition Law (IIC)* 753 at 777.

and especially the 1998 US extension and subsequent constitutional challenge: [9.7], focused analytical attention on the copyright term.[27] This section of the chapter reviews arguments concerning the relationship between the copyright term and the public domain.

Arguments about copyright duration necessarily follow from theoretical perspectives on justifications for copyright: [1.6].[28] From an instrumentalist perspective, perhaps the most prominent contribution has been the amicus brief prepared by seventeen economists, including five Nobel laureates, addressing economic issues in the 2003 constitutional challenge to the 1998 US term extension.[29] The brief separated out issues relating to term extension for existing works from those relating to a longer term for new works.

For existing works, the costs of increased protection, such as above-cost pricing, must outweigh any benefits as, since the work has already been created, there can be no effect on incentives. Extending the term therefore merely results in a transfer of income from users to owners. For works not yet in existence the position is more complex. From an economic perspective, estimating an optimal term involves balancing any positive incentive effect of a longer term against the administrative costs of a longer term and the 'access costs', meaning both the costs of above-cost pricing ('deadweight loss') and transaction costs facing users.[30] Each of these elements requires further consideration.

Where an already long term is extended, the incentive effect is probably negligible. The reasons for this are, first, that for most copyright works economic returns diminish over time (known as 'cultural depreciation') and, second, the need to apply a discount to take into account the diminution in future value of a work.[31] For example, while a twenty-year increase in an already long term will result in only a small increase in incentives, it imposes 'access costs' on users. In this, the transaction costs include the costs in tracing owners and in negotiating to use the work.[32] If, on the other hand, the work had fallen into the public domain, new derivative works could be produced without these costs being incurred. While it is arguable that the effects on the public domain are partly offset by permissible uses under the idea/expression dichotomy and exceptions

---

[27] See, for example, the collection of essays in Volume 36 of *Loyola of Los Angeles Law Review*.
[28] R. Giblin, 'Reimagining copyright's duration', in Giblin and Weatherall (eds.), *What If We Could Reimagine Copyright?*, 177.
[29] Brief of George A. Akerlof et al. as Amici Curiae in support of petitioners in *Eldred v. Ashcroft*, 537 US 186 (2003).
[30] Landes and Posner, 'Indefinitely renewable copyright', 476.
[31] Giblin, 'Reimagining copyright's duration', 181–2.
[32] Landes and Posner, 'Indefinitely renewable copyright', 477–80.

## 9.3 Term of Protection and the Public Domain

(such as fair use),[33] there are often considerable uncertainties about whether or not a use is permitted: Chapters 10–12.

While the incentive effect of a longer term for most works is insignificant, this is not the end of the story. The low threshold for copyright protection means that most works have no or limited commercial value. Moreover, markets for creative works are characterised by a very small percentage of works accounting for the largest share of sales.[34] Therefore, in determining the incentive effect, the longevity of the term may have an effect on the highest value works, which have a long commercial lifespan.[35] Effectively to distinguish works on the basis of commercial value, Landes and Posner proposed a system of copyright renewals, with copyright expiring after an initial term unless the owner takes positive action to renew the copyright.[36] This would help ensure that only the more valuable works have longer terms and reduce tracing costs for those works but, on the other hand, could discriminate against works not owned by large corporations.

Apart from arguments that a longer term may result in more works, a longer term has been supported in that it provides an incentive for copyright owners to invest in existing works, such as by restoring works or making them accessible in new formats (known as the 'old-movies restoration' argument).[37] The economists' brief in *Eldred*, however, concluded that the incentive effects from a longer term for improving existing works are likely to be small, and might be better provided from other areas of the law, such as trade mark law.[38] Apart from questions of whether copyright is the appropriate means for encouraging such activity, a longer term may also create disincentives for investing in existing works, such as where a work becomes an orphan due to difficulties in locating the owner or due to the 'anticommons' effect of coordinating multiple rights holders.[39]

A practical factor which can be overlooked is that because many copyright terms are based on the date of death of the author, if the average lifespan of authors increases, then this longevity also expands the average

---

[33] S. Liebowitz and S. Margolis, 'Seventeen famous economists weigh in on copyright: the role of theory, empirics, and network effects' (2005) 18(2) *Harvard Journal of Law & Technology* 435 at 452–4.
[34] *Ibid.* 454.    [35] *Ibid.* 454–7.
[36] Landes and Posner, 'Indefinitely renewable copyright'.
[37] R. Posner, 'The constitutionality of the Copyright Term Extension Act: economics, politics, law, and judicial technique in *Eldred* v. *Ashcroft*' (2003) 4 *Supreme Court Review* 143 at 156; Landes and Posner, 'Indefinitely renewable copyright', 489–93.
[38] See also W. Gordon, 'Authors, publishers, and public goods: trading gold for dross' (2002) 36 *Loyola of Los Angeles Law Review* 159.
[39] *Ibid.* 166–7; Giblin, 'Reimagining copyright's duration', 189–90.

duration of copyright protection, independently of the expansion of legal copyright terms *pma*. The result is that copyright will now usually protect a work for well over a century.[40]

As Liebowitz and Margolis point out, the information requirements for setting an optimal term are 'severe',[41] as they involve determining and balancing complex costs and benefits. Moreover, as mentioned above, the incentives argument is complicated in that different works require different incentives: some works would be created without copyright, but others might require a significant term for the costs of creation to be recovered.[42] There are good arguments that current terms, such as seventy years *pma*, are excessive, at least for most works, and detrimental to the public domain.[43] That said, it is difficult to disagree with Liebowitz when he observes:

> In truth, there is very little evidence to support either longer or shorter terms for copyright. Nor is there any reason to believe that the copyright terms are near their optimal economic length. It seems that politics tends to drive changes in copyright law more so than changes in the efficient term of copyright.[44]

## 9.4 Copyright Term: The International Framework

International copyright law sets floors on the terms of protection for foreign works and neighbouring rights, constraining the flexibility available for national laws.

The duration of copyright protection was a source of disagreement among Berne members: [4.5], with the minimum fifty years *pma* term being agreed as part of the 1908 Berlin revision. The fifty years *pma* term was made a mandatory minimum at the 1948 Brussels revision,[45] and remains so under Article 7(1) of Berne. Berne sets special minimum terms for anonymous and pseudonymous works, photographs, works of applied art and films; but Article 9 of the WCT effectively provides that photographs are to be protected for the general Berne standard of life plus fifty years: [4.5]. The Berne minima are confirmed by Article 12 of TRIPs.

---

[40] C. Bond and G. Greenleaf, 'Copyright duration in Australia: 1869 to 2014' (2015) 25(3) *Australian Intellectual Property Journal* 155–78.
[41] Liebowitz and Margolis, 'Seventeen famous economists', 438.
[42] See Gordon, 'Authors, publishers, and public goods', 196.
[43] Landes and Posner conclude that, given the importance of 'access costs', an optimal term is 'considerably shorter than the current term of life plus seventy years': Landes and Posner, 'Indefinitely renewable copyright', 476.
[44] S. Liebowitz, 'A critique of copyright's criticisms' (2015) 22(4) *George Mason Law Review* 943 at 945.
[45] Ricketson and Ginsburg, *International Copyright*, [9.24]–[9.25].

The Berne principle of national treatment does not apply to duration of protection: [4.5.3]. In place of this, Article 7(8) adopts the rule of comparison of terms, under which the term must not exceed the term in the country of origin, unless legislation in the country where protection is claimed provides otherwise. Article 4(b) of TRIPs exempts the Berne rule of comparison of terms from the TRIPs most-favoured-nation (MFN) principle. The Berne-TRIPs framework therefore establishes minimum floors for the term of foreign works but, in so doing, allows for considerable variation in terms under national laws that build on the Berne minima.

For neighbouring rights, Article 14 of Rome established minimum terms for phonograms, performances and broadcasts of twenty years: [4.5.4]. While TRIPs extended the minimum terms for phonograms and performances to fifty years, the WPPT set the minimum term for performances fixed in phonograms at fifty years from the year of fixation, and for phonograms at fifty years from the year of publication or (for unpublished phonograms) fifty years from the year of fixation.

## 9.5 EU Term Directive

In the EU the Term Directive,[46] adopted in 1993, completely harmonises copyright terms, prescribing not only minimum but also maximum terms. Prior to the Directive, while all Member States applied the Berne minimum of fifty years *pma*, there were considerable variations, with some jurisdictions providing longer terms, and some establishing exceptions. For example, the general term in Germany was seventy years *pma*, while in Spain it was sixty years *pma* and in France seventy years *pma* for musical works.[47] On the other hand, a 1985 French law assimilated computer programs to works of applied art, with a term of protection of twenty-five years.[48] There was even greater variation in the protection of neighbouring rights with, for example, Belgium and the Netherlands providing no protection for performances, phonograms or broadcasts.[49] In 2011, a further Directive amended the Term Directive to extend the

---

[46] Term Directive. The Directive was amended by InfoSoc Directive, codified in 2006 and amended in 2011. Full titles and citations of all Directives are in the Table of International Instruments.

[47] G. Dworkin and J. Sterling, '*Phil Collins* and the term directive' (1994) 16(5) *European Intellectual Property Review* 187; Goldstein and Hugenholtz, *International Copyright*, [8.3.3]; M. M. Walter, 'Term directive', in Walter and von Lewinski (eds.), *European Copyright Law: A Commentary*, [8.1.3]. Austria, Belgium and Greece also provided for terms of seventy years *pma*.

[48] Walter, 'Term directive', [8.0.5].    [49] Dworkin and Sterling, '*Phil Collins*', 187.

harmonised term to sound recordings and the related rights of performers in sound recordings.[50]

Before the Term Directive, Member States applied the principle of comparison of terms, which meant that different terms could apply to works of foreigners than to those of nationals. In *Phil Collins*,[51] however, the ECJ made it clear that the principle of non-discrimination in the EC Treaty (now the TFEU) applied to prevent discrimination between members on the basis of nationality, so that the principle of national treatment had to be applied. Together with the conclusion that differences in copyright terms were an obstacle to the development of the internal market, the *Phil Collins* ruling, which was handed down almost simultaneously with the Term Directive, provided impetus for harmonisation among Member States.

The Term Directive not only harmonised terms of protection, establishing a general term for works of seventy years *pma*, but harmonised all associated rules, including the event from which the term is to be calculated and the principles for protecting foreign works.

*Term of Protection of Works: Seventy Years pma*   Article 1(1) of the Term Directive established the basic rule, for all categories of works falling within Berne, whether published or unpublished, that the term of protection is seventy years *pma*. As confirmed by Recital (10),[52] the term was set to establish a 'high level' of protection, with the seventy-year term being justified in Recital (5),[53] as being 'intended to provide protection for the author and the first two generations of his descendants', taking into account longer average lifespans since the fifty-year *pma* term was established. As longer lifespans are already taken into account in a term set by reference to the life of the author,[54] the practical explanation for the levelling up to seventy years *pma* was clearly the difficulties, including problems of constitutional law and fundamental rights, in reducing the protection in Member States that already had a term of seventy years *pma*.[55]

Unlike Berne, the harmonised term in the Directive applies to all works, including photographs, works of applied art,[56] computer

---

[50] Term Extension Directive.
[51] Joined cases C-92/92 and C-326/92, *Phil Collins* v. *Imtrat Handelsgesellschaft mbH*, [1993] ECR I-5145.
[52] Recital (11) Codified version.    [53] Recital (6) Codified version.
[54] See, for example, H. Jehoram, 'The EC Copyright Directives, economics and authors' rights' [1994] *International Review of Intellectual Property and Competition Law (IIC)* 821.
[55] Walter, 'Term directive', [8.1.6].
[56] Countries taking advantage of the option in Article 2(7) of Berne to protect works of applied art under industrial designs law do not need to apply the harmonised copyright term.

## 9.5 EU Term Directive

programs and cinematographic and audiovisual works. Where there are two or more joint authors, as under Berne, the term is calculated by reference to the death of the last surviving author.[57] For cinematographic and audiovisual works, Article 2(2) of the Directive specifically confines the joint authors to the principal director, the author of the screenplay, the author of the dialogue and the composer of the music. While databases protected by copyright are entitled to the full term of seventy years *pma*, a database protected under the *sui generis* regime under the Database Directive is protected for only fifteen years.[58] In relation to anonymous and pseudonymous works, the term of protection is set at seventy years after the work is lawfully made available to the public.[59]

*Other Changes to Terms in the Term Directive* The Term Directive made other significant changes in the harmonisation of terms, which were in summary: the duration of protection of related rights was set at fifty years; a twenty-five-year term from publication of unpublished posthumous works; and critical and scientific publications in the public domain may optionally have a term set at up to thirty years from publication. Details of these changes are provided in the Online Supplement.

*Extension of Term for Sound Recordings: Seventy Years* The imminent expiry of copyright in sound recordings of well-known recording artists, such as Paul McCartney, Cliff Richard and Eric Clapton, led to a campaign for extending the term from fifty to ninety-five years.[60] The extension of the term was controversial, being opposed by both the Gowers Review and the Hargreaves Review,[61] with an extension strongly criticised in a 2006 study by the Institute for Information Law (IViR).[62]

Nevertheless, in 2011, the EU adopted the Term Extension Directive, which extended the term for sound recordings (phonograms) to seventy years from fixation, or from first lawful publication or public communication.[63] In addition, the term for performances fixed in

---

[57] Term Directive, Art. 1(2).  [58] Database Directive, Art. 10(1).
[59] Term Directive, Art. 1(3).
[60] S. Atkinson, 'Sir Cliff Richard's victory: an extra 20 years for copyright protection in sound recordings and performers' rights where a sound recording of the performance is released' (2014) 36(2) *European Intellectual Property Review* 75.
[61] A. Gowers, *Gowers Review of Intellectual Property* (December 2006), Recommendation 3, [4.40]; I. Hargreaves, *Digital Opportunity: A Review of Intellectual Property and Growth* (Intellectual Property Office (UK), 2011), [2.16] ('Hargreaves Review').
[62] N. Helberger, N. Dufft, S. van Gompel and P. B. Hugenholtz, 'Never forever: why extending the term of protection for sound recordings is a bad idea' (2008) 30(5) *European Intellectual Property Review* 174.
[63] Term Extension Directive, Art. 1(2)(b).

a sound recording were extended to seventy years from first publication or first public communication, whichever is earlier.[64] However, the term for performances that are fixed otherwise than in a phonogram, such as in a film, remains at fifty years from first publication or first public communication.

The Term Extension Directive also harmonised the term for co-written musical compositions, where the lyrics and music are written by different authors, so that the term expires after seventy years from the death of the last surviving co-author, whether lyricist or composer,[65] and included a 'use it or lose it' clause benefiting performers.[66]

*Duration of Protection of 'Foreign' Works: Comparison of Terms* As the Term Directive harmonises the duration of protection of works and related rights for EU Member States, the problem of how to deal with national differences in terms in the EU does not arise, except where there are gaps in harmonisation, such as for non-original photographs.[67] While Berne generally provides that the rule of comparison of terms applies to works: [4.5.3], applying the non-discrimination principle from *Phil Collins*, an EU Member State cannot apply comparison of terms to works where the country of origin is another EU Member, and must apply national treatment.

Article 7 of the Term Directive sets out rules for determining the duration of protection of works where the country of origin is a third country or the author is not an EU national. By 'third country' the Directive means a country that is neither an EU member nor a Contracting State of the European Economic Area (EEA). Article 7(1) of the Directive mandatorily requires the application of the rule of comparison of terms to third country works, with the proviso that the term must not exceed that provided by the Directive (namely, seventy years *pma*). This means that where the country of origin has a shorter term than that in the EU, that shorter term will be applied (unless the author is an EU national, in which case the EU term must apply). For the related rights dealt with in Article 3, Article 7(2) provides that the rule of comparison of terms must apply where the rights holders are not EU nationals, provided that the terms must not exceed those specified in the Directive (namely, fifty years).

As the mandatory application of the rule of comparison of terms to non-EU works and related rights means that a shorter term of protection would often be applied to works from third countries than to EU works,

---

[64] Term Extension Directive, Art. 1(2). [65] Term Extension Directive, Art. 1(1).
[66] See the Online Supplement. [67] *Ibid.* [8.7.10].

### 9.5 EU Term Directive

this was clearly intended to act as an incentive for non-EU countries to increase their protection to match the longer EU terms.[68] The Term Directive was therefore a contributing factor to the extension of terms in other jurisdictions, notably the United States: [9.7]. It has therefore contributed to the global weakening of the public domain through longer terms of protection.

By mandatorily applying the rule of comparison of terms to foreign works, the Directive complies with Article 7 of Berne, and also falls within the exemption to the MFN principle, allowed under Article 4(b) of TRIPs: [4.5.3]. The mandatory application of comparison of terms to neighbouring and related rights is an innovation. As such, there may be difficulties if, for example, Rome is interpreted as imposing the principle of national treatment.[69]

*Transitional Provisions: Revival of Protection of Public Domain Works* Given differences in terms in EU Member States prior to the Term Directive, at the time the Directive was implemented some works were protected in some EU countries (such as countries applying the seventy-year *pma* term) but were in the public domain in other EU countries (such as countries applying the fifty-year *pma* term). To deal with this, Article 10(2) of the Term Directive provides that the terms established by the Directive apply to works or other subject matter which were still protected in at least one EU Member State on the date the Directive came into effect. As a result, where a work or other subject matter was protected in at least one Member State at the time the Directive came into effect, but was in the public domain in other Member States, copyright was revived in the public domain works for the harmonised term of protection prescribed by the Directive.[70]

*Moral Rights* Given differences in approach to moral rights between EU Member States, the protection of moral rights is not harmonised. Article 9 of the Term Directive expressly preserves the lack of harmonisation of moral rights in relation to copyright duration by providing that the Directive 'shall be without prejudice to the provisions of the Member States regulating moral rights'.

---

[68] *Ibid.* [8.7.7], [8.7.27].
[69] For differences in views on this issue, see *ibid.* [8.7.32]–[8.7.33].
[70] *Ibid.* [8.10.12] ff.; Dworkin and Sterling, *'Phil Collins'*, 188. See also Case C-60/98 *Butterfly* v. *Briciole de Baci* [1999] ECR I-3939; [2000] 1 CMLR 587.

## 9.6 UK Law

The Term Directive was implemented in the UK by amendments to the CDPA made by the Duration Regulations 1995,[71] which came into effect on 1 January 1996. As UK law was required to implement the Directive, this section of the chapter focuses mainly on how UK law differs from the Term Directive.

*Non-Original Photographs?* As the Term Directive applies only to works and related rights for which protection is harmonised, national variations are permissible where protection is not harmonised. Article 6 of the Term Directive provides that the general term of seventy years *pma* is to apply to photographs that are original, in the sense they comply with the EU threshold of being the 'author's own intellectual creation', but expressly preserves the ability of Member States to 'provide for the protection of other photographs'. Although it has been argued that UK law provides for the protection of photographs that do not comply with the 'intellectual creation' standard,[72] as the CDPA does not expressly protect non-original photographs, the better view seems to be, following *Infopaq* and *Painer*: [7.2.10], that photographs are not protected under UK law if they do not meet the harmonised originality threshold.[73]

*Computer-Generated Works and Typographical Arrangements* The CDPA provides for two forms of related rights that do not fall within the Term Directive and for which the UK therefore remains free to set the duration of protection. First, computer-generated works, for which there is no human author, are protected for a period of fifty years from the end of the year in which the work is made.[74] Second, copyright in the typographical arrangement of a published edition is protected for a period of twenty-five years from the end of the calendar year in which the edition was first published.[75]

*Films* The Term Directive sets two terms for films: [9.5] and Online Supplement; first, for cinematographic and audiovisual works, the term is set at seventy years *pma*, and the Directive specifically identifies the authors; second, in relation to the first fixation of a film, the duration is

---

[71] Duration of Copyright and Rights in Performances Regulations 1995 (UK), SI 1995 No. 3297 ('Duration Regulations').

[72] Walter, 'Term directive', [8.6.12]; K. Garnett, G. Davies and G. Harbottle, *Copinger and Skone James on Copyright* (15th edn, Sweet & Maxwell, 2005), [6-45].

[73] T. Margoni, 'The digitization of cultural heritage: originality, derivative works and (non) original photographs', 3 December 2014 https://ssrn.com/abstract=2573104.

[74] CDPA, s. 12(7).   [75] CDPA, s. 15.

fifty years from first fixation, or from first lawful publication or public communication. The CDPA provides that duration of protection for a film is the life of the author plus seventy years with the joint authors, for this purpose, being identified as the principal director, the author of the screenplay, the author of the dialogue and the composer of music specially created for the film.[76] As the CDPA does not provide a separate term for the rights in the first fixation of a film, which would presumably vest in the producer, it is generally assumed that the CDPA does not correctly implement Article 3 of the Term Directive.[77]

*Extension of Protection for Sound Recordings* In 2013, the UK amended the CDPA to implement the Term Extension Directive by extending the term for sound recordings from fifty years to seventy years from the time a recording is first published or communicated to the public, whichever is earlier.[78] The amendments also extended the term for performances fixed in sound recordings to seventy years from when the recording is first 'released', meaning published, played or shown in public, or communicated to the public.[79]

*The 2039 Rule* As previously explained, the former perpetual protection of unpublished works was abolished by the CDPA. In what is known as the '2039 rule', however, transitional provisions applying to categories of unpublished works that were protected when the CDPA came into effect, in 1989, provided that copyright in these works would not expire for fifty years, therefore lasting until 2039.[80] The categories of works to which the 2039 rule applies are: literary, dramatic, musical works and engravings, where the author died before 1969 and the work had not been published, performed in public, offered for sale to the public or broadcast in 1989; anonymous and pseudonymous literary, dramatic, musical or artistic works (other than photographs) that were unpublished in 1989; unpublished photographs that were taken on or after 1 June 1957; sound recordings made on or after 1 June 1957 that were unpublished in 1989; films that were unpublished in 1989; and works granted perpetual copyright by the 1775 Copyright Act including works bequeathed to particular universities and Crown copyright. For

---

[76] CDPA, s. 13B.
[77] P. Kamina, 'Authorship of films and implementation of the Term Directive: the dramatic tale of two copyrights' [1994] *European Intellectual Property Review* 319; P. Kamina, 'British film copyright and the incorrect implementation of the EC Copyright Directives' [1998] *Entertainment Law Review* 109.
[78] Copyright and Duration of Rights in Performances Regulations 2013, SI 2013/1782, reg. 6.
[79] SI 2013/1782, reg. 8.   [80] CDPA, Schedule 1, cl. 12.

unpublished works in which the author died after 1969, under the 1995 term extension regulations, the term is 70 years *pma*, meaning that copyright expires after 2039.

The Enterprise and Regulatory Reform Act 2013 (UK) introduced a power to make regulations to amend the 2039 rule, with the exception of photographs and films,[81] and in 2014 the UK Government consulted on whether the duration of protection of unpublished works subject to the 2039 rule should be reduced to the standard terms.[82] In response to submissions arguing that this would interfere with potential commercialisation of works subject to the rule, in 2015 the government decided against immediately abolishing the rule.[83] Nevertheless, the impact of the rule on old unpublished works, such as diaries held in libraries or archives, continues to make it controversial.

*Publication Right in Unpublished Works* Article 4 of the Term Directive, which establishes a related right for the publication of unpublished works where the term has expired, was implemented by the Copyright and Related Rights Regulations 1996.[84] The right applies in relation to the first publication of unpublished literary, dramatic, musical or artistic works, or films, where the copyright has expired. The publication right gives the first publisher of a previously unpublished work all of the exclusive rights in the copyright, but not the moral rights, for a period of twenty-five years from the end of the year in which the work is first published.

*Revived Copyright* Article 10(2) of the Term Directive required the revival of copyright in works in which the term had expired where they were still protected in at least one EU Member State when the Directive came into effect. Article 10(3), however, gives Member States leeway to 'adopt the necessary provisions to protect in particular acquired rights of third parties'. The Duration Regulations provided for the revival of copyright in works where copyright had expired in the UK but were protected in at least one other EEA state at 1 July 1995,[85] but established special rules about ownership of copyright in revived works, and use of such works. In particular, Regulation 24 provides that where copyright in

---

[81] Enterprise and Regulatory Reform Act 2013 (UK), s. 76.
[82] Intellectual Property Office (UK), 'Consultation on reducing the duration of copyright in unpublished ("2039") works in accordance with section 170(2)of the Copyright, Designs and Patents Act 1988' (IPO, October 2014).
[83] Intellectual Property Office (UK), 'Government response to the consultation on reducing the duration of copyright in certain unpublished works' (IPO, 2015).
[84] SI 1996/2967, regs. 16 and 17.   [85] Duration Regulations, reg. 16(d).

a work has been revived, uses of the work are permitted as if the work was licensed, provided reasonable remuneration is paid (as agreed by the parties or, in default of agreement, as determined by the Copyright Tribunal). As the regime allows permission free use of revived works, subject to the payment of remuneration, on our analysis such works are effectively part of the public domain.

*Perpetual Copyright* The policy of the CDPA was to remove perpetual copyright in certain works that had existed under previous Copyright Acts, such as the perpetual protection previously available for unpublished literary, dramatic and musical works, and unpublished engravings and photographs.[86] As explained above, important categories of unpublished works are subject to the 2039 rule. The remaining form of perpetual protection, introduced by the CDPA, concerns the play, 'Peter Pan' by Sir James Barrie, with the trustees of The Hospital for Sick Children, Great Ormond Street, having an unlimited statutory right to receive royalties for public performances and other specified commercial uses.[87]

## 9.7 Copyright Terms: US Law

The 1976 US Copyright Act, which came into effect on 1 January 1978, extended copyright to all original works that were fixed in a tangible medium of expression, including unpublished works which previously had unlimited protection under state common law copyright, and applied a generally uniform, Berne-compliant term of fifty years *pma*: [9.2].[88]

As a result of concerted lobbying by heirs of music composers, and copyright owners such as the Disney Corporation, and influenced by the term set by the EU Term Directive, the 1998 Copyright Term Extension Act (CTEA)[89] increased the term for works to essentially match the EU term.[90] The CTEA therefore extended the duration of copyright in works created after 1977 to seventy years *pma*.[91] In addition, the CTEA

[86] Copyright Act 1956 (UK), ss. 2(3), 3(4).   [87] CDPA, s. 301 and Sch 6.
[88] See Ochoa, 'Origins and meanings', 228; E. Townsend-Gard, 'January 1, 2003: the birth of the unpublished public domain and its international implications' (2006) 24 *Cardozo Arts & Entertainment Law Journal* 687 at 689.
[89] Sonny Bono Copyright Term Extension Act, Pub L. No. 105-298, tit. I, 112 Stat. 2827 ('CTEA').
[90] See Merges, 'One hundred years of solicitude', 2236; R. Posner, 'The constitutionality of the Copyright Term Extension Act: economics, politics, law, and judicial technique in *Eldred* v. *Ashcroft*' (2003) 4 *Supreme Court Review* 143 at 145; D. Karjala, 'Judicial review of copyright term extension legislation' (2002) 36 *Loyola of Los Angeles Law Review* 199 at 201, 206–8; Martin, 'The mythology of the public domain', 257.
[91] CTEA, §102(3)(a).

extended the term for 'anonymous works, pseudonymous works, and works made for hire' by twenty years, so they are protected for ninety-five years from first publication, or 120 years from creation, whichever is shorter.[92] While the CTEA did not revive copyright for works that were in the public domain at the end of 1997, it extended the term by an additional twenty years for all works in which copyright had not expired from that time;[93] for example, extending the term of works created prior to 1977 from seventy-five years from publication to ninety-five years from publication.[94]

*Eldred v. Ashcroft: Term Extension and the Public Domain* The CTEA term extension met with considerable opposition, resulting in a constitutional challenge before the Supreme Court in *Eldred*,[95] which is the major judicial decision to address duration of protection. In *Eldred*, while the seventy years *pma* term for new works was not challenged, it was claimed both that extending the term for existing works was in breach of the requirement in the Intellectual Property (IP) Clause of the US Constitution that protection be for 'limited Times'[96] and that it failed First Amendment scrutiny: [8.3.1]. The argument was essentially that the IP Clause is aimed at furthering the public interest by both promoting new works and expanding the public domain.[97] The division between the majority and the dissenting judgments in the case focused attention on the relationship between term extension and the public domain.

Noting that US Congress had previously extended the term for existing works, the majority held that the seventy years *pma* term was for a 'limited time' and that it was permissible to confer, as a matter of fairness, the same duration of protection on present as well as future copyright holders. Moreover, the majority effectively held that determining the duration of protection was within the competence of Congress and, especially given the EU term extension, not to be second-guessed by the Court. The majority further held that term extension was compatible with the First Amendment as copyright protection promotes freedom of expression and, while not completely immune from First Amendment challenges, copyright law incorporates internal speech-protective safeguards, especially the idea/expression dichotomy and fair use exception.

---

[92] CTEA, §102(3)(b).
[93] M. Jones, '*Eldred* v. *Ashcroft:* the constitutionality of the Copyright Term Extension Act' (2004) 19 *Berkeley Technology Law Journal* 85 at 91.
[94] CTEA, §102(d).   [95] *Eldred* v. *Ashcroft*, 537 US 186 (2003).
[96] US Constitution, Art. I, §8, cl 8.   [97] Samuels, 'The public domain revisited', 403.

## 9.7 Copyright Terms: US Law

In dissent, Stevens J expressly stated that the 'limited Times' requirement was intended to guarantee that 'innovations will enter the public domain as soon as the period of exclusivity expires'.[98] Rejecting arguments in favour of constitutionality, he held that term extension could not be justified by providing an incentive to restore old movies (the 'old-movies restoration' argument), as this would apply equally to works in which copyright had expired, that extending protection to works already created did not provide an incentive for new works, and that the public were entitled to rely on free access to works in which copyright was scheduled to expire.

In a separate dissent, Breyer J interpreted the IP Clause as being aimed at promoting knowledge and learning by creating incentives for authors to produce works. In this, he read the Clause in light of the First Amendment, as both are aimed at the 'creation and dissemination of information',[99] to require that a copyright statute must be more than minimally rational. As extending the term could not create an incentive to produce works already in existence, and as the extended term (for both existing and new works) imposed costs in the form of additional payments to copyright owners and the costs of obtaining permission to use works, he held that term extension could not be rationally justified. Relatedly, he concluded that the CTEA would cause significant expression-related harms in restricting the dissemination of works and inhibiting dissemination using new technologies.

*Term of Protection: Works Created on or after 1978* For works created on or after 1 January 1978, whether published or unpublished, the US Act establishes a uniform term of seventy years *pma* from creation[100] and, in the event of joint authors, the term is determined by the death of the last surviving author.[101] For works made for hire, and anonymous and pseudonymous works, the duration is ninety-five years from first publication or 120 years from creation, whichever is shorter.[102]

*Term of Protection: Unpublished Works in Existence in 1978* Prior to the 1976 Act, unpublished works were entitled to perpetual protection under state common law copyright. From the time of coming into effect of that Act, such works were protected under statutory copyright and, after the CTEA, have a term of seventy years *pma*.[103] The statute specifically provides, however, that the term for such works could not expire before

---

[98] 537 US 186 at 223 (2003).    [99] 537 US 186 at 244 (2003).    [100] 17 USC §302(a).
[101] 17 USC §302(b).    [102] 17 USC §302(c).    [103] 17 USC §303(a).

31 December 2002; and, in the case of unpublished works published before that date, copyright was extended to December 2047.[104]

*Restoration of Foreign Copyrights* As part of US accession to TRIPs, in 1994 the Copyright Act was amended to restore US copyright to certain foreign works that were in the public domain in the United States (but not as a result of expiry of the copyright term) so as to comply with Article 18(1) of Berne: [4.3.1].[105] Under section 104A of the Act, US copyright was restored in foreign works where: at least one author was a national of a country that is a member of Berne or the WTO; the work was not in the public domain in the source country due to expiry of the term; the work was in the public domain in the United States due to failure to comply with formalities or lack of subject matter protection (for fixed sound recordings); and, if published, the work was first published in an eligible country and not published in the United States during the thirty-day period following first publication.[106] Although copyright was automatically restored for eligible works, copyright owners were required to notify reliance parties, or provide constructive notice by filing with the Copyright Office, of plans to enforce the restored rights.[107]

*Foreign Works: National Treatment* While Article 7(8) of Berne adopts the rule of comparison of terms, it allows deviations from this by legislation that provides otherwise: [4.5.3]. As the US Act does not contain any express provision applying the rule of comparison of terms, however, the rule is not part of US law. Therefore, for almost all foreign works, the United States applies the principle of national treatment, meaning that foreign works are given the same term of protection as domestic works.[108] In practice, this means that US works may have a shorter term of protection in another country than that country's works receive in the United States. The main US exception to the application of national treatment to duration of protection of foreign works applies to the class of works first published before 1964, which were subject to a renewal requirement, and which are subject to the rule of comparison of terms.[109]

---

[104] For works subject to US federal copyright law, state copyright claims are pre-empted: 17 USC §301. There is still, however, scope for claiming state protection for some categories of works, such as unfixed works and pre-1972 sound recordings: 17 USC §301(b).
[105] Uruguay Round Agreements Act, Pub. L. No. 103-465, 108 Stat 4809, 4976 (1994).
[106] 17 USC §104A.  [107] 17 USC §104A(e).  [108] Patry, 'Choice of law', 440.
[109] *Ibid.* 440-1.

## 9.8 Copyright Terms: Australian Law

There are ambiguities concerning the protection of foreign works published without notice prior to 1 March 1989, the effective date of US adherence to Berne, which are discussed in the Online Supplement.

### 9.8 Copyright Terms: Australian Law

As a result of the Australia–United States Free Trade Agreement (AUSFTA), which came into effect on 1 January 2005, Australia extended the term for works from the Berne-compliant fifty years *pma* to seventy years *pma;* and extended the terms for sound recordings and films by twenty years to seventy years.[110] At the same time, the term for photographs was extended from fifty years from publication to the standard term of seventy years *pma*. In a review of the AUSFTA, the Parliamentary Joint Standing Committee on Treaties (JSCOT) indicated that 'Australian negotiators defended the term of copyright protection vehemently, but that the final outcome was necessary to secure the overall package'.[111]

*Term of Protection of Published Works: Seventy Years pma* In accordance with AUSFTA, the term of protection for published works is standardised at seventy years *pma*.[112] As permitted by Berne, however, the term for published anonymous and pseudonymous works is set at seventy years from first publication.[113]

*Terms of Protection of Unpublished Works: Abolition of Perpetual Protection* The terms for unpublished works under Australian law have been more complex than those in jurisdictions such as the UK and United States. Until recently, Australian law distinguished between published and unpublished works such that, in general, for most unpublished works protection was potentially perpetual.

In 2017, amendments were introduced which assimilated the term for unpublished works to that of published works, establishing a standard term of seventy years *pma*.[114] The transitional provisions

---

[110] Australia–United States Free Trade Agreement, signed 18 May 2004 (entered into force 1 January 2005) ('AUSFTA'), Art. 17.4.4. The amendments were introduced by the US Free Trade Implementation Act 2004 (Aus.).
[111] Parliament of Australia, Joint Standing Committee on Treaties (JSCOT), The Australia–United States Free Trade Agreement (June 2004), [16.50].
[112] Copyright Act 1968 (Aus.), s. 33(2). [113] Copyright Act 1968 (Aus ), s. 34(1).
[114] Copyright Amendment (Disability Access and Other Measures) Act 2017 (Aus.). In 2016, the Productivity Commission recommended the abolition of perpetual copyright in unpublished works 'without delay': Productivity Commission (Aus.), 'Intellectual property arrangements', 103.

for unpublished works are, however, complex. A distinction is now drawn between works first made public before 1 January 2019 and those first made public after that date, which allows for copyright owners to obtain longer protection by making an unpublished work public before that date. Making a work public is a broader concept than publishing the work, as it extends to include, for example, publicly performing or communicating a work, or publicly exhibiting an artistic work.[115]

For works first made public before 1 January 2019 there are three rules for determining duration: where the work was first made public before the author died and the identity of the author is generally known, the term is seventy years *pma;* where the work was not first made public before the author died and the identity of the author is generally known, the term is seventy years from the year the work was first made public; and where the identity of the author is not generally known, the term is seventy years from the year the work was first made public.[116] For works that are either never made public or first made public after 1 January 2019, the standard term of seventy years *pma* generally applies.[117] If, however, the identity of the author is not generally known within seventy years after the year the work was made there are two possible rules: where the work is not first made public before the end of fifty years after the year the work is made, the term is seventy years after the year in which the work is made; and where the work is first made public within fifty years of the work being made, the term is seventy years from the year in which the work is first made public.[118]

*Terms of Protection of Related Rights: Sound Recordings, Films and Broadcasts* In accordance with AUSFTA, the terms for published sound recordings and films were set at seventy years from first publication of the sound recording or film.[119] The 2017 amendments referred to above abolished perpetual protection for unpublished sound recordings and films, with the objective of removing the distinction between published and unpublished recordings and films.

As with works, there is now a distinction between sound recordings and films first made public before 1 January 2019 and those that are never made public or are made public after 1 January 2019. For sound recordings and films that are first made public before 1 January 2019, the term is set at seventy years from the year the material is first made public.[120] For

---

[115] Copyright Act 1968 (Aus.), s. 29A.    [116] Copyright Act 1968 (Aus.), s. 33(2).
[117] Copyright Act 1968 (Aus.), s. 33(3), item 1.
[118] Copyright Act 1968 (Aus.), s. 33(3), items 2 and 3.
[119] Copyright Act 1968 (Aus.), ss. 93, 94(1).    [120] Copyright Act 1968 (Aus.), s. 93(2).

## 9.8 Copyright Terms: Australian Law

recordings and films that are never made public or are made public after 1 January 2019, there are two possible rules: if the recording or film is first made public within fifty years of being made, the term is seventy years after the material being first made public, but otherwise the term is seventy years after the recording or film is made.[121]

The duration of protection for broadcasts is set at fifty years from the making of the broadcast,[122] while the term for published editions is twenty-five years from first publication.[123]

*Crown Copyright*  In the past, there were complex rules for determining the term for government works protected by Crown copyright, with different terms for different types of works. The 2017 amendments, however, simplified the term for works and subject matter protected by Crown copyright, setting a standardised term for works, sound recordings and films of fifty years from the year in which the material is made.[124]

*Lack of Harmonisation with US and EU Terms*  While AUSFTA was clearly intended to harmonise the terms of protection with the US terms, this was not achieved for sound recordings and films.[125] As explained above, under US law, the term for works made for hire, which are works where the employer is regarded as the author (and some commissioned works), is ninety-five years from first publication or 120 years from creation, whichever is shorter. As such works will include most sound recordings and films, the Australian terms of seventy years from first being made public are usually shorter than the US terms. Moreover, as further explained above, the EU Term Directive sets two terms of protection for films (seventy years *pma* for cinematographic and audiovisual works, and fifty years for first fixations of films), although the UK CDPA implements only the seventy years *pma* term. The Australian term of seventy years from first being made public for films therefore also differs from both the EU and UK terms. On the other hand, the term of seventy years from a sound recording first being made public is generally consistent with the EU (and UK) term of protection set by the Term Extension Directive.

*Duration of Protection of 'Foreign' Works: National Treatment*  Prior to 22 December 1998, in accordance with Article 7(8) of Berne, Australia

---

[121] Copyright Act 1968 (Aus.), s. 93(3).   [122] Copyright Act 1968 (Aus.), s. 95(1).
[123] Copyright Act 1968 (Aus.), s. 96.   [124] Copyright Act 1968 (Aus.), s. 180.
[125] See Ricketson and Creswell, *The Law of Intellectual Property*, [6.81].

applied the rule of comparison of terms to the term of protection of foreign works.[126] In 1998, however, taking into account that the majority of countries had become members of Berne or the WTO, the regulation implementing the rule of comparison of terms was repealed so that, from that time, the principle of national treatment applies in determining the term for foreign works.[127] The repeal of the rule of comparison of terms means that Australia may protect works even if they are no longer protected in the country of origin, such as US works first published between 1941 and 1950 for which no renewal of registration was obtained.[128] As the term extensions implemented in 2005 to comply with AUSFTA mean that Australia may confer longer protection on foreign works than is conferred in the country of origin, such as for works originating in countries, such as China and Canada, that apply the Berne minimum of fifty years *pma*, there is a case for reintroducing the rule of comparison of terms.[129]

## 9.9  Copyright Terms: China

Following the EU Term Directive, a number of countries extended the term for works from the Berne-compliant fifty years *pma* to seventy years *pma*. Nevertheless, important jurisdictions retain the Berne minimum of fifty years *pma*. In each jurisdiction, however, the basic rule for copyright duration in works is subject to significant variations. China's copyright law is outlined here as an example of a national law that retains the Berne fifty-year *pma* term, but with some important exceptions.

### 9.9.1  Term of Protection for Works: Fifty Years pma

In China, the general term of protection for works, whether published or unpublished, is fifty years *pma*.[130] For works made by employees in the course of employment, however, the term is limited to fifty years after

---

[126] *Ibid.* [16.635] citing former Regulation 5 of the Copyright (International Protection) Regulations 1969 (Aus.).
[127] Copyright (International Protection) Regulations 1969 (Aus.), reg. 4(1); *ibid.* [16.640].
[128] Ricketson and Creswell, *The Law of Intellectual Property*, [16.640].   [129] *Ibid.*
[130] Copyright Law of the People's Republic of China, adopted at the 15th Session of the Standing Committee of the 7th National People's Congress on 7 September 1990, promulgated by Presidential Decree No. 31 of 7 September 1990, effective 1 June 1991 (as amended) ('Copyright Law of the PRC'), Art. 21.

9.9 Copyright Terms: China

publication or creation, whichever occurs first.[131] The basic rules are subject to the following exceptions.[132]

*Photographic and Cinematographic Works* Photographic and cinematographic works are protected for fifty years from the year of first publication or creation, whichever expires earlier.[133] Although the shorter term for photographs complies with Article 7(4) of Berne, it does not comply with Article 9 of the WCT, which China acceded to in 2007, and which effectively requires protection of fifty years *pma*.

*Works of Applied Art* While works of applied art are protected for the general term of fifty years *pma*, a 2014 draft revision to the law proposed reducing the term for such works to twenty-five years,[134] taking advantage of the flexibility allowed by Article 7(4) of Berne.

### 9.9.2 Neighbouring and Related Rights

In general, China's copyright law applies the minimum terms of protection permitted under international law for neighbouring rights in relation to performances, sound recordings and broadcasts. Accordingly, performers' rights are protected for fifty years from the year of the performance;[135] sound recordings (and video recordings) are protected for fifty years from the first fixation (or 'first completion') of the recording;[136] and broadcasts are protected for fifty years from the first broadcasting of a programme.[137]

### 9.9.3 Foreign Works: Rule of Comparison of Terms

It is not entirely clear whether China's copyright law applies the rule of comparison of terms in determining the duration of protection of foreign works. In the absence of specific legislation providing otherwise, however, it is suggested that, in conformity with Article 7(8) of Berne, Chinese law incorporates this rule.[138]

---

[131] *Ibid.*
[132] For further discussion, see Li and Greenleaf, 'China's copyright public domain', 42–4.
[133] Copyright Law of the PRC, Art. 21.
[134] See 'Copyright Law of the People's Republic of China' (Revision draft for solicitation of comments), available from China Law Translate (dated 6 July 2014) http://chinalawtranslate.com/prc-copyright-law-revision-draft-for-solicitation-of-comments/?lang=en ('2014 Draft Revision'), Art. 29.
[135] Copyright Law of the PRC, Art. 39.   [136] Copyright Law of the PRC, Art. 42.
[137] Copyright Law of the PRC, Art. 45.
[138] See Li and Greenleaf, 'China's copyright public domain', 44.

## 9.10 Term of Protection: Other Jurisdictions

Following the EU Term Directive, the majority of countries protect works for one of two general terms of protection: the Berne compliant fifty years *pma* or the longer term of seventy years *pma*. As explained immediately above, China is a significant jurisdiction that protects works for the Berne minimum of fifty years *pma*. Canada is another important jurisdiction that retains the fifty-year *pma* term.[139] Moreover, in relation to foreign works, Canada's law specifically provides that nationals of other countries (other than NAFTA members) are not entitled to a longer term of protection than that available in their own country.[140]

Since the Term Directive was introduced, however, there has been a trend for countries to extend the basic term for works to seventy years *pma*. For example, this term was adopted by the Russian Federation in 2004[141] where it was applied retrospectively to works whose term had expired since 1993 by the 2006 *Civil Code*.[142] Similarly, in Brazil, the 1998 Act extended the term for works to seventy years *pma*.[143] Moreover, even before the Term Directive, some non-EU countries, such as Israel,[144] Switzerland[145] and Nigeria,[146] had adopted the seventy-year *pma* term.

Despite this general trend, however, most countries in the developing world retain the basic term of fifty years *pma*. Over and above this minimum term, however, there is more variation in the term for works than is commonly thought. For example, India has a term of protection for works (except photographs) of sixty years *pma*; and a term for photographs of sixty years from publication.[147] Towards the upper end, the copyright laws of Colombia[148] and Guinea[149] each set the term for works at eighty years *pma*, while Côte d'Ivoire has a term of ninety-nine years *pma*.[150] Meanwhile, the longest basic term of protection for works is provided

---

[139] Copyright Act, RSC 1985, c. C-42 (Canada), s. 6.   [140] *Ibid.* s. 9(2).
[141] Law No. 72 of 20 July 2004, cited in Walter, 'Term directive', [8.1.5].
[142] The Civil Code of the Russian Federation, Pt IV No. 230-FZ of 18 December 2006, Art. 1281.
[143] Law No. 9610 of February 19, 1998, on Copyright and Neighbouring Rights, Art. 41.
[144] See Copyright Act, 2007 (Israel), s. 38.
[145] Federal Act on Copyright and Related Rights of 9 October 1992 (as amended) (Switzerland), Art. 29(2). Protection of computer programs, however, is limited to fifty years *pma*: Art. 29(2)(a).
[146] Copyright Act (Chapter C.28, as codified 2004) (Nigeria), First Schedule.
[147] Copyright Act, 1957 (India), ss. 22, 25.
[148] Law on Copyright (No. 23 of January 28, 1982) (Colombia), Art. 21.
[149] Law Adopting Provisions on Copyright and Neighboring Rights in the Revolutionary People's Republic of Guinea (No. 043/APN/CP, of August 9, 1980) (Guinea), Art. 42.
[150] Law No. 96-564 of July 25, 1996, on the Protection of Intellectual Works and the Rights of Authors, Performers and Phonograms and Videogram Producers (Côte d'Ivoire), Art. 45.

by the Mexican copyright law which since 2003 has been set at 100 years pma.[151]

## 9.11 Moral Rights

Any treatment of the copyright term must take into account not only the term of exclusive economic rights, but also the duration of protection of non-economic moral rights. Moral rights recognise the non-economic interests of authors in works, as an expression of the personality of the creator, by providing creators with control over the treatment and presentation of the work.[152] The three basic moral rights are: the right of authors to disclose their work to the public; the right of attribution, which is a right to be acknowledged as an author; and the right of integrity, which is a right to prevent unauthorised alterations to a work.[153]

Under international copyright law, Article 6*bis*(2) of Berne provides that, after the death of the author, moral rights must be maintained at least until expiry of the economic rights, while permitting countries which upon ratification did not provide protection beyond the life of the author to retain the shorter term for some rights. The minimum term was a compromise between countries supporting a term limited to life of the author, a term lasting for the period of the economic rights, or perpetual protection.[154] As explained above, there is no harmonisation of moral rights in the EU: [9.5].

As international law allows for moral rights to persist following expiry of economic rights, this means that in jurisdictions where the term for moral rights does not expire with termination of the economic rights, the works are not fully in the public domain.[155] While such works may be used without permission, meaning they would strictly be within our public domain definition, as the use is not completely unrestricted, viewing them as not fully in the public domain is consistent with our approach of regarding copyright works as existing on a continuum between the purely 'private' and purely 'public': [2.3.2]. In this respect, there is a fundamental distinction between jurisdictions that apply a monist approach, where moral rights and economic rights are regarded as part of a single set of rights, and those applying a dualist approach, where the

---

[151] Federal Law on Copyright of 24 December 1996 (as amended) (Mexico), Art. 29.
[152] Adeney, *The Moral Rights of Authors and Performers*, [01]; Ricketson and Ginsburg, *International Copyright and Neighbouring Rights*, [10.02].
[153] Ricketson and Ginsburg, *International Copyright and Neighbouring Rights*, [10.02].
[154] *Ibid.* [7.50]–[7.52].
[155] See, for example, debates over perpetual duration of moral rights and the public domain in France: Adeney, *The Moral Rights of Authors and Performers*, [2.53].

two sets of rights are regarded as distinct.[156] The differences can be illustrated by the contrast between German and French law.

German law applies a monist approach which recognises a single author's right (*Urheberrecht*) embodying an author's personality interests in the work as inseparable from the commercial interests.[157] As a result, no distinction is drawn between moral rights and economic rights, with both expiring seventy years *pma*.[158]

France is the main jurisdiction to apply a dualist approach, in which economic rights are a form of property while moral rights protect personality rights.[159] As the work is regarded as a reflection of the author's personality, which lives on in the work after the death of the author, in theory moral rights protection is indefinite.[160] In relation to rights of attribution and integrity, Article L121-1 of the Intellectual Property Code expressly provides that the rights are perpetual and transmissible by will.[161] The right of disclosure is not expressly stated to be perpetual but, as it can be exercised after expiry of the economic rights, would seem to be indefinite.[162] After the death of the author, anyone exercising the right has a duty of fidelity to the author meaning, for example, that it must not be exercised contrary to the author's wishes.[163] The persistence of moral rights following lapse of the economic rights in France clearly represents a restriction on the public domain uses, broadly speaking, in that jurisdiction.

In common law jurisdictions, with few exceptions, moral rights lapse on the expiry of the economic rights. In the UK, for example, the rights of attribution and integrity subsist for the same term as the economic rights, but the right against false attribution is limited to twenty years *pma*.[164] In Australia, the rights of attribution and integrity, and the right against false attribution, all subsist for the same term as the economic rights,[165] subject to one exception. The exception concerns the right of integrity in films, which are treated differently in Australia than other works, and which expires on the death of the author[166] (namely, the director, producer and screenwriter).

The United States has a unique (and limited) moral rights regime, with federal legislation being confined to a *sui generis* regime under the Visual

---

[156] Ibid. [8.24], [9.12]; Ricketson and Ginsburg, *International Copyright and Neighbouring Rights*, [10.05].
[157] Adeney, *The Moral Rights of Authors and Performers*, [9.12].
[158] Law on Copyright and Neighbouring Rights (Urheberrechtsgesetz – UrhG) (Germany), Art. 64.
[159] Adeney, *The Moral Rights of Authors and Performers*, [8.24].    [160] Ibid. [8.19].
[161] Code de la propriété intellectuelle (France), Art. L121-1.
[162] Code de la propriété intellectuelle (France), Art. L121-2; Adeney, *The Moral Rights of Authors and Performers*, [8.133].
[163] Adeney, *The Moral Rights of Authors and Performers*, [8.145].    [164] CDPA, s. 86.
[165] Copyright Act 1968 (Aus.), ss. 195AM(2) (3).    [166] Ibid. s. 195AM(1).

Artists Rights Act (VARA), which is limited to works of visual art.[167] The rights conferred under VARA, which are analogous to moral rights, expire on the death of the author, with the exception of works created prior to the Act coming into effect, where the rights subsist until seventy years *pma*.[168] Moral rights in the United States are, however, also protected under state laws and, where state protection is longer than VARA, the federal statute expressly does not pre-empt the state protection.[169]

## 9.12 Conclusion: A Realist Perspective on Duration

The limited duration of copyright protection has always been at the heart of the boundary between the private and public domains, as once the term has expired works are entirely free to be used. As explained in this chapter, minimum terms have been progressively extended so that, for traditional works, the base standard in most jurisdictions is either fifty years *pma* or seventy years *pma*. Given the 'access costs' imposed by long terms, for most works these terms are too long; and there is no credible case for further term extensions. Where works have already fallen into the public domain through expiry of the term, from our instrumentalist perspective, the case against reviving copyright is even stronger.

A fundamental problem in analysing the copyright term is the difficulty of applying a 'one-size-fits-all' model, given different incentive effects for different works. While the nature of the costs and benefits involved in setting a copyright term are generally accepted, the information demands in estimating these costs and benefits are so severe as to cast doubt on any attempt to propose an 'optimal' term. Applying our realist approach: [1.5], however, we accept the constraints imposed by international copyright law, and make the following suggestions for strengthening the public domain within existing parameters.

First, as illustrated by the national laws surveyed in this chapter, rules on copyright duration are highly technical and complex, with the dense thicket of rules often being a real obstacle to users wishing to determine if a work has conclusively entered the public domain. These complexities arise because of differences in the term for different categories of works, differences in how the terms are calculated, and different terms of protection at different times. The differences are exacerbated where a number of works may subsist in a complex copyright product, such as a film or computer game. Given that use of works is inhibited by difficulties in

---

[167] Visual Artists Rights Act of 1990, Pub L 101-650, 17 USC §§106A, 113(d) (2002) ('VARA').
[168] 17 USC §§106A, 302(a). [169] 17 USC §301(f)(2)(C).

determining if or when copyright expires, the public domain can be supported by measures that reduce tracing costs, such as voluntary registration systems: [6.2.2].[170] In the EU and the UK, the complexity of rules on duration have been addressed by the development of public domain calculators, as part of the Europeana Connect initiative.[171] Applying our realist perspective, while they are not necessarily a magic bullet,[172] initiatives that reduce the information burdens on users, such as properly resourced calculators, are one of the most important practical measures for ameliorating the difficulties arising from complex national rules on duration. There is, in our view, scope for expanding and refining these and related initiatives, such as simplified guides.

Second, the perpetual term for unpublished works that formerly applied in Australia, and which persists under some national laws,[173] and the very long terms for works subject to the 2039 rule under UK law and unpublished works protected until 2047 under US law, prevent valuable uses of works, some of which have considerable cultural and historical value. For example, these terms still prevent museums, libraries and archives from copying and making available unpublished works such as war diaries, poems and letters from the First World War.[174] As the costs of very long terms for unpublished works outweigh any conceivable benefits (incentives for creating works such as diaries are, for example, not an issue), we agree with most commentators that the term for unpublished works should be harmonised with that for published works, and there are no obstacles, at least under international copyright law, preventing this. On a related issue, we are unconvinced of the need for copyright protection for the publication of posthumous unpublished works, as required under the EU Term Directive, especially where there is protection for typographical arrangements of published editions, as under UK and Australian law. We are also sceptical of the case for copyright protection as an incentive for improving existing works (the 'old movies restoration' argument) as this is likely only to be relevant to a small category of

---

[170] See H. Varian, 'Copyright term extension and orphan works' (2006) 15(6) *Industrial and Corporate Change* 965 at 968–9.

[171] See, for example, *Out of Copyright* at www.outofcopyright.eu. See, further, Deazley, 'Copyright and digital copyright heritage: duration of copyright', 45–6.

[172] For example, the European calculators have difficulties in dealing with revived copyrights: *ibid.* 46.

[173] For example, unpublished governmental literary, dramatic and musical works have perpetual protection in Singapore: Copyright Act 1987 (Chapter 63) (Singapore), s. 197(3)(a).

[174] Intellectual Property Office (UK), 'Consultation on reducing the duration of copyright in unpublished ("2039") works', p. 1.

## 9.12 Conclusion: A Realist Perspective on Duration

works,[175] and sufficient incentives can possibly be provided either by the market or other areas of the law, such as trade mark protection.

Third, restriction-free use of works is not fully possible where authors retain moral rights, meaning that where moral rights persist beyond the expiry of economic rights, arguably such works have not fully entered the public domain. From our instrumentalist perspective, we consider there is no case for the terms for moral rights to extend beyond those for economic rights, such as exists with the perpetual protection under French law. Given the significant cultural differences on this question, however, the prospects for greater harmonisation appear remote.

Fourth, given the complexities of navigating complex thickets of national rules on the copyright term, we consider there is scope for simplification and the removal of anomalies. Under UK and Australian law, these anomalies were apparent in the treatment of unpublished works; although there are also questions about the status of photographs failing the 'intellectual creation' threshold under UK law. Furthermore, under UK law, there is no power to amend the 2039 rule for photographs and films. Many of these anomalies would be addressed by the simple expedient of completely harmonising terms for unpublished works with those for published works, and the recent Australian amendments are a welcome reform in this direction.

Fifth, disparities in copyright terms under national laws, such as differences between jurisdictions applying fifty years *pma* and those with terms of seventy years *pma*, mean that rules setting the terms for foreign works are of continuing importance, with some jurisdictions applying the rule of comparison of terms and others applying national treatment. There are also uncertainties under some national laws, such as China, about which principle – comparison of terms or national treatment – applies. Given that international copyright law does not proscribe a single rule, we consider there is scope for greater harmonisation and, from the perspective of the public domain, merit in jurisdictions adopting the rule of comparison of terms, which establishes a ceiling on the term by reference to the term in the country of origin. This rule is more protective of the public domain than the principle of national treatment: where there is a shorter term in the country of origin than the country in which protection is claimed, then the rule requires the application of the shorter term; and where there is a longer term in the country of origin than in the country where protection is claimed, as the rule does not require the longer term, the shorter term will almost invariably be applied. Adopting the rule would therefore ensure that works fall into the public

---

[175] Akerlof et al. as Amici Curiae in support of petitioners in *Eldred* v. *Ashcroft*, p. 5.

domain in the country where protection is claimed at the same time as they do in the country of origin.

While works in which copyright has expired are a category in which there is less flexibility under international copyright law than most other public domain categories, it remains absolutely central to national public domains and the global public domain. As such, it is important for us to explore measures that can clarify or otherwise support this category; and this chapter has not only attempted to capture the complexities and difficulties in this area, but also to make practical suggestions for clarifying when works fall into the public domain and otherwise supporting uses of public domain works.

# 10 Non-Infringing Uses of Protected Works

| 10.1 | Introduction | 279 |
| --- | --- | --- |
| 10.2 | Uses Outside Exclusive Rights | 280 |
| 10.3 | Uses of 'Insubstantial' Parts | 305 |
| 10.4 | Uses of Ideas and Facts | 312 |

## 10.1 Introduction

Our definition of the public domain extends beyond works that are not protected by copyright to include permission-free uses of copyright works: [2.1.4], [2.3.2]. This chapter explains and analyses categories of national public domains that consist of uses of works where the works are protected by copyright, but uses are possible because they do not infringe. Our focus, as with other aspects of the public domain, is the extent to which works may be used without permission. We refer to these uses as public domain uses. The chapter therefore deals with uses of works that fall outside of the copyright exclusive rights (Category 11, [10.2]), non-infringing uses of insubstantial parts of copyright works (Category 9, [10.3]) and the principle that copyright does not protect ideas or facts (Category 10, [10.4]).

In categorising the limits on copyright, Drassinower distinguishes subject matter limitations from scope limitations, with subject matter limitations defining what is or is not a copyright work and scope limitations defining what does or does not fall within the exclusive rights.[1] On this approach, scope limitations are not exceptions, as they define the rights that comprise the copyright or, in other words, acts that *ab initio* fall outside of the exclusive rights: [11.1.1].[2] We generally agree with this categorisation, but with one exception: we deal with the idea/expression dichotomy in this chapter and not in Chapters 7 or 8 (as subject matter limitations), as the dichotomy most commonly arises, under national laws, in determining whether or not a use is infringing, and not in determining whether a work is protected.

[1] Drassinower, 'Exceptions properly so-called', 213.    [2] *Ibid.* 214.

Given the different issues arising from the three categories dealt with in this chapter, we make no attempt at overall analysis of these categories of public domain uses, but confine ourselves to evaluating the implications of the comparative legal analysis of each category at the end of each section of the chapter.

## 10.2 Uses Outside Exclusive Rights

Copyright is a set of limited exclusive rights vested in the copyright owner which are negative, in that they prevent others from doing anything that falls within the rights.[3] As such, uses of works that are outside the scope of the exclusive rights are permitted and, on our analysis, part of the copyright public domain. To identify the scope of public domain uses it is therefore essential to determine what falls within and outside each of the copyright exclusive rights.

There are two aspects to this public domain category: [3.3.11]. First, there are uses that clearly fall outside the exclusive rights in that they are generically different from uses within the exclusive rights and therefore are not uses that would be expected to be prohibited by copyright. Second, there are uses that are not clearly generically different from uses falling within the exclusive rights but, nevertheless, do not fall within any of the rights as a result of uncertainties about the scope of the rights.

### 10.2.1 Uses Clearly Outside Exclusive Rights

The history of the copyright exclusive rights is largely a history of struggles over new uses of copyright works, with rights often expanding to encompass new uses.[4] For example, in the United States, after the Supreme Court held that a mechanical piano roll did not infringe copyright in a musical work,[5] Congress passed legislation that ensured that it did.[6]

Two uses that users have historically expected to be permission free have been, first, reading or browsing and, second, lending hard copies of items such as books. Each of these uses has, however, been complicated by digitisation of copyright content, such as the transition to e-books and digital downloads, and the revolution in online access effected by the

---

[3] See *Pacific Film Laboratories Pty Ltd* v. *Federal Commissioner of Taxation* (1970) 121 CLR 154 at [5] (per Windeyer J).
[4] B. Kaplan, *An Unhurried View of Copyright* (Columbia University Press, (1967), pp. 101–25; J. C. Ginsburg, 'Copyright and control over new technologies of dissemination' (2001) 101 *Columbia Law Review* 1613.
[5] *White Smith Music Publishing Co.* v. *Apollo Co.*, 209 US 1 (1908).
[6] Merges, 'One hundred years of solicitude', 2192–4.

## 10.2 Uses Outside Exclusive Rights

Internet. For example, with analogue content, it was clear that the exclusive rights did not extend to reading, viewing or listening to copyright works. As online access entails reproductions of works, regardless of whether or not a work is downloaded, such as temporary reproductions in Random Access Memory (RAM), an unthinking application of the reproduction right to these uses raised the spectre of a de facto exclusive right to prevent reading, which would contract public domain uses: [10.2.4], [10.2.9].[7]

Similarly, with material in analogue form, users expected that copyright works, such as in the form of books, could be lent to others, or sold in the second-hand market, without requiring permission. Historically, this formed the dividing line between intangible copyright in the work and the property right in the tangible embodiment of the work, such as a book or DVD. For digital content, however, there may be no tangible embodiment, and these uses may infringe the reproduction and public communication rights. In that case, lending and second-hand sale of digital content are not public domain uses, but require permission from the copyright owner: [10.2.7], [10.2.9].[8]

### 10.2.2 Comparative Approaches to Defining Exclusive Rights

National laws adopt three main approaches to defining copyright exclusive rights. First, some laws specify the restricted acts in detail. For example, the UK CDPA in sections 17–21 sets out detailed provisions relating to exclusive rights to copy, issue copies to the public, the public rental or lending of copies, public performance, public communications and the adaptation right. Second, some laws broadly identify the set of exclusive rights without necessarily defining the rights in detail. For example, s. 31(1) of the Australian Act lists the following rights in literary, dramatic or musical works: the reproduction right; publication right; public performance right; public communication right; and adaptation right.[9] Third, some laws generally provide that copyright confers an exclusive right to make economic use of a work, often accompanied by illustrative examples of the exclusive rights. For example, the Italian law

---

[7] See Litman, 'The exclusive right to read'. See also Cohen, 'A right to read anonymously'.
[8] See R. Reece, 'The first sale doctrine in the era of digital networks' (2003) 44 *Boston College Law Review* 577; A. Perzanowski and J. Schultz, 'Digital exhaustion' (2011) 58 *UCLA Law Review* 889; A. Perzanowski and J. Schultz, 'Legislating digital exhaustion' (2014) 29 *Berkeley Technology Law Journal* 1535; S. Karapapa, 'Reconstructing copyright exhaustion in the online world' (2014) 4 *Intellectual Property Quarterly* 307.
[9] Copyright Act 1968 (Aus.), s. 31(1). But note that further provisions relating to the exclusive rights are set out in other provisions of the Act, including s. 21 in relation to the reproduction right and s. 27 in relation to the public performance right.

provides that an author has 'the exclusive right to exploit his work in any form or manner', before specifically referring to the reproduction right, public performance right, diffusion right, distribution right and rental right.[10]

The exclusive economic rights conferred by national laws may, in general, be divided into: reproduction and adaptation rights; communication and performance rights; distribution rights; and rental and lending rights.

### 10.2.3 Reproduction and Adaptation Rights

Although the reproduction right is the most fundamental right, it was not expressly incorporated into Berne until the 1967 Stockholm revision: [4.7.1]. Article 9 of Berne, however, fails to provide guidance on the meaning of 'reproduction'.

In the EU, exclusive economic rights were not harmonised, other than for computer programs and databases, until the InfoSoc Directive,[11] which harmonised the rights of reproduction, distribution and public communication for all other works. Article 2 of the InfoSoc Directive harmonises the reproduction right as follows:

> Member States shall provide for the exclusive right to authorise or prohibit direct or indirect, temporary or permanent reproduction by any means or in any form...

While Article 2 clarifies the extent to which mechanical reproductions, electronic reproductions and temporary reproductions infringe copyright, it provides no assistance in determining whether an altered form is an infringement.[12]

Some national laws set out the right in very general terms. For example, Article 16(1) of the German law defines the right as 'the right to make copies of the work by whatever method and in whatever quantity'.[13] The French law, on the other hand, sets out the right in broad terms, but gives the following detailed examples: 'in particular, by printing, drawing, engraving, photography, casting and all processes of the graphical and plastic arts, mechanical, cinematographic or magnetic recording'.[14]

---

[10] Law for the Protection of Copyright and Neighbouring Rights, Law No. 633 of April 22, 1941 (as amended) (Italy), Art. 12, Arts. 13–19.
[11] Full titles and citations of Directives are in the Table of International Instruments.
[12] S. von Lewinski and M. M. Walter, 'Information society directive', in Walter and von Lewinski (eds.), *European Copyright Law: A Commentary*, [11.2.22].
[13] Law on Copyright and Neighbouring Rights (Urheberrechtsgesetz – UrhG) (Germany), Art. 16(1).
[14] Code de la propriété intellectuelle (France), Art. L122-3.

## 10.2 Uses Outside Exclusive Rights

Most common law jurisdictions broadly define the right but clarify its application by explanatory provisions. In the UK, for example, the reproduction right, known as the right to copy a work, is defined by s. 17(2) of the CDPA to mean 'reproducing the work in any material form', with legislative clarifications, such as extending the right to 'storing the work in any medium by electronic means'.[15] Similarly, under Australian law, the right is the exclusive right to reproduce a work (meaning a literary, dramatic, musical or artistic work) in a material form.[16] While 'reproduction' is not further defined by the Australian Act, its meaning is expanded by s. 21 with, for example, s. 21(1) providing that a 'work shall be deemed to have been reproduced in a material form if a sound recording or cinematograph film is made of the work'.

Under US law, the right is the exclusive right to reproduce the work 'in copies or phonorecords',[17] with 'copies' being defined as 'material objects, other than phonorecords, in which a work is fixed by any method now known or later developed, and from which the work can be perceived, reproduced or otherwise communicated, either directly or with the aid of a machine or device'.[18]

Changes in the form of a work that are not reproductions may infringe the exclusive translation or adaptation rights: [4.7.1]. While the translation right was the first exclusive right to be included in Berne, a separate adaptation right was not incorporated until the 1948 Brussels revision, with Article 12 providing that authors of literary and artistic works have 'the exclusive rights of authorizing adaptations, arrangements and other alterations of their works'. There are considerable national variations in how the right is implemented; some jurisdictions regard adaptation as distinct from the reproduction right,[19] and others regard adaptations as a species of reproduction: [10.2.5].

### 10.2.4 The Reproduction Right

Three main issues arise in determining the scope of the reproduction right and, therefore, of uses outside the right. First, there is the extent to which the right incorporates reproductions in different forms, such as a three-dimensional version of a two-dimensional artistic work. Second, there are questions relating to the requirement, under most copyright laws, that an infringing reproduction must be fixed in a material form. Third, there is

---

[15] Copyright, Designs and Patents Act 1988 (UK) ('CDPA'), s. 17(2).
[16] Copyright Act 1968 (Aus.), ss. 31(1)(a) (b).   [17] 17 USC §106(1).
[18] 17 USC §101.
[19] Although, in some jurisdictions, a particular use may be both a reproduction and an adaptation.

the extent to which temporary reproductions, such as copies stored in caches or RAM, may be infringements.

*Reproduction in Different Forms*  While reproduction in the same medium as the original may be an infringement, reproduction in a different medium is not. But there are complexities.

Most common law jurisdictions specifically provide that transdimensional reproductions of artistic works – that is, a two-dimensional copy of a three-dimensional work, or a three-dimensional copy of a two-dimensional work – may be infringements.[20] As trans-dimensional copying was not an infringement prior to the 1911 UK Act, the extension of copyright to encompass trans-dimensional copying, first by the courts,[21] and subsequently by statutory provisions, reduced public domain uses. Extending copyright in plans or drawings to three-dimensional articles, however, led to the need for exceptions to prevent copyright in plans or drawings extending to designs of useful mass-produced articles, which may be protected under registered designs laws.[22] Similarly, under US law, designs of useful articles are expressly excluded from copyright protection.[23]

Copyright in a literary work, however, cannot be infringed by making a three-dimensional version of that work, such as by using instructions (or a recipe) to produce a three-dimensional article. For example, in *Cuisenaire*,[24] Pape J of the Supreme Court of Victoria held that copyright in a literary work consisting of written tables could not be infringed by manufacturing sets of rods based on the tables.[25] Similarly, a written description of an artistic work will not infringe copyright in the artistic work.[26]

Where a version of a work in a form other than the original is not a reproduction, however, it may still infringe the adaptation right: [10.2.5].

*Reproduction in a 'Material Form'*  With the introduction of works stored electronically on computers, questions arose about whether

---

[20] CDPA, s. 17(3); Copyright Act 1968 (Aus.), s. 21(3); Copyright Act 1957 (India), s. 14 (c)(i); Copyright Act 1987 (Malaysia), s. 3.
[21] See *King Features Syndicate Inc.* v. *Kleeman Ltd* [1940] 3 All ER 484.
[22] CDPA, s. 51; Copyright Act 1968 (Aus.) ss. 74–77A.
[23] 17 USC §113(b); P. Samuelson, 'Why copyright law excludes systems and processes from the scope of its protection' (2007) 85 *Texas Law Review* 1921.
[24] *Cuisenaire* v. *Reed* [1962] VR 719.
[25] See also *Plix Products Ltd* v. *Frank M Winstone (Merchants) Ltd* (1984) 3 IPR 390.
[26] Although a written description of an artistic work might represent a causal link in the indirect reproduction of the work in another artistic work: see *ibid*.

## 10.2 Uses Outside Exclusive Rights

such forms were reproductions. This led to the adoption of an Agreed Statement to the WIPO Copyright Treaty (WCT):

> The reproduction right as set out in Article 9 of the Berne Convention, and the exceptions permitted thereunder, fully apply in the digital environment, in particular to the use of works in digital form. It is understood that the storage of a protected work in digital form in an electronic medium constitutes a reproduction within the meaning of Article 9 of the Berne Convention.[27]

This issue is now largely resolved, with many national laws expressly providing that copyright in a work can be infringed by an electronic copy stored in a computer.[28]

On the other hand, there are questions about whether or not there is a reproduction where, in the process of making a copy, the original ceases to exist. In *Théberge*,[29] for example, the majority of the Canadian Supreme Court held that transfer of a poster to canvas, in which the ink from the original poster was transferred to the canvas, was not a reproduction as, by leaving the original poster blank, it did not multiply copies. The dissent, however, held that fixation of the work in a new medium was a reproduction, even where there was no multiplication of copies. The views of the dissenting judges in *Théberge* were supported, on similar facts, in *Art & Allposters*,[30] where the ECJ rejected the argument that transfer of ink from a poster to canvas was not a reproduction to conclude that there could be a reproduction where the medium is changed. A similar conclusion was reached by a US court in *ReDigi*,[31] which concerned a system in which digital media files were transferred from a user's computer to 'the cloud' and, as part of the process, the original file on the user's computer was deleted. Rejecting an argument that this could not be a reproduction, the Court held that this was not the digital equivalent of a transfer of a physical object embodying the work but, as it resulted in the embodiment of the work in a new material object (the file stored in the cloud), the process produced an infringing reproduction. In other words, in concluding that it was irrelevant that the original file ceased to exist, the Court held this was not a transfer of the file but a reproduction.

---

[27] WCT, Agreed Statement to Article 1(4). Full titles and citations of treaties and Conventions are in the Table of International Instruments.
[28] See CDPA, s. 17(2), Copyright Act 1968 (Aus.), s. 21(1A); Copyright Act (Chapter 63) (Singapore), s. 15(1B).
[29] *Théberge* v. *Galerie d'Art du Petit Champlain Inc.* [2002] 2 SCR 336.
[30] Case C-419/13, *Art & Allposters International BV* v. *Stichting Pictoright*, [2015] All ER (EC) 337.
[31] *Capitol Records, LLC* v. *ReDigi Inc*, 934 F Supp 2d 640 (SDNY 2013).

*Temporary Reproductions* In the lead up to the WCT, there was much debate about whether the reproduction right in Article 9(1) of Berne encompassed temporary reproductions made in using communications networks, such as reproductions made in RAM or on cache-servers.[32] This led to a proposal expressly to incorporate temporary reproductions in the reproduction right, that was defeated, and replaced by the Agreed Statement referred to above. This, however, leaves the status of temporary reproductions under international copyright law uncertain: [4.7.1].

In the EU, Article 4(a) of the Software Directive and Article 5(a) of the Database Directive extended 'reproduction' to encompass temporary reproductions, and this expansive approach is harmonised by Article 2 of the InfoSoc Directive. The effect of this extension is that mere use of a computer attached to an electronic network, such as Internet browsing simply to read content, may infringe the reproduction right. To deal with this, Article 5(1) of the InfoSoc Directive provides a mandatory exception for transient or incidental copies: [11.2], [12.2.1]. In the UK, Article 2 of the InfoSoc Directive is implemented in s. 17(6) of the CDPA, which provides that copying 'includes the making of copies which are transient or are incidental to some other use of the work'; while the Article 5(1) exception is implemented in s. 28A. In practice, therefore, whether a temporary reproduction is an infringement in the EU and UK depends upon whether it falls within the scope of the mandatory exception.

In Australia, temporary reproductions in RAM were considered by the High Court in *Stevens* v. *Sony*,[33] with the majority concluding that such reproductions were not reproductions 'in a material form'. However, as the reasoning depended on a definition of 'material form', which referred to a form of storage from which the work could be reproduced, which has since been amended, it seems that temporary reproductions may now fall within the reproduction right.[34] This interpretation seems confirmed by statutory exceptions introduced in 2005 which provide that copyright is not infringed by the making of a temporary reproduction that is 'incidentally made as a necessary part of a technical process of using a copy of a work'[35]: [12.2.2].

---

[32] Ricketson and Ginsburg, *International Copyright and Neighbouring Rights*, [11.69]–[11.75]; P. Samuelson, 'The US Digital Agenda at WIPO' (1997) 37 *Virginia Journal of International Law* 369.
[33] *Stevens* v. *Kabushiki Kaisha Sony Computer Entertainment* (2005) 221 ALR 448.
[34] There may not, however, be infringements if transient reproductions stored, for example, in RAM do not amount to a substantial part of a work.
[35] Copyright Act 1968 (Aus.), ss. 43B, 111B.

## 10.2.5 The Adaptation (or Derivative) Right

There are considerable variations in how the adaptation right appears in national laws, with some jurisdictions, such as the UK, Australia and the United States, regarding adaptation as distinct from reproduction, and others, such as France and the Netherlands, regarding adaptations as a species of reproduction.

In common law jurisdictions, the adaptation right is a distinct right. For example, s. 21(3) of the CDPA defines an 'adaptation' exhaustively to mean: a translation; a non-dramatic version of a dramatic work or a dramatisation of a non-dramatic work; 'a version of the work in which the story or action is conveyed wholly or mainly by means of pictures'; an arrangement or transcription of a musical work; an arrangement, altered version or translation of a computer program; and an arrangement, altered version or translation of a database. Section 10(1) of the Australian Act defines 'adaptation' in similar terms.

In the United States, the law took a different path. The US Act includes an exclusive right to make a 'derivative work', first introduced in the 1976 Act, and which is defined more expansively than the rights in other common law jurisdictions, to mean 'a work based upon one or more preexisting works, such as a translation, musical arrangement, dramatization, fictionalization, motion picture version, sound recording, art reproduction, abridgement, condensation, or any other form in which a work may be recast, transformed, or adapted'.[36] While the nine enumerated examples are relatively unproblematic, difficulties have arisen with the open-ended nature of the right, which has sometimes been interpreted generously,[37] leading Samuelson to observe that '[m]ysteries abound about the proper scope of the derivative work right'.[38] This has created difficulties, for example, in determining the extent to which a 'reworking' of an artistic work may be caught by the right.[39] Further difficulties arise from the extension of the right to unfixed derivatives, such as unfixed performances.[40]

Under EU law, the adaptation right is not harmonised, leaving the distinction between infringing adaptations and public domain uses to national laws.[41] Civil law jurisdictions take a different approach to

---

[36] 17 USC §101. See P. Goldstein, 'Derivative rights and derivative works in copyright' (1983) 30 *Journal of the Copyright Society of the USA* 209.
[37] Goldstein and Hugenholtz, *International Copyright*, [9.1.3].
[38] P. Samuelson, 'The quest for a sound conception of copyright's derivative work right' (2013) 101 *Georgetown Law Journal* 1505 at 1510.
[39] *Ibid.* 1554–8.
[40] D. Gervais, 'The derivative right, or why copyright law protects foxes better than hedgehogs' (2013) 15(4) *Vanderbilt Journal of Entertainment and Technology Law* 785.
[41] Ohly, 'Economic rights', 218.

whether there is an infringing adaptation to the common law jurisdictions, with infringement depending upon the extent to which the creative elements of the original work have been appropriated.[42] For example, under French law, whether a derivative work is an infringement depends upon the extent to which it is an appropriation of the original features of the primary work.[43] Under German law, in contrast, the doctrine of 'free utilisation' (*freie Banutzung*) draws a distinction between a use of a work that is an impermissible derivation, on the one hand, and a use that is a permissible 'inspiration', on the other, on the basis of whether or not there is 'significant dependence'.[44] In all jurisdictions, however, there are difficulties in determining the extent to which a work based on another work, but which has been 'reworked' or transformed, may be an infringing adaptation or derivative.

### 10.2.6 *Communication and Performance Rights*

The 'non-material' communication and performance rights confer rights over the dissemination of works to the public, with a 'performance' occurring in the presence of the audience and a 'communication' occurring electronically: [4.7.2]. Articles 11 and 11*ter* of Berne provide for exclusive rights of public performance in works, while Article 8 of the WCT provides for a technologically neutral communications right, which includes a 'making available' right: [4.7.2]. The boundary between uses within exclusive rights and public domain uses is set by the distinction between 'public' and 'non-public' performances and communications; and, in the absence of international guidance, there are considerable national variations.[45]

Some national laws incorporate performance and communication rights in a single right. For example, Article 15(2) of the German copyright law establishes a single right of communication to the public, which expressly encompasses: recitation, performance and presentation; broadcasting; communication by means of video or audio recordings; and communication of broadcasts.[46] Most national laws, however, distinguish between public performance and public communication rights.[47] As international copyright law does not prescribe an exclusive exhibition right for artistic works, there is significant divergence, with few

---

[42] *Ibid.*  [43] Gervais, 'The derivative right', 826.  [44] *Ibid.* 829–30.
[45] Ricketson and Ginsburg, *International Copyright and Neighbouring Rights*, [12.02].
[46] Law on Copyright and Neighbouring Rights (Urheberrechtsgesetz – UrhG) (Germany), Art. 15(2).
[47] CDPA, ss. 16(1)(c) (d); Copyright Act 1968 (Cth) ss. 31(1)(a)(iii) (iv); Copyright Act (Chapter 63) (Singapore), ss. 26(1)(a)(iii) (iv).

jurisdictions conferring an exhibition right. Among those that do, the German law includes an exhibition right for unpublished works of fine art and photographs and a presentation right for published works;[48] while the Canadian Act includes a right to present an artistic work at a public exhibition.[49]

*EU Law: The Problematic Public Communication Right*  Article 8 of the WCT is implemented in Article 3 of the EU InfoSoc Directive, which states that:

> Member States shall provide authors with the exclusive right to authorise or prohibit any communication to the public of their works, by wire or wireless means, including the making available to the public of their works in such a way that members of the public may access them from a place and at a time individually chosen by them.[50]

While 'communication' is not defined, it is clearly confined to electronic communications at a distance.[51] Article 3(2) extends the right to fixed performances, phonograms, films and broadcasts.

A controversial series of rulings from the ECJ has considered the meaning of 'the public' in Article 3. Most of the cases have concerned retransmission of communications. In the foundation case, *SGAE*,[52] the Court ruled that retransmission of a broadcast to television sets in hotel rooms of customers was a public communication, despite the rooms being 'private'. In the course of the ruling, the ECJ held that an act would fall within the communication right whenever there was a communication to a 'new public', meaning 'a public different from the public at which the original act of communication of the work was directed'.[53] The Court also held that a communication to the public must be to 'a fairly large number of people',[54] a criterion that has been taken up in subsequent cases which make it clear that it 'excludes from the concept groups of persons which are too small, or insignificant'.[55]

The 'new public' test was refined in cases such as *Premier League*,[56] to mean 'a public which was not taken into account by the authors of the

---

[48] Law on Copyright and Neighbouring Rights (Urheberrechtsgesetz – UrhG) (Germany), Arts. 18, 19.
[49] Copyright Act, RSC 1985, c. C-42 (Canada), s. 3(1)(g).
[50] InfoSoc Directive, Art. 3(1).   [51] See InfoSoc Directive, Recital (23).
[52] Case C-306/05, *Sociedad General de Autores y Editores de España (SGAE)* v. *Rafael Hoteles SL*, [2006] ECR I-11519.
[53] [2006] ECR I-11519 at [40], [42].   [54] *Ibid.* [38]–[39].
[55] Case C-162/10, *Phonographic Performance (Ireland) Limited* v. *Ireland* [2012] CMLR 29 at [35].
[56] Joined Cases C-403/08 and C-429/08, *Football Association Premier League Ltd* v. *QC Leisure* [2011] ECR I-9083.

protected works when they authorised their use by the communication to the original public'.[57] While the Court in *SGAE* had observed that 'the pursuit of profit is not a necessary condition for the existence of a communication to the public',[58] in *Premier League* it held that this consideration was not 'irrelevant'.[59] In *TV Catchup*, the ECJ further complicated matters by ruling that the 'new public' test did not apply where a work is communicated 'under specific technical conditions, using a different means of transmission'.[60] In that case, a 'catch-up' service was provided to subscribers by Internet retransmissions of free-to-air broadcasts, but to subscribe the users had to confirm they were in the UK and entitled to watch UK television. By holding that use of a 'different means of transmission' was a separate communication, the Court held that the transmission infringed the public communication right, even though not made to members of a 'new public'.

In recent cases, the ECJ has ruled on whether a hyperlink may be a public communication. In *Svensson*,[61] the Court extended the 'new public' test to the 'making available' right, applying the test to the question of whether providing a link to works posted with the consent of the rights holder could be a public communication. On the one hand, the ECJ ruled that a link to works that are freely available on the Internet is not a communication to a new public, as it does not expand the public beyond the originally intended recipients. On the other hand, however, a link to a site protected by a form of access restriction, such as a password, will be a communication to a 'new public' where the link circumvents the access restrictions.

In *GS Media*,[62] the ECJ considered links to works that are posted without the copyright owner's consent. In that case, the Court held that the requirements of a communication by a different means of transmission and a communication to a 'new public' are alternatives, so that if the first is satisfied there is no need to establish that the communication is to a 'new public'.[63] In determining whether a link is an infringing communication, the Court further held it was important to take into account the protection of freedom of expression and information under Article 11 of the EU Charter, especially as it is difficult for a person posting a link to ascertain whether the material linked to is infringing. Accordingly, the ECJ held that there would only be a communication to the public where

---

[57] *Ibid.* [197].   [58] [2006] ECR I-11519 at [44].   [59] [2011] ECR I-9083 at [204].
[60] Case C-607/11, *ITV Broadcasting Ltd* v. *TV Catchup Ltd* [2013] FSR 36 at [39].
[61] Case C-466/12, *Svensson* v. *Retriever Sverige AB* [2014] All ER (EC) 609.
[62] Case C-160/15, *GS Media BV* v. *Sanoma Media Netherlands BV*, [2017] 1 CMLR 921.
[63] *Ibid.* [37].

## 10.2 Uses Outside Exclusive Rights

the person posting the link knows, or ought to know, that it provides access to infringing content, such as by notification from the copyright owner.[64] In addition, by analogy with *Svensson*, the ECJ held that there is a communication to the public where a link allows users to circumvent access restrictions to access infringing content.[65] Moreover, if posting hyperlinks is carried out for a profit, there is a rebuttable presumption that the person posting the link knows that the content has been posted without the copyright owner's consent.[66] Finally, if the work is freely available to users on another website with the owner's consent there can be no communication to a 'new public', and therefore the link is not a public communication.[67]

In *Filmspeler*,[68] the ECJ applied the established tests to the novel question of whether sale of a multimedia player, which incorporated links to infringing websites, was a public communication. First ruling that the pre-installation of links was a communication, the Court held that the communication was 'to the public'. In reaching this conclusion, the ECJ applied the established criteria, taking into account that: the player was aimed at a large number of potential recipients; following *GS Media*, the sale of the player was made in the full knowledge that it would give access to unlawful content;[69] and that the player was supplied for a profit.[70]

The 'new public' test adopted by the ECJ is complex and questionable, as a matter both of interpretation and principle.[71] For example, in practice, it is likely that the same outcome would be arrived at in the retransmission cases by applying the simpler test of whether or not the communication is to a 'fairly large number of people' outside of the family circle, or if it was made for a profit. Although the status of hyperlinks raises difficult issues, it may be that a link should generally not amount to an 'act of communication' within the meaning of Article 3(1).[72]

*UK Law* In the UK, the CDPA implements Article 3 of the InfoSoc Directive by establishing a public communication right.[73] Under s. 20(1), the right applies to works, sound recordings, films and broadcasts; and, under s. 20(2), includes the rights of broadcasting and 'making available'. As an implementation of the Directive, the limitation of the right to communications to 'the public' is interpreted consistently with

---

[64] *Ibid.* [49].    [65] *Ibid.* [50].    [66] *Ibid.* [51].    [67] *Ibid.* [52].
[68] Case C-527/15, *Stichting Brein* v. *Jack Frederick Wullems* [2017] 3 CMLR 1027.
[69] *Ibid.* [50].    [70] *Ibid.* [51].
[71] Hugenholtz and van Velze, 'Communication to a new public?', 808–15.
[72] *Ibid.* 813–15.    [73] CDPA, s. 16(1)(d).

ECJ jurisprudence. As the performance right is not harmonised under EU law, however, the limitation that a performance be 'in public' is a matter for UK law.

The performance right is established by s. 16(1)(c) of the CDPA, with the meaning defined in s. 19. In determining if a performance is 'in public', the critical consideration is the character of the audience and its relationship to the copyright owner. If the audience is bound by a purely domestic or private tie, such as family and friends, the performance is not in public.[74] In this, neither payment of a charge for a performance nor the size of the audience is determinative.[75] Another consideration has been whether a performance is to the copyright owner's public, in the sense that the owner might expect payment;[76] although this reasoning is circular.[77] The right has been interpreted expansively with, for example, the playing of music over loudspeakers in a factory[78] and the performance of a play to members of a women's club,[79] being public performances.

*Australian Law* The Australian Act recognises distinct performance and communication rights.[80] In *Telstra* v. *APRA*,[81] in considering the performance right, the High Court endorsed the importance of taking into account the character of the audience and its relationship to the copyright owner; but also acknowledged the test of whether a performance is to the copyright owner's public. In considering the communication right, the Court also applied the 'copyright owner's public' test, with the commercial character of a 'music-on-hold' service being the key consideration in finding it was an infringing communication. In reaching this conclusion, the Court further held that the right to communicate a work 'to the public' was broader than the right to perform a work 'in public', as 'there can be a communication to individual members of the public in a private or domestic setting which is nevertheless a communication to the public'.[82]

---

[74] *Jennings* v. *Stephens* [1936] Ch 469.
[75] *Ibid.* 479–80; *Harms (Inc) Ltd* v. *Martans Club Ltd* [1927] 1 Ch 526.
[76] *Ernest Turner Electrical Instruments Ltd* v. *Performing Rights Society Ltd* [1943] Ch 167; *Jennings* v. *Stephens* [1936] Ch 469; *Performing Right Society Ltd* v. *Harlequin Record Shops Ltd* [1979] 1 WLR 851.
[77] *Australasian Performing Rights Association Ltd* v. *Commonwealth Bank of Australia* (1992) 111 ALR 671 at 684.
[78] *Ernest Turner Electrical Instruments Ltd* v. *Performing Rights Society Ltd* [1943] Ch 167; *Jennings* v. *Stephens* [1936] Ch 469.
[79] *Jennings* v. *Stephens* [1936] Ch 469.
[80] Copyright Act 1968 (Aus.), ss. 31(1)(iii) (iv); 31(1)(iii).
[81] *Telstra Corporation Ltd* v. *Australasian Performing Right Association Ltd* (1997) 191 CLR 140.
[82] (1997) 191 CLR 140 at 295.

## 10.2 Uses Outside Exclusive Rights

The interpretation of a communication 'to the public' under Australian law differs from EU and UK law. The differences are apparent from the treatment of hyperlinks. Under the Australian Act, a communication is defined to mean making a work available online or electronically transmitting it;[83] with the person making a public communication (other than a broadcast) being identified as 'the person responsible for determining the content of the communication'.[84] In *Cooper*[85] it was held that the person responsible for making a work available online was the person who posts an infringing work to a website, not a person linking to that website. That does not, however, mean there is no liability for linking; as in *Cooper*,[86] a person posting a link may be secondarily liable for authorising infringements. The end result may therefore not be significantly different from linking liability under EU law, although the Australian courts place more emphasis on any financial benefit arising from a link.

*US Law* The US Act has a distinctive approach, in which public communication is incorporated within a broad public performance right,[87] with a separate public display right being recognised.[88] Under section 101 of the US Act, to perform or display a work publicly is defined broadly to mean:
(1) to perform or display it at a place open to the public or at any place where a substantial number of persons outside of a normal circle of a family and its social acquaintances is gathered; or
(2) to transmit or otherwise communicate a performance or display of the work to a place specified by clause (1) or to the public ... whether the members of the public capable of receiving the performance or display receive it in the same place or in separate places and at the same time or at different times.

In the United States, downloading a musical work from the Internet is not a public performance, but streaming a work is.[89] The US courts have sometimes drawn fine lines in determining whether a work has been performed 'publicly': in one case a court held that a hotel that rented videodiscs for guests to play in their rooms was not a public performance as a hotel room is a private place,[90] but in another case the transmission of

---

[83] Copyright Act 1968 (Aus.), s. 10(1) (definition of 'communicate')
[84] Copyright Act 1968 (Aus.), s. 22(6).
[85] *Universal Music Australia Pty Ltd* v. *Cooper* (2005) 65 IPR 409 (per Tamberlin J).
[86] *Cooper* v. *Universal Music Australia Pty Ltd* (2006) 71 IPR 1 (Full Federal Court).
[87] 17 USC §106(4).   [88] 17 USC §106(5).
[89] *US* v. *American Society of Composers, Authors and Publishers*, 627 F 3d 64 (2nd Cir 2010).
[90] *Columbia Pictures Industries, Inc.* v. *Professional Real Estate Investors, Inc*, 866 F 2d 278 (9th Cir 1989).

films to guests in hotel rooms infringed, as the guests were 'members of the public'.[91]

The meaning of transmitting a work 'publicly' was considered by the Supreme Court in *Aereo*,[92] where the Court had to consider whether a service that allowed a subscriber to connect to an individualised antenna to receive broadcast transmissions was a public performance of the broadcast. In concluding it was, the majority held that transmission of a large number of discrete communications, even though at different times, to 'a large number of people who are unrelated and unknown to each other', was to transmit the works 'publicly'.[93] Although the US Act does not define 'the public', the Court held that this 'consists of a large group of people outside of a family and friends'.[94] In addition, the majority considered that in determining whether a performance was to 'the public', it was important to take into account the relationship between the members of the audience and the underlying work.[95]

While the US Act includes a display right that can include a right, for example, to display a work in a museum, this is not a general exhibition right for artistic works, as the owner of a copy of the work (or those authorised by the owner) may publicly display the copy.[96]

### 10.2.7 Distribution Rights

Under Berne, the distribution right, which is a right to control the sale and circulation of copies of a work, is limited to cinematographic reproductions or adaptations: [4.7.3]. Article 6 of the WCT, however, provides for a general distribution right which, under Article 6(2), may be confined to the initial sale of a work: [4.7.3]. An Agreed Statement to Article 6 further provides that the right is confined to 'fixed copies that can be put into circulation as tangible objects'.

*EU law: Community-Wide Exhaustion* In the EU, although a distribution right was recognised in the Software and Database Directives, it was not until the InfoSoc Directive that a harmonised, general right was introduced. Article 4(1) of the InfoSoc Directive provides for authors to have an exclusive right 'to authorise or prohibit any form of distribution to the public by sale or otherwise'. The restriction of the right to the distribution of tangible copies of works is confirmed by Recital (28), which provides that it applies to the 'exclusive right to

---

[91] *On Command Video Corp. v. Columbia Pictures Industries*, 777 F Supp 787 (ND Cal 1991).
[92] *American Broadcasting Companies, Inc. v. Aereo, Inc*, 134 S Ct 2498 (2014).
[93] *Ibid.* [54].   [94] *Ibid.*   [95] *Ibid.* [55].   [96] 17 USC §109(c).

## 10.2 Uses Outside Exclusive Rights

control distribution of the work incorporated in a tangible article'. While, unlike Article 6 of the WCT, Article 4(1) is not confined to transfers of ownership, the ECJ has equated distribution with transferring ownership, so mere display of a work or copy is not a distribution.[97] Rental and lending of works are dealt with exclusively by the Rental and Lending Directive, and are not distributions: [10.2.8]. On the other hand, offering for sale is a distribution.[98]

Article 4(2) of the InfoSoc Directive codifies the principle of exhaustion, under which the first sale of copies of a work with consent of the rights holder exhausts the distribution right, meaning that subsequent sales and transfers are permissible without consent.[99] Prior to the codification, the ECJ had developed the principle of 'Community-wide exhaustion', meaning that sale within one Member State of the EU (or the EEA)[100] exhausts the right for the entire EU (and EEA), on the basis that territorial restrictions on the movement of goods are incompatible with the internal market.[101] As is clear from Article 4(2) and Recital (28) of the InfoSoc Directive, the EU does not apply a principle of 'international exhaustion', whereby sale in any part of the world would exhaust the distribution right.[102] Therefore, once a work is put on the market in the EU, the copyright owner loses control over subsequent distribution of copies within the EU, but sale in a non-European country does not affect the distribution right.[103] The principle of exhaustion does not apply to the public communication right nor to rental and lending rights.[104]

Particular difficulties have arisen in applying the principle of exhaustion to electronic distribution of digital works: [10.2.1]. The difficulties arise because the conceptual justification for exhaustion is to balance the property rights in an intangible work with the property rights in a tangible

---

[97] Case C-456/06, *Peek & Cloppenburg KG* v. *Cassina SpA*, [2008] ECR I-2751.
[98] Ohly, 'Economic rights', 220–1.
[99] See also Software Directive, Art. 4(c); Database Directive, Art. 5(c); Rental and Lending Directive, Art. 9(2).
[100] See Art. 2(1) of Protocol 28 to the European Economic Area Agreement: [1994] OJ L 1/1.
[101] See Case 78/70, *Deutsche Grammophon* v. *Metro* [1971] ECR 487; Joined cases C-55 and 57/80, *Musik-Vertrieb Membran* v. *GEMA* [1981] ECR 147. See further, Online Supplement.
[102] This interpretation was confirmed by the ECJ in *Laserdisken*: Case C-479/04, *Laserdisken* v. *Kulturministeriet* [2006] ECR I-8089. On the differences between national exhaustion, international exhaustion and Community exhaustion, see R. Vinelli, 'Bringing down the walls: how technology is being used to thwart parallel importers amid the international confusion concerning exhaustion of rights' (2009) 17(1) *Cardozo Journal of International & Comparative Law* 101.
[103] von Lewinski and Walter, 'Information society directive', [11.4.41] ff.
[104] InfoSoc Directive, Recital (29). See also Art. 4(2) of the Software Directive.

embodiment, such as a physical copy, of the work.[105] The issue seems to be resolved by Recital (29) to the InfoSoc Directive which expressly provides that exhaustion does not apply to the use of online services, 'which should be subject to authorisation where the copyright or related right so provides'. The implication is that whereas a consumer that purchases a tangible item embodying a work, such as a book or DVD, is free to resell it, a consumer who downloads an electronic copy to their computer is not free to resell the copy. This interpretation is supported by the ECJ ruling in *Art & Allposters*:[106] [10.2.5], where the Court held that exhaustion applies to the tangible object into which a copyright work or a copy has been incorporated, and therefore does not apply where the physical medium has been altered.[107] In that case, the Court held that, as the transfer of ink from a poster to canvas altered the physical medium, this was not a sale or transfer of ownership under Article 4(2), meaning that the distribution right would only be exhausted upon first sale or transfer of the canvas.[108]

As a result of the ECJ ruling in *UsedSoft*,[109] a different position applies to downloading of software. In that case, the Court was required to determine whether exhaustion applied to downloading of copies of software that were made available subject to a licence agreement. The Court concluded that, despite the transaction taking the form of a licence agreement, it was in substance a transfer of ownership. Moreover, in reaching this conclusion, the ECJ ruled that it made no difference 'whether the copy of the computer program was made available to the customer by the rightholder concerned by means of a download from the rightholder's website or by means of a material medium such as a CD-ROM or DVD'.[110] In addition, the Court held that the exemption of the communication right from the exhaustion principle in the InfoSoc Directive[111] did not apply given that, as a *lex specialis*, the Software Directive was not subject to the exemption.[112]

Similarly, the ECJ held that Recital (29) to the InfoSoc Directive, which seems to confine exhaustion to tangible copies, had no application to downloads of software, which were governed by Article 4(2) of the Software Directive, which draws no distinction between tangible and

---

[105] S. Karapapa, 'Reconstructing copyright exhaustion in the online world' (2014) 4 *Intellectual Property Quarterly* 307 at 308–9.
[106] Case C-419/13, *Art & Allposters International BV* v. *Stichting Pictoright*, [2015] All ER (EC) 337.
[107] *Ibid.* [45]. [108] *Ibid.* [46].
[109] Case C-128/11, *UsedSoft GmbH* v. *Oracle International Corporation* [2012] 3 CMLR 1039.
[110] *Ibid.* [47]. [111] InfoSoc Directive, Art. 3(3). [112] EU:C:2012:407, [51].

## 10.2 Uses Outside Exclusive Rights

intangible copies.[113] In addition, the Court held that to limit the exhaustion principle so that it did not apply to 'services' would be to 'go beyond what is necessary to safeguard the specific subject-matter of the intellectual property concerned'.[114] Therefore, the right of distribution of software is exhausted if the software is downloaded with the consent of the copyright owner, which results in a transfer of ownership, even if the transfer is free of charge. While a user who purchases a digital copy by downloading it is able to resell it, however, in order to avoid infringing the reproduction right, that user must make the original copy unusable at the time of the resale.[115] Although the *UsedSoft* ruling has been applied to e-books by a Dutch court,[116] it seems that, following the logic of the ruling in *Arts & Allposters*, it should be confined to software.

*UK Law* In the UK, the distribution right takes the form of the exclusive right to issue copies of a work to the public,[117] which is defined by s. 18(2) of the CDPA to mean the act of putting copies into circulation that were not previously in circulation by or with the consent of the copyright owner. The exhaustion principle is implemented in s. 18(3), which provides that the act of issuing copies does not apply to any subsequent distribution, sale, hiring or loan of copies previously put into circulation, or subsequent importation of copies into the UK or another EEA state. While there are problems with the wording of s. 18(3),[118] it seems clear it is intended to implement the principle of 'Community-wide exhaustion'. Thus, if a copy of a work has previously been put into circulation in an EEA state with the permission of the copyright owner, further circulation in the UK is not restricted. On the other hand, if a copy has previously been put in circulation outside the EEA, but not in an EEA state, then putting it into circulation in the UK infringes the distribution right.

*Other Jurisdictions: Australia* Outside of the EU, there is considerable variation in the treatment of distribution rights under national laws, with it being 'impossible to make any generalization that is applicable across the whole range of [Berne] Union membership'.[119]

---

[113] *Ibid.* [55]. [114] *Ibid.* [62]. [115] *Ibid.* [70].
[116] *Nederlands Uitgeversverbond and Groep Algemene Uitgevers* v. *Tom Kabinet*, Case C/13/ 567567/KG ZA 14-795 SP/MV, District Court of Amsterdam, 21 July 2014, discussed in M. Cuevos, 'Dutch copyright succumbs to aging as exhaustion extends to e-books' (2015) 10(1) *Journal of Intellectual Property Law & Practice* 8.
[117] CDPA, s. 16(1)(b).
[118] See J. Philips and L. Bently, 'Copyright issues: the mysteries of section 18' (1999) 21(3) *European Intellectual Property* 133.
[119] Ricketson and Ginsburg, *International Copyright and Neighbouring Rights*, [11.42].

The Australian Act, for example, retains the position that applied in the UK prior to the introduction of an express distribution right, in that copyright owners have an exclusive right to publish a work.[120] Although 'publication' is defined without qualification to mean supply (whether by sale or otherwise) of reproductions of a work to the public,[121] the courts have interpreted the right as being confined to 'first publication', meaning 'to make public that which has not previously been made public in the copyright territory'.[122] The limited scope of the right means that it does not extend to prevent resale or lending of tangible copies of works. As in other jurisdictions, however, online resale or lending of digital copies is restricted to the extent that these activities infringe the public communications or reproduction rights or, particularly in the case of software, are prohibited by licence terms.

*US Law: First Sale Doctrine* Section 106(3) of the US Act gives the copyright owner express rights 'to distribute copies or phonorecords of the copyrighted work to the public by sale or other transfer of ownership, or by rental, lease, or lending'.

While the US distribution right clearly applies to digital copies, courts have differed on whether the right extends to an offer or if a copy must be downloaded.[123] In the United States, the distribution right is limited by the 'first sale' doctrine, the US equivalent of the exhaustion principle which, as codified in section 109(a), provides that:

> the owner of a particular copy or phonorecord lawfully made under this title, or any person authorized by such owner, is entitled, without the authority of the copyright owner, to sell or otherwise dispose of the possession of that copy or phonorecord.[124]

As the first sale doctrine is limited to the 'owner of a particular copy' of a work, it does not apply where a user has obtained a copy under licence, such as a software licence.[125] On the other hand, US courts look to the substance of a transaction and not merely its label to determine whether

---

[120] Copyright Act 1968 (Aus.), ss. 31(1)(a)(ii), 31(1)(b)(ii).
[121] Copyright Act 1968 (Aus.), s. 29(1).
[122] *Avel Pty Ltd* v. *Multicoin Amusements Pty Ltd* (1990) 18 IPR 443 at 445.
[123] See *A&M Records* v. *Napster, Inc*, 239 F 3d 1004, 1014 (9th Cir 2001); *Universal City Studios Productions LLLP* v. *Bigwood*, 441 F Supp 2d 185 (D Me 2006); *Capital Records, Inc.* v. *Thomas*, 579 F Supp 2d 1210 (D Minn 2008). See also P. Menell, 'In search of copyright's lost ark: interpreting the right to distribute in the internet age' (2011) 59 *Journal of the Copyright Society of the USA* 1.
[124] The first sale doctrine was first recognised by the Supreme Court in 1908 in *Bobbs-Merrill Co.* v. *Strauss*, 210 US 339 (1908).
[125] See, for example, *Vernor* v. *Autodesk, Inc*, 621 F 3d 1102 (9th Cir 2010).

## 10.2 Uses Outside Exclusive Rights

or not there has been a transfer of title in a copy, whether by sale or otherwise.[126]

In determining the territorial scope of the first sale doctrine, it is necessary to take into account section 602(a)(1) of the Act, which specifically deems the unauthorised importation of copies of works acquired outside the United States to be an infringement of the distribution right. In *Quality King*,[127] the Supreme Court effectively adopted a principle of international exhaustion, by holding that the distribution right in section 602(a)(1) incorporated a reference to the first sale doctrine, such that if ownership of a particular copy was transferred with the consent of the owner outside of the United States, the copy could be imported without infringing the importation restriction. In other words, once a copy of a work is lawfully sold internationally, the distribution right is exhausted.

In *Kirtsaeng*,[128] the Supreme Court addressed the question of whether the first sale doctrine applied where copies of a work were manufactured outside the United States. By interpreting the words 'lawfully made under this title' in section 109(a) as extending to copies lawfully made outside the United States, the majority held that, once a copy was manufactured abroad under the authority of the copyright owner, such as by a licensee, it could be imported into the United States and subsequently resold without the copyright owner's permission. In reaching this conclusion, the majority observed that:

> reliance upon the 'first sale' doctrine is deeply embedded in the practices of those, such as booksellers, libraries, museums, and retailers, who have long relied upon its protection. Museums, for example, are not in the habit of asking their foreign counterparts to check with the heirs of copyright owners before sending, e.g., a Picasso on tour.[129]

As in other jurisdictions, questions have arisen about the application of the first sale doctrine to digital resales. The issue was addressed in *ReDigi*,[130] which concerned an attempt to establish an online marketplace for resale of digital music. In that case, ReDigi established a system where users were able to upload music files to 'the cloud' and, in the process, deleted the original files from the user's computer. Once a copy was sold, the user no longer had access to it; and ReDigi software continually checked the user's computer to ensure there was no copy. The Court held that uploading a file to 'the cloud' infringed the reproduction right:

---

[126] *UMG Recordings, Inc. v. Augusto*, 628 F 3d 1175 (9th Cir 2011).
[127] *Quality King Distributors Inc. v. L'anza Research International*, 523 US 135 (1998).
[128] *Kirtsaeng v. John Wiley & Sons, Inc*, 133 S Ct 1351 (2013).    [129] *Ibid*. 1354.
[130] *Capitol Records, LLC v. ReDigi Inc*, 934 F Supp 2d 640 (SDNY 2013).

[10.2.4]. In relation to sales of digital files from the ReDigi website, the Court held that absent a defence these would infringe the distribution right, thereby confirming that section 106(3) extends to digital sales.

The *ReDigi* Court, however, rejected the application of the 'first sale' doctrine to digital resales. First, as the doctrine is limited to the distribution right, it cannot be a defence to infringements of the reproduction right. Second, section 109(a) could not apply to copies sold via the ReDigi website as such copies, being infringing reproductions, were not 'lawfully made'. Finally, and significantly, the Court held that the doctrine is limited to distribution of a physical item and, as such, could have no application to digital resales, which did not involve transfers of physical objects but the making of infringing reproductions. Consequently, as appears to be the case in EU law (outside of the Software Directive), digital resale (or other digital transfers) falls outside of the US version of the exhaustion principle.

### 10.2.8 Rental and Lending Rights

Rental rights first became part of international copyright law with TRIPs, with Article 11 requiring Member States to establish a commercial rental right for computer programs and cinematographic works, and Article 14(4) extending the right to phonograms: [4.7.4]. Article 7 of the WCT differs from Article 14(4) in that it applies the right to authors of works embodied in phonograms; and an Agreed Statement to Article 7 provides that the rental right is confined to 'fixed copies that can be put into circulation as tangible objects': [4.7.4]. We discuss here the extension of rental and lending rights under EU and UK law. The implementation of TRIPs and WCT obligations in US and Australian law is provided in the Online Supplement.

*EU Law: Rental and Lending Rights* In the EU, rental and lending rights were the first exclusive rights to be harmonised, in the Rental and Lending Rights Directive ('RLRD'), introduced in 1992. Under the Directive, rental and lending rights are conferred on authors of works, performers (in respect of fixations), producers of phonograms, and producers of the first fixation of a film.[131] The Directive applies to all works protected under Berne, except for buildings and works of applied art.[132] Article 4 of the Software Directive establishes a rental right in computer programs.

---

[131] Rental and Lending Rights Directive, Art. 3(1).  [132] *Ibid.* Art. 3(2).

Article 2(1) of the RLRD defines 'rental' to mean 'making available for use, for a limited period of time and for direct or indirect economic or commercial advantage', and 'lending' to mean 'making available for use, for a limited period of time and not for direct or indirect economic or commercial advantage, when it is made through establishments which are accessible to the public'. An establishment that is 'accessible to the public' clearly includes libraries. According to Recital (10) it is desirable for Member States to exclude certain forms of making available from the rights, namely: making available phonograms or films for the purpose of public performance or broadcasting; making available for the purpose of exhibition; or making available for on-the-spot reference use, such as on-site consultation of reference books.

The incorporation of a public lending right was controversial, as it potentially undermines cultural and social policies, such as access to works in public libraries.[133] To protect these objectives, Article 6 allows for derogations from the public lending right, provided authors obtain remuneration. The Directive does not, however, indicate who is liable to pay the remuneration. In addition, Article 6(3) allows for Member States to exempt categories of establishment from the obligation to pay remuneration. However, in response to attempts by Italy, Portugal, Spain and Ireland to exempt all, or nearly all, libraries from the obligation to pay remuneration, the ECJ has ruled that exempted establishments must be more precisely specified in accordance with the principle that derogations must be restrictively interpreted.[134]

Given the application of Community-wide exhaustion to the distribution right, it is important to establish the relationship between the distribution right and the rental and lending rights. Article 1(2) of the RLRD provides that rental and lending rights are not exhausted by the sale or other distribution of works or copies of works. Therefore, while the distribution right is exhausted by a first sale or transfer of ownership within the EU (or EEA), rental and lending rights continue irrespective of any acts of distribution.[135]

---

[133] S. von Lewinski, 'Rental and lending rights directive', in Walter and von Lewinski (eds.), *European Copyright Law: A Commentary*, [6.1.6]; Ohly, 'Economic rights', 224.

[134] Case C-198/05, *Commission of the European Communities* v. *Republic of Italy* [2006] ECR I-107; Case C-53/05, *Commission of the European Communities* v. *Republic of Portugal* [2006] ECR I-6215; *Commission of the European Communities* v. *Kingdom of Spain* [2006] ECR I-313; Case C-175/05, *Commission of the European Communities* v. *Ireland* [2007] ECR I-3.

[135] See Case C-200/96, *Metronome Musik GmbH* v. *Music Point Hokamp GmbH* [1998] ECR I-1953; [1998] 3 CMLR 919, confirming that the rental right survives exhaustion of the distribution right and is a permissible derogation from the principle of free movement of goods.

*UK Law*  In the UK, the right to rent or lend a work to the public is one of the exclusive rights conferred on works.[136] The RLRD is implemented in s. 18A of the CDPA, which defines the rights consistently with the Directive.[137] Under s. 18A(1), the right applies to literary, dramatic, musical and artistic works, and films or sound recordings; but not to buildings, models of buildings, or works of applied art. Reflecting Recital (10) to the Directive, s. 18A(3) excludes the following:

(a) making available for the purpose of public performance, playing or showing in public, or communication to the public;
(b) making available for the purpose of public exhibition; or
(c) making available for on-the-spot reference use.

The limitation of the right to making a work available 'to the public' excludes rental or lending between private parties.

Pursuant to derogations permitted under Article 6 of the RLRD, s. 40A(1) of the CDPA provides that copyright is not infringed by lending of a book by a public library if the book is within the public lending right scheme. The public lending right scheme, established under the Public Lending Right Act 1979 (UK), is a scheme administered by the British Library which provides for payments to authors for loans of books by public libraries.

Section 66 of the CDPA further provides for the Secretary of State to make an order for public lending of defined categories of works to be treated as licensed subject to payment of a reasonable royalty. Finally, applying the derogation permitted under Article 6(3) of the RLRD, s. 40A(2) provides that copyright in a work is not infringed by the non-profit lending of copies by a prescribed library or archive, that is not a public library. In relation to the lending right, therefore, the CDPA provides that public lending is restricted, except if it involves loans of books within the public lending right scheme or lending by a prescribed library or archive.

### 10.2.9 *Uses Outside Exclusive Rights and the Public Domain*

As public domain uses are uses that fall outside of the scope of exclusive rights (Category 11), they are defined by the scope of each of the exclusive rights. There are, however, significant uncertainties about the scope of each of the exclusive rights. We contend that a contribution can be made to resolving some of the uncertainties by taking into account the value of public domain uses, and we give examples below.

---

[136] CDPA, s. 16(1)(ba).   [137] CDPA, s. 18A(2).

## 10.2 Uses Outside Exclusive Rights

A focus on exclusive rights considers how far uses should extend in the interests of the copyright owner. But what if this is balanced by also asking what uses should be possible without permission? If we consider the reproduction right, there are questions about how far the right extends to encompass changes made to the form of an original work. Some of the limits to the right arise from the boundary between copyright and other intellectual property rights (IPRs). For example, using written instructions to make a three-dimensional article is not an infringing reproduction, but may be prohibited under patent law. Moreover, while making a three-dimensional article based on a design drawing may be an infringing trans-dimensional reproduction, the availability of industrial designs protection for the visual appearance of mass-produced articles may lead to the exclusion, under some national laws, of designs of useful articles from the scope of the reproduction right: [10.2.4]. If, however, we also ask whether, in the absence of another form of IPR, users should generally be able to make versions (such as trans-dimensional versions) of artistic works, this might result in a different boundary between the exclusive right and public domain uses, such as prohibiting only commercial uses. Our argument is that this perspective may be more useful in determining the balance of rights and interests than arid questions of whether a particular form of expression has been copied in a transformed work.

Similar reasoning could assist in clarifying the scope of adaptation and derivative rights. Furthermore, as reproductions that are incidental to a technical process of using a work, such as temporary copies made using the Internet, are essential to facilitate access and use of works, including permissible uses such as browsing, listening and reading, focusing on public domain uses may suggest they should not be regarded as infringing reproductions. In all of these cases, public domain uses can be promoted by clarifications to the scope of the reproduction right rather than, as is often the case, relying on exceptions, such as the exception for transient or incidental copies under EU law: [12.2.1].

Uses of works that involve dissemination by performances or communications are public domain uses where they are 'non-public' uses. While disseminations in a domestic context are public domain uses, in all jurisdictions considerable difficulties have been experienced in distinguishing 'public' from 'non-public' disseminations. These difficulties are exacerbated in the EU, where ECJ rulings have produced overly complex tests for determining whether a communication is 'public', including the unnecessary 'new public' test. The advantages of adding a focus on public domain uses can be illustrated by the difficulties in determining whether or not hyperlinks are infringing public communications. Given the role of links in promoting access and use, including supporting the de facto public domain: Chapter 16, there is a case for most linking to be permission-free public domain uses. That said, there is also a case for copyright owners being able to prevent linking where it is used to circumvent access controls, such as a paywall, or knowingly link to infringing content. From a public domain perspective, these infringing uses of hyperlinks can be regarded as a derogation from a right to permission-free use, rather than permissible linking being a derogation from the public communication right.

The distribution right involves balancing the intangible rights in a work with the property rights in tangible embodiments of the work. The balance is set by doctrines such as the EU exhaustion principle and US first sale doctrine, under which the right is limited to the first sale of a tangible copy. Applying our public domain perspective, the benefits of users, including libraries, booksellers, museums and second-hand dealers, being able to deal with tangible copies without seeking permission from owners favours a principle of national exhaustion. The analysis of international exhaustion is more contentious, given the complexities of market segmentation, but the factors identified by the US Supreme Court in *Kirtsaeng*: [10.2.7], not to mention the realities of global markets in copyright works, are clearly important if not determinative considerations. The application of exhaustion to digital works raises difficult issues, especially given the ease of making digital copies. If the problem of proliferating digital copies can be addressed, however, a public domain perspective suggests that the benefits of second-hand markets, in terms of promoting access and use of works, should be available to users of intangible copies just as much as users of tangible copies. The public domain perspective therefore suggests that it is not so much whether the distribution right should be exhausted following first sale of a digital copy, as the conditions under which the exhaustion doctrine can be implemented in the digital environment that is important.

Exclusive rental rights were introduced to deal with the threat of the reproduction right being undermined by cheap home-copying technologies: [4.7.4]. This right is therefore closely tied to changes in business models for distributing works such as software and films. For example, if a work is distributed online, regardless of whether the work is rented or sold, this involves an exercise of the communication right, so there is less need for a rental right. From a public domain perspective, the key issue is what users can do with a digital work once they have acquired it, regardless of whether the copy is leased or purchased. While the purchase of a hard copy of a book confers the ability to lend or share it with family and friends, this is complicated with digital copies due to the problems of proliferating copies. From a public domain perspective, we suggest that the issue is not so much whether users should have an ability to share a lawfully acquired digital copy with a limited circle of family and friends, but the circumstances in which this may be possible. Regarding a public lending right, which is implemented in the EU, as indicated by the need for broad derogations, this clearly has potential for impeding important public domain uses, including lending by libraries. While we think there is a role for schemes that compensate authors for public lending, we suggest that the best balance is unlikely to be struck by an exclusive lending right. The vital role of libraries and archives in supporting the public domain is taken up further at [12.6].

## 10.3 Uses of 'Insubstantial' Parts

Not all acts within the scope of the copyright exclusive rights are infringements. While literal copying of a whole work is unquestionably infringing, copyright laws must always provide that less than exact copying can also infringe.[138] But difficult questions can arise in determining whether non-literal copying, involving exact copying of part only of a work, or alterations or additions to a work, are infringing uses. This issue is, to an extent, intertwined with the principle that copyright is confined to expression, and does not extend to ideas or facts: [10.4]. But there are also questions of whether copying or other use of a work is sufficient, quantitatively or qualitatively, to be infringing. This section of the chapter deals with the threshold for infringement, which exists under all copyright laws, and which has the effect that uses falling below the infringement threshold are permissible and, therefore, public domain uses. In doing so, to focus the analysis, the section concentrates on the principle in common law jurisdictions that copyright may be infringed by using a 'substantial part' of a work (Category 9).

Berne provides no guidance on the threshold for determining whether a use is infringing, including on matters such as whether the standard is qualitative or quantitative.[139] As, apart from the idea/expression dichotomy, there is no prescribed standard under international copyright law, this is pre-eminently a matter for national laws.

---

[138] Laddie et al., *The Modern Law of Copyright and Designs*, 3rd edn, [3.130]: 'It would be a defective law which denied relief to a copyright owner unless the infringer had made a precise imitation of the whole of the work'.
[139] Ricketson and Ginsburg, *International Copyright and Neighbouring Rights*, [11.26].

### 10.3.1  EU law: Infopaq I and Reproductions 'in Part'

Under EU law, there is also no express statement of a minimum threshold or standard for infringing uses; the InfoSoc Directive, for example, does not define what is meant by a 'reproduction'. The reproduction right in Article 2 of the InfoSoc Directive, however, expressly applies to reproductions 'in whole or in part': [10.2.4]. Moreover, referring to the reproduction right, Recital (21) provides that a 'broad definition of these acts is needed to ensure legal certainty within the internal market'.

In the landmark *Infopaq I* ruling,[140] the ECJ was required to determine whether electronically storing and printing out an extract of eleven words from a newspaper article could be an infringing reproduction of part of a work. In that case, the ECJ harmonised the originality threshold by requiring that a protected work be 'the author's own intellectual creation': [7.2.10]. In relation to the application of the reproduction right to 'part' of a work, the Court held that, as there was nothing in the InfoSoc Directive indicating that parts of a work are to be treated differently from the work as a whole, the parts of a work are to be protected to the extent they share the originality of the work as a whole.[141] Applying this to the facts, the ECJ ruled that an eleven-word extract may be a reproduction 'in part' if it 'contains an element of the work which, as such, expresses the author's own intellectual creation'.[142] In this, the ruling reflects the general approach of both common law and civil law courts of taking originality into account in determining infringement.[143] Nevertheless, the Court also made it clear that parts of a work are entitled to the same protection as the whole, provided they are the 'author's own intellectual creation'.

### 10.3.2  UK Law: Impact of Infopaq I

In the UK, the threshold for infringement is established by s. 16(3) of the CDPA, which provides that reference to any of the acts restricted by the copyright is to the doing of it 'in relation to the work as a whole or any substantial part of it'.[144] The requirement for substantial infringement was established in nineteenth-century cases, but given statutory form in the 1911 Act.[145]

---

[140] Case C-5/08, *Infopaq International A/S* v. *Danske Dagblades Forening*, [2009] ECR I-6569 *(Infopaq I)*.
[141] *Ibid.* [38].   [142] *Ibid.* [48].
[143] Goldstein and Hugenholtz, *International Copyright*, 299.
[144] Copyright, Designs and Patents Act 1988 (UK), s. 16(3)(a).
[145] Copyright Act 1911 (UK), s. 1(2).

10.3 Uses of 'Insubstantial' Parts

In the UK and in other common law countries, 'substantial similarity is at the heart of copyright law, yet it remains one of its most elusive aspects'.[146] The principle that a 'substantial part' may be determined by the qualitative importance of the part taken relative to the work as a whole[147] means that copying of a quantitatively small part of a work may infringe[148] but, as we explain in the Online Supplement, the application of the principle in case law is often complex.[149]

The ECJ ruling in *Infopaq I* has altered the traditional UK approach. In the principal authority, *SAS Institute*,[150] the Court of Appeal first reiterated that a 'substantial part' is to be determined qualitatively and not quantitatively.[151] In determining what is a qualitatively substantial part, however, the Court held that the test was whether the copied parts 'contain elements which are the expression of the intellectual creation of the author of the work'.[152] Therefore, while acknowledging that the basic question involving infringement – that 'the defendant's work must represent the claimant's work in some real sense'[153] – was unchanged, the *Infopaq I* ruling has changed the question to whether 'the form of expression of an intellectual creation' has been taken.[154] This decision does not, however, resolve all uncertainties arising from previous inconsistent UK cases.[155]

### 10.3.3 Australian Law: IceTV

In Australia, the principle that copyright is infringed by doing the acts comprised in the copyright in relation to a substantial part of a work is established by s. 14(1) of the Act.[156] The main authority on the meaning of 'substantial part' is the High Court decision in *IceTV*,[157] which dealt with whether or not copying broadcast time and title information infringed copyright in a weekly programme schedule: [7.2.5]. While the Court held that the information was not a substantial part, there were considerable differences in reasoning between the judgments of French CJ, Crennan and Kiefel JJ, on the one hand, and Gummow, Hayne and

---

[146] *TCN Channel Nine Pty Ltd* v. *Network Ten Pty Ltd (No. 2)* (2005) 216 ALR 631, per Finkelstein J at 634.
[147] See *Ladbroke (Football) Ltd* v. *William Hill (Football) Ltd* [1964] 1 WLR 273 at 276 (Lord Reid); 293 (Lord Pearce); *Designers Guild* v. *Russell Williams* [2000] 1 WLR 2416 at 2422 (Lord Hoffman); 2425–6 (Lord Millet); 2431 (Lord Scott).
[148] *Hawkes & Son Ltd* v. *Paramount Film Service Ltd* [1934] Ch 593.
[149] See the Online Supplement.
[150] *SAS Institute Inc.* v. *World Programming Ltd* [2014] RPC 218.
[151] [2014] RPC 8 at [38]. [152] *Ibid.* [153] *Ibid.* [70]. [154] *Ibid.* [74].
[155] Details are in the Online Supplement. [156] Copyright Act 1968 (Aus.), s. 14(1)(a).
[157] *IceTV Pty Ltd* v. *Nine Network Australia Pty Ltd* (2009) 239 CLR 458.

Heydon JJ, on the other, with the judgments differing primarily on the extent to which originality of a part of a work that has been copied was relevant in determining if it is a 'substantial part'.

For example, according to Gummow, Hayne and Heydon JJ, concentrating on whether there has been a 'misappropriation' of the skill and labour can result in protecting material not properly protected by copyright, overlooking the proposition:

> that the statutory requirement that the part of a work taken must be substantial assumes there may be some measure of legitimate appropriation of that investment.[158]

Lack of clarity in the *IceTV* judgments has led to some difficulties in Australian law about how to determine whether a part of a work is substantial, which are dealt with further in the Online Supplement.

### 10.3.4 US Law: Multiple Tests

Under US law, the elements required to establish infringement were set out as follows by Judge Frank in *Arnstein* v. *Porter*:

> (a) that the defendant copied from plaintiff's copyright work; and (b) that the copying (assuming it to be proved) went so far as to constitute improper appropriation.[159]

Determining what amounts to an 'improper appropriation' involves a finding of 'substantial similarity' between the copyright work and the allegedly infringing copy.[160] The comparison required to establish substantial similarity is known as the 'ordinary observer test' or 'audience test', which Judge Frank explained, in the context of musical works, as follows:

> The question ... is whether defendant took from the plaintiff's works so much of what is pleasing to the ears of lay listeners, who comprise the audience for whom such popular music is composed, that defendant wrongfully appropriated something which belongs to the plaintiff.[161]

The requirement of substantial similarity as the keystone for improper appropriation emerged in the nineteenth century, although the precise

---

[158] *Ibid.* [159] 154 F 2d 464 at 468 (2nd Cir 1946).
[160] A. Latman, '"Probative similarity" as proof of copying: toward dispelling some myths in copyright infringement' (1990) 90 *Columbia Law Review* 1187; B. Stanfield, 'Finding the fact of familiarity: assessing judicial similarity tests in copyright infringement actions' (2001) 49 *Drake Law Review* 489.
[161] 154 F 2d 646 at 473 (2nd Cir 1946).

## 10.3 Uses of 'Insubstantial' Parts

phrase dates from the early twentieth century.[162] As under English law, substantiality is intertwined with whether the copied material is idea or expression, as similarity of ideas is not infringement: [10.4].

In determining substantial similarity, US courts have applied various tests, associated with different Circuits, resulting in some uncertainty. In general, however, a distinction can be drawn between Circuits that apply the 'ordinary observer test', which involves an assessment according to the impressions of ordinary lay persons, and those that apply a 'dissection' analysis, which involves separating out 'non-copyright' aspects of a work before the similarity analysis is undertaken. The Second Circuit applies the 'ordinary observer test', which, in *Peter Pan Fabrics*, was explained as whether 'the ordinary observer, unless he set out to detect the disparities, would be disposed to overlook them, and regard their aesthetic appeal as the same'.[163] The Ninth Circuit, however, following *Sid & Marty Krofft*,[164] applies a two-part test, consisting of an extrinsic test and an intrinsic test. The extrinsic test involves objectively comparing elements of the work and the alleged copy by means of analytic dissection and expert analysis to determine whether there is sufficient factual similarity. If there is, the Court then applies the intrinsic test, which depends upon the observations and impressions of the 'ordinary reasonable person'.[165]

In *Concrete Machinery*,[166] the First Circuit applied a 'dissection' analysis, which entails first dissecting the copyright work to separate protectable expression from unprotectable elements, before analysing only the protectable elements under the 'ordinary observer test'. This form of dissection is fundamentally different from the traditional English approach, which regards dissection of the original work to determine whether copyright would subsist in parts of the work as impermissible.[167] Another distinction between the US approach to substantiality and that applied by other common law courts is that some US courts have adopted a *de minimis* rule, where copying a trivial or trifling amount is not infringing. In *Ringgold*,[168] for example,

---

[162] L. Lape, 'The metaphysics of the law: bringing substantial similarity down to earth' (1994) 98 *Dickinson Law Review* 181 at 187, citing *Chatauqua School of Nursing v. National School of Nursing*, 211 F 1014 at 1015 (WDNY 1914).
[163] *Peter Pan Fabrics, Inc. v. Martin Weiner Corp*, 274 F 2nd 487 at 489 (2nd Cir 1960).
[164] *Sid & Marty Krofft Productions, Inc. v. McDonald's Corp*, 562 F 2nd 1157 (9th Cir 1977).
[165] The two-part test has been further developed in cases such as *Shaw v. Lindheim*, 919 F 2d 1353 (9th Cir 1990).
[166] *Concrete Machinery Co, Inc. v. Classic Lawn Ornaments, Inc*, 843 F 2d 600 (1st Cir 1988).
[167] See *Ladbroke (Football) Ltd v. William Hill (Football) Ltd* [1964] 1 WLR 273 at 277 (per Lord Reid); *Baigent v. Random House Group* [2007] FSR 579.
[168] *Ringgold v. Black Entertainment Television, Inc*, 126 F 3d 70 (2nd Cir 1997).

the Second Circuit applied both a quantitative and qualitative analysis to the question of substantiality, but accepted a *de minimis* rule where 'copying has occurred to such a trivial extent as to fall below the quantitative threshold of substantial similarity'.[169] Applying this analysis, in *Sandovel*,[170] the Second Circuit held that use of a photograph as part of a scene in a movie fell below a *de minimis* use.

If anything, the analysis of substantiality by US courts is more convoluted than in other common law jurisdictions. In part, this arises from differences between Circuits, which can only be summarised here. In part, it follows from a closer link than in other common law jurisdictions between the analysis of substantiality and the principle that copyright does not protect ideas. In addition, the strength of the fair use doctrine in the United States: [11.3] has led some courts to address issues that would be dealt with in substantiality analysis in other jurisdictions as part of the analysis of whether the use falls within the fair use exception.[171]

### 10.3.5 Insubstantial Uses and the Public Domain

Determining whether or not part of a work that is used is a 'substantial part' is at the heart of infringement analysis in common law jurisdictions, but is far from straightforward. While courts cannot be expected to apply an all-purpose 'bright line' rule, such as a quantitative standard, there has been a tendency in jurisdictions dealt with in this book for the infringement inquiry to be obscured by overly complex analysis. For example, there are now questions in both the UK and the United States of the extent to which a work may be dissected into protected and non-protected parts before the analysis of whether a part is a substantial part of a work. There is no doubt that difficulties in determining whether or not a part of a work that is used is insubstantial can, from the point of view of potential users, inhibit public domain uses in Category 9.

From a public domain perspective, it is arguable that the value of uses made of part of a protected work should be taken into account in the analysis of substantiality. There are sometimes suggestions of this, such as the statement by Gummow, Hayne and Heydon JJ in *IceTV* that the substantiality threshold assumes a 'measure of legitimate appropriation'. Moreover, as pointed out in *IceTV*, too much focus on the originality of

---

[169] 126 F 3d 70, 74 (2nd Cir 1997).
[170] *Sandoval* v. *New Line Cinema Corp*, 147 F 3nd 215 (2nd Cir 1998).
[171] See, for example, L. Lape, 'The metaphysics of the law', 188–90.

## 10.3 Uses of 'Insubstantial' Parts

the part that is used can lead to the conclusion that use of any original expression, no matter how insignificant, is an infringement. On the other hand, focusing too much on the extent to which a user has added to, or transformed, a copyright work can easily create incentives for 'colourable alterations', or users adding to a work to disguise infringement.

The conventional history of infringement in English law prior to the 1911 Act is that, starting with *Gyles* v. *Wilcox*,[172] the courts adopted a doctrine of fair abridgement, or fair use, to protect the public benefits of uses of copyright works that produced new works.[173] For example, in *Cary* v. *Kearsley*, the Court stated:

> That part of the work of one author is found in another, is not in itself, piracy, or sufficient to support an action; a man may fairly adopt part of the work of another: he may so make use of another's labours for the promotion of science, and the benefit of the public.[174]

According to the conventional account of UK law, the focus, in infringement cases, on the 'fairness' of the use ended with the introduction of the limited fair dealing defence in the 1911 Act: [11.4]. Although this account has been questioned,[175] the history of fair abridgement/fair use under English law raises the question of the extent to which the use to which a work is put should be taken into account in the analysis of infringement or as an exception to infringement.

While the extent of the use is clearly relevant to the substantiality analysis, and while greater focus on the use to which part of a work has been put can correct tendencies to protect any part of a copyright work, there are dangers associated with too much focus on the nature of the use, including potential for overly complicating infringement analysis. It may be that greater clarity is possible if considerations relating to the nature of the use are taken into account more in the analysis of exceptions than of infringement. Regardless, in our view, public domain uses can be supported and promoted by introducing greater clarity to the substantiality test, possibly through statutory codification of relevant factors, and potentially by introducing a *de minimis* principle, which would better ensure that insignificant parts of works are available for re-use.

---

[172] (1741) 2 Atk 141.
[173] See W. Patry, *The Fair Use Privilege in Copyright Law* (2nd edn, Bureau of National Affairs, 1995), p. 7; N. Snow, 'The forgotten right of fair use' (2011) 62(1) *Case Western Reserve Law Review* 135 at 142–4.
[174] (1802) 170 ER 679 at 680.
[175] R. Burrell, 'Reining in copyright law: is fair use the answer?' (2001) 4 *Intellectual Property Quarterly* 361.

## 10.4 Uses of Ideas and Facts

The principle that copyright does not protect ideas or facts (our category 10), but extends only to expression – commonly referred to compendiously as the 'idea/expression dichotomy' – is one of the most important, but complex, safeguards of copyright public domains. It means that once material is classified as 'idea' or 'fact' it is free to be used and an indispensable part of the public domain. As Gorman put it, the dichotomy mitigates 'what might be an overreaching monopolistic control by the copyright owner, thus promoting society's interest in enriching the public domain'.[176]

The principle is easy to state, but notoriously difficult to explain and apply. In the oft-cited words of Lord Hailsham in *LB (Plastics)*:

> Of course, it is trite law that there is no copyright in ideas.... But, as the late Professor Joad used to observe, it all depends on what you mean by 'ideas'.[177]

Much of the difficulty arises from the multiple meanings given to the terms 'idea', 'fact' and 'expression', with courts at times slipping between different meanings in the one judgment.[178]

For example, the 'idea' of a work may be regarded, amongst other things, as a 'thought' in the mind of the author before it is expressed in a material form; as the 'meaning' of a work at a higher level of abstraction than the particular form of expression used to convey the meaning; as the functions of a utilitarian work, such as a computer program; or as the basic elements that form the building blocks of a work, such as the words that make up a literary work or geometrical shapes used in an artistic work.[179] The relative indeterminacy of the dichotomy poses difficulties for mapping the public domain, which are best explained through examples drawn from the law in selected jurisdictions, which is the approach adopted in this chapter.

Although the principle that copyright does not protect facts is often assimilated to the idea/expression dichotomy, it is best regarded as an allied principle that raises distinct issues. In relation to the characterisation of 'facts' and 'expression', identifying what is meant by a 'fact' is as

---

[176] R. Gorman, 'Fact or fancy? The implications for copyright' (1982) 29 *Journal of the Copyright Society of the US* 560 at 560–61.

[177] *LB (Plastics) Ltd* v. *Swish Products* [1979] RPC 551 at 629.

[178] E. Samuels, 'The idea–expression dichotomy in copyright law' (1989) 56 *Tennessee Law Review* 321; A. Rosen, 'Reconsidering the idea/expression dichotomy' (1992) *UBC Law Review* 263; S. Ang, 'The idea–expression dichotomy and merger doctrine in the copyright law of the US and the UK' (1994) 2(2) *International Journal of Law and Information Technology* 111.

[179] Ang, 'The idea–expression dichotomy', 116–23.

## 10.4 Uses of Ideas and Facts

complex as identifying an 'idea'. For example, questions arise about whether the term 'fact' is confined to something that corresponds to a 'truth' about the world, or if it extends to 'social facts', such as credit ratings or predictions of future market values.[180] Moreover, there are ongoing legal issues concerning the protection of compilations of facts and factual databases, and especially their protection against appropriation of resources expended in collecting data. Again, these complexities are best illustrated by court decisions in selected jurisdictions, with the following sections focusing on EU, UK, Australian and US law.

### 10.4.1 Idea/Expression: International and EU Law

The idea/expression dichotomy is implied in Berne and expressly incorporated in Article 9(2) of TRIPs: [4.6.3]. The principle is, moreover, incorporated in Article 2 of the WCT, with Agreed Statements to Articles 4 and 5 emphasising its importance in the context of computer programs and compilations of data. Although an accepted part of international copyright law, the ambiguities in interpreting and applying the principle mean that, in practice, it is left to implementation in national laws: [4.6.3].

With one exception, the dichotomy is not codified in EU law. The exception is the Software Directive, which, in Article 1(2), provides:

> Protection in accordance with this Directive shall apply to the expression in any form of a computer program. Ideas and principles which underlie any element of a computer program, including those which underlie its interfaces, are not protected by copyright under this Directive.

This provision addresses a particular issue that arises in the protection of computer programs in that the form of expression of a program has functional effects, as it causes a computer to operate. Conferring protection on the non-literal elements of a computer program in a way that protects the functioning of a program would therefore effectively create a monopoly over those functions.

ECJ rulings indicate that, for computer programs, expression will not be protected where the effect of doing so would be to confer protection over the functioning of a program.[181] In applying ECJ rulings in *SAS Institute*, the English Court of Appeal held that a uniform approach

---

[180] J. Hughes, 'Created facts and the flawed ontology of copyright law' (2007) 83 *Notre Dame Law Review* 43.
[181] See Case C-393/09, *Bezpečnostní softwarová asociace – Svaz softwarové ochrany v. Ministerstvo kultury* [2010] ECR I-13971; Case C-406/10, *SAS Institute Inc. v. World Programming Ltd* [2012] 3 CMLR 55.

should be applied to separating idea from expression in both the Software Directive and the InfoSoc Directive, explaining that:

> What is protected is the form of expression of an intellectual creation. The intellectual creation itself is not protected; and the functionality of a computer program does not count as a form of expression. The functionality of a computer program (in the sense of what it does and how it responds to particular inputs) falls on the ideas side of the line. It falls on that side of the line whether one is considering the Software Directive or the Information Society Directive.[182]

### 10.4.2 Idea/Expression under UK Law

In the UK, the idea/expression dichotomy emerged through case law addressing infringements by non-literal copying. As early as 1854, Erle J explained the principle as follows:

> The subject of property is in the order of words in the author's composition; not in the words themselves ... nor in the ideas expressed by those words, they existing in the mind alone, which is not capable of appropriation.[183]

This formulation already conveyed inconsistent meanings of 'idea' and 'expression', including that an idea, unlike expression, is something yet to be embodied in a tangible form, but that expression can be a non-material form of a work, such as the arrangement of words in a literary work. These meanings are also apparent from the statements of principle by Farwell J in *Donoghue*.[184] In that case, Farwell J first explained that a person who has an idea but fails to reduce it to material form is not an author:

> A person may have a brilliant idea for a story, or for a picture, or for a play ... [but the work] which is the result of the communication of the idea to the author or the artist or the playwright is the copyright of the person who clothed the idea in form, whether by means of a picture, a play, or a book, and the owner of the idea has no rights in that product.[185]

While this seems to equate expression with the tangible embodiment of an idea, later in the judgment Farwell J observed that, in a literary work, 'that in which copyright exists is the particular form of language by which the information which is to be conveyed is conveyed'.[186] As Ang points out, the latter construction understands expression as 'a mentally constructed relationship between elements in a given medium'.[187]

---

[182] *SAS Institute Inc.* v. *World Programming Ltd* [2014] RPC 218.
[183] *Jefferys* v. *Boosey* (1854) 10 ER 681 at 702.
[184] *Donoghue* v. *Allied Newspapers Ltd* [1938] 1 Ch 106.   [185] *Ibid.* 109.   [186] *Ibid.* 110.
[187] Ang, 'The idea/expression dichotomy', 115.

## 10.4 Uses of Ideas and Facts

Much of the concern behind confining copyright to the relationship between elements of a work, such as the order of words, is to avoid conferring exclusivity on subject matter by allowing others to deal with that subject matter by means of their own expression. This is clear from cases dealing with simple works, such as the basic pictorial expression involving a square and a cross on a ballot paper in *Kenrick v. Lawrence*.[188] In rejecting the claim for infringement in that case, Wills J stated that:

> A square can only be drawn as a square, a cross can only be drawn as a cross, and for such purposes as the plaintiffs' drawing was intended to fulfil there are scarcely more ways than one of drawing a pencil or the hand that holds it. If the particular arrangement of square, cross, hand, or pencil be relied upon it is nothing more than a claim of copyright for the subject, which in my opinion cannot possibly be supported.[189]

This might seem to support the proposition that there can be no copyright when to confer it would be to protect the subject matter, which is known as the merger doctrine under US law: [10.4.4]. Although it has been suggested that *Kenrick* supports a form of merger doctrine,[190] most courts have interpreted it as accepting that copyright may subsist in works depicting simple subject matter while denying protection to all but exact reproductions.[191] The English approach therefore applies idea/expression in determining whether there has been an infringement, not in determining whether copyright subsists in a simple work.

In *Designers Guild*, Lord Hoffman attempted to rationalise the idea/expression principle by relating it to two fundamental propositions.[192] The first is that copyright must have a connection to the categories of protected subject matter, such that it is related to the literary, dramatic, musical or artistic nature of a work. From this, subject matter not related to protected categories, such as a system or invention, is unprotectable idea. Second, he interpreted cases such as *Kenrick* as standing for the proposition that ideas falling within copyright subject matter would not be protected if they are insufficiently original to be a substantial part of the work. This led to the well-known statement that '[c]opyright law protects foxes better than hedgehogs',[193] meaning that the simpler the work the

---

[188] (1890) 25 QBD 99.  [189] (1890) 25 QBD 99 at 104.
[190] *Total Information Processing Systems Ltd* v. *Daman Ltd* [1992] FSR 171 at 181.
[191] *John Richardson Computers* v. *Flanders* [1993] FSR 497; *Ibcos Computers Ltd* v. *Barclays Mercantile Highland Finance Ltd* [1994] FSR 275.
[192] *Designers Guild* v. *Russell Williams* [2000] 1 WLR 2416 at 2422–3.
[193] *Ibid*. 2423  The quote refers to a fragment from the Greek poet, Archilochus, which says, 'The fox knows many things, but the hedgehog knows one big thing': see I. Berlin, *The Hedgehog and the Fox: An Essay on Tolstoy's View of History* (Weidenfeld & Nicolson, 1953).

less expression there is and, therefore, the more exact the copying must be to amount to an infringement.

The problem of distinguishing idea from expression commonly arises where literal elements of a work, such as the words of a literary work, have not been copied, but structural elements have been. It is well established that where sufficient structural elements have been used this can amount to copying expression rather than permissible use of ideas. For example, in literary and dramatic works, the use of a combination of incidents, plot structure and character may reach the level of substantial copying of expression.[194]

In *Designers Guild*, there was, similarly, no literal copying of any part of an original artistic work, but a combination of features were taken. While Lord Hoffman reasoned that the answer depended on the originality of the features taken, with the more detail taken the more likely for this to be substantial copying, the reasoning is circular. As the originality of a work lies only in expression, and not in ideas, a distinction must be drawn between ideas and expression before originality is assessed. Lord Hoffman's attempt at reductionism is therefore not convincing: in practice, the inquiry resolves into how much of the non-literal elements of a work have been copied. In this, the English courts commonly conclude that this is a matter of impression or, as Lord Lloyd put it in *Baigent*:

> No clear principle is or could be laid down in the cases in order to tell whether what is sought to be protected is on the ideas side of the dividing line, or on the expression side.[195]

In this sense, idea/expression often seems little more than a ratification of conclusions the courts have reached on other grounds, often meaning little more than that an impermissible amount of detail of a work has been used.

The application of the fact/expression principle in the UK has been influenced by the EU Database Directive and the EU harmonisation of the originality threshold: [7.2.10]. Prior to that development, English law applied 'sweat of the brow', effectively to protect resources expended in collecting facts: [7.2.2]. Following the Directive, however, a distinction is drawn in the scope of protection given to a 'database' depending upon whether it is entitled to copyright protection or *sui generis* rights to prevent extraction or reutilisation of its contents: [7.2.8]. Applying the harmonised EU originality threshold, databases are protected by copyright only if they are the author's own intellectual creation 'by reason of the selection or arrangement of the contents of the database': [7.2.10]. This means that

---

[194] See *Baigent* v. *Random House Group* [2007] FSR 579.   [195] *Ibid.* [5].

## 10.4 Uses of Ideas and Facts

infringement of database copyright will occur only if a substantial part of the selection or arrangement of data is copied, so there can be no copyright infringement merely by extracting raw data. The application of the *sui generis* rights, which can effectively mean that 'facts' are protected, is explained in the Online Supplement.

### 10.4.3 Idea/Expression under Australian Law

While there are similarities in the application of idea/expression under English and Australian law, there are also differences. The principle that the dichotomy prevents the acquisition of exclusive rights in the subject matter of a work was first endorsed by Latham CJ in *Victoria Park*:[196]

> The law of copyright does not operate to give any person an exclusive right to state or describe particular facts. A person cannot by first announcing that a man fell off a bus or that a particular horse won a race prevent other people from stating those facts.[197]

The main Australian authority on the application of the dichotomy to non-literal copying is *Zeccola*.[198] In that case, the Full Federal Court accepted that a literary work, the novel *Jaws*, can be infringed by a film incorporating sufficient elements of plot, incidents or characters, with Lockhart and Fitzgerald JJ stating that:

> Originality, when dealing with incidents or characters familiar in life or fiction, lies in the association, grouping and arrangement of those incidents and characters in such a manner that presents a new concept or a novel arrangement of those events and characters. We accept that where a story is written based on various incidents which, in themselves, are commonplace, a claim for copyright must be confined closely to the story which has been composed by the author.[199]

In applying this analysis, the Court rejected the 'dissection' analysis[200] adopted by some US courts: [10.4.4]. *Zeccola* therefore endorses the traditional English approach by, first, undertaking idea/expression analysis in the context of infringement and, second, focusing on the originality of non-literal elements that are used.

The main Australian authority on fact/expression is *IceTV*: [7.2.5], [10.3.3]. Prior to this, in *Desktop Marketing*, the Full Federal Court had applied the 'sweat' principle: [7.2.5], to protect the information compiled in a telephone directory from extraction and re-use. In *IceTV*, the High

---

[196] *Victoria Park Racing and Recreation Grounds Company Limited* v. *Taylor* (1937) 58 CLR 479.
[197] *Ibid.* 498.   [198] *Zeccola* v. *Universal City Studios* (1982) 46 ALR 189.   [199] *Ibid.* 192.
[200] It was also rejected in *Elwood Clothing Pty Ltd* v. *Cotton On Clothing Pty Ltd* (2008) 80 IPR 566: see the Online Supplement.

Court rejected this approach, but there were significant differences in the two judgments delivered in the case: [10.3.3]. For example, while both judgments endorsed the fact/expression dichotomy, the judgment of Gummow, Heydon and Hayne JJ seemed to adopt a version of the US merger doctrine: [10.4.4], in concluding that information is not protected where 'baldly stated matters of fact or intention are inseparable from and co-extensive with their expression'.[201]

The differences in the judgments have resulted in much uncertainty about the extent of protection of factual compilations and databases under Australian law, which are explained in the Online Supplement. Despite the uncertainties, it is now clear that, where such compilations are protected, infringement is confined to appropriating a substantial amount of the selection or arrangement of the data, and not the data itself.

### 10.4.4 Idea/Expression under US Law

The idea/expression dichotomy under US law is conventionally traced to the Supreme Court's decision in *Baker* v. *Selden*,[202] which held that copyright in a book of accounting forms did not confer protection on the accounting system. Although the result in the case has never been doubted, there are difficulties in the reasoning. Like other cases in this area, the judgment incorporates multiple readings of idea/expression.[203] At its heart, it stands for the proposition that copyright in a book including a collection of accounting forms does not extend to protect a method or system which, if anything, must be protected by patent law. This can also be seen as an instance of the more general proposition that copyright in a work does not confer rights over the subject matter of the work.

*Baker* v. *Selden* has, however, also been interpreted as the origin of the US merger doctrine, which denies protection where ideas are so inseparably connected to their expression that it is impossible to protect expression without also protecting the ideas. On the facts, merger arose from the extent to which the accounting system could not be used without using the forms, meaning that the forms could not be protected as they were 'necessary incidents to the art'.[204] In addition, the judgment implies that copyright could not subsist at all in the book of forms, as it was not proper subject matter for copyright protection.[205]

Drawing from *Baker* v. *Selden*, idea/expression is codified in section 102(b) of the US Copyright Act, which provides:

---

[201] *Elwood Clothing Pty Ltd* v. *Cotton On Clothing Pty Ltd* (2008) 80 IPR 566 at 512.
[202] 101 US 99 (1880).   [203] See Samuels, 'The idea–expression dichotomy'.
[204] 101 US 99 at 103 (1880).   [205] 101 US 99 at 107 (1880).

## 10.4 Uses of Ideas and Facts

In no case does copyright protection for an original work of authorship extend to any idea, procedure, process, system, method of operation, concept, principle, or discovery, regardless of the form in which it is described, explained, illustrated or embodied in such work.

US courts conventionally address idea/expression in determining whether an allegedly infringing copy is substantially similar to an original work, the dichotomy being described as an 'indispensable corollary' of substantiality.[206]

The most influential US approach to applying the dichotomy to traditional works is Judge Learned Hand's 'abstractions' test, set out in his judgment in *Nichols*.[207] The case involved the basic question of when copying non-literal elements of a literary or dramatic work amounts to copying protected expression. In addressing this problem, Judge Hand framed the question as follows:

Upon any work, and especially upon a play, a great number of patterns of increasing generality will fit equally well, as more and more of the incident is left out. The last may be no more than the most general statement of what the play is about, and at times might consist only of its title; but there is a point in this series of abstractions where they are no longer protected, since otherwise the playwright could prevent the use of his 'ideas', to which, apart from their expression, his property is never extended.[208]

While the abstractions test more explicitly directs attention to whether non-literal elements are ideas or expression than comparative approaches, it does little more than point out that idea/expression is more a continuum than dichotomy, and provides no guidance of when copying might slip from idea to expression. This therefore remains a matter of judgment for the court, and, as Judge Hand himself said, '[n]obody has ever been able to fix that boundary, and nobody ever can.'[209]

*Merger and Scènes à faire Doctrines*  Unlike other common law jurisdictions, US law has two specific doctrines that apply in determining whether similarities between works are attributable to permissible similarities of idea or impermissible similarities in expression: the merger and *scènes à faire* doctrines. The merger doctrine applies where, as a result of there being only limited ways of expressing an idea, the expression is not protected. For example, in *Morrisey*,[210] the First Circuit held that the rules for a sweepstakes competition were not protected as their idea

---

[206] A. Cohen, 'Copyright law and the myth of objectivity: the idea–expression dichotomy and the inevitability of artistic judgments' (1990) 66 *Indiana Law Review* 175 at 197.
[207] *Nichols* v. *Universal Pictures Corporation*, 45 F 2d 119 (2nd Cir 1930).
[208] 45 F 2d 119 at 121 (2nd Cir 1930).   [209] *Ibid.*
[210] *Morrisey* v *Proctor & Gamble Co.*, 379 F 2d 675 (1st Cir 1967).

merged with the expression. Potentially more significantly, in *Kern River Gas*,[211] the Fifth Circuit held that maps, which were unoriginal except for the location of a gas pipeline, were not protected as to confer protection would have been to protect the idea of the location of the pipeline.

The *scènes à faire* doctrine, which is allied to the merger doctrine, means that copyright does not extend to common settings or sequences of events which are a necessary part of the treatment of certain subject matter. As one court put it, the doctrine applies to prevent protection of 'incidents, characters or setting which are as a practical matter indispensable, or at least standard, in the treatment of a given topic'.[212] For example, in *Walker*,[213] the Second Circuit held that in stories dealing with police life in the Bronx certain elements of the setting, such as 'drunks, prostitutes, vermin and derelict cars', and stock themes, such as '[f]oot chases and the morale problems of policemen, not to mention the familiar figure of the Irish cop', were unprotectable as *scènes à faire*.[214]

Although the doctrines are disarmingly simple, considerable difficulties arise in applying them. In relation to 'merger', there are problems in determining when an idea is inseparable from expression, as there is usually leeway in how an idea can be expressed. It is therefore unsurprising that there has been inconsistency in US court decisions applying the doctrines. Moreover, different circuits take different approaches to how the doctrines fit within infringement analysis: some circuits hold that the doctrines apply to prevent copyright subsisting, some apply the doctrines in the context of infringement and others apply them as defences.[215]

*Fact/Expression* Compared with other common law jurisdictions, US courts have more explicitly addressed some difficult issues relating to the principle that copyright does not protect facts, especially in applying the merger doctrine and determining whether selections of facts can be protected without extending protection to facts. The case law is dealt with in more detail in the Online Supplement.

---

[211] *Kern River Gas Transmission Company v. Coastal Corporation*, 899 F 2d 1458 (5th Cir 1990).
[212] *Alexander v. Haley*, 460 F Supp 40 at 45 (SDNY 1978).
[213] *Walker v. Time Life Films, Inc*, 784 F 2d 44 (2nd Cir 1986). [214] *Ibid.* 50.
[215] The First, Third, Fifth and Eleventh Circuits hold that the doctrines are bars to protection, while the Second, Seventh, Eighth and Ninth Circuits, that they are defences to infringement: see A. Hebl, 'A heavy burden: proper application of copyright's merger and *scène à faire* doctrines' (2007) 8 *Wake Forest Intellectual Property Law Journal* 128; S. Ocasio, 'Pruning paracopyright protection: why courts should apply the merger and *scène à faire* doctrines at the copyrightability stage of the copyright infringement analysis' (2006) 3 *Seton Hall Circuit Review* 303.

## 10.4 Uses of Ideas and Facts

The principal US authority on fact/expression is the Supreme Court judgment in *Feist*,[216] which rejected the application of 'sweat' to the originality threshold: [7.2.3]. In that case, the Supreme Court further held that the Intellectual Property Clause prohibited the protection of facts as they do not originate from an author: [8.3.1].

The Court's approach to originality means that the elements of a factual compilation that are protected under US law are confined to selection and arrangement of facts, and not the facts themselves. As the Court put it, this approach:

> inevitably means that the copyright in a factual compilation is thin. Notwithstanding a valid copyright, a subsequent compiler remains free to use the facts contained in another's publication to aid in preparing a competing work, so long as the competing work does not feature the same selection and arrangement.[217]

In *Feist*, the Court therefore held that a 'White Pages' telephone directory did not have sufficient creativity in selection, being an exhaustive collection, or arrangement, being prosaically arranged alphabetically, to be protected.[218] Cases since *Feist* illustrate some difficulties in interpreting and applying the judgment.

In applying *Feist*, particular problems have arisen with the protection of compilations based on selections of 'facts' that are 'created' by the compiler. For example, in *Maclean Hunter*,[219] the Second Circuit addressed the application of fact/expression to a compilation of predicted car valuations for regions of the United States. The Court first held there was sufficient originality in the selection of regions and car models for the compilation to be protected. Turning to the predicted valuations, Judge Leval held they were 'original creations',[220] in that they originated from the compiler, before addressing the argument that a valuation could not be protected as the idea merged with its expression. Acknowledging the difficulty, the Court identified the idea of the work as making some valuation of a particular car, with the expression being the particular valuation. In his analysis, Judge Leval distinguished between two sorts of 'ideas': ideas that are the 'building blocks' for future knowledge, such as the symptoms for identifying a disease, and ideas infused with opinion or evaluation, such as a selection of statistics. As the car valuations fell into the category of evaluative or opinion-infused ideas, the Court held

---

[216] *Feist Publications, Inc. v. Rural Telephone Services Co*, 499 US 340 (1991).
[217] *Ibid.* 349.
[218] See J. C. Ginsburg, 'No "sweat"? Copyright and other protection of works of information after *Feist v. Rural Telephone*' (1992) 92 *Columbia Law Review* 338.
[219] *CCC Information Services, Inc. v. Maclean Hunter Marketing Reports, Inc.*, 44 F 3d 61 (2nd Cir 1994).
[220] *Ibid.* 67.

that the merger doctrine could be applied less strictly than to 'building block' ideas, as protecting the valuations would not 'restrict access to the kind of idea that illuminates our understanding of the phenomena that surround us or of the useful processes to solve our problems'.[221]

### 10.4.5 Idea/Expression and the Public Domain

The idea/expression and fact/expression dichotomies are fundamental to copyright public domains, as once material is categorised as 'idea' or 'fact' it is free to be used without permission. In addition to being a distinct public domain category (category 10), the principles are essential to other categories: as copyright protects only original expression, ideas or facts fail the minimum threshold for protection (category 1); in some jurisdictions, copyright subsists only in works fixed in a material form: [7.2.14]; and, as infringement involves using protectable expression, ideas or facts cannot be a substantial part of a work (category 9). As the principles usually arise in determining whether or not material is an infringing use of expression or a permissible use of ideas or facts, we deal with them in this chapter as permissible uses of protected works.

The principles, while underpinning copyright, are among the most difficult areas of copyright law. The multiple meanings of the terms 'idea' and 'fact', and slippage between meanings in judicial reasoning, create considerable difficulties in identifying 'ideas' or 'facts' in a work, and distinguishing them from protected expression. The diverse meanings given to 'idea', 'fact' and 'expression' suggest that the dichotomies should be best understood as a collection of related principles for denying copyright, rather than a single homogenous concept. The principles include that copyright does not protect: the function of utilitarian works, such as computer programs; the building blocks of works, such as particular words or shapes; the 'meaning' of works, beyond the medium, such as particular words, used to express that meaning; material that is not properly copyright subject matter, such as a mathematical formula or laws of nature; in some jurisdictions, material not fixed in a material form; and mere collections of data. Individually and collectively, these principles support essential public domain values, including the importance of material being freely available for use in producing new works and new knowledge, and the availability of material for freedom of expression and cultural participation: [1.7].

To address the risk that idea/expression can be used simply to justify conclusions reached on other grounds, such as that a use is insufficient to

---

[221] *Ibid.* 72.

## 10.4 Uses of Ideas and Facts

support a finding of infringement, we suggest that greater attention should be paid to identifying and applying the principles underpinning the dichotomy. In Chapter 7, we argued that, in determining the threshold for protection, greater clarity was possible by more focus on when works should not be protected, and that the public domain could be supported by greater precision in identifying underlying rights and interests rather than formulaic approaches to threshold tests: [7.2.16]. While idea/expression and fact/expression direct attention to uses which can be made of elements of copyright works, too often recourse to the dichotomies can be formulaic and obscure fundamental issues. For example, while whether the use of non-literal elements of a literary work or play may infringe copyright involves value judgements, the question can be reduced to how much of a work should be free for others to use: asking whether the elements used are idea or expression is often an arid or abstract exercise that does not necessarily assist the court in reaching a conclusion. Furthermore, given our argument that public domain uses can be supported by greater judicial clarity, we also suggest that, in some jurisdictions, there is scope for explicit adoption of sub-principles that may assist the reasoning process, such as the US merger and *scènes à faire* doctrines.

Just as difficulties in establishing a consistent approach to the originality threshold have created problems in determining the extent of protection for 'low authorship' works, especially where factual material originates from an author: [7.2.16], significant difficulties arise in distinguishing 'facts' from 'expression'. Especially as illustrated by US case law, these difficulties are acute with 'evaluative' facts, such as valuations of cars, coins or real estate. Fundamental problems underpinning the protection of 'low authorship' works include the extent to which they incorporate building blocks (sometimes called 'facts') essential to creating future works and that full copyright protection is not necessarily appropriate for these works. Applying our 'realist' and public domain perspectives: [1.5], however, we suggest that a focus on whether or not 'facts' originate from an author often fails to address more fundamental issues, including the extent to which material categorised as facts should be in the public domain. In general, we think there is scope for further development of sub-principles, which incorporate the importance of public domain uses, and which might avoid overly formulaic or mechanistic approaches to the fact/expression dichotomy.

Given how far 'idea/expression' and 'fact/expression' are entrenched in copyright law, and the degree to which the principles pervade the law, we do not suggest abandoning the dichotomies as fundamental principles. Furthermore, especially given the rhetorical power of the principles that

324  Non-Infringing Uses of Protected Works

'ideas' and 'facts' are free to be used, the principles remain essential to protecting copyright public domains. Consistently with the pragmatic or 'realist' approach adopted in this book, however, we claim the law can be improved by clearer focus on the specific public domain uses of works, including in disaggregating the functions performed by the general principles, and by better incorporating considerations such as the extent to which material should be free to be used to create new works and the importance of permission-free uses for freedom of expression.

# 11 Copyright Exceptions and Limitations – Comparative Approaches

| | | |
|---|---|---|
| 11.1 | Introduction | 325 |
| 11.2 | The EU Framework | 329 |
| 11.3 | Fair Use | 333 |
| 11.4 | Fair Dealing | 339 |
| 11.5 | *Droit d'auteur* Jurisdictions Outside the EU | 345 |
| 11.6 | Comparative Approaches to Exceptions and the Public Domain | 347 |

## 11.1 Introduction

This book conceives copyright as a holistic system for encouraging creativity and innovation, in which property rights are one part, but exceptions to those rights are an equal and integral part: [1.3], [1.5.1]. This chapter and the following focus on uses of works that are protected by copyright, and which would be infringing but are not as they are expressly excused or justified,[1] and are, as such, exceptions (**Category 12**). This chapter explains general approaches to exceptions under national laws, while Chapter 12 compares national approaches to selected categories of exceptions. This chapter and the next are mainly concerned with free use exceptions, with Chapters 14 and 15 dealing with remunerated use exceptions; but some exceptions that can be implemented as either free or remunerated use are introduced in Chapter 12.

As explained in Chapter 2, on our positive view of the public domain, exceptions form part of the copyright public domain, even though they may be limited to certain classes of uses or contexts: [2.2.1]. As will become clear from this chapter, and especially the next, copyright exceptions have similar objectives and justifications to those of traditional public domain categories.

---

[1] W. Gordon, 'Excuse and justification in the law of fair use: commodification and market perspectives', in N. Elkin-Koren and N. Netanel (eds.), *The Commodification of Information* (Kluwer Law International, 2002), pp. 149–92.

The previous chapter, in dealing with three categories involving permissible uses of copyright works, also addressed limitations on the scope of the copyright exclusive rights. While uses within those categories (Categories 9, 10 and 11) do not infringe, uses within Category 12 are copyright infringements but are, nevertheless, excepted on some public interest ground. From this, it might be assumed that Chapter 10 deals with limitations, while Category 12 deals with exceptions. The distinction between limitations and exceptions is, however, more complex: [11.1.1].

Copyright exceptions are extraordinarily important parts of the public domain, both from the viewpoint of the important uses permitted and the symbolic power of excepting a use from infringement. From a property-centric perspective, as reflected in the minimum protections required under international copyright law, exceptions are the most important mechanism for national laws to balance copyright with other public policy objectives; or, as Hugenholtz and Senftleben put it, exceptions are 'the main instruments of flexibility' in copyright law.[2] Nevertheless, there is limited harmonisation of exceptions, with this area of copyright being marked by very considerable variations in national laws. These two factors explain why issues relating to exceptions, such as whether national laws should introduce a fair use exception, are flashpoints for copyright policy debates. They also justify us allocating two chapters to this category.

### 11.1.1 Terminology: 'Exceptions' and 'Limitations'

As a matter of legal terminology, the terms 'exceptions' and 'limitations' are sometimes used interchangeably. For example, under EU law, Article 5 of the InfoSoc Directive[3] is headed 'exceptions and limitations' without further defining the terms;[4] and a distinction between the two terms is commonly not drawn in civil law systems, such as under German law.[5]

---

[2] P. B. Hugenholtz and M. Senftleben, 'Fair use in Europe. In search of flexibilities', Amsterdam, 4 March 2012 http://ssrn.com/abstract=1959554, p. 6.

[3] InfoSoc Directive, Art. 5. Full titles and citations of all Directives are in the Table of International Instruments.

[4] In *VG Wort*, however, the ECJ distinguished the two terms on the basis that an 'exception' totally excludes the relevant exclusive right while a 'limitation' on a right 'may include ... in part an exclusion, a restriction, or even the retention of that right': Joined Cases C-457/11 and C-460/11, *Verwertungsgesellschaft Wort (VG Wort)* v. *Kyocera* [2013] ECLI:EU:C:2013:426 at [34].

[5] T. Dreier, 'Thoughts on revising the limitations on copyright under Directive 2001/29' (2015) 11(2) *Journal of Intellectual Property Law & Practice* 138 at 139.

## 11.1 Introduction

The terminology, however, can have significant consequences.[6] On the one hand, the term 'limitation' may be used to define the scope of the rights comprised in the copyright, such as the limitations dealt with in Chapter 10.[7] An exception, on the other hand, does not define the scope of the right but is a 'divergence' or derogation from the right.[8] As Drassinower suggests, the distinction may depend upon the generality at which the right is defined: for example, the exclusive right may be defined as either 'the right to reproduce the work or any substantial part of the work' or 'the right to reproduce the work or any substantial part of the work for purposes other than criticism or review'.[9] In the first formulation, permitted uses for the purpose of criticism or review are an 'exception' to the right, but in the second formulation they are a 'limitation'.

The distinction is not entirely semantic. At the conceptual level, if a use is a limitation then it is an integral part of the copyright system, and not merely a defence. If, on the other hand, a use is regarded as an exception, this is likely to reflect a property- or author-centric model of copyright, with permissible uses relegated to the periphery of the copyright system.

The proper characterisation of exceptions and limitations has been a prominent issue in debates concerning the US fair use doctrine. In particular, considerable attention has been given to the question of whether fair use is a 'right' or a 'privilege': [2.4.2]. Snow, for example, has argued that, over time and as a result of misreadings of precedents, fair use was transformed from a right to free speech that defined the scope of copyright to an affirmative defence that excused infringement, with the burden of proof shifting to the defendant.[10]

As we start with the assumption that the public domain consists of positive public rights: [2.4.2], it follows that what are commonly called 'exceptions' should be more precisely regarded as 'limitations' on the scope of the exclusive rights. This seems to be the view adopted by the Canadian Supreme Court in applying a users' rights perspective to fair dealing exceptions: [11.4.3]. As this chapter demonstrates, however, in most jurisdictions, and even in Canada, there is ambiguity in the treatment of exceptions and limitations, which results in them commonly sitting uneasily between limitations on exclusive rights and exceptions to, or derogations from, those rights; and with courts sometimes

---

[6] Drassinower, 'Exceptions properly so-called', 207–38.  [7] *Ibid.* 214–17.
[8] See Dreier, 'Thoughts on revising the limitations on copyright', 139; C. Geiger and F. Schönherr, 'The Information Society Directive (Articles 5 and 6(4))', in Stamatoudi and Torremans (eds.), *EU Copyright Law: A Commentary*, [11.64].
[9] Drassinower, 'Exceptions properly so-called', 216.
[10] N. Snow, 'The forgotten right of fair use' (2011) 62(1) *Case Western Law Review* 135.

switching between the two perspectives. For the sake of consistency, and reflecting the most common usage, we generally refer to copyright 'exceptions' in this book, but revisit this issue in the concluding section to the chapter.

This chapter first reviews the international framework for copyright exceptions before explaining the main national approaches. Most of the chapter deals with general approaches to exceptions in the EU, United States, UK, Australia, Canada and selected non-EU civil law jurisdictions, namely China and South Korea.

### 11.1.2 International Copyright Law

International copyright law provides for both free use and remunerated use exceptions: [5.2]. In relation to free use exceptions, Berne provides for one mandatory and four voluntary express free use exceptions. The mandatory exception requires Member States to introduce an exception for quotation, while the permissible exceptions relate to: education and teaching; press and media uses of media reports; press and media uses of lectures and addresses; and ephemeral recordings by broadcasting organisations: [5.4.2]. While the three-step test cannot extend the scope of exceptions expressly provided for under Berne, national laws may introduce additional exceptions that comply with the test: [5.4.1].

In relation to neighbouring rights, Rome expressly allows for exceptions for: private use; short excerpts in reporting current events; ephemeral fixation of broadcasts; and uses solely for the purposes of teaching or scientific research: [5.4.3]. In addition, under Rome and the WPPT, national laws may provide for the same kinds of exceptions for performers and producers of phonograms as permitted for works under Berne.

### 11.1.3 Three Main Approaches in National Laws

Exceptions to copyright infringement must balance the benefits of certainty that would allow rights holders and users to know whether or not uses are permissible with the need for flexibility, especially to deal with new uses and technological change. While there is much variation in the details, there are three main approaches to striking the balance between certainty and flexibility under national laws.[11] First, most civil law jurisdictions have closed lists of permissible exceptions. This approach is

---

[11] While Burrell and Coleman distinguish two main approaches, generally worded exceptions, and specific exceptions, we believe it is preferable to distinguish fair use from fair dealing, and therefore identify three approaches: Burrell and Coleman, *Copyright Exceptions*, 4.

reflected in EU law, with Article 5 of the InfoSoc Directive including a closed list: [11.2]. The closed list approach is, however, ameliorated in that civil law jurisdictions codify exceptions at a high level of abstraction, leaving it to courts to refer to high-level principles, such as 'reasonableness and fairness', in applying the exceptions.[12]

Second, at the other end of the spectrum, US law includes a general, open-ended exception in the form of fair use. The US fair use exception is not confined to uses for specific purposes, but requires the courts to engage in case-by-case analysis of whether the use, taking into account its purpose, complies with identified 'fair use factors': [11.3]. The US fair use model has influenced the laws of other jurisdictions, being adopted in some national laws, but also finding support in official recommendations for law reform, especially given its potential for flexibly dealing with technological change.

Third, in Commonwealth common law jurisdictions, the dominant approach is based on 'fair dealing' exceptions: [11.4]. Fair dealing exceptions are more flexible than the 'closed list' approach, but differ from fair use in that they are confined to uses for specified purposes. There are variations in 'fair dealing' exceptions under national laws, with the courts in some jurisdictions adopting an expansive interpretation and others a more restrictive interpretation: [11.4]. As a generalisation, there has been a recent tendency for fair dealing exceptions to be extended, partly in response to expansion of copyright protection and partly to introduce flexibility. It is also important to bear in mind that, apart from fair dealing and fair use exceptions, national laws in common law jurisdictions include many more specific exceptions, which are commonly more detailed and more specific than exceptions listed in civil law codes.

## 11.2 The EU Framework

In EU law, exceptions and limitations are dealt with in four directives: the Software Directive, Database Directive, Rental and Lending Rights Directive and the InfoSoc Directive. This leads to fragmentation in the treatment of exceptions, depending on the subject matter. For example, exceptions under the Software Directive are tailored to computer programs and, therefore, include exceptions for back-up copies and observing, studying or testing the functioning of a computer program.[13]

Leaving aside exceptions for specific subject matter, exceptions and limitations are partially, but imperfectly, harmonised by Article 5 of the

---

[12] Hugenholtz and Senftleben, 'Fair use in Europe', 6.
[13] Software Directive, Art. 5(2), (3).

InfoSoc Directive and the *acquis communautaire*. By referring to 'exceptions and limitations', Article 5 follows the traditions of Member States in conceptualising these as carve outs from exclusive rights, rather than as positive users' rights.

Article 5 provides for one mandatory and twenty facultative exceptions, with the exceptions being further subject to the three-step test.[14] The mandatory exception, in Article 5(1), applies to transient or incidental reproductions as part of technological processes for the purpose of electronic transmissions or lawful use: [12.2.1]. The optional exceptions are set out in two groups. First, Article 5(2) allows for five facultative exceptions to the reproduction right: reprographic copying; private copying; non-profit copying by public libraries, educational establishments or museums; ephemeral copying by broadcasters; and reproductions of broadcasts by social institutions. Second, Article 5(3) lists fifteen facultative exceptions to the reproduction and public communication rights, including exceptions for: teaching and scientific purposes; reporting current events; caricature, parody or pastiche; and research or private study. Article 5(4) further provides that Member States may introduce exceptions or limitations to the distribution right where they do so in relation to the reproduction right.

### 11.2.1 Partial Harmonisation within the EU

Recital (32) to the InfoSoc Directive states that 'Member States should arrive at a coherent application of these exceptions and limitations'. Read together, however, it is clear from Recitals (31) and (32) that the Directive does not aim at complete harmonisation of exceptions. For example, Recital (31) states that:

> In order to ensure the proper functioning of the internal market, such exceptions and limitations should be defined more harmoniously. The degree of their harmonisation should be based on their impact on the smooth functioning of the internal market.

Recital (32) makes it clear that the exceptions listed in Article 5 are exhaustive. Nevertheless, the Recital goes on to state:

> This list takes due account of the different legal traditions in Member States while, at the same time, aiming to ensure a functioning internal market. Member States should arrive at a coherent application of these exceptions and limitations.

In addition, the flexible drafting of the optional exceptions confers discretion on Member States in interpreting them. Nevertheless, in *TV2*

---

[14] InfoSoc Directive, Art. 5(5).

## 11.2 The EU Framework

*Danmark*, the ECJ referred to the need for a 'coherent application' set out in Recital (32) to rule that Member States were not free to limit an exception in an un-harmonised manner.[15] This means that a Member State that decides to implement an optional exception must apply the same 'substantive scope' to the exception as the relevant exception under the Directive.[16]

There are conflicting indications in the Recitals to the Directive about how restrictively exceptions should be interpreted. On the one hand, Recital (4) states that a harmonised legal framework should provide 'for a high level of protection of intellectual property'. On the other hand, Recital (31) states that:

> A fair balance of rights and interests between the different categories of rightholders, as well as between the different categories of rightholders and users of protected subject-matter must be safeguarded.

The ECJ, reflecting the legal traditions of most Member States,[17] initially interpreted exceptions restrictively. In *Infopaq I*, in interpreting the exception for temporary reproductions, the Court applied the rule that provisions of a directive derogating from a general principle, such as exceptions to exclusive rights, must be interpreted strictly.[18] In *Premier League*, however, while acknowledging this rule, the ECJ held that Article 5(1) must be interpreted to allow for the effectiveness and purpose of the exception. Taking into account Recital (31), which provides that a 'fair balance of rights and interests ... must be safeguarded', the Court ruled that the exception 'must allow and ensure the development and operation of new technologies and safeguard a fair balance between the rights and interests of rights holders, on the one hand, and of users of protected works who wish to avail themselves of those technologies, on the other'.[19] Similarly, in *Painer*, the ECJ ruled that, in interpreting the exception for quotations: [12.3.1], a fair balance must be struck 'between the right to freedom of expression of users of a work and other protected subject-matter and the reproduction right conferred on authors'.[20]

---

[15] Case C-510/10 *DR and TV2 Danmark A/S* v. *NCB – Nordisk Copyright Bureau* [2012] 2 CMLR 1280 at [36].

[16] E. Rosati, 'Copyright in the EU: in search of (in)flexibilities' (2014) 9(7) *Journal of Intellectual Property Law & Practice* 585 at 593; Dreier, 'Thoughts on revising the limitations on copyright', 139.

[17] Geiger and Schönherr, 'The Information Society Directive', [11.79].

[18] Case C-5/08 *Infopaq International A/S* v. *Danske Dagblades Forening*, [2009] ECR I-6569 at [56]–[57].

[19] Joined Cases C-403/08 and C-429/08 *Football Association Premier League Ltd* v. *QC Leisure* [2011] ECR I-9083 at [163].

[20] Case C-145/10 *Eva-Maria Painer* v. *Standard VerlagsGmbH* [2011] ECR I-12533.

This approach was confirmed in *Deckmyn*, where, in interpreting the parody exception, the Court held that a fair balance was required between the rights of authors and the freedom of expression of users: [12.4.1].[21] Therefore, despite earlier contrary statements, and at least where the principle of proportionality applies to ensure a balance between the rights of authors and rights such as the freedom of expression of users, there appears to be no general principle requiring a narrow interpretation of exceptions.[22]

### 11.2.2 EU Reform Proposals

Although Article 5 was never meant to achieve complete harmonisation, the optional nature of the exceptions and their flexible drafting led to concerns about national variations.[23] Furthermore, the closed list of exceptions has given rise to concerns about flexibility of EU copyright law, especially in the face of technological change.[24] In September 2016, the European Commission released a proposal for a new copyright Directive,[25] which, in part, responded to some of the uncertainties of existing exceptions, including problems with cross-border uses arising from lack of harmonisation. Better to accommodate technological change, and facilitate cross-border uses within the EU, the proposed Directive included exceptions for: digital and cross-border uses in the field of education; text and data mining in the field of scientific research; and preservation of cultural heritage. To enhance harmonisation, the proposed exceptions are mandatory. This development further illustrates the centrality of exceptions for contemporary debates about public domain uses.

---

[21] Case C-201/13 *Johan Deckmyn* v. *Helena Vandersteen* [2014] All ER (D) 30.
[22] C. Geiger, J. Griffiths, M. Senftleben, L. Bently and R. Xalabarder, 'Limitations and exceptions as key elements of the legal framework for copyright in the European Union – opinion of the European Copyright Society on the judgment of the CJEU in Case C-201/13 *Deckmyn*' (2015) 46 *International Review of Intellectual Property and Competition Law (IIC)* 93.
[23] Geiger and Schönherr, 'The Information Society Directive', [11.74]; P. B. Hugenholtz, 'The dynamics of harmonization of copyright at the European level', in C. Geiger (ed.), *Constructing European Intellectual Property: Achievements and New Perspectives* (Edward Elgar, 2013), pp. 273–91.
[24] A. Strowel, 'Towards a European copyright law: four issues to consider', in Stamatoudi and Torremans (eds.), *EU Copyright Law: A Commentary*, 1127–54.
[25] European Commission, Proposal for a Directive of the European Parliament and of the Council on copyright in the Digital Single Market, COM (2016) 593 final, Brussels, 14 September 2016.

## 11.3 Fair Use

The US fair use exception has attracted considerable attention as a model that is more flexible and adaptable than either a closed list of exceptions or circumscribed fair dealing exceptions.[26] While fair use has been described as a 'uniquely American doctrine',[27] apart from the United States, where it originated, it has been adopted, in versions resembling the US exception, in six other jurisdictions: Israel,[28] Liberia,[29] the Philippines,[30] Sri Lanka,[31] Taiwan[32] and South Korea,[33] In addition to countries that have expressly adopted a fair use exception, there has been movement towards greater flexibility in countries with fair dealing exceptions. For example, Singapore,[34] Malaysia[35] and the Bahamas[36] have adopted open-ended fair dealing exceptions, with the list of permitted purposes being indicative.[37] While a number of jurisdictions, such as Bangladesh[38] and Uganda,[39] have exceptions that are called 'fair use', in fact the provisions are confined to a closed list of permitted purposes, so they are, in practice, more like fair dealing exceptions. In a significant development, the Canadian Supreme Court has adopted an expansive interpretation of fair dealing under Canadian law, which moves Canada closer to a fair use model: [2.4.2], [11.4.3].

---

[26] Productivity Commission (Aus.), 'Intellectual property arrangements'; Australian Law Reform Commission, *Copyright and the Digital Economy*; Copyright Review Committee (Ireland), Department of Jobs, Enterprise and Innovation, *Modernising Copyright* (Dublin, 2013). Proposals for introducing a fair use exception in Commonwealth common law jurisdictions have a long history: Burrell, 'Reining in copyright law'.

[27] P. Goldstein, 'Fair use in context' (2008) 31 *Columbia Journal of Law & the Arts* 433 at 433.

[28] Copyright Act, 2007 (Israel), s. 19. The provision empowers the Minister of Justice to issue regulations specifying the conditions for a use to amount to a fair use: O. Afori, 'An open standard "fair use" doctrine' (2008) 30(3) *European Intellectual Property Review* 85; G. Pessach, 'The new Israeli Copyright Act: a case-study in reverse comparative law' (2010) 41 *International Review of Intellectual Property and Competition Law (IIC)* 187.

[29] Copyright Law of Liberia (Liberia), s. 2.7.

[30] Intellectual Property Code of the Philippines, Republic Act No. 8293 (the Philippines), s. 185.

[31] Intellectual Property Act, No. 36 of 2003 (Sri Lanka), ss. 11–12.

[32] Copyright Act, 2007 (Taiwan), s. 65.

[33] Copyright Act, 2011 (South Korea), Art. 35*ter*.

[34] Copyright Act (Chapter 63) (Singapore), s. 35.

[35] Copyright (Amendment) Act 2012 (Malaysia), s. 13(2).

[36] Copyright Act, 1998 (Ch 323) (Bahamas), ss. 58–60. See J. Band and J. Garafi, *The Fair Use/Fair Dealing Handbook* (policybandwidth, March 2013), p. 1.

[37] M. Geist, 'Fairness found: how Canada quietly shifted from fair dealing to fair use', in M. Geist (ed.), *The Copyright Pentology: How the Supreme Court of Canada Shook the Foundations of Canadian Copyright Law* (University of Ottawa Press, 2013), pp. 157–86.

[38] Copyright Act 2000 (No. 28 of 2000) (Bangladesh), s. 72.

[39] The Copyright and Neighbouring Rights Act, 2006 (Uganda), s. 15.

## 11.3.1 The US Fair Use Exception

The US fair use exception is codified in section 107 of the Copyright Act.[40] The exception, which supplements more specific exceptions,[41] was a codification of the US common law doctrine, and is conventionally traced to the 1841 judgment of Justice Story in *Folsom v. Marsh*,[42] which first established what are known as the 'fair use factors'. While the judgment built upon English common law precedent relating to 'fair abridgements',[43] it was a watershed in distinguishing US from English law: [10.3.5].

The codification of fair use was not intended to change the common law, but was intended to provide the courts with flexibility to adapt US copyright law, especially to deal with technological change.[44] The provision establishes the principle that a use does not infringe copyright if it is 'fair', with two parts to the inquiry. First, there is a list of illustrative purposes, which provide examples of uses that may be fair, namely: 'criticism, comment, news reporting, teaching (including multiple copies for classroom use), scholarship, or research'. As the list is illustrative, the doctrine leaves it open for additional uses to be considered fair. Merely because a use falls within a listed purpose, however, does not mean the exception applies: the use must also be 'fair'. The second part of the inquiry, the most important part, is the determination of the fairness of the use, which requires the application of four non-exhaustive criteria, or 'fair use factors':

(1) The purpose and character of the use, including whether such use is of a commercial nature or is for non-profit educational purposes;
(2) The nature of the copyrighted work;
(3) The amount and substantiality of the portion used in relation to the copyrighted work as a whole; and
(4) The effect of the use upon the potential market for or value of the copyrighted work.

Due mainly to its open-textured nature, and potential indeterminacy, the fair use doctrine has been called 'the most troublesome in the whole law of copyright'.[45] Despite the Supreme Court holding, in *Campbell*, that fair

---

[40] 17 USC §107.  [41] 17 USC §§108–118.
[42] 9 F Cas 342 (CCD Mass 1841). L. Ray Patterson points out that it is a myth that *Folsom v. Marsh* created fair use, arguing instead that it 'merely redefined infringement': '*Folsom v. Marsh* and its legacy' (1998) 5 *Journal of Intellectual Property Law* 431 at 431.
[43] M. Sag, 'The prehistory of fair use' (2011) 76(4) *Brooklyn Law Review* 1371.
[44] United States House of Representatives, Committee on the Judiciary, Copyright Law Revision (House Report No. 94-1476) (1976) 5680.
[45] *Dellar v. Samuel Goldwyn, Inc*, 104 F 2d 661 at 662 (CA2 1939), cited by Blackmun J in *Sony Corporation of America v. Universal City Studios, Inc*, 464 US 417 at 474 (1984).

## 11.3 Fair Use

use is an affirmative defence,[46] there is uncertainty even concerning its legal status. Relying on legislative history, Loren, for example, argues that fair use is a defence, but not an affirmative defence, meaning that the burden of establishing there has been an infringement and no fair use should fall on the plaintiff.[47] There has, moreover, been considerable disagreement about the extent to which the doctrine is incoherent and/or unpredictable. On the one hand, some argue that the case-by-case, fact sensitive reasoning in fair use cases, and the absence of any agreement on principles underpinning the factors, lead to unpredictability.[48] On the other hand, empirical analysis of case law going beyond the contentious judgments of the Supreme Court, has suggested that outcomes are more predictable than often thought.[49] Furthermore, Samuelson has suggested that uncertainty can be reduced by distilling common patterns, or 'policy-relevant clusters', from the case law.[50]

### 11.3.2 The Four Fair Use Factors

The malleable nature of the four fair use factors, and inconsistencies between courts in their application, led David Nimmer to lament that reliance on the factors 'often seems naught but a fairytale'.[51] Nevertheless, as the courts must address the factors, their interpretation by courts, especially the Supreme Court, sets the parameters for application of the doctrine. This section of the chapter explains the way in which US courts have interpreted and applied the factors.

*Purpose and Character of the Use* The first factor, the purpose and character of the use, has become the key consideration in whether or not the exception applies. There are two main issues in applying the factor: whether the use is commercial and whether it is 'transformative'. As Netanel has argued, there has been a historical shift in focus from emphasis on the commerciality of a use to whether it is

---

[46] *Campbell* v. *Acuff-Rose Music, Inc,* 510 US 569 at 590 (1994).
[47] L. Loren, 'Fair use: an affirmative defense?' (2015) 90 *Washington Law Review* 685.
[48] B. Sites, 'Fair use and the new transformative' (2016) 39(4) *Columbia Journal of Law & the Arts* 514; M. Carroll, 'Fixing fair use' (2007) 85 *North Carolina Law Review* 1087; D. Nimmer, '"Fairest of them all" and other fairy tales of fair use' (2003) 66 *Law & Contemporary Problems* 263; Goldstein, 'Fair use in context'; D. Hunter, 'American lessons: implementing fair use in Australia' (2014) 24 *Australian Intellectual Property Journal* 192.
[49] B. Beebe, 'An empirical study of US copyright fair use opinions, 1978–2005' (2008) 156 *University of Pennsylvania Law Review* 549; M. Sag, 'Predicting fair use' (2012) 73 *Ohio State Law Journal* 47.
[50] Samuelson, 'Unbundling fair uses'.    [51] D. Nimmer, '"Fairest of them all"' 287.

transformative,[52] with the latter often being the touchstone of whether a use is fair.

While the commercial nature of a use has never meant it cannot be a fair use, in *Sony*, the Supreme Court stated that 'every commercial use of copyrighted material is presumptively an unfair exploitation of the monopoly privilege'.[53] In *Harper & Row*, the Court stepped back from the claim that a commercial use is presumptively unfair, but concluded that the fourth factor, the effect of the use on the market for the work, was 'the single most important element of fair use'.[54] In *Campbell*, however, the Supreme Court rejected any presumption that a commercial use might lead to market harm in cases involving more than slavish copying effectively to elevate the main inquiry into whether or not a use is transformative, meaning whether it 'adds something new, with a further purpose or different character, altering the first with new expression, meaning or message'.[55] In this, the Court adopted the analysis from a 1990 article by Judge Leval, who found an underlying justification for fair use in the extent to which 'the secondary use adds value to the original – if the quoted matter is ... transformed in the creation of new information, new aesthetics, new insights and understanding'.[56] Although following *Campbell* there is a greater chance of a court finding fair use if the use is transformative,[57] this does not rule out a multi-factor approach, particularly where the use is not transformative. Moreover, following *Campbell*, the *Sony* presumptions that a commercial use is unfair and causes market harm still seem to apply to non-transformative uses.[58]

*The Nature of the Work* In considering the second factor, the nature of the work, there is less inconsistency in approaches applied by the courts than in relation to other factors. The analysis is also more sparing, with the relevant considerations often being incorporated into the other factors.[59] Following the Supreme Court decision in *Harper & Row*, a key consideration in applying the second factor is whether or not a work is published, with the use of an unpublished work less likely to be

---

[52] N. Netanel, 'Making sense of fair use' (2011) 15(3) *Lewis & Clark Law Review* 715.
[53] *Sony Corporation of America* v. *Universal City Studios, Inc*, 464 US 417 at 451 (1984).
[54] *Harper & Row, Publishers, Inc.* v. *Nation Enterprises*, 471 US 539 at 566 (1985).
[55] *Campbell* v. *Acuff-Rose Music, Inc*, 510 US 569, 591 (1994). The decision on the facts in the case was remanded to the Sixth Circuit and subsequently settled.
[56] P. Leval, 'Toward a fair use standard' (1990) 103 *Harvard Law Review* 1105 at 1111.
[57] Netanel, 'Making sense of fair use', 730.
[58] P. Samuelson, 'Possible futures of fair use' (2015) 90 *Washington Law Review* 815 at 819–20.
[59] R. Kasunic, 'Is that all there is? Reflections on the nature of the second fair use factor' (2008) 31(4) *Columbia Journal of Law & the Arts* 529.

## 11.3 Fair Use

fair.[60] The other significant consideration in treatment of the second factor is whether the work is creative or factual, with uses of creative works less likely to be fair as they form the core of works intended to be protected by copyright, while there is a greater case for dissemination of factual works.[61] Overall, however, the second factor has been less important in the outcome of fair use cases than the other factors.

*The Amount and Substantiality of the Part Used* The third factor, the amount and substantiality of the part used, includes considerations relating to both the amount of the work that is taken and its qualitative significance in relation to the original work as a whole.[62] In *Campbell*, the Supreme Court pointed out that assessment of the importance of the amount taken depended upon the purpose and character of the use, with the Court concluding that a use 'does not become excessive in relation to parodic purpose merely because the portion taken was the original's heart'.[63] In addition, this factor is related to the fourth factor in that the more that is taken the more likely there is an adverse effect on the market for the original work.[64] The highly contextual nature of this factor means that it is difficult to draw generalisations, beyond saying that the less that is used the more likely there is to be a finding of fair use.

*The Effect of the Use on the Potential Market* The fourth factor, the effect of the use on the potential market for the work, was, until *Campbell*, considered the most important factor and, despite the increased importance of transformative use, remains influential.[65] A problem identified with the fourth factor is its potential circularity: if a use is found to be fair then this pre-empts the development of a market for that use of the work, leaving it open for rights holders to argue that most findings of fair use can adversely affect a potential market.[66] This is illustrated by the decision of the Second Circuit in *Texaco*,[67] where employees of a scientific research company, Texaco, photocopied articles from a scholarly journal for use in research, and the company claimed this

---

[60] *Salinger v. Random House, Inc*, 811 F 2d 90 (2nd Cir 1987); *New Era Publications International ApS v. Henry Holt and Co, Inc*, 873 F 2d 576 (2nd Cir 1989).
[61] Beebe, 'An empirical study', 610. See also *Peter Letterese and Associates, Inc. v. World Institute of Scientology Enterprises, International*, 533 F 3d 1287 (11th Cir 2008).
[62] *Harper & Row, Publishers, Inc. v. Nation Enterprises*, 471 US 539 at 564–566 (1985).
[63] *Campbell v. Acuff-Rose Music, Inc*, 510 US 569 at 591 (1994).
[64] Sag, 'Predicting fair use', 63.
[65] Beebe, 'An empirical study'; Netanel, 'Making sense of fair use'.
[66] Hunter, 'American lessons', 200–1; Samuelson, 'Unbundling fair uses', 2620.
[67] *American Geophysical Union v. Texaco Inc*, 60 F 3d 913 (2nd Cir 1994).

was a fair use. Even though there was no traditional market for individual articles, the Court took into account the extent to which the publishers of the journal had established a mechanism for licensing photocopying to hold that failure to pay for the photocopying had adversely affected a potential market.

Following *Campbell*, US courts have tended not to apply this form of circular reasoning, and especially not in 'transformative use' cases.[68] In *Bill Graham Archives*,[69] for example, the Second Circuit was required to rule on whether use of reduced size concert posters in a history of the *Grateful Dead* was a fair use. Pointing to the circularity of holding that a potential market is forestalled whenever a payment is not made, the Court distinguished *Texaco* on the basis that use of the images was transformative. Moreover, the Court rejected the proposition that merely because some users were willing to pay a licence fee the use could not qualify as a fair use.[70]

Where it is unlikely that a rights holder will license use of a work, as in transformative uses such as parody, US courts will not find harm to a potential market. In *Blanch* v. *Koons*,[71] for example, the Second Circuit considered the use of images of legs taken by a fashion photographer as part of a painting by appropriation artist, Jeff Koons. After concluding that the use was transformative, as it had a different purpose from the original work, the Court referred to the fact that the photographer had never licensed any works in reaching the conclusion that the use had no deleterious effect on a potential market.[72] The case confirmed the importance of finding that a use is transformative, which it referred to as '[t]he heart of the fair use inquiry',[73] in analysing the fourth factor.

While US courts are reluctant to find there has been an adverse effect on derivative markets where a use has been transformative, there are ongoing difficulties both in defining what amounts to a transformative use and in identifying potential markets. In some respects, moreover, it seems that concerns about circularity in analysis of hypothetical derivative markets has led the courts to focus almost entirely on the actual markets exploited by the rights holder, rather than on potential markets.

---

[68] Samuelson, 'Unbundling fair uses', 2620. This is sometimes referred to as a 'transformative market': *Bill Graham Archives* v. *Dorling Kindersley Ltd*, 448 F 3d 605 at 615 (2nd Cir 2006).
[69] *Bill Graham Archives* v. *Dorling Kindersley Ltd*, 448 F 3d 605 (2nd Cir 2006).
[70] *Bill Graham Archives* v. *Dorling Kindersley Ltd*, 448 F 3d 605 at 615 (2nd Cir 2006).
[71] *Andrea Blanch* v. *Jeff Koons*, 467 F 3d 244 (2nd Cir 2006).   [72] *Ibid.* 258.
[73] *Ibid.* 251.

## 11.4　Fair Dealing

Unlike fair use, fair dealing exceptions allow for uses for specific purposes only. Just as fair use has its roots in English common law cases dealing with whether a fair abridgement infringed, the fair dealing exceptions, first introduced in the 1911 UK Act, can be traced to the same line of cases.[74] The 1911 UK Act, apparently intending partially to codify the common law, introduced an exception for fair dealing with a work 'for the purposes of private study, research, criticism, review, or newspaper summary'.[75]

The introduction of the statutory exception transformed the reasoning in infringement cases so that 'fairness' was no longer taken into account in analysis of infringement but was relegated to the application of the fair dealing defence, which, furthermore, tended to be interpreted restrictively.[76] The result of the introduction of a statutory exception was summed up by members of the Australian High Court in *TCN Channel Nine*:

> It would be quite wrong to approach an infringement claim on the footing that the question of taking a substantial part may be by-passed by going directly to the fair dealing defences.[77]

It has been suggested that, as a result of courts restrictively interpreting fair dealing, by the end of the twentieth century there was a noticeable split between 'an omnipresent, flexible fair use regime in the United States, and a seemingly rigid and restrictive fair dealing tradition in the Commonwealth countries'.[78] While there is some truth in this, there is also exaggeration: the position was always more complex[79] and, as explained below, there has been movement towards more expansive approaches to exceptions in Commonwealth jurisdictions, especially Canada.

---

[74] See Burrell, 'Reining in copyright law'; K. Bowrey, 'On clarifying the role of originality and fair use in nineteenth century UK jurisprudence: appreciating "the humble grey which emerges as the result of long controversy"', in L. Bently, C. Ng and G. d'Agostino (eds.), *The Common Law of Intellectual Property: Essays in Honour of Professor David Vaver* (Hart Publishing, (2010), pp. 45–69; A. Katz, 'Fair use 2.0: the rebirth of fair dealing in Canada', in Geist (ed.), *The Copyright Pentology*, 93–156.

[75] Copyright Act 1911 (UK), s. 2(1)(i).　　[76] Burrell, 'Reining in copyright law', 369–73.

[77] *Network Ten Pty Ltd* v. *TCN Channel Nine Pty Ltd* (2004) 218 CLR 273 at [21] (per McHugh ACJ, Gummow and Hayne JJ).

[78] Katz, 'Fair use 2.0', 93–4.

[79] As Katz acknowledges, a rigid dichotomy between fair dealing and fair use is false: *ibid.* 95.

## 11.4.1 The UK

The CDPA includes fair dealing defences for: research and private study;[80] criticism, review, quotation and reporting of current events;[81] and caricature, parody or pastiche.[82] The purposes of the permitted dealings are dealt with in Chapter 12 in sections addressing categories of exceptions, while this section explains the general approach of UK courts to interpreting fair dealing.

In *Pro Sieben*, the Court of Appeal held that the purpose of 'criticism or review' and 'news reporting' could not be precisely defined, but 'should be interpreted liberally', so that 'criticism' could extend not just to a work but to the ideas found in a work.[83] Moreover, the introduction of the Human Rights Act 1998 (UK) reinforced a flexible approach to interpreting fair dealing, especially where freedom of expression is implicated. In the principal authority, *Ashdown*, the Court of Appeal held that, following the introduction of the Human Rights Act, it is 'essential not to apply inflexibly tests based on precedent, but to bear in mind that considerations of public interest are paramount'.[84] In that case, however, the outcome depended mainly on an assessment of whether the dealing, consisting of the verbatim reproduction of one-fifth of a politician's secret minute in a newspaper, was 'fair', which the Court assessed by drawing on three factors identified by *Laddie*: whether the dealing commercially competes with the copyright owner's exploitation of the work, whether the work was published or unpublished, and the amount and importance of the part taken.[85] Giving most weight to the potential for the newspaper report to compete with the politician's memoirs, the Court held that the publication was not 'fair'. Therefore, although the judgment acknowledges the importance of taking into account freedom of expression in interpreting fair dealing, this did not affect its application of the 'fairness factors', which were applied mechanically.[86]

The English approach to fair dealing therefore applies a liberal approach to interpreting the statutory purposes, but has been less expansive in applying the 'fairness factors'.

---

[80] Copyright, Designs and Patents Act 1988 (UK) ('CDPA'), s. 29.  [81] CDPA, s. 30.
[82] CDPA, s. 30A.
[83] *Pro Sieben Media AG* v. *Carlton UK Television Ltd* [1999] 1 WLR 605 at 625.
[84] *Ashdown* v. *Telegraph Group Ltd* [2002] Ch 149 at [71].
[85] Ibid. [70]–[77], citing Laddie et al., *The Modern Law of Copyright and Designs*, 3rd edn, [20.16].
[86] J. Griffiths, 'Copyright law after *Ashdown* – time to deal fairly with the public' (2002) 3 *Intellectual Property Quarterly* 240.

## 11.4.2 Australia

The Australian Act incorporates fair dealing defences for: research or study;[87] criticism or review;[88] parody or satire;[89] and reporting news.[90] In 2017, as part of a package of new exceptions, a fair dealing exception was introduced for the purpose of persons with a relevant disability having access to copyright material.[91] While the Australian exceptions are similar to the UK exceptions, there are differences: for example, the exception for research or study is not limited to 'private' study,[92] and news reporting is not confined to current events. Like the UK courts, Australian courts have tended to be flexible in interpreting the statutory purposes, such as 'criticism or review' and 'reporting news'. For example, the courts have consistently held that news and entertainment are not mutually exclusive, and that 'criticism and review' should be interpreted liberally.[93]

Australian courts have, however, been more mechanical in interpreting the purposes than other common law courts, with the main authority, *De Garis*,[94] rigidly applying dictionary definitions to delimit terms such as 'research', 'study', 'criticism' and 'review'. In addition, in *De Garis*, Beaumont J restrictively interpreted who is entitled to the fair dealing defence, holding that the relevant purpose is that of the person making the use and not that of a person on whose behalf the use is made, so that an intermediary assisting a person is not entitled to the defence.[95] A fair dealing for the purpose of access by persons with a disability may, nevertheless, be made by a person on behalf of the person with a disability. Furthermore, disagreements over the application of the purposes to particular facts, which are attributed to differences of 'impression',[96] have led to ongoing uncertainty about the scope of the Australian defences.[97]

---

[87] Copyright Act 1968 (Aus.), ss. 40, 103A.
[88] Copyright Act 1968 (Aus.), ss. 41, 103AA.
[89] Copyright Act 1968 (Aus.), ss. 41A, 103B.
[90] Copyright Act 1968 (Aus.), ss. 42, 103C.
[91] Copyright Act 1968 (Aus.), s. 113E. The Act defines a 'person with a disability' to mean 'a person with a disability that causes the person difficulty in reading, viewing, hearing or comprehending copyright material in a particular form': s. 10(1).
[92] The word 'private' was deleted by the Copyright Amendment Act 1980 (Aus.).
[93] *Nine Network Australia Pty Ltd* v. *Australian Broadcasting Corporation* (1999) 48 IPR 333; *TCN Channel Nine Pty Ltd* v. *Network Ten Ltd* (2002) 55 IPR 112.
[94] *De Garis* v. *Neville Jeffress Pidler Pty Ltd* (1990) 95 ALR 625.
[95] J. McCutcheon and S. Holloway, 'Whose fair dealing? Third party reliance on the fair dealing exception for parody or satire' (2016) 27(2) *Australian Intellectual Property Journal* 53.
[96] See, especially: *TCN Channel Nine Pty Ltd* v. *Network Ten Ltd* (2002) 55 IPR 112.
[97] D. Brennan, 'Copyright and parody in Australia: some thoughts on *Suntrust Bank* v. *Houghton Mifflin Company*' (2002) 13 *Australian Intellectual Property Journal* 161.

In response to proposals for introducing a fair use exception, in 2006 additional exceptions were introduced, in s. 200AB, which were intended to 'provide some of the benefits that the fair use doctrine provides in the United States'.[98] Section 200AB is, however, far from open-ended, being originally confined to uses by bodies administering libraries or archives, bodies administering educational institutions and by or for persons with a disability.[99] Moreover, the exception is confined to uses that satisfy the three-step test, with the terms used in the exception given the same meaning as those used in Article 13 of TRIPs.[100] In addition, the exceptions in s. 200AB do not apply where a use would not be an infringement under other statutory exceptions, including exceptions under statutory licences.[101] The limitations on s. 200AB have meant that the exceptions are rarely used in practice,[102] and were acknowledged by the replacement of the exception for persons with a disability with a fair dealing defence.[103]

## 11.4.3 Canada

The landmark 2004 judgment of the Canadian Supreme Court in *CCH*[104] is arguably the most significant judicial interpretation of fair dealing exceptions, in that it recognised fair dealing as a users' right and not merely a defence: [2.4.2].[105] Since then, the 'users' rights' perspective on fair dealing has been applied and clarified in two Supreme Court decisions, *SOCAN*[106] and *Alberta (Education)*.[107]

---

[98] Commonwealth Attorney-General, Hansard, 19 October 2006, p. 2.
[99] Copyright Act 1968 (Aus.), ss. 200AB(2)-(4).
[100] Copyright Act 1968 (Aus.), ss. 200AB(1) (7).
[101] Copyright Act 1968 (Aus.), s. 200AB(6).
[102] E. Hudson, 'Implementing fair use in copyright law' (2013) 25 *Intellectual Property Journal* 201.
[103] Copyright Amendment (Disability Access and Other Measures) Act 2017 (Aus.), Schedule 1, item 56.
[104] *CCH Canadian Ltd* v. *Law Society of Upper Canada* (2004) 1 RCS 339; 236 DLR (4th) 395.
[105] G. D'Agostino, 'Healing fair dealing? A comparative analysis of Canada's fair dealing to UK fair dealing and US fair use' (2008) 53 *McGill Law Journal* 309. The first reference to the term 'user rights' was in Linden JA's Court of Appeal judgment in *CCH*: G. Reynolds, 'The limits of statutory interpretation: towards explicit engagement, by the Supreme Court of Canada, with the *Charter* Right to freedom of expression in the context of copyright' (2016) 41 *Queen's Law Journal* 455 at 468.
[106] *Society of Composers, Authors and Music Publishers of Canada (SOCAN)* v. *Bell Canada* [2012] 2 SCR 326.
[107] *Alberta (Education)* v. *Canadian Copyright Licensing Agency (Access Copyright)* [2012] 2 SCR 345.

## 11.4 Fair Dealing

The Canadian Act includes fair dealing exceptions for: research, private study, education, parody or satire;[108] criticism or review;[109] and news reporting.[110] The *CCH* judgment built upon earlier *obiter* comments from Binnie J in *Théberge*,[111] explaining the relationship between exceptions and the public domain as follows:

> Excessive control by holders of copyrights and other forms of intellectual property may unduly limit the ability of the public domain to incorporate and embellish creative innovation in the long-term interests of society as a whole, or create practical obstacles to proper utilization. This is reflected in the exceptions to copyright infringement enumerated in ss. 29 to 32.2, which seek to protect the public domain in traditional ways such as fair dealing for the purpose of criticism or review...[112]

In *CCH* the Supreme Court held that provision of single copies of material, such as law reports, by the Law Society library to its members was a fair dealing for the purpose of research or study. In reaching this conclusion, McLachlin CJ interpreted fair dealing as a user's right and an 'integral part of the scheme of copyright law'.[113] As such, the Court held that the exception should not be interpreted restrictively, and therefore held that 'research' was not limited to 'non-commercial or private contexts'.[114] Drawing on both US and UK law, the Court identified six non-exhaustive factors relevant to whether a dealing is 'fair': (1) the purpose of the dealing; (2) the character of the dealing; (3) the amount of the dealing; (4) alternatives to the dealing; (5) the nature of the work; and (6) the effect of the dealing on the work.[115] Applying an expansive approach to the factors, McLachlin CJ characterised the purpose of fair dealing as 'to ensure that users are not unduly restricted in their ability to use and disseminate copyrighted works'.[116]

By placing fair dealing within a broader context of copyright policy, in which the exceptions safeguard users' positive rights and not merely excuse infringement, the Canadian jurisprudence endorses the view that fair dealing is a limitation rather than an exception. As Gervais has pointed out, however, while the Court appears to have raised fair dealing to a level equivalent to the rights of the copyright owner, there are inconsistencies in the judgment. For example, McLachlin CJ at times refers to

---

[108] Copyright Act, RSC 1985, c. C-42 (Canada), s. 29.
[109] Copyright Act, RSC 1985, c. C-42 (Canada), s. 29.1.
[110] Copyright Act, RSC 1985, c. C-42 (Canada), s. 29.2.
[111] *Galerie d'Art du Petit Champlain Inc.* v. *Claude Théberge* [2002] 2 RCS 336
[112] *Ibid.* [32].    [113] (2004) 1 RCS 339; 236 DLR (4th) 395 at [48].    [114] *Ibid.*
[115] *Ibid.* [53].    [116] *Ibid.* [62].

users having 'interests' rather than 'rights'.[117] Furthermore, the *CCH* Court may have established a hierarchy of exceptions, in which the fair dealing exceptions are privileged over other exceptions. This seems to follow from the Court's treatment of the exception for libraries, established under s. 30.2(1) of the Canadian Act, in which it concluded that, as the use was a fair dealing for research or study, there was no need for the Law Society to rely on the specific exception.[118] This might be compared with the more restrictive approach in Australia, where exceptions are not regarded as 'rights', and where, in *Haines*,[119] for example, it was held that fair dealing exceptions could not be relied upon where a use fell within a statutory licence.[120]

Following *CCH*, the Canadian Supreme Court has expansively interpreted the statutory purposes. In *SOCAN*, the Court applied a liberal approach to the meaning of 'research' to conclude that previews of musical works provided by commercial online music services were fair dealings for the purpose of research. In reaching this conclusion, the Court held that, as the exceptions safeguard users' rights, whether the dealing amounted to 'research' should be analysed from the perspective of the end-user, not the online service provider.[121] In *Alberta (Education)*, the majority of the Court extended the user-centric perspective to hold that copies of works made by teachers for instructing students were permissible fair dealings for the purpose of research or study. In that case, the key issue was whether the purpose was that of the copier, namely the teacher, or the end-user students. On this, the Court held that the purposes of instruction and study were so intertwined as to be inseparable, such that 'there is no separate purpose on the part of the teacher'.[122] On this point, the Canadian analysis can again be contrasted with the Australian approach where, in *De Garis*, the Court held that the relevant purpose was that of the intermediary copier, a commercial news-clipping service, and not that of end-users.[123]

As Geist has pointed out, the Canadian approach has shifted the focus of the analysis from the purpose of the dealing, which is interpreted flexibly, to its fairness; and, in the process, has transformed fair dealing in Canada to something more like fair use.[124] On the other hand, as he

---

[117] D. Gervais, 'Canadian copyright law post-*CCH*' (2004) 18 *Intellectual Property Journal* 131.
[118] (2004) 1 RCS 339; 236 DLR (4th) 395 at [84].
[119] *Copyright Agency Ltd* v. *Haines* (1982) 40 ALR 264.
[120] See also *Copyright Licence Ltd* v. *University of Auckland* (2002) 53 IPR 618.
[121] [2012] 2 SCR 326 at [29].   [122] [2012] 2 SCR 345 at [23].
[123] McCutcheon and Holloway, 'Whose fair dealing?', 53.
[124] Geist, 'Fairness found: How Canada quietly shifted from fair dealing to fair use', 157–86.

further points out, since *CCH*, and especially in the majority judgment in *Alberta (Education)*, Canadian courts have mechanistically applied the six fairness factors identified in *CCH*, treating them as an exhaustive statutory code rather than applying the open-ended and flexible analysis suggested in *CCH*.[125] Adherence to such an approach could threaten the user-centric perspective introduced in *CCH*, by excluding potentially important factors from consideration and introducing undue rigidity.

## 11.5 *Droit d'auteur* Jurisdictions Outside the EU

Although civil law, or *droit d'auteur*, systems apply closed lists of permissible exceptions: [11.1.3], there is diversity in how that approach is applied. To illustrate further the diversity, this section of the chapter explains exceptions in two non-EU jurisdictions, China and South Korea.

### 11.5.1 China

China's Copyright Law applies a closed list approach, listing twelve exceptions[126] to protection of published works,[127] most of which have been adapted to the network environment.[128] The list of exceptions in Article 22 appears to be exhaustive. Some are, however, very different from those found in other countries; for example, one exception provides that appropriate specified types of works, for the purpose of eradicating poverty, can be made accessible free of charge to the public in rural areas via any information network (although the copyright owner may opt out within thirty days of receiving notice).[129]

Only one of the twelve exceptions uses a concept similar to fairness, namely the requirement that only an 'appropriate' quotation for specified purposes may be made from published works.[130] Cases on this exception have considered 'fairness factors', including the purpose of the use,

---
[125] *Ibid.* 190-7.
[126] Copyright Law of the People's Republic of China (China), adopted at the 15th Session of the Standing Committee of the 7th National People's Congress on 7 September 1990, Art. 22.
[127] All these exceptions apply to copyright in 'published' works and to such neighbouring rights in performances, sound and video recordings, broadcasts, and editions; that is, to protected works and media productions that have already been made public.
[128] Articles 6 and 7 of the Internet Regulations (China), and Articles 16 and 17 of the Computer Software Regulations (China). See Y. Li, 'China', in P. Geller, M. Nimmer and L. Bently (eds.), *International Copyright Law and Practice* (LexisNexis, 2016), §8(1)(c)(iii)(B).
[129] Internet Regulations (China), Art. 9.   [130] Copyright Law (China), Art. 22(1).

amount of use, and effect of use on the market.[131] Some authors argue that the Chinese courts may also exempt some uses outside of the Article 22 list of exceptions, utilising concepts similar to 'fair use', at least when the public interest is in issue. However, such arguments are not clearly supported by the legislation or court decisions.[132]

The 2014 draft Revision to China's law appears to adopt a slightly more 'open-ended' approach to exceptions, moving closer to a 'fair use' approach. After listing twelve exceptions, draft Article 43(13) adds 'other circumstances',[133] but such additional exceptions are subject to criteria based on the three-step test.[134]

### 11.5.2 South Korea: From Fair Dealing to Fair Use

South Korea is a civil law jurisdiction that has introduced greater flexibility to a law previously based on a closed list of exceptions. The 2016 amendment to South Korea's law of Article 35*ter*, entitled, 'Fair Use of Works etc.' previously stated that '[i]t is permissible to use works for news reporting, critique, education and research when such use does not conflict with the normal exploitation of works and does not unreasonably prejudice the legitimate interests of rights holders.' It now states that (with some exceptions) 'where a person does not unreasonably prejudice an author's legitimate interest without conflicting with the normal exploitation of works, he/she may use such works.'[135] The exception's wording still reflects parts of the three-step test. Four factors, based on the US 'fair use factors', are considered in determining fairness, namely:

> 1. Purposes and characters of use, including whether such use is for or not for nonprofit. 2. Types and natures of works, etc. 3. Amount and substantiality of portion used in relation to the whole works, etc. 4. Effect of the use of works, etc. on the current or potential market for or value of such work etc.[136]

In a number of decisions, uses which have not qualified under South Korea's quotation exception – the most frequently used Korean

---

[131] *Yang Luo-Shu* v. *China Pictures Press* (Shandong High Court, 2007) at 94, discussed by S. Song, 'Reevaluating fair use in China – a comparative copyright analysis of Chinese fair use legislation, the US fair use doctrine, and the European fair dealing model' (2011) 51 *IDEA* 453 at 481–2.
[132] *Ibid.* 481. See also Li and Greenleaf, 'China's copyright public domain', 51–5.
[133] 2014 Draft Revision (China), Art. 43(13).
[134] 2014 Draft Revision (China), Article 43 provides, following paragraph (13): 'When using works in ways provided by the previous Paragraph, it is prohibited to influence the regular use of the work, and it is prohibited to unreasonably harm the lawful rights and interests of the copyright holder.'
[135] Copyright Act (South Korea), Art. 35*ter* (1).
[136] *Ibid.* Art. 35*ter* (2); see Online Supplement.

exception – have, nevertheless, been upheld as fair uses under the new provision.[137] In one case, a Korean company intending to import an overseas-manufactured drug submitted to the Korean Food and Drug Agency, as part of an approval process, an academic article about the drug that it had downloaded from the Internet.[138] As Jong explains, the Suwon District Court held that this was a 'fair use', emphasising the public nature of the academic article, and that the use was non-profit, and narrowly interpreting 'for profit' purposes as limited to where profit flows directly from the infringing act.[139]

## 11.6 Comparative Approaches to Exceptions and the Public Domain

Exceptions are the main means by which copyright expressly balances rights of owners and competing public interests, by permitting uses mainly for particular purposes or in particular contexts. Exceptions define both the scope of copyright exclusive rights and the scope of permissible uses (or, using our terminology, public rights). As this chapter has explained, there are three general approaches to exceptions under national laws: the *droit d'auteur* 'closed list' approach, the US fair use model and the Commonwealth fair dealing approach.

While an open-ended fair use exception is more flexible than other approaches, national exceptions are not as clear-cut as this division into three approaches suggests. In the EU, there is a closed list of exceptions, but the broad drafting of exceptions confers considerable discretion in their application and interpretation; and, despite indications that exceptions should be narrowly interpreted, ECJ jurisprudence requires the interpretation of exceptions to apply a 'fair balance' between the rights and interests of owners and users: [11.2.1]. Moreover, reform proposals would introduce greater flexibility through new mandatory exceptions. Outside of the EU, South Korea has introduced flexibility by an exception, similar to a flexible fair dealing exception, permitting 'fair' uses for four statutory purposes; and China is proposing a new open-ended exception, subject to the three-step test.

Fair dealing and fair use exceptions can be traced to English case law, in which fair abridgements (or fair uses) were not regarded as infringing. The exceptions therefore, strictly speaking, originated as a limitation on exclusive rights. In Chapter 10 we argued that, while there is

---

[137] S. Jong, 'Fair use in Korea', Presentation at *Australian Digital Alliance Copyright Forum*, 24 February 2017, Canberra http://infojustice.org/archives/37819.
[138] Suwon District Court decision (2016) GoJung 432, decided 18 August 2016.
[139] Jong, 'Fair use in Korea'.

a case for greater attention to be paid to the nature of the use of a work in analysing infringement, there are dangers this could overly complicate the analysis: [10.3.5]. Nevertheless, following the codification of fair dealing and fair use, their status as limitations or exceptions continues to be unclear. Applying a public domain perspective, it is arguable that fair dealing and fair use are both limitations, in that they establish the scope of exclusive rights, and exceptions, in that the uses are excused or justified. In this, it is arguable that the status of these general exceptions is distinguishable from the more specific exceptions in common law systems. Overall, it seems to us that public domain uses can be supported and promoted by more clarity in the interpretation of the exceptions.

Although most common law jurisdictions have interpreted the limited fair dealing purposes flexibly, there are considerable variations in the interpretation of fair dealing exceptions. By applying a 'users' rights' perspective to interpret fair dealing as aimed at ensuring permission-free uses, the Canadian Supreme Court effectively raised user rights and interests to an equivalent status to the copyright exclusive rights. The practical implications of this approach include allowing recourse to a general fair dealing exception even where a more specific exception might apply, and identifying the purpose of the use from the point of view of the end-user rather than an intermediary that directly exercises an exclusive right. While the Canadian jurisprudence is not entirely internally consistent or problem-free, the Canadian Supreme Court has illustrated how a perspective that fully takes into account the public objectives of permission-free uses can lead to greater flexibility in applying and interpreting fair dealing exceptions, and avoiding overly rigid or mechanistic approaches that have characterised the approaches of courts in some jurisdictions, such as Australia.

The user-oriented Canadian approach also shows the difficulty in drawing overly rigid distinctions between fair dealing and fair use. While considerable attention has been given to the advantages of a fair use exception, and especially in its potential to flexibly apply to new uses, there are problems in both the formulation and interpretation of the US fair use exception. For example, there are fundamental uncertainties about whether it is an affirmative defence, about the relative importance of the fair use factors, and about what may amount to a 'transformative use'. An open-ended exception, such as fair use, clearly has the potential to promote public domain uses, but it is, in and of itself, not a magic bullet. As Jaszi, for example, has argued, the weaknesses of the fair use approach, and a balanced understanding of approaches to exceptions and limitations in other jurisdictions, dispels

## 11.6 Comparative Approaches to Exceptions & Public Domain 349

any knee-jerk perception that the US exception is necessarily superior.[140] Difficulties, and inconsistencies, with the application of the fair use factors also suggest there is potential for reform of US law, including considering if the four statutory factors are the best guide for determining whether a use should be permitted, as well as potential mechanisms for improving certainty in applying the exception.[141]

While flexible exceptions may promote public domain uses, to the extent they may create new uncertainties or indeterminacies, they may also inhibit uses, especially by risk averse users. On balance, we consider that an open-ended exception has potential to support public domain uses, including by avoiding the undue rigidity of more specific exceptions. This conclusion, however, is subject to two qualifications. First, it is not clear to us that the US fair use factors direct attention to the most relevant public interest considerations in determining whether a use should be permitted, and we consider there is scope for development of clearer, better targeted factors. Second, there is also scope for any flexible exception to be accompanied by measures that clarify the interpretation and operation of the exception, such as the development of 'best practice' guidelines.[142] In this, we acknowledge the collective action problems facing industry and user groups, which are likely to result in less than optimal interpretations of an open-ended exception, suggesting that guidelines may be best produced by a neutral third party.

While this chapter has introduced and evaluated the main approaches to exceptions in national laws, understanding the public interests underpinning this public domain category depends upon the particular categories of exceptions, which we introduce in the next chapter.

---

[140] P. Jaszi, 'Public interest exceptions in copyright: a comparative and international perspective', Paper presented to Correcting Course: Rebalancing Copyright for Libraries in the National and International Arenas, Columbia University, 5–7 May 2005 http://correctingcourse.columbia.edu/paper_jaszi.pdf. Jaszi provocatively argues that there may be potential in exploring a hybrid approach that combines some of the best features of national approaches to exceptions and limitations.

[141] For some suggested reforms aimed at improving the US doctrine, see Carroll, 'Fixing fair use'; M. Madison, 'Rewriting fair use and the future of copyright reform' (2005) 23 *Cardozo Arts & Entertainment Law Journal* 391.

[142] See, for example, W. Fisher and W. McGeveran, 'The digital learning challenge: obstacles to educational uses of copyrighted material in the digital age: a foundational white paper', Berkman Center for Internet & Society, 10 August 2006; P. Hirtle, E. Hudson and A. Kenyon, *Copyright and Cultural Institutions: Guidelines for Digitization for US Libraries, Archives, and Museums* (Cornell University Library, 2009); D'Agostino, 'Healing fair dealing?', 352.

# 12 Copyright Exceptions and Limitations – Categories

12.1 Introduction: Categories of Exceptions and Limitations 350
12.2 Temporary, Transient or Incidental Copies 351
12.3 The Quotation Exception 357
12.4 Parody or Satire 363
12.5 Education and Research 369
12.6 Libraries and Archives 379
12.7 Conclusions: Exceptions as a Key Contributor to the Public Domain 389

## 12.1 Introduction: Categories of Exceptions and Limitations

Copyright exceptions are the main means for expressly balancing rights of owners and the public interest in permission-free uses of works, but the difficulties in establishing this balance has resulted in complex exceptions in national laws. The contemporary importance of exceptions is evidenced by the attention given to them by WIPO's Standing Committee on Copyright and Related Rights (SCCR), which since 2004 has focused on exceptions for educational activities, libraries and archives, and disabled persons.[1] There are, however, significant disagreements between the developing world and developed countries about both the scope of exceptions and whether there should be an exceptions treaty or treaties.

To date, Marrakesh is the sole international copyright agreement to be concerned principally with exceptions: [4.2.1]. There have, however, been proposals before the SCCR for new international instruments for exceptions for educational uses: [12.5] and libraries and archives: [12.6]. In 2010, for example, the African Group presented a draft treaty to the SCCR on 'Exceptions and limitations for the disabled,

---

[1] World Intellectual Property Organization (WIPO, various dates), 'Limitations and exceptions' www.wipo.int/copyright/en/limitations/.

educational and research institutions, libraries and archive centers'.[2] Since then, however, there has been disagreement between some developing countries that have supported binding exceptions treaties and the United States, which has advocated non-binding agreements on high-level principles.

Given the diversity of exceptions in national laws, it is impossible for categories of exceptions to be treated comprehensively in this book. We have therefore selectively chosen the following categories of exceptions: temporary or transient copies; quotations; parody or satire; educational uses; and libraries and archives. In addition to these categories, exceptions for 'news', political speeches and related exceptions are dealt with in our chapter on copyright exclusions (which are often implemented as exceptions): [8.2]. For each category of exception covered, we introduce the exception, explain how it is dealt with under international copyright law, give examples drawn from selected national laws, and draw conclusions about implications of the exceptions for copyright public domains. Our selection of categories of exceptions should not be interpreted as suggesting we consider these exceptions are more important than others; they were chosen simply for their ability to illustrate broader principles. In addition, we deal with two other important categories of exceptions – private use exceptions and exceptions to assist visually impaired and print-disabled people under Marrakesh – in the Online Supplement. We regard these (and other) exceptions as extremely important, and deal with them in the Supplement purely due to space constraints.

## 12.2 Temporary, Transient or Incidental Copies

The combination of digitisation and online access gave rise to questions about whether transient copies, such as temporary reproductions stored in RAM or on cache-servers, were infringing reproductions. An Agreed Statement to the WCT fails to resolve these questions, which are left to national laws: [10.2.4]. The potential application of the reproduction right to transient copies, however, led to the introduction of exceptions in most national laws. Given the importance of transient or incidental copying for facilitating access to and use of Internet content, and that the sole mandatory exception under EU law applies to such copies, this is the first category of exceptions selected for this chapter.

---

[2] WIPO SCCR, 'Draft WIPO Treaty on exceptions and limitations for the disabled, educational and research institutions, libraries and archive centers', Proposal by the African Group, SCCR/20/11 (15 June 2010).

### 12.2.1 The EU and the UK

In the EU, Article 2 of the InfoSoc Directive takes an expansive approach to the reproduction right, extending it to all 'temporary reproductions': [10.2.4]. However, the one mandatory exception under the InfoSoc Directive applies to ensure that transient copies made to access Internet content are not infringing reproductions. Article 5(1) requires an exemption for temporary reproductions which are 'transient or incidental' and 'which are an integral and essential part of a technological process whose sole purpose is to enable:

(a) a transmission in a network between third parties by an intermediary; or
(b) a lawful use.

In addition, to be entitled to the exception, the reproductions must 'have no independent economic significance'.

In *Infopaq I*, which involved printing out eleven word extracts from newspaper articles: [10.3.1], the ECJ held that the exception imposed five cumulative conditions, namely that: the act is temporary; is transient or incidental; is an integral and essential part of a technological process; the sole purpose of that process is to enable a transmission in a network between third parties by an intermediary of a lawful use of a work or protected subject matter; and the act has no independent economic significance.[3] Significantly, the Court ruled that a reproduction could only be 'transient' if a copy is automatically deleted without human intervention.[4] As the extracts were printed in paper form, the Court ruled that this step was neither transient nor incidental, so the exception did not apply.

Subsequently, in *Premier League*,[5] the ECJ ruled that for a temporary reproduction to have 'independent economic significance' it must have a distinct and separable economic advantage beyond that obtained from lawful use of the work. In *Infopaq II*, the Court elaborated on this to rule there would be a distinct and separable advantage where either a profit was made from the economic exploitation of the temporary copies or the temporary reproductions modified the work.[6] In relation to the fourth condition, that the purpose of the transmission is to allow a lawful use, the Court held that as drafting a summary of newspaper articles was not an

---

[3] Case C-5/08, *Infopaq International A/S* v. *Danske Dagblades Forening*, [2009] ECR I-6569 at [54].
[4] *Ibid.* [64].
[5] Joined Cases C-403/08 and C-429/08, *Football Association Premier League Ltd* v. *QC Leisure* [2011] ECR I-9083.
[6] Case C-302/10, *Infopaq International A/S* v. *Danske Dagblades Forening* [2012] ECLI:EU:C:2012:16 at [52]–[54].

## 12.2 Temporary, Transient or Incidental Copies

infringement, this use was not unlawful. In *Filmspeler*,[7] however, the ECJ held that, as use of links to infringing websites that were pre-installed on a multimedia player was an unlawful use, temporary reproductions on the player made by streaming from the websites were not protected by the exception.

In the UK, Article 5(1) is transposed in s. 28A of the CPDA[8] and, in *Meltwater*,[9] the UK Supreme Court considered the application of the exception to a news monitoring service made available from a website. The issue before the Court was the application of the exception to acts of an end-user where the reports were not downloaded but, in accessing them, copies were made in the cache of a user's computer and on screen. As one purpose of Article 5(1) is 'to authorise the making of copies to enable the end-user to view copyright material on the internet',[10] the Supreme Court held that the copies were automatically made as part of using the Internet but, as the issue had a 'transnational dimension', referred questions concerning the interpretation of Article 5(1) to the ECJ.

Concerning the third condition, that reproductions must be part of a technological process, the ECJ ruled that the technological process could be activated by human intervention, such as browsing by an Internet user.[11] On the second condition, that the reproduction must be transient or incidental, the Court noted the difficulties in finding that copies stored in the user's cache are 'transient', as they are retained after browsing has been terminated. As the cached copies could not exist independently of the technological process of browsing, however, the Court ruled that the copies were 'incidental' to web browsing.[12] While there remain some uncertainties about the scope of the exception, such as the precise meaning of 'transient' reproductions, the ECJ ruling in *Meltwater* makes it clear that it applies to exclude copies automatically made as an integral part of browsing, apparently regardless of how long the copies are retained.

### 12.2.2 Australia

The Australian Act incorporates a number of specific exceptions for temporary reproductions. First, there are exceptions for temporary

---

[7] Case C-527/15, *Stichting Brein* v. *Jack Frederick Wullems* [2017] 3 CMLR 1027.
[8] Copyright, Designs and Patents Act 1988 (UK) ('CDPA'), s. 28A.
[9] *Public Relations Consultants Association Limited* v. *The Newspaper Licensing Agency Limited* [2013] UKSC 18; [2013] 2 All ER 852.
[10] *Ibid.* [28].
[11] Case C-360/13, *Public Relations Consultants Association Ltd* v. *Newspaper Licensing Agency Ltd* [2014] 2 All ER (EC) 959 at [32].
[12] *Ibid.* [50].

reproductions made 'as part of the technical process of making or receiving a communication'.[13] Second, there are exceptions for temporary reproductions 'incidentally made as a necessary part of a technical process of using a copy' of the work or subject matter.[14] To be entitled to these two exceptions, however, the temporary copies must not be of infringing material.[15] Third, as part of the safe harbour regime for Internet intermediaries, some intermediaries are insulated from liability for the automated caching of copyright material, provided they comply with certain conditions.[16] Fourth, there is an exception allowing automatic caching by educational institutions where copies 'are made by the system merely to facilitate efficient later access to the works and other subject-matter by users of the system'.[17]

There are many uncertainties arising from the drafting of the complex exceptions, which create doubts about the status of common forms of caching.[18] For example, the exceptions for 'temporary reproductions' may not cover cached copies that may be held for more than a limited period. Moreover, the effectiveness of the exceptions for Internet intermediaries is limited by the exclusion of reproductions of infringing material from the scope of the exceptions: caching by an ISP, for example, will commonly include both non-infringing and infringing material, without the ISP being able to distinguish between the two. The uncertain application of the exceptions, together with the need for flexibility for analogous new uses, led the Australian Law Reform Commission to recommend repealing the exceptions and replacing them with a general fair use, or expanded fair dealing, exception.[19]

### 12.2.3 The United States

The US Act includes a specific exception that applies to copyright in a computer program, where making a copy is an 'essential step' in using the program or the copy is for archival (or back-up) purposes only.[20] The courts have, however, restrictively interpreted the exception so it is confined to copies made in RAM that are deleted when the computer is

---

[13] Copyright Act 1968 (Aus.), ss. 43A, 111A.
[14] Copyright Act 1968 (Aus.), ss. 43B, 111B.
[15] Copyright Act 1968 (Aus.), ss. 43A(2), 43B(2), 111A(2), 111B(2).
[16] Copyright Act 1968 (Aus.), ss. 116AB, 116AD, 116AG, 116AH.
[17] Copyright Act 1968 (Aus.), s. 200AAA.
[18] K. Weatherall, 'Internet intermediaries and copyright: an Australian agenda for reform', Policy paper prepared for Australian Digital Alliance, April 2011.
[19] Australian Law Reform Commission, *Copyright and the Digital Economy*, Recommendation 11-1, p. 260.
[20] 17 USC §117.

## 12.2 Temporary, Transient or Incidental Copies

turned off.[21] In the absence of other applicable exceptions, under US law temporary or incidental copies may be exempted under the fair use exception.

A number of significant fair use cases have concerned liability for search engine activities, such as automated caching of web content. In *Field*,[22] for example, the Court held that copies of material stored in Google's cache, and snippets returned in response to user-initiated searches, fell within the fair use exception. In concluding that the use was transformative, the Court held that 'Google serves different and socially important purposes in offering access to copyrighted works through "Cached" links'.[23] Similarly, in *Perfect 10*,[24] the Ninth Circuit held that storage and return of thumbnail images by the Google search engine was a fair use as it was 'highly transformative'.[25] In reaching this conclusion, the Court emphasised that a search engine 'provides social benefit by incorporating an original work into a new work, namely, an electronic reference tool'.[26] In holding that wholesale copying of works to facilitate access by search engines is a transformative use, US courts have effectively shifted the focus from whether a use is transformative to whether there is a 'transformative purpose' for the use.[27]

The US 'transformative purpose' cases therefore provide broad scope for excluding uses that facilitate access to works, that go beyond the specific exclusions for temporary or incidental uses under other national laws. In particular, as the key consideration is the purpose of the use, there is no need for US courts to consider issues such as the length of time a work may be stored in a cache.

### 12.2.4 Other Approaches: South Korea and India

The diversity of national approaches to exceptions for temporary copies is illustrated by the laws of two additional jurisdictions, South Korea and India.

South Korea's law provides that:

> If a work is used on a computer, the work may be temporarily reproduced on the computer to the extent deemed necessary for smooth and efficient information

---

[21] *Sega Enterprises Ltd* v. *Peak Computer, Inc*, 977 F 2d 1510 (9th Cir 1992).
[22] *Field* v. *Google Inc*, 412 F Supp 2d 1106 (D Nev 2006).   [23] *Ibid.* 1119.
[24] *Perfect 10, Inc.* v. *Amazon.com, Inc*, 508 F 3d 1146 (9th Cir 2007).   [25] *Ibid.* 1165.
[26] *Ibid.*
[27] See J. C. Ginsburg, 'Google Books and fair use: from implausible to inevitable?', *SociallyAware*, 17 November 2015 www.sociallyawareblog.com/2015/11/17/google-books-and-fair-use-from-implausible-to-inevitable/.

processing: *Provided,* That the foregoing shall not apply if the use of the work infringes copyright.[28]

The key consideration in this potentially broad exception is clearly when a reproduction is 'necessary for smooth and efficient information processing', which has yet to be addressed by the courts.

India, on the other hand, has two relevant exceptions. First, the Indian Act excepts 'the transient or incidental storage of a work or performance purely in the technical process of electronic transmission or communication to the public'.[29] Second, there is an exception for 'transient or incidental storage of a work or performance for the purpose of providing electronic links, access or integration, where such links, access or integration has not been expressly prohibited by the rights holder, unless the person responsible is aware or has reasonable grounds for believing that such storage is of an infringing copy'.[30]

One thing that seems clear from the Indian Act is that, if a website uses the Robot Exclusion Protocol[31] to tell search engines that the pages on its website are not to be made searchable, then the rights holder has prohibited linking or access, so the exception is not available.

### 12.2.5 'Temporary' Copies and the Public Domain

Making temporary, incidental or transient copies of works is an essential part of accessing and using content by means of the Internet and, therefore, requiring permission for all such copies would substantially inhibit public domain uses of works. The reasons for excluding intermediary liability for cached copies were addressed by the Canadian Supreme Court in its 2004 decision on ISP liability:

> there is a public interest in encouraging intermediaries who make telecommunications possible to expand and improve their operations without the threat of copyright infringement. To impose copyright liability on intermediaries would obviously chill that expansion and development, as the history of caching demonstrates.[32]

The necessity of making 'temporary' copies in the course of a communication might suggest there is a case for the reproduction right to be interpreted so that these uses are not infringements, removing the need

---

[28] Copyright Act, 2011 (South Korea), Art. 35*bis.*
[29] Copyright Act 1957 (India), s. 52(1)(b).   [30] Copyright Act 1957 (India), s. 52(1)(c).
[31] 'A standard for robot exclusion' www.robotstxt.org/orig.html.
[32] *Society of Composers, Authors & Music Publishers of Canada (SOCAN)* v. *Canadian Association of Internet Providers* [2004] SCR 427 at 472.

for exceptions.[33] The variety of reproductions that may be made to assist communications, however, means that the position is more complex. For example, material must be able to be removed from a mirror server, or a proxy cache, that hosts infringing content even though these copies may facilitate communications. Moreover, if an end-user who accesses an infringing streaming service does not infringe the communications right, there is a case for copies stored in the user's client cache to be infringements. It is therefore important to identify circumstances in which making temporary copies should be permissible.

All jurisdictions have found it difficult to devise criteria for excepting temporary copies. The exceptions in the EU and Australia are cumbersome and overly complex, and those in South Korea and India not much better. While an open-ended exception, such as fair use, can flexibly apply to existing and new uses, the application of 'transformative purpose' analysis under US law has created uncertainties. We acknowledge the potential advantages of an open-ended exception: [11.6], but also suggest that public domain uses can be promoted by improving specific exceptions in national laws. One constant issue has been determining how long a 'temporary' or 'transient' copy can be stored while being entitled to an exception. If making a copy is truly incidental to a communication, as suggested by the ECJ in *Meltwater*, there may be no need also to require the copy to be 'transient' or 'temporary'. Moreover, as intermediaries are often not in a position to distinguish infringing from non-infringing content, they could be better protected by removing any limitation restricting the exception to non-infringing content.

## 12.3 The Quotation Exception

Article 10 of Berne provides for one mandatory exception under international copyright law, an exception permitting quotations: [5.4.2]. The Article sets out three conditions for the exception to apply: that the work has been made available to the public; that the quotation is compatible with 'fair practice'; and that it must not 'exceed that justified by the purpose' of the quotation. There is, however, much diversity in how the exception is implemented in national laws.

---

[33] Hugenholtz, for example, has argued that the reproduction right should be interpreted 'normatively' so it does not include all copies 'in a purely technical sense': P. B. Hugenholtz, 'Caching and copyright: the right of temporary copying' (2000) 22(10) *European Intellectual Property Review* 482 at 485.

## 12.3.1 EU Law

In the EU, Article 5(3)(d) of the InfoSoc Directive provides for an optional exception for quotations 'for purposes such as criticism or review', which tracks the conditions applicable under Berne. Article 5(3)(d) therefore requires that the work must have been lawfully made available to the public, that the quotation must acknowledge the source and it must be 'in accordance with fair practice'. In *Painer*, the ECJ interpreted the exception as 'intended to strike a fair balance between the right to freedom of expression of users of a work ... and the reproduction right conferred on authors'.[34] While the balance is struck through the conditions attached to the exception, the Court also ruled that expressive rights of users had to be taken into account in interpreting the exception to ensure the effectiveness of the quotation right and safeguard its purpose.[35]

Given the flexibility allowed by Article 5(3)(d), there are significant variations in quotation exceptions in EU Member States, with some jurisdictions implementing the exception restrictively and others liberally. At one end of the spectrum, French law applies a restrictive approach, allowing short quotations for a closed list of purposes, including critical, polemical, educational, scientific or informatory works, or press reviews or reports of current events.[36] At the other end, Scandinavian laws are liberal, with the exception being subject only to a general 'rule of reason'.[37] For example, Article 22 of the Swedish law simply provides that:

> Anyone may, in accordance with proper usage and to the extent necessary for the purpose, quote from works which have been made available to the public.[38]

While broad exceptions such as this are subject to general principles of 'fairness', they provide scope for the exception to extend beyond purposes such as criticism or review to include 'creative' uses of quotations in derivative works, analogous to a 'transformative use' exception.[39] In some *droit d'auteur* jurisdictions the flexibility of the exception is such that it may perform similar functions to fair dealing or fair use, although

---

[34] Case C-145/10 *Eva-Maria Painer* v. *Standard VerlagsGmbH* [2011] ECR I-12533 at [134].
[35] *Ibid.* [133]; Geiger et al., 'Limitations and exceptions', 97.
[36] Code de la propriété intellectuelle (France), L 122-5(4); Adeney, 'Appropriation in the name of art?', 146–7.
[37] See Hugenholtz and Senftleben, 'Fair use in Europe', Amsterdam, 4 March 2012, p. 15.
[38] Act on Copyright in Literary and Artistic Works (Law No. 729 of 30 December 1960, as amended), Art. 22.
[39] Adeney, 'Appropriation in the name of art?', 147.

## 12.3 The Quotation Exception

the conditions for applying the exceptions are quite different.[40] This can be illustrated by the scope of the German exception.

### 12.3.2 German Law

Under German law the quotation exception, in Article 51, is one of the two most important copyright exceptions.[41] This reflects the policy of the law of promoting cultural and scientific progress, which requires authors to accept some uses of a work by others. As the German Constitutional Court put it in the principal case, *Germania 3*:

> Other artists have interests, protected by the 'freedom of art', in being able to engage in an artistic dialogue and creation process in relation to existing works without the danger of financial consequences or consequences for the content of their art.[42]

Although 'quotation' is not defined, German courts have held that there must be some relationship, or engagement, between the quotation and the quoting work, so that use of the quotation is justified, such as by providing evidence of a point made in the quoting work.[43] Moreover, the parts used must retain their separate character as quotations, and cannot be merged into the quoting work.[44]

In *Germania 3*, the Constitutional Court was required to assess the status of two substantial extracts from Brecht plays that were used in another play: [8.3.3]. In concluding that the use fell within the quotation exception, the Court acknowledged it went beyond the function of providing evidence, and therefore was outside the strict terms of Article 51. Nevertheless, as the quoting work was an 'artistic work', taking into account the guarantee of the right to artistic freedom in Article 5(3) of the Basic Law (*Grundgesetz*), the Court held that, in such cases, there must be a broader inquiry into the balance between the commercial interests of an author and the creative freedom of other artists. As any commercial disadvantage to Brecht was insubstantial, the Court ruled that the balance favoured the creative use of the work 'for the purposes of artistic engagement'.[45]

---

[40] *Ibid.* 148.
[41] Law on Copyright and Neighbouring Rights (Urheberrechtsgesetz – UrhG) (Germany), Art. 51. The other important exception is the 'free use' exception in Article 24: see [12.4.3].
[42] German Federal Constitutional Court, 29 June 2000, *Germania 3*, 2001 GRUR 149. For a translation of the decision, see Adeney and Antons, 'The *Germania 3* decision translated', 654.
[43] Adeney, 'Appropriation in the name of art?', 150.   [44] *Ibid.* 151.
[45] Adeney and Antons, 'The *Germania 3* decision translated', 654.

This broad interpretation of the exception is, however, qualified by subsequent decisions that have restrictively interpreted the requirements, first, for there to be a 'quotation' and, second, that the quoting work be a 'work of art'.[46] In June 2017, the German Federal Court of Justice referred to the Constitutional Court the question of whether an unauthorised musical sample could be a permissible quotation under Article 5(3)(d) of the Infosoc Directive, with the defendants arguing that quotation is a 'right' and not an 'exception'.[47] At present, however, while the German exception applies to some 'transformative uses', the extent to which it does so should not be overstated.

### 12.3.3 UK Law

Until recently, there was no express quotation exception in the UK. In 2014, however, implementing recommendations from the Hargreaves Review, an express fair dealing exception permitting quotations was introduced.[48] The conditions that apply to the exception generally mirror those under Article 5(3)(d) of the InfoSoc Directive, but in place of the requirement that a quotation accord with 'fair practice', the exception was implemented as a fair dealing exception.

The new exception may address problems, such as the need for historians or biographers to obtain permission to use extensive excerpts from personal letters (provided that the works have been made available to the public, such as by public exhibition).[49] Nevertheless, the exception is untested and its scope uncertain. For example, as the term 'quotation' is not defined, there are questions about which uses fall within the exception. Moreover, although the exception applies to all works, there are questions about what might be a fair quotation from musical or artistic works. For example, while the exception applies to photographs, guidance from the UK Intellectual Property Office suggests that use of a photograph in a news report would not be a fair dealing, as this would conflict with normal exploitation of the work.[50]

---

[46] *Ibid.* 657.
[47] Bundesgerichtshof, Vorlage des Bundesgerichtshofs an den Europäischen Gerichtshofs zur Zulässigkeit des Tonträger-Samplings, 1 June 1017.
[48] CDPA, s. 30(1ZA), introduced by the Copyright and Rights in Performances (Quotation and Parody) Regulations 2014 (UK).
[49] A. Herman, 'The year of living exceptionally: new copyright exceptions in UK law' (2014) 19(4) *Art Antiquity and Law* 303 at 309.
[50] Intellectual Property Office (UK), 'Exceptions to copyright: guidance for creators and copyright owners' (IPO, October 2014), p. 7.

## 12.3 The Quotation Exception

### 12.3.4 South Korea: An Expansive Approach

South Korea's law provides that '[i]t is permissible to quote a work already made public for purposes of news reporting, critique, education and research, etc. within a reasonable limit and in compliance with fair practices'.[51] The quotation exception is the most frequently used Korean exception, and the 'purpose of quotation and the reasonable extent of quotation have both been interpreted very broadly by courts'.[52] For example, the exception has been applied by the Seoul High Court to non-commercial use of a musical work where an Internet user uploaded a video of his daughter singing and dancing with the song used as background music.[53] The Korean Supreme Court has also held that a commercial use involving thumbnail images made by a search engine is a legitimate quotation.[54]

In applying the exception, the Korean courts take into account factors similar to the US 'fair use factors': [11.3.2], namely: the purpose of the quotation; the nature of the quoted work; the content and amount of the quoted portion; the interactive relationship between the quoted and quoting works; the general notion of readers; and the possibility of displacing market demand for the quoted work.[55]

### 12.3.5 Australia: No Express Exception

Like traditional English law, there is no express exception for quotations in Australia. The use of quotations therefore depends upon whether the quoted material is too insubstantial to infringe and, if it is a substantial part, whether it falls within a fair dealing exception, such as the exceptions for criticism or review, or parody or satire.[56] In its 2013 report on copyright exceptions, the ALRC raised the possibility of a specific quotation exception, but concluded it was preferable for quotations to be dealt with as part of a fair use or extended fair dealing exception.[57] The ALRC further pointed out that the need for a 'quotation' to reference the quoted work would mean that some transformative uses would not fall within

---

[51] Copyright Act, 2011 (South Korea), Art. 28.
[52] S. Jong, 'Fair use in Korea', Presentation at Australian Digital Alliance Copyright Forum, Canberra, 24 February 2017 http://infojustice.org/archives/37819.
[53] Seoul High Court Decision 2010na35260, decided 13 October 2010, cited in Jong, 'Fair use in Korea'.
[54] (South Korea) Supreme Court Decision 2005Do7793, 9 February 2006; Supreme Court Decision 2009Da4343, 11 March 2010, cited *ibid*.
[55] See (South Korea) Supreme Court Decision 2012Do10777, 26 August 2014, cited *ibid*.
[56] Adeney, 'Appropriation in the name of art?', 142–4.
[57] Australian Law Reform Commission, *Copyright and the Digital Economy*, Recommendation 9-1, p. 225.

a fair dealing exception for the purpose of quotation, but might be protected by a fair use exception.[58]

### 12.3.6 US Law: Is Quotation a Fair Use?

As there is no express quotation exception in US law, assuming it is an infringement, whether or not a quotation is permissible depends upon the application of the fair use exception. There is, however, little case law on whether 'iterative uses of other author's works', such as direct quotations or paraphrases, are a fair use.[59]

In *Harper & Row*,[60] the main Supreme Court precedent, it was claimed that copyright in the unpublished manuscript of President Ford's memoirs was infringed by a news article which included 300 to 400 words of direct quotations: [8.3.1]. Finding that the quotations were substantial, the majority placed considerable weight on the commercial nature of the use and the effect on the potential market for rights in the memoir, as well as the fact the manuscript was unpublished, to hold that the quotations were not a fair use. As a result of the Supreme Court decision in *Campbell*, which, in the case of transformative uses, rejected the presumption that commercial uses are always unfair, some of the reasoning in *Harper & Row* must be doubted. While, following *Campbell*, it is more likely that quotations that are 'transformative' will be protected as a fair use, *Harper & Row* may still present an obstacle to extensive use of quotations, especially in a commercial context.[61]

### 12.3.7 Quotations and the Public Domain

The importance of the right to quote for the copyright public domain is illustrated by quotation being the one mandatory exception in international copyright law. Exceptions for quotation are one of the most important safeguards of public domain uses in some civil law jurisdictions, where they promote the freedom of expression of users, but also support creative uses and may extend to some transformative uses. For example, under German law, taking into account the constitutional right to artistic freedom, it is clear that relatively extensive use can be made of quoted works in 'artistic works'. Nevertheless, to fall within the exception the use must still be for the purpose of 'quotation', which is subject to varying interpretations, and there must be some relationship between the quoting

---

[58] *Ibid.* 224.   [59] Samuelson, 'Unbundling fair uses', 2577.
[60] *Harper & Row, Publishers, Inc.* v. *Nation Enterprises Inc*, 471 US 539 (1985).
[61] Samuelson, 'Unbundling fair uses', 2565.

work and the quoted work. These limitations, not to mention the conditions imposed by Article 10 of Berne, mean that even under a liberal interpretation, a quotation exception is not a general purpose 'transformative use' exception. The US Supreme Court's judgment in *Harper & Row*, however, indicates that there may also be difficulties in applying a fair use exception to quotations, with the extent to which fair use applies to transformative uses also presenting challenges: [11.3].

Applying our realist perspective: [1.5], there is scope for greater use of the flexibility allowed by international copyright law for national laws to introduce relatively broad quotation exceptions, such as the South Korean exception, which can extend to some transformative uses. For example, in jurisdictions such as Australia, which do not have a specific exception, public domain uses could be bolstered by introducing an express exception, such as the fair dealing exception that has been introduced in the UK. While a broadly drafted exception could promote public domain values, such as 'freedom of art', as Adeney has pointed out, a number of significant issues need to be addressed, including whether the exception is confined to published works, the scope of a 'quotation', the conditions applied to an exception, and its relationship with other copyright exceptions.[62]

## 12.4 Parody or Satire

As parodies are often critical of or even derogatory towards an original work, they are unlikely to be licensed by the copyright holder.[63] Although there is no exception for parody under international copyright law, it is widely assumed that exceptions for legitimate parodies will satisfy the three-step test.[64] An exception is needed, as there is no rule that a parody cannot amount to a substantial reproduction.

The law in this area tends to distinguish between the humorous treatment of the original work itself, which may be referred to as 'parody' or 'target parody', and the use of a work to criticise other works or social practices, referred to as 'satire' or 'weapon parody'.[65] There has, increasingly, been an international shift towards recognising satire or weapon parodies as legitimate exceptions. While exceptions for parody can be justified by the need to resist attempts by owners to suppress

---

[62] Adeney. 'Appropriation in the name of art?', 158.
[63] R. Deazley, 'Copyright and parody: taking backwards the Gowers Review?' [2010] 73(5) *Modern Law Review* 785.
[64] Goldstein and Hugenholtz, *International Copyright*, [11.4.1].
[65] A. Spies, 'Revering irreverance: a fair dealing exception for both weapon and target parodies' (2011) 34(3) *UNSW Law Journal* 1122.

criticism, exceptions for satire promote broader objectives of freedom of expression, including encouraging social criticism in a democratic society.[66]

### 12.4.1 EU Law and the Balance of Rights

In the EU, Article 5(3)(k) of the InfoSoc Directive provides for an optional exception permitting 'use for the purpose of caricature, parody or pastiche'. In *Deckmyn*,[67] the main ECJ ruling, the Court emphasised the importance of an exception for parody in establishing a 'fair balance' between the rights and interests of authors, on the one hand, and freedom of expression of users, on the other.[68] In that case the ECJ held parody must be given 'its usual meaning in everyday language'[69] and that the essential characteristics of a parody are 'first, to evoke an existing work, while being noticeably different from it, and secondly, to constitute an expression of humour or mockery.'[70]

By affirming there are just two general requirements for a parody, the ECJ rejected a distinction drawn by the Advocate General between a 'parody of' the evoked work, in which the work is the object of the parody, and a 'parody with' the evoked work, in which something or someone else is the object of the parody (that is, the distinction between target and weapon parodies).[71] By this expansive approach, the ECJ recognised the importance of humour in promoting freedom of expression.

There are, nevertheless, some limits on the exception. For example, given the need for a fair balance between freedom of expression and the right to non-discrimination, the exception does not extend to discriminatory speech. The Court further held that in any particular case a fair balance must be struck between the rights of the rights holder and the freedom of expression of the parodist, suggesting that the exception does not automatically apply merely because the two essential prerequisites are present.[72] Moreover, it is unclear from *Deckmyn* whether, in determining if a treatment is parodic, the 'effect' must be humorous or mocking, or simply the 'intent'.[73]

---

[66] *Ibid.* 1143.
[67] Case C-201/13, *Johan Deckmyn* v. *Helena Vandersteen* [2014] All ER (D) 30 ('*Deckmyn*').
[68] *Ibid.* [27], [34].   [69] *Ibid.* [19].   [70] *Ibid.* [20].
[71] E. Rosati, 'Just a laughing matter? Why the decision in *Deckmyn* is broader than parody' (2015) 52 *Common Market Law Review* 511.
[72] *Deckmyn*, [34].   [73] Rosati, 'Just a laughing matter?', 518–19.

## 12.4.2 French and German Exceptions

As an autonomous concept of EU law,[74] the meaning of 'parody' must be interpreted uniformly in accordance with ECJ guidance in national exceptions. The wording of Article 5(3)(k) was influenced by the exception for the 'purpose of caricature, parody or pastiche' under the French Code.[75] Following *Deckmyn*, however, there are questions about the extent to which the French exception is consistent with EU law. For example, the French exception requires a parody to comply with the 'rules of the genre', which includes that it is not confusing, and is not intended personally to harm the author of the evoked work.[76] As these requirements are additional to the two essential characteristics identified by the ECJ, they may not survive *Deckmyn*.[77]

Under German law, there is no specific exception for parodies; but they are protected by the second of the two important general exceptions, the doctrine of 'free use' (*freie Benutzung*) or 'adaptation', in Article 24 of the German law.[78] Article 24 'gives authors breathing room to draw on themes and ideas in earlier works'[79] and, as such, is analogous to, but narrower than, 'transformative use'.[80] This doctrine allows for adaptations or derivative works where the essential aspects of the original work 'are sufficiently attenuated, or faded away, within the later work'.[81] In June 2017, the German Federal Court referred the question of whether the 'free use' doctrine is compatible with EU law to the ECJ.[82]

## 12.4.3 The UK Exception

In the UK, until recently there was no express exception for parody. Previously, while there were early indications that courts were more lenient with parodies than other alleged infringements,[83] later decisions

---

[74] *Deckmyn*, [27].   [75] Code de la propriété intellectuelle (France), Art. L112-5(4).
[76] R. Jacob, 'Parody and IP claims: a defence?', in R. Dreyfus and J. C. Ginsburg (eds.), *Intellectual Property at the Edge: The Contested Contours of IP* (Cambridge University Press, 2014), p. 431.
[77] Rosati, 'Just a laughing matter?', 517.
[78] Law on Copyright and Neighbouring Rights (Urheberrechtsgesetz – UrhG) (Germany), Art. 24.
[79] Goldstein and Hugenholtz, *International Copyright*, [11.4.1].
[80] D. Mendis and M. Kretschmer, *The Treatment of Parodies under Copyright Law in Seven Jurisdictions: A Comparative Review of the Underlying Principles* (Intellectual Property Office (UK), 2013), p. 32.
[81] P. Geller, 'A German approach to fair use: test cases for TRIPs criteria for copyright limitations?' (2010) 57 *Journal of the Copyright Society of the USA* 553 at 555.
[82] Vorlage des Bundesgerichtshofs an den Europäischen Gerichtshofs zur Zulässigkeit des Tonträger-Samplings, Federal Court of Justice (Bundesgerichtshof – BGH) 1 June 1017.
[83] *Joy Music Ltd* v. *Sunday Pictorial Newspapers Ltd* [1960] 2 QB 60.

confirmed that a parodic purpose was irrelevant to whether a substantial part of a work had been taken.[84] In 2014, a new exception was introduced for 'caricature, parody or pastiche'.[85] While the excepted purposes mirror those in Article 5(3)(k) of the InfoSoc Directive, the exception is, like the quotation exception, implemented as a fair dealing exception. Therefore, in addition to being for a permitted purpose, the exception applies only if the dealing is fair, which may be difficult to satisfy, for example, if the parodied work is unpublished.

Apart from French and UK law, the terms 'caricature, parody or pastiche' appear in a number of other laws of EU Member States.[86] Nevertheless, to date, only the term 'parody' has been interpreted by the ECJ. Presumably, following *Deckmyn*, 'parody' as it appears in the UK Act must be interpreted expansively, so as to encompass 'satire'.

### 12.4.4 Common Law Jurisdictions: Australia and Canada

Prominent common law jurisdictions, namely Australia and Canada, have introduced express fair dealing exceptions for both parody and satire.

In Australia, fair dealing exceptions for the purpose of 'parody or satire' were introduced in 2006.[87] The Australian Act does not attempt to define the terms 'parody' or 'satire', but the available secondary sources suggest the exceptions should be interpreted expansively,[88] at least to cover both target and weapon parodies. While it has been argued that comparative approaches to interpreting the scope of a parody exception, such as the EU approach, might inform interpretations of the Australian exception,[89] the distinction drawn between parody and satire may mean the two terms should be given distinct meanings; so caution may be required in applying the approach taken by the ECJ in *Deckmyn*.

---

[84] *Schweppes Ltd* v. *Wellingtons Ltd* [1984] FSR 210; *Williamson Music Ltd* v. *Pearson Partnership Ltd* [1987] FSR 97.

[85] CDPA, s. 30A introduced by The Copyright and Rights in Performances (Quotation and Parody) Regulations 2014 (UK).

[86] See Copyright Act 1912 (as amended) (Netherlands), Art. 18b; Law on Copyright and Neighbouring Rights of 30 June 1994 (as amended) (Belgium), Art. 22(1)(6).

[87] Copyright Act 1968 (Aus.), ss. 41A, 103AA. See M. Sainsbury, 'Parody, satire and copyright infringement: the latest addition to Australian fair dealing law' (2007) 12 *Media and Arts Law Review* 292; J. McCutcheon, 'The new defence of parody or satire under Australian copyright law' [2008] *Intellectual Property Quarterly* 163.

[88] The Second Reading Speech stated that the exceptions were intended to protect Australia's 'fine tradition of satire': Commonwealth, Parliamentary Debates, House of Representatives, 19 October 2006, 2 (Philip Ruddock, Attorney-General).

[89] G. Austin, 'EU and US perspectives on fair dealing for the purpose of parody or satire' (2016) 39(2) *UNSW Law Journal* 684.

12.4 Parody or Satire

Although Canadian courts, in cases such as *CCH*, have adopted a flexible approach to fair dealing exceptions: [11.4.3], an express exception for parody was not introduced until 2012, when 'parody or satire' was added as a fair dealing exception.[90] In *United Airlines*,[91] the first Canadian parody case, Phelan J held that alterations made to the United Airlines logo and website on a criticism site did not fall within the exception as, although the use was a parody, it was not a 'fair' dealing. In reaching this conclusion, the Court adopted the two-part meaning given to 'parody' in *Deckmyn*: that the use evokes the original and is an expression of humour or mockery.[92] Applying the six Canadian fairness factors, however, Phelan J held that the dealing was not fair as the purpose was to defame or punish the airline, the entirety of the airline's website had been substantially copied, and the use was potentially confusing. Therefore, the Court applied an expansive approach to the meaning of 'parody', but undercut this by restrictively applying the fairness factors, including inconsistently holding that the purpose of the dealing was to embarrass or punish the airline, after previously finding the use was parodic.[93]

### 12.4.5 The United States: Parody as Fair Use

In *Campbell*[94] the US Supreme Court clearly established that parody, including a commercial parody, is a transformative use that can amount to a fair use. In this, Souter J confined parody to 'target parody', stating that the essence of a parody 'is the use of some elements of a prior author's composition to create a new one that, at least in part, comments on the author's works'.[95] The Court, however, rejected a contention that a parodic use should be presumptively fair.

Souter J's judgment is the source of the distinction, drawn under US law, between parody and satire, with satire (or weapon parody) receiving less favourable treatment as it does not need to 'mimic an original to make its point'.[96] In the case of both parodies and satires, however, US courts must engage in case-by-case analysis of the fair use factors, with satires unlikely to be a fair use if they act as a market substitute for the original work.

---

[90] Copyright Act, RSC 1985, c. C-42 (Canada), s. 29, as amended by Copyright Modernization Act (Bill C-11).
[91] *United Airlines Inc.* v. *Jeremy Cooperstock* (2017) FC 616.   [92] *Ibid.* [119].
[93] S. Jacques, 'First application of the parody exception in Canadian law – long live Deckmyn!', The IPKat, http://ipkitten.blogspot.com.au/2017/07/first-application-of-parody-exception.html, 3 July 2017.
[94] 510 US 569 (1994).   [95] *Ibid.* 580.   [96] *Ibid.*

Since *Campbell*, US courts have almost invariably found parodies (as opposed to satires) are protected by the fair use exception.[97] While courts have also found satires to be fair uses, there has been inconsistency in how rigidly the distinction drawn in *Campbell* has been applied. In *Dr Seuss*,[98] for example, the Ninth Circuit held a book which used the style of Dr Seuss to retell the story of the OJ Simpson trial was not a fair use because it did not comment on or criticise the original work, *The Cat in the Hat*. In *Suntrust Bank*,[99] however, the Eleventh Circuit took a broader view of parody in finding that a retelling of *Gone with the Wind* from the point of view of the slaves was a fair use.

### 12.4.6 Parodies, Satires and the Public Domain

While the above jurisdictions have exceptions for parody or satire, many countries, including China and India, do not. Nevertheless, exceptions for parody clearly promote the fundamental public domain value of freedom of expression: [1.7], by preventing copyright being used as an instrument for suppressing speech, especially speech critical of the parodied work. In addition, exceptions for satire encourage speech that, by criticising political and social practices, promotes democratic processes. Both forms of expression assist in supporting a vibrant, creative culture, as well as broad participation in cultural practices. The recent trend to recognise satire as an exception in a number of jurisdictions is therefore a welcome addition to the copyright public domain.

Nevertheless, in all jurisdictions, difficult questions arise in distinguishing permissible uses for parody or satire from impermissible uses. It is, for example, important to prevent uses where a facade of parody or satire is adopted merely to disguise a use that competes with the original work, making it necessary for some balancing of the rights of owners and users. Under EU law, therefore, while the ECJ has interpreted 'parody' broadly, there is still a need for a 'fair balance' to be struck between competing rights, including the rights of owners and freedom of expression of parodists. In the UK, Canada and Australia, the balance has been struck by introducing fair dealing exceptions and, as a result, making the exception subject to the 'fairness factors'.

In a number of jurisdictions, exceptions for parody or satire are part of broader exceptions. In Germany, for example, the 'free use' exception allows certain adaptations or derivative works, including parodies or satires

---

[97] Samuelson, 'Unbundling fair uses', 2550.
[98] *Dr Seuss Enterprises* v. *Penguin Books USA, Inc*, 109 F 3d 1394 (9th Cir 1997).
[99] *Suntrust Bank* v. *Houghton Mifflin Co*, 268 F 3d 1257 (11th Cir 2001).

and, following *Deckmyn*, is applied less restrictively to parodies and satires than in the past. In the UK, the fair dealing exception extends beyond parodies to include caricatures and pastiche. The US fair use exception protects parodies, as well as other transformative uses, but there is uncertainty or inconsistency in how it applies to 'satire'. These examples suggest that exceptions for parody and satire may be a subset of a broader category involving transformative use of copyright works, which may at least extend to include caricature and pastiche. On the other hand, the extent to which general copyright exceptions, such as the 'free use' exception under German law or US fair use, may be narrower in their application to parodies or satires than more specific exceptions, focuses attention on the need for clarity in defining the purpose and scope of copyright exceptions. Irrespective of which approach best fits a country's legal culture, exceptions for satire and parody are in our view essential for a public domain that pays due regard to freedom of expression and civic engagement.

## 12.5 Education and Research

With roots in the Enlightenment, copyright law has always been associated with 'encouragement of learning', involving production of new knowledge and access to works for the purpose of education.[100] Yet, although most national laws traditionally have exceptions for educational purposes,[101] the Berne system never recognised encouragement of education as a core objective.[102] Furthermore, while there were historical proposals for introducing a right to use works for education under international law, these were not accepted, and educational exceptions under Berne were narrowed to their current form.[103]

The public interest in education and access to information is, however, specifically acknowledged in the Preamble to the WCT, which refers to 'the need to maintain a balance between the rights of authors and the larger public interest, particularly education, research and access to information'. Article 10(2) of Berne allows for a free use exception for use of works 'by way of illustration' in teaching, provided such use is compatible with 'fair practice': [5.4.2]. Further exceptions for education and research may be permissible if they comply with the three-step test.

Since 2004, educational use has been one of the focuses of the programme on exceptions and limitations of the WIPO SCCR: [12.1].

---

[100] M. Tawfik, 'History in the balance: copyright and access to knowledge', in Geist (ed.), *In the Public Interest*; Bannerman, *International Copyright and Access to Knowledge*, 53–79.
[101] S. Ricketson, 'The birth of the Berne Union' (1986) 9 *Columbia-VLA Journal of Law & the Arts* 11 at 12.
[102] Bannerman, *International Copyright and Access to Knowledge*, 58.   [103] *Ibid.* 62–5.

In 2010, the African Group presented a draft international treaty on exceptions, which included mandatory exceptions for educational and research institutions.[104] Subsequently, however, the United States announced that it did not support work towards a treaty[105] and, instead, proposed a set of non-binding high-level objectives and principles on educational exceptions, which emphasised the importance of commercial markets and licensing for educational content.[106]

Within the limits of international copyright law, as illustrated by the comprehensive study of educational exceptions in WIPO Member States, published in 2016, national models for exceptions for educational and research uses are extraordinarily varied.[107] This book does not attempt to duplicate this study but, instead, focuses on analysing existing law in selected jurisdictions. A general distinction can be drawn between approaches taken in common law and civil law jurisdictions. In common law jurisdictions, there are usually detailed exceptions for uses for specific educational purposes, as well as collective licensing arrangements, which operate alongside fair dealing (or fair use) exceptions.[108] In civil law jurisdictions, on the other hand, there are a variety of specific exceptions, ranging from general exceptions for educational use to fragmented exceptions for specific acts or specific works.[109] In addition, in these jurisdictions, there is considerable variation in whether exceptions are unremunerated or subject to compensation by compulsory licences. In all jurisdictions, exceptions for private copying and quotation must be taken into account for a complete understanding of permissible educational uses.[110]

### 12.5.1 EU Law

In the EU, Article 5(3)(a) of the InfoSoc Directive provides for an optional exception permitting 'use for the sole purpose of illustration for teaching or scientific research, ... to the extent justified by the non-commercial purpose to be achieved'.

---

[104] WIPO SCCR, *Draft WIPO Treaty on Exceptions and Limitations*, Arts. 5–7.
[105] United States of America, *Intervention on Exceptions and Limitations for Educational Activities*, SCCR/26, 20 December 2013.
[106] WIPO SCCR, 'Objectives and principles for exceptions and limitations for educational, teaching, and research institutions', Submitted by the United States of America, SCCR/27/8 (26 May 2014).
[107] D. Seng, 'Study on copyright limitations and exceptions for educational activities', Prepared for WIPO SCCR, SCCR/33/6, 9 November 2016.
[108] R. Xalabarder, 'Study on copyright limitations and exceptions for educational activities in North America, Europe, Caucasus, Central Asia and Israel', WIPO SCCR, Nineteenth Session, SCCR/19/8 (Geneva, 14–18 December 2009), SCCR/19/8, p. 40.
[109] *Ibid.* 61–2.   [110] Seng, 'Study on copyright limitations and exceptions', 15.

## 12.5 Education and Research

Article 5(3)(a) does not limit the nature of the works that may be used, the two main limitations being that the use must be only to the extent justified by teaching or research, and must be non-commercial. Merely because payment is made for teaching instruction does not mean that the use is disqualified as commercial use, as otherwise it could not extend to commercial institutions, which it clearly does.[111] In addition to Article 5(3)(a), Article 5(2)(c) provides for an optional exception for specific acts of reproduction made by institutions, including educational establishments, which are not for direct or indirect commercial advantage. Moreover, Article 5(3)(n) provides for an exception to the public communications right for use of dedicated terminals in institutions, including educational establishments, for the purpose of research or private study. While the exceptions do not mandate 'fair compensation', Recital (36) states this does not prevent the payment of compensation, such as under a compulsory licence.

The 2016 European Commission proposal for a new copyright Directive includes exceptions to provide for digital and cross-border uses in the field of education, especially to support distance education: [11.2.2]. The proposed Directive therefore includes a mandatory exception for digital use of works for the sole purpose of teaching provided the use takes place on the premises of an educational establishment or through a secure electronic network.[112] The proposed harmonised exception would, however, be limited, including to uses to the extent justified by the non-commercial use of teaching. Moreover, Member States would be able to exclude the exception where adequate licences are 'easily available in the market'.[113]

The flexibility in the wording of the EU exceptions allows for much diversity in national implementation, with Member States implementing teaching exceptions, but in quite different ways. For example, while some jurisdictions, such as Germany and Belgium, use the terms of the Directive in setting out the purpose of permitted uses as 'illustration for teaching',[114] others, such as Italy, use broader terms, such as 'teaching

---

[111] Xalabarder, 'Study on copyright limitations and exceptions', 64.
[112] European Commission, Proposal for a Directive of the European Parliament and of the Council on copyright in the Digital Single Market, COM (2016) 593 final, Brussels, 14 September 2016, Art. 4.
[113] Proposal for a Directive of the European Parliament and of the Council on copyright in the Digital Single Market, COM (2016) 593 final, Brussels, 14 September 2016, Art. 4(2).
[114] Law on Copyright and Neighbouring Rights (Urheberrechtsgesetz – UrhG) (Germany), Art. 52a; Law on Copyright and Neighbouring Rights of June 30, 1994 (Belgium), Art. 22.1.4bis, 4ter.

purposes' or 'teaching uses'.[115] Moreover, while exceptions in Belgium, France, Germany and the Netherlands require payment of compensation under compulsory licensing schemes elsewhere, apart from the Nordic countries, exceptions are uncompensated. In the Nordic countries, copying for educational activities (and, in some cases, public communications) are generally subject to extended collective licences: [13.5]. In addition to differences in the scope of the exceptions, there are variations in how the limitation to 'non-commercial uses' is implemented. While some jurisdictions, such as Belgium, specify that the use must not be for a commercial or 'for-profit' purpose,[116] in other jurisdictions, such as Germany, the non-commercial purpose is linked to the nature of the institutions entitled to an exception.[117]

### 12.5.2 UK Exceptions

In the UK, in 2014, amendments were introduced to existing exceptions to take advantage of the flexibility permitted by the InfoSoc Directive and provide greater scope for use of technology in teaching.[118] The reforms replaced an exception for non-reprographic copying by a fair dealing exception for the 'sole purpose of illustration for instruction' provided the dealing is for a non-commercial purpose, by a person giving or receiving instruction, and accompanied, if possible, by acknowledgement of the source.[119] The purpose of 'giving or receiving instruction' is to be interpreted broadly as including setting examination questions, communicating questions to students and answering questions.[120]

While the fair dealing exception is not confined to educational institutions, another exception permits copying and use of extracts of works by educational establishments.[121] The exception is confined to copying and use of extracts for the purposes of instruction for a non-commercial purpose and must, if possible, be accompanied by acknowledgement of the source.[122] Moreover, a permissible 'extract' is limited to no more than 5 per cent of a work over a twelve-month period.[123] In addition, the

---

[115] Law for the Protection of Copyright and Neighbouring Rights (Law No. 633 of April 22, 1941 as amended) (Italy), Art. 70(1).
[116] Law on Copyright and Neighbouring Rights of June 30, 1994 (Belgium), Art. 22.1.4*bis*, 4*ter*.
[117] Law on Copyright and Neighbouring Rights (Urheberrechtsgesetz – UrhG) (Germany), Art. 52a.
[118] Introduced by The Copyright and Rights in Performances (Research, Education, Libraries and Archives) Regulations 2014 (UK).
[119] CDPA, s. 32.   [120] CDPA, s. 32(2).
[121] 'Educational establishments' are schools or other institutions specified by order of the Secretary of State: CDPA, ss. 36, 174.
[122] CDPA, s. 36(1).   [123] CDPA, s. 36(5).

## 12.5 Education and Research

reforms provided for recording and communication of broadcasts by educational establishments for non-commercial educational purposes, provided any communications are limited to pupils or staff of the establishment.[124] The exceptions permitting use of extracts and recording of broadcasts do not apply where licences are available authorising the acts and the educational establishment knew or ought to have been aware of the licence.[125] This effectively means that educational institutions must have licences for activities falling outside of the fair dealing exception, such as photocopying for students.[126] The Copyright Licensing Agency provides a variety of licences authorising copying by schools, universities and other educational institutions,[127] while the Educational Recording Agency operates a licensing scheme for broadcasts for non-commercial educational purposes.[128]

Alongside these exceptions, the UK has a limited exception permitting the inclusion of short passages from literary or dramatic works in anthologies for educational use.[129] Furthermore, the performance, playing or showing of works, including sound recordings, films or broadcasts, in the course of activities of an educational establishment, is exempted from the public performance right.[130] Finally, an exception permits lending of copies of a work by an educational establishment.[131]

### 12.5.3 The Australian Exceptions

In Australia, apart from the fair dealing exceptions, there is a patchwork of unremunerated use exceptions that permit uses for educational purposes. While the Australian Act includes a fair dealing exception for research or study, the exception protects only the person engaged in research or study and not, for example, an educational institution making copies for students: [11.4.2].[132] Moreover, the exception does not apply where a use falls under a statutory licence for uses by educational institutions, with the educational statutory licences being substantially amended and simplified in 2017: [14.2].[133] The specific exceptions are limited in scope, each being subject to detailed conditions, and are poorly drafted.

In addition to fair dealing and the specific exceptions, s. 200AB of the Australian Act includes a general exception for uses by educational

---

[124] CDPA, s. 35.   [125] CDPA, ss. 35(4), 36(6).
[126] Intellectual Property Office (UK), 'Exceptions to copyright: education and teaching' (IPO, October 2014), p. 4.
[127] See www.cla.co.uk.   [128] See www.era.org.uk.   [129] CDPA, s. 33.
[130] CDPA, s. 34.   [131] CDPA, s. 36A.
[132] *De Garis v. Neville Jeffress Pidler* (1990) 95 ALR 625.
[133] *Haines v. Copyright Agency Limited* (1982) 42 ALR 549.

institutions made for the purpose of giving educational instruction provided they are not made partly for the purpose of obtaining a commercial advantage or profit.[134] The limitations on the exception, including that it is subject to the three-step test, have meant that the exception is rarely used in practice: [11.4.2].

The inflexible, limited and patchwork nature of the Australian exceptions mean that minor activities, such as a teacher printing a webpage, are not permitted. Given these difficulties, the ALRC recommended the wholesale repeal of the educational exceptions and replacing them with a fair use or extended fair dealing exception.[135] The ALRC also recommended amending the Act so that the educational statutory licences do not apply where a use falls within a free use exception.[136]

## 12.5.4 The Canadian Approach

The Australian exceptions can be contrasted with permitted uses for educational and research purposes in Canada. In *Alberta (Education)*[137] the Canadian Supreme Court held that the fair dealing exception for research or study extended to allow teachers to make use of short excerpts of works for the purposes of instructing students: [11.4.3]. Moreover, as part of reforms introduced in 2012, the Canadian fair dealing exception was extended to include fair dealing for the purpose of education,[138] which lowered the threshold for applying fair dealing exceptions to educational uses.[139] Following introduction of the fair dealing exception for education there was considerable disagreement on uses that are permitted and those that require a licence.[140] On the one hand, in 2012, the Council of Ministers of Education, Canada (CMEC) and Universities Canada issued fair

---

[134] Copyright Act 1968 (Aus.), s. 200AB(3).
[135] Australian Law Reform Commission, *Copyright and the Digital Economy*, Recommendation 14-1, p. 327.
[136] *Ibid.* Recommendation 8-1, p. 195.
[137] *Alberta (Education)* v. *Canadian Copyright Licensing Agency (Access Copyright)* [2012] 2 SCR 345.
[138] Copyright Act, RSC 1985, c. C-42 (Canada), s. 29, as amended by Copyright Modernization Act (Bill C-11).
[139] S. Trosow, 'Fair dealing practices in the post-secondary education sector after the pentalogy', in Geist (ed.), *The Copyright Pentalogy*, 213–33.
[140] See R. Levy, 'Access copyright has the infrastructure and expertise to best serve universities', *Academic Matters* (January 2016) www.academicmatters.ca/2016/01/access-copyright-addressing-the-needs-and-concerns-of-both-creators-and-users-in-a-changing-copyright-landscape/; M. Geist, 'Fair access: strikes the right balance on education and copyright', *Academic Matters* (January 2016) www.academicmatters.ca/2016/01/2279/.

dealing content usage guidelines.[141] On the other, Access Copyright, the Canadian collecting society, issued new licences which, in response to the greater scope for free educational uses, attempted to be more flexible.[142]

In *Access Copyright*,[143] Phelan J held that copying in accordance with fair dealing guidelines produced by York University did not fall within the fair dealing exception as the guidelines allowed for mass, systematic copying of works, including in course packs or digital formats, and therefore failed to satisfy the Canadian fairness factors. As a result, the educational uses were subject to a form of compulsory licence, known as a mandatory tariff, with the remuneration to be determined by the Copyright Board.[144]

### 12.5.5 US Exceptions and Fair Use

In the United States, educational uses are dealt with by both specific statutory exceptions and the fair use exception.[145]

The specific exceptions allow for in-classroom performances and displays, and for distance education. First, section 110(1) allows for performances or displays of works 'in the course of face-to-face teaching activities of a non-profit educational institution, in a classroom or similar place devoted to instruction',[146] but does not extend to making copies. The requirement that the teaching be 'face-to-face' separates the exception from the second exception, in section 110(2), which applies to distance education. This exception, which was extended to online digital uses by the 2001 TEACH Act,[147] allows for the performance or displays of works in the course of electronic transmissions, but does not apply to works 'produced or marketed primarily for ... mediated instructional activities transmitted via digital networks'.[148] The exception is subject

---

[141] Council of Ministers of Education, Canada (CMEC) and Universities Canada, *Fair Dealing Guidelines* www.cmec.ca/docs/copyright/Fair_Dealing_Guidelines_EN.pdf.
[142] M. Geist, 'Too little, too late?: Access Copyright finally acknowledges the reduced value of its licences', Michael Geist blog, 10 December 2014 www.michaelgeist.ca/2014/12/little-late-access-copyright-finally-acknowledges-reduced-value-licence/.
[143] *The Canadian Copyright Licensing Agency ('Access Copyright')* v. *York University* (2017) FC 669.
[144] Copyright Act, RSC 1985, c. C-42 (Canada), s. 66.
[145] J. M. Besek, J. C. Ginsburg, P. Loengard and Y. Lev-Aretz, 'Copyright exceptions in the United States for educational uses of copyrighted works', The Kernochan Center for Law, Media and the Arts, Columbia University School of Law, 29 April 2013 www.screenrights.org/sites/default/files/uploads/Attachment_A_Kernochan_Ctr_Report.pdf.
[146] 17 USC §110(1).
[147] Technology Education and Copyright Harmonization (TEACH) Act of 2002, Pub L. No. 107-273, §13301, 116 Stat 1758 (2002).
[148] 17 USC §110(2).

to significant limitations designed to ensure that it is no broader than the 'face-to-face' exception. For example, it applies only where instruction is provided exclusively to enrolled students and the performance or display must be essential to the class, not merely supplementary. There is continuing uncertainty concerning the relationship between the specific exceptions and the fair use exception, although in *HathiTrust*,[149] the Second Circuit held that, due to a specific savings clause in section 108, the failure of a use to fall within a specific exception did not prevent it being a fair use.

Educational activities are specifically mentioned in the list of illustrative purposes for the fair use exception, which refers to uses for the purposes of 'teaching (including multiple copies for classroom use), scholarship, or research': [11.3.1]. Given the relative indeterminacy of fair use analysis, Congress encouraged stakeholders in the education sector to develop guidelines clarifying the application of fair use to classroom activities.[150] As a result, fair use guidelines were produced by the Copyright Office for classroom photocopying, educational uses of music and off-air recordings of broadcasts.[151] The guidelines allow, for example, for making of single copies of short items for research or class preparation; as well as multiple copies of short excerpts for classroom use. The guidelines provide that multiple copies must comply with the tests of 'brevity, spontaneity and cumulative effect', and expand on these tests. More recently, the Center for Social Media and user groups have developed codes or standards for fair use best practices in a number of areas, such as academic and research libraries and media literacy.[152] Although there has been some involvement of rights holders in the creation of these codes, they lack official approval.

### 12.5.6 India

Access to works for educational purposes is particularly important for developing countries, and has been a source of contention between the developed and developing world in international forums.[153] It is therefore important to take into account how educational exceptions are

---

[149] *Authors Guild* v. *HathiTrust*, 755 F 3d 87 (2nd Cir, 2014).
[150] Besek et al., 'Copyright exceptions in the United States', 25.
[151] See US Copyright Office, *Circular 21, Reproduction of Copyrighted Works by Educators and Librarians*, www.copyright.gov/circs/circ21.pdf.
[152] See *Best Practices*, Center for Social Media www.centerforsocialmedia.org/fair-use/best-practices; J. Rothman, 'Best intentions: reconsidering best practices statements in the context of fair use and copyright law' (2010) 57 *Journal of the Copyright Society of the USA* 371.
[153] Bannerman, *International Copyright and Access to Knowledge*, 65–6.

## 12.5 Education and Research

implemented in jurisdictions such as India, which has a constitutional right to education.[154]

India's free use exceptions for educational purposes are comparatively broad, and complement educational compulsory licences: [14.2].[155] There are two main exceptions. First, there is an exception permitting the reproduction of any work by a teacher or a pupil in the course of instruction, or as part of examination questions or answers.[156] Unlike similar exceptions in other national laws, there are no quantitative limits on the amount of copying that is permitted, and the exception is not limited by a 'fairness' test, raising questions of compatibility with Article 10(2) of Berne. On the other hand, as the exception does not extend to the communication right, it is limited in its application to distance education.[157] Second, an exception is provided for performances of works, films or sound recordings, in the course of the activities of an educational institution, by its staff or students to an audience limited to them, their families or persons connected with the institution, and for the communication of sound recordings and films to such an audience.[158] As the exception provides only for the public communication of sound recordings and films, like the other exception, it provides limited protection for distance education activities.

### 12.5.7 Education, Research and the Public Domain

Public education and research have always had a special status in national copyright laws, which promote these public domain uses by diverse means including unremunerated exceptions and compulsory licences. The public interest in education and research is not fully recognised under Berne but, even so, most jurisdictions have not introduced exceptions that take full advantage of existing flexibilities under international copyright law.[159]

The importance of markets for educational uses for authors, however, means that balancing the interests of owners and users in the context of uses for education and research is challenging. These difficulties are evident in differences in the WIPO SCCR between developing countries that favour a binding agreement on educational exceptions, and the United States, which has supported non-binding objectives and

---

[154] Mullin v. The Administrator, Union Territory of Delhi [1981] AIR 746; Mohini Jain v. State of Karnataka [1992] SC 1858; L. Liang, 'Exceptions and limitations in Indian copyright law for education: an assessment' (2010) 3 Law and Development Review 197.
[155] Copyright Act 1957 (India), ss. 32, 32A.  [156] Copyright Act 1957 (India), s. 52(i).
[157] Liang, 'Exceptions and limitations', 224–5.
[158] Copyright Act 1957 (India), s. 52(j).
[159] Bannerman, International Copyright and Access to Knowledge, 60.

principles: [12.5]. The differences are not about whether there is a need for educational use exceptions, which is acknowledged by all parties, but on where the line between supporting markets for educational works and public interest exceptions should be drawn. Our analysis of differences in national laws suggests that uniformity, clarity and the public interest could be served by an appropriate international agreement on educational exceptions. But, accepting the difficulties of reaching agreement, our realist approach leads us to focus on what is possible under current international constraints.

The examples of educational and research exceptions under national laws given above suggest there are three important issues that must be confronted by any regime for educational exceptions. First, while many national laws confine exceptions to non-commercial or non-profit uses, the extent to which education is a major business, and the provision of educational services by private entities in many jurisdictions, makes this restriction problematic. Second, there are questions about whether educational uses should be permitted as free use exceptions or remunerated exceptions, with uncertainty in some jurisdictions about whether uses may be uncompensated or must be remunerated. Related to this, in some cases, such as permissible extracts under UK law and digital uses under the proposed EU Directive, a free use exception applies only if a commercial licence is not available. Third, there are fundamental challenges facing all jurisdictions in adapting exceptions to changing educational practices, including digital uses and distance education.

Applying our realist and public domain perspectives, there is much potential for national exceptions for education and research to be extended and clarified. For example, international copyright law does not require quantitative limitations on the copying of extracts for educational purposes, especially if such uses are subject to a fairness test, such as applies under the UK and Canadian fair dealing exceptions. Moreover, if, as under Canadian law, the purpose of a dealing is interpreted as being the purpose of the end-user, this would permit uses made by an educational institution on behalf of students. That said, to encourage provision of educational content such as digital course packs, there seems scope for some uses to be covered by remunerated exceptions. Regarding digital uses and distance education, which are now standard educational practices, in principle there is no reason for exceptions to be less extensive than traditional permitted uses, provided there are safeguards to prevent widespread unauthorised reproductions and disseminations, such as limiting electronic dissemination to communications to a secure electronic network, as under the proposed EU copyright Directive. Whatever the precise national exceptions, given the scale and complexity of educational uses, there are considerable advantages in guidelines, such as best practice statements, that provide stakeholders with clarity about the scope of permissible uses, while acknowledging inherent problems of guidelines produced by owner or user groups.

## 12.6 Libraries and Archives

Libraries, archives and comparable institutions, such as museums and art galleries, are the main cultural institutions responsible for providing public access to, and preserving, copyright works. These institutions face significant challenges as a result of digitisation, with libraries and archives, on the one hand, and publishers and collecting societies, on the other, holding divergent views on permissible uses of digital content.[160] As international copyright law does not provide for specific exceptions for libraries or archives, all such exceptions must satisfy the three-step test in Article 9(2) of Berne.[161]

As with educational use exceptions, there are competing proposals for an international instrument on exceptions for libraries; but these are more developed than those for educational exceptions. Following presentation of a draft treaty on exceptions by the African Group to the WIPO SCCR in 2010: [12.1], the International Federation of Library Associations (IFLA), supported by WIPO members such as Brazil, prepared a comprehensive proposed treaty on exceptions for libraries and archives.[162] The United States, however, supported the development of a non-binding agreement on high-level principles aimed at 'maintaining the balance between the rights of authors and the larger public interest, particularly education, research, and access to information'.[163] As part of the SCCR programme on exceptions, a series of comparative studies has been prepared,[164] the most recent of which found that 156 Berne

---

[160] E. Hudson and A. Kenyon, 'Digital access: the impact of copyright on digitisation practices in Australian museums, galleries, libraries and archives' (2007) 30(1) *UNSW Law Journal* 12; L. Guibault, 'Why cherry-picking never leads to harmonisation: the case of the limitations on copyright under Directive 2001/29/EC' (2010) 1 *Journal of Intellectual Property, Information Technology and Electronic Commerce Law (JIPITEC)* 55.

[161] Bannerman, *International Copyright and Access to Knowledge*, 65.

[162] International Federation of Library Associations (IFLA), 'Treaty proposal on copyright limitations and exceptions for libraries and archives', Version 4.4, 6 December 2013; WIPO SCCR, 'The case for a treaty on exceptions and limitations for libraries and archives: background paper by IFLA, ICA, EIFL and INNOVARTE', Document presented by Brazil, WIPO Doc. SCCR/23/3 (18 November 2011).

[163] WIPO SCCR, 'Objectives and principles for exceptions and limitations for libraries and archives', Document presented by the United States of America, WIPO Doc. SCCR/26/8 (10 January 2014).

[164] See K. Crews, 'Study on copyright limitations and exceptions for libraries and archives', WIPO SCCR, Seventeenth Session, Geneva, 2008; K. Crews, 'Study on copyright

members had at least one library exception, with most having multiple, more specific exceptions, although thirty-two countries have no specific exception.[165] Persistent uncertainties with the scope of the exceptions have increasingly led to rights holders imposing contractual restrictions on uses by libraries and archives.[166]

In general, there are three kinds of exceptions for libraries and archives that allow for: making copies for users; making copies for the purposes of preservation; and making of copies for replacing works that have been damaged or destroyed.[167] National exceptions, however, take a variety of forms, including a general library exception and exceptions for: making copies for users for research or study; making available digital works; preservation or replacement; and interlibrary loans or document delivery.[168]

### 12.6.1 EU Law

In the EU, Article 5(2)(c) of the InfoSoc Directive provides for an optional exception for specific acts of reproduction made by 'publicly accessible libraries, educational establishments or museums, or by archives', provided such uses are 'not for direct or indirect economic or commercial advantage'. According to Recital (40), the exception 'should not cover uses made in the context of online delivery of protected works or other subject-matter'. The limitation that the permitted uses not be for direct or indirect commercial advantage is taken from the Rental and Lending Directive,[169] which provides that it should not be interpreted as extending to libraries charging user fees to cover operational costs.[170] The requirement that exceptions be confined to 'specific acts' of reproduction mirrors the first condition of the three-step test, and requires national laws to define precisely the permitted acts.[171] While an exception for copies made for preservation would satisfy this condition, for copies made for individual users there is an overlap with private copying

---

limitations and exceptions for libraries and archives', WIPO SCCR, Twenty-Ninth Session, Geneva, 2014. For a comparative study of exceptions for museums, see J. Canat, L. Guibault and E. Logeais, 'Study on copyright limitations and exceptions for museums', WIPO SCCR, Thirtieth Session (Geneva, 2015) www.wipo.int/edocs/mdocs/copyright/en/sccr_30/sccr_30_2.pdf.

[165] Crews, 'Study on copyright limitations and exceptions for libraries and archives', WIPO SCCR, Twenty-Ninth Session, Geneva, 2014, 6.
[166] Guibault, 'Why cherry-picking never leads to harmonisation', 61.
[167] Crews, 'Study on copyright limitations and exceptions for libraries and archives', WIPO SCCR, Twenty-Ninth Session, Geneva, 2014, 6.
[168] *Ibid.* 8–9.   [169] Rental and Lending Directive, Art. 1(3).
[170] Rental and Lending Directive, Recital (14).
[171] See von Lewinski and Walter, 'Information society directive', [11.5.39].

## 12.6 Libraries and Archives

exceptions: see the Online Supplement. In that case, it seems that, applying the rule *lex specialis*, the more specific private copying exceptions should apply to copies made for users to the exclusion of the library exceptions.[172]

Apart from Article 5(2)(c), Article 5(3)(n) provides for an optional exception for communication or making available of works for the purpose of research or private study to members of the public by dedicated terminals on the premises of establishments listed in Article 5(2)(c). This exception is narrow. First, it is confined to use by individual members of the public on dedicated terminals on premises of the establishment. Second, the works can only be used if they are contained in the establishment's collection. Third, and importantly, the exception is only available for works that are not already subject to purchase or licensing terms.[173] In *Darmstadt*,[174] the ECJ was required to interpret Article 5(3)(n) where an academic library made electronic versions of a book available from terminals but had refused an offer to purchase the text as an e-book. The Court first ruled that a mere offer to sell or license a work does not mean that the work is subject to purchase or licensing terms, meaning there must be an actual agreement setting out the conditions under which the work may be used.[175] Second, the ECJ held that the exception extends to allowing libraries to make digital reproductions for the purpose of making copies available from terminals.[176] Third, the Court ruled that the exception cannot be extended to allow users to make copies by printing out or storing to a USB stick, meaning that the exception is confined to viewing at terminals.[177] To be permissible, therefore, the provision of copies to library users must comply with the private copying exceptions.[178]

Digitisation and online accessibility of cultural material has received considerable attention in Europe. The 2016 European Commission proposal for a new directive includes a new mandatory exception, designed to allow for digital technologies, for cultural heritage institutions (CHIs) to make copies of works in their collections for the purposes of preservation to address, for example, technological obsolescence or degradation. The exception would be available to CHIs, defined to mean publicly accessible libraries or museums, and archives or film or audio heritage institutions;[179] and would allow for the making of copies permanently in

---

[172] *Ibid.* [11.5.27].    [173] *Ibid.* [11.5.70].
[174] Case C-117/13, *Technische Universität Darmstadt* v. *Eugen Ulmer* [2015] 1 WLR 2017.
[175] *Ibid.* [35].    [176] *Ibid.* [49].    [177] *Ibid.* [57].    [178] See Online Supplement.
[179] European Commission, Proposal for a Directive of the European Parliament and of the Council on copyright in the Digital Single Market, COM (2016) 593 final, Brussels, 14 September 2016, Art. 2.

their collections, in any format or medium, for the sole purpose of preservation.[180]

Not all EU Member States have implemented the optional exceptions for libraries and cultural institutions; and, among those that have, there are considerable variations in how they have been implemented.[181] For example, some have implemented Article 5(2)(c) by allowing only analogue reproductions, others have extended this to digital reproductions, and yet others do not distinguish between analogue and digital reproductions.

### 12.6.2 UK Law

In the UK, the CDPA includes detailed exceptions for uses of works by libraries and archives, all subject to substantial restrictions.[182] First, libraries, archives or museums may make copies of items in their permanent collections to preserve or replace an item, provided the item is not on loan to the public (such as reference-only material) and it is not reasonably practicable to purchase it.[183] Second, not-for-profit libraries may make single copies of an article in a periodical or a reasonable proportion of a published work in response to a written declaration from a user that includes a statement that the person requires the copy for non-commercial research or private study.[184] A similar exception allows for single copies to be made of entire unpublished works in response to a written declaration from a user, but does not apply if the copyright owner has prohibited copying and the librarian should have been aware of this.[185] Third, Article 5(3)(n) is implemented by an exception that allows for libraries, archives, museums and educational establishments to communicate works by dedicated terminals on their premises subject to relevant conditions.[186] Fourth, an inter-library loan exception allows libraries to make single copies of works to supply to another not-for-profit library, provided the copy is made in response to a request and the librarian cannot reasonably identify the rights holder.[187]

### 12.6.3 Australian Law

The Australian Act includes exceptions for public libraries, parliamentary libraries and archives that were substantially amended in 2017 to provide

---

[180] Proposal for a Directive of the European Parliament and of the Council on copyright in the Digital Single Market, COM (2016) 593 final, Brussels, 14 September 2016, Art. 5.
[181] Guibault, 'Why cherry-picking never leads to harmonisation', 60.
[182] See The Copyright and Rights in Performances (Research, Education, Libraries and Archives) Regulations 2014 (UK).
[183] CDPA, s. 42.    [184] CDPA, s. 42A.    [185] CDPA, s. 43.    [186] CDPA, s. 40B.
[187] CDPA, s. 41.

## 12.6 Libraries and Archives

'greater flexibility in copying and digitisation of copyright material'.[188] The exceptions allow for the making of preservation copies, administrative uses, and document delivery for research and study.

First, a library or archives may use copyright material for the purpose of preserving its collection, or the collection of another library or archives, if the material is: held by the library in original form; and/or cannot be obtained in the required version or format consistent with best practice for preservation of such collections.[189] Under this exception, a library or archives can make multiple copies in a version or format that complies with best practice preservation policy, provided the material cannot be obtained in that version or format. Moreover, where a preservation copy is in electronic form, it may be made available for access at the library or archives provided reasonable steps are taken to ensure that copyright in the preservation copy is not infringed.[190] The library or archives does not need to wait for material to be damaged or suffer deterioration, and can make a preservation copy from an earlier copy. Similar provisions allow use of copyright material for preserving collections of key cultural institutions, and making electronic preservation copies available for access, provided the material is of historical and cultural significance to Australia.[191] Key cultural institutions include, but are not confined to, libraries and archives that have a statutory function of developing or maintaining a collection.[192]

Second, a library or archives may use copyright material, including making copies, where the material is held in its collection in original form and the use is for the purpose of research carried out at the library or archives, or at another library or archives.[193] Where a research copy is in electronic form, the library or archives may make it available for access at the library or archives, provided reasonable steps are taken to ensure the person accessing the copy does not infringe copyright.[194] As the exception is confined to research carried out at a library or archives, it does not extend to providing remote access to copies, which must comply with the document delivery exceptions explained below. Third, a library or archives is able to use copyright material for administrative purposes directly related to care or control of its collection including, for example, back up copying, record keeping and training.[195]

---

[188] Copyright Amendment (Disability Access and Other Measures) Bill 2017 (Aus.), Explanatory Memorandum, p. 17.
[189] Copyright Act 1968 (Aus.), s. 113H(1). [190] Copyright Act 1968 (Aus.), s. 113H(2).
[191] Copyright Act 1968 (Aus.), s. 113M. [192] Copyright Act 1968 (Aus ), s. 113L.
[193] Copyright Act 1968 (Aus.), s. 113J(1). [194] Copyright Act 1968 (Aus.), s. 113J(2).
[195] Copyright Act 1968 (Aus.), s. 113K.

The exceptions introduced in 2017 left unchanged existing exceptions for documentary delivery, under which a library or archive may reproduce or communicate an article contained in a periodical or a published work in response to a request from a user.[196] The request must include a declaration that the copy is required solely for research or study. Moreover, where a request is made for the whole or more than a 'reasonable portion' of a published work, the library must be satisfied that the work cannot be obtained within a reasonable time at an ordinary commercial price.[197] Where a library acquires a work in electronic form it may make the work available online, but only on the library premises, and in such a way that users cannot copy or communicate it.[198] Furthermore, where a request has been made for an electronic reproduction to be communicated to a user, the exception does not apply unless the electronic copy held by the library is destroyed as soon as practicable after the communication.[199]

There are further detailed exceptions that apply to: uses by parliamentary libraries;[200] reproduction and publication of unpublished works and theses by libraries or archives;[201] publication of unpublished works kept in libraries or archives;[202] and reproduction and communication of works in the care of the National Archives of Australia.[203] In addition, s. 200AB includes a general exception for bodies administering libraries or archives: [11.4.2], but the uncertainties associated with the exception have restricted its use by libraries and archives.[204]

While exceptions for preservation, research and administration introduced in 2017 have considerably enhanced the flexibility available for these purposes, the exceptions for research and document delivery remain complex and limited. In relation to these exceptions, in its 2013 report the ALRC recommended that library or archive use should be one of the permitted purposes for a proposed fair use or extended fair dealing exception,[205] but also concluded that there was scope for redrafting and simplification of the document delivery exceptions.[206]

## 12.6.4 Canadian Law

The most important development for libraries in Canada was the Canadian Supreme Court decision in *CCH*, where the Court ruled that providing single copies of material, such as law reports, by a library to its

---

[196] Copyright Act 1968 (Aus.), s. 49.   [197] Copyright Act 1968 (Aus.), s. 49(5AB).
[198] Copyright Act 1968 (Aus.), s. 49(5A).   [199] Copyright Act 1968 (Aus.), s. 49(7A).
[200] Copyright Act 1968 (Aus.), s. 48A.   [201] Copyright Act 1968 (Aus.), s. 51.
[202] Copyright Act 1968 (Aus.), s. 52.   [203] Copyright Act 1968 (Aus.), s. 51AA.
[204] Australian Law Reform Commission, *Copyright and the Digital Economy*, [12.10]–[12.6].
[205] *Ibid.*, Recommendation 12-1, p. 278.   [206] *Ibid.* [12.90]–[12.91].

members was a fair dealing for the purpose of research or study. Furthermore, the Court held that, as the use was a fair dealing there was no need for the library to rely on the specific library exception in s. 30.2(1) of the Canadian Act. As part of reforms introduced in 2012, important extensions were made to the specific library exceptions.

In Canada, there are two main specific exceptions for libraries, archives and museums. First, s. 30.1 of the Canadian Act allows these institutions to make a copy of a work in a permanent collection in particular circumstances.[207] The exception is not available, however, where a copy of the work is commercially available in a form appropriate to the purpose of the exception. The second exception, in s. 30.2, specifically allows libraries, archives and museums to do anything for a person that is permissible under the fair dealing exception for research or study.[208] In particular, it is an exception for these institutions to make a copy of an article in a periodical or newspaper in response to a request from a user.[209] The exception, however, allows only for making of a single copy and the institution must inform the user that it is to be used solely for research or private study.

### 12.6.5 US Law

In the United States, apart from the fair use exception, the Copyright Act includes specific exceptions for uses by libraries and archives, which apply to both non-profit and for-profit institutions.[210] The main exceptions are established by section 108 of the Act and provide for: making three copies of unpublished works solely for the purpose of preservation, or for research use in another library or archives;[211] making three copies of published works solely for the purpose of replacement of works that are damaged, deteriorating, lost, stolen or in obsolete formats;[212] reproduction of no more than one copy of an article from a periodical or a small part of a work in response to a request from a user;[213] reproduction of entire works, or substantial parts of works, in response to a request from a user if, after reasonable investigation, the library is satisfied that the copy cannot be obtained at a fair price;[214] and making copies for inter-library loans.[215]

---

[207] Copyright Act, RSC 1985, c. C-42 (Canada), s. 30.1.
[208] Copyright Act, RSC 1985, c. C-42 (Canada), s. 30.2(1).
[209] Copyright Act, RSC 1985, c. C-42 (Canada), s. 30.2(2).
[210] Hirtle, Hudson and Kenyon, *Copyright and Cultural Institutions*.
[211] 17 USC §108(b).   [212] 17 USC §108(c).   [213] 17 USC §108(d).
[214] 17 USC §108(e).   [215] 17 USC §108(g)(2).

The specific exceptions are restricted in scope and detailed.[216] For example, each of the exceptions is subject to a condition that the library or archives is: (i) open to the public or (ii) accessible to non-affiliated researchers working in a specialised field.[217] In addition, all exceptions are subject to conditions that uses must not be for direct or indirect commercial advantage, and that any copies made include a copyright notice.[218] Moreover, the particular exceptions are subject to further limitations; for example, the exceptions allowing for reproduction of works in response to user requests do not apply to musical works, pictorial, graphic, or sculptural works, motion pictures, and other audiovisual works.[219] Other limitations on the exceptions for providing a copy to users include that the copy must become the property of the user and that the library or archives must have no notice that the copy will be used for a purpose other than 'private study, scholarship, or research'. On the other hand, copies can be provided to users in any format, including digital copies.

In addition, the US Act includes even more specific exceptions. For example, libraries and archives are permitted to make copies of audiovisual news programmes and to lend copies of the broadcasts to users.[220] Furthermore, non-profit organisations operating for scholarly, educational or religious purposes can import to the United States no more than five copies of works (other than audiovisual works) for library or archival purposes, where importation would otherwise be prohibited.[221]

Where the section 108 exceptions do not apply, uses of works may still be permitted under the fair use exception.[222] For example, while pictorial, graphic and photographic works are excluded from the exceptions allowing reproductions for library users, copying these works may be permitted as fair use.[223] Moreover, in the absence of a general exception allowing reproduction of published works for the purpose of preservation, libraries and archives must rely on fair use for preservation activities.[224] As most library uses are not 'transformative', the fourth fair use factor, the effect of the use upon the potential market, is particularly important. For example, in *Texaco*,[225] the Second Circuit held that photocopying scholarly articles in a commercial context was not a fair use, as permitting it would prevent the development of a market for licensing copies: [11.3.2].

---

[216] 17 USC §108(e).   [217] 17 USC §108(a)(2).   [218] 17 USC §108(a)(1) (3).
[219] 17 USC §108(i).   [220] 17 USC §108(f)(3).   [221] 17 USC §602(a)(3).
[222] §108(f)(4) provides that nothing in the section affects the right of fair use under §107.
[223] Hirtle, Hudson and Kenyon, *Copyright and Cultural Institutions*, 101.   [224] *Ibid.*
[225] *American Geophysical Union* v. *Texaco Inc*, 60 F 3d 913 (2nd Cir 1994).

## 12.6 Libraries and Archives

The US library exceptions have been under revision for some time, with the Copyright Office establishing an independent 'Section 108 Study Group' in 2008.[226] In June 2016, the Copyright Office published draft revisions to section 108 that incorporated many of the Study Group's recommendations, which include: adding museums as eligible institutions; expanding preservation exceptions to published works; creating a new exception to permit reproduction and distribution of publicly available Internet content for preservation and research; and reforming the three-copy limit to the preservation exception.[227]

### 12.6.6 Indian Law

As with educational use exceptions, India has simpler and possibly more expansive exceptions for libraries compared with other jurisdictions dealt with in this book.

Under Indian law, there are two exceptions for the benefit of a 'noncommercial public library'. The first excepts the storing of a work in any medium by electronic means, for preservation, if the library already possesses a non-digital copy.[228] The second excepts the making of not more than three copies of a book by such a library for its own use, but this is subject to the condition that the book is not available for sale in India.[229]

An unusual exception allows for reproduction of unpublished works held by a public library, museum or similar institution for purposes of research or private study, or for publication.[230] This exception is, however, subject to the condition that, where the identity of an author is known, it applies only where copyright would have expired if the work had been published, in effect, making this a form of orphan works exception.

### 12.6.7 Libraries, Archives and the Public Domain

Libraries, archives and similar institutions perform essential public domain functions of preserving works and making them available, with all the attendant benefits for vibrant and creative cultures. The significant challenges facing libraries, in particular, from the transition to digital and

---

[226] See Section 108 Study Group, *The Section 108 Study Group Report* (2008) www.section108.gov/docs/Sec108StudyGroupReport.pdf.
[227] Library of Congress, 'Section 108: Draft Revision of the Library and Archives Exceptions in US Copyright Law', Federal Register 81(109) (7 June 2016).
[228] Copyright Act 1957 (India), s. 52(n). [229] Copyright Act 1957 (India), s. 52(o).
[230] Copyright Act 1957 (India), s. 52(p).

online content has placed them at the centre of debates about the scope of digital copyright. While libraries play an important role in facilitating access to works, there are concerns that overly expansive exceptions may interfere with copyright markets, especially for digital content. These concerns have contributed to the detail and complexity of national exceptions.

As is clear from the above, there are significant differences in national exceptions for libraries and archives, with most laws having an unsatisfactory patchwork of exceptions. Moreover, uncertainty about the scope of exceptions has resulted in self-help by stakeholders, often involving contractual restrictions that override copyright exceptions.[231] There is therefore a strong case for refining and clarifying exceptions that apply to the three main categories of library uses, namely making preservation copies, replacement copies and uses undertaken for users. Ideally, we think this would take the form of a binding international agreement but, acknowledging the difficulties of reaching agreement, there is still scope for reforming national exceptions consistently with the three-step test.

Broad exceptions for preserving works, including migrating content from obsolete formats, are essential for accessibility. In crafting exceptions, it would seem counter-productive to limit the number of preservation copies that can be made, such as under US or Indian law, as a more appropriate safeguard would be to require compliance with best professional preservation practice.[232] Similarly, in principle, appropriate exceptions allowing libraries and archives to make replacement copies is unobjectionable, especially if accompanied by safeguards, such as requiring compliance with best practices. Recent reforms to the Australian exceptions go some way towards meeting these objectives.

The extent to which exceptions should allow for libraries to make and disseminate copies of works for users is more contentious, as unconstrained digital copying and online dissemination may impact copyright markets. In our view, it is helpful to distinguish two categories of uses that libraries may undertake for users. First, there are activities connected with the traditional function of lending works, which are challenged by digital content delivery. Provided lending-related activities are not conducted for a profit, and there are safeguards, such as the deletion of digital copies on expiry of the loan period, creating appropriate exceptions does not

---

[231] One study of contracts offered to the British Library found that over 90 per cent override exceptions under UK law: see WIPO SCCR, 'The case for a treaty on exceptions and limitations for libraries and archives', p. 3.

[232] For preservation standards, see http://libguides.wits.ac.za/digitisation_preservation_ and_digitalcuration.

seem to present insurmountable difficulties.[233] Second, there are activities such as making digital copies, and online dissemination, conducted by libraries for use in private research or study by users. In principle, we think that, as under Canadian law, libraries should be able to engage in uses on behalf of users which would fall under an exception for research or study, such as fair dealing. The potential for unconstrained copying and dissemination to undermine copyright markets, however, suggests a need for reasonable safeguards. While restricting the public communication of works to dedicated terminals on the premises of an institution, as under the InfoSoc Directive, seems excessive, there is scope for a legal standard, such as a 'fairness' standard, to support technological limits on copying and dissemination by users.[234] Getting the balance right is admittedly difficult; but retaining the public domain functions of libraries and archives is, in our view, essential to preserving public rights in access to and use of digital works.

## 12.7 Conclusions: Exceptions as a Key Contributor to the Public Domain

The breadth of copyright protection, including the extent of protectable subject matter, the scope of exclusive rights and duration of protection, gives rise to the need for protection for public domain uses of works which, in this book, we refer to as public rights: [2.4.2]. Exceptions are therefore one of the key components of copyright public domains, as they provide a key corrective to the strength of copyright protection. While flexible, open-ended exceptions may promote public domain uses, problems with existing exceptions, such as fair use, must also be acknowledged: [11.6]. Even where, as under US law, there is a broad, flexible exception, this inevitably coexists with more specific exceptions.

In this chapter, and in Chapter 8 dealing with exclusions from copyright protection, we have attempted to capture the complexities in establishing exceptions for public domain uses. At the heart of these complexities lies the dilemma of maximising permissible uses, while not unduly undermining copyright markets. Once the case is made for an exception, this inevitably leads to difficulties in determining its scope, which often involves establishing limits on the exception in an attempt to

---

[233] See, for example, IFLA, *Treaty Proposal on Copyright Limitations and Exceptions*, Art. 7(2).
[234] Article 8(1) of the IFLA proposed treaty would restrict reproduction and supply of works for education, research or private use to activities undertaken in accordance with 'fair practice'.

protect copyright markets. This exercise is complicated by the issues arising from digital copying and online distribution.

The exceptions dealt with in this book protect public rights in freedom of expression (exceptions for 'news of the day', political speeches, quotation, parody and satire), access to information (exceptions for government information, educational uses, libraries and archives, and visually impaired and print-disabled people), user autonomy and privacy (for example, private copying), and creative and cultural practices (exceptions for quotation, parody and satire but, broadly speaking, all exceptions). Moreover, the categories of exceptions should be seen as a whole, in that it is often impossible to consider exceptions in one category, such as exceptions for libraries and archives, without taking into account exceptions in other categories, such as exceptions for private copying or quotation. The diversity in national approaches to exceptions, which we have explained in some detail, reflects the extent to which exceptions are the least harmonised area of international copyright law, but also reflect significant cultural differences in approaches to copyright and public domain values. That said, the general orientation of international copyright law, which foregrounds authors' rights, tends to relegate exceptions to the margins, playing down important public rights. To counteract this tendency, we argue there would be considerable value in proposals for greater international consensus on exceptions, potentially taking the form of a treaty or treaties, as supported by some developing countries. While there seems scope for agreement concerning particular uses that pose little threat to copyright owners, such as some transient uses and preservation copying by libraries, over and above this, the nature and scope of exceptions is invariably vigorously contested. The studies undertaken for the WIPO SCCR: [12.5] and [12.6], can clearly assist with providing richer information on national exceptions, as a step in this direction, but fundamental differences in approaches dictated by national self-interest will doubtless persist. The continuing difficulties faced in forging international agreement, we argue, further illustrates the value of our realist approach of asking what is currently possible under international copyright law.

In each of the categories of copyright exceptions addressed in this chapter, the exceptions under national laws are, as a rule, complex and cumbersome and, we suggest, far too much so. Furthermore, most jurisdictions have not taken full advantage of the flexibility under current international law to introduce exceptions to the extent permitted. A good example is the failure of many jurisdictions fully to implement an exception for quotation, as mandated by Article 10 of Berne. One major conclusion from this chapter is therefore that there is much scope for

## 12.7 Conclusions

exceptions to be both clarified and extended under national laws, up to the extent permitted by international copyright law. In our view, the lack of clarity in existing exceptions is a significant constraint on public domain uses. This is nowhere more evident than in the failure of many national laws sufficiently to adapt exceptions to the digital environment. While the potential for unconstrained copying and dissemination arising from digital content raises challenges for copyright exceptions, such as exceptions for private copying, educational uses and libraries and archives, from our public domain perspective, it is vital for laws to be adapted to support online access and uses of digital content. For each of the categories of exceptions dealt with in this chapter, we have therefore made practical suggestions for how public domain uses can be strengthened by clarification, adaptation and, where appropriate, expansion of exceptions within the constraints of international copyright law.

In this chapter, and Chapter 11, we have focused on free or unremunerated use exceptions. For some categories of exception, however, such as exceptions for educational uses exceptions and private copying, compensation is often payable to copyright owners, whether under a compulsory licence or a private copying levy scheme. Applying our approach to the public domain, uses requiring payment remain an essential part of the public domain, provided the use may be undertaken without permission: [2.2.3]. The public domain status of compensated exceptions, and their relationship with uncompensated exceptions, is taken up further in Chapters 14 and 15, which deal with public domain uses under compulsory licences.

# 13 Compulsory Licensing – Variations

| | | |
|---|---|---|
| 13.1 | Introduction | 392 |
| 13.2 | Public Domain Definition and Compulsory Licences | 392 |
| 13.3 | International Copyright Law and Compulsory Licences | 399 |
| 13.4 | National Applications of Statutory Licences | 408 |
| 13.5 | Extended Collective Licensing (ECL) Systems | 421 |
| 13.6 | Governance of Compulsory Licensing: A Public Domain Perspective | 429 |
| 13.7 | Conclusions: A Flexible and Important Part of the Public Domain | 430 |

## 13.1 Introduction

It is unusual to discuss 'compulsory licences' and the activities of collecting societies in the context of the public domain, so in this chapter we discuss what we mean by a 'compulsory licence', its variants, and how it relates to our overall concept of the copyright public domain. The following chapter provides a comparative national analysis of the main subject matters with which compulsory licences deal. We conclude from these chapters that, in practice, various forms of compulsory licensing now constitute some of the most important components of the public domain in many countries **(Category 13)**, that this seems likely to increase, and that there is much scope for more countries to use the various forms of compulsory licences, within the tolerances of international copyright law, in order to achieve net social benefits.

## 13.2 Public Domain Definition and Compulsory Licences

For our purposes, 'compulsory licences' are where rights holders are required to allow their works to be used by parties specified by the licence terms, on conditions and for a fee set by a neutral party on public interest grounds, and on equal terms for licensees. In other words, rights holders are compelled to allow what would otherwise be copyright infringements, in return for remuneration. From the perspective of copyright owners, the

## 13.2 Public Domain Definition and Compulsory Licences

distinguishing feature of compulsory licences (compared with free use exceptions) is that they involve a right to receive remuneration. Compulsory licences are the only aspect of the public domain in relation to which rights owners are entitled to receive payment. They have a long history in copyright law, from 1842 onwards.[1] On our analysis, compulsory licences are part of the public domain because of the negative liberty to use works without permission [2.2.3], whether or not copyright owners are entitled to opt out in relation to specific works or classes of works, and whether or not there are some owners who participate voluntarily although others are compelled. Compulsory licences are distinct from fully voluntary collective licences, which, under our definition, are not part of the public domain.

We use 'statutory licence' to distinguish between licences created and made mandatory by statutory provisions, as distinct from extended collective licences (ECLs) and some similar compulsory licences which only come into existence on the basis of a determination by a tribunal.[2] We will also use 'CS' to refer generically to a 'collecting society', an organisation representing groups of copyright rights holders, also known as collective management organisations (CMOs).[3]

On our definition, 'compulsory licences' have the following features:

(1) **Compulsion of rights-owners is involved** – Compulsion may be by statutory provisions, or according to the determination of a neutral body (for example, a tribunal for some extended collective licences). The licence may exist before any uses of the works are made (as in a new statutory licence scheme), or it may be imposed by the neutral body after voluntary licensing of some works have been made, but the scope of the licence is then extended to all works within the subject matter of the licence, by the decision of a neutral body. For example, a Minister or a Tribunal may impose terms and fees on uses of all works within this extended scope. This is the case with the Nordic-influenced Extended Collective Licensing (ECL) system, which is compulsory for large groups of rights holders, although voluntary for

---

[1] The Copyright Act 1842 (UK) containing the first example, intended to prevent book suppression *post mortem* was never used: D. Brennan 'The first compulsory licensing of patents and copyright' (2017) 17 *Legal History* 1.

[2] There is no uniform use of terminology in this field. For example, although the result will usually be the same as the distinction we make, *Copinger* considers that the distinguishing feature is that 'in the case of a statutory licence the rate [fee] is set by law, in the case of a compulsory licence the rate is left to be negotiated': K. Garnett, G. Davies and G. Harbottle, *Copinger and Skone James on Copyright* (16th edn, Sweet and Maxwell, 2010), [28–02] ('*Copinger*, 16th edn'). We do not consider this distinction useful, or applicable in all countries.

[3] For usage of 'CMO', see chapters throughout D. Gervais (ed.), *Collective Management of Copyright and Related Rights* (3rd edn., Wolters Kluwer, 2016).

some. This aspect of ECL is sufficient for these licences to fall within our definition of a compulsory licence, as discussed in [13.4.1].

(2) **Fees are paid to or for rights holders** – Compulsory licences are the only part of the public domain where the uses not requiring permission are intended to result in revenue flowing to the copyright owner.[4] For this reason alone, they constitute a distinct category of the public domain. 'Licence' is used here in the sense of a 'licence-for-fee', as distinct from the kind of voluntary licences considered in Chapter 15, which are of the 'licence-for-free' variety.

(3) **Set by a neutral body** – To fit our definition of the public domain, the licence conditions and the fee for a compulsory licence must be set by a neutral body, whether a public tribunal such as Australia's Copyright Tribunal, or a private arbitrator, or directly by the legislature, on public interest grounds. Copyright owners or their representatives may not set conditions or fees based solely on private interest considerations through market mechanisms and they should be uniform for all users entitled to make use of the licence. The point is that neither the conditions nor the fee must be set, or revocable, by the copyright owners, or bodies acting on their behalf (CSs). Many licences administered by CSs such as collective, voluntary licences negotiated directly between a CS and potential licensees, are therefore excluded from this definition.

(4) **Uses may be limited to a class of users** – Only certain classes of the public may be allowed to make use of the works in the ways allowed by the compulsory licence, as is the case with some free use exceptions: Chapter 12. For example, in some countries only a radio broadcaster can utilise the (statutory) compulsory licence for public broadcasting of sound recordings (and pay for that), but the listening public as a whole benefits. Similarly, there are free use exceptions that can only be exercised by educational institutions, but any students of that institution may benefit. By contrast, a statutory licence which allows any person to republish, or translate, a work after a period of time, and on compliance with certain conditions, including payment, is an open licence, in the sense that it is not limited to a class of the public (a closed licence).

---

[4] 'Copyright levies', where very indirect payments to rights holders results from levies imposed on copying equipment and/or blank media as compensation for private copying, are in our view not compulsory licences because of the indirectness of the remuneration to copyright owners, but are supports for the private use exceptions that are part of the public domain. They are allowed by Article 5(2) of the Infosoc Directive, and used extensively in the laws of EU Member States. They are discussed in the Online Supplement.

(5) ***May allow non-operation in some situations*** – Some compulsory licences do not operate if there is a voluntary licensing scheme covering the same field (for example, some educational licences in the UK), but the voluntary licence is then made 'in the shadow' of the compulsory licence, effectively removing the right to exclude. In rare cases compulsory licences include provision for copyright owners to 'opt out' of the licence by notice (for example, in China). This does not stop these compulsory licences coming within our definition of the public domain, because the copyright owner is not able to choose which users are able to use the work, but only to choose (in the UK) negotiated licence terms, or (in China) which of their works, if any, will come within the compulsory licence. The neutral voluntary licences discussed in Chapter 15 are 'opt-in', whereas these compulsory licences may be described as 'opt-out'.

### 13.2.1 Why Compulsory Licences are Part of the Public Domain

The essence of the public domain, on our approach, is that it includes all situations where users of works do not have to seek the permission of copyright owners (or their representative CS) in order to make use of one or more of their exclusive rights in the works, so that what would otherwise be infringing uses are permitted. While copyright essentially involves three main forms of rights – rights that are good against all the world, rights to control uses, and rights to receive payment[5] – compulsory licences transform this by converting the absolute rights into a limited right to receive reasonable remuneration. From the point of view of the user, the nature of copyright changes from being based on permission to being based on freedom to use coupled with an obligation to pay reasonable compensation, as set by a neutral party, an example of a change from a property rule to a liability rule.[6] As Geiger puts it, in the case of a compulsory licence:

> 'sailing on the ocean of freedom' is still available to everyone, but subject to the payment of a fair remuneration to the creator, just like the use of highways in some countries is open to all car drivers but requires the buying of a sticker, or how the use of the underground is open to all passengers but requires the buying of a ticket.[7]

---

[5] Goldstein and Hugenholtz, *International Copyright*, [4.2.3.1].

[6] See Merges, 'Contracting into liability rules'.

[7] C. Geiger, 'Promoting creativity through copyright limitations: reflections on the concept of exclusivity in copyright law' (2010) 12(3) *Vanderbilt Journal of Entertainment and Technology Law* 515, 521 n. 15.

As explained in [2.2.3], we consider that theories of the public domain should include within them compulsory licences involving reasonable remuneration set by a neutral party. As the costs to licensees, and indirectly to end-users, under a compulsory licence are constrained – such as by the 'equitable remuneration' standard – and as they are commonly more moderate than commercially negotiated fees, they are, in a sense, a 'half way house'[8] to free use exceptions.

The inclusion of compulsory licences as part of the public domain is confirmed by the treatment of compulsory licences under international copyright law and EU law. Under Berne, certain specific exceptions provide for compulsory remuneration, while the permissible uses under Article 9(2) include both free uses and remunerated uses: [14.3]. International copyright law therefore does not draw a hard and fast distinction between free uses and remunerated uses, meaning that both free use exceptions and compulsory licences can be regarded as limitations or exceptions to copyright. Similarly, Article 5 of the EU InfoSoc Directive, providing for exceptions and limitations, does not distinguish between free use exceptions and remunerated uses. Therefore, while three of the permissible exceptions require the payment of 'fair compensation', a requirement to pay such compensation may also be imposed on any of the optional exceptions or limitations under Article 5: [13.3.2]. Moreover, the application of the general three-step test may mean that an exception or limitation is available for particular uses if it is accompanied by remuneration or compensation.[9]

This general grouping of free use exceptions and remunerated use exceptions under international and EU copyright law is based on a coherent understanding of the need for limitations and exceptions on exclusive rights to promote broader public interest objectives. As these objectives may be promoted, depending upon the circumstances, by either free use exceptions or compulsory licences, it makes no sense to exclude uses permitted under compulsory licences from the public domain. Geiger argues that, in relation to both free use and remunerated use exceptions:

> It is indisputable that copyright law must create free spaces that enable the creative use of existing works. Through these free spaces, common constitutional values like the freedom of expression, freedom of information, and freedom of art shall be secured, and the public interest in a comprehensive cultural life shall be served.[10]

---

[8] Ricketson and Ginsburg, *International Copyright and Neighbouring Rights*, [13.25].
[9] von Lewinski and Walter, 'Information society directive', [11.5.23].
[10] Geiger, 'Promoting creativity', 524.

## 13.2 Public Domain Definition and Compulsory Licences

For many members of the public, many uses they will make of works in the public domain may be via compulsory licences, whether through photocopying, music broadcast on radio or TV, or exhibitions in museums and galleries. Compulsory licensing may be the genesis of whole new industries which would not have flourished, or perhaps existed, in the absence of an imposed uniform cost structure. It has, for example, been argued that these compulsory licences are the principal reason for the financial success of the recorded music, radio and cable TV industries of the United States.[11] In recent years, compulsory licences are becoming one of the preferred ways to deal with some persistent problems, such as the under-utilisation of orphan works, and the lack of sufficient access to works in developing countries. Globally, their considerable social importance means that they should not be ignored as a distinctive and vital part of the public domain.

*Why Include Extended Collective Licences (ECLs)?* With ECLs there is a starting point of a negotiated licence between a CS and a group of potential licensees, usually in a situation where a CS already broadly represents a class of rights holders: [13.4]. The obligations of the licence are then compulsorily extended (by legislation or a tribunal decision) to all rights holders whose content is relevant to the licence, whether or not they are CS members. Such non-members may be local, foreign, missing or dead. From the perspective of these unrepresented rights holders, this is therefore a compulsory licence, as they lose the ability to control uses. From the perspective of the licensees, it is also a compulsory licence in relation to all of these unrepresented rights holders, as there is no need to obtain permission. Although ECLs are a hybrid between compulsory licences and traditional collective rights management,[12] these perspectives make ECLs part of our concept of compulsory licences, and of the public domain. Some conditions of use are usually set by neutral parties, including remuneration questions (as between rights holders and the CS), and are subject to neutral arbitration, and requirements of equal treatment. These external controls further reduce the extent to which the conditions of the licence are under the control of the CS and its members.

---

[11] L. Lessig, *Free Culture: How Big Media Uses Technology and the Law to Lock Down Culture and Control Creativity* (Penguin USA, 2004), chap. 4.

[12] T. Riis and J. Schovsbo, 'Extended collective licenses and the Nordic experience: it's a hybrid but is it a Volvo or a lemon?' (2010) 33(4) *Columbia Journal of Law & the Arts* 471, 472.

### 13.2.2 Main Varieties of Public Domain Compulsory Licences

We consider that there are five types of compulsory licences that are part of the public domain. The distinctions drawn here will become clearer from examples in this and the following chapter. In all cases the licensees are required to pay a licence fee of some type (or have a contingent liability to pay compensation), usually to a CS, but sometimes to individual rights holders. The terminology we use to discuss each type of licence is as follows:

(1) ***Statutory licences to a class of licensee*** are where a statute specifies a compulsorily allowed use of a class of materials (such as reproducing materials for university teaching, or playing sound recordings on radio stations), and an adjudicative method for the setting of fees (or a fixed fee), and provides for a collecting society (CS) to collect fees from licensees and distribute them to rights holders.

(2) ***Extended collective licensing (ECL) systems*** involve the compulsory extension of the repertoire of a CS, and thus the compulsory use of the works of 'unrepresented rights holders', as explained above.

(3) ***Statutory licences to the public*** are where any member of the public may, without application, use works, subject to payment of remuneration. An example is the right, in some countries, to make 'cover versions', sound recordings of songs that have already been published (or recorded).

(4) ***Compulsory licences to individual applicants*** are where individuals may, by application, obtain a licence from some neutral body, such as a copyright Board or Tribunal (for example, uses of orphan works, or translation of works). Payment of remuneration may be contingent upon a rights holder appearing, as in some orphan works schemes.

(5) ***Statutory permission, subject to a contingent payment*** are where an individual user, or a class of users, such as cultural heritage institutions, is given permission (without need for any application) to use a particular class of subject matter, subject to a contingent liability to compensate rights owners if and when they request compensation.

In categories (1)–(3) a licence fee is always paid to a CS, whereas in (5) and sometimes in (4) a fee (or fair compensation) is payable only if and when a rights holder makes a claim.

By contrast, the following types of collective licensing are not, in our view, part of the public domain, because they allow individual copyright owners, or their representatives, to set and change the terms of a licence, and the uses made of works are not 'permission free':

(1) **Purely voluntary collective licences** are where a CS sets conditions and fees for uses of a class of materials, acting only for its members, and collects and distributes royalties according to its rules, even if there is some level of supervision by a Tribunal of these conditions and fees. However, some voluntary collective licensing shares many features of compulsory licensing, for example, Australian 'blanket licensing': [13.4]
(2) **Voluntary 'click wrap' and other licences by adhesion** are where an individual rights holder sets the licence terms and fees (if any) of a licence to use a particular item of content, but (unlike the voluntary licensing discussed in Chapter 15) these are not chosen from predetermined conditions set by a neutral party.

The basis for our distinction is simply that, under a compulsory licence, rights holders do not have the ability to prevent or control uses, whereas under voluntary licences rights holders retain this ability. Where there is full, or at least predominant, control over the creation and terms of a licence by some neutral party acting in the public interest, we consider that rights holders do not retain this ability. That said, there are forms of collective licensing which involve some but not all the aspects of compulsion found in a statutory licence or ECL, which we do not classify as a compulsory licence but are at the borderline. These include Australia's system of 'blanket licences' to a class of licensee, established by a tribunal which is empowered to decide that an existing system of voluntary licences for a particular purpose (for example, playing of music in gyms) should be brought within fees and conditions determined by the tribunal.

Where a CS is involved, we therefore see a spectrum relating to the level of compulsion imposed on rights holders, ranging from statutory licences, to ECLs, to voluntary collective licences with some degree of neutral supervision, to purely voluntary collective licensing.

## 13.3 International Copyright Law and Compulsory Licences

International copyright law does not provide carte blanche for national laws to create compulsory licences. Instead, they are permissible only if they fit within the internationally allowable limitations or exceptions to exclusive rights. Some national licences do not comply fully with these requirements, but the limited enforcement of international copyright law means that their practices may be tolerated [5.7]. We discuss here where compulsory licences are permissible, under international copyright law, pursuant to provisions of the Berne and Rome Conventions[13] that allow

---

[13] Full titles and citations of all conventions are in the Table of International Instruments.

for specific remunerated exceptions and in accordance with the general three-step test under Article 9(2) of Berne.

### 13.3.1 Specific Provisions Enabling Compulsory Licences

International copyright law provides for certain exceptions to copyright infringement that are available only upon payment to the copyright owner: [5.5]. The Berne Convention specifically permits three kinds of remunerated use exceptions, the first two of which are commonly found under national copyright laws, and are important: mechanical recording of musical works under Article 13(1): [5.5.1]; rebroadcasting and cable retransmissions under Article 11*bis*: [5.5.2]. The third type specifically permitted by Berne is compulsory licensing allowing translation and reproduction in developing nations under the Paris Appendix to Berne, of limited importance: [5.5.3] and [14.3].

Article 10*bis*(2) of Berne also leaves it to national laws to determine the 'conditions' under which works may be reproduced or made available in certain forms for the purpose of 'reporting current events': [5.5.4]. Article 2*bis*(2) leaves it to national laws to determine the 'conditions' under which public lectures, addresses and like works may be reproduced by the press and broadcast or communicated to the public where this is justified by the 'informatory purpose' of the use. In both cases, the use of the term 'conditions' implies not only that Berne members may introduce free use exceptions but also that they have a discretion to introduce remunerated use exceptions, such as compulsory licences. Neither is of great importance.

Three broadcasting-related compulsory licences are also permitted under the Rome Convention in relation to: fixations of performances for broadcasting purposes; broadcasting and public communications of phonograms; and communication to the public of certain broadcasts.

### 13.3.2 'Equitable Remuneration' and 'Fair Compensation'

Remuneration to copyright owners is central to compulsory licences, and distinguishes them from unremunerated exceptions, so the required payment must be considered. The Berne Convention requires Member States to provide, when implementing two Berne provisions, for the payment of 'equitable remuneration, which, in the absence of agreement, shall be fixed by competent authority'. The two provisions are made in Article 11*bis* ('Broadcasting and other wireless communications, public communication of broadcast by wire or rebroadcast,

## 13.3 International Copyright Law and Compulsory Licences 401

public communication of broadcast by loudspeaker or analogous instruments",[14] and Article 13 ('the Right of Recording of Musical Works and Any Words Pertaining Thereto').[15] Referring to the Article 11*bis* provision, Brennan concludes[16] that, in that regime, equitable remuneration 'is best understood as fair market value', and that what this 'actually means can be understood in both economic and restitutionary terms as a "fair share of the subjective value of the use of copyright in the hands of the user"'.

Equitable remuneration, at the EU level, is required by Article 8(2) of the Rental and Lending Rights Directive,[17] but the concept is not further defined there. The ECJ has, however, held that the concept of equitable remuneration in Article 8(2)[18] is an autonomous concept of EU law, to be interpreted uniformly in all the Member States. Nevertheless, 'it is for each Member State to determine, in its own territory, the most appropriate criteria for assuring, within the limits imposed by Community law and Directive 92/100 in particular, adherence to that Community concept.'[19] The Court held that it was not its role to lay down the criteria for determining what constitutes equitable remuneration, but only to ensure that the national criteria applied were consistent with EU law. Here, the approach taken by the Netherlands legislature was held to be consistent, particularly as it required the parties first to attempt to resolve the question themselves by establishing a tariff which (at least for the initial years following the Directive) was not less than amounts previously paid (unless the need for equitable remuneration required an increase), and only in the absence of such agreement left the matter to be determined by the Dutch court. The ECJ referred to the need for the parties to take account, in particular, of the methods used in the other Member States, because of the need for uniform interpretation of the requirement. 'Equitable remuneration' in EU law is therefore very particular to circumstances within the EU. As an autonomous concept of EU law, it cannot be assumed to have the same meaning as in the Berne Convention.

---

[14] Berne Convention, Art. 11*bis*(2).   [15] Berne Convention, Art. 13(1).
[16] D. Brennan, *Retransmission and US Compliance with TRIPs* (Springer, 2003), pp. 329–30.
[17] Full titles and citations of all EU Directives are in the Table of International Instruments.
[18] Rental and Lending Rights Directive (EU), Art. 8(2): 'Member States shall provide a right in order to ensure that a single equitable remuneration is paid by the user, if a phonogram published for commercial purposes, or a reproduction of such phonogram, is used for broadcasting by wireless means or for any communication to the public, and to ensure that this remuneration is shared between the relevant performers and phonogram producers. Member States may, in the absence of agreement between the performers and phonogram producers, lay down the conditions as to the sharing of this remuneration between them.'
[19] Case C-245/00, *Stichting ter Exploitatie van Naburige Rechten (SENA)* v. *Nederlandse Omroep Stichting (NOS)* [2003] ECLI:EU:C:2003:68.

The concept of 'fair compensation', referred to in the EU InfoSoc Directive, Article 5 and Recital (36), is not the same as the concept of 'equitable remuneration' in Berne. As von Lewinski and Walter explain,[20] the term 'compensation' was used because the UK and Ireland do not have the familiarity with statutory remunerations found in most Continental European countries. They argued that 'some other form of compensation should be sufficient to comply with the three-step test and to take account of the interest of the right holders', and so 'the term "fair compensation" allows for other forms of compensation than remuneration'.[21]

The text of the Directive does not provide any details of what is meant by 'fair compensation', but Recital 35, while stating that 'account should be taken of the particular circumstances of each case', lists some criteria that may be used in evaluating the circumstances, including that if 'the prejudice to the rightholder would be minimal, no obligation for payment may arise'.[22]

The ECJ has stated a number of principles concerning fair compensation in the context of copying levies, which should also be applicable in relation to compulsory licences. The concept of 'fair compensation' is, like equitable remuneration, an autonomous concept of EU law, which must be interpreted uniformly in Member States.[23] 'Fair compensation' must be calculated on the basis of the harm caused to the author.[24] While the concept should be interpreted consistently in all exceptions, because it must be based on the harm to the author, it is appropriate for national laws to distinguish between compensation payable for private uses by natural persons and compensation for non-private or commercial uses.[25] As a derogation from a right, the exception must be strictly interpreted, and it is also necessary to comply with the three-step test in Article 5(5).[26] 'Fair compensation' is not a concept that is used outside EU law.

---

[20] von Lewinski and Walter, 'Information society directive', [11.5.24].   [21] Ibid.
[22] InfoSoc Directive, Recital (35): 'When evaluating these circumstances, a valuable criterion would be the possible harm to the rightholders resulting from the act in question. In cases where rightholders have already received payment in some other form, for instance as part of a licence fee, no specific or separate payment may be due. The level of fair compensation should take full account of the degree of use of technological protection measures referred to in this Directive. In certain situations where the prejudice to the rightholder would be minimal, no obligation for payment may arise.'
[23] Case C-467/08, *Padawan SL v. Sociedad General de Autores y Editores de España (SGAE)* [2011] ECDR 1; [2011] FSR 17.
[24] *Ibid.*
[25] Case C-572/13, *Hewlett-Packard Belgium SPRL v. Reprobel SCRL* [2016] Bus LR 73.
[26] Case 435/12, *ACI Adam BV v. Stichting de Thuiskopie* [2014] All ER (D) 83 (Apr).

### 13.3.3 The Three-Step Test and Compulsory Licences

The most important provision of international copyright law which allows for the introduction of remunerated use exceptions, or compulsory licences, is the three-step test, which, under Berne Article 9(2), is confined to exceptions to the reproduction right, but was extended to all exclusive rights under copyright by Article 13 of TRIPs: [5 4.1].

Although questions have arisen, the consensus is that the Berne test allows for free use exceptions and compulsory licences.[27] As Ricketson and Ginsburg explain, reference in the drafting history of Article 9(2) to national legislation requiring 'equitable remuneration' clearly envisaged that exceptions under the test could 'take the form of either absolute exceptions or compulsory licences, depending essentially on the number of copies made'.[28] Moreover, as some national laws preceding the introduction of Article 9(2) already had compulsory licences, and as the general test was intended to cover all exceptions under national laws other than those falling within the specific exceptions under Berne, it is clear that the test does not preclude compulsory licences.[29] This further suggests that pre-existing compulsory licences were grandfathered as passing the test, with the permitted uses being presumed to satisfy the first two steps.

Nevertheless, in order to comply with the test, compulsory licences must satisfy the third step, namely that the permitted uses do not 'unreasonably prejudice the legitimate interests of the author'. The effect of the third step, which assumes that some prejudice is acceptable provided it is not 'unreasonable', seems to be that more copying or other uses may be permissible under a compulsory licence than under a free use exception, due to the requirement of payment.[30] Ricketson and Ginsburg conclude, as the test is not a 'bright line' rule, there is a need for some 'care, moderation, and constraint in constructing any compulsory licensing scheme under national law'.[31] In other words, payment of remuneration does not automatically ensure that a compulsory licence complies with the test.

While the interpretation of the three-step test, in light of the WTO Panel 'Homestyle' decision, is discussed in [5.4.1], it is worth adding some general comments on the relevance of the decision to compulsory licensing in relation to each step.[32]

---

[27] Ricketson and Ginsburg, *International Copyright and Neighbouring Rights*, [13.25]; Goldstein and Hugenholtz, *International Copyright*, [11.1].
[28] Ricketson and Ginsburg, *International Copyright and Neighbouring Rights*, [13.25].
[29] *Ibid.* [13.25].   [30] Goldstein and Hugenholtz, *International Copyright*, [11.1].
[31] Ricketson and Ginsburg, *International Copyright and Neighbouring Rights*, [13.25].
[32] Compare the more detailed summary of academic perspectives on each leg, in T. G. Agitha, 'International norms for compulsory licensing and the Indian copyright

Although the first step, the limit to 'certain special cases', was interpreted by the WTO Panel to require exceptions narrow in scope and reach, as the case was not about a compensated use, different factors may be relevant. The Panel did not find it was relevant to consider public policy reasons for an exception,[33] so public policy or public interest factors that are otherwise raised to justify a compulsory licence are not relevant here.

To comply with the second step and avoid conflicting with the normal exploitation of a work it is necessary, according to the Panel, to avoid depriving rights holders of 'significant or tangible commercial gains'. This does not, however, prevent licensees from making commercial gains, which often occurs under compulsory licences, as these may be offset by the payment of licence fees. This was already the case when Article 9(2) was adopted,[34] and could be considered a factor that has been grandfathered. Furthermore, if only 'normal' exploitation by rights holders, and not all exploitation, is protected, then it becomes relevant to ask whether it is likely that the exploitation would have been carried out, absent the compulsory licence.[35] While the Panel applied a predominantly economic approach to what amounts to 'normal exploitation', it did not necessarily rule out non-economic considerations, which could mean that some socially valuable uses, such as uses for scientific research or education, do not fall within the 'normal exploitation' of a work.[36] Other authors argue that 'normal' does not include unlimited or exorbitant commercial exploitation.[37]

To avoid unreasonably prejudicing the legitimate interests of rights holders under the third step, statutory requirements for equitable remuneration (or the like) via a compulsory licence will often suffice, although Article 9(2) gives no guidance about how the avoidance of unreasonable prejudice is to be measured. Laws establishing CSs can have different rules concerning the relative positions of CS members vis-à-vis

---

law' (2012) 15(1) *Journal of World Intellectual Property* 26–50; at 29–33; see also Ricketson and Ginsburg [1311]–[1325].

[33] This is contested by some authors: see Agitha, 'International norms for compulsory licensing and the Indian copyright law', 30 for the views of Senftleben, 2004, Ricketson, 1987, and others; contra Ricketson and Ginsburg [13.14].

[34] Ricketson and Ginsburg, *International Copyright and Neighbouring Rights*, [13.9].

[35] *Ibid.* [13.17].

[36] See, for example, J. C. Ginsburg, 'Toward supranational copyright law? The WTO panel decision and the "three-step test" for copyright exceptions' (2001) 187 *Revue internationale du droit d'auteur* 3; see also Ricketson and Ginsburg, *International Copyright and Neighbouring Rights*, [13.20]–[13.21] questioning whether every potential type of exploitation of a work (such as scientific research or education) is a 'market' that authors should expect to have under their sole control as 'normal exploitation'.

[37] Agitha, 'International norms for compulsory licensing and the Indian copyright law', 31.

non-members (local, foreign, missing or deceased) in relation to distribution of funds, and these rules could potentially raise issues of unreasonable prejudice. However, perfect compensatory systems are unlikely to be required, especially if in reality the relevant comparison is between receiving some compensation or none.

In summary, there are significant unresolved issues in the application of the three-step test to compulsory licences. Consequently, there is leeway for a potentially broad range of compulsory licences to comply with the test, particularly because, in practice, the interpretation of the steps will be left largely to national legislatures to resolve when fashioning compulsory licences.

### 13.3.4 International Law, Practice and Reality

The international copyright law provisions discussed above, originating in Berne and consolidated through other treaties, are restrictive because of the need to comply with the three-step test or a specific enabling provision. But the three-step test might possibly allow a wide range of compulsory licensing practices to be compliant. We argue that extensive and appropriate use of compulsory licensing broadens and enriches the public domain. International copyright law obviously raises the question of how broad is the range of Berne-compliant compulsory licences? However, there is a degree of implied tolerance found in the enforcement of international copyright law of divergences in national laws which are not strictly Berne-compliant: [5.7]. The range of compulsory licensing practices found in national jurisdictions may disclose some compulsory licences in national legislation more permissive than is strictly justifiable under Berne, but which are accepted and valued by parties to them.

### 13.3.5 EU InfoSoc Directive and other Directives

The European Union has the most significant regional multilateral requirements that affect compulsory licensing. EU Member States, particularly those in the Nordic countries (and Norway, outside the EU), are also the most common location for extended collective licensing (ECL) schemes.

The InfoSoc Directive of 2001 includes modest steps toward the harmonisation of exceptions in copyright laws in the Member States of the EU, some of which affect compulsory licensing, including an exhaustive list of twenty optional exceptions or limitations, as discussed in [11.2.1]. Article 5 confirms that all such exceptions and limitations must satisfy the 'three-step test'. Compensated and uncompensated exceptions are dealt with together in Article 5. Recital (36) explains that the optional exceptions under the Directive do not rule out a requirement that they may be subject to 'fair compensation'.[38] Three exceptions require payment of 'fair compensation', so compulsory licences are in effect optional in implementations of the other seventeen exceptions: [13.3.2]. The EU has therefore given broad recognition to the use of compulsory licensing as a means of satisfying public interest considerations in relation to access to works. Examples from EU national laws are in the following chapter.

The three exceptions concerning the reproduction right which are subject to the compulsory proviso that 'the rightholders receive fair compensation' are: (i) reprographic reproductions (not including sheet music); (ii) any reproduction by natural persons for private use and non-commercial ends; and (iii) reproductions of broadcasts by social institutions (e.g., hospitals or prisons) for non-commercial purposes.[39] In (ii), the compensation provisions must take account of any use or non-use of technological measures for protective purposes.[40] So, in three situations, the only limitations on rights that are allowed are those involving compulsory licences and payments to rights holders.

A 2015 Report on the implementation of the InfoSoc Directive[41] by the European Parliament's Committee on Legal Affairs, made sixty-eight recommendations for its improvement, including calling on the Commission to examine the application of minimum standards across the exceptions and limitations; and to examine 'the possibility of making certain exceptions mandatory where the purpose is to protect fundamental rights', with fair compensation.[42] The Report recommended that where free use exceptions exist, compensatory schemes such as compulsory licences should not override them.[43]

There are also compulsory licensing provisions for retransmissions under the EU Satellite & Cable Directive (1993), and a non-waivable

---

[38] InfoSoc Directive (EU), Recital (36): Member States may 'provide for fair compensation for rightholders also when applying the optional provisions on exceptions or limitations which do not require such compensation'.
[39] InfoSoc Directive (EU), Arts. 5(2) (a) (b) and (e), respectively.
[40] InfoSoc Directive (EU), Art. 6(3).
[41] EU Parliament, Committee on Legal Affairs, Report on the implementation of Directive 2001/29/EC of the European Parliament and of the Council of 22 May 2001 on the harmonisation of certain aspects of copyright and related rights in the information society, 24 June 2015 ('Report on the implementation of the InfoSoc Directive').
[42] 'Report on the implementation of the InfoSoc Directive', Recommendations 38 and 49.
[43] Ibid. Recommendation 58.

## 13.3 International Copyright Law and Compulsory Licences

right to equitable remuneration for rental under the Rental and Lending Rights Directive.

*Implications of Soulier and Doke* In 2012, France enacted an 'unavailable books' law,[44] which provides for a CS (SOFIA)[45] that will issue licences for republication or other digital exploitation of such books. It specifies that 'an out-of-print book means a book published in France before 1 January 2001 which is no longer commercially distributed by a publisher and is not currently published in print or digital format.'[46] A database register of 'unavailable books', known as ReLIRE, was established by the Bibliothèque nationale de France,[47] to be updated annually. The author or publisher then had six months to object to management of the book's digital rights by SOFIA. Detailed procedures, no longer relevant,[48] set out the circumstances under which SOFIA could license other commercial publishers, and after ten years, libraries and archives would be allowed to digitise and provide access to the book free of charge.

However, the ECJ held in 2016 in *Soulier and Doke*[49] that aspects of this law were inconsistent with the InfoSoc Directive. In particular, the Court held that the legislation does not fall within the scope of any of the Directive's exceptions and limitations in Article 5. The Court pointed out that Articles 2(a) and 3(1) provide that the Member States are to grant authors the exclusive rights to authorise or prohibit direct or indirect reproduction of their works, and communication to the public of their works, and that these provisions must be given a broad interpretation,[50] being preventative in nature. Therefore (in the absence of an Article 5 exception) 'any reproduction or communication to the public of a work by a third party requires the prior consent of its author.'[51] Because Articles 2(a) and 3(1) do not state

---

[44] 'Law on the digital exploitation of out-of-print books of the twentieth century' (LOI n° 2012-287 du 1ᵉʳ mars 2012 relative à l'exploitation numérique des livres indisponibles du xxᵉ siècle) (France).
[45] SOFIA (Société française des intérêts des auteurs de l'écrit) www.la-sofialivresindisponibles .org/2015/index.php.
[46] Intellectual Property Code (France), Art. L. 134-1
[47] Register of orphan works http://relire.bnf.fr/.
[48] The details are not relevant due to the ECJ's invalidation of the law, but are summarised in the Online Supplement.
[49] Case C-301/15 *Soulier and Doke* v. *Prime Minister of France and French Minister for Culture and Communication* [2017] 2 CMLR 267.
[50] Case C-508 *Infopaq International*, [2009] ECR I-6569 [43], and Case C-145/10 *Painer* [2011] ECR I-12533 [96].
[51] *Soulier and Doke*, C-301/15, [33].

that consent must be explicit, implicit consent is possible. However, the Court held that 'the circumstances in which implicit consent can be admitted must be strictly defined in order not to deprive of effect the very principle of the author's prior consent' and 'every author must actually be informed of the future use of his work by a third party and the means at his disposal to prohibit it if he so wishes.'[52] Moreover, the Court ruled that 'a mere lack of opposition on their part cannot be regarded as the expression of their implicit consent to that use.'[53] The ECJ concluded[54] that these Articles precluded national legislation such as the French 'unavailable books' law which gave a CS the right to authorise reproduction of such books 'while allowing the authors of those books, or their successors in title, to oppose or put an end to that practice, on the conditions that that legislation lays down'.

The significant implication of this decision is that any digitisation schemes, where the consent of individual authors (express or implied) cannot be demonstrated, are likely to conflict with the InfoSoc Directive unless they can be made to fit within one of the Article 5 exceptions, or be authorised by another Directive such as the Orphan Works Directive. The application of this decision to schemes limited to orphan works is questionable: [14.2.4]. However, *Soulier and Doke* may have additional implications for the general operation of extended collective licensing (ECL) schemes within the EU: [13.5.3].

## 13.4 National Applications of Statutory Licences

This section sets out the basic structures under which a number of countries make relatively extensive use of statutory licensing. These include 'developed' countries (Australia and the UK) and 'developing' countries (India and China). The licences discussed here include examples of all five types of compulsory licences: [13.2.2], except ECL schemes, discussed in the next section. Examples of specific licences are in the next chapter.

### 13.4.1 Australia

In Australia, all compulsory licences are statutory licences. Australia does not have ECL schemes, but it does have a system of 'blanket' licences, administered by the Copyright Tribunal, which share many but not all

---

[52] *Soulier and Doke*, [37]–[38].    [53] *Soulier and Doke*, [43].    [54] *Soulier and Doke*, [52].

## 13.4 National Applications of Statutory Licences

features of an ECL scheme. These blanket licences are not part of the pubic domain, but are in something of a 'grey area' on the spectrum between ECL schemes and completely voluntary collective licensing. The Australian compulsory licensing system, as amended in 2017, will be used as a detailed illustration of how such systems can work, and how they relate to the public domain.[55]

### Statutory Licences

Statutory licences are where the Copyright Act creates and defines the licence and such matters as the fee mechanism. The statutory licences, following the 2017 amendments, are as follows: the 'educational licence', for copying or communication by educational institutions of works and broadcasts (Part IVA, Division 4);[56] for government use, 'for the services of the Crown' (including by contractors) (Pt VII, Division 2); for recording of 'cover versions' of musical work (by any person) (ss. 54–64); and for broadcasting / causing to be heard in public sound recordings (ss. 108–9). The breadth of both the users (licensees) and uses that are regulated, shows how significant statutory licences are in Australia. The 'end users' of the uses permitted by these licences include all those attending educational institutions, all listeners to recorded music, all those who hear broadcasts of recordings, and all public servants. Some of these licences are discussed in more detail, and compared with compulsory licences in similar subject areas, in Chapter 14. Since the early 1980s, the Australian legislature frequently created new statutory licences (and CSs) to resolve copyright problems, and their significance will probably continue to grow. However, the 2017 amendments have also seen the replacement of the statutory licences relating to persons with intellectual disabilities by a fair dealing exception in relation to persons with a disability: [14.8.1].

Five key features of the Australian statutory licences, arising from provisions in the Copyright Act, can be summarised as follows.[57]

---

[55] Amendments by the Copyright Amendment (Disability Access and Other Measures) Act 2017 (Aus.), in effect from December 2017, are assumed for the purposes of the following discussion.

[56] Prior to the 2017 amendments, these licences for educational institutions were in Parts VA and VB, and also covered institutions assisting those with intellectual disabilities.

[57] Further details concerning some of these licences are in Chapter 14. For the pre-2017 position, see part 2.2.1 of K. Lindgren 'The jurisdiction of the Copyright Tribunal of Australia: the 2006 Amendments' (2007) 70 *Intellectual Property Forum: Journal of the Intellectual and Industrial Property Society of Australia and New Zealand* 6–15.

Copyright is not infringed, by a user or through authorisation by a CS, if the statutory conditions of the particular licence are satisfied.[58] In each case the statutory licence is in relation to specific acts comprised in the copyright of particular categories of works or other subject matter.[59] Both the user of the copyright material and the purpose of its use must satisfy the relevant statutory description.

In most licences,[60] a CS can apply to the Minister to be declared to be a CS for works (either for all or specified classes of eligible rights holders), or as the CS for broadcasts (including works contained in a broadcast).[61] In general, only one CS is 'declared' to administer each type of licence concerning works[62] (and only ever one for broadcasts). Declarations are by the Minister, unless referred to the Tribunal.

The scope of the licence is in relation to *any* work that falls within the defined subject matter of the licence, so it can apply to any 'eligible rights holders'. It is not limited to works owned by members of the relevant CS, or repertoire otherwise controlled by the CS. These statutory licences share that aspect of an extended repertoire with ECLs: they are comprehensive. Therefore, they cover works owned by local non-members of the relevant CS, by foreign rights owners, and by rights owners (local or foreign) who cannot be identified or located.

The user must notify the declared CS of the use being made of the copyright material, for most licences, or under the educational licence simply provide a 'remuneration notice' that uses are occurring.[63] The user must undertake to pay[64] a fee to the declared CS for the use. The amount paid (described as 'equitable remuneration' or in similar terms), is either as agreed between the CS and users, or, failing agreement, as determined by the Tribunal, including by substitution of a new scheme proposed by one of the parties.[65] Generally, there are prescribed

---

[58] For example, in relation to the educational statutory licence, s. 113P(1) provides, 'The body administering an educational institution does not infringe copyright in a work by copying or communicating the whole or a part of the work if ...'.

[59] There is an exception in that the statutory licence for government uses of works is generic, in that it applies to any of the exclusive acts applicable to any types of subject matter.

[60] The licences under Copyright Act 1968 (Aus.), Pt 3, Div 6 and s. 108 are not based on declared societies.

[61] Copyright Act 1968 (Aus.), s. 113V.

[62] In some cases, more than one CS may be declared for a particular licence. Under Copyright Act 1968 (Aus.), s. 153F, the Tribunal declared that, for the purposes of the Pt VII Div 2 licence, both Copyright Agency Ltd (CAL) and Screenrights were CSs.

[63] Copyright Act 1968 (Aus.), s. 113P(1)(a): an educational institution must have provided a remuneration notice to the relevant CS agreeing to pay equitable remuneration.

[64] Where the user is the Commonwealth or State Government, there is simply a statutory requirement to pay.

[65] The 2006 Amendments allowed the Tribunal to decide to substitute for an existing licence scheme 'another scheme proposed by one of the parties'; see Lindgren,

## 13.4 National Applications of Statutory Licences

procedures for determining the extent of copying that takes place under some statutory licences, so that fees may be determined, but in the case of educational licences these procedures such as record-keeping are settled by agreements reached between the parties, or the Tribunal if there is failure to agree.

The Act imposes four types of restrictions on an organisation eligible to be declared as a CS under these licences:[66] (i) it must be an incorporated company limited by guarantee; (ii) it must allow all eligible rights owners, or their agents, relevant to the scheme for which it is declared, to be entitled to become members of the CS; (iii) it must prohibit payment of dividends to its members; and (iv) its rules must contain such prescribed provisions as are necessary to ensure that the interests of these members of the CS are protected adequately.

### Allocation of Royalty Shares – Members and Non-Members

These rules must include[67] provisions concerning the collection of amounts of equitable remuneration; the payment of the administrative costs of the CS out of it; the distribution of amounts collected by the CS; 'the holding on trust by the CS of amounts for relevant copyright owners who are not its members'; and access to records of the CS by its members. This final requirement is not an obligation to be transparent to non-members, despite Australia's Productivity Commission noting that many participants in its enquiry 'consistently raised concerns about the lack of transparency of CSs, and in particular, the lack of information and disclosure around the distribution of funds to rights holders'.[68]

The Guidelines under the Copyright Act applying to these declared CSs[69] are important to a public domain perspective on compulsory licences because they indicate the difficult issues involved in ensuring equity in distribution of royalties to non-members as well as CS members, which is essential in justifying the use without permission of a copyright owner's works, as a matter of policy.

The Guidelines provide that a CS's rules which determine a 'scheme of allocation' to distribute amounts collected 'should not be such as to discriminate between members and non-members, or between relevant

---

'The jurisdiction of the Copyright Tribunal of Australia', [4.1] for the numerous provisions of the Act reflecting this change.

[66] Copyright Act 1968 (Aus.), s. 113W.   [67] Copyright Act 1968 (Aus.), s. 113W.
[68] Productivity Commission (Aus.), 'Intellectual property arrangements', 156.
[69] Attorney-General's Department, Declaration of Collecting Societies – Guidelines (Copyright Act 1968), April 2001 ('CS Guidelines'); These Guidelines apply to CSs declared under Parts VA, VB and VC.

copyright owners from Australia and those from other countries', and that the CS and its directors should act with similar impartiality.[70] However, although the allocation to qualified persons must be impartial between members and non-members, royalty shares can only be distributed to members of the CS, and shares due to non-members must be placed in the trust account for this purpose.[71]

Where another organisation is a member of the declared CS and has the right to receive royalties for many copyright owners, such as a professional society or an overseas CS, the declared CS need only concern itself with an aggregate allocation of funds to them, and not with how they redistribute it. Overseas CSs can therefore become members of an Australian declared CS, receiving royalty shares for many rights holders from their country, although they do not have all rights holders as their members. Such royalty shares do not go into the trust fund for undistributed shares. They can, however, be held in the trust account, 'under mutual arrangements', 'pending acquittal with a foreign society'.

The undistributed funds held on trust by CSs, for qualified non-members, or for other reasons preventing immediate distribution,[72] are to be held for a 'trust period' of at least four years and then 'fall into general revenue for distribution in respect of the then current accounting period' among the members of the CS.[73]

Despite the stated objective of impartiality, its achievement in practice would seem to depend upon the CS being very energetic in identifying and contacting qualified non-members, both local and overseas (where not represented by a CS with which there are reciprocal arrangements), and in convincing them of the benefits of CS membership. Otherwise, the royalty shares rightly due to them would just be redistributed to existing CS members after a few years. To what extent the declared CSs are assiduous in this matter is beyond the scope of this book.

Australia's Productivity Commission has, however, been unpersuaded as to the merits of the current arrangements, and has recommended, in relation to such undistributed funds, that '[a]ny funds that cannot be paid to rights holders (for example, because the works are orphaned) should be returned to government, rather than distributed to other rights holders who have no connection with the work used.' 'Orphan works' in this context simply means copyright owners who have not yet been located.

---

[70] CS Guidelines, paras. 11 and 23.   [71] CS Guidelines, para. 16.
[72] CS Guidelines, para. 17 suggest eight categories of such reasons.
[73] There are complaints from user organisations in Australia that the CS Copyright Agency Limited (CAL) has retained such funds for purposes including its advocacy, rather than distributing them to members.

13.4 National Applications of Statutory Licences    413

User organisations have strong objections to paying a CS for use of orphan works, rather than being able to rely on an exception such as fair use. It also seems clear that the prospect of a CS having to pay out its undistributed funds after four years to the government, rather than distribute it to its members according to its next allocation (or keep it for its own purposes), would act as a strong incentive to the CS to identify missing rights holders, distribute funds to them, and perhaps convince them of the benefits of membership, so as to reduce undistributed funds as close to zero as possible.

*Blanket Licences – At the Margins of the Public Domain*

'Blanket licences' are where, by virtue of provisions in the Copyright Act,[74] an existing licensing practice *empowers* the Copyright Tribunal to set uniform conditions and licence fees across an industry. These powers of the Tribunal were introduced in 2006 with the principal aim of regulating potential anti-competitive conduct. By the definition of 'licence scheme',[75] these licences arise from 'anything in the nature of a scheme ... formulated by a licensor or licensors' which sets out the terms under which they are willing to grant licences, and are in that sense 'voluntary' in origin. The role of the Copyright Tribunal is to add various types of compulsion or regulation to such licences, in the situations provided by the Act. However, these elements of compulsion in blanket licensing still fall short of what we would describe as a form of compulsory licence. This is primarily because, unlike an ECL, there is no compulsory extension of the works covered by the licence beyond that of CS members.

Although these blanket licences are not compulsory licences, they share many features of ECLs, and it is valuable to give a brief account[76] to differentiate them from such compulsory licensing.

Blanket licences determined by the Copyright Tribunal from 2006 to 2016 are for use of sound recordings for: 'background music' in retail outlets; in nightclubs and at dance parties; for broadcasts by commercial

---

[74] Copyright Act 1968 (Aus.), primarily Part VI Copyright Tribunal of Australia, ss. 154–159 concerning 'References and applications relating to licences and licence schemes', and s. 136 concerning definitions.
[75] Definition of 'licence scheme', Copyright Act 1968 (Aus.), s. 136: '"*licence scheme*" means a scheme (including anything in the nature of a scheme, whether called a scheme or tariff or called by any other name) formulated by a licensor or licensors and setting out the classes of cases in which the licensor or each of the licensors is willing, or the persons on whose behalf the licensor or each of the licensors acts are willing, to grant licences and the charges (if any) subject to payment of which, and the conditions subject to which, licences would be granted in those classes of cases.'
[76] For details, see the Online Supplement.

television; for provision of downloading by digital music; in fitness classes; in radio simulcasts; and by subscription television broadcasters. These licences involve the three CSs which represent songwriters, music publishers and record companies. As with statutory licences, the breadth of the users and the range of licensees of the Australian blanket licences is clear. Although all licences to date concern sound recordings, the Tribunal's powers extend to all types of copyright subject matter. The process by which licences are created is a dynamic one, and its range can be expected to expand.

Key aspects of the Act relevant to blanket licences can be summarised as follows.[77] The relevant CS must satisfy the definition of 'licensor', but is not a declared CS for these purposes. The key differentiator from an ECL (or a statutory licence) is that its scope is limited to what can be granted by CS members: it does not cover all works which fall within the subject matter of the licence. The effect of an order by the Tribunal approving a licence scheme is that licensees are protected against actions for copyright infringement, and incur debts for licence fees recoverable by the licensor. A licensor CS must allow any relevant copyright owners to become members and receive royalties. Licensors and would-be licensees, and organisations representing them, can refer either a proposed or an existing licence scheme to the Tribunal, which has wide powers as to who can be parties before it. The Tribunal may confirm or vary a licence scheme or proposed scheme, and may substitute a new scheme for the one referred to it. The Tribunal may also make orders concerning reasonableness of charges and conditions in a licence. These last four elements demonstrate that these blanket licences are very different from completely voluntary collective licensing, and involve significant elements of compulsion: statutory immunity against infringement actions; CS 'open membership' obligations; ability of parties other than existing licensees to become parties to disputes; and ability of the Tribunal to change licence terms.

Because these blanket licences are not ECLs, the CS need only distribute licence fees collected to its members. From the perspective of a licensee, such as the operator of a retail outlet, nightclub or gym, they must have confidence that all of the music that they are using is within the repertoire controlled by the relevant CS, if they are to be operating within the terms of the licence, and paying licence fees for all music that they use. Otherwise, as a matter of practice, although not as a matter of law, there would be no difference between these blanket licences and an ECL. These are voluntary collective licences that are located, on our view, close to the dividing line from compulsory licences.

---

[77] This summary draws in part on Lindgren, 'The jurisdiction of the Copyright Tribunal of Australia', [2.1].

### The Public Domain Aspects of Australian Compulsory Licensing

In Australia, statutory licences are one of the largest and most important limitations on the right of copyright owners unilaterally to determine the conditions of use of their works. They are a distinctive part of Australian public rights, crucial to the operation of major intermediary institutions, and benefit large classes of users. The voluntary blanket licences in relation to uses of sound recordings are also of considerable public importance, not as part of the public domain, but on its boundary, and with many similar elements.

Statutory licences in Australia are public domain aspects of works, primarily because copyright owners, whether or not they are members of the relevant CS, have no option but to allow the statutorily permitted uses of their works. Neither the terms nor the fee is set unilaterally by copyright owners or their CSs, because various 'neutral parties' (the Copyright Tribunal, the Minister and the Australian Competition and Consumer Commission) can all have significant roles in setting terms and fees. The conditions of use of works (including the basis of licence fees) in statutory licences are set by the legislature in the Copyright Act, and are therefore set by a neutral party for public interest reasons. Any parties in the relevant class of users, such as libraries, universities and radio stations, are able to benefit from the licence as licensees. End-users of the works in question, such as students, library users and radio listeners as part of the general public, usually benefit indirectly from these licences, so there is a significant element of public benefit to the licences. Copyright owners also benefit a great deal from rights to collect fees for large-scale uses of their work in contexts where individual licensing would not be practicable. CSs benefit from this, and also from exemptions from anti-competition protections. There are, however, always questions concerning whether the licences work equitably in relation to non-members of CSs whose works are in fact used because of the licences.

### Reforms and Conclusions

The Australian Law Reform Commission (ALRC) made various recommendations relevant to statutory licences and orphan works in its 2013 Report 'Copyright and the digital economy',[78] which were subsequently endorsed by the Productivity Commission.[79] Some of these

---

[78] Australian Law Reform Commission, *Copyright and the Digital Economy*.
[79] Productivity Commission (Aus.), 'Intellectual property arrangements', Recommendation 6.2 (orphan works), and re statutory licences, p. 163.

recommendations were enacted in 2017, at least in relation to education licences, including that they should be made less prescriptive concerning how records are kept and payments are calculated. A simple obligation to pay equitable remuneration, by procedures agreed between the relevant parties, or failing agreement, determined by the Copyright Tribunal, was introduced.[80] The ALRC's other recommendations concerning statutory licences, orphan works, and their relationship to free access exceptions, are discussed in Chapter 14.

By making use of two types of licences – compulsory statutory licences that have comprehensive coverage of subject matter, and voluntary collective 'blanket' licences which emerge from existing licensing practices, but do not have comprehensive coverage of subject matter – Australia has developed a complex but flexible approach to licensing that shares some but not all of the features of an ECL. As a result, use of copyright works is available on a large scale in many situations, without the need for negotiation of individual licences. The CS involved, and copyright owner representatives in Australia, generally support the continued operation and reform of these schemes, for the benefits they bring to rights holders.

### 13.4.2 The United Kingdom

Until recently, the UK legislation has included quite a range of compulsory licensing,[81] each relatively narrow in scope, and less significant when compared with those in a country like Australia. Some of these licences are discussed in the following chapter, including where the Secretary of State has made an order regarding lending of works;[82] cable retransmissions of works included in wireless broadcasts;[83] broadcast schedules;[84] broadcast or cable transmission of sound recordings,[85] reprographic copying in educational establishments (providing ECL-like power to extend the scope of an existing licensing scheme)[86] and some other very specific licences.[87] The Secretary of State can impose a compulsory

---

[80] Australian Law Reform Commission, *Copyright and the Digital Economy*, pp. 200–8.
[81] See *Copinger*, 16th edn, chap. 28 for a comprehensive survey.   [82] CDPA (UK), s. 66.
[83] CDPA (UK), s. 73(4).   [84] Broadcasting Act (UK).   [85] CDPA (UK), ss. 135A–H.
[86] CDPA (UK), s. 137. This licence involves a choice between collectively licensing the right or losing the right, in that rights holders outside the collecting society membership are subject to a free use exception. It is therefore a hybrid of mandatory collective administration and a free exception. A similar approach has been taken in New Zealand.
[87] These miscellaneous licences include where copyright has lapsed but is revived by the EU Term Directive; documents embodying a design in existence on 1 Jan 1989; works of 'enemy origin'; and where there are statutory powers in relation to competition held by the Office of Fair Trading, Competition Commission or Secretary of State which require

licence in relation to reprographic copies made for the purposes of instruction by educational establishments, where previous recommendations concerning licensing have not been followed.[88]

Some compulsory licences (for example, licences concerning lending of works, or the above-mentioned reprographic licences) cannot be ordered by the Secretary of State if there is in force a voluntary licence scheme which has been certified by the Secretary of State as one that 'enables the works to which it relates to be identified with sufficient certainty by persons likely to require licences', and 'sets out clearly the charges (if any) payable and the other terms on which licences will be granted'.[89] In other words, the existence of a certified voluntary licence stops a compulsory licence being ordered.

From 2014, the UK has introduced two new compulsory licences: a potentially very broad ECL scheme applicable to all types of works: [13.5.3], and a similarly broad compulsory licence, available on application, for orphan works: [14.2.6]. The UK also introduced a permitted use scheme (with contingent liability for compensation) for use of orphan works by cultural heritage institutions: [14.2.6]. The UK does therefore now make reasonably broad use of compulsory licences or other remunerated schemes.

The statutory licence allowing 'cover versions' (recordings of musical works previously recorded with the owner's consent), first included in the 1911 Act, was not included in the 1988 Act, as it was considered that risks of monopolistic practices no longer existed.[90]

### 13.4.3 The United States

Compulsory licences are significant in the United States in relation to many aspects of the entertainment industries, but unlike many other countries they are not significant in relation to education or cultural institutions such as museums or libraries. The US free use exception for 'fair use' will in some cases allow what in other countries would be covered by compulsory licences. The main compulsory licences in the United States[91] concern 'cover versions' of musical works in sound recordings already distributed to the public, whether by physical recordings, permanent downloads or ringtones,[92] TV and radio public

---

the exercise of powers in relation to conditions in licences or refusal to issue licences: *Copinger*, 16th edn, [28-04].

[88] CDPA (UK), s.141.   [89] CDPA (UK), s.143.   [90] *Copinger*, 16th edn, [28-04].
[91] Parts of this summary are derived from Strong, *The Copyright Book: A Practical Guide*, 6th edn, chap. 7: 'The Compulsory Licences'.
[92] 17 USC §115

(non-commercial) broadcasting of a very limited range of works (published non-dramatic musical works and certain published artistic works),[93] satellite transmission of TV broadcasts,[94] retransmission of broadcasts by cable systems,[95] subscription digital audio transmission,[96] and non-subscription digital audio transmission,[97] including Internet radio but not including background music for other commercial transactions. All of these licences are subject to very complex conditions.[98]

In general, these licences allow industry organisations to negotiate voluntarily to set licence terms and fees, in the absence of which agreement the provisions of the compulsory licence will apply. The determination of fees payable, and some other matters, will then be made by the Copyright Office or the Copyright Royalty Judges. With some licences, royalties may be held by the Copyright Office in escrow, and divided between classes of recipients by the Copyright Royalty Board. Closely related to these compulsory licences is the so-called 'digital audiotape licence', which is a levy on the sales of both digital audio recording equipment and recording media, with royalties paid by the Copyright Office. Royalties are distributed to affected copyright owners 'using the same rough justice as already applies to cable royalties and the like'.[99]

## 13.4.4 China[100]

In China the Copyright Law 2010 allows specified uses of certain works without the prior consent of the authors or owners of rights, but subject to the obligation to pay remuneration.[101] China has at present five approved[102] copyright CSs, also called 'collective management organizations' (*jítǐ guǎnlǐ zǔzhī*). They are regarded as 'non-profit' social organisations,[103] but their establishments and operations are subject to the approval and management of the National Copyright Administration of China (NCAC),[104] unauthorised CCSs are

[93] 17 USC §118    [94] 17 USC §119    [95] 17 USC §111    [96] 17 USC §114(d)(2)
[97] 17 USC §114(d)(1)    [98] For a survey, see Strong, *The Copyright Book*, chap. 7.
[99] *Ibid.* 222.
[100] This section is based on Li and Greenleaf, 'China's copyright public domain', 147–80, Part II (13), where further details may be found.
[101] In accordance with Article 22 of the Implementing Regulations (China), the NCAC is to establish interim regulations, and eventually more permanent standards, concerning remuneration for statutory licences.
[102] Music Copyright Society of China (MCSC); China Copyright Society of Written Works (CCSWW); Audio-Visual Copyright Association (AVCA); China Film Copyright Association (CFCA); and China Photographic Association (CPA)
[103] Copyright Law (China), Art. 8(2).
[104] Regulations on Collective Management of Copyright (China), Arts. 3 and 5.

## 13.4 National Applications of Statutory Licences 419

prohibited,[105] and foreign CSs are subject to the approval of the NCAC and registration with the SAIC.[106] Their fee schedules are subject to the approval of the NCAC.[107] It is common for China's compulsory licences to include provision for copyright owners to 'opt out' of the licence by notice.

The main compulsory licences in current use cover: compulsory and distance education; free access publication 'to the public in rural areas'; reprinting items in newspapers and periodicals; and a statutory licence for State-commissioned software.[108] One unusual licence, proposed for reform, allows continuing use of infringing software under some circumstances, on payment of a licence fee.[109]

The 2014 draft Revisions of the Copyright Law published by the State Council,[110] with an explanatory document,[111] propose the introduction of significant new types of compulsory licences for orphan works: [14.2.9], and an extended collective licence (ECL) in relation to karaoke establishments. A consistent set of administrative provisions is proposed to apply to all existing and proposed licences, requiring conformity to three conditions: filing details with the corresponding CS before the first time of use; indicating details of the author, the work, and its source (if possible); paying use fees, within one month of using a work, either directly to the rights holder or to the CS on their behalf, according to remuneration standards formulated by the State Council. Such details filed, and fees paid, must be made searchable by the CS. The proposals

---

[105] Regulations on Collective Management of Copyright, Arts. 6, 41, 44; Implementing Regulations on the Copyright Administrative Punishment, Art. 3(4).
[106] Reply of the NCAC to the Inquiry from Hainan Provincial Copyright Administration Regarding the Issues of Copyright Licenses, No. 22, 4 June 2003.
[107] Regulations on Collective Management of Copyright (China), Arts. 7(4), and 9.
[108] See Law for Advancement of Science and Technology 2007 (China), Art. 20 (allowing a computer program developed in a project funded by state funds to be used, free of charge, for national security, national interests or public interests by the state or by a party licensed by the state).
[109] Under the Software Regulations (China), software end-users are strictly liable for infringement for using pirated software. However, they can continue to use the pirated copy after paying a fee to the copyright owner if they can prove that ceasing to use it would cause them serious harm. Proposed reforms will discontinue the licence for illegal software provision, although such users will still not be liable to pay compensation for past uses.
[110] 'Copyright Law of the People's Republic of China' (Revision draft for solicitation of comments), available from China Law Translate (dated 6 July 2014) http://chinalaw translate.com/prc-copyright-law-revision-draft-for-solicitation-of-comments/?lang=en ('2014 Draft Revision').
[111] State Council (China), 'Explanatory document concerning the 2014 Draft Copyright Law, 18 June 2014' (unofficial translation by R. Creemers), https://chinacopyrightand media.wordpress.com/2014/06/18/state-council-publishes-new-copyright-law-revision -draft/ ('2014 State Council explanation (China)').

also set out detailed rules on collective-rights management organisations,[112] applicable to both voluntary and compulsory licensing.[113] A State Council agency is given extensive powers to set licence fees and to arbitrate in licensing disputes. Among the State Council's reasons for wanting to reform the Copyright Law are that 'it insufficiently stimulates the vigour of creators; copyright licensing mechanisms and trading rules are not smooth, it is difficult to guarantee that users are able to gain authorization lawfully, conveniently and effectively, and to disseminate and use works.'[114]

Since 2014, progress on enacting a new *Copyright Law* seems very limited. If China does enact reforms which resemble those proposed it will have both strengthened existing provisions and extended its already reasonably broad scope of compulsory licensing.

## 13.4.5 India

Chapter VI 'Licences', in India's Copyright Act 1957, provides an extensive range of compulsory licences. India amended the Act in 1983 'so as to avail of the benefits of the compulsory rights' of the 1971 Paris Appendix,[115] by inserting sections 31A, 32(1A), 32A and 32B, and amending sections 31 and 32 (which have a longer lineage). However, India did not renew its initial declaration, as required under the Paris Appendix.[116] Some of these provisions were expanded significantly when Chapter VI was amended by the Copyright (Amendment) Act 2012 (effective June 2015), particularly by the broadening of some of the provisions beyond 'Indian works'. The 2012 amendments added statutory licences for sound recording 'cover versions', and for broadcasting of works and recordings thereof (ss. 31C and 31D), as found in some other countries: [14.7]. There is also a compulsory licence for the benefit of persons with a disability (s. 31B).

The result is that, at least in theory, India has one of the broadest arrays of compulsory licences of any country. In summary, the main Indian compulsory licences now cover these areas, in order of their legislative appearance: republication, performance and broadcast of works withheld from the public where previously published or performed (s. 31); publication or translation of orphan works, unpublished or published (s. 31A); publication of works by deceased authors in the national interest (s. 31A(6)); publication of works for the benefit of persons with a disability

---

[112] 2014 Draft Copyright Law (China), Arts. 61- 67.
[113] 2014 Draft Copyright Law (China), Art. 61.
[114] 2014 State Council explanation (China): 'Concerning the necessity of the revision'.
[115] Agitha, 'International norms for compulsory licensing and the Indian copyright law', 34 and n. 53, quoting the objects clause of the 1983 Amendment Act.
[116] *Ibid.* n. 53.

(s. 31B); cover versions of published sound recordings (s. 31C); broadcasting of published literary and musical works and sound recordings (s. 31D); translations of literary or dramatic works, and their publication, where there is no translation or it is out of print (s.32(1)); translations for the purpose of teaching, education or research, where there is no translation or it is out of print (s. 32(1A)); reproduction and publication of works, not available to the public, for systematic instructional activities (s. 32A). Most of these licences are discussed in Chapter 14.

The Copyright Board[117] plays a key role in the administration of compulsory licences. Its responsibilities include adjudication of disputes relating to the grant of compulsory licences in respect of republication of works withheld from the public; publication of 'orphan works'; translation and publication of translations of works; and publication of works for 'systematic instructional activities'. The Board has existed since enactment of the 1957 Act, but was a part-time body until 2012 amendments[118] provided for a full-time Board,[119] not yet appointed. There are no provisions for appeals against the Board's decisions, but judicial review is available.[120] Because the major changes to the compulsory licence provisions have only been in force since June 2015, it is too early to assess how widespread will be their uses, or how the Board and the courts will interpret key terms.

## 13.5 Extended Collective Licensing (ECL) Systems

Extended collective licensing (ECL) systems are related closely to other forms of compulsory licences, but have significant differences. We consider them to be part of the copyright public domain, despite these differences. The Nordic countries (Denmark, Finland, Iceland, Norway and Sweden) first developed extended collective licensing, also known as the Extended Repertoire System (ERS), in the 1960s, originally in relation to broadcasting but later expanding to many other subject matters. The basic principles of an ECL system are as follows.[121]

---

[117] Copyright Board (India) website http://copyright.gov.in/frmCopyrightBoard.aspx.
[118] Copyright (Amendment) Act, 2012 (India), which came into force on 21 June 2015.
[119] Copyright Act 1957 (India), s. 11 now provides for a Chairman and two other members, with headquarters in Delhi.
[120] R. Singh et al., *Iyengar's Commentary on The Copyright Act* (7th edn, Universal Law Publishing Company, 2010), p. 86.
[121] This summary draws on Riis and Schovsbo, 'Extended collective licenses and the Nordic experience'; D Gervais, 'Collective management of copyright', chap. 1 in Gervais (ed.), *Collective Management of Copyright and Related Rights*, 23–9; T. Koskinen-Olsson and V. Sigurdardóttir, 'Collective management in the Nordic countries', chap. 8, *ibid.* 249–53; Wikipedia, 'Extended collective licensing', 'ECL in Nordic countries' https://en.wikipedia.org/wiki/Extended_collective_licensing#ECL_in_Nordic_countries.

A CS representing a substantial number of rights holders[122] voluntarily negotiates with a class of users the conditions and fees for licensing particular rights in relations to works owned by its members. The ECL legislation in force in Nordic countries then allows the CS to obtain 'a legal extension of the [CS]'s repertoire to encompass non-member rights-holders',[123] and their works. 'It is thus a basic feature of the [Danish] model that the *Copyright Act* does not affect the concrete ECL agreements but only "extends" such agreements to unrepresented rights holders'.[124]

This 'extension' applies to those non-members of the CS in the same country, those overseas and those deceased ('unrepresented rights holders').[125] A variety of legal mechanisms have been used to achieve this, in the Nordic countries and elsewhere.[126] The ECL law provides legal protection against legal actions by these unrepresented rights holders to both the user of the works licensed, and to the CS (for authorising such uses). The unrepresented rights holders are only entitled to take action against the CS to the copyright Tribunal about the remuneration agreed in the ECL agreement, or (at least in theory) to demand an individually calculated fee.[127]

ECL laws require the CS to treat unrepresented rights holders the same as their members, particularly in relation to remuneration. However, there are many factors mitigating against this in practice. It may be extremely difficult for foreign rights holders, including representatives of deceased rights holders, to be aware that their works are being used, or make effective claims for remuneration.[128] In relation to orphan works, payments that would be due to unknown rights holders are used for the benefit of members of the (national) CS. Riis and Schovsbo argue

> that in various situations foreign rights holders do not receive any remuneration for the use of their work under ECL. Remuneration is distributed to foreign organizations only if the organization that administers the ECL has entered into a so-called A-agreement with the foreign organization and that is the case for only a limited number of foreign organizations.[129]

---

[122] Now a legal requirement in all Nordic countries: see Koskinen-Olsson and Sigurdardóttir, 'Collective management in the Nordic countries', 254.
[123] Gervais, 'Collective management of copyright', 24.
[124] Riis and Schovsbo, 'Extended collective licenses and the Nordic experience', 5.
[125] *Ibid.* 4.
[126] For the range of alternatives, see Koskinen-Olsson and Sigurdardóttir, 'Collective management in the Nordic countries', 252–3.
[127] Riis and Schovsbo, 'Extended collective licenses and the Nordic experience', 5.
[128] *Ibid.* 19.
[129] *Ibid.* 20; see n. 11 noting that the Danish organisation Copydan has reciprocal A-agreements only with CSs in Australia, Canada, Sweden, the United States, Spain, the UK, Ireland, Italy and Germany.

## 13.5 Extended Collective Licensing (ECL) Systems

ECL laws sometimes provide that unrepresented rights holders can opt out and exclude their works from an ECL (in Finland, for example[130]), but although this is often assumed to be a standard feature of an ECL, Riis and Schovsbo insist that it is not.[131] Also, in practice, if unrepresented rights holders are unaware that their works are being used in an ECL, they will not opt out, so the effect is one of compulsory use.[132]

CSs participating in ECL schemes must be approved by government (except in Sweden), and there is provision for mediation (and arbitration) of disputes between a CS and licensees, but there is no need for a Tribunal or other body to approve the terms of each ECL scheme, or power to insert alternative sets of terms.

The scope of ECL varies between Nordic countries, and may cover many specific areas, as illustrated below. However, commencing with Denmark in 2008, 'general ECL provisions for a delimited area' have been introduced, allowing potential users to negotiate with a CS in a particular field, and then to apply for the extension effect to operate.[133] New legislation is therefore not needed. The effect of this 'general ECL rule' in Article 50(2) of the Danish Act has been, according to Riis and Schovsbo, that 'all areas of copyright licensing which involves a multitude of rights holders may fall prey to ECL agreements'.[134]

In Denmark, the uses of ECL have been broadened to encompass the following:[135] reproduction within educational institutions or by business enterprises; digital reproduction by libraries; recordings of works in broadcasts for the visually impaired etc.; reproduction of works of art which have been made public; broadcasts by certain national Danish TV companies; broadcast by certain national TV companies of works in their archives; cable retransmission to more than two connections; and 'other forms of use' within specific areas covered by an agreement between an organisation which represents a significant number of rights holders and users.

Across all Nordic countries, uses of ECL include reproduction in educational activities, in administration, and in businesses; archives, libraries and museums; various uses in radio and television; uses of visual

---

[130] See *ibid.* n. 65.
[131] *Ibid.* 5, noting certain provisions in the Danish Copyright Act where this is possible, but that it is not in other cases
[132] *Ibid.* 6.
[133] Koskinen-Olsson and Sigurdardóttir, 'Collective management in the Nordic countries', 249.
[134] Riis and Schovsbo, 'Extended collective licenses and the Nordic experience', 6.
[135] This list is from Riis and Schovsbo, with references to the Danish Copyright Act omitted.

art and photography; and certain uses for the disabled.[136] 'Many mass digitisations of in-copyright works by universities and libraries in Scandinavia are based on ECL'.[137] The breadth and significance of ECL is clear.

### ECL and Our Approach to Compulsory Licensing

ECL schemes, as described above, obviously provide advantages to licensees and end-users in making available to them a far wider repertoire, including what might otherwise be orphan works, but they do not fit entirely within our definition of a public domain compulsory licence, because – seen from the perspective of the licensee/user – the terms of the licence and the fees are not necessarily set by any neutral body, but must be negotiated with the rights-owners' representative, the CS. From the perspective of the non-member rights holder, this is of course a compulsory licensing of their work (and one which may benefit them). From the perspective of the licensees, it is a compulsory licence in relation to all of these unrepresented rights holders.

An ECL scheme will usually involve a tribunal or similar body overseeing at least some aspects of the terms and fees of the ECL, and particularly its distribution of revenues, with fair treatment of unrepresented rights holders, before the CS could obtain the extension of the repertoire. This involvement of a neutral body makes ECL much closer to other public domain compulsory licences. The extent of such control appears to be relatively low in Nordic countries in comparison with the powers of the Copyright Tribunal in relation to Australia's blanket licences. However, the effect of ECL in the compulsory licensing of non-member, foreign and deceased rights holders means that ECL cannot be ignored in relation to compulsory licensing.

The fact that ECL involves a CS which does *not* represent non-member, foreign and deceased rights holders, but does negotiate with licensees in relation to their rights, also points to why there needs to be more control of the governance of such licences than other 'voluntary' collective licences. For all these reasons, it makes sense to consider ECL at the same time as other compulsory licences. All of these factors make ECL part of our concept of compulsory licences.

---

[136] Koskinen-Olsson and Sigurdardóttir, 'Collective management in the Nordic countries', 249.
[137] Wikipedia, 'Extended collective licensing', 'Examples of extended collective licensing' https://en.wikipedia.org/wiki/Extended_collective_licensing#Examples_of_Extended_Collective_Licensing.

## 13.5.1 ECL and International Copyright Law

As with some other aspects of compulsory licensing, the compatibility of ECL practices with international treaties is somewhat contentious. ECL approaches will normally have to satisfy the three-step test under Article 9(2), although in areas where Berne specifically allows compulsory licences (such as broadcast rights under Article 11*bis*(2) this is not necessary.

Riis and Schovsbo argue, unconvincingly, that ECL can avoid the three-step test.[138] They argue that most ECL schemes would pass the three-step test in any event, which seems a more realistic approach. In summary, they argue that Nordic ECL schemes are usually sufficiently specific as to constitute 'certain special cases'; they do not conflict with 'normal exploitation' because they are usually initiated by CSs representing rights holders (though they admit these are only some, local, rights holders), and they have now become commonplace in these countries; and there is 'no unreasonable prejudice' to rights holders because they receive remuneration (while admitting that this depends on equitable arrangements for both members and non-members).[139] Ficsor[140] has suggested unjustifiably narrow interpretations.[141]

The basis of ECL schemes is the extension of the repertoire managed by a CS to include content owned by non-members of the CS, which may include content owned by foreign rights owners represented by a CS which has reciprocal relations with the national CS concerned. Ficsor argues that the principle of national treatment in Berne and other treaties must be observed in the operation of ECL schemes, particularly in the distribution of revenues collected.[142] In practice, this 'requirement' is not observed in relation to most foreign rights holders. Riis and Schovsbo argue that 'a closer examination of the copyright organizations' allocation practices reveals that in various situations foreign right holders do not receive any remuneration for the use of their work under ECL', at least

---

[138] Riis and Schovsbo, 'Extended collective licenses and the Nordic experience', 14–15 point out that the three-step test only applies to 'limitations or exceptions to exclusive rights', so if the rights holder's ability to deal exclusively with their works is preserved then the test has no application. So in their view if an ECL provides for opt-outs (as they admit most do not), it can be Berne-compliant without passing the three-step test. Given that 'unrepresented authors', particularly those foreign, missing or dead, will have no realistic opportunity to opt out, this seems like a very artificial approach, as well as one only occasionally applicable.
[139] Riis and Schovsbo, 'Extended collective licenses and the Nordic experience', 16–17.
[140] M. Ficsor, 'Collective rights management from the viewpoint of international treaties, with special attention to the EU "acquis"', chap. 1 in Gervais (ed.), *Collective Management of Copyright and Related Rights*, 66–8.
[141] See the Online Supplement for discussion.
[142] Ficsor, 'Collective rights management', 77–9.

not unless they are in the privileged category of members of CSs from a few foreign countries with 'A-agreement' reciprocity.[143] Furthermore, their royalties are more likely to fall foul of minimum thresholds for payment, and are subject to a typical 10 per cent withholding fee, both of which benefit only the local CS and its members. It seems that in many cases the principle of national treatment, and equitable distribution between all rights holders, are convenient fictions.

ECL systems have been operating for many decades, although mainly in Nordic countries, for almost as long as the three-step test, but have not been challenged under international copyright law, except by the views of a minority of commentators. Arguments that they are not 'limitations or exceptions', or that their validity depends on opt-out provisions or strict observance of equitable distribution to all affected rights holders, are unconvincing. Even on a relatively narrow interpretation of the three-step test, ECL schemes can be argued to be Berne-compliant. To the extent that this compliance is uncertain or unproven, the best answer is that they have stood the test of time, are well regarded, and are expanding. However, under the different standards of EU copyright law, *Soulier and Doke* may imply difficulties.

### 13.5.2 *ECL Provisions in EU Law after Soulier and Doke*

'Even though no EU copyright Directives contain specific ECL-rules EU legislation has embraced both collectivization and ECLs', argue Riis and Schovsbo.[144] The EU Satellite and Cable Directive (1993) did so first by establishing a system of mandatory collective rights management, including a provision (Article 9(2)) which extended such agreements to non-members, like an ECL, in order to prevent 'hold-up problems' in uses of content. Recital 18 to the InfoSoc Directive (2001) says it 'is without prejudice to the arrangements in the Member States concerning the management of rights such as extended collective licences'. Recital 12 to the EU CRM Directive (2014), on collective management of copyright, similarly states that it 'does not interfere with arrangements concerning the management of rights in Member States such as ... mandatory collective management'. Ficsor regards these laissez-faire approaches toward ECL as 'strange lacunae'.[145]

These provisions are now brought into sharp focus by the ECJ's reasoning in *Soulier and Doke* concerning the lack of opportunity for rights

---

[143] Riis and Schovsbo, 'Extended collective licenses and the Nordic experience', 20.
[144] Riis and Schovsbo, 'Extended collective licenses and the Nordic experience', 7
[145] Ficsor, 'Collective rights management', 56.

## 13.5 Extended Collective Licensing (ECL) Systems

holders to consent to use of their works, which can be read as potentially applying to any ECL scheme. An ECL in any EU Member State might therefore now be subject to challenge[146] unless it fits within an exception under Article 5 of the InfoSoc Directive, or the terms of the Orphan Works Directive, or the new ECL limited to some CHI uses of out-of-commerce works, to be created by the proposed Directive on Copyright in the Digital Single Market: [14.3.1]. However, such a result would fly in the face of Recital 18 to the InfoSoc Directive stating that it 'is without prejudice to the arrangements in the Member States concerning the management of rights such as extended collective licences'.

Potentially relevant to all of these issues is the argument that, if authors are considered to be deprived of their ability to authorise the making of acts restricted by copyright, 'this could amount to a deprivation of authors' fundamental right to intellectual property protection, as per Article 17(2) of the Charter of Fundamental Rights'.[147] A notable omission in the *Soulier and Doke* ruling is that the ECJ did not consider fundamental rights issues.

### 13.5.3 Examples of ECL Systems

ECL schemes are being applied in jurisdictions outside the Nordic region in which they originated, both within and outside Europe. The new broad-based ECL in the UK, and some uses outside Europe, are considered here, and, in the following chapter, Germany's ECL limited to ICH uses of 'out of commerce works' [14.3.1], orphan works uses in Hungary [14.2.7], and proposed uses in karaoke establishments in China [14.7].

#### The UK's Broad-Based ECL Provisions

In 2013, UK legislation[148] introduced ECL into its copyright law, allowing CSs approved by the Secretary of State under regulations to operate an ECL scheme, described as 'copyright licences in respect of works in which copyright is not owned by the body or a person on whose behalf the

---

[146] M. Lopez, 'CJEU ruling in Doke & Soulier case emphasizes the need for a real solution to the out-of-commerce problem', COMMUNIA, 23 November 2016 www.communia-association.org/2016/11/23/cjeu-ruling-doke-soulier-case-emphasizes-need-real-solution-commerce-problem/.
[147] E. Rosati, 'The CJEU decision in Soulier: what does it mean for laws other than the French one on out-of-print books?', IPKAT blog, 17 November 2016 ipkitten.blogspot.com.au/2016/11/the-cjeu-decision-in-soulier-what-does.html.
[148] Enterprise and Regulatory Reform Act 2013 (UK), s. 77, inserting ss. 116A–116D in the Copyright, Designs and Patents Act 1988 (UK).

body acts'.[149] The 'ECL Regulations'[150] have been in force since 2014, but as yet no UK collecting society has obtained approval to operate a CS.[151] An ECL scheme can be approved for any type of works, and must specify the 'permitted use' to which it applies,[152] but it seems that such uses should not include uses for which a free use exception already exists.[153] Opt-out provisions must be provided and the scope of the licence is limited to the UK. The ECL Regulations include detailed provisions concerning the external governance of ECL schemes. In the English-speaking world, the UK is now a very significant jurisdiction for compulsory licensing, because it has both ECL schemes and two orphan works provisions (one being a compulsory licence), but it is too early to assess what benefits, and what problems, will arise in practice, so this significance is as yet more theoretical than practical.

*ECL Provisions outside Europe*

Although still very unusual elsewhere, ECL systems are not limited to the EU and Europe. Seng notes that Brunei[154] and Fiji[155] have legislation extending licences offered by a CS to works of non-represented rights holders.[156] In his study of library and archive exceptions in the laws of all 188 WIPO member countries, Crews only found ECL provisions in the Nordic countries and in the UK used for those purposes.[157] Other laws may use ECLs but limit their uses to different purposes, as in the following example of Fiji's use for educational purposes.

Fiji's law illustrates the diversity of arrangements that may apply to such ECL schemes. Where there is an existing licence authorising educational establishments to make reprographic copies of works for the purposes of instruction, and it appears to the Minister that 'works of a description similar to those covered by the scheme or licence are unreasonably excluded from it' so that 'making them subject to the scheme or licence would not conflict with the normal exploitation of the works or unreasonably prejudice the legitimate interests of the

---

[149] CDPA 1988 (UK), s. 116B, and ss. 116C-D (also applying to orphan works schemes).
[150] The Copyright and Rights in Performances (Extended Collective Licensing) Regulations 2014 (UK) ( 'ECL Regulations').
[151] See the Online Supplement for details.
[152] ECL Regulations (UK), reg. 4(2)(a) and (b).
[153] The CDPA (1988) (UK), s. 116A(4) refers to 'licences to do ... any act restricted by copyright that would otherwise require the consent of the copyright owner'.
[154] Copyright Order (Brunei), reg. 148.   [155] Copyright Act (Fiji), s. 159.
[156] 'WIPO Study on the Copyright Exceptions for the Benefit of Educational Activities', 12.
[157] K. Crews, 'Study on copyright limitations and exceptions for libraries and archives: updated and revised'. The database used in the study includes a category 'Extended collective license', which enables checking.

copyright owners', 'the Minister may by order provide that the scheme or licence extends to those works'.[158] The legislation requires the Minister to give notice to 'the copyright owners', the relevant CS ('licensing body'), and educational establishments, all of which have rights to make representations to the Minister before the order is made, to apply for variations of it, to appeal against it to the Copyright Tribunal and to have disputes concerning equitable remuneration settled by the Tribunal.[159] The Fijian legislation also includes a statutory implied indemnity in such licences for reprographic copying, borne by licensing bodies (CSs), in favour of licensees, for any infringements which are within the 'apparent scope of the scheme'.[160] This extended licence is very similar to the provisions for extending licences in similar circumstances in the UK legislation.[161]

## 13.6 Governance of Compulsory Licensing: A Public Domain Perspective

If compulsory licensing, in its various forms, is part of the public domain, this should have implications for the governance of CSs. It affects the interests of numerous parties: authors who are CS members; local authors who are non-members of CSs; foreign authors who are non-members of the relevant CS, but are sometimes represented by a CS with reciprocal relationships; the CSs themselves (in so far as they have interests separate from those of their members); licensees of all types of compulsory licences; and the members of the public who are end-users of such licences. Other parties in this ecology are regulators (including copyright Tribunals or Boards, and competition regulators) and the management bodies of CSs. Since compulsory licensing is the only aspect of the public domain which results in revenue flowing to copyright owners, revenue flows are part of the ecology within which licensing operates. To put it simply, licences flow in one direction in this ecology, and fees flow in the other direction.

A public domain perspective on the management of CSs, in relation to compulsory licensing, starts from the consideration that, since compulsory licences are created by legislation with underlying public

---

[158] Copyright Act (Fiji), s. 159(2).
[159] Copyright Act (Fiji), ss. 159, 160 and 161, respectively.
[160] Copyright Act (Fiji), s. 162, stated more specifically as applying 'if the scheme or licence does not specify the works to which it applies with such particularity as to enable a licensee to determine whether a work falls within the scheme or licence by inspection of the scheme or licence and the work'.
[161] CDPA (UK), s. 137.

interest motivations, some aspects of CS operation have potential to harm the public interest and the public domain – or at least not to maximise those interests. We argue that each CS administers *part* of the public domain: some public rights in some works. The governance of such compulsory licences, including at least some aspects of the operation of CSs, should therefore take into account the interests of parties other than members of CSs, including those of non-members, licensees and public end-users of licensed content. Such perspectives are considered only rarely. For example, the EU Directive on Collective Management of Copyright 2014 has aims limited to 'ensuring that rightsholders have a say in the management of their rights', and therefore does not take a public domain perspective. Nor does a 2017 review underway in Australia.[162]

The main question we ask is how these other interests can be best, or even adequately, protected? Is it sufficient to have 'top-down' protections through requirements in legislation, codes of conduct for CSs (possibly mandatory), or periodic reviews by supervisory bodies? To what extent is it necessary to have opportunities for interested NGOs (including 'public domain NGOs' with a particular interest in copyright), or representatives of licensees, to participate in governance structures 'external' to CSs? These can include periodic reviews of the conduct of specific licences, reviews of codes of conduct, or the opportunity to make complaints (both to CSs and to external regulators). Finally, is there any value or justification in 'internal' CS reforms, for representatives of public domain interests being required on the management bodies of those CSs that administer part of the public domain? Substantive issues affecting all parties include whether the expenses to collection ratio of the CS is low enough. Comprehensive discussion is not possible here.[163]

## 13.7 Conclusions: A Flexible and Important Part of the Public Domain

We have seen that the core reason compulsory licences (or remunerated exceptions) are part of the public domain is that they require copyright owners to allow what would otherwise be copyright infringements. With ECLs, this compulsion applies to large groups of copyright owners,

---

[162] Bureau of Communications and Arts Research (Aus.), 'Discussion Paper: Review into the efficacy of the Code of Conduct for Australian Copyright Collecting Societies', August 2017, 22–4.
[163] See the Online Supplement for examples of how such issues have been dealt with in Australia.

## 13.7 A Flexible and Important Part of the Public Domain

although not for all, but that is enough. Although fees are paid to copyright owners (though, in practice, probably not all of them), the fees and other licence conditions may be determined by a neutral body, and do not discriminate between eligible licensees. Such licences are always subject to conditions, and may be limited to certain classes of licensees, both matters being neutrally determined. Some licences may allow copyright owners to opt out. None of these variations detracts significantly from the core public domain feature of compulsory licences, according to our approach: they enable copyright works to be used without first obtaining the permission of the copyright owner. They enable freedom of use, but not free use.

Brennan suggests that compulsory licensing is more likely to represent good public policy if it is responsive to an actual need, can be effectively administered without excessive cost to rights holders, and enforceable against those obliged to pay the royalty or fee.[164] We would add that it should result in an equitable distribution of royalties to affected rightsholders.

The general structure of the two main types of compulsory licences – extended collective licences (ECLs) and statutory licences – has been shown to have many common features, with their main differentiating factor being that ECLs originate from voluntary proposals to license by copyright owners represented by a CS (even though they are subsequently created by legislation or a tribunal). Both ECLs and statutory licences allow use of works owned by copyright owners not represented by the CS. Both share the problems of ensuring that such unrepresented rights holders are compensated for use of their works.

International law places fewer impediments against countries enacting compulsory licensing schemes than might be assumed. The Berne Convention specifically permits certain remunerated use exceptions to copyright, as does the Rome Convention. However, the most important source of justification for compulsory licences is Berne Article 9(2) and the three-step test. Each step may readily be satisfied for a wide range of licensing purposes, but difficult borderline cases will still arise. No compulsory licence has been challenged before the WTO. EU law has also given support to the use of remunerated exceptions, requiring them for some purposes, and making it clear that Member States have a choice between free use exceptions and remunerated exceptions. With all compulsory licences, requirements for 'equitable remuneration' or 'fair compensation', whether express or implied, must be observed but these do not provide major hurdles if carried out in good faith.

---

[164] Brennan, 'The first compulsory licensing of patents and copyright': 'Conclusions'.

ECLs have in effect been endorsed by EU legislation, reflecting that they have been operating for over five decades in parts of Europe, without significant challenge (though subject to the as yet uncertain effect of *Soulier and Doke*). The UK's broad-based and flexible ECL provision, which can be progressively extended to new subject matters and users, has been operative only since 2014, but indicates that ECLs are becoming more widespread, and increasingly used alongside statutory licences. The general schemes for statutory licences in China, India and Australia illustrate the approach to compulsory licensing found more commonly than ECL schemes. The 'blanket licensing' system in Australia shows how voluntary collective licensing schemes can share so many aspects of compulsory licensing that they are on the borderline of compulsory licensing.

When these various forms of compulsory licensing are viewed from the perspective of the public domain, it is apparent that they involve the interests of far more parties than copyright owners (and their CSs) and licensees. For that reason, their governance should be a matter of serious interest to all those who wish to advance and protect the public domain.

This chapter has demonstrated the importance to the copyright public domain of compulsory licences, and their potential flexibility. This is reinforced in the following chapter by examples in the main subject-areas in which their use is common. The significance of compulsory licences does vary considerably between national jurisdictions, from countries at the high end such as the Nordic countries (as ECLs) and Australia (as statutory licences). It is also of growing scope and importance in China and India. Globally, the overall importance of compulsory licensing is increasing.

# 14 Compulsory Licensing – Subject Areas

| | | |
|---|---|---|
| 14.1 | Introduction: Subject Areas of Compulsory Licensing | 433 |
| 14.2 | Orphan Works | 434 |
| 14.3 | Mass Digitisation Licences | 454 |
| 14.4 | Educational Compulsory Licensing | 458 |
| 14.5 | Educational Licences in Developing Nations: The Paris Appendix | 462 |
| 14.6 | Translation Licences | 465 |
| 14.7 | Libraries, Archives, Other Cultural Heritage Institutions (CHIs) and Licensing | 467 |
| 14.8 | Other Subject Areas of Compulsory Licensing | 469 |
| 14.9 | Conclusions: The Underused Potential of Compulsory Licensing | 473 |

## 14.1 Introduction: Subject Areas of Compulsory Licensing

The role of copyright exceptions as the main means for expressly balancing the rights of copyright owners and the public interest in permission-free uses of works finds expression both in free use exceptions [12.1] and in remunerated exceptions, or 'compulsory licensing' as we refer to them in general terms. The previous chapter explained the main types of compulsory licences [13.2.2], particularly statutory licensing and extended collective licences (ECLs), and the role that collecting societies (CSs) play in both. The recent focus of WIPO's Standing Committee on Copyright and Related Rights (SCCR) on exceptions, has resulted in only one binding agreement, the Marrakesh Treaty for visually impaired persons and persons with print disabilities, but work on other possible treaties continues: [12.1]. Some compulsory licences are specifically allowed under international law. Others need to be justified under Berne Convention[1] Article 9(2) and the three-step test, but this must be

---
[1] Full titles and citations of all international agreements are in the Table of International Instruments.

considered against the constraints on enforceability and acceptance of national variations in international copyright law: [5.7] and [13.3].

This chapter examines a selection of the main subject areas in which compulsory licensing is used, but, as with free-access exceptions, it is not possible to cover all subject areas. Much of the chapter concerns approaches to orphan works, and licences for mass digitisation projects. We also discuss compulsory licensing in relation to: education and translation (including special provisions applicable only to developing countries); cultural institutions; and works unavailable to the public. Examples selected demonstrate the variety of approaches taken in national laws. As with free use exceptions, for each category covered, we consider any effect of international copyright law, give examples of the exceptions from individual jurisdictions and conclude with any implications for the copyright public domain. Brief mention is made of other areas of compulsory licensing.

## 14.2 Orphan Works

'Orphan works' are those works protected by copyright where the rights holders are either unknown or, if known, unable to be located. The category includes where authors or their assignees are known to be dead but it is impracticable to identify or locate those who have succeeded to the rights to their works. It also includes those works where it is not known where or when the author died so it is not possible to determine whether the copyright term has expired.

### 14.2.1 Orphan Works Problems

The principal problem caused by orphan works is that of 'blockage' of uses of the work by third parties, because they cannot identify a rights owner with whom they could negotiate a licence to use the work. The problem, as Favale et al. describe it is:

> that people refrain from using them, as for example for inclusion in another work, or for digitization and distribution over the internet, for fear of liability. This is how mass digitisation projects aimed at preserving cultural heritage and granting unprecedented access to forgotten works are facing a gridlock.[2]

Even where potential users have a high degree of confidence that a work is no longer within copyright, or that an unidentifiable or non-locatable

---

[2] M. Favale, F. Homberg, M. Kretschmer, D. Mendis and D. Secchi, 'Copyright, and the regulation of orphan works: a comparative review of seven jurisdictions and a rights clearance simulation', CREATe working paper 2013/7 (July 2013) https://zenodo.org/record/8377/files/CREATe-Working-Paper-2013-07.pdf.

rights owner would have no objection to the proposed use and would probably welcome it, fear of liability is significant, because its consequences are so uncertain, potentially involving damages, litigation costs (including potentially the other party's costs), and destruction or cessation of products or processes using the work.

There is consensus about the significance of the problem, variously described as 'the starkest failure of the copyright framework to adapt' (Hargreaves Report)[3] and 'perhaps the single greatest impediment to creating new works' (US Copyright Office report).[4] The potential magnitude of the problem supports such comments. For example, UK impact assessments have estimated that orphan works amount to at least 20 per cent of the collections of its major cultural institutions,[5] or up to 50 million orphan works.

Elements of international copyright law which exacerbate the extent of orphan works problems include: the long minimum lengths of copyright terms; the extensions of terms by bilateral and multilateral treaties; the prohibition of formalities (such as registration) for subsistence of copyright (which would assist identification and perhaps location of rights holders); and the prohibition of a registration requirement after an initial period of protection, as a condition of copyright continuing.

*14.2.2 Orphan Works Schemes and the Public Domain*

Orphan works schemes fit within the public domain because, under all variations, licensees are able to use works without obtaining the permission of a copyright owner, and the conditions under which they do so are set by a neutral body (an official licensing body, or the legislature) which balances the interests of the parties. The unusual factor is that, in some jurisdictions, the licence obtained may be contingent upon the rights holder not reappearing. Such a reappearance may result in the licence terminating and the full exclusive rights applying once again. At that point, the work's public domain aspects as an orphan work cease. Most works classified as orphans remain so, with few ever 'reclaimed' by reappearing rights owners. This possibility needs to be reflected in our

---

[3] Hargreaves, *Digital Opportunity: A Review of Intellectual Property and Growth* ('Hargreaves Review'), 38

[4] US Copyright Office, 'Orphan works and mass digitization: a report of the register of copyrights', June 2015, p. 1, quoting Congressional testimony by M. Donaldson of the International Documentary Association.

[5] See Favale et al., 'Copyright, and the regulation of orphan works', 6–8 for tables from Department of Business, Innovation and Skills (UK), 'Impact Assessment BIS1063, Orphan Works', 15 June 2012, on which this estimate is based.

full definition of the public domain, but is not a reason to exclude orphan works schemes from it.

Limited liability orphan works schemes (no licensing, but limited remedies) are within our concept of the public domain, because users are free to use works without obtaining unobtainable permission, and free of the normal liabilities for infringement of copyright, if they have conducted a diligent search and complied with other conditions. By legislation, copyright owners no longer have all of their remedies against infringement as copyright owners, but must accept reasonable compensation, determined by arbitration if necessary.

*Compulsory Licences and ECL Schemes Overlap with Orphan Works Schemes* All statutory licences, and ECLs, will allow use of some orphan works, because they allow use of all subject matter covered by particular schemes (usually with a CS as licensor). However, because they only allow uses of all works in particular categories for particular purposes, they are not general solutions to orphan works problems. They do not usually allow reappearing rights holders to claim compensation as such (as may occur with orphan works schemes), but may allow them to claim a share of past distributions, according to the rules governing the CS concerned. These regimes and their distribution mechanisms must be kept in mind in any discussion of the position of orphan works within a jurisdiction: Chapter 13. Where they exist, they are a part of the available public domain solutions to orphan works problems.

### 14.2.3 *International Law and Orphan Works*

Although orphan works problems are exacerbated by aspects of international copyright, there are likely to be fewer difficulties under Berne Article 9(2) in justifying compulsory licences that focus on orphan works than there are for some other categories of works. If orphan works schemes do require credible steps (diligent searches) to determine that rights holders are in fact not identifiable or not locatable, then it is easier to show that such a licence is the only way to make the works usable by potential licensees, and to provide remuneration to rights holders who are subsequently identified or located. Other potential issues in relation to the three-step test include the provision of fair remuneration to foreign rights holders, and the continuation of licences (or revival of exclusive rights) if and when a rights holder reappears.

## 14.2 Orphan Works

*Unpublished Works, Compulsory Licences and Orphan Works* Berne Article 9(2) makes no reference to the works within its scope being published or otherwise made available to the public. Ricketson and Ginsburg conclude that unpublished works can be included, subject to the three-step test, when the Convention is read as a whole,[6] which implies they can be within both free and remunerated exceptions. Moral rights must, nevertheless, still be observed.[7] However, they consider that exceptions that include unpublished works will rarely satisfy the second step (removing opportunity to exploit), and will find it impossible to satisfy the third step (deprivation of opportunity to divulge).[8] We query the applicability of these factors where authors are missing or deceased, particularly if a diligent search has been undertaken which would, if successful, have provided an opportunity to exploit or to refuse publication. Some types of compulsory licences dealing with orphan works, such as museum collections of century-old letters from soldiers or complaints to organisations, are likely to include unpublished works still in copyright, and this may be a significant part of their value.

### 14.2.4 EU Orphan Works Directive 2012 – A Solution for Cultural Institutions?

Following the 2010 'Digital Libraries Initiative', EU institutions developed proposals,[9] including a Commission draft Directive and 'impact assessment' working paper in 2011,[10] which rapidly became the EU Orphan Works Directive of 2012. The Commission considered and rejected other options including a general ECL solution which was rejected because it lacked a diligent search requirement; provided no mechanism for mutual recognition of orphan works across EU countries; and had uncertain fee mechanisms which might result in very large licensing fees payable by cultural institutions.[11]

The Directive required EU Member States to legislate by 29 October 2014 to provide for a permitted use exception, following a diligent search, with a contingent liability for fair compensation to reappearing rights

---

[6] Ricketson and Ginsburg, *International Copyright and Neighbouring Rights*, [12.28].
[7] *Ibid.* [12.30].  [8] *Ibid.* [12.29].
[9] For summary histories of EU developments, see Favale et al., 'Copyright, and the regulation of orphan works', 30–2; US Copyright Office, 'Orphan works and mass digitization', 19–22.
[10] EU Commission Staff Working Paper, 'Impact assessment on the cross-border online access to orphan works', Accompanying the Proposal for a Directive of the European Parliament and of the Council on certain permitted uses of orphan works, COM (2011) 289 final (24 May 2011) ('EU Impact Assessment').
[11] EU Impact Assessment, 27–9.

holders. The exception applies only to the use of some categories of orphan works for some purposes (making available to the public, and reproduction 'for the purposes of digitisation, making available, indexing, cataloguing, preservation or restoration')[12] by specified types of public institutions,[13] and only in relation to their public interest missions. By February 2015, twenty of the twenty-eight EU Member States had legislated.[14] This EU-wide scheme is now a significant element in the global approach, adding international reciprocity via its mutual recognition requirement.

The Directive does not therefore require Member States to legislate a general solution, as it does not provide for uses of orphan works by individuals, or by commercial organisations, or for purposes beyond those listed. Some existing legislation in EU states, like ECL regimes [13.5], may already provide some of the elements required by this Directive, and be modifiable to comply with it.

The Directive sets out how 'orphan work status' is to be determined, by providing that:

> A work or a phonogram shall be considered an orphan work if none of the right-holders in that work or phonogram is identified or, even if one or more of them is identified, none is located despite a diligent search for the rightholders having been carried out and recorded in accordance with Article 3.[15]

Article 3 sets out a diligent search procedure, which need only be carried out where the work is first published or broadcast. A work found to be an orphan work in one Member State shall be considered to be an orphan work in all Member States, and may be used and accessed in any of them,[16] so national legislation must provide for this. The mechanisms of identification and location are to some extent specified by the Directive,[17] and otherwise left to Member States.

No tribunal or approval process is specified by the Directive, this being left to Member States. Some laws, such as in the UK's 'permitted uses' scheme, do not require licences, so national approaches can take the form of a specific limited liability scheme, where the remedies are limited to 'fair compensation' as understood in EU law (see [13.3.2]).

---

[12] Orphan Works Directive (EU), Art. 6(1).
[13] Orphan Works Directive (EU), Art. 1(1): 'publicly accessible libraries, educational establishments and museums, as well as by archives, film or audio heritage institutions and public-service broadcasting organisations ...'.
[14] K. Herlt, 'ACE survey on the implementation of the Orphan Works Directive', Project FORWARD, 3 April 2015 (Project initiated by Association of European Film Archives and Cinematheques (ACE)). The exceptions were Cyprus, Portugal, Luxembourg, Poland, Belgium, Romania, Slovenia and Lithuania.
[15] Orphan Works Directive (EU), Art. 2(1).   [16] Orphan Works Directive (EU), Art. 4.
[17] Orphan Works Directive (EU), Art. 3(1)–(5).

## 14.2 Orphan Works

However, states must collaborate to establish one EU-wide database of works affected, 'diligent searches', and uses made of works by each institution.[18] This database, which has been established at EUIPO,[19] sometimes referred to as the 'OHIM database',[20] may be used as evidence that a work is an orphan work in all Member States. It could also be used by those rights holders who have succeeded in 'putting an end to the orphan work status' of a work[21] in order for them to proceed to obtain the 'fair compensation' for the prior use of their work which Member States must provide.[22] However, registration, or lack of it, has no legal impact on the orphan status of a work.

*Effectiveness of the Directive*  One analysis of the Directive's implementation, by the film sector, considers that it 'goes more or less smoothly [and in general] the law has been transposed in the spirit of the Directive'.[23] Their survey showed that national legislation required diligent searches to use sources 'almost the same' as those listed in the Directive, often literally, but sometimes in more detail. The study concluded that Denmark was a 'best practice example' because 'no binding list is specified and beneficiaries can decide for themselves' what should be consulted.[24]

Nevertheless, commentary[25] on a 2016 preliminary analysis of the operation of the Directive in three countries (the UK, the Netherlands and Italy)[26] is less sanguine, claiming to show that the diligent search requirements in the Directive have been implemented by these countries 'in such a way that the cost of undertaking a diligent search is prohibitive'.[27] While this study is perhaps premature, with the Directive requiring transposition only two years earlier, it indicates the need for

---

[18] Orphan Works Directive (EU), Art. 3(6).
[19] European Union Intellectual Property Office (EUIPO), Orphan Works Database https://euipo.europa.eu/ohimportal/en/web/observatory/orphan-works-database.
[20] Office for Harmonisation of the Internal Market (OHIM).
[21] Orphan Works Directive (EU), Art. 5.   [22] Orphan Works Directive (EU), Art. 6(3).
[23] Herlt, 'ACE survey on the implementation of the Orphan Works Directive'.   [24] *Ibid.*
[25] M. Borghi, 'Report backs up the overly burdensome nature of the "Diligent Search" requirement in UK, Italy and Netherlands', Diligent Search website, 9 February 2016 diligentsearch.eu/2016/02/09/endow-research-backs-up-the-overly-burdensome-nature-of-the-diligent-search/; M. Zeinstra, 'Research: Orphan Works Directive does not work for mass digitisation', COMMUNIA, 16 February 2016 www.communia-association.org/2016/02/16/orphan-works-directive-does-not-work/
[26] M. Favale, S. Schroff and A. Bertoni, *Requirements for Diligent Search in the United Kingdom, the Netherlands, and Italy*, EnDow, February 2016.
[27] Zeinstra, 'Research: Orphan Works Directive does not work for mass digitisation': over 210 sources requiring checking in the UK alone, 357 in Italy and 87 in the Netherlands. This may be one cause of only 1,435 works being registered in the OHIM Orphan Works Database, by that time, half coming from one Netherlands database.

further empirical work to determine the effectiveness of legislation, and how bureaucratic impediments must be avoided.

Deazley concludes that while many aspects of the Directive are welcome, the result is 'generally unsatisfactory', considering that only seventy items per month on average for the first thirty months are being lodged in the OHIM database, across all of Europe,[28] and very few CHIs have registered. He identifies the limited scope of works covered, with exclusion of unpublished works and risks of uncertain compensation to reappearing rights holders, as limiting factors.[29]

The purpose of the Directive was limited to providing a partially uniform procedure to assist digitisation projects by CHIs across the EU, rather than to provide a more general legislative solution to orphan works problems. Legislation in individual EU states may go beyond the scope of the Directive, subject to other limits in EU law such as the InfoSoc Directive Article 5.

*Implications of* Soulier *and* Doke *for Orphan Works Schemes*   The application of *Soulier and Doke*'s invalidation of France's 'unavailable books' law [13.3.5] to schemes limited to orphan works is questionable. The rationale of *Soulier and Doke*, the protection of the rights of authors to consent to third party uses of their works, is understandable in relation to the broader class of 'unavailable' or 'out-of-print' works. However, it makes little substantive sense when applied only to the narrower class of orphan works, because by definition the consent of the author is impossible to obtain. The French legislation was not restricted to orphan works, did not require a diligent search before use of works, although it did imply it in relation to distribution of royalties, and the ECJ never mentioned orphan works or unlocatable rights holders. Nevertheless, it is difficult to see how legislation similar to the French law but limited solely to orphan works would fare any better, as non-locatability cannot be equated with implied consent. Therefore, unless the ECJ distinguishes orphan works from the *Soulier and Doke* reasoning, legislation addressing orphan works problems in EU Member States must be confined to complying with the narrow scope of the Orphan Works Directive, unless it is able to fit within Article 5 limitations or exceptions.

---

[28] R. Deazley, 'Copyright and digital cultural heritage: orphan works', Copyright 101, Copyright Codex, May 2017, p. 7 https://copyrightcortex.org/.
[29] *Ibid.*

## 14.2.5 National Approaches

Orphan works legislation has been enacted with increasing frequency in national jurisdictions, particularly since 2010. Orphan works schemes fall into four main categories: (i) licensing of individual applications relating to specified works by an official body ('official licensing schemes'); (ii) an ECL scheme applying only to categories of works where orphan works are common ('ECL orphan scheme'); (iii) limits on the remedies (but no licences) available against any diligent user concerning any work ('general limited liability scheme'); and (iv) limits on the remedies (but no licences) available against specific institutional diligent users, for specific purposes ('specific limited liability scheme'). The 'limited remedies' could include a requirement of reasonable compensation. We have coined this combination of category names, but others use similar terms for particular categories.[30] Official licensing schemes are by far the most common national approach, followed by ECL orphan schemes. There is, however, at least one operating specific limited liability scheme (in the UK), but general limited liability schemes are, to date, proposals only (in the United States and Australia). These schemes have many common elements.[31]

There have been several orphan works official licensing schemes for some time (Japan (1970); Canada (1988); Korea (2008); Hungary (2008); India (2012); France (2012); Germany (2013); and the UK (2014)). In 2006, a US Copyright Office report proposing a general limited liability scheme stimulated considerable interest internationally, but it has not been enacted, although essentially reiterated in 2015. Australia in 2013 and China in 2014 also proposed laws. The laws of many of the EU countries go beyond the requirements of the EU Directive. These eleven jurisdictions are not a complete list of those with orphan works provisions,[32] but give a reasonable representation of national approaches, adopted or proposed.

*Early Official Licensing Schemes Show Few Results* Two of the earliest schemes involving official licensing systems (Japan and Canada) do not appear to have been very successful; and nor does a similar more

---

[30] For example, Favale et al., 'Copyright, and the regulation of orphan works', 62 refer to 'limited liability' schemes.
[31] See Online Supplement, Chapter 14: 'Common characteristics of orphan works schemes'.
[32] In a 2010 survey by WIPO, Albania, Algeria, Guinea, Ghana, Jamaica and Singapore, and various EU members, claimed to have provisions dealing with orphan works: WIPO, 'Summary of the responses to the questionnaire for survey on copyright registration and deposit systems' (WIPO, 2010), para. 21.

recent scheme in Korea. We discuss them in more detail in the Supplement.[33]

Japan enacted the earliest explicit orphan works legislation in 1970,[34] an official licensing scheme operated by the Commissioner of the Agency for Cultural Affairs (ACA). It has only resulted in eighty-two licences over more than forty years, about two per year, mainly to the National Diet Library, although these licences are often for large numbers of works.[35]

A 1988 amendment to section 77 of Canada's Copyright Act established an orphan works scheme.[36] The Copyright Board is empowered to issue licences to applicants, including setting the licence royalty, and licence term. The Canadian system gives applicants the option to pay the royalties only if the copyright owner reappeared (a contingent royalty), or to pay the royalty up front on approval of the application, and 70 per cent of royalties are paid up front.[37] Such royalties are paid to the relevant Canadian CS. The Board granted 230 licences from 1990 to 2008, about half of all applications.[38] From 1990 to 2016, it made 294 decisions, an average of just eleven per year, but declining to about eight per year since 2008.[39] Almost all decisions have been in relation to a handful of works, typically only one work per decision. Royalties only amounted to CAN$70,000 in the first two decades of the scheme,[40] less than $4,000 per year. These decisions may give certainty to applicants that they would not breach copyright law, but the Act's provisions seem to have done little to address orphan works problems or allow mass digitisation projects.

Korea's orphan works provision,[41] in effect since 2008, is an official licensing system, operated by a Ministry, requiring prior 'considerable efforts' to locate copyright owners before a licence is issued. It does not apply to 'foreigners' works'.[42] As of 2015, only ten licences had been approved,[43] so the Korean system provides little evidence of success.

[33] For discussion of these and other orphan works schemes, see Favale et al., 'Copyright, and the regulation of orphan works'.
[34] Copyright Act 1970 (Japan), s. 67.
[35] See the Online Supplement and Favale et al., 'Copyright, and the regulation of orphan works', part 7, 'Japan'.
[36] Copyright Act (Canada), s. 77.
[37] J. de Beer and M. Bouchard, 'Canada's "orphan works" regime: unlocatable copyright owners and the Copyright Board' [2010] 10(2) *Oxford University Commonwealth Law Journal* 38–9.
[38] *Ibid.* 215–56.
[39] Copyright Board of Canada, 'Decisions – unlocatable copyright owners, de Beer and Bouchard, Canada's "Orphan Works" Regime' www.cb-cda.gc.ca/unlocatable-introuvables/licences-e.html.
[40] de Beer and Bouchard, 'Canada's "orphan works" regime', 38.
[41] Copyright Act (Korea), Art. 50.   [42] Copyright Act (Korea), Art. 50(1).
[43] US Copyright Office, 'Orphan works and mass digitization', 33.

### 14.2.6 United Kingdom – Official Licence Plus Permitted Cultural Heritage Institution (CHI) Use (2014)

The UK introduced two orphan works regulations in 2014, by which it both complied with the EU Orphan Works Directive of 2012 in relation to CHIs[44] and also created a more generally applicable orphan works compulsory licence.[45] The extended collective licensing (ECL) scheme introduced by the UK at the same time (discussed in [13.5.3]) also catches orphan works within the extended repertoire covered by ECL licences, so there are in fact three UK regimes affecting orphan works. The two UK orphan works regulations, together with the ECL regulation, comprise the most sophisticated and comprehensive example of an orphan works scheme in a common law country, and are therefore considered in some detail.

*Compulsory Licence Regulations* The Intellectual Property Office (IPO) is the UK licensing body for the compulsory licence for orphan works. Applicants for an 'orphan licence' must carry out a 'diligent search' (or demonstrate a valid search exists).[46] A diligent search must comprise a 'reasonable search' of relevant sources, and include as a minimum a search of the OHIM database,[47] and the relevant sources for the class of work, as specified in Part 2, Schedule ZA1 of the CDPA.[48] The IPO may also issue guidance on what constitutes a 'reasonable search',[49] and has done so.[50] It is required to take reasonable steps to ensure that the search relied upon is a diligent search.[51] Comprehensive searches of all Schedule ZA1 sources are not required.[52]

Alternatively, an applicant may show that a 'valid' search already exists, comprising either a search accepted by the IPO, on the basis of which an

---

[44] The Copyright and Rights in Performances (Certain Permitted Uses of Orphan Works) Regulations 2014 (UK), in force October 2014 ('Orphan Works Permitted Use Regulations').
[45] The Copyright and Rights in Performances (Licensing of Orphan Works) Regulations 2014 (UK), in force October 2014 ('Orphan Works Licensing Regulations').
[46] Orphan Works Licensing Regulations (UK), reg. 4(1).
[47] The relationship of UK institutions to the EU's OHIM database post-Brexit needs clarification.
[48] Orphan Works Licensing Regulations (UK), reg. 4(2) and (3).
[49] Orphan Works Licensing Regulations (UK), reg. 4(4).
[50] IPO, 'Orphan works diligent search guidance for applicants: guidance on searching for right holders in copyright works to obtain permission to reproduce the work' (IPO, September 2014) www.gov.uk/government/publications/orphan-works-diligent-search-guidance-for-applicants.
[51] Orphan Works Licensing Regulations (UK), reg. 4(9).
[52] For examples of searches and compliance costs, see Deazley, 'Copyright and digital cultural heritage: orphan works'.

orphan licence was granted within the past seven years, or a diligent search of works made public in the OHIM database within the past seven years.[53] Whichever approach an applicant takes, the IPO must maintain a register of the orphan works in respect of which applications are being considered (on the basis of a diligent search), or licences that have been granted or refused.[54] These provisions underline the non-exclusivity of orphan licences, by allowing later applicants to rely upon previous diligent searches.

The licence granted by the IPO may permit only non-exclusive use, within the UK, for seven years or less, and 'has effect as if granted by the right holder'.[55] Licences may be refused by the IPO on any 'reasonable ground' including that the proposed use, as set out in the application, would be inappropriate (for example, due to derogatory treatment).[56] A licence may be granted subject to conditions, and its terms may be varied by the IPO.[57] Licences may be renewed for a further seven years, but applications must be supported by a diligent search,[58] and it seems that this must be a new diligent search rather than reliance on a previous, but still valid, diligent search.

The IPO charges[59] the orphan licensee a 'reasonable licence fee' for the period of the licence, calculated with regard to relevant factors such as fees obtained for similar uses of similar (non-orphan) works, plus additional amounts for its costs, and for processing an application.[60] While licence fees for commercial uses take account of market rates (such as the number of items on which a work is intended to be printed), for non-commercial uses there is a nominal fee of £0.10 per work.[61] Licence fees are to be held in a designated 'ring fenced' account by the IPO.[62] Any licence fees unclaimed by a rights holder after eight years may be applied by the IPO to the operational costs of the orphan works scheme, with any surplus being applied to 'social, cultural and educational activities'.[63]

A rights holder may apply to the IPO, with evidence of ownership of an orphan work, within eight years of an orphan licence being granted, and is

---

[53] Orphan Works Licensing Regulations (UK), reg. 4(5).
[54] Orphan Works Licensing Regulations (UK), reg. 5.
[55] Orphan Works Licensing Regulations (UK), reg. 6(2).
[56] Orphan Works Licensing Regulations (UK), reg. 6(5).
[57] Orphan Works Licensing Regulations (UK), reg. 6(3) and (6).
[58] Orphan Works Licensing Regulations (UK), reg. 8.
[59] Orphan Works Licensing Regulations (UK), reg. 9 and 10(1).
[60] In practice, applications may be for up to 30 works and as many uses as desired, with application fees on a sliding scale from £20 (1 work) to £80 (30 works).
[61] Intellectual Property Office (UK), 'Orphan works: review of the first twelve months' (IPO, 2015), p. 4.
[62] Orphan Works Licensing Regulations (UK), reg. 10(2).
[63] Orphan Works Licensing Regulations (UK), reg. 13.

## 14.2 Orphan Works

entitled to be paid a sum equivalent to the licence fees paid in relation to the work. The licensee is then informed, but entitled to continue use of the work for the unexpired period of the licence, or any notice period included in the licence.[64] The IPO may pay such payments to a rights holder 'as it considers reasonable in all the circumstances' if an application is made later than eight years after grant of the licence.[65]

The IPO is required to report on the operation of the licence scheme annually.[66] In its first report,[67] the Minister stated:

> The first twelve months have provided an incredibly varied range of licences. One licence was for the poem read at the 100 year anniversary of the Battle of Gallipoli in April; others have enabled the republishing of old novels as ebooks. Some licences have provided support for academic research, and other orphan works have featured on TV programmes. There have been licences with a local interest as well as those with national importance.

Despite this limited initial uptake, Deazley sees this licence system as 'more progressive and enabling' than the permitted use exception for CHIs arising from the Directive.[68]

*Permitted Use Exception for Cultural Heritage Institutions (CHIs)*
The Orphan Works Permitted Use Regulations[69] implements the EU Orphan Works Directive. It applies to designated CHIs, namely publicly accessible libraries, educational establishments or museums, archives, film or audio heritage institutions, or public service broadcasting organisations.[70] Ten CHIs registered in the first year of operation.[71] The exception applies to most types of works, except stand-alone artistic works such as photographs, in the collections of CHIs.[72] It also applies to some unpublished (or unbroadcast) works held by CHIs, and made publicly available with the permission of rights holders, if it is reasonable to assume they would not object to the uses allowed by the exception.[73] The exception therefore goes beyond orphan works to encompass some other works in CHI collections (as does the Directive).

---

[64] Orphan Works Licensing Regulations (UK), reg. 12.
[65] Orphan Works Licensing Regulations (UK), reg. 13(3).
[66] Orphan Works Licensing Regulations (UK), reg. 11.
[67] Intellectual Property Office (UK), 'Orphan works: review of the first twelve months'.
[68] Deazley, 'Copyright and digital cultural heritage: orphan works', 12.
[69] Schedule ZA1, 'Certain permitted uses of orphan works' ('Schedule ZA1'), inserted by Orphan Works Permitted Use Regulations (UK), r. 3(5) before Schedule A1 to the CDPA 1988 (UK).
[70] Orphan Works Permitted Use Regulations (UK), reg. 2.
[71] Intellectual Property Office (UK), 'Orphan works: review of the first twelve months', 5.
[72] Schedule ZA1 (UK), para. 2(2), definition of 'relevant work'.
[73] Schedule ZA1 (UK), para. 2(4).

Designated CHIs do not infringe copyright in orphan works provided they only make specified restricted uses of such works in their collections,[74] namely making the work available to the public, or reproducing it for the purposes of digitisation, making available, indexing, cataloguing, preservation or restoration. The CHI does not have to apply to the IPO for a licence, but must make a diligent search for rights holders before a work becomes an orphan work and the CHI can use it.[75] The requirements for a diligent search are specified separately[76] from those for the orphan works compulsory licence, although they require the same Schedule ZA1 list of sources to be used. For this diligent search, the IPO[77] may issue guidance on appropriate sources to consult,[78] but, in contrast with the licence scheme, it does not check the validity of searches recorded with it. Alternatively, the CHI can rely upon the designation of a work as an orphan work in another Member State of the EU,[79] as provided by the Orphan Works Directive, and this can be ascertained from the OHIM database.[80] CHIs making use of orphan works must provide details of diligent searches and uses of orphan works to the OHIM database,[81] in accordance with the Directive. In the first year, fifty-seven records were lodged.[82]

To avoid infringing copyright, a CHI must use orphan works to achieve aims relevant to its public interest mission, and use revenues generated by use of orphan works to digitise such works and make them available to the public.[83]

A rights holder may put an end to the orphan works status of a work by providing evidence of ownership to the OHIM or the first CHI to have established the work's orphan work status. Any CHI that has been using the orphan work must pay 'fair compensation' to the rights holder 'within a reasonable period', with information on how it has been calculated. Either party may apply to the Copyright Tribunal to determine the amount if there is no agreement.[84] This scheme is a specific limited liability scheme, with similarities to the proposals by the US Copyright Office: [14.2.9].

---

[74] Schedule ZA1 (UK), para. 1(1); also CDPA 1988 (UK), s. 44, inserted by Orphan Works Permitted Use Regulations (UK), reg. 3.
[75] Schedule ZA1 (UK), para. 3.   [76] Schedule ZA1 (UK), para. 5.
[77] Technically, the Comptroller-General of Patents, Designs and Trade Marks, for which IPO is an operating name.
[78] Schedule ZA1 (UK), para. 5(4).   [79] Schedule ZA1 (UK), para. 4.
[80] Schedule ZA1 (UK), para. 5(3) then means that no further searches are necessary.
[81] Schedule ZA1 (UK), para. 5(9).
[82] Intellectual Property Office (UK), 'Orphan works: review of the first twelve months', 16.
[83] Schedule ZA1 (UK), para. 6.   [84] Schedule ZA1 (UK), para. 7.

### 14.2.7 Hungary – Multiple Approaches (2008)

Hungary was one of the first EU countries to address orphan works issues, and now does so in four ways, all of which are relevant to the public domain: (i) a free use exception (2003); (ii) an ECL; (iii) an official licensing system (2008); and (iv) an implementation of the Orphan Works Directive for beneficiary cultural institutions (2013).[85] Hungary's approach exemplifies multiple responses to orphan works issues within a jurisdiction. Details are in the Online Supplement. In 2013, Favale et al. concluded that the

> combined system of centrally administered compulsory licensing and extended collective licensing, whilst on the one hand seems to guarantee legal certainty and reward for rights holders, on the other hand seems to be not suitable for mass digitization, and ultimately seems to be rather expensive.[86]

### 14.2.8 Orphan Works Schemes in Developing Countries

In the two most significant developing countries, India in 2012 extended a very limited official licensing scheme, and China is proposing to implement a scheme limited to digital uses but otherwise potentially broad.

*India – Official Licence Scheme Extended to Foreign Works (2012)*
India's Copyright Act 1957, section 31A was previously limited to 'unpublished Indian works', until amendments introduced in 2012 removed both the limitation to Indian works and to unpublished works, effectively making it a new provision. Now the Copyright Board may authorise a compulsory licence if two cumulative conditions are satisfied: (a) a work is 'withheld from the public in India' (whether it is unpublished, or it is published or communicated to the public); and (b) either, the 'author is dead or unknown or cannot be traced' or 'the owner of the copyright ... cannot be found'.[87] The Board may approve a 'licence to publish or communicate to the public such work or a translation thereof in any language', and 'subject to such other terms and conditions as the Copyright Board may determine'.[88] The licence conditions, which are not discussed in detail here,[89] are quite prescriptive, involving advance payment of licence fees, publication of proposed uses, and limits to one

---

[85] The following summaries are derived from US Copyright Office, 'Orphan works and mass digitization', pp. 23–5; and Favale et al., 'Copyright, and the regulation of orphan works', part 2, 'Hungary'.
[86] Favale et al., 'Copyright, and the regulation of orphan works', 24.
[87] Copyright Act 1957 (India), s. 31A.    [88] Copyright Act 1957 (India), s. 32A(4).
[89] Details are included in the Online Supplement.

work per licence. The provision has only been in force since 2015, so any evaluation of effectiveness is as yet premature.

*China – Proposed Orphans Works Reforms for Digital Uses Only (2014)* The 2014 (and most recent) revision draft of China's Copyright Law [13.4.4] proposes an 'orphan works' regime[90] which would apply where users have 'tried their best ... without result' to find the rights holders of works in which copyright has not yet expired, and either (i) 'the identity of the copyright holder is unclear'; or (ii) 'it is impossible to establish contact'. A user would then be permitted to use the work 'in digital form' (but not otherwise) after applying to a body appointed by the State Council administrative copyright management department (and subject to its administrative regulations), and 'posting a use fee'. The proposal, however, says nothing about what is to occur if the copyright holder subsequently appears (including compensation payable from use fees). No CS is involved, only a State Council agency. The State Council explains that this change is 'in order to resolve the reality that under specific circumstances, searching for copyright holders is fruitless but works still need to be used'.[91]

### 14.2.9 United States – Limited liability Proposals (2006 and 2015)

Much international interest in orphan works legislation was provoked by a 2006 Report by the US Copyright Office[92] proposing that if a 'good faith, reasonably diligent search' failed to locate a copyright owner, then use could be made of a work, subject to a form of limited liability to pay reasonable compensation, for commercial use, to a rights holder who subsequently came forward. There would therefore be no monetary liability for non-commercial uses. Injunctive relief would not be available if derivative uses had been made of the work, but could be in other cases 'so long as due allowance is made for any loss caused by reliance upon the remedial limitation'.[93] Despite the Report's influence, its approach has

---

[90] 2014 Draft Copyright Law (China), Art. 51.
[91] State Council (China) 'Explanation of the "Copyright Law of the People's Republic of China" (Submission Version of the Revision Draft)', 6 June 2014 (unofficial translation by Rogier Creemers, 18 June 2014), https://chinacopyrightandmedia.wordpress.com/2014/06/18/state-council-publishes-new-copyright-law-revision-draft/: 'Concerning the limitation of rights', para. 4.
[92] US Copyright Office, 'Report on orphan works: a report of the Register of Copyrights', 2006 www.copyright.gov/orphan/orphan-report.pdf ('2006 Report on orphan works').
[93] D. Brennan and M. Fraser 'The use of subject matter with missing owners: Australian copyright policy options', Screenrights commissioned paper, Communications Law Centre, UTS, 2011.

## 14.2 Orphan Works

not yet been enacted in any country. However, the Australian Law Reform Commission's 2013 proposals are similar.

In 2015, the US Copyright Office revisited the issue,[94] and concluded that its 2006 approach was still preferable for the United States. It rejected official licensing schemes because experience had shown 'they tend to be either rarely used or extremely limited in terms of the scope of users and uses covered'.[95] The Office therefore recommended the introduction of a modified version of the 2008 Shawn Bentley Orphan Works Bill, a limited liability scheme to apply to both commercial and non-commercial uses of works, which had been unanimously passed by the US Senate,[96] plus an ECL scheme for non-commercial mass digitisation projects: [14.7].

In the event of action taken by a reappearing copyright owner, a user would be required to prove that they had undertaken a good faith diligent search without success. Minimum elements of a diligent search would be defined, and it would otherwise be required to be reasonable and appropriate under the circumstances, with the Copyright Office providing Recommended Practices. A US court could take into account a foreign jurisdiction's certification of a diligent search, provided it extended reciprocal treatment to US searches. Users would be required to file a Notice of Use with the Copyright Office, and provide appropriate attribution when works were used. If a reappearing copyright owner filed a notice of claim for infringement, the user would also be required to enter good faith negotiations for reasonable compensation. If these conditions were satisfied, a court would only be able to award reasonable compensation (defined as 'the amount a willing buyer and a willing seller would have agreed upon immediately before the use began'), instead of the normal remedies for copyright infringement (including damages, and costs). Injunctive relief against continued use of the work(s) would only be available in limited circumstances.[97] No monetary compensation would be payable by most non-profit entities for non-profit uses,[98] in effect converting this into a free use exception in such situations, consistent with the Copyright Office's ECL proposal: [14.3.2].

The proposals for international reciprocity of diligent searches, and for filed Notices of Use, are significant innovations that increase the practicality of the proposal. The allowance for both commercial and non-commercial uses means there are no limitations on its scope of application.

---

[94] US Copyright Office, 'Orphan works and mass digitization', 23–5   [95] *Ibid.* 3.
[96] *Ibid.* 40.   [97] *Ibid.* 3–4 (summary of proposals), 50–72 (detailed proposals).
[98] *Ibid.* 4.

*Australian Proposals Similar to the United States (2013)* The Australian Law Reform Commission (ALRC) proposed in 2013 that the issue of orphan works should be addressed by limiting available remedies where a reasonably diligent search (subject to statutory guidelines) has not found a rights holder, provided reasonable attribution has been made in any uses.[99] Australian copyright law does not include any specific provisions concerning orphan works, but they may incidentally be included under other exceptions (for example, s. 200AB: [12.5.3]) and would often fall under other compulsory licences. The ALRC's main proposal, to provide for limited remedies in relation to orphan works,[100] would leave many elements yet to be resolved through further investigation.[101] The ALRC's proposal, like those of the US Copyright Office, have some characteristics of a compulsory licence (potential for payment of fees; possible continuation of use of a work after a rights owner reappears), but wherever a work continues to be an orphan they will operate in effect as a free use exception, with liability for reasonable compensation contingent on the reappearance of a rights holder. There is no government commitment to enact these proposals. The Australian government has announced support for the ALRC approach, but that it will consult further on 'the most appropriate way to limit liability'.[102]

### 14.2.10 Conclusions: Orphan Works and the Public Domain

Orphan works are described as 'the starkest failure of the copyright framework to adapt' and 'perhaps the single greatest impediment to creating new works' [16.1]. They are the most urgent instance where expansions of national public domains are needed, so that copyright law can serve the needs of copyright owners, users and society generally. The significance of the orphan works issue is increasing, due to factors such as the constantly improving technical capacity for mass digitisation projects by institutions, and the growing ability of publishers small and large to create new sources of value, often innovative ones, from orphan works. This means that 'the inability to use orphan works means that their beneficial uses are lost to both users and copyright owners.'[103] However, while the need is clear, the

---

[99] Australian Law Reform Commission, *Copyright and the Digital Economy*, chap. 13.
[100] *Ibid.* 302–7, and summarised on p. 310.
[101] Details are included in the Online Supplement.
[102] Australian Government, 'Response to the Productivity Commission Inquiry', 7.
[103] Australian Law Reform Commission, *Copyright and the Digital Economy*, p. 298

most desirable solution is not, nor is it necessarily uniform between countries.

While elements of international copyright law exacerbate the orphan works problem, there are several potential solutions, including compulsory licence elements, in addition to possible free use exceptions (such as fair use). All four options identified in this chapter have been enacted, or proposed by official bodies, in the past decade: (i) official licensing schemes open to all applicants (Japan, Canada, Korea, Hungary, UK, India, China); (ii) ECL schemes incidentally covering orphans (UK, United States, Hungary, Germany, France and other EU countries); (iii) general limited liability schemes (United States, Australia); and (iv) limited liability schemes for specific institutions (UK permitted uses).

*Official Licensing Schemes* Licensing by an official authority has been adopted, with many variations, in seven of the eleven jurisdictions discussed, including in recent years (China, India and the UK since 2012). One of their common elements, and attractions, is that the liability of licensees is limited to licence fees paid (or owed), when a copyright owner reappears, provided always that a preventative search has been undertaken, thus giving more certainty than a contingent liability to pay 'reasonable compensation'.

Australia's ALRC argued against any official licensing scheme, or one involving up-front payments. It argued that where 'there is no guarantee or little likelihood that a copyright owner will appear', protecting copyright is poor policy,[104] and up-front payments are 'problematic' because the funds collected will not go to a rights holder, but will be 're-distributed to other copyright owners [with] no connection with the orphan work'.[105] This is 'not consistent with copyright's purpose of providing an incentive to create by remunerating the author of a work'.[106] The same argument could apply to schemes such as the UK orphan works licence, where unclaimed funds are used for 'social, cultural and educational activities'.[107]

Although incentive theories are not the only justification for copyright, this objection has weight. Centralised licensing schemes for orphan works

---

[104] *Ibid.* 296, quoting Maria Pallante, Director of the US Copyright Office
[105] *Ibid.* 297: The ALRC rejects arguments from author representatives that 'without upfront payment, the market for other non-orphan works would be harmed', pointing out that where a work is an orphan 'there is little difference between it and one in which the copyright holder would allow free use, such as through a creative commons licence'.
[106] *Ibid.*
[107] This argument has less application to broader statutory licences and ECL schemes where, although some funds collected may be redistributed by a CS, most funds collected do go to CS members, and can therefore be considered as incentives.

can operate without up-front payment of royalties or licence fees (but not without payment of administrative costs by applicants), but the costs of establishing and operating such a licensing system may be disproportionate to the payments received by rights holders.[108] Even small per-item licence fees could easily be prohibitive to licensees for mass digitisation proposals, at least for public and non-profit institutions,[109] and would be exacerbated if periodic renewals were required.[110]

A major objection is that no existing official licence scheme demonstrates clearly that it has delivered use of orphan works on a large scale for diverse applications. Schemes in Japan, Canada, Korea and the UK all have low levels of use. Even so, the elements of certainty provided both to individual applicants (concerning both fees, and that no breach of copyright will occur), and to third parties such as publishers, should not be discounted. The real questions appear to be, first, whether this certainty is provided at a justifiable cost, and, second, could the obstacles of official applications be reduced by other approaches?

*Limited Liability Schemes*   The US Copyright Office proposals, and ALRC proposals, favour a system of liability to pay reasonable compensation, if and when a copyright owner reappears, provided a diligent search has been undertaken. This approach obviates the need for a licensing body. The UK 'permitted use' system for CHIs, subject to a contingent liability for fair compensation but without a diligent search obligation, is also a liability-based scheme. In our view, a general limited liability (compensation) scheme deserves serious consideration, and the 2015 US Copyright Office proposals may present a reasonable starting point.

With such schemes, the likely advantages because of lack of bureaucracy must be offset against the greater uncertainty to users of contingent reasonable compensation, compared with fixed licence fees, and the lack of any official certification that the use is legal. The potential problem of a lack of registers or other records of the use of the orphan works to assist copyright owners find if their works have been used is potentially addressed by the notice requirements in the US 2015 proposals. Similarly, the Australian ALRC proposals could be made to operate more fairly to copyright owners by adding a requirement of notification

---

[108] Australian Law Reform Commission, *Copyright and the Digital Economy*, pp. 299–300.
[109] *Ibid.* 299.
[110] *Ibid.* It is pointed out that Favale et al. ('Copyright, and the regulation of orphan works') found in their study of six jurisdictions that there was 'no systematic recognition of the need for permanent licences'.

to a public register of sufficient details of the work, the missing copyright owner, intended use and user contacts. Such a register could be maintained by a national deposit library, or a government office responsible for copyright, at only a moderate cost, and could possibly be funded by a lodgement fee. Alternatively, the relevant CS could maintain the register. Such a register would assist development of a market to reunite orphan works with their lost owners. There is no logical necessity for such schemes to be coupled with fair use; they can coexist with any system of exceptions.

*ECL Schemes* ECL schemes are not suited for dealing with all orphan works, but may provide a solution for specific categories of subject matter or institutional users, provided they incorporate limiting factors which bring the proposed scheme within the requirements of the three-step test. The EU Orphan Works Directive, the current German legislation and the proposed US legislation are all examples of ECL schemes that support greater uses of orphan works. Because they do not provide a means for all individuals to make justified uses of orphan works, only for specific categories of licensees, ECL schemes are not a generalised solution.

*Hybrid Approaches are Worth Consideration* Expert opinion on the best option for countries to implement is mixed. Gompel and Hugenholtz, for example, considered that the two best approaches were 'the Nordic model of extended collective licensing, and the Canadian system of compulsory licensing'.[111] Favale et al. concluded from their comparative study 'that different regulatory approaches should be taken for commercial and non commercial uses (and users)', and made specific suggestions to improve schemes, but did not reach any general conclusion about whether an official licensing system or a 'liability' system was preferable.[112]

Hungary has implemented a hybrid approach including an official licensing scheme, an ECL for institutional users, a free use exception and the EU scheme for CHIs. The UK has also adopted a combination of approaches: an official licensing system, plus permitted use for CHIs, with a limited liability approach, plus an ECL which would also catch orphan works.

---

[111] S. van Gompel and P. B. Hugenholtz, 'The orphan works problem: the copyright conundrum of digitizing large-scale audiovisual archives, and how to solve it' (2010) 8 (1) *Popular Communication: The International Journal of Media and Culture* 61.

[112] Favale et al., 'Copyright, and the regulation of orphan works', 1.

If achievable, a low-cost official licensing scheme, operated by an existing institution, could be a useful supplement to a limited liability scheme, to provide certainties to those applicants that need it. Experience has shown it cannot be the centrepiece of a solution. No single approach is likely to provide a sufficient response to this complex problem.

## 14.3 Mass Digitisation Licences

Overlapping, but separate from the problems of orphan works, is the desire by many organisations, both non-profit CHIs and commercial, to be able to carry out mass digitisation projects in situations where it is impracticable to obtain individual consents from rights holders, and where there is not a CS representing all relevant rights holders. Orphan works are the extreme instance, with 'out-of-commerce' works also under consideration in some jurisdictions. This leads to efforts to identify those situations where there is sufficient justification for a compulsory licence (usually some form of ECL), and both protective mechanisms (including opt-out provisions) and fair remuneration for rights holders. Under international copyright law, such proposals must be justified under Berne Article 9(2) and the three-step test.

### 14.3.1 Mass Digitisation Licences within the EU

The position is more complicated in the EU Member States because if legislation for digitisation projects is not within the limited scope of the Orphan Works Directive [14.2.4], then it must be within the exceptions allowed by Article 5 of the InfoSoc Directive [13.3.5]. French legislation which went beyond orphan works to deal with all 'unavailable books' was held invalid by the ECJ in *Soulier and Doke* in 2016, as being inconsistent with the InfoSoc Directive: [13.3.5]. German legislation concerning all out-of-commerce works is consequently of questionable validity, but a proposed new Directive on copyright in the Digital Single Market may provide a partial solution.

*Germany – An ECL for CHI Uses of 'Out of Commerce Works' (2013)* In 2013, Germany enacted an orphan works ECL scheme applying to 'out of commerce works' (OOCW). A CS established to administer the rights of reproduction and make available such works is presumed by the law to have the right to do so for any OOCW published before 1 January 1966 'in books, scientific journals, newspapers, magazines or other writings' (but not, for example, in newspapers) if they are currently 'in the collections of publicly accessible libraries, educational

## 14.3 Mass Digitisation Licences 455

institutions, museums, and institutions concerned with film or audio heritage'.[113] The CS is entitled to so administer works owned by non-members, provided that the relevant work has been listed in the Register of Out of Commerce Works maintained by the German Patent and Trademark Office[114] by the CS, and a rights holder has not objected within six weeks of the listing, and the licensed uses do not serve commercial purposes.[115] A non-member rights holder 'shall have the same rights and obligations towards the CS as if he had transferred his rights for administration'.[116] Any rights holder can opt out of CS administration of their work under this scheme at any time.[117] Anyone, not CHIs, may apply for a licence from the CS, provided it is for non-commercial purposes. If the CS sets licence fees, this is borderline public domain.

This legislation is therefore broader than is necessary to achieve the aims of the narrow EU Orphan Works Directive. In light of the ECJ's decision in *Soulier and Doke*, this is now a considerable problem: [13.3.5]. The ECJ's conclusion in *Soulier and Doke* seems to apply squarely to the German legislation, and the terms of the Orphan Works Directive are not broad enough to justify the German 'out of commerce works' legislation.

*EU Proposed Directive – An ECL for some CHI Uses of Out-of-Commerce Works* The result of the ruling in *Soulier and Doke* is that, although the French and German laws are examples of a way for EU jurisdictions to deal constructively with both orphan works and with more general issues of mass digitisation projects, this now seems illusory.

In September 2016, the European Commission proposed a new Directive on copyright in the Digital Single Market[118] which includes, as well as non-remunerated exceptions [11.2.2], a requirement on Member States to enable an ECL which would support digitisation of the existing collections of a CHI, similar to the German OOCW legislation, but not the broader French legislation. The proposed provision is

---

[113] Law on the Administration of Copyright and Neighboring Rights 1965 (Germany), Art. 2, §13d(1); unofficial translation of Article 2, §13d and §13e www.vgwort.de/fileadmin/pdf/allgemeine_pdf/out_of_commerce_law_2013.pdf.
[114] Law on the Administration of Copyright and Neighboring Rights 1965 (Germany), Art. 2, §13e.
[115] Law on the Administration of Copyright and Neighboring Rights 1965 (Germany), Art. 2, §13d(1).
[116] Law on the Administration of Copyright and Neighboring Rights 1965 (Germany), Art. 2, §13d(4).
[117] Law on the Administration of Copyright and Neighboring Rights 1965 (Germany), Art. 2, §13d(2).
[118] European Commission, Proposal for a Directive of the European Parliament and of the Council on copyright in the Digital Single Market, COM (2016) 593 final, Brussels, 14 September 2015 ('Proposed copyright in the DSM Directive').

that when a [CS] on behalf of its members, concludes a non-exclusive licence for non-commercial purposes with a cultural heritage institution for the digitisation, distribution, communication to the public or making available of out-of-commerce works or other subject-matter permanently in the collection of the institution, such a non-exclusive licence may be extended or presumed to apply to right-holders of the same category as those covered by the licence who are not represented by the [CS].[119]

Three conditions would be required: (a) a CS broadly representative of rights holders in the category of works concerned; (b) equal treatment guaranteed to all rights holders; and (c) rights holders to have the right to opt out.[120] Other proposed provisions would require: OOC works to be defined broadly to encompass whole collections where reasonable, thus facilitating mass digitisation; publicity measures, including concerning opt-out rights; ensuring licences are sought from an appropriate CS; and limiting application to works of third-country nationals in some cases.[121] EU-wide use of the licensed content by the cultural institution is also to be enabled.[122] If the CS sets licence fees, this is borderline public domain.

Such a regime, if adopted and transposed, may resolve the problems raised by *Soulier and Doke* for legislation limited in ways similar to the current German legislation, but broader legislation such as the French 'unavailable books' law would still be impermissible because it extends to books which are not 'permanently in the collection of the institution' concerned (France's national library). A more fundamental issue is that the Court's reasoning in *Soulier and Doke* might potentially apply to any ECL scheme [13.5.3] unless it could fit within an exception under Article 5 of the InfoSoc Directive, or the terms of the Orphan Works Directive, or (if enacted) the new Directive discussed above.

### 14.3.2 US Proposal for an ECL for Non-Profit Mass Digitisation (2015)

The US Copyright Office has concluded that neither its proposed limited liability legislation [14.2.9], nor the fair use exception, would be likely to result in mass digitisation projects that many institutions (and businesses) now wish to undertake. It has therefore proposed, partly to encourage dialogue among stakeholders and in Congress,[123] legislation to establish an ECL 'pilot program'[124] subject to a five-year sunset clause. The ECL would operate in three subject areas: literary works; pictorial or graphic

---

[119] Proposed copyright in the DSM Directive, Art. 7(1).
[120] Proposed copyright in the DSM Directive, Art. 7(1).
[121] Proposed copyright in the DSM Directive, Art. 7(2)–(5).
[122] Proposed copyright in the DSM Directive, Art. 8.
[123] US Copyright Office, 'Orphan works and mass digitization', 5.
[124] *Ibid.* 5–7 (summary of proposals), 72–105 (detailed proposals).

## 14.3 Mass Digitisation Licences

works published as illustrations, diagrams or similar adjuncts to literary works; and photographs, and only in relation to published works.[125] Licences could only be for non-profit educational or research purposes, 'without any purpose of direct or indirect commercial advantage',[126] and with security measures required.

The proposed legislation would permit the Register of Copyrights to authorise a CS meeting eligibility criterion to issue licences covering the use of works by both members and non-members of the CS. An eligible CS seeking authorisation of an ECL must be able to demonstrate its sufficient level of representation of authors in the relevant field, that its members consent to the proposal, and transparency in its operations. Copyright owners, whether members of the CS or not, could opt out of the ECL. Licence rates would be subject to a dispute resolution procedure. The CS would be required to conduct diligent searches to identify non-members in relation to whose works it has collected royalties, to include them in distributions and to distribute unclaimed royalties after a period.

The Copyright Office claims that its ECL proposal complies with the Berne three-step test.[127] It argued that the ECLs of Nordic countries have been unchallenged for decades, and that the UK's ECL legislation is broader than what it is proposing.[128] While recent EU developments [13.5.3] raise questions concerning ECLs, these arise from provisions in EU law, and are not related directly to the three-step test.

*Fair Use and Mass Digitisation* The fair use exception in US copyright law is an essential part of the Copyright Office's proposal, with users having a legislatively preserved option of relying on it under either of its proposals.[129] However, the question of whether mass digitisation of orphan works, or other works, might be a fair use within US copyright law has not yet been resolved. In *Authors Guild* v. *HathiTrust*, the University of Michigan's orphan works digitisation project was one of the issues in the original litigation, but the university suspended the project in 2011, the Second Circuit Court of Appeals in its 2014 decision indicated that the issue was not ready for resolution[130] and the parties in 2015 settled outstanding issues. In *Authors Guild* v. *Google*,[131] while holding that Google's provision of 'snippets' from digitised books was fair use, the Court emphasised that the limited access to the works

---

[125] *Ibid.* 84.  [126] *Ibid.* 8, 101.  [127] *Ibid.* 102–4.  [128] *Ibid.* 103–4.
[129] *Ibid.* 3, 4, 40–4.  [130] *Authors Guild v. HathiTrust*, 755 F.3d 87 (2nd Cir 2014).
[131] *Authors Guild, Inc. v. Google, Inc*, 804 F 3d 202 (2nd Cir, 2015).

involved in this meant that Google's use did not substitute for the original book [12.2.3].

Favale et al. concluded in relation to the 2006 Copyright Office proposal that

> the US approach ... reflects the typical market-driven American stance on copyright matters. For the same reason, collective management of rights (either 'extended' or not) do not find a viable place among the proposed solutions to the Orphan Works problem in the US.[132]

The US Copyright Office's 2015 proposals were a major change in emphasis, with an ECL being expressly supported. However, it was influenced in this choice by the fact that 'three key U.S. trading partners – France, Germany, and the United Kingdom – have adopted versions of ECL to allow for digitization of copyrighted works for certain purposes'.[133] But that is also in flux.

*Conclusions* The proposed EU directive may provide a model for the digitisation of works held by CHIs, but acceptable solutions of broader scope, such as 'unavailable books' have not yet been found.

## 14.4 Educational Compulsory Licensing

Berne Convention Article 10(2) allows exceptions for the use of literary and artistic works 'to the extent justified by the purpose ... by way of illustration in publications, broadcasts or sound or visual recordings for teaching, provided that such utilization is compatible with fair practice': [5.4.2]. This is a very limited exception. As Bannerman explains, while education was a major purpose of many countries' copyright laws, it was never a major purpose of the Berne Convention, and earlier broader educational exceptions in Berne were in successive revisions cut back to the very limited 'by way of illustration' remnant.[134] The wording of Article 10(2) may exclude some forms of adult education, but probably not distance education per se, including via the Internet.[135] The only other Berne exception explicitly allowing educational licensing is the Paris Appendix exception, limited to developing countries: [14.5]. Rome allows exceptions 'for use solely for the purposes of teaching or scientific research': [5.4.2].

---

[132] Favale et al., 'Copyright, and the regulation of orphan works', 17–18.
[133] US Copyright Office, 'Orphan works and mass digitization', 83.
[134] Bannerman, *International Copyright and Access to Knowledge*, 61–6.
[135] Ricketson and Ginsburg, *International Copyright and Neighbouring Rights*, [13.43].

## 14.4 Educational Compulsory Licensing

A wide variety of approaches is used in national jurisdictions to assist educational activities. Some countries rely on free use exceptions [12.5]; others on statutory licences based on Berne Article 9(2). Others such as Australia and Canada rely on both. ECL is used in educational activities across all Nordic countries.[136] Some countries such as the United States do not have any compulsory licences for educational purposes. Berne's Paris Appendix exception for educational purposes is also used by some developing countries, but is of very limited value, given its restrictions [14.5].

The studies carried out for WIPO SCCR by Seng[137] and by Xalabarder[138] demonstrate the wide variety of approaches taken. Seng's review of 2,048 pieces of copyright legislation, of all 189 WIPO Member States, found 77 provisions from 37 Member States relating to compulsory licences for reproduction and translation which 'corresponded to' the Berne 'Paris Appendix': [14.5]. But Seng also found that there were many other types of educational exceptions that included statutory licences and required some form of remuneration to the copyright owner. He identified 215 instances from dozens of countries.[139] While the remunerated provisions were in the minority in all categories of exceptions, these figures nevertheless demonstrate that statutory licences are being used to allow permission-free use of works for educational purposes in dozens of countries, separate from the Paris Appendix licences.

The countries considered in this section exemplify differences in approach to compulsory licensing.

*Australia – Licence Arising from Notice* Australia has a statutory licence applying automatically to all educational institutions, with a post-2017 'flexible' licence for copying or communication by educational institutions of works and broadcasts.[140] The general principles under

---

[136] Koskinen-Olsson and Sigurdardóttir, 'Collective management in the Nordic countries', 249.
[137] Seng, 'Study on copyright limitations and exceptions'.
[138] Xalabarder, 'Study on copyright limitations and exceptions for educational activities in North America, Europe, Caucasus, Central Asia and Israel'.
[139] Seng, 'Study on copyright limitations and exceptions', 29–49: these included education broadcasts, communications and recordings (29 provisions in 23 states), school performances (7 provisions), educational publications, anthologies and the like (38 provisions in 27 states), educational reproductions (44 provisions), quotations (7 provisions), and personal use (90 provisions).
[140] Part IVA, Division 4, Copyright Act 1968 (Aus.), inserted by the Copyright Amendment (Disability Access and Other Measures) Act 2017 (Aus.), and replacing Parts VA and VB, the previous statutory licences. The amendments are intended to be in effect from December 2017, and are assumed for the purposes of the following discussion.

which such statutory licences operate are set out in [13.4.1]. The new 'flexible' licence implements some of the 2013 recommendations of the Australian Law Reform Commission (ALRC). Despite the preference of many educational institutions for voluntarily negotiated licences, rights holder representatives, including CSs, generally preferred to retain the statutory licences.[141] A statutory licence has been retained, but with much greater flexibility for negotiation between the parties.

The new licence has the following main features. It operates once an educational institution provides a 'remuneration notice' to the relevant CS agreeing to provide 'equitable remuneration' for uses made under the licence. It applies to all works, except computer programs or compilations thereof, or works included in a broadcast.[142] A licence with equivalent features operates for broadcasts and works included in them, but is not discussed here. A copy or communication may then be made by or on behalf of the educational institution solely for its educational purposes, or those of another educational institution (which has a remuneration notice in force). The Act simply provides that 'the amount of the work copied or communicated does not unreasonably prejudice the legitimate interests of the owner of the copyright',[143] replacing previously prescriptive provisions concerning amounts that could be copied. The educational institution must comply with any relevant agreement between it and the CS, and with any relevant determinations made by the Copyright Tribunal.[144] It is expected that this will cover record-keeping requirements and similar matters. The Tribunal has broad powers to resolve any questions 'relating to copyright or communicating' under the licence.[145] The policy basis underlying this approach 'differs from the previous scheme because it does not mandate a particular method for determining remuneration, such as sampling or record keeping' but leaves this for the parties to negotiate, and the Tribunal to resolve if negotiation fails.[146] Educational institutions are required, by the terms of the remuneration notice, and also by statutory provisions, to assist CSs to review compliance.[147]

As the ALRC proposed, copyright owners and performers (or CSs representing them) will remain free to negotiate licences directly with

---

[141] Australian Law Reform Commission, *Copyright and the Digital Economy*, pp. 187–93.
[142] Copyright Act 1968 (Aus.), s. 113P(1) and (2) provide for each of the 'works' licence and the 'broadcast' licence.
[143] Copyright Act 1968 (Aus.), s. 113P(1)(d).
[144] Copyright Act 1968 (Aus.), s. 113P(1)(e).
[145] Copyright Act 1968 (Aus.), s. 113P(4).
[146] Copyright Amendment (Disability Access and Other Measures) Act 2017 – Explanatory Memorandum (Aus.), 23.
[147] Copyright Act 1968 (Aus.), s. 113S.

## 14.4 Educational Compulsory Licensing

educational institutions.[148] If this occurs, the statutory licence will not apply where the educational institutions instead relies on the alternative licence. However, it continues to be entitled to rely on the statutory licence. Also, as recommended by ALRC,[149] any applicable free use exceptions will still operate, and the statutory licence will not apply where such an exception applies.[150] Educational institutions can therefore rely on unremunerated exceptions. The Copyright Tribunal would also take into account the right of such institutions to rely on unremunerated exceptions when determining disputes concerning equitable remuneration.[151]

*The EU and the UK* The EU InfoSoc Directive[152] limits the types of exceptions open to EU Member States to those provided by Article 5. While states may make any allowed exceptions subject to payment of compensation,[153] in two of the allowed exceptions which are likely to be used for educational purposes, fair compensation to rights holders is required: reprographic reproductions (excluding sheet music),[154] and other reproductions for non-commercial private uses (which could include study).[155]

In the UK, the Secretary of State can impose a compulsory licence in relation to reprographic copies made for the purposes of instruction by educational establishments, where previous recommendations concerning licensing have not been followed.[156] The UK's attempt to implement a private use exemption was held in BASCA to be invalid: [12.5.2]. The UK's other educational exceptions do not involve remuneration: [12.5.2].

*China – Compulsory and Distance Education Licence, with Opt-Out*
China has an automatically applying compulsory licence for nine-year compulsory education (and national education planning), covering 'passages' of published works or short literary texts, musical works or single works of fine art or photography which may be copied, compiled and published in textbooks, with provision for opt-out by express notice on

---

[148] Copyright Act 1968 (Aus.), s. 113T.
[149] Australian Law Reform Commission, *Copyright and the Digital Economy*, pp. 193–5.
[150] Copyright Act 1968 (Aus.), s. 113Q(2).
[151] Australian Law Reform Commission, *Copyright and the Digital Economy*, pp. 193–5.
[152] Full titles and citations of all EU Directives are in the Table of International Instruments.
[153] InfoSoc Directive (EU), Recital (36). [154] InfoSoc Directive (EU), Art. 5(2)(a).
[155] InfoSoc Directive (EU), Art. 5(2)(b). [156] CDPA (UK), s.141.

publication.[157] This approach is extended to a compulsory licence for the use of information networks by 'distance education institutions'.[158] The 2014 proposed reforms retain the statutory licensing framework for textbooks compiled for national compulsory education.[159]

*India – Grants of Licences for Systematic Instructional Activities*
India allows the grant by the Copyright Board (as the relevant 'competent authority') of a compulsory licence for reproduction of works to be made for use in 'systematic instructional activities' where copies are not distributed at a 'normal price' after five years from first publication (or different periods in some cases).[160] Section 32A was inserted in 1983 in response to the Paris Appendix, Article III (with the deficiencies discussed in the next section), and was not amended in the 2012 reforms. Evidence of any use of these licences is lacking. Some other Indian compulsory licences may also be relevant to education: [13.4.5].

*Conclusions: Education and the Public Domain*  Efficient licensing for educational purposes must be a high priority for any country. Compulsory licences which can be invoked by any educational institutions, with terms and procedures that can be resolved by a neutral Tribunal, in the event that licensing cannot be settled between the relevant stakeholders, and which remain subordinate to any non-remunerated exemptions, seem to offer a very good result from a public domain perspective. Licences dependent upon applications (India), or subject to opt-outs (China) are less desirable.

## 14.5  Educational Licences in Developing Nations: The Paris Appendix

Special provisions for compulsory licensing in developing nations resulted from a compromise reached at the Paris revision conference, the 'Paris Appendix' to the Berne Convention: [5.5.3]. The Paris Appendix allows developing countries[161] to subject the translation right and reproduction right to compulsory licences for educational purposes.

---

[157] Copyright Law (China), Art. 23.
[158] Regulations on Protection of the Right of Communication through Information Network, State Council (China), 2006 ( 'Internet Regulations (China)') www.wipo.in t/edocs/lexdocs/laws/en/cn/cn064en.pdf, Arts. 8, 10, 11.
[159] 2014 Draft Copyright Law (China), Art. 47.
[160] Copyright Act 1957 (India), s. 32A.
[161] 'Any country regarded as a developing country in conformity with the established practice of the General Assembly of the United Nations ...': Berne Convention, Paris Appendix, Art. 1(1).

## 14.5 Educational Licences in Developing Nations

At the Berne revision conferences,[162] two issues consumed a decade of negotiations in the 1960s: the ability of developing countries to translate foreign works into their own national languages for educational purposes; and the ability of developing countries to republish books published overseas, within their own country, when no local publication had occurred, but such books were needed for educational purposes.

*The Paris Appendix Conditions* In relation to the translation right, Article II provides that the exclusive rights in published works may be replaced with non-exclusive, non-transferable licences, granted by a competent authority under numerous detailed conditions.[163] The most significant conditions include: the licences may only be granted for 'the purpose of teaching, scholarship or research'; a period of three years or longer has elapsed from the date of first publication during which an authorised translation has not been published in a 'language in general use' in the developing country; or if such a translation has been published but all editions of it are out of print; a 'grace period' of six to nine months before a licence may be granted (during which the owner of the translation right may publish and obviate the need for a licence); and that the licence may be subsequently terminated by the owner of the translation right publishing at a reasonable price. The translation licence only applies to 'works published in printed or analogous form',[164] so there are uncertainties about its application to digital works and online access.[165]

In relation to the reproduction right, Article III provides that a compulsory licence may be granted to permit copies of works to be made for use in 'systematic instructional activities' where copies are not distributed at a 'normal price' after five years from first publication (which, depending on the subject matter of the work, may be reduced to three years or extended to seven years). Numerous restrictions similar to those affecting translation licences also apply, including grace periods and termination provisions.[166]

To take advantage of the Paris Appendix, a developing country must deposit a declaration with WIPO declaring that it will take advantage of either or both of the compulsory licences for translations and reproductions, and must renew such declarations every ten years.[167] There are

---

[162] See Ricketson and Ginsburg, *International Copyright and Neighbouring Rights*, [14.01]–[14.110]; Bannerman, *International Copyright and Access to Knowledge*, 133.

[163] For details, see Ricketson and Ginsburg, *International Copyright and Neighbouring Rights*, [14.60]–[14.77].

[164] Berne Convention, Appendix, Art. II(2)(a).   [165] *Ibid.* 607–12.

[166] For details, see Ricketson and Ginsburg, *International Copyright and Neighbouring Rights*, [14.78]–[14.91].

[167] For the complexities of timing of renewal declarations, see *ibid.* 928.

numerous further complexities concerning preconditions for the grant of a licence (including denial of requests by the relevant rights owners), and subsequent restrictions on the uses of translations or reproductions.[168]

*Deficiencies and Influence*  The Paris Appendix has been condemned frequently by scholars as useless, and attempts by developing countries to comply with it as a waste of time. Ricketson and Ginsburg conclude that, although the Paris Revision Conference 'brought to an end the crisis in international copyright that had arisen around the demands by developing countries',[169] they found it 'hard to point to any obvious benefits that have flowed directly to developing countries from the adoption of the Appendix'.[170] Agitha, informed by Indian experience, condemns its 'irrational and complex procedures ... to the verge of absurdity', and concludes that its provisions 'are commercially so deterrent that no sensible person who means business shall venture to make any application'.[171] Okediji and Cerda Silva reached similar conclusions of failure.[172]

Although nineteen countries have lodged Declarations/Notifications with the Paris Appendix by 2017,[173] there is little evidence of national laws complying strictly with the Appendix or its Declaration requirement,[174] as Cerda Silva's study demonstrates.[175] Seng found that seventy-seven provisions (forty-four for translations, thirty-three for reproductions) from thirty-seven Member States (nearly 20 per cent of all Member States) provide for compulsory licences for educational purposes that 'corresponded' to the two Paris Appendix licences. However, he found that of these thirty-seven states only six had renewed their required declarations under the Appendix, whereas seven had allowed their declarations to lapse (calling into question the validity under Berne of their statutory provisions).

---

[168] For details, see *ibid.* [14.92]–[14.102]    [169] *Ibid.* [14.103].    [170] *Ibid.* [14.106].
[171] Agitha, 'International norms for compulsory licensing and the Indian copyright law', 28, footnotes to Berne Convention provisions, and to Okediji, omitted.
[172] For details of further criticisms, see the Online Supplement.
[173] Including Kuwait, Cuba, Bangladesh, United Arab Emirates, Viet Nam, Thailand, Yemen, Algeria, Sri Lanka, Syria, Sudan, Mongolia, UAR, Philippines, Oman, Jordan, Egypt, India and Mexico.
[174] Ricketson and Ginsburg, *International Copyright and Neighbouring Rights*, [14.106] in 2006 found eleven currently valid notifications, but only one country which had enacted resulting laws (Thailand); Okediji regarded thirteen notifications by 2004 as evidence of failure.
[175] A. Cerda Silva, 'Beyond the unrealistic solution for development provided by the Appendix of the Berne Convention on copyright' (2013) 60 *Journal of the Copyright Society of the USA* 581 at 590.

*Conclusions and Alternatives* The Paris Appendix is a failure, rarely if ever, implemented in full. Nevertheless, it seems that numerous developing countries have enacted 'idiosyncratic' non-compliant exceptions, often including compulsory licences, for both translation and reproductions for educational purposes. The studies by Cerda Silva, Seng and Crews[176] make it clear that there is much legislation in developing countries dealing with translation and reproduction for teaching, although it does not comply fully with the Paris Appendix text and Declaration requirements.

Given that Berne has not been amended since 1971, hopes for reform of the Paris Appendix seem unduly optimistic, though some scholars advance them. Agitha takes a different approach that, although the Paris Appendix is free from the constraints of the three-step test, its unrealistic procedural requirements mean that reliance on Berne Article 9(2), available to any country, is preferable. As she illustrates in relation to the Indian compulsory licences resulting from 2012 amendments to the Indian law [13.4.5], extensive compulsory licences (in developing countries and elsewhere) are capable of being justified under the three-step test in a wide range of circumstances.

The existence of the Paris Appendix indicates that the Berne Convention contemplates compulsory licensing as one solution to problems experienced by developing countries. Numerous countries in the developing world have implemented legislation that does not comply with the Appendix requirements, but does provide compulsory licences or other exceptions concerning translations and republication for teaching purposes, possibly influenced by its terms. Retaliatory actions, if they exist, are not well known. Developing countries may be best off relying on Berne Article 9(2) and the three-step test to justify exceptions which have far fewer technicalities that the Paris Appendix licences. Development of a new international copyright instrument to deal with these needs may be desirable, but is probably an unrealistic option.

## 14.6  Translation Licences

Although the use and value of the Paris Appendix translation provisions may be limited, the question of access to translations has played a major and contentious role in the history of the public domain aspects of the Berne Convention.[177] Strategies have changed from initial attempts to

---

[176] For details of these studies, see the Online Supplement.
[177] Bannerman, *International Copyright and Access to Knowledge*, chap. 6, 'Access to translations', sets out this history and significance of the disputes around it.

deny a right of translation; then to have the term of protection for the translation right less than for other rights;[178] and then (after that was lost) to obtaining compulsory licence provisions. As Bannerman puts it '[t]he role of translation in copyright resonated to the very core of the linguistic impact of colonialism.'[179] Other than the Paris Appendix provisions, Berne has no explicit provisions dealing with translations. It is difficult to see exceptions involving translation coming within any of the EU's allowed exceptions under the InfoSoc Directive, Article 5. The need for the right to translate, facilitated by exceptions, is still predominantly felt in developing countries.

India's compulsory licences, where a 'translation is required for the purposes of teaching, scholarship or research', are subject to most of the limitations required by the Berne Paris Appendix, Article II.[180] They allow translations of works 'other than an Indian work, in any language in general use in India after a period of three years from the first publication of such work' (instead of seven years, where there is no 'teaching, scholarship or research' requirement[181]), or even after only one year if the translation is to be in 'a language not in general use in any developed country' (in accordance with UN practices).[182] Agitha argues it would be in India's public interest if it removed many of the restrictions resulting from the Berne Appendix, but retaining the reduced three-year period, and that such a compulsory licence scheme would be justifiable under Berne Article 9(2).[183]

Some types of translations that might elsewhere be the subject of compulsory licences, are free use exceptions in China, such as the translation of works by Chinese citizens in the Han language into minority nationality languages,[184] and transliterations of (any) published works into braille.[185]

*Conclusions: Translations and the Public Domain* Given the significant numbers of translation statutory licences that Seng's survey found, but which may well be non-compliant with the Paris Appendix, perhaps developing countries would be best served by modifying its most

---

[178] The Copyright Act 1905 (Aus.) provided in s. 28 an immediate right to make translations for private purposes and in s. 30 the ability to apply to the Minister for a licence to translate a book into another language after ten years.
[179] Bannerman, *International Copyright and Access to Knowledge*, 112.
[180] Copyright Act 1957 (India), s. 32, with the conditions set out in s. 32(2)–(4) generally applying to each of the various licences arising from ss. 32(1), 32(1A) and 32(5).
[181] Copyright Act 1957 (India), s. 32(1).   [182] Copyright Act 1957 (India), s. 32(1A).
[183] Agitha, 'International norms for compulsory licensing and the Indian copyright law', 34–6.
[184] Copyright Law (China), Art. 22(11).   [185] Copyright Law (China), Art. 22(12).

counter-productive conditions, and instead aim at a compulsory licence which could comply with Berne Article 9(2). Cooperation between developing countries might well be productive in developing and defending a robust licence.

## 14.7 Libraries, Archives, Other Cultural Heritage Institutions (CHIs) and Licensing

There are no specific Berne provisions concerning assistance to cultural heritage institutions (CHIs) such as galleries, libraries, archives and museums (also called the 'GLAM sector') to enable them to undertake tasks such as preservation, cataloguing, display and digitisation of their enormous collections of works. National provisions will generally need to rely on Berne Article 9(2) and the three-step test, and usually provide free use exceptions, rather than remunerated exceptions (compulsory licences). In Europe, ECLs may be applicable (providing remuneration). In some cases, specific orphan works statutory licences may also apply to orphan works held by CHIs: [14.2.2], and there may be statutory licences concerning out-of-print / out-of-commerce works: [14.2.4]. The rest of this section is applicable to where no such specific statutory licences apply.

Most countries have no compulsory licence provisions expressly to benefit cultural institutions. For example, the United States has no such provisions, but its fair use provisions may often provide free use exceptions, and it has many specific free access exceptions to benefit CHIs: [12.6.5]. In Australia, there is a broad range of free access exceptions for public libraries, parliamentary libraries and archives: [12.6.3]. In Canada, specific free use exceptions available to CHIs are supported by Canada's flexible fair dealing provisions: [12.6.4]. However, there are some exceptions where remunerated licences may be appropriate or necessary in relation to cultural institutions, examples of which follow.

*Europe and the UK – ECL Provisions*  There is use of ECL in all Nordic countries in archives, libraries and museums.[186] Denmark uses ECL for purposes of cultural institutions such as digital reproduction by libraries and reproduction of works of art that have been made public.[187] UK CHIs have generally welcomed the UK's ECL Regulation, discussed in [13.5.2], although it has significant limitations in relation to

---

[186] Koskinen-Olsson and Sigurdardóttir, 'Collective management in the Nordic countries', 249.
[187] Riis and Schovsbo, 'Extended collective licenses and the Nordic experience', section 2.1.

digitisation. As Mendis and Stobo point out, there may well not be any CS which can claim to have any existing representation for many of the types of materials in archival collections, such as correspondence, archival records or unpublished manuscripts. Further, if collections consist primarily of non-commercial materials, and rights holders do not usually expect payment for digitisation, negotiating use with a fee-oriented CS might not be desirable. On the other hand, an ECL scheme can license materials without the necessity for a licensee to carry out a diligent search as required by orphan works provisions. But the CS must carry out the equivalent of a diligent search in order to contact non-member rights holders for purpose of distribution of fees.[188]

*The UK – Lending of Works* As required by EU law, the UK includes the right to rent as one of the exclusive rights of the copyright owner. The legislation also gives the Secretary of State the power to order that renting to the public of copies of most types of copyright subject matter[189] (as specified in the order) 'shall be treated as licensed by the copyright owner subject only to the payment of such reasonable royalty or other payment as may be agreed or determined in default of agreement by the Copyright Tribunal'.[190] Orders may vary depending on the type of work, 'any factor relating to the work, the copies lent, the lender or the circumstances of the lending'.[191] Non-profit lending by prescribed libraries or archives is also exempted: [10.2.8].

*China's Licence Aiding Poverty-Stricken Areas* China has a very unusual compulsory licence, which allows free access publication 'to the public in rural areas through information network, for the purpose of aiding poverty-stricken areas', by publication of works relating to poverty reduction, but also 'which satisfies the basic needs for culture'.[192] Authors are to be notified in advance of publication, including with details of fees payable, and have thirty days in which to opt out. The licence applies only to 'a published work of a Chinese citizen', which avoids problems of international agreements.[193]

---

[188] D. Mendis and V. Stobo, 'UK: Extended Collective Licensing', Kluwer copyright blog, 3 December 2014 http://kluwercopyrightblog.com/2014/12/03/uk-extended-collective-licensing/.
[189] CDPA (UK), s. 66: 'copies of literary, dramatic, musical or artistic works, sound recordings or films'.
[190] CDPA (UK), s. 66(1).   [191] CDPA (UK), s. 66(3).
[192] Internet Regulations (China), Art. 9.
[193] Wan Yong, 'Copyright limitation for the benefit of poverty alleviation: is Chinese copyright provision to be a model for developing countries?' (2015) 3 *China Legal Science* 129.

*Conclusions – Compulsory Licences and Cultural Heritage Institutions (CHIs)* In [12.6.7] we set out the types of free access exceptions that it would be desirable for national legislation to include in relation to CHIs. Proposals to WIPO SCCR for a treaty on exceptions to benefit CHIs have not included proposals for remunerated exceptions.[194] Opt-out provisions, as in China, add an extra layer of bureaucracy and transaction costs, and in our view should be avoided.

The need for all TRIPS and WTC members to accommodate rental rights [10.2.8] makes it essential that all countries exercise the option to exclude non-commercial rentals (or subject them to a compulsory licence) so as to protect the operation of CHIs and minimise the deleterious effects of rental rights on the public domain. In some cases, a compulsory licence where an independent tribunal sets what is a 'reasonable royalty' may be appropriate, preferably with exceptions for hardship, as well as support for copyright owners, such as public lending rights.

## 14.8 Other Subject Areas of Compulsory Licensing

There are many other subject areas of compulsory licensing, which, while they can only be mentioned here,[195] indicate the variety of uses to which such licences are put.

### 14.8.1 Assistance to the Disabled

The 2013 Marrakesh Treaty to Facilitate Access to Published Works by Visually Impaired Persons and Persons with Print Disabilities (Marrakesh Treaty) requires contracting states to establish a standard set of limitations and exceptions: [5.4.4]. Implementation can be either by a free use exception or by a remunerated licence.[196] On 10 May 2017, the EU reached a compromise position on the terms of a proposed Directive to implement the Treaty. Controversially,[197] Member States will retain the option in the Treaty to implement it by statutory licences, not only free use exceptions. The proposed Directive has not yet been made. The European Union has exclusive competence to ratify the

---

[194] WIPO SCCR. 'The case for a treaty on exceptions and limitations for libraries and archives: background paper by IFLA, ICA, EIFL and INNOVARTE', Document presented by Brazil, WIPO Doc. SCCR/23/3 (18 November 2011).
[195] See the Online Supplement for further details. [196] Marrakech Treaty, Art. 4(5).
[197] European Bureau of Library, Information and Documentation Associations (EBLIDA), 'EU Compromise on Marrakesh Treaty Directive Comes with a Sting in the Tail', 15 May 2017 www.eblida.org/news/eu-compromise-on-marrakesh-treaty-directive-comes-with-a-sting-in-the-tail.html.

Marrakesh Treaty on behalf of all Member States.[198] The InfoSoc Directive already allows exemptions for uses of a non-commercial nature to benefit disabled people.[199]

The Marrakech Treaty also allows for exceptions in national laws to be limited 'to works which, in the particular accessible format, cannot be obtained commercially under reasonable terms for beneficiary persons in that market'.[200] Of the twenty-nine parties that have ratified or acceded, Australia is the only party to have utilised this option,[201] but it did not exercise the compulsory licence option.

India has a free use exception for non-profit assistance (including cost recovery) to persons with a disability.[202] It also has a provision for applications to the Copyright Board, by 'any person working for the benefit of persons with disability on a profit basis or for business' for a remunerated licence,[203] which appear to be compliant with the three-step test.[204] Such applications must be decided 'expeditiously', preferably within two months. This provision pre-dates the Marrakesh Treaty, which India was the first country to ratify.

### 14.8.2 Sound Recordings, Performances, Broadcasts and Related Matters

Other significant compulsory licences relate to sound recordings, broadcasts and performances, often based in exceptions explicitly allowed under international copyright agreements. In addition to the cover version and broadcasting licences discussed below, there are many other licences addressing technical aspects of communications. All Nordic countries make various uses of ECL in relation to radio and television.[205]

Article 13(1) of Berne allows, but does not require, Member States to permit mechanical recordings of musical works including accompanying lyrics, and provide 'equitable remuneration': see [5.5.1]. Laws allowing such 'cover versions' were previously more widespread, but today are said to 'exist in relatively few Berne countries'.[206] Such licences are restricted

---

[198] Opinion 3/15: Opinion of the Court (Grand Chamber) of 14 February 2017 – European Commission
[199] Infosoc Directive (EU), Art. 5(3)(b). [200] Marrakech Treaty, Art. 4(4).
[201] WIPO 'Marrakech Treaty Status List' (as at 16 July 2017) www.wipo.int/treaties/en/ShowResults.jsp?lang=en&treaty_id=843.
[202] Copyright Act 1957 (India), s. 52(1)(zb).
[203] Copyright Act 1957 (India), s. 31B, and Copyright Rules 2013 (India), Chapter VI.
[204] Agitha, 'International norms for compulsory licensing and the Indian copyright law', 40.
[205] Koskinen-Olsson and Sigurdardóttir, 'Collective management in the Nordic countries', 249.
[206] Goldstein and Hugenholtz, *International Copyright*, 400.

14.8 Other Subject Areas of Compulsory Licensing                471

to where recordings of the work have already been published or imported with the licence of the copyright owner, and notice is given to the copyright owner, such as in the United States[207] or Australia.[208] India introduced a cover version statutory licence only in 2012, restricted to covers made at least five years after original publication, in the same medium as the prior publication, and with royalties on 50,000 copies per year paid in advance.[209] China's cover version provisions allow for copyright owners to opt out.[210] Canada, in contrast, does not have a compulsory licence for cover versions. Nor does the EU InfoSoc Directive include it as a permissible exception for EU countries.[211] Commentators are divided as to whether it is an 'open question' whether Berne Article 13(1) applies irrespective of this omission,[212] or whether the closed list in Article 5 'leaves member states no room for such a general statutory licence'.[213] The UK has no such compulsory licence, although it did prior to 1988.

Berne Article 11*bis* allows for a compulsory licence for broadcasting of literary and artistic works: [5.5.2]. Rome permits a compulsory licence for broadcasting and public communications of phonograms: [5.5.4]. Many countries have enacted a statutory licence for radio or television broadcasting of sound recordings (and in some cases for causing them to be heard in public), such as in Australia,[214] China[215] and India.[216] In some countries, such licences are limited to free-to-air broadcasts. The EU InfoSoc Directive does not include it as a permissible exception for EU countries.[217]

### 14.8.3 Government Uses

Australia has a statutory licence for government use, 'for the services of the Crown' (including by contractors), subject to fees either negotiated or set by the Copyright Tribunal.[218] In contrast, in China, uses by government organs necessary for their work are a free use exception.

### 14.8.4 Works Unavailable to the Public

There is no provision in Berne specifically allowing countries to republish books (or other subject matter) which are available in other countries

---

[207] 17 USC §115.  [208] Copyright Act 1968 (Aus.), ss. 54–64.
[209] Copyright Act 1957 (India), s. 31C.
[210] Copyright Law (China), Art. 40(3); Implementing Regulations (China), Art. 31.
[211] InfoSoc Directive (EU), Art. 5(3).
[212] Walter and von Lewinski, *European Copyright Law: A Commentary*.
[213] Goldstein and Hugenholtz, *International Copyright*, 400.
[214] Copyright Act 1968 (Aus.), ss. 108–109.  [215] Copyright Law (China), Art. 44.
[216] Copyright Act 1957 (India), s. 31D.  [217] InfoSoc Directive (EU), Art. 5(3).
[218] Copyright Act 1968 (Aus.), ss. 182B-183E (Pt VII, div 2).

but which copyright owners have chosen not to make available in the country in question, to satisfy public demand there. While Article III of the Paris Appendix to Berne allows such a compulsory licence in developing countries, it is restricted to publication for use in 'systematic instructional activities' [14.5], and countries wishing to enact compulsory licences for other purposes must therefore rely on Berne Article 9 (2) and satisfy the three-step test. No such remunerated use is possible in EU countries.[219]

India is very unusual in legislating such an exception for works so withheld.[220] The s. 31(1) licence is only for use by an individual applicant, on application, not for a class of licensees. It may apply if the owner of a work which has been published or performed in public has refused to republish the work, or allow performances of it,[221] or allow communication of the work or recordings of it,[222] 'and by reason of such refusal the work is withheld from the public' [in India, we must assume]. Upon receiving a complaint, the Copyright Board may, 'if it is satisfied that the grounds for such refusal are not reasonable', after giving the owner an opportunity to be heard, 'direct the Registrar of Copyrights to grant to the complainant a licence to republish the work' (etc.) 'subject to payment to the owner of the copyright of such compensation and subject to such other terms and conditions as the Copyright Board may determine'.[223]

Prior to 2012, s. 31(1)(a) referred only to 'any Indian work' (works by Indian citizens or which were first published in India), but now it refers to 'any work'. Agitha considers that no such restriction to 'Indian works' was required by Berne, and that it is 'paradoxical' that India so limited herself in this way.[224] Prior to the 2012 amendments, little use was made of the section to obtain compulsory licences of literary, dramatic, musical or artistic works.[225] It is now a provision allowing compulsory licences to be granted for republication in relation to 'works withheld from the public', with no inherent limitation on the purpose of republication, nor any limitation to 'Indian works'. Such a compulsory licence needs to be justified under Berne Article 13(2), in terms of the three-step-test. Agitha notes that section 31(1)(a) requires the extreme situation of refusal

---

[219] InfoSoc Directive (EU), Art. 5.     [220] Copyright Act 1957 (India), s. 31(1).
[221] Copyright Act 1957 (India), s. 31(1)(a).
[222] Copyright Act 1957 (India), s. 31(1)(b). See details in the Supplement.
[223] Copyright Act 1957 (India), s. 31.
[224] Agitha, 'International norms for compulsory licensing and the Indian copyright law', 34.
[225] *Ibid.* 36.

to republish resulting in 'withholding from the public', and argues that such a compulsory licence is a special case, which cannot conflict with the author's normal exploitation (as there is none, and a request to publish has been refused), and will not prejudice the author's interests because compensation is paid. The provision does not cover non-availability at an affordable price.[226]

## 14.9 Conclusions: The Underused Potential of Compulsory Licensing

There is considerable variation among countries in relation to the subject matters where they utilise compulsory licences, as might be expected given differences in the histories of development of copyright law, and the different social conditions faced by countries considering utilising compulsory licensing. Other than free use exemptions, compulsory licences compliant with international law (particularly Berne Article 9(2)) are the principal instruments available to countries that wish to allow certain permission-free uses of works to specified classes of users or to the general public. Given the challenges facing most countries in providing effective access to educational resources, in finding answers to the universally admitted problems of orphan works, in making the most effective use of the potential of digitisation of content of all forms, and in providing new and equitable revenue streams for creators – compulsory licensing needs to be considered as one potential answer. From a public domain perspective, there is no inherent aversion to compulsory licensing, which also provides equitable remuneration. It is under-utilised.

Developing countries have additional historically rooted needs for better access to educational materials, and to translations. The Paris Appendix, the one Berne compulsory licensing provision which ostensibly aimed to assist developing countries, is an over-restrictive and over-technical failure, such that resort to Berne Article 9(2) is more useful. Some countries enact provisions resembling aspects of the Paris Appendix, but do not adhere to it.

Overall, while the potential public domain benefits of compulsory licensing are constrained by international copyright law, countries are nevertheless finding creative ways to extend the ambit of compulsory licensing without yet coming into collision with these constraints. There is a need for good legislative models of compulsory licensing provisions, which, if challenged, stand good prospects of satisfying international law

---

[226] See discussion in Online Supplement.

474    Compulsory Licensing – Subject Areas

requirements, and which deliver solutions to the above problems. A valuable form of international cooperation, falling short of attempting to modify existing international agreements, would be for interested countries, and IGOs and NGOs assisting them, to collaborate on drafting such provisions.

# 15  Voluntary Licensing Creating Public Rights

| 15.1 | 'Neutral' Voluntary Licensing and the Public Domain | 475 |
| 15.2 | Free and Open Source Software (FOSS) Licensing | 482 |
| 15.3 | Creative Commons and Other Open Content Licensing | 493 |
| 15.4 | Legal Issues and Open Content Licensing | 501 |
| 15.5 | Government Supports for Open Content Licences | 505 |
| 15.6 | 'Relinquishment' or 'Public Domain Dedications' | 509 |
| 15.7 | Conclusions: Legal Certainty Desirable | 516 |

## 15.1  'Neutral' Voluntary Licensing and the Public Domain

Normally, the use of works enabled by a voluntary licence from a copyright owner should not be considered to be 'public rights', and such uses are not part of the public domain, no matter how generous the terms of the licence: [2.4.2]. Our short definition of the public domain as the ability of users to use works without first obtaining the consent of a copyright owner indicates why: obtaining a licence means obtaining consent from the copyright owner.

This chapter discusses two exceptions where voluntary acts by copyright owners do create potential for use of works which fits our definition of 'public rights': voluntary licensing of works by copyright owners, using pre-designed licences written by some independent third party on public interest grounds (which we call 'neutral voluntary licensing') (**Category 6**); and 'relinquishment' of copyright (also called 'public domain dedications') (**Category 14**). These voluntary licences are at no cost to licensees, and are usually grants of licences to the public at large, but the uses are subject to compliance with conditions set out in the particular licence. The result can be described as a 'contractually constructed commons'. Major expansions of public rights in copyright in the last two decades have been because of such voluntary licensing.

We explain when voluntary licensing should be regarded as part of the public domain. There are two main types of such licensing: free and open source software (FOSS) licensing and open content licensing, including

475

the Creative Commons suites of licences. We also consider public domain dedications (relinquishment of copyright). Finally, we examine the need to strengthen these aspects of the public domain.

### 15.1.1 Relevance of International and National Copyright Laws

The significance of voluntary licences to the public has not arisen because of international copyright agreements, nor because of provisions in national copyright laws, nor because of government initiatives or international organisations. It has developed primarily because of the efforts of individuals and non-government organisations, particularly from the United States, which have used the mechanisms of copyright law to ensure that various types of copyright content are available for access and use by the public, that it remains available, and that the content expands.

International agreements say nothing about voluntary licensing, nor impede it. Voluntary licences are antecedent to the creation of the work which is licensed, so the Berne Convention's prohibitions on formalities for the subsistence of copyright are irrelevant. They are not restrictions or conditions on copyright. National copyright legislation usually also has little to say about non-exclusive voluntary licensing agreements. These voluntary licences are not assignments or exclusive licences, so laws that require formalities for such dispositions are not relevant. It is unusual for national copyright laws to include any positive provisions which assist the enforceability (or other aspects of validity) of voluntary licences to the public or public domain dedications.

### 15.1.2 When Does Voluntary Licensing Create Public Rights?

The theoretical background to why voluntary licensing should in some cases be considered to be part of the copyright public domain is set out in [2.2.4]. We argue that some contractually constructed use regimes are forms of privately managed common resources ('neutral voluntary licences'). From a user's perspective, it is the positive freedom to use a work without permission that is important, and not whether the source of the freedom is a statutory limitation on copyright law, or private ordering by means of a predefined contract or copyright licence. We argued that the initial voluntary act of the copyright owner to 'permit' the use of their work by applying a neutral licence to it is outweighed by numerous other factors that distinguish neutral voluntary licensing which put the terms of use and identity of users of works under one of these licences far removed from the influence of the copyright owner. These

## 15.1 'Neutral' Voluntary Licensing and the Public Domain

attributes give neutral voluntary licences a close 'family resemblance' to other aspects of the copyright public domain.

As discussed in brief in Chapters 2 and 3, the factors listed below put the terms of use and identity of users of works under one of these licences so far beyond the influence of the copyright owner that the initial 'permission' involved by the copyright owner's preceding decision to utilise one of these licences should not be the determining factor. Neutral licence schemes exist, in our view, where copyright owners grant licences allowing uses of their works which would otherwise be within the exclusive rights of the copyright owner, on the basis of the following conditions:

1. *The terms of the licence have been determined by a 'neutral' body.* A neutral body is one which is independent of individual copyright owners or users (or their representatives) and can reasonably be considered as not acting on behalf of any particular owner but neutrally on behalf of all potential licensors and licensees.
2. *The terms may impose restrictions on the uses that may be made of the work.* Such restrictions must not be inconsistent with the following conditions (3)–(9). It is common in other categories of the public domain that the uses allowed of works may be limited, and fundamental to our understanding of the relationship between the public and private domains: [2.3.2]. As well as 'non-commercial uses only' conditions, conditions such as 'for educational uses only' would satisfy this condition. Such conditions would require adoption by a neutral licensing body.
3. *The terms must allow reproductions of the work licensed to be distributed by the licensee.* Licences may and do differ concerning conditions imposed on the making of modifications (derivative works), and on commercial uses, but must adhere to the core requirement of allowing distribution of reproductions of the licensed work. To be part of the public domain, there must be a permission-free use (in the extended sense discussed below) of at least some of the exclusive rights of a copyright owner.
4. *The terms do not allow any variation of terms by the copyright owner, but may include some choices of included terms set by the neutral body.* The copyright owner decides whether or not they will apply the licence to a work that they own, but their control through permissions then ceases.
5. *The licence cannot be revoked, in relation to any licensee already using the work under the licence.* It can, however, be denied in relation to its use by future licensees. This provides a necessary but minimal loss of control by the copyright owner, and is all that is possible in some jurisdictions: [15.2.4].

6. *The licence is granted to the public, or to a significant class of the public, on equal terms.* The intent of this condition is that the copyright owner cannot exercise any discretion about which individuals are eligible to become licensees, but can restrict the class of users to, for example, 'all University teachers'. Such restrictions would require adoption by a neutral licensing body.
7. *Copies of the licence are freely available.* Consequently, an intended licensor need not obtain the assistance of any party to access and apply the licence. There is no requirement that either the licensor or licensees must make any works freely available, but licensees cannot be prevented from doing so if they choose. While no licence fees are allowed, there is no prohibition on licensors or other parties charging associated costs, as is often done for some 'distributions' of software under such licences.
8. *The licence is not granted in response to the licensee expressing interest in using the work.* It is a standard-form, pre-existing licence, not bespoke and thus does not require an act by another party, including the neutral licensing body.
9. *The terms of the licence do not require remuneration to the copyright owner (a licence fee).* Such a requirement does not prevent a copyright owner or a third party selling a copy of the work, or providing services to assist with its use, but it must be open to any other party to provide copies of the work (in accordance with the licence) with no remuneration at all. This non-remuneration condition is consistent with both the main strands of FOSS licences, and with Creative Commons licences.

These conditions, except the last, are based on the touchstone of our definition of the copyright public domain: the absence of the need for permission to use a work. The other key element of these conditions is the necessity for a neutral licensing body. Subject to conditions 2–9, the terms of neutral voluntary licences are those that are set by one or more neutral licence schemes. On our approach, any licensing schemes fitting these criteria are such that works licensed under them become part of the public domain.

By taking this approach, we allow some flexibility in what terms may or may not be allowed in particular neutral voluntary licence schemes, by relying mainly on the neutrality of the parties drawing up the licences.

We stress that, since this part of the public domain is constructed by voluntary actions (licences and dedications), rather than by international agreements and national legislation, it is essential that these licences are enforceable. Unlike legislation, enforceability cannot be assumed, and needs more thorough examination than do other aspects of the public domain.

## 15.1 'Neutral' Voluntary Licensing and the Public Domain

*Licences Not Included* We do not include in the public domain those voluntary licences which do not meet all the above criteria. This is not a value-judgement: the public domain has no monopoly on socially valuable content. It is a result of application of our key criterion of the absence of the need for permission to use a work from a copyright owner.

Individual copyright owners may create licences under which they make their works freely available to the public (or which other copyright owners can also use), and these may be on generous terms. However, there is no practicable and objective way to distinguish such licences from those that are simply private licensing of works. Even if such a licence met our criteria 3–9 above, criterion 2 allows imposition of other restrictions. Because these restrictions are open-ended, and in our view cannot be specified exhaustively as various licence conditions, it is necessary to interpose a neutral party to specify which conditions are and are not desirable, thereby creating independence from the self-interest of individual copyright owners. In practice, the existence of such neutral parties is a key element of the success of FOSS licensing and Creative Commons. Licences crafted by individual copyright owners with generous free use terms can best be described as 'on the border' of this category of the public domain, but still as essentially proprietary licences. Licences may also be implied by conduct, and such licences may support the public domain but are not part of it: [16.2.2].

An example of a family of licences not within the definition of 'neutral' licences is some 'shareware' licences which allow some forms of distribution of licensed content by anyone, and which have many variations concerning free use and licence fees. They are not included primarily because they are not drawn up by a neutral party, for the reasons stated above, and (in some cases) because they require a licence fee.

As will become apparent later in this chapter, our permission-focused criteria for when licensed works are part of the public domain are not exactly the same as the conditions for the applicability of various strands of FOSS licences, nor for Creative Commons licences. Their conditions are in some respects more restrictive but within our criteria.

*Borderline Cases* Our categories of the copyright public domain are united more by their family resemblance than by an a priori strict definition, so arguments about borderline cases may sometimes change the categories and the definition. Two examples arise from neutral voluntary licences.

Some long-standing licences originally developed by a copyright owner, not by a neutral party (nor subsequently taken over by one), which have subsequently been adopted by very large numbers of licensors and licensees, may be a borderline case of what should be regarded as part of the public domain. But this is the exception, not the rule. Some licences early in FOSS history may be in this category.

If the condition of non-remuneration to copyright owners did not apply, it would be very difficult to distinguish from the public domain commercial licensing of works via an independent third party (for example, an app store) on prices, terms and conditions set by it. All categories of the copyright public domain other than compulsory licensing are non-remunerated. It could be argued by analogy that licences should not be excluded where the neutral body has decided that the copyright owner should be remunerated and sets the remuneration. We have excluded them because it is not possible to distinguish commercial licensing via a third party, unlike compulsory licensing.

### 15.1.3 Causes of Global Consistency

Neutral voluntary licensing has contributed much to the expansion of the public domain since the 1990s. Despite public domains being essentially national in character, this aspect of the public domain is essentially global. This is because a relatively small number of standardised licences have come to be used worldwide and to dominate the application of licences to works, and because a high percentage of works licensed are under licences which have a 'viral' character which assists their international spread. The creation of neutral voluntary licences has had many advantages, especially the reduction of the transaction costs involved in using copyright works,[1] but these two factors have influenced their global consistency.

*Uniformity in Voluntary Licences through Global Standards* While most of the significant neutral voluntary licences originate in the United States and most reflect the categories and terminology of US law to some extent, their usage has been global. The Creative Commons (CC) licensing organisation originated in the United States, but has affiliates in seventy-nine jurisdictions.[2] CC claims that over 1.2 billion works are licensed under its licences: [15.3.1], and its licence suite is the most commonly used globally.

---

[1] N. Elkin-Koren, 'Exploring creative commons: a skeptical view of a worthy pursuit', in Guibault and Hugenholtz (eds.), *The Future of the Public Domain*, 325–45.
[2] Creative Commons, CC Affiliate Network https://wiki.creativecommons.org/wiki/CC_Affiliate_Network.

## 15.1 'Neutral' Voluntary Licensing and the Public Domain

From 2002, the CC licence suite was available in an 'international' version (although influenced by US law), but the licences were subsequently modified ('ported') into country-specific versions to better suit the legal systems and terminologies of many countries (as well as translation into national languages), nevertheless retaining all the essential elements of the original. The most recent version of the CC licensing suite (v. 4.0) has been 'internationalised' further to make it consistent with international conventions, and ported versions will only be available in 'compelling circumstances': [15.3.2]. None of the significant FOSS licences for software have been 'ported' to local versions, but they are used globally, and alternative 'national' licences do not seem to have become significant: [15.2.2]. Licences primarily used in a particular country or region are the exception and not the rule, and some previously popular national licence schemes have not survived, although many works licensed under them continue to be available.[3] The neutral voluntary licences in use globally are fairly uniform across most countries. The global nature of the Internet both inspires and propagates this uniformity, thereby reinforcing the global public domain of voluntary licensing. The effectiveness of this voluntary licensing is supported by many Internet-based mechanisms which assist both these licences, and works licensed under them, to be found: [6.2.2].

*Viral Character of Some Licences* Viral licences are neutral voluntary licences of works that allow the software, text or other content to which they apply to be modified to create a new derivative work (in US terminology), but only on the basis that the derivate work is available for distribution under the same licence conditions. As a result, where such a viral licence is adopted, the software or content available under the licence will expand with the distribution of any derivative works, thereby reinforcing the public domain. Viral, or 'share-alike', licences are the most significant aspect of voluntary licensing for the public domain, because they contain an in-built mechanism to expand the public domain.

The global effects arise because, if a work is under a viral licence developed in country A, but that work is used to produce a derivative work in country B, the licence developed in country A will then be in use in country B, and its use is likely to spread further there, and to other countries. Global enforceability of these licences is therefore a significant

---

[3] For example: the Australian TVET/AESN licences for educational materials; the European Commission's European Public Licence (EUPL), which is still in active use https://joinup.ec.europa.eu/community/eupl/home.

issue, but the viral nature of these licences is the source of their importance.

In practice, the most effective viral licences create a significant and expanding global public domain in certain types of information, especially software. The most obvious and important example is open source software created by the viral GNU General Public License (GPL), as well as some other Free and Open Source (FOSS) licences. There are now many instances of such licences being used globally. In relation to content other than software, the outstanding example is that of the Creative Commons (CC) suite of licences, from which (as detailed in [15.3.3]) the two licences with viral characteristics are applied to 50 per cent of all CC-licensed content, comprising an estimated half billion items of content globally by 2016.[4] The creation and propagation of viral licences, the terms of which are uniform across legal borders, are, like other neutral voluntary licences, obviously enabled and facilitated by global Internet practices.

## 15.2 Free and Open Source Software (FOSS) Licensing

Computer software is inherently more an unfinished product than other literary works, because changes which will objectively improve its performance are possible, and because practices of team development and acceptance of iterative improvements by different individuals have been widespread and approved by the community of software developers in the seventy years or so of its development.

Out of this culture of collaboration, what we now call free and open source software (FOSS) licensing started to develop thirty years ago. GNU software for UNIX was released under the GNU General Public License (GPL) v.1.0 by Richard Stallman in February 1989, and later that year other UNIX software was released by Bill Joy under the University of California's Berkeley Software Distribution (BSD) licence.[5] The GPL and BSD licences represent two strains of what have subsequently come to be known as free and open-source software (FOSS) licensing. Licences that comply with one definition will usually comply with the other: the differences are primarily philosophical.[6]

---

[4] Creative Commons, 'State of the Commons', 2016 report https://stateof.creative commons.org/.

[5] L. Rosen, *Open Source Licensing: Software Freedom and Intellectual Property Law* (Prentice Hall, 2004), p. xix.

[6] For general discussions of FOSS licensing, see *ibid.*; N. Shemtov and I. Walden (eds.), *Free and Open Source Software: Policy Law and Practice* (Oxford University Press, 2013); M. Schellekens, 'Free and open source software: an answer to commodification', chap. 13, in Guibault and Hugenholtz (eds.), *The Future of the Public Domain*; H. Meeker,

## 15.2.1 The Conditions for FOSS Licences

The two predominant strains of FOSS licences are those that comply with the Open Source Initiative's 'Open Source Definition', and those that comply with the Free Software Foundation's 'Free Software Definition', each of which is explained in this section.

*Open Source Definition* The Open Source Initiative (OSI) uses the 'Open Source Definition'[7] which defines open-source software as requiring not only access to the source code, but that the distribution terms of open-source software must comply with ten criteria, which we have abbreviated slightly:

'1. Free Redistribution – The license shall not restrict any party from selling or giving away the software as a component of an aggregate software distribution containing programs from several different sources. The license shall not require a royalty or other fee for such sale.
2. Source Code – The program must include source code, and must allow distribution in source code as well as compiled form. Where some form of a product is not distributed with source code, there must be a well-publicized means of obtaining the source code for no more than a reasonable reproduction cost, preferably downloading via the Internet without charge. The source code must be the preferred form in which a programmer would modify the program. [...]
3. Derived Works – The license must allow modifications and derived works, and must allow them to be distributed under the same terms as the license of the original software.
4. Integrity of The Author's Source Code – The license may restrict source code from being distributed in modified form only if the license allows the distribution of "patch files" with the source code [...]
5. No Discrimination Against Persons or Groups – The license must not discriminate against any person or group of persons.
6. No Discrimination Against Fields of Endeavor – The license must not restrict anyone from making use of the program in a specific field of endeavor. [...]
7. Distribution of License – The rights attached to the program must apply to all to whom the program is redistributed without the need for execution of an additional license by those parties.

---

*The Open Source Alternative: Understanding and Leveraging Opportunities* (John Wiley & Sons, 2008).
[7] Open Source Initiative, 'Open source definition', 2007 https://opensource.org/osd.

8. License Must Not Be Specific to a Product – The rights attached to the program must not depend on the program's being part of a particular software distribution. [...]
9. License Must Not Restrict Other Software – The license must not place restrictions on other software that is distributed along with the licensed software. [...]
10. License Must Be Technology-Neutral – No provision of the license may be predicated on any individual technology or style of interface.'

All licences meeting the OSI definition will meet our conditions in [15.1.2] for a neutral voluntary licence, and, therefore, in our view, software licensed under them are part of the public domain. Some of the OSI conditions are more strict than the minimum conditions we have proposed for works to be part of the public domain, particularly condition 3 (derived works must be allowed, not merely reproductions), 5 and 6. Software can expand the permission-free uses that are our key criterion for the public domain, and still be within our definition, even though there may be good arguments favouring these additional OSI conditions.

It is significant that condition 3 ('Derived Works'), while it 'must allow' derived works to be distributed on the same conditions as the original software, does not require that either the original software or the derivative must include a 'share-alike' or viral condition. So OSI-compliant licences may include both viral and non-viral licences.

*Free Software Definition* The Free Software Foundation (FSF)[8] uses the Free Software Definition[9] which requires that a program 'is free software if the program's users have the four essential freedoms', which are:

> The freedom to run the program as you wish, for any purpose (freedom 0).
> The freedom to study how the program works, and change it so it does your computing as you wish (freedom 1). Access to the source code is a precondition for this.
> The freedom to redistribute copies so you can help your neighbor (freedom 2).
> The freedom to distribute copies of your modified versions to others (freedom 3). By doing this you can give the whole community a chance to benefit from your changes. Access to the source code is a precondition for this.

---

[8] Free Software Foundation (FSF) website www.fsf.org/.
[9] Free Software Definition www.gnu.org/philosophy/free-sw.html.

## 15.2 Free and Open Source Software (FOSS) Licensing

The FSF's own licences, particularly the GPL and the LGPL, implement these four freedoms, and are discussed in [15.2.3]. All licences meeting the FSF's definition will meet our above conditions for a neutral voluntary licence, and, therefore, in our view, all software licensed under them is part of the public domain. The Free Software Definition, as with the Open Source Definition, allows both viral and non-viral licences, and does not allow licences to prevent derivative works, nor to be limited to particular uses or classes of users (all of which restrictions are allowed by our public domain definition). In Creative Commons terminology, all OSD-compliant and FSD-compliant licences may be the equivalent of either BY licences, or BY-SA licences, but cannot be the equivalent of any of the other three CC licence variations because they are too restrictive: [15.3.2].

The FSF argues that it is important to refer to 'free software' rather than 'open-source', because '[t]he two terms describe almost the same category of software, but they stand for views based on fundamentally different values. Open source is a development methodology; free software is a social movement'.[10] FSF considers that the Open Source Definition agrees with the Free Software Definition in most cases,[11] but that common usages of 'open-source' are misleading, partly because they often imply that access to source code is sufficient to constitute 'open source', whereas usage of 'free software' is less likely to mislead.

Merely providing source code as part of the provision of software does not satisfy the OSI definition (even if this is often misunderstood, as FSF claims), nor does it meet the FSF definition, nor does it meet our criteria for neutral voluntary licensing. Software that is 'open source' only in this simple sense is therefore not part of the public domain.

### 15.2.2 Utilisation of FOSS Licences

The list of 'open source' licences kept by the OSI,[12] and of 'free' software licences kept by the FSF,[13] are together called FOSS (free and open-source software) licences. All FOSS licences, because they meet the requirements of either OSI or FSF, should also meet our criteria for neutral voluntary licences and thus software licensed under them is part of the public domain.

---

[10] Richard Stallman, 'Why open source misses the point of free software', FSF website, undated www.gnu.org/philosophy/open-source-misses-the-point.html.
[11] Ibid.
[12] Open Source Initiative website https://opensource.org/; see under 'Licenses' for licences categorised in various ways.
[13] FSF, 'Various licenses and comments about them' www.gnu.org/licenses/license-list.html.

The use of FOSS-licensed software has proliferated. A survey in 2015 showed that 78 per cent of companies used it for part or all of their operations (and less than 3 per cent did not use it at all), an increase from 42 per cent in 2010.[14] A few examples of the most widely used software so distributed should suffice to demonstrate how important this aspect of the public domain has become to all aspects of commerce, government and other sectors: the Linux kernel for operating systems; GNU utilities and compilers; RedHat and Ubuntu distributions of Linux; BSD operating systems; MYSQL database server; Apache web server; Samba networking protocol; SendMail mail transfer agent; Firefox web browser; Wordpress blog software; and BIND (Berkeley Internet Name Domain Server) DNS server software.[15]

The most widely used FOSS licences, according to one industry classification,[16] are: MIT License (32 per cent); GNU General Public License (GPL) 2.0 (18 per cent); Apache License 2.0 (14 per cent); GNU General Public License (GPL) 3.0 (7 per cent); BSD License 2.0 (3-clause, New or Revised) License (6 per cent); ISC License (5 per cent); Artistic License (Perl) (4 per cent); GNU Lesser General Public License (LGPL) 2.1 (4 per cent); GNU Lesser General Public License (LGPL) 3.0 (2 per cent). The Mozilla Public License (MPL) 1.1 was ranked 14th, with less than 1 per cent. This analysis claimed twenty licences account for almost the entire market. These licences have enabled FOSS software to become at least as important as proprietary software, and to become indispensable to the operation of the Internet.

*Governance of FOSS Licences* All of the licences which have more than 1 per cent of market take-up are developed and/or revised by organisations which qualify as 'neutral parties' for the purposes of our definition of neutral voluntary licensing, particularly universities and non-profit foundations. Furthermore, there is a 'meta-level' of something similar to accreditation in that these licences are listed by either OSI or

---

[14] S. Vaughan-Nichols, 'It's an open-source world: 78 percent of companies run open-source software', ZDNet, 16 April 2016 www.zdnet.com/article/its-an-open-source-world-78-percent-of-companies-run-open-source-software/. These results are from the 9th annual industry survey by Black Duck Knowledge Base www.blackducksoftware.com/technology/knowledgebase.

[15] For examples of such lists, and justifications for inclusions, see www.linux.com/blog/top-10-best-open-source-softwares-rocks-world-wide-web and http://royal.pingdom.com/2009/05/29/the-8-most-successful-open-source-products-ever/.

[16] Black Duck Knowledge Base, 'Top Open Source Licenses', undated www.blackducksoftware.com/top-open-source-licenses. Black Duck claims 'This open source licensing data reflects analysis of over two million open source projects from over 9,000 global forges and repositories.' Links to details of most of the licences mentioned are available from this table.

## 15.2 Free and Open Source Software (FOSS) Licensing

FSF as complying with their definitions of open source software or free software. However, not all 'open source' licences meet our definition. For example, the Microsoft Public Licence, ranked 11th with 1 per cent of market share, is not developed by a neutral party.

The FSF has modified the two GPL licences in Version 3, by defining 'convey' and other minor changes, in order to make the GPL more compatible with non-US laws.[17]

*Classification of FOSS Licences: 'Copyleft' Variations*  All FOSS licences come within our definition of the public domain, so the main purpose of further classification is to assist in understanding the significance of this licensing to the public domain, and in particular which licences are viral licences. This distinction between 'no copyleft' and 'copyleft' (or viral) licences is important,[18] but further distinction between 'weak copyleft' and 'strong copyleft' licences is unnecessary.[19] There are many other substantial differences between FOSS licences[20] that are not necessary for our purposes.

McDonagh's classification, with each category's total market share of all software licences indicated, is as follows.[21]

*No copyleft licences* – 'No copyleft' refers to the lack of provisions restricting how the software can be redistributed, including no requirement to distribute derivative works under copyleft licences.[22] Licences which have no copyleft provisions include Apache 2.0, BSD and MIT licences (total 52 per cent uptake). These licences allow any party 'to modify the source code and release, commercially or non-commercially, a free/open or commercial/closed version' of the software.[23] These are not

---

[17] GNU General Public License, Version 3, 29 June 2007 www.gnu.org/licenses/gpl-3.0.en.html; 'A quick guide to GPLv3: A global license' www.gnu.org/licenses/quick-guide-gplv3.html.

[18] L. McDonagh, 'Copyright, contract and FOSS', chap. 3, in Shemtov and Walden (eds.), *Free and Open Source Software: Policy Law and Practice*, 73–87; A. Guadamuz, 'Free and open source software', in L. Edwards and C. Waelde (eds.), *Law and the Internet* (3rd edn, Hart, 2009), pp. 367–8.

[19] McDonagh, 'Copyright, contract and FOSS', 73. This distinction is based on some licences distinguishing between static and dynamic linking of code modifications, in relation to such licensing of derivative works. Static linking incorporates modifications through compilation to produce a merged object file that is a stand-alone executable, whereas with dynamic linking additional components are incorporated only when the program is loaded, or when it is executed, and no static object code combining the modifications with the original code results. The FSF argues that dynamic linking does create a derivative work, but McDonagh's view is that only static linking would be held to constitute a derivative work, if the matter was litigated.

[20] See *ibid.* 74–6 for other distinctions that we do not discuss.

[21] The following paragraphs are derived from *ibid.* 73–87, with percentages added from Black Duck Knowledge Base, 'Top open source licenses'.

[22] McDonagh, 'Copyright, contract and FOSS', 78–9.

[23] *Ibid.* 77. These comments apply equally to all of these licences.

viral licences: modifications may be issued under any other licence, including weak or strong copyleft licences.[24] Larger GPL-licensed projects may contain non-copyleft-licensed components.

*Copyleft licences* – Both strong and weak copyleft licences are viral licences, in that, in relation to 'modifications to the code', they 'require that this derivative material must be licensed under the same licence as the first work in the chain'.[25] Licences with only weak copyleft provisions include MPL and LGPL (total 7 per cent uptake). 'LGPL code must be left open and accessible. The LGPL is suitable for the distribution of derivative works, but crucially the LGPL requires that derivative content must be licensed under LGPL/GPLv2'.[26] Licences with the strongest copyleft provisions include GPLv2 and GPLv3 (total 25 per cent uptake). The GNU General Public Licenses (GPL v2 and v3) from the FSF, and similar licences, 'maintain that derivative works cannot be distributed under any other licence and that the full source code must be provided'.[27] These licences aim to capture the widest possible range of software-related 'material' as possible within the licence, and to have many types of distributions triggering the copyleft requirements of providing source code modifications to other parties.[28] GPL-licensed software may not be included in a larger non-copyleft licensed projects.

Therefore, about one-third of software under FOSS licences is licensed under viral licences, but about two-thirds of software so licensed does not have this 'share-alike' requirement.

### 15.2.3 Legal Status of FOSS Licences

Decided cases on basic legal questions concerning FOSS licences, including questions of whether they are contracts or bare licences (or something in between), and resulting questions of enforceability, are infrequent and largely insignificant, even though it is well over twenty-five years since use of FOSS became widespread and commercially important. McDonagh considered that, in 2013, 'case law in all jurisdictions is still in its infancy' and that 'assessment of the enforceability of FOSS licences must be greeted with a degree of caution'.[29] It has been claimed that, as of 2017, no court in any country has yet ruled on whether there must be distribution of the source code of a derivative work because of a breach of the GPL.[30] Given the differences between contract, consumer and copyright laws around the world, it may be that the answers to these fundamental

---

[24] *Ibid.* 73.   [25] *Ibid.* 73.   [26] *Ibid.* 82.   [27] *Ibid.* 82.   [28] *Ibid.* 83–7   [29] *Ibid.* 99.
[30] M. von Haller, 'Enforcement of open source licenses?', *Digital Business Law* (Bird & Bird), 24 January 2017 http://digitalbusiness.law/2017/01/enforcement-of-open-source-licenses/#page=1.

## 15.2 Free and Open Source Software (FOSS) Licensing

questions will vary between jurisdictions, even though the licences are very often used globally.[31]

One of the potential problems of FOSS licences is when FOSS-licensed software is used without adherence to its licence conditions, in particular without the copyleft requirements of disclosure of source code of derivative works. This could occur because, unlike with proprietary software, there is no one with a sufficient economic interest to enforce the licence conditions. However, there are organisations such as FSF which have taken on the role of representing the diffuse community of code authors by pursuing enforcement actions. The FSF has taken a very active role in enforcing the GPL and similar licences, where it holds the copyright,[32] based on a set of enforcement principles.[33] FSF obtains assignments of copyright of GNU-licensed software, so that it is able to take enforcement actions.[34] Similar actions in Europe are discussed below.

Despite these legal uncertainties, it seems from the extensive commercial, governmental and other uptake of FOSS-licensed software over the past quarter century, that large organisations are not deterred from making major investments in utilisation of FOSS-licensed software: [15.2.2]. Legal issues have not impeded the growth of this significant new component of the public domain.

The potential legal issues concerning FOSS licences that go to the question of their legal validity and enforceability, and are thus critical to their position as part of the public domain, include whether they are a contract or bare licence or a hybrid, how privity of contract arises between the original copyright owner and successive licensees, and the role of estoppel in relation to enforcement. This first issue is discussed here, and the latter issues in [15.4].

*Contract or Bare Licence?* Although there has been 'a tremendous amount of academic debate'[35] concerning when FOSS licences will constitute a 'bare' licence (not involving a contract), or a 'contractual licence' (a licence created by and coupled with a contract), there is little consensus. From a public domain perspective, the issue is important

---

[31] McDonagh, 'Copyright, contract and FOSS', 96.
[32] FSF, 'Violations of the GNU licenses' www.gnu.org/licenses/gpl-violation.html.
[33] J. Gay, 'Principles of community-oriented GPL enforcement', Free Software Foundation, 30 September 2015 www.fsf.org/licensing/enforcement-principles.
[34] FSF, 'Copyright & compliance' www.fsf.org/licensing/.
[35] McDonagh, 'Copyright, contract and FOSS', 87; see his discussion at 87–99; A. Guadamuz, 'The license/contract dichotomy in open licenses: a comparative analysis' (2009) *University of La Verne Law Review* 30(2) 101–16; Guadamuz, 'Free and open source software', 377–82.

because FOSS licences must be valid on either one, or both, grounds, or this aspect of the public domain will be without foundations.

A bare licence (in the copyright context) is a unilateral permission by the licensor, to the licensee, allowing the licensee to use the work in a way that would otherwise infringe copyright.[36] Guadamuz explains that in most civil law and mixed jurisdictions, unlike in common law jurisdictions, such unilateral acts can constitute contracts if offer and acceptance are present, without the necessity for consideration.[37] It is arguable that if a FOSS licence is considered to be a contract, it might fail to be valid in common law countries because of lack of consideration by the licensee, but the counter-argument is raised that a promise to observe licence conditions is sufficient consideration.[38] Moglen of the FSF, for example, has argued that the GPL is not a contract, but that it is sufficient that it is a bare licence coupled with copyright law: 'Licenses are not contracts: the work's user is obliged to remain within the bounds of the license not because she voluntarily promised, but because she doesn't have any right to act at all except as the license permits'.[39] Those taking such an approach argue that, if the conditions of the licence are broken, the licence simply ceases to exist, and the rights of copyright owners under copyright law (not under contract) are enforced. One reason that Moglen prefers to rely upon copyright law is the perception that it is more uniform internationally than contract law. However, unlike a contract, a bare licence can be revoked at the will of the licensor. A clause in a FOSS licence stating that the licence is irrevocable provided the licence conditions are adhered to 'is merely a promise', unless it is part of a binding contract.[40] Despite the forty-year history of FOSS licences, this basic issue of 'contract or bare licence' has yet received relatively little clarification through litigation.

*Enforcement of FOSS Licences in the United States and Common Law Countries* In the United States, the leading case is now more than a decade old but is reinforced by recent cases. In *Jacobsen* v. *Katzer*,[41] Jacobsen released software under the Artistic License

---

[36] McDonagh, 'Copyright, contract and FOSS', 93.
[37] Guadamuz, 'Free and open source software', 378.
[38] *Ibid.*; contra. N Shemtov, 'FOSS licence: bare licence or contract', Centre for Commercial Law Studies Queen Mary University of London presentation https://web.ua.es/es/contratos-id/documentos/itipupdate2011/shemtov.pdf.
[39] E Moglen, 'Enforcing the GNU GPL', 10 September 2001 www.gnu.org/philosophy/enforcing-gpl.html. See also P. Jones, 'The GPL is a license, not a contract' [2003] *Linux Weekly News* 3 December http://lwn.net/Articles/61292/.
[40] McDonagh, 'Copyright, contract and FOSS', 93.
[41] *Jacobsen* v. *Katzer*, 2007 US Dist. LEXIS 63568 (ND Cal 2007); *Jacobsen* v. *Katzer*, 535 F.3d 1373 (Fed Cir 2008).

## 15.2 Free and Open Source Software (FOSS) Licensing

(AL).[42] The licence allowed anyone to distribute the software with modifications, provided the modifications were clearly documented, and accompanied by the original copyright notices. Katzer distributed the software without complying with these terms. Concerning consideration, the Court of Appeals for the Ninth Circuit held that '[t]he choice to exact consideration in the form of compliance with the open source requirements of disclosure and explanation of changes, rather than as a dollar denominated fee, is entitled to no less legal recognition.' The Court therefore found that the AL was a contractual licence (not a mere covenant), but that the licence was of a 'hybrid' nature and Katzer's actions had also breached copyright, by reproducing the software contrary to the terms of the licence. Consequently, injunctive relief was available, which is more likely for a copyright infringement than for a breach of contract. McDonagh notes Menon's conclusion that the conditional language ('provided that') in the licence which was crucial to the decision here is also found in most other major FOSS licences such as Apache 2.0, BSD, MIT, GPLv2 and GPLv3, and so they are in his view likely to be enforceable in the United States, and result in copyright remedies being available.[43]

In 2017 in *Artifex Software* v. *Hancom*,[44] the plaintiff offered commercial licences for its Ghostscript PDF interpreter software, but also offered an open source licence under the open source GNU GPL, section 9 of which stated that users were not required to accept the licence in order to run it, but

> nothing other than this License grants you permission to propagate or modify any covered work. These actions infringe copyright if you do not accept this License. Therefore, by modifying or propagating a covered work, you indicate your acceptance of this License to do so.

The defendant distributed its own software incorporating the Ghostscript software, but did not include the source code and therefore breached the terms of the GPL. It had advertised on its website that its use of Ghostscript was so licensed. The court held that the defendant's use of Ghostscript, and its public representations concerning the GPL, sufficiently demonstrate the mutual assent necessary for a contract.

In *Versata* v. *Ameriprise*,[45] in 2014, the court rejected Versata's argument that the GPL 'amounts to nothing more than a promise to not

---

[42] 'Open Source Initiative – Artistic Licence 2.0' https://opensource.org/licenses/Artistic-2.0.
[43] McDonagh, 'Copyright, contract and FOSS', 98.
[44] *Artifex Software* v. *Hancom* 2017 US Dist. LEXIS 62815 (ND Cal, Apr 25, 2017).
[45] *Versata Software, Inc.* v. *Ameriprise Financial, Inc.* (2014), US D. Ct, W. D. Texas, Austin Div., unreported WestLaw 950065.

commit copyright infringement, and Ameriprise's claim is therefore preempted'. Instead, the court considered that the GPL 'imposes an affirmative obligation on any license holder to make the code of any derivative work freely available and open source', and this '"viral" component of the GPL is separate and distinct from any copyright obligation'.

The use of FOSS software components without adherence to FOSS licensing conditions is alleged to be widespread,[46] and these recent cases demonstrate the considerable risks of such misuse.

We have not found cases concerning the validity of FOSS licences in the UK[47] or other common law jurisdictions.[48]

*Enforcement of FOSS Licences in Civil Law Countries* Since European civil law countries do not share common law contract doctrines such as distinctions between conditions and covenants,[49] or the requirement of consideration for contract formation, it is not surprising that cases before European courts have consistently found FOSS licences to be valid and enforceable.[50] In the early 2000s, Harald Welte and gpl-violations.org[51] took a successful series of actions in German courts to enforce the GPL, obtaining injunctions in three decisions for various failures by licensees to distribute copies of GPL-licensed software without the necessary copyright information, and distribution of derivative works without the requisite copies of the source code.[52] Guadamuz notes that 'the Munich District Court recognised that the GPL is a valid contract in accordance with German law [and] it upheld the contractual validity of the main clauses, including the copyleft clause.'[53] The gpl-violations.org organisation is again active, reporting 2013 litigation success against distribution of firmware containing GPL-licensed code, without distribution of source code.[54] The first ruling on the GPL v.3,[55] in 2015, found an educational institution in breach for failure to provide to students either

---

[46] Jeff Luszcz, '*Artifex* v. *Hancom*: open source is now an enforceable contract', 31 August 2017, *Linux.com* www.linux.com/print/473842.
[47] McDonagh, 'Copyright, contract and FOSS', 98. This was stated as at 2013.
[48] In the Australian case *Trumpet Software* v. *OzEmail Pty Ltd*. [1996] FCA 560; (1996) 34 IPR 481 Heerey J held that a shareware licence is revocable at the will of the licensor and characterised a shareware licence as a bare licence. However, in this case there was neither any licence with terms similar to a FOSS licence, nor any contractual relationship between the parties, so it is of little relevance.
[49] McDonagh, 'Copyright, contract and FOSS', 98.   [50] *Ibid*. 99.
[51] The gpl-violations.org project http://gpl-violations.org/.
[52] Guadamuz, 'Free and open source software', 383–4.   [53] *Ibid*. 384.
[54] H. Welte, 'Regional court Hamburg judgement against FANTEC', 26 June 2013 http://gpl-violations.org/news/ concerning a decision of the Regional Court of Hamburg [Landgericht Hamburg] against FANTEC Gmb.r.
[55] 'SBV v. a German University', Regional Court Halle, Ref. 4 O 133/15, 27 July 2015 www.jbb.de/Docs/LG_Halle_GPL3.pdf.

the licence text or the source code with the software.[56] The European affiliate of FSF has started workshops on licence enforcement actions,[57] so it appears that FOSS licensing in Europe, as in the United States, is unlikely to fail because of want of advocacy.

### 15.2.4 Government Supports for FOSS Licensing

While FOSS software has many competitive advantages that account for its success in commercial environments, within the public sector it is also being supported by explicit government policies in many countries. For example, the Indian government has adopted a policy[58] that it (and state governments that wish to do likewise) will endeavour to adopt Open Source Software (OSS) in all e-Governance systems implemented by Indian government agencies, in preference to 'closed' commercial software. Tenders must require bidders to consider OSS and must 'provide justification for exclusion of OSS in their response'. It is difficult for FOSS to be excluded from tenders in the EU.[59]

## 15.3 Creative Commons and Other Open Content Licensing

We use 'open content' generally to refer to works other than software, including text, music, videos and artistic works, which are licensed under neutral voluntary licences. As with FOSS software licences, there are a variety of open content licences, of which the Creative Commons (CC) suite of licences has become the most widely used and best known globally. Other open content licences with significant global use include the GNU Free Documentation License (GNU FDL or GFDL) and the Open Data Commons (ODC) suite: [15.3.3].

---

[56] JBB Lawyers, 'Open Source Software: preliminary injunction based on violation of GPL-3.0', 27 November 2015 www.jbb.de/en/news/open-source-software-preliminary-injunction-based-violation-gpl-30.

[57] P. Brown, 'Enforcement and compliance for the GPL and similar licenses', 11 May 2016 https://lwn.net/Articles/686768/ (report on 2016 EFSF Free Software Legal & Licensing Workshop).

[58] Ministry of Communication & Information Technology (India), 'Policy on adoption of open source software for government of India', 2014 http://meity.gov.in/sites/upload_files/dit/files/policy_on_adoption_of_oss.pdf.

[59] In EU procurement law, because of principles derived from EU treaties, it is very difficult for FOSS software to be excluded from tenders, but 'seemingly absolute rules suffer exception where the contracting authority's reasons for departing from them are objectively justifiable, and one may be slow to state ... that the exclusion of open source can never be justified': I. Mitchell, 'Public sector and open source', in Shemtov and Walden (eds.), *Free and Open Source Software*, 417.

494    Voluntary Licensing Creating Public Rights

There are various definitions of 'open content', one of which is the Open Definition (previously the Open Knowledge Definition), the most succinct version of which is that 'open data and content can be freely used, modified, and shared by anyone for any purpose'.[60] It defines Open Works and the Open License under which they must be licensed unless they are already free of all copyright restrictions. The Open Knowledge Definition was initially derived from the Open Source Definition, and is consistent with the Free Software Definition.[61] Licences and public domain dedications conforming to the Open Definition are only those that are limited to having attribution (BY) and share-alike (SA) conditions, and no others.[62] Non-conforming licences therefore include some CC licences such as NonCommercial or No-Derivatives conditions: [15.3.2].[63] Our definition of neutral public licensing is therefore broader than the Open Definition.

### 15.3.1   Creative Commons Licensing: Extent and Significance

Since 2002, Creative Commons (CC) has provided a suite of licences that are now the most widely used open content licences. CC is a US non-profit corporation governed by a board of thirteen directors,[64] including non-US directors. It is a 'neutral party' in relation to licence development as required by our definition. Its deliberative processes concerning version 4 of its licence suite, discussed below, demonstrate this.

CC claims that there are 1.2 billion CC licensed works as of 2016, and average annual expansion per year exceeds 10 per cent over the past few years,[65] so the rate of increase is still significant at around 100 million works per year. CC licensed works are distributed across millions of websites,[66] but a large proportion are located on major Internet content platforms that distribute user-generated content (UGC), and which either offer CC licences to users or require their use. These platforms include flickr, Wikipedia, YouTube, the Internet Archive, 500px, FMA and the Public Library of Science (PLOS).[67] The range of media and volume of works which are CC licensed content available from these

---

[60] The Open Definition http://opendefinition.org/.
[61] Open Definition 2.1 http://opendefinition.org/od/2.1/en/.
[62] Open Definition, 'Conformant licenses' http://opendefinition.org/licenses/.
[63] Open Definition, 'Non-Conformant licenses' http://opendefinition.org/licenses/nonconformant/.
[64] Creative Commons, 'Our board' https://creativecommons.org/about/team/#our-board.
[65] Creative Commons, 'State of the Commons', 2016 Report.
[66] Creative Commons, 'Creative Commons platforms', undated https://creativecommons.org/about/platform/.
[67] *Ibid.*

15.3 Creative Commons and Other Open Content Licensing     495

platforms is described in CC's 2016 'State of the Commons' Report,[68] including 381 million images in flickr, 45.5 million articles in Wikipedia and 29.4 million files in the Wikimedia Commons media file repository, 30 million videos in YouTube, 27.7 million digital objects in the *Europeana* digital library, 5.8 million videos in vimeo, 1.6 million 3D designs in *Thingiverse*, 858,000 high-quality images from independent photographers in 500px, 532,000 musical tracks in Jamendo Music, 160,000 research articles in PLOS, and 108,000 musical tracks in FMA. CC claims that over 92 million works are 'marked with' CC's public domain tools, particularly the CC0 licence.[69]

An important development was that in 2009 the Wikipedia community and Wikimedia Foundation board approved the adoption of the Creative Commons Attribution-ShareAlike (CC BY-SA) licence as the main content licence for Wikipedia and other Wikimedia sites.

### 15.3.2  *The CC Licence Suite: Varieties of Freedom*

The CC licence suite offers what it describes as 'six main licences', but these arise from only four conditions of licences, the combination of which provides six distinct licences. The four attributes, and their customary abbreviations, with brief descriptions as provided by CC,[70] are:

- Attribution (BY) – 'All CC licenses require that others who use your work in any way must give you credit the way you request, but not in a way that suggests you endorse them or their use.'
- ShareAlike (SA) – 'You let others copy, distribute, display, perform, and modify your work, as long as they distribute any modified work on the same terms.'
- NonCommercial (NC) – 'You let others copy, distribute, display, perform, and (unless you have chosen NoDerivatives) modify and use your work for any purpose other than commercially'. Permission must be obtained for commercial use.
- NoDerivatives (ND) – 'You let others copy, distribute, display and perform only original copies of your work. If they want to modify your work, they must get your permission first.'

The six compatible combinations are: (i) BY (acknowledgment required, but no restrictions on re-use, including commercial and derivative uses,

---

[68] Creative Commons, 'State of the Commons', 2016 Report (undated) https://stateof.creativecommons.org/.
[69] *Ibid.*
[70] Creative Commons, 'Licensing types', undated https://creativecommons.org/share-your-work/licensing-types-examples/.

and no requirement of 'share-alike'); (ii) BY-SA (share-alike required, but no other restrictions on use); (iii) BY-NC-ND (no commercial or derivate uses allowed, but share-alike is not required); (iv) BY-NC-SA (derivatives are allowed, but not commercial uses, and share-alike is required); (v) BY-NC (no commercial uses allowed); and (vi) CC BY-ND (no derivative uses allowed). In addition, there is the CC 'public domain' dedication, CC0, discussed later, which has no licence conditions, and is thus more permissive than the BY licence.

The BY condition is required in all the licences, including the stand-alone BY licence. The SA condition only applies to the modified version of a work, so there is no possible SA-ND combination. The result is six compatible licence combinations, plus the CC0 dedication.

No licence in the CC suite allows licences to be limited to use of a work for particular purposes, or by a particular class of users (e.g., 'for education only' uses, or use only by educational institutions). This is similar to FOSS licences. The most significant differences between the CC licence suite and FOSS licences are that neither the NonCommercial (NC) nor the NoDerivatives (ND) conditions are compatible with FOSS licences. Our definition of neutral voluntary licences allows all of these limitations. All of the licences within the CC suite come within our public domain definition, although some of the CC licences are more strict than our definition requires.

Content licensed under 'open content' licences will almost always be available for free access via the Internet, but it is not a requirement under any CC licence that free access be provided to licensed content. Control over access is not an exclusive right of the copyright owner, and the principal focus of CC licences is on issues concerning exclusive rights. However, no licensee can be prevented from making any CC-licensed content freely available.

As at 2016, CC claims that 65 per cent of CC-licensed works are under the most permissive forms of licences or dedications (which it describes as 'free culture' licences): CC0 6 per cent; 'other public domain tools' 2 per cent; CC BY 20 per cent; CC BY-SA 37 per cent. Distribution of the 35 per cent of licensed works under the other less permissive types of licences is: CC BY-NC-ND 14 per cent; CC BY-NC-SA 13 per cent; CC BY-NC 6 per cent; CC BY-ND 2 per cent.[71] Another perspective is that the combination of CC-BY-SA (37 per cent) and CC BY-NC-SA (13 per cent) indicates that 50 per cent of works licensed under the CC suite are licensed under viral licences.

---

[71] Creative Commons, 'State of the Commons', 2016 Report.

15.3 Creative Commons and Other Open Content Licensing    497

Elkin-Koren was critical of the wide range of CC licences, which stand in contrast to the GPL, saying that under CC '[e]very license that goes beyond absolute exclusion is considered to be a sufficient instrument for promoting sharing and reuse', and arguing that this diversity of licensing options would make CC less effective.[72] Elkin-Koren's criticisms that a proliferation of licence types could result in confusion to users[73] seems to have been shared by CC: a lengthy list of once-available licence types have been 'retired',[74] commonly because of 'inadequate demand'.

While Elkin-Koren is correct that CC 'is completely dependent upon a proprietary regime and derives its force from its existence',[75] CC's utilisation of copyright law to expand the public domain is often regarded as its key innovation and its major strength. Her fears that by encouraging creators to become more proprietary about their works they would give less value to free distribution of their works[76] has not been borne out in practice: the dominance of use of 'free culture' licences suggests that, in fact (in her words), authors 'armed with user-friendly licensing schemes, will exercise their legal powers with self-restraint, authorizing free access to their creative works'.[77]

Corbett is very critical of CC for similar reasons, arguing that 'any kind of quasi-alternative which claims to "enhance the public domain" and "facilitate creativity", but which at the same time is offered from within the constructs of traditional copyright law will be unable to attain those objectives', and 'is doomed'.[78] Some of Corbett's criticisms are addressed by the changes to Version 4.0 discussed below. However, the main problem with this criticism is that it expects too much of CC: it is not an alternative to copyright, but only one of many contributing parts of the public domain. Corbett considers that copyright laws must first be 'more aligned with community norms and expectations' before something like CC could work.[79] In our view, CC's method of voluntary expansion of the public domain, is at least as realistic an approach as to expect such legislation.

*Internationalisation of CC Licences in Version 4*   CC continues to move away from 'porting' its suite of licences better to fit local legal systems, although over fifty ported licence suites currently exist, because

---

[72] Elkin-Koren, 'Exploring creative commons', 331.   [73] *Ibid.* 342.
[74] Creative Commons, 'Retired legal tools' https://creativecommons.org/retiredlicenses/. Other than the sampling licences, most of the other retired licences lacked the BY condition, which became compulsory in CC v.2.0 in 2004.
[75] Elkin-Koren, 'Exploring creative commons', 333–4.   [76] *Ibid.* 337.   [77] *Ibid.* 338.
[78] S. Corbett, 'Creative Commons licences, the copyright regime and the online community: is there a fatal disconnect?' (2011) 74(4) *Modern Law Review* 503 at 531.
[79] *Ibid.*

it intends to adhere as much as possible to one 'international licence suite'. It says the Version 4.0[80] licence suite 'will not be ported absent compelling circumstances' and that the licences are 'written to conform to international treaties governing copyright [and] are all intended to be effective anywhere in the world, with the same effect'.[81]

Numerous policy decisions influenced the development of the CC Version 4.0 licence suite[82] and demonstrate CC's active governance of this aspect of the public domain. They included strengthening of the licences by: (i) applying them to copyright-like rights of licensors, such as database rights; (ii) increasing compatibility with other licences, by removal of two of three compatibility conditions; (iii) requiring licensors who have the capacity to waive or not assert moral rights (or publicity, privacy or personality rights), not to exercise those rights so as to make the CC licensed rights meaningless;[83] (iv) affirmatively granting permission to circumvent effective technological measures 'in order to exercise the rights CC licences grant'. They give licensees more flexibility by (v) allowing under a NoDerivates licence, creation and use of adaptations provided they are not publicly shared; and (vi) allowing licensees thirty days in which to remedy breaches, upon which their licence (which has terminated upon breach) is automatically reinstated, so they do not have to seek a new licence from the licensor, but the licensor is still able to pursue damages if aware of the breach; and by (vii) adhering to the 'NonCommercial' option, despite criticisms of its imprecision,[84] because of user familiarity.

### 15.3.3 Implications of CC Licences for the Public Domain

All of the CC licence suite is within our definition of neutral voluntary licences, and thus part of the public domain. The Creative Commons organisation is the requisite 'neutral party' responsible for drafting the licences, and none of the four conditions which may apply to a licence is outside our definition: [15.1.2]. In particular, there is no inconsistency

---

[80] Version 4.0 (2013) follows Version 1.0 (2001), Version 2.0 (2004) and Version 3.0 (2007).
[81] Creative Commons, 'The Licensing Suite', 19 July 2016 https://wiki.creativecommons.org/wiki/CC_Affiliate_Network.
[82] These points summarise aspects of Creative Commons: 'Version 4: Policy Decisions and Versioning Notes', 18 February 2014 https://wiki.creativecommons.org/wiki/Version_4. For a more detailed summary, see the Online Supplement.
[83] Derivative works licensed under CC licences will be bound by moral rights requirements, in countries where they apply in national laws, and have not been waived (where they can be waived). See Corbett, 'Creative Commons licences, the copyright regime and the online community', 520–2.
[84] See, for example, ibid. 522–5.

## 15.3 Creative Commons and Other Open Content Licensing 499

with our definition where content in the copyright public domain is able to be used for commercial purposes (absence of NC), nor where such commercial use is prohibited (NC), which is a factor which also varies between some free use exceptions and some compulsory licences. Also, while the BY condition requires attribution of authorship, it prohibits author promotion as a condition of the licence. The NoDerivatives condition is uncontentious (at least where software is not the subject matter); it is the same as a free use exception allowing reproductions but nothing more.

The policy decisions concerning CC V 4.0 discussed above demonstrate a number of important factors about CC licences and their significance for the public domain. They are now more intentionally 'global' than in Versions 1–3, because of the policy decision to avoid porting wherever possible, and because of the numerous policy decisions to make them more relevant in important jurisdictions, particularly the EU. The licences are not static, as they evolve between versions in reaction to both experience and global developments in copyright and related laws. CC pays considerable attention to the relationship between this aspect of the public domain (contractually constructed neutral licences) to prevent it diminishing other aspects of the public domain, particularly free use exceptions, and to counteract factors constraining the public domain such as DRMs. These explanations of how the Creative Commons organisation actively manages the public domain resources comprised by its licence suite, including by active engagement with the CC community, is a powerful illustration that Hess and Ostrom and other theorists were correct that successful means of managing commons could be developed: [2.2.4]. Because this aspect of the public domain is contractually constructed, rather than made by legislative fiat, it has to gain and hold adherents who choose to use its licences as licensors, and to comply with them as licensees. CC aims to be adopted globally, rather than relying on national legislation. The CC suite of licences must therefore be curated actively and from a global perspective. While all aspects of the public domain benefit from supportive contexts [6.2], this aspect is different because voluntary organisation is essential to it.

Perhaps the most significant implication of the take-up of CC licences for the future of the copyright public domain is that two of the CC licences use the ShareAlike (SA) condition, and these have 50 per cent of CC's measured usage of licences: BY-SA (37 per cent); and BY-NC-SA (13 per cent).[85] These are viral licences[86]. Therefore, based on CC's

---

[85] Creative Commons, 'State of the Commons', 2016 report https://stateof.creative commons.org/.
[86] M. Radin, 'Humans, computers and binding commitment' (2000) 75 *Indiana Law Journal* 1125 at 1132–3; Elkin-Koren, 'Exploring creative commons', 330.

usage statistics, as at 2016, over half a billion works are licensed under viral licence conditions, such that anyone making use of their content to create a derivative work must, if they distribute that work, do so on the same viral conditions (which may or may not allow commercial uses). This is a powerful engine for future growth of this part of the public domain.

### 15.3.4 Other Open Content Licences

There are many open content licences,[87] but since the availability of the CC licences in 2002 only a few have continued to be significant, including those noted here, and some government-developed licences for open government data (see [15.5]).

*GNU Free Documentation License (GFDL)* The GFDL was designed by the FSF for instructional materials and documentation, giving readers rights to reproduce and modify a textual work, but requiring all copies and derivatives to be available under the GFDL. It is therefore a viral licence. If more than 100 copies are sold commercially, the original source document must also be distributed to recipients. All text contributed to Wikipedia is under the GFDL, and since 2009 has been co-licensed with the CC Attribution Share-Alike License (CC-BY-SA).[88]

*Open Data Commons (ODC) Suite* The Open Data Commons (ODC)[89] project's suite of licences was developed in 2007 as open content licences which would cover both copyright exclusive rights and the *sui generis* database rights existing in the EU, because the CC 3.0 suite of licences did not deal with database rights. ODC provides two licences (equivalents of CC-BY and CC-BY-SA) and a public domain dedication (equivalent to CC0).[90] The CC 4.0 suite has, since 2014, aimed to include database rights. Since the 2010 release of the ODC-BY licence there seems to have been no active development of the ODC project.[91]

---

[87] A partial list, with links to details, is at Wikipedia, 'Open Content License' https://en.wikipedia.org/wiki/Open_Content_License.
[88] 'GNU Free Documentation License', 'List of projects that use the GFDL' https://en.wikipedia.org/wiki/GNU_Free_Documentation_License#List_of_projects_that_use_the_GFDL.
[89] Open Data Commons https://opendatacommons.org; ODC was developed under the Open Knowledge Foundation by J. Hatcher and C. Waelde; see J.-A. Lee, 'Licensing open government data' (2017) 13(2) *Hastings Business Law Journal* 207–40.
[90] ODC, 'Licenses' https://opendatacommons.org/licenses/.
[91] ODC, 'News' https://opendatacommons.org/news/.

## 15.4 Legal Issues and Open Content Licensing

Although there are potential legal issues with the interpretation and enforcement of open content licences and CC, after more than two decades of operation few have been litigated.

### 15.4.1 Enforcement Actions

A few decisions by lower level courts have enforced the conditions of CC licences or enabled their use as a defence against other claims.[92] Issues considered significant in relation to FOSS licences, such as differences between contracts and bare licences, have not been significant in these CC cases. These cases, although small-scale, are significant, because without credible enforceability this aspect of the public domain would lack legal foundations and might not be sustainable in the long term. They illustrate that CC licences have been resistant to litigation which would undermine their effectiveness.

In *Curry* v. *Audax*,[93] stated to be the first court decision on a CC licence,[94] a Dutch court found in 2006 that a commercial magazine had breached both the Attribution and NoCommercial conditions of the CC licences under which the plaintiff made four photos of his family public via flickr. The court prohibited the magazine from further publication of the photos unless in compliance with the licence, on penalty of 1,000 euros per violation. However, it found that there was no justification for damages beyond the 1,000 euros compensation already paid by the defendants. A German court decision also held that a profit-making publication that created hypertext links to photographs published under a CC-licence which did not allow commercial use could be required to remove the hypertext links.[95] A Belgian court awarded 4,500 euros in damages to a band that had released the song 'Abatchouck' under a CC BY-NC-ND 2.0 Belgium licence. A theatre company used twenty seconds of the song in a commercial, and in doing so had violated all three of the licence terms. Both modification of the original work, and use in

---

[92] For lists of known cases, see Creative Commons, 'Case Law' https://wiki.creativecommons.org/wiki/Case_Law.
[93] *Curry* v. *Audax*, District Court of Amsterdam, 9 March 2006, Case no. 334492/ KG 06-176 SR (trans. N. Steijger and N. Hendriks, Institute for Information Law, University of Amsterdam) https://wiki.creativecommons.org/images/3/38/Curry-Audax-English.pdf.
[94] *Curry* v. *Audax* (summary) https://wiki.creativecommons.org/wiki/Curry_v._Audax.
[95] Decision of the Regional Court of Hamburg (Landgericht Hamburg) 16 November 2016 https://wiki.creativecommons.org/wiki/Spirit.

a commercial, violated the No Derivatives provision, and the attribution requirement was also breached.[96]

In *SGAE* v. *Fernandez*,[97] a bar owner successfully defended a claim by a Spanish collecting society (CS) on the basis that all the music played in his bar was under CC licences.

In the US case of *Drauglis* v. *Kappa Map Group*,[98] a professional photographer placed a photo on flickr under a CC-BY-SA-2.0 licence. Kappa used it as the cover photo on a commercial atlas of maps. Drauglis claimed that although the licence permitted commercial use, this use went beyond the scope of the licence. The court rejected his three arguments on this point. First, the SA condition did not require the whole atlas to be distributed free of charge, as the atlas was not a derivative work. Second, the requirement of the BY condition to provide adequate information about the licence did not require the URL of the licence to be printed on the atlas, it was sufficient that it stated the photo was licensed under a 'Creative Commoms [*sic*] CC-BY-SA-2.0' licence. Third, the licence requirement of attribution as prominent as comparable material referred to each individual map, not the whole atlas, and was satisfied.

In *Great Minds* v. *FedEx Office*, it was held that for FedEx to charge its normal duplication fee for schools to obtain copies of materials for non-commercial use did not breach the NonCommercial condition (required under a US federal government grant) under which the materials were created and licensed by Great Minds.[99] Creative Commons supported FedEx, noting that this assisted public schools 'that did not have the means or resources to make the tens of thousands of copies of the publicly funded materials needed for use in the classroom'.[100]

---

[96] Summary of *Lichôdmapwa* v. *L'asbl Festival de Théâtre de Spa*, Le Tribunal de première instance de Nivelles, Belgium, 28 October 2010 https://wiki.creativecommons.org/wiki/09-1684-A_(Lich%C3%B4dmapwa_v._L%27asbl_Festival_de_Theatre_de_Spa).

[97] *SGAE* v. *Fernandez*, Lower Court number six of Badajoz (Spain), 17 February 2006; Decision in Spanish http://wiki.creativecommons.org/File:Sentencia_metropoli.pdf.

[98] *Drauglis* v. *Kappa Map Grp.*, 128 F. Supp 3d 46 (DDC 2015); see J. Butler, 'Proof that using creative commons material is not risk-free', 12 October 2015 www.guidethroughthelegaljungleblog.com/2015/10/proof-that-using-creative-commons-material-is-not-risk-free.html#page=1.

[99] *Great Minds* v. *Fedex Office and Print Services*, US DC E. Dist. NY (Hurley, Snr Dist J), Order on Motion to Dismiss, 24 February 2017 https://drive.google.com/file/d/0B0HBOY8b2doEdmpkMU4ya2dKM28/view.

[100] See R. Merkeley, 'Why we're fighting to protect noncommercial uses', 9 September 2016 https://creativecommons.org/2016/09/09/why-were-fighting-to-protect-noncommercial-uses/.

## 15.4.2 Potential Legal Issues

Relatively early in the history of CC licensing, Loren identified potential legal issues in an extensive review,[101] but few of the issues she identified have resulted in court decisions. She identified two main types of potential issues: first, whether the 'some rights reserved' by CC licences can be enforced effectively and so protect the position of copyright owners who choose to make their works available under CC licences, thus encouraging other copyright owners to do similarly; and, second, to protect the public's confidence that content licensed under CC licences will remain permanently so available, thus encouraging the public to use it. Both forms of assurance are necessary for the 'reliability' of what she describes as a 'semicommons', and was a category of the public domain.[102] The arguments Loren put forward in favour of both aspects of 'reliability' of earlier versions of CC licences continue to be sound in relation to the current versions of the licences. They are however, not beyond argument under US law, and other arguments may be raised in other jurisdictions. These issues are also relevant to FOSS software, so much of the following discussion is relevant to both.

*CC as Contracts and Licences* Loren argues that, under US law, CC licences may be enforced both as licences under copyright law, and as contracts. As a licence, the termination provisions in all CC licences state that the licence and all rights granted under it 'terminate automatically upon any breach' by the licensee. Defence against consequent claims of infringement based on[103] enforcement through breach of contract claims will also be effective, she argues.[104] All CC licences include clauses in which can be found an argument that there is consideration for the licence. This was previously an explicit assertion,[105] but the 'international' licences now simply state that the grant of the licence is 'Subject

---

[101] L. Loren, 'Building a reliable semicommons of creative works: enforcement of creative commons licenses and limited abandonment of copyright' (2007) 14 *George Mason Law Review* 271–328.
[102] Loren, 'Building a reliable semicommons', 298.
[103] *Ibid.* 306–9: the US doctrine of abandonment will not apply because the copyright owner has not abandoned the whole copyright. A defence based on the US copyright misuse doctrine will not apply because copyright owners do not use their rights granted by copyright law in a manner contrary to the public interest. In particular, the ShareAlike provisions in two of the licences will not constitute misuse because 'misuse has never been extended to a clause that prevents different business models, so long as the clause does not attempt to reach beyond the scope of the rights granted by the Copyright Act.'
[104] Loren, 'Building a reliable semicommons', 309–14.
[105] Earlier versions of CC licences stated: 'The licensor grants you the rights contained here in consideration of your acceptance of such terms and conditions.'

to the terms and conditions of this Public Licence'.[106] All CC licences require attribution of both the author's identity and the conditions under which the work is licensed, and some require share-alike licensing of derivative works, all of which are 'promises by the user to engage in activity that would be beneficial to the licensor', and are not merely conditions on a gift.[107]

*Privity and Acceptance* As Merges puts it, because CC licences are copyright licences, they operate by way of contract, and the whole CC system depends on the assumption that the contract terms 'run with the content'. This means 'there must be an unbroken chain of privity of contract between each successive user of the content', and that this is particularly important for the licences with the share-alike conditions (as with FOSS copyleft licences) because of the strength of the restrictions they aim to pass on.[108] Radin put it similarly, without committing to the validity of such 'attempted' viral licensing.[109]

Loren finds the 'unbroken chain' was satisfied by the terms found in all CC licences at that time.[110] Similarly, in the current CC licences, every 'downstream recipient' of licensed material 'automatically receives an offer from the Licensor to exercise the Licensed Rights under the terms and conditions of this Public License'.[111] However there must be acceptance, not only an offer, which raises the question of whether the licence runs with the content regardless of whether the user/licensee has manifested assent to the licence terms, other than by use of the content (such as by republication). This must at least require that the licensee have notice of the licence terms. Both CC licences and FOSS licences require that such notice be provided with the content licensed.

*Revocation and Estoppel* Concerning the permanence of CC licences, Loren noted that all CC licences previously stated that they are 'perpetual' (for the duration of the applicable copyright in the Work). They now state in Version 4.0, to similar effect, that the licence is 'irrevocable'[112] and 'applies for the term of the Copyright and Similar

---

[106] Creative Commons Attribution 4.0 International licence, Legal Code, s. 2(a)(1); see similarly, in s. 3.
[107] Loren, 'Building a reliable semicommons', 313 and 318.
[108] Merges, 'A new dynamism in the public domain', 183, 198–9.
[109] Radin, 'Humans, computers and binding commitment', 1125. Similar hesitation about effectiveness is found in B. Fitzgerald and G. Bassett, 'Legal issues relating to free and open source software' (2001) 12 *Journal of Law and Information Science* 159 [4.5.2].
[110] Loren, 'Building a reliable semicommons', 313–14.
[111] Creative Commons Attribution 4.0 International licence, Legal Code, s. 2(a)(5)(A).
[112] Creative Commons Attribution 4.0 International licence, Legal Code, s. 2(a)(1).

## 15.5 Government Supports for Open Content Licences

Rights licensed here'.[113] The termination clause also continues to make clear that while a licensor can cease to offer to license the work under the licence this will not affect existing licensees:

> For the avoidance of doubt, the Licensor may also offer the Licensed Material under separate terms or conditions or stop distributing the Licensed Material at any time; however, doing so will not terminate this Public License.[114]

Estoppel is also relevant. Although bare licences can be revoked, the same uses as are relevant to consideration are also 'induced by reliance on the Creative Commons status of the work', and at least such users who have acted in such reliance should be able to rely on this detriment so that 'a court would enforce the licence as a contract and prohibit any attempt to terminate the licence'.[115]

### 15.5 Government Supports for Open Content Licences

As discussed in [6.2.5], an important support for various categories of the public domain is official requirements for (or simply endorsement of) the provision of various types of information as open content or free access content. We consider here two areas where official support for neutral licensing is vital, Open Government Data and re-use of publicly funded research.

*Open Government Data (OGD)* It is not new for government-generated works or data to be considered part of the public domain. Many countries have adopted the option provided by Berne to exempt laws and other texts from copyright: [8.2.2]. Some government data collections fall short of the requirements for copyright protection, and most jurisdictions outside the EU do not have *sui generis* database protection. However, exemption from copyright does not make such works widely available for re-use, which is made most effective and affordable when governments provide the data online in standard formats, with no barriers to access. Formal licences are not essential for re-use because governments can simply make works available online under circumstances which make clear that they may be re-used. In these situations, government could use a CC0 public domain declaration or equivalent (where the content is copyright), or a Public Domain Mark or equivalent (where the content is already in the public domain):[116] [15.6.1]. However, where investments

---
[113] Creative Commons Attribution 4.0 International licence, Legal Code, s. 6(a).
[114] Creative Commons Attribution 4.0 International licence, Legal Code, s. 6(c).
[115] Loren, 'Building a reliable semicommons', 318.
[116] Lee, 'Licensing open government data', 240.

506    Voluntary Licensing Creating Public Rights

are to be made in re-use of government data, many users may prefer the perceived greater certainty of formal licences.

National and other governments in many countries have adopted policies to facilitate re-use of government data, now regarded as an international OGD movement. A significant development is the Open Government Partnership (OGP), formed in 2011,[117] which signed the Open Government Declaration, to which seventy-five governments have now subscribed.[118] It involves a commitment by governments 'to pro-actively provide high-value information, including raw data, in a timely manner, in formats that the public can easily locate, understand and use, and in formats that facilitate reuse.'[119] It does not involve a commitment to license data for public use. Lee, in an extensive survey,[120] finds that the licences most commonly considered by governments for open government data are the CC suite, the ODC suite: [15.3.3] and the UK GLF suite (and equivalent government-developed licences in some countries).

*Government OGD Licences, including the UK GLF Suite and Canada*   Rather than adopting CC licences for government data, some governments have devised their own licences in order to make public sector information (PSI) 'open government data'. These 'OGD licences' include those developed by the governments of France, Germany, Italy, the UK [121] and Canada. Although it could be argued that such 'whole of government' licences are not 'neutral licences' because they have been drawn up by the owner of the copyright works to be licensed, a more realistic view is that the government is acting as a neutral party to bring consistency in the practices of the many government agencies that will utilise the licence over works they create, with public interest considerations in mind, and for a non-profit purpose. The position is analogous to the legislature acting as a neutral party when it creates compulsory licences. We therefore consider that government OGD licences are neutral voluntary licences, creating part of the

---

[117] Brazil, Indonesia, Mexico, Norway, the Philippines, South Africa, UK and United States.
[118] Open Government Partnership, 'About' www.opengovpartnership.org/about/about-ogp.
[119] 'Open Government Declaration', September 2011 www.opengovpartnership.org/open-government-declaration.
[120] Lee, 'Licensing open government data', 240.
[121] See Lee, 'Licensing open government data', 222–3 for sources for the OGD licences developed by France (Licence ouverte), Germany (Datenlizenz Deutschland), Italy (Italian Open Data License) and the UK (UK Government Licensing Framework for Public Sector Information).

## 15.5 Government Supports for Open Content Licences

public domain. However, they are on the borderline of the proprietary domain.

The UK's Re-use of Public Sector Information Regulations 2015 (the 'PSI Regulations') establish principles and rules for public sector bodies responding to requests for re-use of public sector information, making re-use, at marginal cost, mandatory in most cases. The UK Government Licensing Framework (UKGLF)[122] for Public Sector Information 'mandates the Open Government Licence (OGL) as the default licence for Crown bodies and recommends OGL for other public sector bodies'. UK government policy is that 'public sector information should be licensed for use and re-use free of charge under the OGL with only a few prescribed exceptions'; in particular it is not to be used for content that includes personal data. The OGL[123] superseded the PSI Click-Use Licence in 2010. Users of OGL-licensed content do not need to apply or register in order to use the content. The OGL requires attribution and allows commercial use and derivative uses. An OGL symbol is used to facilitate searching. Its terms are compatible with both the CC Attribution (BY) License and the ODC Attribution License, which compatibility is often necessary where government data is to be combined in applications with data from other sources.

There are special licences[124] which UK licensing bodies can have delegated authority[125] to use instead of the OGL where they also comply with the PSI regulations.[126] These include the Non-Commercial Government Licence (like a CC-NC licence), the Charged Licence (some datasets outside the scope of the PSI Regulations 2015), the Developer Licence (charging for some non-Crown copyright data held by government) and the Open Supreme Court Licence (some uses of court data). These special UK licences illustrate that governments usually cannot or do not license all data they hold under a minimal-restrictions licence like the OGC, even when that is the default.

In 2014, the Canadian federal government adopted the Directive on Open Government, which is designed to maximise the release of

---

[122] The National Archives (UK), 'UK Government Licensing Framework for public sector information', version 5.0, January 2016 www.nationalarchives.gov.uk/documents/information-management/uk-government-licensing-framework.pdf.
[123] 'Open Government Licence for public sector information' (OGLv3.0) www.nationalarchives.gov.uk/doc/open-government-licence/version/3/.
[124] The National Archives (UK), 'Other licences' www.nationalarchives.gov.uk/information-management/re-using-public-sector-information/uk-government-licensing-framework/open-government-licence/other-licences/.
[125] A Delegation of Authority from the Controller of Her Majesty's Stationery Office.
[126] Re-use of Public Sector Information (PSI) Regulations 2015 (UK) www.nationalarchives.gov.uk/information-management/re-using-public-sector-information/psi-directive-transposition-and-re-use-regulations/.

government information and data, as part of its Action Plan on Government 2.0.[127] In accordance with this Directive, free access to government information is provided by the Open Government Licence – Canada.[128] Like the UK Open Government Licences, these are not CC Licences, but are compatible with them.[129]

*Australian Use of the CC Licence Suite for OGC*  Australia is an example of a country that still has Crown Copyright in legislation and government documents: [8.2.2], but has adopted neutral licensing to make government data available for public re-use. Unlike the UK, it has not developed its own licence to do so. Since 2002, there has been consistent advocacy from Creative Commons Australia, and individuals and organisations associated with it, to have CC licences adopted by Australian governments for public sector information (PSI),[130] resulting in initial successes with the Australian federal and Queensland state governments in adoption of CC licensing. Following the 2009 Government 2.0 Taskforce recommendations,[131] the Australian government adopted a Declaration of Open Government[132] and a policy that public sector information (PSI) would, by default, be released free of charge under a Creative Commons 'BY' (attribution) licence. PSI includes legislation and legislative instruments, and Parliamentary documents such as Hansard and Parliamentary reports.[133] The result is the Australian Governments Open Access and Licensing Framework (AusGOAL),[134] which provides support and guidance to government and related sectors to facilitate open access to publicly funded information, based on a set of open access principles formulated by the Australian Information Commissioner. The Commissioner recommended that the default condition for PSI should be the Creative Commons

---

[127] Government of Canada, Directive on Open Government, 9 October 2014.
[128] Government of Canada, 'Open Government Licence – Canada' (OGL- C 2.0) http://open.canada.ca/en/open-government-licence-canada.
[129] K. Mewhort, 'Creative Commons Licenses: options for Canadian open data providers', Canadian Internet Policy and Public Interest Clinic (CIPPIC), 1 June 2012 https://cippic.ca/sites/default/files/Creative%20Commons%20Licenses%20-%20Options%20for%20Canadian%20Open%20Data%20Providers.pdf.
[130] For a detailed history, see G. Greenleaf and C. Bond, 'Re-use rights and Australia's unfinished PSI revolution' (2011) 1(2) *Informatica e diritto – Rivista internazionale* 341 http://papers.ssrn.com/sol3/papers.cfm?abstract_id=1951625.
[131] Government 2.0 Taskforce, 'Engage: Getting on with Government 2.0', Report of the Government 2.0 Taskforce (December 2009).
[132] Department of Finance, 'Declaration of Open Government', 16 July 2010 www.finance.gov.au/blog/2010/07/16/declaration-open-government/.
[133] Department of Communications and the Arts, 'Guidelines on Licensing Public Sector Information for Australian Government Entities' (September 2016).
[134] AusGoal www.ausgoal.gov.au/.

BY licence.[135] The resources provided include a licence suite including the Creative Commons Version 4.0 licences, the AusGOAL Restrictive Licence Template (relevant for content including, for example, personal data) and the BSD 3-Clause software licence, and licensing tools such as a Licence Chooser tool, and 'Licence Manager' licence injector software. AusGOAL is aligned with international open government initiatives, such as the Open Government Partnership.[136]

## 15.6 'Relinquishment' or 'Public Domain Dedications'

A category of the copyright public domain related closely to voluntary licensing arises from this question: can works enter the public domain under the general law through a formal and intentional forfeiture of copyright, sometimes called a 'public domain dedication' or 'abandonment of copyright', or 'relinquishment'? The effects of both statutory provisions which create such facilities, and voluntary facilities such as Creative Commons Zero (CC0), must also be considered.

### 15.6.1 *International Copyright Agreements*

International copyright agreements do not address this question directly. Berne has nothing directly to say about relinquishment through intentional actions by copyright owners, or about national legislation on the topic, but Johnson argues that a public domain dedication 'simply makes copyright come to an end earlier in time', and so may be inconsistent with the minimum term of copyright set by Berne.[137] He concedes, however, that it could be argued that 'dedications are not related to term in principle'. This is also the approach adopted by Hudson and Burrell, who argue that the issue here is about ownership of copyright, not about its duration: 'the effect of abandonment is not to shorten the copyright term per se but to divest the abandoning owner of title to the work such that copyright remains technically in existence but is unowned and hence incapable of enforcement.'[138] As a result, they argue, 'any objection to abandonment based on its conflict with treaty obligations falls away

---

[135] Australian Information Commissioner, 'Open Access Principles', May 2011 www.oaic.gov.au/images/documents/information-policy/information-policy-agency-resources/principles_on_psi_short.pdf.
[136] Open Government Partnership www.opengovpartnership.org/.
[137] P. Johnson, '"Dedicating" copyright to the public domain' (2008) 71 *Modern Law Review* 587 at 598.
[138] E. Hudson and R. Burrell, 'Abandonment, copyright and orphaned works: what does it mean to take the property nature of intellectual property rights seriously?' (2011) 35 *Melbourne University Law Review* 971, 988.

because the treatment of ownership remains largely unharmonised at the international level and countries continue to maintain very different rules in this regard.'[139] We consider that this is the better view, and that there can be differing national approaches to this question.

Johnson raises a second argument, applicable only to EU Member States, that the uniform term set by the Term Directive: [9.5],[140] and the purpose of that Directive to avoid distortions to the internal market, means that a dedication would have to be effective throughout the EU: 'harmonisation requires copyright to cease to exist in every Member State, or in none'.[141] The problem with this argument is, as identified by Hudson and Burrell, that it depends whether the issue is characterised as one of ownership or duration.

### 15.6.2 National Case Law on Relinquishment

International copyright law therefore leaves the question of abandonment or dedications to national laws, whether case law or legislation.

Under English law, accidental abandonment of copyright was rejected[142] in the *British Leyland Motor* case[143] and other cases,[144] and while it does not seem that a defendant has ever successfully established such a defence, UK commentators consider that 'the point has not been definitively settled'.[145] Concerning intentional and formal abandonment, either in the form of a legal document or a simple statement, the views of commentators in common law countries differ. Johnson argues that copyright in works cannot be abandoned under English law, and that dedications purporting to do so may simply amount to bare licences that can be revoked at will.[146] Johnston considers a succession of English cases that have touched on this issue,[147] as do Hudson and

---

[139] *Ibid.*
[140] The full titles and citations of all Directive are in the Table of International Instruments.
[141] Johnson, '"Dedicating" copyright to the public domain', 598.
[142] *British Leyland Motor Corporation v. Armstrong Patents Co. Ltd* [1982] FSR 481, 492; Foster J found that '[t]his is a legal right and no case was cited to me in which in English law it was held or even suggested that a copyright had been abandoned. It is extremely difficult in my experience to divest oneself of a legal right.'
[143] *British Leyland Motor Corporation v. Armstrong Patents Co. Ltd* [1982] FSR 481.
[144] *Copinger*, 16th edn, [6-88]. See *Plix Products v. Frank M. Winstone (Merchants)* [1986] FSR 63 (High Court of NZ); *Australian Olympic Committee v. Big Fights* [1999] FCA 1042. This argument occurs primarily in litigation where a defendant who, in response to an allegation of copyright infringement, argues that the plaintiff has previously abandoned their copyright and as such infringement cannot have occurred.
[145] J. A. L. Sterling and T. Cook, *Sterling on World Copyright* (4th edn, Sweet & Maxwell, 2015), [12.27], citing *Copinger and Skone James on Copyright* (14th edn), para. 6-85.
[146] Johnson, '"Dedicating" copyright to the public domain', 591-6.   [147] *Ibid.* 594-6.

## 15.6 'Relinquishment' or 'Public Domain Dedications' 511

Burrell,[148] but they do not find any significant authorities. Hudson and Burrell find some support for abandonment both in Australasian cases and general principles.[149] Johnson considers UK copyright legislation but, other than the inclusion of a provision for waiver of moral rights perhaps implying that other rights cannot be waived, finds nothing conclusive.[150] Other authors are also divided. Sterling considers the position unsettled.[151] Deazley considers that abandonment of copyright can occur.[152] Commentators also argue that 'it is difficult to say what amount of evidence the courts would require of a dedication of a copyright to the public.'[153] In Australia there are no relevant provisions in the Copyright Act 1968, but Rothnie, in a discussion on the waiver of moral rights in Australia, believes that case law indicates 'the general principle that a person may waive a statutory right for his or her own benefit'.[154] The position is further complicated by moral rights provisions.[155]

In the United States, although there is no statutory provision concerning dedication of a work to the public domain, there is a judicially developed doctrine permitting abandonment.[156] Walden points out that the doctrine 'requires a defendant to show that the copyright owner intends to surrender his rights in the work and has overtly acted in a manner evidencing his intention'. He considers that 'such intent could be easily manifest in an open source software context through appropriate notices dedicating the work to the public',[157] even though such complete abandonment of copyright is not the practice or purpose of most open source software. Some US commentators suggest that works can enter the public

---

[148] Hudson and Burrell, 'Abandonment, copyright and orphaned works', 938.
[149] *Ibid.* 985.   [150] Johnson, '"Dedicating" copyright to the public domain', 596–7.
[151] Sterling and Cook, *Sterling on World Copyright* (4th edn), [12.27].
[152] Deazley, *Rethinking Copyright*, 107 n. 26, Deazley does not include abandonment as part of the legal public domain. He includes works where owners 'dedicate their work to the public' as part of his 'de facto public domain' (he may not have included it in his list for this reason).
[153] *Copinger*, 16th edn, [6-88].
[154] Warwick A. Rothnie, 'Moral rights: consents and waiver' (2002) 20 *Copyright Reporter* 145, 152.
[155] The three moral rights provided by the Copyright Act 1968 (Cth) in Australia – the right of attribution, the right against false attribution, and the right of integrity – cannot be waived by the author, although a breach of moral rights can be consented to in *limited* circumstances: see Copyright Act 1968 (Cth), s. 195AW.
[156] *National Comics Publications Inc.* v. *Fawcett Publications Inc.* 191 F 2d 594 (2nd Cir, 1952); see Loren, 'Building a reliable semicommons', 319; M. W. Turetsky, 'Applying copyright abandonment to the digital age' (2010) 19 *Duke Law & Technology Review* 22.
[157] I. Walden, 'Open source as philosophy, methodology and commerce: using law with attitude', chap. 1, in Shemtov and Walden (eds.), *Free and Open Source Software*, 17.

domain through an accidental or unintentional abandonment of copyright.[158]

European civil law jurisdictions generally do not accept abandonment of copyright, according to Hudson and Burrell.[159] The German Federal Court has stated that authors' rights cannot be abandoned.[160] The position under national laws therefore varies widely, from being uncertain, as in the UK and some other common law countries, to allowing intentional abandonment (as in the United States), or to rejecting it (as in Germany).

### 15.6.3  Statutory Provisions Allowing Relinquishment

The idea of a legislative provision facilitating abandonment was rejected by the UK Whitford Committee in its 1977 report on copyright and designs law, although no reasons were given beyond this statement:[161]

> It has been suggested to us that a copyright owner ought to be able to place a work irrevocably in the public domain, for example, by publishing a renunciation of his copyright in a suitable journal. At first sight the idea seems attractive, but most of us feel that legislation to cover renunciation would not be practicable.

There are, however, statutory provisions in some countries providing for such relinquishment, including in Kenya, India, Chile and Colombia. India's Copyright Act 1957 has long provided[162] that an author 'may relinquish all or any of the rights comprised in the copyright in the work by giving notice ... and thereupon such rights shall ... cease to exist.' The relinquishment does not affect any rights subsisting in any other person at the time of notice.[163] Notice was previously required to be in a prescribed form[164] to the Registrar of Copyrights, with such notice Gazetted, and is now required to be published on the Registrar's website for at least three years.[165] Amendments in 2012 now allow authors to effect relinquishment 'by way of public notice'.[166]

---

[158] See Loren, 'Building a reliable semicommons', 320.
[159] Hudson and Burrell 'Abandonment, copyright and orphaned works'.
[160] Sterling and Cook, *Sterling on World Copyright* (4th edn), [12.27], citing *Berlin Wall Pictures*, BGH 23 February 1995 (1995) GRUR 673; (1997) 28 IIC 282.
[161] J. Whitford, Committee to Consider the Law on Copyright and Designs, *Copyright and Designs Law: Report of the Committee to Consider the Law on Copyright and Designs* (HMSO, 1977), [655], Renunciation of Copyright.
[162] Copyright Act 1957 (India), s. 21.   [163] Copyright Act 1957 (India), s. 21(3).
[164] The prescribed form is located at http://copyright.gov.in/frmformsDownload.aspx.
[165] Copyright Act 1957 (India), s. 21(2A), as amended in 2012.
[166] Copyright Act 1957 (India), s. 21(1), as amended in 2012.

## 15.6 'Relinquishment' or 'Public Domain Dedications'  513

The Copyright Act of Kenya takes a similar approach, stating that 'works in respect of which authors have renounced their rights' 'shall belong to the public domain'[167] and 'may be used without any restriction' (subject to any fees the Minister may prescribe).[168] As for formalities, 'renunciation by an author or his successor in title of his rights shall be in writing and made public but any such renunciation shall not be contrary to any previous contractual obligation relating to the work.'[169] The allowance of relinquishment by successors in title is not found in other provisions.

The Chilean Intellectual Property Law is brief, simply stipulating that, among the circumstances in which a work will pass into the public domain, are works 'whose owners gave up the protection provided by this law',[170] but without providing details of how such renunciation may occur.[171] The Colombian Copyright Law specifies that those 'works whose authors have waived their rights' are in the public domain,[172] and also that 'the waiver by the authors or heirs to property rights of the work shall be in writing and published.'[173] Guadamuz considers that the publication required is a notice in one of the official journals.[174]

In the five other jurisdictions studied by Guadamuz (Brazil, China, Egypt, France and the Republic of Korea), the relevant legislation does not authorise relinquishment. In some laws (namely Egypt, France), provisions preventing assignment of future copyrights may imply that relinquishment is not possible.[175]

The Indian reference to renunciation of 'all or any of the rights comprised in the copyright' may also provide a legislative basis for something like the 'some rights reserved' approach taken by Creative Commons and other voluntary licensing approaches. However, the Indian provision only authorises an author to 'relinquish' rights, and does not say anything about doing so on the basis of conditions such as the 'share-alike' condition on which viral licensing is based.

Hudson and Burrell suggest in passing, following from their argument that copyright continues to exist but that abandonment relates to

---

[167] Copyright Act, CAP 130, Rev. 2014 (Kenya), s. 45(1).
[168] Copyright Act, CAP 130, Rev. 2014 (Kenya), s. 45(3).
[169] Copyright Act, CAP 130, Rev. 2014 (Kenya), s. 45(3).
[170] Ley 17.336 sobre la Propiedad Intelectual (Chile), Art. 11(c).
[171] A. Guadamuz, 'Comparative analysis of national approaches on voluntary copyright relinquishment', Report presented to WIPO Committee on Development and Intellectual Property (CDIP), 13th Session (2014), section 3.2, 'Chile'.
[172] Ley 23 de 1932 Sobre derechos de autor (Colombia), Art. 187.3.
[173] Ley 23 de 1932 Sobre derechos de autor (Colombia), Art. 188.
[174] Guadamuz, 'Comparative analysis of national approaches on voluntary copyright relinquishment', section 3.4, 'Colombia'.
[175] Ibid. 15–22.

ownership, that it could not be objectionable under international law if 'a country would ... legislate to the effect that a dedication to the public domain serves to vest copyright in a public body and then to direct that trustee make the work freely available for use by the public.'[176] It is not obvious what the role of such a trustee would add, beyond the advantage that there would then be an identifiable copyright owner for the term of copyright in the work.

### 15.6.4 CC Public Domain Dedications (CC0), and Equivalents

Creative Commons provides two tools in relation to the public domain: a public domain dedication (CC0); and a 'mark' for indicating works by others believed to be in the public domain. CC claims these have resulted in '92.9 million public domain works', such as in 2016 the release of 375,000 digital works from the Metropolitan Museum of Art under CC0.[177] Guadamuz provides numerous examples of institutions using CC0 in relation to parts of their collections or their metadata.[178] Irrespective of the legal position in some countries, it seems that these practices are causing significant global changes in relation to which works are treated as if they are in the public domain.

The purpose of the Creative Commons 'CC0' (CC Zero) facility[179] is to give copyright owners 'a way to waive all their copyright and related rights in their works to the fullest extent allowed by law [as] a universal instrument that is not adapted to the laws of any particular legal jurisdiction, similar to many open source software licenses.'[180] This replaced an earlier public domain dedication facility based on US law.[181] Given that few countries have statutory provisions for relinquishment of copyright, and case law in others is uncertain, CC0 plays a significant role in the public domain. Aside from its legal effect, its use gives a clear indication that a copyright owner is unlikely to enforce any rights they may have in a work.

---

[176] Hudson and Burrell, 'Abandonment, copyright and orphaned works', 989.
[177] Creative Commons, 'State of the Commons' https://creativecommons.org/2017/04/28/state-of-the-commons-2016/.
[178] Guadamuz, 'Comparative analysis of national approaches on voluntary copyright relinquishment', section 4.1, 'Examples of copyright relinquishment'.
[179] Creative Commons, 'CC0 1.0 Universal – Public Domain Dedication' https://creativecommons.org/publicdomain/zero/1.0/ (summary version) and https://creativecommons.org/publicdomain/zero/1.0/legalcode (legal text).
[180] Creative Commons, 'CC0 – "No rights reserved"' https://creativecommons.org/share-your-work/public-domain/cc0/.
[181] Creative Commons, 'Public Domain Dedication' http://creativecommons.org/licenses/publicdomain/ [at 28 October 2008].

## 15.6 'Relinquishment' or 'Public Domain Dedications' 515

CC0 declarations state that, in relation not only to copyright exclusive economic rights, but also to a wide range of other related rights including moral rights, database rights, 'publicity and privacy rights',

> To the greatest extent permitted by, but not in contravention of, applicable law, Affirmer hereby overtly, fully, permanently, irrevocably and unconditionally waives, abandons, and surrenders all of Affirmer's Copyright and Related Rights and associated claims and causes of action . . .

The CC0 dedication also contains a 'fall back' provision which aims to ensure that, if a relinquishment of copyright is for any reason ineffective in a particular jurisdiction, then the CC0 dedication will instead operate as an 'unconditional license to exercise' the same rights, to the maximum extent possible in the jurisdiction.[182] The intended global operation of CC0 may mean that its use in those jurisdictions which are believed not to support public domain dedications will test and clarify the law, although this has not yet occurred.

In the Open Data Commons (ODC) licence suite, the Public Domain Dedication and License (PDDL) plays a similar role to CC0, including covering database rights in the EU and other jurisdictions with such rights.

### 15.6.5 CC Public Domain Mark for Content by Others

The CC Public Domain Mark[183] is intended to be used on works not owned by the user, but which are 'free of known copyright restrictions' (i.e., believed to be in the public domain), so as clearly to convey that status, and to make such works more easily found.[184] It enables an 'identifying individual or organisation' to identify such works, including by the URL where they can be found,[185] so that the reliability of the 'marking' is to some extent based on the reputation of the party applying the mark (for example, a museum or similar cultural institution). Wrongly applying such a mark to a work could in theory lead to actions being available in some countries against the person applying the mark, but such problems are hypothetical. Works to which such a mark are applied are not necessarily part of the public domain, and we regard the

---

[182] See Guadamuz, 'Comparative analysis of national approaches on voluntary copyright relinquishment', 25.
[183] Creative Commons, 'Public Domain Mark 1.0' https://creativecommons.org/publicdo main/mark/1.0/.
[184] Creative Commons, 'Public Domain Mark' https://creativecommons.org/choose/mark/.
[185] Creative Commons, 'Public domain mark generation tool' https://creativecommons.org /choose/mark/details?lang=en.

Public Domain Mark as a support mechanism for the public domain (see Chapter 6). Related issues arise with orphan works: [14.1].

## 15.7 Conclusions: Legal Certainty Desirable

The absence of significant court decisions undermining either neutral voluntary licensing or public domain dedications means that it is tempting to conclude that 'if it isn't broken, don't fix it.' However, this is perhaps too sanguine an approach, given that there is theoretical uncertainty, in many countries, concerning some of the legal underpinnings of these voluntary methods of expanding the public domain. This is particularly so when the quantities of content being licensed or dedicated are taken into account, the critical role that free and open source software plays in the Internet-based economy and society, and that the whole output of some governments is being put under CC licences. Voluntary licensing and public domain dedications now need and deserve legal certainty.

Merges argues for greater certainty, in comments applicable to both neutral voluntary licensing and public domain dedications:

> So how best to balance autonomy with the desire of many creators to share their works? The answer is simple: create a straightforward mechanism that allows individual creators to waive their IP rights. This is the essence of the Creative Commons organization, which promotes various licenses that have the effect of allowing creators to share their works widely. The problem is that these licenses are only contracts. A better mechanism would be to build the waiver mechanism directly into copyright (and patent) law, and to create a central online registry that would record waivers and allow them to be searched and verified easily. This would solve some of the technical problems that accompany the use of contracts to signal a waiver of rights (concerns with notice, privity, and so on).[186]

Such a legislative solution does not necessitate a registration system, which might be a bureaucratic impediment to widespread use. It should be sufficient that a licence or dedication be in writing, coupled with public notice.

As Merges also points out, effective methods of waiving IP rights are entirely consistent with supporting individual autonomy as a central feature of copyright, but bring that principle 'into the era of shared content and collaborative creativity'. 'Traditional legal structures, in service of desirable practices facilitated by the new digital technology – this sounds like a good combination.'[187]

---

[186] Merges, *Justifying Intellectual Property*, 229.    [187] *Ibid.* 230.

## 15.7 Conclusions: Legal Certainty Desirable

### 15.7.1 Voluntary Licensing Could Benefit from Certainty

Walden concludes that 'although open source has existed for nearly three decades, there is scant case law available to provide an additional layer of legal certainty to code-users, whether FOSS advocates or opponents.'[138] In our view, countries should legislate to remove uncertainties in relation to enforcement of neutral voluntary licensing. Legislation to assist certainty could, for example, state that where there is a purported licence, the reproduction of the licensed content, or the exercise of any other exclusive right in the content, will constitute consideration for the licence; and that such licences must be in writing to be effective. In jurisdictions where case law gives clear support to non-economic consideration, or where consideration is irrelevant, this would not be necessary.

Where countries do not wish completely to remove copyright in official documents, a valuable alternative is to provide exceptions allowing the use of those documents under conditions, or to make those documents available under neutral voluntary licences.

### 15.7.2 Statutory Provisions for Public Domain Dedications are Needed

It is desirable, in our view, that copyright owners have the capacity to provide works that they own for public use, in a way which provides both legal certainty to future users and protection to copyright owners against unfounded claims that they have relinquished their rights. It is common for copyright law to require that assignments or exclusive licences of copyright works must be made in writing,[189] so at least a similar degree of protection to copyright owners, and clarity for potential users of such content, should be required, as it is in Kenya and India.

Given the continuing uncertainty at common law, it seems that a statutory provision to this effect is desirable in (most) common law countries, whether as part of the copyright legislation or otherwise, and would be effective. In civil law countries, the author's rights tradition makes such legislation necessary. Legislation should provide that authors or successors in title may relinquish copyright, including of part of the exclusive rights, and that such dedications must be in writing to be effective.

---

[188] Walden, 'Open source as philosophy, methodology and commerce'.
[189] For example, Copyright Act 1968 (Australia), s. 10, definition 'exclusive licence'.

# 16 The De Facto Public Domain – Internet-Enabled Public Rights

| 16.1 | Internet-Enabled Global Public Rights | 518 |
| 16.2 | De Facto Public Rights in Internet-Published Content | 519 |
| 16.3 | 'Spillover' Effects of National Public Domains on Other Countries | 537 |
| 16.4 | Conclusions: The Significance of the Global Internet Public Domain | 540 |

## 16.1 Internet-Enabled Global Public Rights

In the 1990s, debates about copyright policy were focused on the effects of digital technology in destabilising the copyright balance. On the one hand, digitisation enabled cheap, unlimited copying and distribution of protected works, thereby threatening copyright. On the other hand, it provided the basis for copyright owners to apply technological measures to control content which, together with contractual agreements, potentially allowed greater control than the balances struck by copyright law.[1] This was the so-called 'digital dilemma'.[2] From this perspective, it became common to see the combination of technological protection and contractual overrides as threats to the public domain.[3]

---

[1] See, for example, N. Elkin-Koren, 'Cyberlaw and social change: a democratic approach to copyright in cyberspace' (1996) 14 *Cardozo Arts & Entertainment Law Journal* 215; C. Clark, 'The answer to the machine is in the machine', in Hugenholtz (ed.), *The Future of Copyright in a Digital Environment*, 139; K. Koelman, 'A hard nut to crack: the protection of technological measures' (2000) 22 *European Intellectual Property Review* 272.

[2] Committee on Intellectual Property Rights and the Emerging Information Infrastructure and Computer Science and Telecommunications Board, National Research Council, *The Digital Dilemma: Intellectual Property in the Information Age* (National Academy Press, 2000).

[3] See P. B. Hugenholtz, 'Copyright, contract and code: what will remain of the public domain' (2000) 26 *Brooklyn Journal of International Law* 77; P. Samuelson, 'Intellectual property and the digital economy: why the anti-circumvention regulations need to be revised' (1999) 14 *Berkeley Technology Law Journal* 519; K. Koelman, 'The public domain commodified: technological measures and productive information use', in Guibault and Hugenholtz (eds.), *The Future of the Public Domain*, 105–20.

In retrospect, it seems clear that this paradigm underestimated the positive effects of the Internet, and general Internet practices (or Internet norms), in enhancing the public domain. Given its border-transgressing character, these Internet-enabled practices have contributed to what we regard as an Internet-enabled global public domain. It exists somewhat separately from, and in addition to, the global copyright public domain shaped predominantly by international law. It is essential to take this Internet-enabled public domain fully into account in order to determine the parameters of the global public domain.

Two aspects of this Internet-enabled public domain were dealt with in the previous chapter on voluntary licensing: uniformity in voluntary licences through global standards and the dramatic effects of viral licences. In distinct ways they have each contributed enormously to the expansion of content which is now subject to expanded public rights, and they have created substantial global uniformity in the licence terms which create such public rights.

This chapter is predominantly concerned with another aspect of the copyright public domain arising most often from Internet-published content: de facto public rights arising from benign uses of such content and the acquiescence of copyright owners in its use because of benefits to them (**Category 15**). We also consider another closely related 'Internet effect' on the copyright public domain: 'spillover' effects of national public domains on other national public domains. While this is neither part of the de facto public domain nor a separate public domain category, it is in effect an Internet-enabled partial equalisation of public domains across jurisdictions, effectively expanding the public domain in countries that benefit from these spillovers. As a result, some aspects of public rights become more global, despite national boundaries.

Each of these four influences may have relatively complex effects, and may apply to more than one form of content. Together, they create the powerful effect the Internet has had on expanding the global copyright public domain.

## 16.2  De Facto Public Rights in Internet-Published Content

The Internet is an unparalleled engine for publishing and accessing content, and this brute fact cannot be discounted in understanding the global public domain. It is fundamental to appreciate that the Internet facilitates effective de facto user rights that go beyond the formal legal rights arising from copyright law. After setting out our definition and indicia of the de facto copyright public domain, we examine the most significant examples of de facto public domains to date: the browsable commons of the web;

and the searchable commons created by Internet-wide search engines. From this, we hypothesise the conditions most conducive to creation of a de facto copyright public domain. We consider some other examples of when de facto public domains are likely to arise, not necessarily Internet-related, and we note some borderline examples falling short of de facto copyright public rights.

### 16.2.1 Definition and Indicia of the De Facto Public Domain

We propose that a de facto public right exists when the vast majority of affected copyright owners in a jurisdiction (or, more often, globally) consider that they should not attempt to prevent what would be an otherwise infringing use of their work, because the use is sufficiently in their own interests (a benign use), and the minority who do not hold this view are dissuaded from litigating.

For such a public right to be effective, there must also be sufficient disincentives to dissuade those copyright owners who do not hold this opinion from litigating against the breaches of copyright involved, and thus potentially destroying the tolerated practice. One of the most significant 'disincentives', the provision of easily used opt-out facilities, is more accurately a risk-reduction strategy. For example, most copyright owners who do not wish their works to be indexed by search engines, if given an easy opportunity to opt out from such indexing, will not wish to take the matter any further. As a matter of law, neither the provision of opt-out facilities, nor making use of them, stops actions for infringements, but, in practice, if uses of works are otherwise by and large seen as benign by copyright owners, an opt-out is an important factor in reducing risk.

We therefore define the de facto public domain as comprising those situations where the public (or a class of intermediaries) is able to make significant uses of works without obtaining the explicit consent of copyright owners, where the uses concerned are (at least arguably) contained in the copyright owner's exclusive rights, but which, as a matter of practice or custom, go unchallenged because copyright owners recognise that to do so is in their interests, and they have the ability to opt out of the practice.

This reference to a practice or custom which goes unchallenged obviously implies that an example of this category of the public domain does not arise overnight, but there must be some period of time during which the non-contestation becomes apparent.

A variation on the above is that, in particular cases (particularly with old content) there may be very little likelihood of there being very many copyright owners who are alive, locatable, or likely to become aware of

## 16.2 De Facto Public Rights in Internet-Published Content

the uses made of the work but, nevertheless, the uses are overt and will be known to some copyright owners. The age and nature of the works and the public benefit of the uses (such as in museums, archives or libraries) may also greatly reduce the likelihood of any objections, but the capacity of rights holders to object (and opt out) does exist.

The above complex definition can be summed up as 'non-objection to benign uses of works coupled with opt-outs'. In the following, we use the expression 'public rights in benign uses', rather than a 'commons by friendly appropriation',[4] which has been used by one of us previously. This category is clearly not within the legal public domain, so we describe it as the de facto public domain. Other public domain theorists have, however, been ambivalent about such de facto rights.[5] These de facto public rights can also be regarded as examples of 'tolerated uses' of works; but we stress that most tolerated uses do not constitute de facto public rights: [16.2.3].

*Conditions for Creating De Facto Public Rights for Benign Uses*
When are such de facto rights most likely to arise in relation to some part of the exclusive rights of a class of copyright owners? Extrapolating from the limited but very important example of search engines [16.2.3], and its consistency with other examples [16.2.4], here is a set of ten particular circumstances (often Internet-related) which make this more likely:

1. The practice organises the content better through some innovation (technical, organisational or artistic).
2. Obtaining prior consent from all copyright owners is not practicable, and unlikely to occur.
3. The public benefits from the use (usually unremunerated) being made of the exclusive rights.
4. Copyright law is unclear whether the use of the exclusive rights constitutes infringement, at least in relation to some works or under some common circumstances.
5. Many of the relevant class of copyright owners will benefit from the use being made.
6. Few (if any) of the relevant class of copyright owners will suffer significantly from the use being made, including through direct competitive use of the content by the intermediary.
7. Many of the copyright owners are not likely to be aware of the details of copyright infringements, even though they are aware of the end-result of the use of their works.

---

[4] G. Greenleaf, 'Creating commons by friendly appropriation' (2007) 4(1) *SCRIPTed* 117.
[5] See R. Deazley's references to the 'perceived public domain' in [3.6.3].

8. An opt-out mechanism is provided, and is reasonably effective.
9. Opting out is unattractive so only a minority do so.
10. Litigation is unlikely to result in positive public relations or significant benefit to the copyright owner.

These factors contribute to a situation where a significant number of copyright owners are aware of uses being made of their works, but by and large they do not object because they perceive benefits from the use, and no objections to the use are sufficiently strong to result in litigation which could bring the practice to an end. Overall, there is acquiescence in the use because it is benign, with advantages for all parties involved.

Where the above conditions apply, we consider that de facto public rights are likely to result from such benign use and acquiescence, but we do not suggest that all ten conditions are necessary. For example, perhaps the copyright position (4) may be clear, but the other factors may override that. Moreover, few copyright owners may benefit (5), but, provided few are disadvantaged (6), the use may still become part of the de facto public domain.

Factors other than those listed can also be significant. For example, if many copyright owners are not aware of the use at all, objections are not likely, but this can easily become mere unknown use (which is something else) and not a known benign use. If a significant portion of the copyright owners are professionally represented by authors' associations, publishers or collecting societies, the benefits to the copyright owners will have to be high (as is the case with many uses by and enabled by search engines), otherwise litigation is more likely.

There is therefore no bright line between what we consider to be examples of the de facto public domain and similar situations which could be classified merely as 'tolerated uses', or which are essentially 'unknown uses', so there are borderline examples: [16.2.4].

### 16.2.2 What are not De Facto Public Rights?

The de facto public domain must be distinguished from both tolerated uses and implied licences.

*'Tolerated Uses' and the 'Rights Cushion' Distinguished* De facto public rights are distinct from, and narrower than, Wu's concept of 'tolerated use',[6] which he describes as:

---

[6] Wu, 'Tolerated use'.

## 16.2 De Facto Public Rights in Internet-Published Content

a giant 'grey zone' in copyright, consisting of millions of usages that do not fall into a clear category but are often infringing. These usages run the gauntlet, from PowerPoint presentations, personal web sites, social networking sites, church services, and much of Wikipedia's content to well-known fan guides. Such casual and often harmless uses of works comprise the category of tolerated use.[7]

To qualify as de facto public rights, the vast majority of affected copyright owners must consider that it is in their interest to tolerate otherwise infringing uses, and there must be some mechanism for owners to 'opt out' of the relevant uses. It is not sufficient that some significant uses of copyright works go undetected or that copyright owners do not think that enforcement action is worthwhile, or even that uses are 'harmless'. To include all instances of tolerated uses would make the boundary between the proprietary domain and the public domain impossible to define, as it would depend on the individual decisions of millions of copyright owners, without any underlying principle as to why they have decided one way or the other. Furthermore, our conditions for the de facto public domain ensure some certainty and permanence in this category, such that it is not vulnerable to the wishes of individual copyright owners.

De facto public rights are also narrower than Merges' concept of 'non-enforcement' (or the 'rights cushion'), which he regards as important in the context of digital remixes:

> Widespread nonenforcement has brought a new set of de facto rights to the users of digital works.... They are not on a par with the true rights held by original creators... Yet they are significant; users do take the quasi norm of nonenforcement into account when deciding whether making and distributing a remix is a good idea.[8]

Although Merges directs attention to a significant issue, like Wu's analogous concept of 'tolerated use', it is insufficiently precise, and depends too much on the subjective decisions of rights holders to delineate this part of the public domain.

In some circumstances, what may once have been merely a 'tolerated use' is given statutory recognition, such as with regimes limiting the liability of Internet intermediaries. These 'safe harbour' or 'notice-and-takedown' regimes recognise the advantages of 'benign' third party uses. They are distinguished from the public domain at [6.2.3].

*Implied Licences Distinguished* De facto public rights in benign uses may sometimes be difficult to distinguish from, and may even overlap, implied licences. The conduct of copyright owners will often result in an implied licence to some individuals to use a work for a particular

---

[7] *Ibid.*  [8] Merges, *Justifying Intellectual Property*, 256–7.

purpose without the need to obtain explicit permission from the copyright owner. Wu gives the example of newspapers that place an icon above online stories to assist users to email copies of the article to others,[9] and there are plenty of offline examples, such as an implied licence to use architectural plans to construct a building.[10]

Implied licences do not, by themselves, fit into any of our categories of the copyright public domain. Although they allow for permission-free uses, and their terms are set by business practices, as determined by a court (at least in some jurisdictions),[11] they can, in general, be altered by the copyright owner either by creating an express licence (on different terms) or revoking the implied licence. They therefore do not fit within our concept of 'neutral' voluntary licences: Chapter 15.[12] The other notable difference is that the implied licensee, if sued for infringement, has a legal defence unless and until the implied licence is revoked.

Given these difficulties, rather than establishing a distinct public domain category, we consider it is better to say that some implied licences may be part of the de facto public domain, but only if they fit the conditions set out above for the de facto public domain. The role of an implied licence then becomes an occasional 'effectiveness support' for the de facto public domain category: [6.2]. There is, in short, no doubting the practical importance of some implied licences to the public domain, but that does not mean that they are a separate category.

### 16.2.3 The Public Domain of Internet-Published Content: Browsing and Searching[13]

Intuitively, Internet applications, especially the World Wide Web (the web), seem like some form of copyright public domain, but how is that public domain created? Our view is that from the early 1990s, the creation of and mass public access to the World Wide Web created global de facto public rights for *browsing* and private use (including reproduction by downloading) of works that authors made accessible on the Internet, irrespective of the legal position in particular countries. Similarly, since 1996, the development of search engines has created global de facto public rights enabling the *searching* of such works, irrespective of

---

[9] Wu, 'Tolerated use', 617–18.
[10] *Blair* v. *Osborne & Tomkins* [1971] 2 QB 78; *Concrete Pty Ltd* v. *Parramatta Design & Developments Pty Ltd* (2006) 70 IPR 468.
[11] See *Copyright Agency Ltd* v. *New South Wales* (2008) 233 CLR 279.
[12] In addition, obtaining a copy of the work is also not necessarily available to all free of charge or at the same price.
[13] A longer version of this section is available in the Online Supplement, chap. 16, 'The public domain of Internet-published content: browsing and searching'.

## 16.2 De Facto Public Rights in Internet-Published Content

copyright considerations in particular countries. Taken together, the access enabled by Internet browsing and searching may be the largest practical expansion in the effectiveness of the public domain ever to occur, at least since the developments of low-cost printing and public libraries turned the right to read physical copies of works into an effective public domain.

These developments have expanded the copyright public domain. We use the expressions 'browsable commons' and 'searchable commons' for readability, but the term 'commons' is used here in the same sense as 'copyright public domain': see further [2.4.1].

*The Browsable Commons of the Web* Up to the mid-1990s, the World Wide Web grew quickly to millions of pages of content, most of it available for free access. From inception, this did affect authors' exclusive rights. To use any content, even to read it on screen, it was necessary for the user's browser software to download a copy of the work into the web cache of their PC and to retain it for a period. Web browsing therefore involved users exercising what was arguably part of the copyright owner's exclusive rights, the right to reproduce the work.

Temporary reproduction for the purpose of access, however, was obviously what the owner intended by making the work freely available on the web. The legal status of such temporary reproductions was uncertain, including under EU law,[14] where an Agreed Statement to the WCT failed to resolve the issue, leaving this to national laws: [10.2.4]. Depending on the jurisdiction, such temporary reproductions may be permissible under statutory exceptions: [12.2]; or, potentially, as an implied licence. At [12.2.5], we explained how excepting such temporary or transient copies from infringement is essential to the copyright public domain, and suggested measures for clarifying the legal status of temporary copies.

In addition, owners were also giving users a de facto ability to make a permanent copy of the file, and to print it out for their private purposes. Such uses were advantageous to copyright owners, as likely to strengthen their reputation (commercial, academic or otherwise) and with no likely harm, provided copies were not exploited commercially. Globally, all members of the public therefore had, in effect, a de facto right to make such reproductions of works made available on the web as were necessary for them to view, store and print those works, irrespective of the position

---

[14] For the uncertain position as at 2000, particularly in relation to client caching, see Hugenholtz, 'Caching and copyright: the right of temporary copying', 482.

under the copyright law of their country. The tacit acceptance by copyright owners of such infringements as were necessary to create this result, which was advantageous to them, despite its often uncertain legal status, created a more valuable body of public rights to use content than any development since public libraries: the 'browsable commons' of the early web.

*The Searchable Commons of the Web vs Exclusive Rights*  Browsing web pages was assisted by catalogues of websites (the basis of the original Yahoo! system), or by memorable domain names, but there were initially no effective web wide search engines. From 1996, search engines made it possible to search a progressively increasing proportion of all content available via the web, originally via Digital's AltaVista search engine, but from 1998 by the eventually dominant Google search engine.[15] 'Search' became, and has remained, central to the operation of the web.

To what extent are uses of works which are prima facie within the exclusive rights of copyright owners necessary for search engines to add to the pre-existing browsable commons? In non-technical terms,[16] the following key aspects of typical search engine operation have copyright implications:

- *Location of web content is usually far faster and more effective* than browsing catalogues, only because a web robot makes a copy (reproduction) of every web page it locates in order to create a word-occurrence location index of every word on each page, and for other purposes such as analysis of links between pages. The search engine uses this index to find all pages satisfying a user's search request.
- *Displays of search results help the user assess relevance*, including reproduction of the 'document' title, plus in some cases a few lines of text from the original web page ('snippets'), and 'thumbnail' copies of original images. These may be reproductions of substantial parts of the original.
- *Pages that are temporarily inaccessible from the web can still be viewed*, because most, but not all, search engines allow users to display the 'cached' copy of the page held by them. This may involve reproducing, 'making available' or 'communicating' works.
- *Documents may be displayed with features additional to the original.* For example, cached documents presented with the user's search terms may be highlighted, or converted from their original formats into HTML

[15] J. Battelle, *The Search – How Google and its Rivals Rewrote the Rules of Business and Transformed our Culture* (Nicholas Brealey Publishing, 2005) and D. Vise, *The Google Story* (Macmillan, 2005).
[16] For more detailed explanations, synonyms and references, see the Online Supplement.

## 16.2 De Facto Public Rights in Internet-Published Content

format for easier use. Such transformations may constitute infringing reproductions of the original work, or other forms of infringement, depending on the national copyright law concerned.

The revolution that search engines brought to the web was therefore only possible because their operators have been able to exercise, as a practical matter, multiple aspects of what might normally be the exclusive rights of copyright owners all over the world. Aspects of those exclusive rights are now exercised by intermediaries, especially search engine operators, for the benefit of all Internet users.

*Law and Search Engines: Twenty Years, Many Countries* How did the above situation occur? Was it because search engine operators were able to rely upon limits on the exclusive rights of copyright owners or exceptions to them (in other words, the broad notion of the *de jure* public domain), or was it because of some other factor?[17]

In the first decade of search engine operations, from 1996 to 2006, legal challenges to search engine practices were intermittent and marginal. However, their position under copyright law was uncertain, even in the United States. In most countries there were no serious legal challenges at all. This may be explained in part by the fact that the major search engines were based in the United States but the first legal challenge to Google's caching practices, *Field*,[18] was decided in its favour only in January 2005, a decade after search engines commenced: [12.2.3]. During the prior decade, when the legality of search engine operations was uncertain, they became the core utility of Internet commerce, throughout the world, without any authoritative support in case law even in the United States.

From 2006 onwards, US law progressively clarified that the normal operations of search engines were protected against copyright infringement actions, primarily through the fair use exception: [12.2.3], but also because of the 'safe harbour' provisions concerning 'intermediate and temporary storage' of the Digital Millennium Copyright Act.[19] The 'transformative use' aspect of the fair use exception was adopted in 2007 by the Ninth Circuit Court of Appeals in *Perfect 10*,[20] holding that the storage and return of thumbnail images by the Google search engine was a fair use as it was 'highly transformative',[21] emphasising that a search engine 'provides social benefit by incorporating an original work into a new work, namely, an electronic reference tool', and shifting the focus from whether a use is transformative to whether there is a 'transformative

---

[17] For a more detailed account of this legal history, see the Online Supplement.
[18] *Field* v. *Google Inc*, 412 F Supp 2d 1106 (D Nev 2006).    [19] 17 USC s512(b)(1)
[20] *Perfect 10, Inc.* v. *Amazon.com, Inc*, 508 F 3d 1146 (9th Cir 2007).
[21] *Perfect 10, Inc.* v. *Amazon.com, Inc*, 1165.

purpose' by finding that a use may be transformative, even if it does not add new expression, provided it gives the work 'new meaning'.[22] The breadth of the 'transformative purpose' analysis was confirmed in 2013 by the Second Circuit Court of Appeals in *Authors Guild*:[23] [12.3.2]. By then, it was clear that the normal operation of search engines (including practices such as spidering, creating concordances, caching and snippets) was part of the *de jure* copyright public domain of the United States, with no need to rely on a de facto public domain.

Outside the United States, the operations of search engines, particularly in their first decade, was less likely to be clearly protected by copyright law. Some protections result from statutory changes, such as exceptions for transient reproductions, post-dating the 1996 start of search engine operations. Even now, it is difficult to be certain about some aspects of the operation of search engines (differing between jurisdictions), because there is little case law testing their operations. However, copyright owner beliefs concerning the operation of search engines is influenced by both their legitimacy in the United States and uncertainty about which country's law is applicable. In some jurisdictions, the meaning of 'reproduction' may exclude certain types of temporary reproductions broadly enough to protect search engine practices, or there may be explicit statutory exceptions that protect the core elements of searching. Many jurisdictions do not have any free use exceptions which specifically protect such Internet uses. In the EU, the InfoSoc Directive requires EU Member States provide that the reproduction right extends to all 'temporary reproductions', but with a mandatory exception to ensure that transient copies made to access Internet content, such as copies made by browsing or caching, do not fall within the reproduction right. After a series of CJEU cases there remain uncertainties, such as the precise meaning of 'transient' reproductions, but it is clear that the exception applies to exclude copies automatically made as an integral part of Internet browsing, apparently regardless of how long the copies might be retained: [12.2.1]. Nevertheless, the exception is very technical, imposing five cumulative conditions, and does not have the breadth and flexibility available under US law. In other countries that have purported to deal with these issues, the position is even more uncertain. In Australia, for example, relatively complex exceptions for temporary reproductions 'incidentally made as a necessary part of a technical process' give rise to doubts about their application to all common forms of caching, including

---

[22] See J. Ginsburg, 'Google Books and fair use: from implausible to inevitable?', *SociallyAware*, 17 November 2015 www.sociallyawareblog.com/2015/11/17/google-books-and-fair-use-from-implausible-to-inevitable/.

[23] *Authors Guild, Inc. v. Google, Inc*, 804 F 3d 202 (2nd Cir, 2015).

## 16.2 De Facto Public Rights in Internet-Published Content

those that may be held for more than a limited period. This is made worse by the exceptions for Internet intermediaries not applying to reproductions of infringing material: [12.2.2]. Other countries such as Korea and India introduced exceptions after 2010, but with no greater clarity: [12.2.3]. Only a handful of jurisdictions have a fair use exception such as in the US. Fair dealing exceptions are unlikely to cover search engine operations, except in Canada's 'flexible' version: [11.4.3]. Other doctrines are unlikely to come to the rescue of search engine operations.

We can therefore conclude that, more than twenty years after search engines commenced operations, the legal positions of search engines outside the United States is still unclear and complicated, although the paucity of relevant case law makes the extent of problems uncertain.

*Why Search Engines Were Able to Create a Global Commons*
Despite uncertainties and variations in local laws, the normal operations of search engines have gone largely unchallenged. Given this international history, how then do we explain the global achievement of the 'searchable commons of the web', particularly in the early years of search engines? As explained above, we cannot do so simply by saying that the law provides sufficient exceptions to or limitations on copyright protection to ensure that search engines could function within the law. In our view, many of the factors contributing to the successful operation of search engines can be identified. These observations now only apply to countries other than the United States, because, from around 2006, US law has clarified that when US law applies, the searchable commons is part of the *de jure* public domain, arising primarily from fair use exceptions but also from other statutory provisions such as 'safe harbour' legislation.

We identify eight factors[24] which resulted in the global acceptance of search engines, despite their unprecedented copyright infringement.

(i) They contribute *a significant innovation* to the pre-existing Internet, not achievable by individual content owners.
(ii) They contribute something of *general public benefit*. Gratis use by Internet users enables them to find content more effectively, creating expectations of continuation.
(iii) They contribute *benefit to most copyright owners*, making findable content they have already made available for free access, often resulting in commercial dependence.[25]

---

[24] See the Online Supplement for a more detailed statement of these factors.
[25] There is a 'search engine optimisation' (SEO) industry because businesses have become dependent on their websites obtaining high rankings in search engine result displays.

(iv) They *cause harm to few copyright owners and actively minimise some possible harms.*[26]
(v) In many countries, the *copyright position of search engines is (or at least was) neither clear-cut nor widely understood.*
(vi) It is *not practicable for search engines to obtain prior consent* of all websites they make searchable.
(vii) They provide an *effective ability to opt out from searching* for those who don't want their content to be searchable.
(viii) *The rate of opting-out has not been sufficient in practice to threaten their viability.*

The result has been the creation of a global de facto searchable commons.

While copyright owners who make copies of their own works available for free access on the Internet have considered it a benign practice that search engines should make those copies searchable, it does not follow that they would take a similar view of search engines making searchable other copies of their works put on the Internet without their permission (infringing or 'pirate' content). Copyright owners have resisted this, and legal controversy in many countries has resulted in search engines being required to implement various forms of 'notice and takedown' schemes, usually with 'safe harbour' protections in return [6.2.3]. Some search engine providers have published 'transparency reports' detailing how they process take-down requests.[27] As is the case here, the use of infringing content has little to do with the copyright public domain.

### 16.2.4 Examples on the Borderline of the De Facto Public Domain

The conditions that we have suggested are conducive to de facto public domain examples [16.2.1], and found applicable to search engines, do occur in other contexts, and are not limited to the Internet, even though not widely applicable. Examples follow, of varying strengths.

*A De Facto Public Domain for Private Use Machine Translations* International law requires that national laws provide that copyright owners have an exclusive right over translations of copyright works: [4.7.1]. Translations are variously described in national copyright laws, including as adaptations (Australia) or derivative works (United States).

---

[26] Claims that search results are manipulated to favour some websites, if sustained, would weaken this position.
[27] For example, see Google's 'transparency reports': 'Requests to remove content due to copyright' www.google.com/transparencyreport/removals/copyright/. For a study of these practices, see J. M. Urban, J. Karaganis and B. L. Schofield, *Notice and Takedown in Everyday Practice*, version 2 (American Assembly, 2017).

## 16.2 De Facto Public Rights in Internet-Published Content

Automated translation by machine ('machine translation' or MT) has become far more reliable in very recent years, and is now used very widely. The free use Google Translate facility is perhaps the most broadly known and used example.[28]

The legal position varies considerably between jurisdictions on whether the product of MT will be in the public domain, or alternatively might constitute a work in its own right, or might constitute an infringement of the work that has been translated. Which is the case will depend primarily on whether the law requires a human author in order to meet the criterion of originality. The position in the United States is uncertain concerning the need for human authorship.[29] In some jurisdictions, such as Australia, all computer-generated works, such as MT, are part of the public domain,[30] but in others, such as the UK, statutory provisions mean there is no bar to copyright protection of computer-generated works: [7.2.12]. However, differences between jurisdictions on that question might not make a difference to the question of whether an MT is an infringement, just as a photocopy may still be an infringing reproduction even though it has no originality. It would be unwise to be dogmatic outside the specifics of individual laws. In some countries only, use of translators might come within private use exceptions [12.3], and in other countries exceptions such as fair use may apply [11.3]. In short, the global legal position is confused, but (as with search engines) the most-used facilities are global and Internet-based.

If translations by any MT facility of any works which are considered by authors to be of commercial value are reproduced for commercial purposes, or made available via the Internet, or used for large-scale teaching purposes, or used for other purposes which affect the interests of copyright owners, then such practices could not be regarded as part of the de facto public domain, even if they are beyond the legal reach of copyright owners in some cases.

At the other end of the spectrum of uses, Internet users in all countries now have access to facilities such as Google Translate. It seems reasonable to assume that most uses are private uses that do not result in reproductions for others, and are done for such purposes as learning another language, travel (websites of institutions, hotels and restaurants), and research into

---

[28] Google Translate https://translate.google.com/.
[29] E. Ketzan, 'Rebuilding Babel: copyright and the future of machine translation online' *Tulane Journal of Technology & Intellectual Property*, Spring 2007.
[30] This is provided the software is primarily responsible for the expression, as is likely with MT: J. McCutcheon, 'The vanishing author in computer-generated works: a critical analysis of recent Australian case law' (2013) 36 *Melbourne University Law Review* 915 at 931–4.

such matters as laws or customs of other countries. Given the extent of English-language content on the web, significant translation may be from English into other languages. Google Translate includes a facility described as 'automatically view any web page in your preferred language', which would greatly increase the quantity of private use translations. These MT facilities are also free to use although they cannot be described as 'non-profit' because of associated advertising revenues. These uses largely satisfy the ten indicative factors listed above although Google Translate does not seem to include an opt-out facility.[31]

On balance, we suggest there is now a global de facto public domain for private use machine translations. It is, in fact, the clearest example other than the browsable and searchable Internet public domains.

*Reproduction of Legislation and Case Law* Quite a few countries still have Crown copyright in case law and legislation, particularly in the common law world, although some common law countries do not [8.2.2]. By 2005, many significant common law countries had free access legal information institutes (LIIs), and these LIIs received active assistance from courts and legislation offices to reproduce cases and legislation for free access. However, this was not the case in many other countries, in the Caribbean, Africa and Asia, even though there was often official free access Internet publication of cases and legislation. The Australasian Legal Information Institute wished to build a Commonwealth-wide free access service (with the cooperation of the existing LIIs), but could not obtain replies to requests for consent from those countries not involved in the existing LIIs and where Crown copyright applied. Nevertheless, it went ahead and reproduced case law and legislation from official sites in those countries (not commercial sites), as part of the free access Commonwealth Legal Information Institute (CommonLII). No website concerned excluded web spiders through the Robot Exclusion Protocol, and such an 'opt-out' would have been respected. Since 2005, no court or legislation office has requested any content removed from CommonLII. At its launch in 2005, the Chief Justice of one of the countries concerned said it made her very proud that her court's decisions were included, consistent with AustLII's expectations that such reproductions would be considered as benign. By 2010, CommonLII included sixty-nine

---

[31] Although the same Robot Exclusion facility that allows opting out from search engines is stated also to facilitate opting out from translations of websites (B. Clay, 'Robots exclusion protocol guide', 2015 www.bruceclay.com/seo/robots-exclusion-guide.pdf indicates that the protocol prevents web spiders used by 'Translation services (e.g., Bing Translator, Google Translate)'), tests indicate this does not prevent machine translation from URLs blocked from robots.

databases from twenty-five countries not included in other LIIs, and many of these were included on that assumption of a de facto public domain.[32]

*Non-Commercial Mass Digitisation of Sets of Orphan and Non-Orphan Works* Mass digitisation projects by cultural institutions are based on complex calculations of benefits and risks, and consideration of the interests of numerous stakeholders.[33] They are sometimes carried out on the basis of risk assessments which predict that, even though the results of digitisation will be overt (displayed online, or displayed in galleries, or reproduced in catalogues), it is unlikely that there will be significant complaints or litigation. Factors contributing to such risk assessments are similar to the ten factors we list above. Digitisation and cataloguing organise material otherwise unseen. Consent may be impossible to obtain for many genuine orphans in a collection, but the cost of diligent searching may also make that impracticable even if it might reveal owners in a few cases. The institution concerned may be non-profit, even if entrance fees are charged. Harms to owners can be avoided (for example, by deletion of potentially sensitive content) and opt-outs can be publicised. The use of individual works would need to be of little commercial value before the de facto public domain would be relevant.

Such an approach is unlikely to be successful if the uses made of individual works are of significant commercial value, even if they may be orphans, as this is likely to attract the understandable interest of organisations representing copyright owners. Free access reproductions on a museum website, even though it involves dissemination, may be less likely to attract objections than licensing by a museum to third parties for commercial purposes.[34] We do not suggest that positive risk assessments necessarily indicate the existence of a de facto public domain, because such risk assessment may depend on factors such as almost all works involved being likely to be out of copyright.

Where cultural institutions proceed with digitisation of non-commercial works with otherwise low risk factors, in our view such

---

[32] For background, see G. Greenleaf, A. Mowbray and P. Chung, 'Building a Commons for the Common Law – The Commonwealth Legal Information Institute (CommonLII) after four years' progress' (2010) 36(1) *Commonwealth Law Bulletin* 127–34.

[33] US Copyright Office, 'Legal issues in mass digitization: a preliminary analysis and discussion document', October 2011, III B: 'The nature of existing mass digitization projects'.

[34] For permutations of uses of digitisation by CHIs, see J. McCutcheon, 'Digital access to culture: copyright in photographs of two-dimensional art under Australian copyright law' *Queen Mary Intellectual Property Journal* (forthcoming).

projects, when well-managed with risk assessments and opt-outs, should often be regarded as examples of the de facto public domain.

*Digitisation of Non-Profit Journals* A related example is where non-profit journals, previously available only in print, become online journals, and in the process digitise their back-issues and put them online. In many jurisdictions the legal position as between the journal publisher and many of its content authors will be unclear, with no assignments of copyright held, or no licences covering online publication. Nevertheless, thousands of journals in many countries have been so digitised, and can usually expect that their non-profit status, the benefits to their authors in increased exposure, and the sensible provision of opt-outs for authors, will bring such publication within the de facto public domain. This may also apply to third-party digitisers, where the institutions responsible for the journals give consent.

*Fan Fiction, including Japan's* Doujinshi *Culture* 'Dōjinshi' is a shorthand reference to Japanese self-published graphic stories, in the form of magazines or books (*manga*), that cater to the interests of specific groups of people. One version (*niji sousaku*, or derivative works) is based on characters that appear in commercially produced graphic stories: a form of fan-fiction comics. They are primarily sold through fan conventions (*dōjinshi sokubaikai*). The largest, from over 1,000 such events, Comiket, attracts up to 600,000 people. Although relatively few *dōjinshi* authors make significant money, the total amount is significant, given the multi-billion-dollar *manga* market.[35] Nevertheless, the only known example of litigation being completed is a prosecution concerning a *dōjinshi* version of a Nintendo character which may have been more to do with pornography than *dōjinshi*.[36]

Six factors have been put forward to explain why the commercial manga houses have been content to leave the *niji sousaku dōjinshi* culture alone, despite its very substantial size: (i) many professional manga artists started their careers in the same way as these amateurs, and their publishers may wish to hire new talents in future; (ii) artists and publishers fear litigation will alienate their customer base; (iii) 'borrowing' characters is a long-established practice in Japan, prior to more recent emphasis on copyright; (iv) the legal position of *dōjinshi* is somewhat confused, with

---

[35] R. Richey and M. Richey, 'Japan's doujinshi culture of creativity through theft and the monster trying to destroy it', 6 September 2016 www.tofugu.com/japan/doujinshi-definition/.

[36] S. Mehra, 'Copyright and comics in Japan: does law explain why all the cartoons my kid watches are Japanese imports?' (2002) 55 *Rutgers Law Review* 59.

## 16.2 De Facto Public Rights in Internet-Published Content

the Prime Minister declaring during Trans-Pacific Partnership (TPP) negotiations that it constituted parody;[37] (v) *dōjinshi* attract new readers to the works from which they are derived; and (vi) Japanese society discourages unnecessary litigation.[38] Other suggested factors are that *doujinshi* are usually only published in small volumes, and sold primarily at conventions, to reduce litigation risks. There may also be effective opting out by artists or publishers that have a strong aversion to a particular *dōjinshi*: one publisher's warning letter to an artist resulted in cessation of *doujinshi* publication and voluntary payment of damages, and the complaint was probably against passing off rather than *dōjinshi* publication, as such.[39] Mehra concluded that 'the benefits to the industry as a whole likely outweigh' any costs to affected publishers and authors.[40]

Of the ten conditions we suggest are favourable to de facto rights emerging [16.2.1], factors 1, 3, 4, 5, 6, 8, 9 and 10 are arguably present with *niji sousaku dōjinshi*. In many cases it might be unlikely that *dōjinshi* authors could obtain replies from commercial studios (factor 2), or that those studios would be aware of *dōjinshi* works (factor 7). Although Mehra concluded that it 'would not be surprising if the tolerance of *dōjinshi* markets in Japan changed as Japanese copyright holders became more invested in U.S. markets',[41] fifteen years later, *niji sousaku dōjinshi* still thrive. This is far more likely to be a de facto public domain than tolerated use caused by a shortage of lawyers.[42]

It is arguable that the same can be said about fan fiction generally, outside Japan. This is only relevant to fan fiction which arguably is an infringement of copyright, not examples where it is clear that a defence such as fair use (in the United States) or satire/parody may apply.[43] We would need to assume it only attracts a relatively small audience, whether online or offline, and that the uses do not conflict with the copyright owner's commercial interests.[44] Country-specific investigation would be needed.

---

[37] 'Japanese Prime Minister Shinzo Abe: Doujinshi safe under TPP', SG Cafe, 11 April 2016 http://sgcafe.com/2016/04/japanese-prime-minister-shinzo-abe-doujinshi-safe-tpp/.

[38] Richey and Richey, 'Japan's doujinshi culture'; paraphrase of the authors' six reasons; Mehra reached similar conclusions in 2004.

[39] F. Makoto, 'Doraemon fanzine ignites copyright alarms', *Daily Yomiuri*, 17 June 2007.

[40] Mehra, 'Copyright and comics in Japan', 56.   [41] *Ibid.* 59.

[42] Contra Lessig, *Free Culture*, 27.

[43] For examples either side of the line in the US, see D. Kluft, '10 copyright cases every fan fiction writer should know about', Trademark and Copyright Law Blog, 18 October 2016 www.trademarkandcopyrightlawblog.com/2016/10/10-copyright-cases-every-fan-fiction-writer-should-know-about/.

[44] Unlike in *Warner Brothers v. RDR Books*, 575 F.Supp.2d 513 (SDNY 2008), where this line was crossed.

*The Wrong Side of the Border: Mass Digitisation of Books Still in Copyright*    A few of the factors we say indicate where a de facto public domain for benign uses exist [16.2.1] have some similarity with the factors that US courts have taken into account in deciding that a 'fair use' exception exists (mainly, our factors 1, 3 and 6), but taken together they are far narrower than the key factor in recent US cases, transformative use or purpose.

Examples show that digitisation of books still in copyright is not likely to constitute a de facto public domain, and that those undertaking such projects will need to rely upon exceptions (whether remunerated compulsory licences or non-remunerated exceptions). Some aspects of the mass digitisation of books in the circumstances of *Authors Guild* v. *Google*,[45] specifically the provision of 'snippets' to the public, are within the fair use exception in US law as a transformative use [12.2.3]. However, the litigation surrounding Google's actions makes it clear that most copyright owners (or their representatives) do not regard Google Books as a benign use of their works nor have they acquiesced in it. There is little reason to believe that similar mass digitisation projects in other jurisdictions would be met with acquiescence as a benign use elsewhere. For example, the litigation by French publishers in *Soulier and Doke* resulted in the invalidation of France's 'Law on the digital exploitation of out-of-print books of the twentieth century', because aspects of it were inconsistent with the InfoSoc Directive: [13.3.5]. These uses are therefore, as yet, on 'the wrong side of the border' of the de facto public domain.

*'Fuzzy Borders' Distinguished*    Similar examples of the 'wrong side of the border' can be found where libraries or other free-access providers digitise materials such as newspapers or commercially published law reports up to a period (for example, seventy years ago) earlier than which the publishers concerned may have few records of ownership of copyright of individual items, or dates of death of individual contributors. These are more likely to be instances of 'tolerated use', not examples of publishers accepting practices because they see them to be in their interest. Tolerated uses like these are often desirable and prudent, but not part of the de facto public domain.

### 16.2.5 Conclusion: No Panacea, but the De Facto Public Domain Must Not be Ignored

Despite the uncertain borderline between the de facto public domain and uses falling short of this which are merely 'tolerated uses' or 'unknown

---

[45] *Authors Guild, Inc.* v. *Google, Inc*, 804 F 3d 202 (2nd Cir, 2015).

uses', we are insistent that this aspect of the public domain should not be ignored. The above examples of the browsable web, the public domain of search engines, the private use of machine translation, fan fiction in Japan and perhaps elsewhere, republication of legislation and case law in common law countries, non-profit journal archives, and some other carefully managed non-commercial mass digitisation projects, when taken together, demonstrate the vast scale of these aspects of the de facto public domain. In terms of social utility as well as scale, they may be just as important as free use exceptions, compulsory licensing or neutral voluntary licences. They should not be ignored, because together they comprise the most significant moderating factor on copyright of the past few decades. They are likely to become even more important in future, though only very rarely of global significance comparable to the rise of search engines. Of course, changes to legislation in relation to fair use, orphan works exceptions and the like may convert them from the de facto to the *de jure* public domain. Wu correctly claims that 'copyright lacks a vocabulary to describe what is happening in the 21st century',[46] and part of that vocabulary should be the de facto public domain.

## 16.3 'Spillover' Effects of National Public Domains on Other Countries

With some qualifications relating, for example, to geo-blocking or filtering of content, the Internet allows access to content irrespective of its physical location. The territorial nature of copyright, however, means that some countries have broader national public domains than other countries.

In the physical world of books and CDs, parallel importation restrictions in copyright laws may place a general prohibition on the import into countries of items which are legitimately accessible under the copyright laws of a country of origin, but where there is a different copyright owner in the country in which the user is located: [10.2.7].[47] These restrictions can also apply to works which are in the public domain under one country's laws, but not in the destination country, due, for example, to differences in statutory exceptions or copyright terms. Parallel importation restrictions, where they exist, may be subject to exceptions which, by allowing legitimate importation of content that might otherwise be infringing, constitute part of the national public domains as statutory

---

[46] Wu, 'Tolerated use', 617.
[47] See, for example, Copyright Act 1968 (Cth), ss. 37, 102; *Avel Pty Ltd v. Multicoin Amusements Pty Ltd* (1991) 18 IPR 443; *Polo/Lauren Company v. Ziaani Holdings Pty Ltd* (2008) 173 FCR 266.

exceptions to exclusive rights.[48] The existence of Internet-based commerce now allows copyright goods to be ordered from overseas providers such as Amazon, Book Depository and other merchants, efficiently, at competitive prices, and often for content not available locally. Over and above the legal issues, market segmentation may be circumvented by online trading, where consumers can readily order legitimate physical copies of works through globally available services such as Amazon, and where technical forms of geo-blocking are often relatively easily circumvented.[49] The extent to which such imports do in fact comply with available local statutory exceptions is contentious.

All of these issues are multiplied by the direct accessibility of digital content, via the Internet without need for physical copies. This applies equally to access to proprietary content through purchase, but with no customs posts to enforce local statutory exceptions, even in theory, and to content which is in the public domain in other jurisdictions but not in the jurisdiction to which it is imported. Imports of both proprietary content and public domain content are in practice unstoppable, in the absence of geo-blocking or region-coding of digital content: [6.3.3]. However, circumvention of both geo-blocking and region-coding is also common. This increased global accessibility of copyright content places considerable strain on the continued viability of parallel importation restrictions. Details of parallel importation laws, including issues relating to exceptions to those laws, and the viability of such restrictions, only tangentially concern the public domain. One aspect requires brief discussion.

What we refer to as the 'spillover' effect occurs where the combination of a broader public domain in some jurisdictions, together with global accessibility via the Internet, allows practical access to, and use of, copyright works in jurisdictions where they are not in the public domain. For example, an author's work may still be within its copyright term in country A, but (for various reasons) its copyright term may have expired in country B, and it may be available for free access on an Internet server located in country B without any geo-blocking. Internet users in country A may therefore download it free of charge, instead of purchasing a copy in country A. Under these circumstances, the unconstrained access to these works can be said to result in effect in a partial equalisation of the public domains across jurisdictions, resulting in an expansion of the public domain in destination countries. It is in effect an Internet-enabled expansion of public rights, lawful or unlawful, depending on

---

[48] See, for example, in Australia, Copyright Act 1968 (Aus.), ss. 44A, 44C, 44D, 44E, 44F, 112A, 112C, 112D, 112DA.
[49] M. Fornaro, 'Parallel problem: grey market goods and the Internet' (2003) 8 *Journal of Technology Law & Policy* 69.

the destination country, but not a separate category of public rights. Nor does it fit within our definition of the de facto public domain, because acquiescence of copyright owners is not involved. Similarly, imports of proprietary content via Internet or post, outside the scope of local statutory exceptions to parallel import restrictions, have nothing to do with the de facto public domain. From our perspective, while the weakness of parallel import restrictions is generally not relevant to the public domain, 'Internet spillovers' between the public domains of various countries can be regarded as a support for the global public domain.

### 16.3.1 Conclusions on Internet Spillovers

What steps in relation to Internet spillovers are desirable to protect and expand public domains? First, consumers and others in a country should not be prevented from circumventing geo-blocking technologies which would prevent them from accessing content which is in the public domain. Australia's Productivity Commission has recommended that the Copyright Act should be amended to clarify such perceived ambiguity, and state it is not an infringement for consumers to circumvent geo-blocking technology,[50] and the government is considering doing this through a new exception in the regulations governing TPMs.[51] It also recommended that Australia 'should avoid any international agreements that would prevent or ban consumers from circumventing geo-blocking technology'.[52] Such a recommendation is somewhat broader than is necessary to support the public domain, but it avoids the necessity to distinguish between content in the public domain and other content legitimately obtained.

Second, if particular content is within the public domain in a country because, for example, the term of copyright has expired, it has no obligation to prevent that content from being obtained by persons in another country where the same content may still be protected by copyright. Countries should not impose some form of geo-blocking technology on content providers in order to prevent such spillovers of public domain content, and nor should they enter international agreements requiring such imposition.

---

[50] This was also recommended in the Australian House of Representatives Standing Committee on Infrastructure and Communications' report, 'At what cost? IT pricing and the Australia tax', 2013.
[51] Australian Government, 'Response to the Productivity Commission Inquiry', 5.
[52] Productivity Commission (Aus.), 'Intellectual property arrangements', Recommendation 5.2.

## 16.4 Conclusions: The Significance of the Global Internet Public Domain

The extent and importance of the public domain created by voluntary licensing and public domain dedications, including FOSS licensing and CC and other open content licences, has been explained in Chapter 15, and recommendations made for legal changes that would strengthening them: [15.7]. To appreciate the full extent and significance of the global public domain made possible by the Internet it is necessary to add the examples of the de facto public domain created by Internet browsing, searching and machine translation, and some limited instances of derivative fiction and mass digitisation, plus the 'equalisation effect' of 'Internet spillovers' of national public domains. Together, these factors which operate by and large outside international and national copyright laws, have been responsible for the most significant expansions of public domains in the past forty years since FOSS licensing first started, vastly accelerated by what is now a quarter-century of mass access to the Internet.

*Part IV*

# Conclusions

# 17 Reform Agendas for the Copyright Public Domain

| 17.1 | Achievable Reforms and Future Goals | 543 |
| 17.2 | A New Perspective on Public Domains | 543 |
| 17.3 | Exclusive Rights and Public Domains: Complex Relationships | 544 |
| 17.4 | Main Innovations in Public Domain Categories | 546 |
| 17.5 | Constraints on and Supports for Copyright Public Domains | 548 |
| 17.6 | Reforms to Strengthen Copyright Public Domains | 551 |
| 17.7 | Contemporary Values and the Future of Public Rights | 560 |
| 17.8 | Future Reforms | 562 |

## 17.1 Achievable Reforms and Future Goals

In this chapter, we conclude by reviewing the main arguments we have presented, and the main conclusions we have reached concerning achievable reforms to strengthen national public domains. Finally, we consider some directions in which we hope the public domain may develop in the future.

## 17.2 A New Perspective on Public Domains

We have argued for a positive view of the public domain, as the full complement of copyright's exclusive rights: [1.3]. More expressly taking the public domain into account gives us a broader perspective on copyright law that can elucidate issues overlooked by the orthodox approach of seeing copyright almost entirely through the lens of exclusive rights. Such traditional approaches to copyright law can easily lead to overbroad proprietarianism, where greater protection is automatically assumed desirable: [1.5.1]. The freedom (or negative liberty) to use works without permission, which in our view lies at the heart of the diverse values that support the public domain, forms the essence of a user-centric approach to the public domain: [1.6.3]. We propose and justify a working definition of the public domain, which can be summarised as 'the public's ability to use works on equal terms without seeking permission', but we also give a longer more technical definition: [2.3]. We use this technical definition comprehensively to identify fifteen legal categories of the public domain which we argue can also be regarded as 'public rights': [2.4.2]. These categories are based on analysis of laws in the jurisdictions selected for study and are therefore a working hypothesis, subject to modification by further research. This attempt comprehensively to identify the legal categories of the public domain is the main conceptual innovation of Part I and forms the basis for the detailed comparative analysis of each of the categories in Part III.

Copyright law is territorial, so public domains are necessarily jurisdiction-specific or national. In Part II, we therefore identified and explained the supports for and constraints on national public domains arising first from international copyright law and, second, from national practices and laws other than copyright law. From what we call a 'realist' approach: [1.5], we do not focus on or propose reforms to international copyright law, but accept it as a fundamental constraint within which national regimes must pragmatically work, using whatever flexibilities are possible. That does not mean that unreflective public domain 'maximalism' – the automatic privileging of public domain values – should be the rubric for copyright law reform: it would raise as many problems as unreflective copyright proprietarianism: [1.6.1]. We consider it is enough to argue that taking a positive and broad view of the public domain and of public domain values can help us to understand better the complexities of the interlocking rights and interests that comprise the copyright system. We argue that this approach also helps to identify issues that may be overlooked and to suggest reforms with the potential to improve the law for both authors and users.

## 17.3  Exclusive Rights and Public Domains: Complex Relationships

It is a mistake to conceive of copyright as consisting of mutually exclusive private and public domains. The copyright system should instead be seen as a continuum with shadings or gradations between the purely 'private' and the purely 'public', including gradations within the one work: [2.3.2]. From this perspective, and using a comprehensive definition of the public domain based on permission-free use, we pursue the insight that the public domain, far from being simply what is left after exclusive rights are exhausted, should be seen as permeating the entire copyright system.

## 17.3 Exclusive Rights and Public Domains

We systematically track its implications for each of the fifteen identified legal categories of the copyright public domain.

There is already considerable complexity in copyright law in determining precisely whether a use falls within the exclusive rights of copyright owners, requiring permission, or whether it is a public right, which may be exercised without permission. Accepting the proposition that the public domain is found within each work may seem to add to the complexity. Our doctrinal analysis of the public domain categories, with a focus on the decisions of superior courts in difficult cases which define the public/private boundary, while necessary, can appear to overstate the complexities in determining whether or not a particular use of a work is permissible. However, the application of flexible copyright doctrines, such as the originality/creativity threshold, idea/expression dichotomy and substantial infringement, is necessarily both contested and complex.

We argue that to take public domain considerations into account in defining the main elements of copyright law has great advantages. First, by reflecting the reality that the legal limits of protectable works and exclusive uses also set the limits of the public domain, it more accurately indicates the complex rights and interests implicated by the copyright system. Second, by expressly taking account of the public domain and values supporting it (public domain values), we argue that the issues at stake in setting the limits of copyright protection can be clarified. Third, by introducing considerations overlooked or obscured in traditional approaches, there is an increase in analytical clarity.

Because our analysis of the fifteen public domain categories is based on doctrinal law, our descriptions of the categories in Part III often reflects the orthodox focus on exclusive property rights in both legislation and case law, and makes it necessary to engage with the complexity (and vagaries) of the law in each category. However, expressly inserting a public domain perspective into each of the categories delivers insights which help us to understand better the categories, and provides the basis for suggesting reforms for strengthening copyright public domains, summarised at [17.6] below.

The traditional values that support the public domain – uses of works in creative endeavours, to further freedom of expression and access to knowledge, and to promote broader cultural participation – lead us to view the public domain as supporting the negative liberty of users to use works without permission: [1.6.3]. But a focus on permission-free uses of works in the abstract is inadequate and must be firmly grounded in the specific legal contexts in which permission-free uses of works are possible. Most of the book therefore deals with the identification and detailed analysis (both descriptive and normative) of the fifteen categories, each of which allows for permission-free uses of works, but in different contexts. A comprehensive understanding of the public domain, as we define it, is possible only if all categories are fully taken into account. What emerges is a complex web or network of uses, which can be regarded as a bundle of public rights to use works, and which are ultimately referable to the values which support the public domain.

While the public rights that make up the categories of the public domain (and the values supporting them) are, in our view, of equal importance to the exclusive property rights of authors and owners, they are both more diffuse and diverse, and can be easily overlooked in favour of proprietarianist approaches. This can make it more difficult definitively to set out (and defend) these values and rights than it is to delineate exclusive property rights (which, in any case, draw on long-established, if contested, jurisprudential traditions).

The first type of innovation coming from our approach is therefore that we take the public domain, and the values on which it is based, expressly into account in our analysis of the central doctrines of copyright law.

## 17.4   Main Innovations in Public Domain Categories

The second innovation in our approach is seen in the final three of our fifteen categories of the copyright public domain, which best illustrate how our expansive conception of the public domain goes beyond previous attempts at defining or mapping it: neutral compulsory licensing; neutral voluntary licensing; and the de facto public domain of benign uses. Each is based on permission-free uses of copyright works, and each furthers public domain values by enhancing the autonomy of either licensees or the end-users of the works licensed. They all demonstrate the gradations between purely private and purely public rights, by being on the border between the two in varying ways involving the participation of copyright owners: respectively, receipt of remuneration; deciding to utilise a voluntary licence; and refraining from enforcement action. Their inclusion gives us a more complete understanding of the public domain than conventional approaches.

We argue that the public domain extends to uses that do not require permission, although payment may be required, and therefore includes uses under **compulsory licences**. The element of permission-free use in all its variants brings it within our concept of the public domain. To form part of the public domain, however, the terms of use must be determined by a neutral party and be available on equal terms for all licensees. Many of the most important values that support the public domain are promoted by regarding it as freedom from constraints, regardless of whether

## 17.4 Main Innovations in Public Domain Categories

or not payment is required. Although a requirement to pay may inhibit or restrict some users from using works, we consider this is less important than the positive ability to use works without obtaining permission, particularly because of how this supports both creativity and use on a mass scale, whether in digitisation projects, educational materials or otherwise. Furthermore, many categories of copyright exceptions may be implemented in national laws as either unremunerated or remunerated uses. As common values are reflected in both approaches, both should be considered part of the copyright public domain. Compulsory licences are therefore best seen as part of the public domain, but as the part closest to its boundary with the proprietary domain.

Uses of works enabled by voluntary licences, even if there is no licence fee, are not normally part of the copyright public domain, on our definition, because they require a form of a priori permission from a copyright owner. However, we argue that what we call *'neutral voluntary licensing'*, where copyright owners use pre-designed licences written by an independent third party on public interest grounds, creates a 'contractually constructed commons'. Works licensed under such licences are part of the public domain, because control of the use of the work is so far removed from the rights holder that it effectively amounts to a form of permission-free use. We set out nine conditions demarcating those licences which we consider should be regarded as creating this part of the public domain, based on our touchstone of the public domain, the absence of the need for permission to use a work. Major expansions of public rights in copyright in the last two decades have been because of such voluntary licensing, particularly FOSS licensing and Creative Commons licensing. 'Viral' conditions in these licences are of particular importance, because they have an inherent character of expanding the public domain, and have done so on a large scale. These licensing practices have arisen largely via the Internet, and have resulted, particularly because of viral expansion, in an important part of the technological infrastructure, including the Internet, which would not have developed in the way it has without these permission free uses. A distinctive contribution of this category to our understanding of the public domain is that it illustrates the importance of uses effectively beyond the control of numerous copyright owners, especially for incremental and continuous improvements of products such as software, and new forms of aggregated content such as Wikipedia.

We propose that *'benign uses'*, a de facto category of the copyright public domain, exist when the vast majority of affected copyright owners consider that they should not attempt to prevent what would otherwise be an infringing use of their work, because the use is sufficiently in their own interests, and the minority who do not hold this view are dissuaded from litigating. These 'benign uses' are distinct from other tolerated uses of works. We identify ten factors which indicate when they are likely to arise. This category of the public domain explains both the initial 'browsable commons' created by the World Wide Web from 1995, and subsequently the far more important 'searchable commons' created by search engines. These are developments of enormous social and economic importance, and we consider they must not be overlooked by a comprehensive account of the copyright public domain, because they have the defining public domain characteristic of permission-free use. Other examples of such benign uses being accepted by copyright owners include the private use of machine translation, fan fiction in some situations, republication of legislation and case law in common law countries, non-profit journal archives, and some other carefully managed non-commercial mass digitisation projects. These examples are very diverse, but they share all or most of the ten factors we identify as common to 'benign uses'. Taken together, these developments are a major part of the very significant expansion of the copyright public domain in recent decades, arising primarily because of the Internet. This category further illustrates the importance of rights holders refraining from using their ability to control uses to the full extent of the law, when it is not in their interest to do so.

By taking these last two categories into account, we better understand the extent to which the reality of the copyright system is not determined solely by laws and international agreements, but also by emergent social practices – voluntary licensing and benign uses – which can create new public domain categories. This is also the case with some varieties of compulsory licences, where it is the initiatives of the users of various compulsory licensing systems that determine the form and scope of licensing, not the copyright owner or their CS.

## 17.5 Constraints on and Supports for Copyright Public Domains

Copyright laws and copyright public domains are inherently national, but they do not exist in a legal vacuum. The most important legal constraints on national copyright laws derive from international copyright law, a complex series of nested international agreements, centred on the Berne Convention: [4.2]. As we explain in Chapters 4 and 5, international copyright law imposes significant constraints on national copyright laws, in the form of minimum levels of protection and ceilings on permissible exclusions and exceptions. We argue that, largely in a

## 17.5 Constraints on and Supports for Copyright Public Domains

negative sense, the international framework constitutes a global public domain: [4.1].

While international copyright law should not be regarded as immutable, we are concerned mainly with identifying the flexibilities for national laws to support public domains, given our realist perspective: [1.5]. The historical trajectory of international copyright law has been towards expanding copyright, with the main structural features of international copyright law biased in favour of protection: [4.2.2]. For example, the twin pillars of the Berne regime, national treatment and minimum levels of protection, result in a 'levelling up' of protection under national laws, with public domain considerations marginalised. The structural effects of Berne are reinforced by the combination of post-TRIPs agreements and the TRIPs MFN principle, which have ratcheted up protection.

Nevertheless, international copyright law is not an exhaustive code and therefore leaves room for measures under national laws that may support national public domains. For example, while the rule against formalities is a major constraint on public domains, there remains scope for national measures such as voluntary systems of recordation or registration, with the potential to counter some of the effects of the rule: [6.2.1]. In addition, while international copyright law provides for broad minimum categories of protectable subject matter, there are flexibilities under national laws for defining what falls within protected categories, as well as in the interpretation and application of copyright principles relating to protected works, such as the originality threshold and the idea/expression dichotomy. Similarly, international harmonisation of exclusive rights at a general level of expression provides flexibilities in determining the scope of exclusive rights under national laws.

The structural biases of international copyright law mean that public interest considerations are most expressly taken into account in setting copyright exceptions, which are potentially the most significant element of international copyright law for supporting national public domains. For example, specific exceptions under international copyright law can be seen as promoting public domain values of freedom of expression, access to public information (laws and official documents), democratic processes and education: [5.6]. Nevertheless, the role of exceptions in safeguarding public domains is limited by the structural preference of international copyright law for exclusive rights over exceptions: the Berne system sets ceilings on exceptions and makes most exclusions and exceptions permissive not mandatory. Furthermore, the general ceiling on exceptions – the three-step test – is characterised by ambiguities and inconsistencies, which can limit the flexibility for introducing exceptions (especially broad exceptions) under national laws. While there are some indications of a greater emphasis on exceptions under international copyright law, with the Marrakesh Treaty being the first international agreement to be concerned principally with exceptions: [4.2.1], and with proposals for new international instruments for exceptions for educational uses: [12.5], and libraries and archives: [12.6], so far these developments have been tentative and limited.

The introduction of an international enforcement regime, in the form of the WTO dispute resolution procedure, has potentially decreased the discretion for national laws flexibly to implement international copyright standards: [5.7]. Nonetheless, factors such as the complexity of the international regime and the strategic and selective use of the enforcement mechanism effectively mean there is a degree of implied tolerance of diversity of national laws, with more flexibility for national laws to interpret and apply international copyright law than commonly thought.

Public domains are constrained and supported not only by international copyright law, but also by laws and practices outside copyright at the national level: Chapter 6. Statutory deposit requirements are essential to the public domain, so that works are preserved to allow public rights to be exercised. They need now to cover digital works, and should allow anyone to obtain a copy of the work once the copyright term expires: [6.2.1]. Systems for registering, recording and locating works can be invaluable for identifying and locating authors and other rights holders, facilitating the operation of compulsory licensing, including orphan works schemes: [6.2.2]. 'Safe harbour' provisions are a valuable 'buffer zone' for reasonable exercise of public rights, but need to be sufficiently broad in their coverage: [6.2.3], as are forms of limited remedies for 'innocent infringer' defences: [6.2.4]. Access to copyright works is important for public domain uses, but in this book we focus on analysing copyright law's use rights from a public domain perspective, not on access rights per se: [2.1.2]. However, some of the main non-copyright supports for access to works (including unpublished works) are considered, particularly laws and practices supporting free access to government works: [6.2.5].

On the other hand, national laws outside copyright law can impose major constraints on the effectiveness of the public domain, and at present these constraints are generally more powerful than national supports. Contractual overrides of public rights are potentially the most significant constraint on the public domain (though not yet so in practice), but can be appropriately regulated by national laws. We support legislative differentiation between those exceptions (and other public rights) where contractual overrides should be prohibited, and those where they should be allowed, but favour a default position of disallowance: [6.3.1].

17.6 Reforms to Strengthen Copyright Public Domains 551

Technological protection measures, and their protection by law, present a similar threat (again, not realised in full) of 'digital lock-up'. Countries need to be more precise in undertaking the difficult task of specifying the circumstances in which circumvention should be allowable and should, consistent with our views on contractual overrides, extend this to cover all types of exception where overrides are prohibited: [6.3.2]. Where surveillance is built into systems delivering access to works, the public domain uses of that content are inhibited or threatened. Such measures should be proportional to the protection of the interests of rights holders, but national laws rarely guarantee this: [6.3.3]. Finally, other laws such as confidentiality law may well constrain the copyright public domain: [6.3.4], but are largely outside the scope of this book.

## 17.6 Reforms to Strengthen Copyright Public Domains

We summarise here those reforms to national copyright public domains which our analyses in Part III suggest are desirable (particularly in light of public domain values), which are achievable, within the constraints of international copyright law, and which are intended to take due account of the interests of all relevant parties. The justifications and details of the proposals summarised here are set out in each chapter. For consistency and comprehensiveness, we adhere to the fifteen categories of the public domain around which this book is structured. The justifications for what we recommend are not restated here, only the conclusions. Reference is therefore needed to the relevant sections of the substantive chapters for the complete explanation of our recommendations.

*1 Works Failing Minimum Requirements* Under national copyright laws, works may fail to satisfy the minimum requirements for protection because: they do not meet the originality threshold; they are insufficiently substantial; or, in some jurisdictions, are not fixed. For each of these subcategories, courts generally ask whether the works should be protected, but less frequently whether they should not be protected. Greater clarity is achievable from more precise focus on when works should not be protected, taking into account public domain considerations.

Concerning originality, we argue that an exclusively author-centric focus can obscure key considerations relating to drawing the line between protected and unprotected works, especially the value of unprotected material as a source for new works. A lack of precision in formulating the originality threshold, as well as diversity in national thresholds, could be addressed by paying more explicit attention to the value of leaving some works unprotected. This same reasoning can counteract tendencies to formulaic approaches to the originality threshold, as well as to the application of the related principles that 'ideas' or 'facts' are not protected.

Insubstantial works, such as titles, slogans or headlines, are not protected by copyright in most jurisdictions, but there is no consistency in the principles for denying protection. There would be merit in the adoption of an express *de minimis* rule that applies a multi-factor test, as well as taking into account the value of permission-free uses.

Whether fixation is imposed as a condition for protection is not mandated by international copyright law, being therefore left to national laws. There are important, but complex, differences in national approaches, with common law systems generally requiring fixation and civil law systems protecting unfixed works. In general, given the importance of unprotected works in producing new works, we consider there is value in imposing a fixation requirement. Moreover, where fixation is a prerequisite, equating fixation with authorship, as under US law, has the advantage that works fixed otherwise than under the authority of the author are part of the public domain.

*2 Works Impliedly Excluded from Copyright* By defining protected works, copyright laws necessarily impliedly exclude some works from protection. In 'closed list' jurisdictions, a work is protected only if it falls within a statutory 'pigeonhole', whereas 'open list' jurisdictions do not exhaustively define protected categories of works. Given the potential breadth of copyright-protected works, overall, we consider that a 'closed list' approach is preferable, especially as it leaves the definition of the boundary between the private and public domains to the legislature, but with scope for judicial interpretation. Whether a closed or open list approach is taken, there is potential for improvements in the criteria, whether explicit or implicit, applied by courts in determining whether 'creations' fall within protected categories.

*3 Works Expressly Excluded* Most jurisdictions have not taken full advantage of flexibilities allowed by mandatory and permitted exclusions under international law. There is, in particular, a strong case for exclusion of government information, including legislation and legal judgments, from copyright to the full extent permitted by international law, such as by abolishing Crown and Parliamentary copyright in relevant common law jurisdictions.

*4 Constitutional and Treaty Exclusions* Courts in the United States and the EU have been cautious in applying constitutional limitations on copyright where there are potential conflicts between copyright and competing rights. There is, in our view, considerable scope for further development of the jurisprudence in this area, whether in applying 'rights-based' analysis in interpreting existing exceptions, or in the analysis of the circumstances in which rights, such as the right to freedom of expression, might require permission-free uses beyond established exceptions.

*5 Public Policy Refusals against Enforcement* Public policy exceptions are, in most jurisdictions, of marginal practical relevance to the public domain, given the contemporary reluctance of courts to deny copyright on the basis of the nature of the content.

*6 Public Interest Exceptions to Enforcement* This public domain category is relevant mainly due to the broad interpretation of the public interest exception under UK law under the influence of Article 10 of the ECHR. In our view, the protection of the public domain value of freedom of expression is more likely to be advanced by rights-based jurisprudence and, even more so, the further development of copyright exceptions, than by the exclusive rights of copyright owners being subordinated to a general, relatively indeterminate public interest exception.

*7 Works in which Copyright has Expired* Given the already long copyright terms, there is no credible case for further term extensions (whether the base standard in a jurisdiction is fifty years *pma*, seventy years *pma*, or otherwise). The case against reviving copyright that has expired is even stronger. For most works the existing terms are too long, but because of the constraints imposed by international copyright law, and the difficulties in establishing a single acceptable term, we make the following suggestions for strengthening copyright public domains.

The public domain can be supported by measures that reduce tracing costs, such as voluntary registration systems and public domain calculators. Initiatives that reduce the information burdens on users, such as properly resourced calculators, are important practical measures for ameliorating the difficulties arising from overly complex national rules on duration.

The perpetual term for unpublished works in some jurisdictions, and the very long terms in others, such as the UK and United States, prevent valuable uses of works, some of which have considerable cultural and historical value. The term for unpublished works should be harmonised with that for published works, as has occurred recently in Australia.

From our perspective, there is no case for the terms for moral rights to extend beyond those for economic rights, but given the significant cultural differences on this question, the prospects for greater harmonisation appear remote. There is, however, scope for simplification and the removal of anomalies.

*8 Insubstantial Parts* Determining whether or not there is a 'substantial' infringement is at the heart of infringement analysis, but substantiality analyses are marred by inconsistencies and indeterminacies. In our view, there is a need for greater clarity in the substantiality test, possibly through statutory codification of relevant factors, and potentially by introducing a *de minimis* principle, which would better ensure that insignificant parts of protected works are available for re-use.

*9 Ideas or Facts* The idea/expression and fact/expression dichotomies, while underpinning copyright, are among its most difficult principles. We argue that greater attention should be paid to identifying and applying the principles underpinning the dichotomy. In addition, in some jurisdictions, there is scope for adopting sub-principles that may assist the reasoning process, such as the US merger and *scènes à faire* doctrines. A singular focus on whether or not 'facts' originate from an author potentially fails to address more fundamental issues, including the extent to which material categorised as facts should be in the public domain. The law can be improved by clearer focus on the specific public domain uses of works, including in disaggregating the underlying functions performed by the principles, such as the extent to which material should be free to be used to create new works and the importance of permission-free uses for freedom of expression.

*10 Uses Outside Exclusive Rights* Uses of works falling outside of exclusive rights are an important, but often overlooked, part of copyright public domains. Uncertainties about the scope of each of the exclusive rights are also uncertainties about the scope of the public domain as, on our analysis, public domain uses include uses that fall outside of the scope of exclusive rights. Consistent with our rejection of copyright maximalism, much caution is required in introducing new rights (such as the EU lending right), and in ensuring that exclusive rights are not expansively interpreted. Taking into account the value of public domain uses can assist in resolving uncertainties in the scope of existing exclusive rights, as in the following examples.

A clear example of how taking public domain values into account can assist in appropriately limiting the application of exclusive rights to new technologies is the application of the reproduction right to temporary copies made using the Internet. Focusing on public domain uses might

## 17.6 Reforms to Strengthen Copyright Public Domains

result in allowing reproductions that are incidental to a technical process of using a work, such as temporary copies made using the Internet, in so far as these copies are essential to facilitate access to and use of works, including permissible uses such as browsing, listening and reading. Excluding such uses from the right removes the need for introducing a complex exception (or exceptions), as under EU law.

All jurisdictions have experienced difficulties in distinguishing 'public' from 'non-public' disseminations, whether performances or communications. The advantages of adding a focus on public domain uses can be illustrated by the treatment of linking: given the importance of hyperlinks for facilitating access, most linking should be regarded as permission-free public domain uses. Applying this perspective, infringing uses of hyperlinks (such as where used to circumvent access controls, or knowingly linking to infringing content) should be regarded as a derogation from a right to permission-free use, rather than permissible linking being a derogation from the public communication right.

The distribution right involves difficult balances between intangible rights in a work and property rights in tangible embodiments of the work. A public domain perspective, however, supports the benefits of users, including libraries, booksellers, museums and second-hand book dealers, being able to deal with tangible copies without seeking permission from owners and, consequently, favours a principle of national exhaustion. This perspective also suggests that, provided difficult problems of proliferation of digital copies can be resolved, the benefits of second-hand markets, in terms of promoting access to and use of works, should be available to users of intangible copies as much as to users of tangible copies.

*11 Statutory Exceptions* Exceptions have become the main means by which copyright expressly balances rights of owners and competing public interests, by permitting uses mainly for particular purposes or in particular contexts. As such, exceptions are potentially the most important element of copyright law in defining the scope of exclusive rights and of public domain uses, especially in controversial cases.

Our overall approach is that, given immutable elements of international copyright law – the irreducible length of copyright terms, the breadth of protected subject matter, minimum levels of protection and the prohibition on formalities – there are inevitably works, and uses of works, that are protected by copyright where the public interest favours permission-free use. The structural biases of international copyright law, reflected in national laws, result in issues concerning the types of uses that should be permission free (and within our concept of the public domain) being dealt with mainly by means of exceptions. Our proposals for incorporating public domain considerations in substantive areas of copyright – in relation to both copyright subsistence and infringement – have some potential to alleviate over-reliance on exceptions as a safety valve for public domain uses. But, nevertheless, contests about whether or not there is a public interest in promoting uses are likely to be mostly fought out in the context of particular uses or users entitled to exceptions, whether free use or compensated.

Our conclusions concerning selected categories of free use exceptions follow.

On balance, we consider that an *open-ended exception* (such as the US 'fair use' doctrine or Canadian 'flexible fair dealing') can support public domain uses, especially by avoiding the undue rigidity of specific exceptions. This does not, however, mean that such an exception is a panacea or trouble-free, particularly given problems identified with the US fair use doctrine. There is, in our view, scope for development of more targeted factors than the US fair use factors, which could better direct attention to the most relevant public interest considerations. There is also scope for any flexible exception to be supplemented by measures that clarify the interpretation and operation of the exception, such as the development of 'best practice' guidelines.

All jurisdictions have found it difficult to determine criteria for excepting *temporary copies*. As suggested above, we generally support excluding temporary copies made by means of the Internet from the scope of the reproduction right. In so far as exceptions are relied upon, however, permitted uses could be dealt with by an appropriate open-ended exception, but there is also scope for simplifying and streamlining existing complex exceptions in ways that could both promote public domain uses and protect rights holders.

Exceptions for *quotations*, required by international copyright law, can be one of the most important safeguards of public domain uses, as they support freedom of expression of users as well as creative uses of works, potentially extending to some transformative uses. But even under the most liberal interpretations applied in some civil law jurisdictions, a quotation exception is not a general purpose 'transformative use' exception. There is, however, scope for greater use of the flexibility allowed under international copyright law, which not only requires a quotation exception, but clearly permits it to extend to some creative and transformative uses.

Exceptions for *parody* promote the essential public domain value of freedom of expression by preventing copyright from being used to suppress speech. Further, exceptions for *satire*, which have been increasingly

## 17.6 Reforms to Strengthen Copyright Public Domains

recognised, encourage speech that, by criticising political and social practices, promotes democratic processes. While some countries allow such exceptions as part of more general exceptions, in others there are specific statutory exceptions. Irrespective of which approach best fits a country's legal culture – and difficulties have arisen in applying both broad exceptions and more targeted exceptions – exceptions for satire and parody are essential for a public domain that pays due regard to freedom of expression and civic engagement, and should be introduced where they are not already part of national copyright laws.

Although the public interest in *education and research* is not fully recognised under Berne, most jurisdictions have not introduced exceptions that take advantage of existing flexibilities available under international copyright law (not only for unremunerated exceptions, but also for remunerated exceptions). For example, there is no requirement of quantitative limitations on the copying of extracts for educational purposes (which are applied under some national laws), especially if such uses are subject to a fairness test, such as under the UK and Canadian fair dealing exceptions. There is, furthermore, no reason for exceptions regarding digital uses and distance education, which are increasingly standard educational practices, to be less extensive than traditional permitted uses, provided there are safeguards to prevent widespread unauthorised reproductions and disseminations. Given the scale and complexity of educational uses, there are considerable advantages in guidelines and best practice statements for clarifying the scope of permissible uses.

Exceptions for *libraries, archives and similar institutions* perform essential public domain functions of preserving works and making them available, with attendant benefits for vibrant and creative cultures. Concerns that expansive exceptions may interfere with markets for copyright works, especially digital content, have resulted in detailed and complex national exceptions. Broad exceptions for the purpose of preserving works, including migrating content from obsolete formats, are essential to ensure accessibility of works. Desirable elements of such exceptions are requirements to comply with best professional preservation practice (rather than arbitrary limits on the number of copies made). Exceptions for making and disseminating digital copies for lending purposes are more controversial, but, in our view, it is possible to craft reasonable exceptions, provided lending-related activities are not conducted for a profit, and there are safeguards, such as the deletion of digital copies on expiry of the loan period. Overriding 'fairness' standards can also potentially limit abuse of such exceptions.

*12 Neutral Compulsory Licensing* Compulsory licensing plays a major role in the copyright systems of some countries, and because it involves remuneration to copyright owners it is often the most practical and efficient way of allowing use of copyright works on a mass scale. International law places fewer impediments on countries enacting compulsory licensing schemes (including extended collective licensing) than is often assumed. The Berne Convention permits specific remunerated use exceptions to copyright, as does Rome. However, the most important source of justification for compulsory licences is Berne Article 9(2) and the three-step test. Each step may readily be satisfied for a wide range of licensing purposes, but difficult borderline cases often arise. EU law has given particular support to the use of remunerated exceptions, requiring them for some purposes, and making it clear that, in general, Member States have a choice between free use exceptions and remunerated exceptions. Countries are finding creative ways to extend the ambit of compulsory licensing without coming into collision with international copyright law. Interested countries, and parties assisting them, could usefully collaborate on drafting legislative models of compulsory licensing provisions, which, if challenged, stand good prospects of satisfying international law requirements.

Compulsory licensing involves the interests of more parties than licensees, collecting societies (CSs) and their member copyright owners. Its cost-effective and fair operation affects the general public and non-member rights holders as well, so good governance of compulsory licences and of CSs is an important, but often neglected, support for the protection of the public domain.

Our conclusions concerning some of the most common uses of compulsory licensing follow.

*Orphan works* are potentially the most important example of where compulsory licences can play a role in promoting public domain uses. Leaving aside the possibility of some uses of orphan works falling within broad exceptions, such as fair use, providing for permission-free uses subject to the possibility of payment seems a good general model for addressing this problem. In our view, a general limited liability (compensation) scheme, such as the 2015 US Copyright Office proposals, deserves serious consideration. The main elements of this approach involve a system of liability to pay reasonable compensation, if and when a copyright owner reappears, provided a diligent search has been undertaken, which obviates the need for a licensing body. However, if it is achievable, a low-cost official licensing scheme could be a useful supplement to a limited liability scheme to provide certainties to those applicants that need it. Official licensing schemes have not proven to be

## 17.6 Reforms to Strengthen Copyright Public Domains

successful as a stand-alone solution. Overall, however, no single approach is likely to provide a sufficient response to this admittedly complex problem.

Many organisations, including non-profit cultural heritage institutions (CHIs) and commercial entities, want compulsory licences to be able to carry out *mass digitisation projects* in situations where it is impracticable to obtain individual consents from rights holders, and where there is no CS that represents all relevant rights holders. Under international copyright law, however, such proposals must be justified under Berne Article 9(2) and the three-step test. A proposed EU directive may provide a model for the digitisation of works held by CHIs, but acceptable solutions of broader scope, such as enabling digitisation of 'unavailable books' have yet to be found.

Efficient licensing for *educational purposes* should be a high priority for any country. Compulsory licences which can be invoked by any educational institutions, with terms and procedures that can be resolved by a neutral Tribunal, are the minimum legal requirements for protecting educational uses. In our view, compulsory licences should not be able to derogate from non-remunerated educational use exceptions. Further, it is undesirable for licences to be dependent on applications, or to be subject to opt-outs by rights holders.

Developing countries have historically rooted needs for better access to educational materials and, in particular, to *translations*. The Paris Appendix, the one Berne compulsory licensing provision ostensibly aimed at assisting developing countries, is an over-restrictive and over-technical failure, such that reliance on Berne Article 9(2) is more useful.

Berne does not provide for compulsory *licences to assist CHIs* such as galleries, libraries, archives and museums. Such licences are unusual, but may be appropriate where remuneration is justified. For example, some Nordic countries have established compulsory licences where reproductions of works of art are published. Due to the introduction of rental rights, provisions are now essential in all countries enabling either exceptions or remunerated licensing of non-commercial rental/lending of works by CHIs.

*13 Neutral Voluntary Licensing* Voluntary licensing of works by copyright owners, using pre-designed licences written by an independent third party on public interest grounds ('neutral voluntary licensing'), has resulted in major expansions of public rights in copyright, particularly in the last two decades. It would be valuable for national legislation to remove, where necessary, uncertainties in relation to enforcement of neutral voluntary licensing. For example, laws could state that where there is a purported licence, the reproduction of the licensed content (or the exercise of any other exclusive right in the content) will constitute consideration for the licence, and that such licences must be in writing to be effective.

*14 Public Domain Dedications* It is desirable that copyright owners have the capacity to provide works that they own for public use, in a way which provides both legal certainty to future users and protection to copyright owners against unfounded claims that they have relinquished their rights. Legislation should provide that authors or successors in title may relinquish copyright, and that such dedications must be in writing to be effective.

*15 De Facto Public Domain of Benign Uses* In our view, one further aspect of the copyright public domain, arising primarily but not solely from Internet-published content, are the de facto 'public rights' arising from benign uses of copyright content and the acquiescence of copyright owners in its use because of benefits to them. Our conclusion is only that it should not be ignored, because it has been one of the most significant factors expanding the effective public domain, particularly over the last two decades.

## 17.7 Contemporary Values and the Future of Public Rights

In this book we have deliberately limited our discussion of desirable reforms by accepting current international copyright law, and focusing on realistic proposals for reform to national copyright laws and practices. In our discussions of 'public domain values' that we consider support both existing public domains and proposals for reform, we have by and large restricted ourselves to traditional values that support the public domain, including uses of works in creative endeavours, to further freedom of expression and access to knowledge, and to promote broader cultural participation. However, public domain values, and the objectives of those who support a broader understanding of copyright public domains, necessarily change over time as circumstances change. In this concluding section of the book, we therefore sketch what could be called contemporary public domain values, and what they might imply for the public rights that could provide the basis for future reform of national laws, institutions and practices – even extending to international copyright law.

Over the past two decades, 'contemporary circumstances' have been conditioned by widespread Internet access, technology and associated

## 17.7 Contemporary Values and the Future of Public Rights

social practices. These technologies and practices have broken down many (but not all) of the previous distinctions between creators and 'mere users'. For example, the ubiquity of the many forms of 'user generated content' (UGC) has been a major social development, and one accelerated by the innovations of voluntary licensing. Moreover, users have become accustomed to ubiquitous and near instantaneous access to content, through a variety of largely interchangeable devices. In our view, these highly practical considerations cannot be ignored.

As a starting point, we tentatively propose eight main objectives or values of public rights and public domains, derived from and adapted to contemporary circumstances, namely: (i) accessibility (including access to knowledge), (ii) transferability/sharing, (iii) preservation and authenticity, (iv) free access, (v) re-usability, (vi) privacy, (vii) locatability / retrievability, and (viii) 'play of culture' (or space for creativity/ experiment).[1] The first three of these overlap: while a vibrant public domain depends upon the primary value of user accessibility, once there is access, users should be able to transfer or share content appropriately. Moreover, for content to be accessed and used over time, it must achieve some permanence and consistency. The second three public domain values – 'free' access, locatability/retrievability and privacy – are also linked by the extent to which they are directly related to the everyday lived experience of Internet users. The final two public domain values, 'reusability' and what we call 'play of culture' are linked through the concept of users as creators of works. We believe that each objective is part of what users of works would ideally like to achieve, particularly in the Internet context – at least some of the time. They are contemporary values that animate what many would like public rights to achieve, and achieve more of in future. They are additional to the more traditional public domain values that we have discussed throughout this book. We cannot set out the full explanations and arguments for each here, but have discussed them in more detail in the Online Supplement.

Reconciling these contemporary values with the legitimate interests of creators and owners will and should require many compromises. They should not be read as suggesting some 'public domain maximalism': they only refer to values, not reform proposals, much less demands. Nor is any universal applicability suggested: often, that would not make sense, particularly for transferability, preservation or free access. Copyright law reform must always deal with achievable compromise and balancing of interests, but those interests and the values supporting them change over time.

[1] Cohen, *Configuring the Networked Self*, 50–104; see also Online Supplement.

## 17.8 Future Reforms

As we have argued throughout this book, public domain values need to be more explicitly recognised in copyright law and policy-making, because by more expressly taking them into account, a more accurate and complex picture of the rights and interests at stake in the copyright system is possible. Reconciling these values with the legitimate rights and interests of creators and owners is at the heart of the recommendations and reform proposals made in this book, and summarised above.

To achieve a more valuable copyright public domain in the future, we need to articulate and debate the values and objectives that we want it to achieve. The public domain should not continue to be something desirable but vague and ill-defined. Its rationale, its categories and the values on which it is based should be as well-defined and defended as the exclusive rights that make up the other half of copyright, and should develop with contemporary circumstances and values. In this book, we hope that we have contributed toward a process for achieving these goals by providing material for future investigation of copyright, public domains and public rights.

# Bibliography

Adeney, E., 'Appropriation in the name of art? Is a quotation exception the answer?' (2013) 23 *Australian Intellectual Property Journal* 142.
  'Authorship and fixation in copyright law: a comparative comment' (2011) 35 *Melbourne University Law Review* 677.
  *The Moral Rights of Authors and Performers: An International and Comparative Analysis* (Oxford University Press, 2006).
Adeney, E. and Antons, C., 'The *Germania 3* decision translated: the quotation exception before the German Constitutional Court' (2013) 35(11) *European Intellectual Property Review* 646.
Afori, O., 'An open standard "fair use" doctrine: a welcome Israeli initiative' (2008) 30(3) *European Intellectual Property Review* 85.
  'Proportionality – a new mega standard in European copyright law' (2015) *International Review of Intellectual Property and Competition Law (IIC)* 889.
Agitha, T., 'International norms for compulsory licensing and the Indian copyright law' (2012) 15(1) *Journal of World Intellectual Property* 26.
Alexander, I., *Copyright Law and the Public Interest in the Nineteenth Century* (Hart Publishing, 2010).
Ang, S., 'The idea–expression dichotomy and merger doctrine in the copyright law of the US and the UK' (1994) 2(2) *International Journal of Law and Information Technology* 111.
Aplin, T., 'Subject matter', in E. Derclaye (ed.), *Research Handbook on the Future of EU Copyright* (Edward Elgar, 2009).
Arnold, R., Bently, L. A. F., Derclaye, E. and Dinwoodie, G. B., 'The legal consequences of Brexit through the lens of IP law' (2017) 101(2) *Judicature* (forthcoming).
Atkinson, S., 'Sir Cliff Richard's victory: an extra 20 years for copyright protection in sound recordings and performers' rights where a sound recording of the performance is released' (2014) 36(2) *European Intellectual Property Review* 75.
Attorney-General's Department (Aus.), *Declaration of Collecting Societies – Guidelines (Copyright Act 1968)*, April 2001.
  *Extending the Legal Deposit Scheme to Digital Material: Regulation Impact Statement* (2014).
Austin, G., 'EU and US perspectives on fair dealing for the purpose of parody or satire' (2016) 39(2) *UNSW Law Journal* 684.

Australian Government, 'Response to the Productivity Commission inquiry into intellectual property arrangements', Commonwealth of Australia, August 2017.

Australian Information Commissioner, 'Open access principles', Office of the Australian Information Commissioner (OIAC), May 2011.

Australian Law Reform Commission, *Copyright and the Digital Economy*, ALRC Report 122, November 2013.

Australian Research Council, *Open Access Policy*, v. 2015.1, Australian Research Council (ARC), 2015.

Baker, E., 'First Amendment limits on copyright' (2002) 55 *Vanderbilt Law Review* 891.

Band, J. and Garafi, J., *The Fair Use/Fair Dealing Handbook* (policybandwidth, March 2013).

Bannerman, S., *International Copyright and Access to Knowledge* (Cambridge University Press, 2016).

Battelle, J., *The Search – How Google and its Rivals Rewrote the Rules of Business and Transformed our Culture* (Nicholas Brealey Publishing, 2005).

Beebe, B., 'An empirical study of US copyright fair use opinions, 1978–2005' (2008) 156 *University of Pennsylvania Law Review* 549.

Beldiman, D., 'Utilitarian information works – is originality the proper lens?' (2010) 14(1) *Marquette Intellectual Property Law Review* 1.

Benabou, V.-L. and Dusollier, S., 'Draw me a public domain', in P. Torremans (ed.), *Copyright Law: A Handbook of Contemporary Research* (Edward Elgar, 2007).

Benkler, Y., 'Coase's penguin or, Linux and the nature of the firm' (2002) 112 *Yale Law Journal* 369.

'Free as the air to common use: First Amendment constraints on enclosure of the public domain' (1999) 74 *New York University Law Review* 354.

'Through the looking glass: Alice and the constitutional foundations of the public domain' (2003) 66 *Law and Contemporary Problems* 173.

Bently, L., 'Bently slams "very disappointing" ruling in Meltwater', 27 July 2011, The IPKat http://ipkitten.blogspot.com/2011/07/bently-slams-very-disappointing-ruling.html.

"Harmonisation by stealth: copyright and the ECJ', unpublished paper presented at the Fordham IP Conference, 8 April 2012 http://fordhamipconference.com/wp-content/uploads/2010/08/Bently_Harmonization.pdf.

Berlin, I., *The Hedgehog and the Fox: An Essay on Tolstoy's View of History* (Weidenfeld & Nicolson, 1953).

'Two concepts of liberty', in *Four Essays on Liberty* (Oxford University Press, 1969).

Besek, J. M., Ginsburg, J. C., Loengard, P. and Lev-Aretz, Y., 'Copyright exceptions in the United States for educational uses of copyrighted works', The Kernochan Center for Law, Media and the Arts, Columbia University School of Law, 29 April 2013 www.screenrights.org/sites/default/files/uploads/Attachment_A_Kernochan_Ctr_Report.pdf.

Birnhack, M., 'The copyright law and free speech: making-up and breaking-up' (2003) 43 *IDEA* 233.

'Copyrighting speech: a trans-Atlantic view', in P. Torremans (ed.), *Copyright and Human Rights – Freedom of Expression – Intellectual Property – Privacy* (Kluwer Law International, 2004).

'More or better? Shaping the public domain', in L. Guibault and P. B. Hugenholtz (eds.), *The Future of the Public Domain: Identifying the Commons in Information Law* (Kluwer Law International, 2006).

'The Dead Sea Scrolls case: who is an author?' (2001) 23 *European Intellectual Property Review* 128.

Birrell, A., *Seven Lectures on the Law and History of Copyright in Books* (Cassell & Co., 1899).

Bitton, M., 'Trends in protection for informational works under copyright law during the 19th and 20th centuries' (2006) 13 *Michigan Telecommunications and Technology Law Review* 115.

Black Duck Knowledge Base, 'Top open source licenses', undated www.blackducksoftware.com/top-open-source-licenses.

Bogsch, A., 'WIPO views of Article 18' (1995) 43 *Journal of the Copyright Society of the USA* 181.

Bond C. and Greenleaf, G., 'Copyright duration in Australia: 1869 to 2014' (2015) 25(3) *Australian Intellectual Property Journal* 155.

Borghi, M., 'Report backs up the overly burdensome nature of the "Diligent Search" requirement in UK, Italy and Netherlands', Diligent Search website, 9 February 2016.

Bowrey, K., 'On clarifying the role of originality and fair use in nineteenth century UK jurisprudence: appreciating "the humble grey which emerges as the result of long controversy"', in L. Bently, C. Ng and G. d'Agostino (eds.), *The Common Law of Intellectual Property: Essays in Honour of Professor David Vaver* (Hart Publishing, 2010).

Boyle, J., 'Foreword: the opposite of property?' (2003) 66 *Law and Contemporary Problems* 1.

'The second enclosure movement and the construction of the public domain' (2003) 66 *Law and Contemporary Problems* 33.

*Shamans, Software, and Spleens: Law and the Construction of the Information Society* (Harvard University Press, 1996).

Brennan, D., 'Copyright and parody in Australia: some thoughts on *Suntrust Bank v. Houghton Mifflin Company*' (2002) 13 *Australian Intellectual Property Journal* 161.

'The first compulsory licensing of patents and copyright' (2017) 17 *Legal History* 1.

*Retransmission and US Compliance with TRIPs* (Springer, 2003).

'The three-step test frenzy – why the TRIPS panel decision might be considered *per incuriam*' [2002] 2 *Intellectual Property Quarterly* 212.

Brennan, D. and Christie, A., 'Spoken words and copyright subsistence in Anglo-American law' (2000) 4 *Intellectual Property Quarterly* 4.

Brennan, D. and Fraser, M., 'The use of subject matter with missing owners: Australian copyright policy options', Screenrights commissioned paper, Communications Law Centre, UTS, 2011.

Brown, P., 'Enforcement and compliance for the GPL and similar licenses', LWN.net, 11 May 2016 https://lwn.net/Articles/686768/.

Bureau of Communications and Arts Research (Aus.), Discussion paper, 'Review into the efficacy of the Code of Conduct for Australian Copyright Collecting Societies', August 2017.

Burrell, R., 'Reining in copyright law: is fair use the answer?' (2001) 4 *Intellectual Property Quarterly* 361.

Burrell, R. and Coleman, A., *Copyright Exceptions: The Digital Impact* (Cambridge University Press, 2005).

Burrell, R. and Weatherall, K., 'Exporting controversy? Reactions to the copyright provisions of the US–Australia Free Trade Agreement: lessons for US trade policy' (2008) 2 *University of Illinois Journal of Law, Technology and Policy* 259.

Calabresi, G. and Melamed, A., 'Property rules, liability rules, and inalienability: one view of the cathedral' (1972) 85 *Harvard Law Review* 1089.

Canat, J., Guibault, L. and Logeais, E., 'Study on copyright limitations and exceptions for museums', WIPO SCCR, Thirtieth Session (Geneva, 2015) www.wipo.int/edocs/mdocs/copyright/en/sccr_30/sccr_30_2.pdf.

Carpenter, M. and Hetcher, S., 'Function over form: bringing the fixation requirement into the modern era' (2014) 82 *Fordham Law Review* 2221.

Carroll, C., 'Fixing fair use' (2007) 85 *North Carolina Law Review* 1087.

Carter, J., Peden, E. and Stammer, K., 'Contractual restrictions and rights under copyright legislation' (2007) 23 *Journal of Contract Law* 32.

Cerda Silva, A., 'Beyond the unrealistic solution for development provided by the Appendix of the Berne Convention on copyright' (2013) 60 *Journal of the Copyright Society of the USA* 581.

Chander, A. and Sunder, M., 'The romance of the public domain' (2004) 92 *California Law Review* 1331.

Chander, A., Sunder, M. and Le, U., '*Golan v. Holder*' (2012) 106 *American Journal of International Law* 637.

Choisy, S., *La Domaine public et droit d'auteur* (Litec, 2002).

Christie, A., 'A proposal for simplifying United Kingdom copyright law' [2001] *European Intellectual Property Review* 26.

Clark, C., 'The answer to the machine is in the machine', in P. B. Hugenholtz (ed.), *The Future of Copyright in a Digital Environment* (Kluwer Law International, 1996).

Clay, B., 'Robots exclusion protocol guide' (2015), Bruce Clay, Inc. internet marketing optimization company www.bruceclay.com/seo/robots-exclusion-guide.pdf.

Cohen, A., 'Copyright law and the myth of objectivity: the idea–expression dichotomy and the inevitability of artistic judgments' (1990) 66 *Indiana Law Review* 175.

Cohen, J., *Configuring the Networked Self: Law, Code, and the Play of Everyday Practice* (Yale University Press, 2012).

'Copyright, commodification, and culture', in L. Guibault and P. B. Hugenholtz (eds.), *The Future of the Public Domain: Identifying the Commons in Information Law* (Kluwer Law International, 2006).

'A right to read anonymously: a closer look at "copyright management" in cyberspace' (1996) 28 *Connecticut Law Review* 981.

Committee on Intellectual Property Rights and the Emerging Information Infrastructure and Computer Science and Telecommunications Board, National Research Council, *The Digital Dilemma: Intellectual Property in the Information Age* (National Academy Press, 2000).

Committee on the Law of Copyright, *Report, with minutes of evidence, appendix and table of contents* (Printed for H.M. Stationery Office by Eyre and Spottiswoode, 1909).

Coombe, R., 'Fear, hope, and longing for the future of authorship and a revitalized public domain in global regimes of intellectual property' (2002–3) 52 *DePaul Law Review* 1171.

Copyright Board of Canada, 'Decisions – unlocatable copyright owners, de Beer and Bouchard, Canada's "Orphan Works" Regime' www.cb-cda.gc.ca/unlo catable-introuvables/licences-e.html.

Copyright Law Review Committee (CLRC) (Aus.), *Copyright and Contract* (Copyright Law Review Committee, Canberra, 2002).

*Computer Software Protection*, Office of Legal Information and Publishing, Attorney-General's Department, Canberra, April 1995.

*Crown Copyright*, Copyright Law Review Committee, Barton, ACT (2005).

Copyright Review Committee (Ireland), Department of Jobs, Enterprise and Innovation, *Modernising Copyright* (2013).

Corbett, C., 'Creative Commons licences, the copyright regime and the online community: is there a fatal disconnect?' (2011) 74(4) *Modern Law Review* 503.

Council of Ministers of Education, Canada (CMEC), *Fair Dealing Guidelines* (2012) www.cmec.ca/docs/copyright/Fair_Dealing_Guidelines_EN.pdf.

Crews, K., 'Study on copyright limitations and exceptions for libraries and archives', WIPO SCCR, Seventeenth Session, Geneva, 2008.

'Study on copyright limitations and exceptions for libraries and archives', WIPO SCCR, Twenty-Ninth Session, Geneva, 2014.

Cuevos, M., 'Dutch copyright succumbs to aging as exhaustion extends to e-books' (2015) 10(1) *Journal of Intellectual Property Law & Practice* 8.

D'Agostino, G., 'Healing fair dealing? A comparative analysis of Canada's fair dealing to UK fair dealing and US fair use' (2008) 53 *McGill Law Journal* 309.

Daum, F., 'Copyright, European competition law, and free movement of goods and services', in M. M. Walter and S. von Lewinski (eds.), *European Copyright Law: A Commentary* (Oxford University Press, 2010).

de Beer, J. and Bouchard, M., 'Canada's "orphan works" regime: unlocatable copyright owners and the Copyright Board' [2010] 10(2) *Oxford University Commonwealth Law Journal* 38.

de Zwart, M., 'Technological enclosure of copyright: the end of fair dealing?' (2007) 18 *Australian Intellectual Property Journal* 7.

Deazley, R., 'Copyright and digital copyright heritage: duration of copyright', *Copyright 101, Copyright Codex* https://copyrightcortex.org/copyright-101/chapter-6, May 2017.

'Copyright and digital cultural heritage: orphan works', *Copyright 101, Copyright Codex*, May 2017 https://copyrightcortex.org/copyright-101/chapter-9.

'Copyright and parody: taking backwards the Gowers Review?' [2010] 73(5) *Modern Law Review* 785.

*Rethinking Copyright: History, Theory, Language* (Edward Elgar, 2006).

Denicola, R., 'Copyright and free speech: constitutional limitations on the protection of expression' (1979) 67 *California Law Review* 283.

Department of Communications and the Arts (Aus.), 'Guidelines on Licensing Public Sector Information for Australian Government Entities' (September 2016).

Department of Finance (Australia), *Declaration of Open Government*, 16 July 2010.

Derclaye, E., 'Assessing the impact and reception of the Court of Justice of the European Union case law on UK copyright law: what does the future hold?' [2014] 240 *Revue internationale du droit d'auteur* 5.

'Infopaq International A/S v. Danske Dagblades Forening (C-5/08): wonderful or worrisome? The impact of the ECJ ruling in *Infopaq* on UK copyright law' (2010) 32(5) *European Intellectual Property Review* 247.

Directorate General for the Internal Market and Services (European Union), Working Paper: 'First evaluation of Directive 96/9/EC on the legal protection of databases', European Commission, 12 December 2005.

Donner, W., 'Mill's utilitarianism', in J. Skorupski (ed.), *The Cambridge Companion to Mill* (Cambridge University Press, 1998).

Drahos, P., 'Freedom and diversity – a defence of the intellectual commons', in P. Jayanthi Reddy (ed.), *Creative Commons: International Perspectives* (ICFAI University Press, 2008–9).

*A Philosophy of Intellectual Property* (Aldershot, 1996).

Drassinower, A., 'Exceptions properly so-called', in Y. Gendreau and A. Drassinower (eds.), *Language and Copyright* (Carswell/Bruylent, 2009).

'A rights-based view of the idea/expression dichotomy in copyright law' (2003) 16 *Canadian Journal of Law and Jurisprudence* 1.

'Taking user rights seriously', in M. Geist (ed.), *In the Public Interest: The Future of Canadian Copyright Law* (Irwin Law, 2005).

Dreier, T., 'Balancing proprietary and public domain interests: inside or outside of proprietary rights?', in R. Dreyfus, D. Zimmerman and H. First (eds.), *Expanding the Boundaries of Intellectual Property: Innovation Policy for the Knowledge Society* (Oxford University Press, 2001).

'Thoughts on revising the limitations on copyright under Directive 2001/29' (2015) 11(2) *Journal of Intellectual Property Law & Practice* 138.

Dusollier, S., 'Scoping study on copyright and related rights and the public domain', WIPO, 30 April 2011 www.wipo.int/edocs/mdocs/mdocs/en/cdip_7/cdip_7_inf_2.pdf.

Dworkin, G. and Sterling, J., '*Phil Collins* and the term directive' (1994) 16(5) *European Intellectual Property Review* 187.

Elkin-Koren, N., 'Can formalities save the public domain? Reconsidering formalities for the 2010s' (2013) 28 *Berkeley Technology Law Journal* 1537.

'Cyberlaw and social change: a democratic approach to copyright in cyberspace' (1996) 14 *Cardozo Arts & Entertainment Law Journal* 215.

'Exploring creative commons: a skeptical view of a worthy pursuit', in L. Guibault and P. B. Hugenholtz (eds.), *The Future of the Public Domain* (Kluwer Law International, 2006).

Epstein, R., 'The dubious constitutionality of the Copyright Term Extension Act' (2002) 36 *Loyola of Los Angeles Law Review* 123.

European Commission, 'Proposal for a Directive of the European Parliament and of the Council on copyright in the digital single market', COM (2016) 593 final (14 September 2016).

European Commission, Staff Working Paper, 'Impact assessment on the cross-border online access to orphan works', Accompanying the Proposal for a Directive of the European Parliament and of the Council on certain permitted uses of orphan works, COM (2011) 289 final (24 May 2011).

Farley, C., 'Judging art' (2005) 79 *Tulane Law Review* 805.

Favale, M., Homberg, F., Kretschmer, M., Mendis, D. and Secchi, D., 'Copyright and the regulation of orphan works: a comparative review of seven jurisdictions and a rights clearance simulation', CREATe working paper 2013/7 (July 2013) https://zenodo.org/record/8377/files/CREATe-Working-Paper-2013-07.pdf.

Favale, M., Schroff, S. and Bertoni, A., *Requirements for Diligent Search in the United Kingdom, the Netherlands, and Italy*, EnDow, February 2016.

Feather, J., 'The book trade in politics: the making of the Copyright Act of 1710' (1980) 8 *Publishing History* 39.

'Publishers and politicians: the remaking of the law of copyright in Britain 1775–1842. Part II: the rights of authors' (1989) 25 *Publishing History* 45

Fernández-Diez, I., 'Comparative analysis on national approaches to the liability of internet intermediaries for infringement of copyright and related rights', WIPO, 2010 www.wipo.int/export/sites/www/copyright/en/doc/liability_of_internet_intermediaries_garrote.pdf.

Ficsor, M., 'Collective rights management from the viewpoint of international treaties, with special attention to the EU "acquis"', in D. Gervais (ed.), *Collective Management of Copyright and Related Rights* (3rd edn, Wolters Kluwer, 2013).

'How much of what? The three-step test and its application in two recent WTO dispute settlement cases' (2002) 192 *Revue internationale du droit d'auteur* 111.

*The Law of Copyright and the Internet: The 1996 WIPO Treaties, their Interpretation and Implementation* (Oxford University Press, 2002).

Ficsor, M. and WIPO, 'Guide to the copyright and related rights treaties administered by WIPO and glossary of copyright and related rights terms', WIPO, 2003 www.wipo.int/edocs/pubdocs/en/copyright/891/wipo_pub_891.pdf.

Fisher, W. and McGeveran, W., 'The digital learning challenge: obstacles to educational uses of copyrighted material in the digital age: a foundational white paper', Berkman Center for Internet & Society, 10 August 2006.

Fitzgerald, B. and Bassett, G., 'Legal issues relating to free and open source software' (2001) 12 *Journal of Law and Information Science* 159.
Fornaro, M., 'A parallel problem: grey market goods and the internet' (2003) 8 *Journal of Technology Law & Policy* 69.
Gangjee, D., 'Copyright formalities: A return to registration?', in R. Giblin and K. Weatherall (eds.), *What If We Could Reimagine Copyright?* (Australian National University Press, 2017).
Garnett, K. and Davies, G., *Copinger and Skone James on Copyright*, 2 vols. (14th edn, Sweet & Maxwell, 1998).
Garnett, K., Davies, G. and Harbottle, G., *Copinger and Skone James on Copyright*, 2 vols. (15th edn, Sweet & Maxwell, 2005).
*Copinger and Skone James on Copyright*, 2 vols. (16th edn, Sweet & Maxwell, 2010).
Gasser, U. and Girsberger, M., 'Transposing the Copyright Directive: legal protection of technological measures in EU Member States: a genie stuck in the bottle?', Berkman Publication Series No. 2004-10 (2004).
Gay, J., 'Principles of community-oriented GPL enforcement', Free Software Foundation (30 September 2015).
Geiger, C., '"Constitutionalising" intellectual property law? The influence of fundamental rights on intellectual property in the European Union' [2006] *International Review of Intellectual Property and Competition Law (IIC)* 371.
'Copyright's fundamental rights dimension at EU level', in E. Derclaye (ed.), *Research Handbook on the Future of EU Copyright* (Edward Elgar, 2009).
'Intellectual property shall be protected? – Article 17(2) of the Charter of Fundamental Rights of the European Union: a mysterious provision with an unclear scope' (2009) 31(3) *European Intellectual Property Review* 113.
'Promoting creativity through copyright limitations: reflections on the concept of exclusivity in copyright law' (2010) 12(3) *Vanderbilt Journal of Entertainment and Technology Law* 515.
Geiger, C. and Izyumenko, E., 'Copyright on the human rights trial: redefining the boundaries of exclusivity through freedom of expression' (2014) 45 *International Review of Intellectual Property and Competition Law (IIC)* 316.
Geiger, C. and Schönherr, F., 'The Information Society Directive (Articles 5 and 6(4))', in I. Stamatoudi and P. Torremans (eds.), *EU Copyright Law: A Commentary* (Edward Elgar, 2016).
Geiger, C., Griffiths, J., Senftleben, M., Bently, L. and Xalabarder, R., 'Limitations and exceptions as key elements of the legal framework for copyright in the European Union – opinion of the European Copyright Society on the judgment of the CJEU in Case C-201/13 *Deckmyn*' (2015) 46 *International Review of Intellectual Property and Competition Law (IIC)* 93.
Geist, M., 'The case for flexibility in implementing the WIPO internet treaties: an examination of the anti-circumvention requirements', in M. Geist (ed.), *From 'Radical Extremism' to 'Balanced Copyright': Canadian Copyright and the Digital Agenda* (Irwin Law Inc., 2010).
'Fair access: strikes the right balance on education and copyright' (*Academic Matters*, January 2016) www.academicmatters.ca/2016/01/2279/.

'Fairness found: how Canada quietly shifted from fair dealing to fair use', in M. Geist (ed.), *The Copyright Pentalogy: How the Supreme Court of Canada Shook the Foundations of Canadian Copyright Law* (University of Ottawa Press, 2013).

'Too little, too late?: Access Copyright finally acknowledges the reduced value of its licences', Michael Geist blog, 10 December 2014 www.michaelgeist.ca /2014/12/little-late-access-copyright-finally-acknowledges-reduced-value-li cence/.

Geller, P., 'A German approach to fair use: test cases for TRIPs criteria for copyright limitations?' (2010) 57 *Journal of the Copyright Society of the USA* 553.

'From patchwork to network: strategies for international intellectual property in flux' (1998) 31 *Vanderbilt Journal of Transnational Law* 553

Gendreau, Y., 'The criterion of fixation in copyright law' (1994) 159 *Revue internationale du droit d'auteur* 110.

Gendreau, Y., Nordemann, A. and Oesch, R. (eds.), *Copyright and Photographs: An International Survey* (Kluwer Law International, 1999).

Gervais, D., 'Canadian copyright law post-*CCH*' (2004) 18 *Intellectual Property Journal* 131.

'China – measures affecting the protection and enforcement of intellectual property rights' (2009) 103(3) *American Journal of International Law* 549.

'Collective management of copyright', in D. Gervais (ed.), *Collective Management of Copyright and Related Rights* (3rd edn, Wolters Kluwer, 2016).

'The derivative right, or why copyright law protects foxes better than hedgehogs' (2013) 15(4) *Vanderbilt Journal of Entertainment and Technology Law* 785.

'*Feist* goes global: a comparative analysis of the notion of originality in copyright law' (2002) 49 *Journal of the Copyright Society of the USA* 949.

'*Golan v. Holder*: a look at the constraints imposed by the Berne Convention' (2011) 64 *Vanderbilt Law Review En Banc* 147.

*(Re)structuring Copyright: A Comprehensive Path to International Copyright Reform* (Edward Elgar, 2017).

'Towards a new core international norm: the reverse three-step test' (2005) 9(1) *Marquette Intellectual Property Law Review* 1.

*The TRIPs Agreement: Drafting History and Analysis* (2nd edn, Sweet & Maxwell, 2003).

(ed.), *Collective Management of Copyright and Related Rights* (3rd edn, Wolters Kluwer, 2016).

Gervais, D. and Renaud, D., 'The future of United States copyright formalities: why we should prioritize recordation, and how to do it' (2013) 28 *Berkeley Technology Law Journal* 1459.

Giblin, R. and Weatherall, K. (eds.), *What If We Could Reimagine Copyright?* (Australian National University Press, 2017).

Gibson, J., 'Once and future copyright' (2005) 81 *Notre Dame Law Review* 167.

Ginsburg, J. C., '"Une chose publique"? The author's domain and the public domain in early British, French and US copyright law', in P. Torremans (ed.), *Copyright Law: A Handbook of Contemporary Research* (Edward Elgar, 2007).

'Copyright and control over new technologies of dissemination' (2001) 101 *Columbia Law Review* 1613.

'Creation and commercial value: copyright protection of works of information' (1990) 90 *Columbia Law Review* 1865.

'Exceptional authorship: the role of copyright authorship in promoting creativity', in S. Frankel and D. Gervais (eds.), *Evolution and Equilibrium: Copyright this Century* (Cambridge University Press, 2013).

'From having copies to experiencing works: the development of an access right in US copyright law' (2003) 50 *Journal of the Copyright Society of the USA* 113.

'Google Books and fair use: from implausible to inevitable?' *SociallyAware*, 17 November 2015 www.sociallyawareblog.com/2015/11/17/google-books-and-fair-use-from-implausible-to-inevitable/.

'International copyright: from a "bundle" of national copyright laws to a supranational code' (2000) 47 *Journal of the Copyright Society of the USA* 265.

'No "sweat"? Copyright and other protection of works of information after *Feist v. Rural Telephone*' (1992) 92 *Columbia Law Review* 338.

'A tale of two copyrights: literary property in revolutionary France and America' (1990) 64(5) *Tulane Law Review* 991; also in B. Sherman and A. Strowel (eds.), *Of Authors and Origins: Essays in Copyright Law* (Clarendon Press, 1994).

'Toward supranational copyright law? The WTO panel decision and the "three-step test" for copyright exceptions' (2001) 187 *Revue internationale du droit d'auteur* 3.

'"With untired spirits and formal constancy": Berne compatibility of formal declaratory measures to enhance copyright title-searching' (2013) 28 *Berkeley Technology Law Journal* 1583.

Ginsburg, J. C. and Treppoz, E., *International Copyright: US and EU Perspectives* (Edward Elgar, 2015).

Goldstein, P., 'Derivative rights and derivative works in copyright' (1983) 30 *Journal of the Copyright Society of the USA* 209.

'Fair use in context' (2008) 31 *Columbia Journal of Law & the Arts* 433.

Goldstein, P. and Hugenholtz, P. B., *International Copyright: Principles, Law, and Practice* (Oxford University Press, 2010).

Gordon, W., 'Authors, publishers, and public goods: trading gold for dross' (2002) 36 *Loyola of Los Angeles Law Review* 159.

'Excuse and justification in the law of fair use: commodification and market perspectives', in N. Elkin-Koren and N. Netanel (eds.), *The Commodification of Information* (Kluwer Law International, 2002).

'Fair use as market failure: a structural and economic analysis of the *Betamax* case and its predecessors' (1982) 82(8) *Columbia Law Review* 1600.

'On owning information: intellectual property and the restitutionary impulse' (1992) 78 *Virginia Law Review* 149.

Gorman, R., 'Fact or fancy? The implications for copyright' (1982) 29 *Journal of the Copyright Society of the USA* 560.

Gotzen, F., 'The right of destination in Europe' (1989) 25 *Copyright* 218.

# Bibliography 573

Government 2.0 Taskforce (Australia), 'Engage: getting on with government 2.0', Report of the Government 2.0 Taskforce (Australian Government, December 2009).

Government of Canada, *Directive on Open Government* (Canadian Government, 9 October 2014).

Gowers, A., *Gowers Review of Intellectual Property* (UK Government, December 2006).

Greenleaf, G., 'Creating commons by friendly appropriation' (2007) 4(1) *SCRIPTed* 117.

'IP, phone home: privacy as part of copyright's digital commons in Hong Kong and Australian law', in L. Lessig (ed.), *Hochelaga Lectures 2002: The Innovation Commons* (Sweet & Maxwell Asia, 2003).

'National and international dimensions of copyright's public domain (an Australian case study)' (2009) 6(2) *SCRIPTed* 259.

Greenleaf, G. and Bond, C., '"Public rights", in copyright: what makes up Australia's public domain?' (2013) 23 *Australian Intellectual Property Journal* 111.

'Re-use rights and Australia's unfinished PSI revolution' (2011) 1(2) *Informatica e diritto – Rivista internazionale* 341.

Greenleaf, G., Mowbray, A. and Chung, P., 'Building a commons for the common law – the Commonwealth Legal Information Institute (CommonLII) after four years' progress' (2010) 36(1) *Commonwealth Law Bulletin* 127.

Greenleaf, G., Paramaguru, A., Bond, C. and Christou, S., 'Legal deposit's role in the public domain', UNSW Law Research Paper No. 2008-38 (2008).

Griffiths, J., 'Constitutionalising or harmonising? – the Court of Justice, the right to property and European copyright law' (2013) 38 *European Law Review* 65.

'Copyright law after *Ashdown* – time to deal fairly with the public' (2002) 3 *Intellectual Property Quarterly* 240.

'The United Kingdom's public interest "defence" and European Union copyright law', in N. Lee, G. Westkamp, A. Kurr and A. Ohly (eds.), *Intellectual Property, Unfair Competition and Publicity* (Edward Elgar, 2014).

Guadamuz, A., 'Comparative analysis of national approaches on voluntary copyright relinquishment', Report presented to WIPO Committee on Development and Intellectual Property (CDIP), 13th Session (2014).

'Free and open source software', in L. Edwards and C. Waelde (eds.), *Law and the Internet* (3rd edn, Hart, 2009).

'The license/contract dichotomy in open licenses: a comparative analysis' (2009) *University of La Verne Law Review* 30(2).

Guibault, L., *Copyright Limitations and Contracts: An Analysis of the Contractual Overridability of Limitations on Copyright* (Kluwer Law International, 2002).

*The Reprography Levies Across the European Union* (Institute for Information Law, University of Amsterdam, March 2003).

'Why cherry-picking never leads to harmonisation: the case of the limitations on copyright under Directive 2001/29/EC' (2010) 1 *Journal of Intellectual Property, Information Technology and Electronic Commerce Law (JIPITEC)* 55.

'Wrapping information in contract: how does it affect the public domain?', in L. Guibault and P. B. Hugenholtz (eds.), *The Future of the Public Domain: Identifying the Commons in Information Law* (Kluwer Law International, 2006).

Hardin, G., 'The tragedy of the commons' (1968) 162 *Science* 1243.

Hargreaves, I., *Digital Opportunity: A Review of Intellectual Property and Growth* (Intellectual Property Office (UK), 2011).

Harnad, S., 'The green road to open access: a leveraged transition' (2004) http://users.ecs.soton.ac.uk/harnad/Temp/greenroad.html.

Hebl, A., 'A heavy burden: proper application of copyright's merger and *scène à faire* doctrines' (2007) 8 *Wake Forest Intellectual Property Law Journal* 128.

Helberger, N., Dufft, S., van Gompel, S. and Hugenholtz, P. B., 'Never forever: why extending the term of protection for sound recordings is a bad idea' (2008) 30(5) *European Intellectual Property Review* 174.

Helfer, L., 'Regime shifting: the TRIPs Agreement and the new dynamics of international intellectual property making' (2004) 29 *Yale Journal of International Law* 1.

'Regime shifting in the international intellectual property system' (2009) 7(1) *Perspectives on Politics* 39.

Heller, M. and Eisenberg, R., 'Can patents deter innovation? The anticommons in biomedical research' (1998) 280 *Science* 698.

Herlt, K., 'ACE survey on the implementation of the Orphan Works Directive', Project FORWARD, 3 April 2015 http://project-forward.eu/2015/04/03/ace-survey-on-the-implementation-of-the-orphan-works-directive/.

Herman, A., 'The year of living exceptionally: new copyright exceptions in UK law' (2014) 19(4) *Art Antiquity and Law* 303.

Hess, C. and Ostrom, E., 'Ideas, artefacts, and facilities: information as a common pool resource' (2003) 66 *Law and Contemporary Problems* 111.

Hirtle, P., Hudson, E. and Kenyon, A., *Copyright and Cultural Institutions: Guidelines for Digitization for US Libraries, Archives, and Museums* (Cornell University Library, 2009).

House of Representatives Standing Committee on Infrastructure and Communications (Australia), 'At what cost? IT pricing and the Australia tax' www.aphref.aph.gov.au/house/committee/ic/itpricing/report/fullreport.pdf.

Hudson, E., 'Implementing fair use in copyright law' (2013) 25 *Intellectual Property Journal* 201.

Hudson, E. and Burrell, R., 'Abandonment, copyright and orphaned works: what does it mean to take the property nature of intellectual property rights seriously?' (2011) 35 *Melbourne University Law Review* 971.

Hudson, E. and Kenyon, A., 'Digital access: the impact of copyright on digitisation practices in Australian museums, galleries, libraries and archives' (2007) 30(1) *UNSW Law Journal* 12.

Hugenholtz, P. B., 'Caching and copyright: the right of temporary copying' (2000) 22(10) *European Intellectual Property Review* 482.

'Copyright, contract and code: what will remain of the public domain' (2000) 26 *Brooklyn Journal of International Law* 77.

'The dynamics of harmonization of copyright at the European level', in C. Geiger (ed.), *Constructing European Intellectual Property: Achievements and New Perspectives* (Edward Elgar, 2013).
(ed.), *The Future of Copyright in a Digital Environment* (Kluwer Law International, 1996).
'Is harmonization a good thing? The case of the copyright *acquis*', in A. Ohly and J. Pila (eds.), *The Europeanization of Intellectual Property Law* (Oxford University Press, 2013).
Hugenholtz, P. B. and Senftleben, M., 'Fair use in Europe. In search of flexibilities', VU Centre for Law and Governance, Amsterdam http://ssrn.com/abstract=1959554.
Hugenholtz, P. B. and van Velze, S., 'Communication to a new public? Three reasons why EU copyright law can do without a "new public"' (2016) 47(7) *International Review of Intellectual Property and Competition Law (IIC)* 797.
Hughes, J., 'Created facts and the flawed ontology of copyright law' (2007) 83 *Notre Dame Law Review* 43.
'Locke's 1694 Memorandum (and more incomplete copyright historiographies)' (2010) 27 *Cardozo Arts & Entertainment Law Journal* 555.
'Size matters (or should) in copyright law' (2005) 74 *Fordham Law Review* 575.
Hughes, J. and Merges, R. P., 'Copyright and distributive justice' (2016) 92 *Notre Dame Law Review* 513.
Hunter, D., 'American lessons: implementing fair use in Australia' (2014) 24 *Australian Intellectual Property Journal* 192.
Intellectual Property Office (UK), 'Consultation on reducing the duration of copyright in unpublished ("2039") works in accordance with section 170(2)of the Copyright, Designs and Patents Act 1988' (IPO, 2014).
'Exceptions to copyright: education and teaching' (IPO, 2014)
'Exceptions to copyright: guidance for creators and copyright owners' (IPO, 2014).
'Government response to the consultation on reducing the duration of copyright in certain unpublished works' (IPO, 2015).
'Orphan works diligent search guidance for applicants: guidance on searching for right holders in copyright works to obtain permission to reproduce the work' (IPO, 2014).
'Orphan works: review of the first twelve months' (IPO, 2015)
International Federation of Library Associations (IFLA), 'Treaty proposal on copyright limitations and exceptions for libraries and archives', version 4.4 (IFLA, 6 December 2013).
Jacob, R., 'Parody and IP claims: a defence?', in R. Dreyfus and J. C. Ginsburg (eds.), *Intellectual Property at the Edge: The Contested Contours of IP* (Cambridge University Press, 2014).
Jarrah, E., 'Victory for the public: West Publishing loses its copyright battle over star pagination and compilation elements' (2000) 25 *University of Dayton Law Review* 163.
Jaszi, P., 'Public interest exceptions in copyright: a comparative and international perspective', Paper presented to Correcting Course: Rebalancing Copyright

for Libraries in the National and International Arena, Columbia University, 5–7 May 2005.

Jehoram, H., 'The Dutch Supreme Court recognises copyright in the scent of a perfume. The Flying Dutchman: all sails, no anchor' (2006) 28 *European Intellectual Property Review* 629.

'The EC Copyright Directives, economics and authors' rights' [1994] *International Review of Intellectual Property and Competition Law (IIC)* 821.

Johnson, P., '"Dedicating" copyright to the public domain' (2008) 71 *Modern Law Review* 587.

Jones, M., *'Eldred* v. *Ashcroft:* the constitutionality of the Copyright Term Extension Act' (2004) 19 *Berkeley Technology Law Journal* 85.

Jones, P., 'The GPL is a License, not a Contract', *Linux Weekly News*, 3 December 2003.

Jong, S., 'Fair use in Korea', Presentation at Australian Digital Alliance Copyright Forum, Canberra, 24 February 2017 http://infojustice.org/archives/37819.

Judge, E., 'Crown copyright and copyright reform in Canada', in M. Geist (ed.), *In the Public Interest: The Future of Canadian Copyright Law* (Irwin Law, 2005).

Judge, E. and Gervais, D., 'Of silos and constellations: comparing notions of originality in copyright law' (2009) 27 *Cardozo Arts & Entertainment Law Journal* 375.

Kamina, P., 'Authorship of films and implementation of the Term Directive: the dramatic tale of two copyrights' [1994] *European Intellectual Property Review* 319.

'British film copyright and the incorrect implementation of the EC Copyright Directives' [1998] *Entertainment Law Review* 109.

Kaplan, B., *An Unhurried View of Copyright* (Columbia University Press, 1967).

Karapapa, S., 'Reconstructing copyright exhaustion in the online world' (2014) 4 *Intellectual Property Quarterly* 307.

Karjala, D., 'Federal preemption of shrinkwrap and online licenses' (1997) 22 *University of Dayton Law Review* 511.

'Judicial review of copyright term extension legislation' (2002) 36 *Loyola of Los Angeles Law Review* 199.

Karp, I., 'Final report, Berne Article 18 study on retroactive United States copyright protection for Berne and other works' (1996) 20 *Columbia-VLA Journal of Law & the Arts* 157.

Kasunic, R., 'Is that all there is? Reflections on the nature of the second fair use factor' (2008) 31(4) *Columbia Journal of Law & the Arts* 529.

Katz, A., 'Everything open', in N. Shemtov and I. Walden (eds.), *Free and Open Source Software: Policy Law and Practice* (Oxford University Press, 2013).

'Fair use 2.0: the rebirth of fair dealing in Canada', in M. Geist (ed.), *The Copyright Pentalogy: How the Supreme Court of Canada Shook the Foundations of Canadian Copyright Law* (University of Ottawa Press, 2013).

Ketzan, E., 'Rebuilding Babel: copyright and the future of machine translation online' *Tulane Journal of Technology & Intellectual Property*, Spring 2007.

Koelman, K., 'Fixing the three-step test' (2006) 28 *European Intellectual Property Review* 407.

'A hard nut to crack: the protection of technological measures' (2000) 22 *European Intellectual Property Review* 272.

'The public domain commodified: technological measures and productive information use', in L. Guibault and P. B. Hugenholtz (eds.), *The Future of the Public Domain: Identifying the Commons in Information Law* (Kluwer Law International, 2006).

Koskinen-Olsson, T. and Sigurdardóttir, V., 'Collective management in the Nordic countries', in D. Gervais (ed.), *Collective Management of Copyright and Related Rights* (3rd edn, Wolters Kluwer, 2016).

Krasilovsky, M., 'Observations on the public domain' (1967) 14 *Bulletin of the Copyright Society* 205.

Kretschmer, M., Derclaye, E., Favale, F. and Watt, R., 'The relationship between copyright and contract law', Research commissioned by the Strategic Advisory Board for Intellectual Property Policy (UK) (2010) http://eprints.bournemouth.ac.uk/16091/1/_contractlaw-report.pdf.

Kurlantzick, L. and Pennino, J., 'The Audio Home Recording Act and the formation of copyright policy' (1998) 45 *Journal of the Copyright Society of the USA* 497.

Ladas, S., *The International Protection of Literary and Artistic Property* (The Macmillan Company, 1938).

Laddie, H., Prescott, P. and Vitoria, M., *The Modern Law of Copyright and Designs* (Butterworths, 1980).

*The Modern Law of Copyright and Designs* (2nd edn, Butterworths, 1995).

Laddie, H., Prescott, P., Vitoria, M., Speck, A. and Lane, L., *The Modern Law of Copyright and Designs* (3rd edn, Butterworths, 2000).

Landes, W. and Posner, R., 'Indefinitely renewable copyright' (2003) 70 *University of Chicago Law Review* 471.

Lange, D., 'Recognizing the public domain' (1981) 44(4) *Law and Contemporary Problems* 147.

'Reimagining the public domain' (2003) 66 *Law and Contemporary Problems* 463.

Lape, L., 'The metaphysics of the law: bringing substantial similarity down to earth' (1994) 98 *Dickinson Law Review* 181.

Latman, A., '"Probative similarity" as proof of copying: toward dispelling some myths in copyright infringement' (1990) 90 *Columbia Law Review* 1187.

Lee, E., 'The public's domain: the evolution of legal restraints on the Government's power to control public access through secrecy or intellectual property' (2003) 55 *Hastings Law Journal* 91.

Lee, J., 'Licensing open government data' (2017) 13(2) *Hastings Business Law Journal* 207.

Lemley, M., 'Beyond preemption: the law and policy of intellectual property licensing' (1999) 87 *California Law Review* 111.

'Faith-based intellectual property' (2015) 62 *UCLA Law Review* 1328.

Lessig, L., 'The architecture of innovation' (2002) 51 *Duke Law Journal* 1783.

*Free Culture: How Big Media Uses Technology and the Law to Lock Down Culture and Control Creativity* (Penguin USA, 2004).

*The Future of Ideas: The Fate of the Commons in a Connected World* (Random House, 2001).

'Re-crafting a public domain' (2006) 18 *Yale Journal of Law & the Humanities* 56.

Leval, P., 'Toward a fair use standard' (1990) 103 *Harvard Law Review* 1105.

Levy, R., 'Access Copyright: Addressing the needs and concerns of both creators and users in a changing copyright environment'.

Li, Y., 'China', in P. Geller, M. Nimmer and L. Bently (eds.), *International Copyright Law and Practice* (LexisNexis, 2016).

Li, Y. and Greenleaf, G., 'China's copyright public domain: a comparison with Australia' (2017) 27(3) *Australian Intellectual Property Journal* 34.

Liang, L., 'Exceptions and limitations in Indian copyright law for education: an assessment' (2010) 3 *Law and Development Review* 197.

Library of Congress, 'Section 108: Draft Revision of the Library and Archives Exceptions in US Copyright Law', Federal Register 81(109) (7 June 2016).

Liebowitz, S., 'A critique of copyright's criticisms' (2015) 22(4) *George Mason Law Review* 943.

Liebowitz, S. and Margolis, S., 'Seventeen famous economists weigh in on copyright: the role of theory, empirics, and network effects' (2005) 18(2) *Harvard Journal of Law & Technology* 435.

Lindgren, K., 'The jurisdiction of the Copyright Tribunal of Australia: the 2006 Amendments' (2007) 70 *Intellectual Property Forum: Journal of the Intellectual and Industrial Property Society of Australia and New Zealand*.

Lindsay, D., 'Copyright and freedom of expression', in K. Bowrey, M. Handler and D. Nicol (eds.), *Emerging Challenges in Intellectual Property* (Oxford University Press, 2011).

*The Law and Economics of Copyright, Contract and Mass Market Licences* (Centre for Copyright Studies Ltd, 2002).

'Protection of compilations and databases after *IceTV*: authorship, originality and the transformation of Australian copyright law' (2012) 38(1) *Monash University Law Review* 17.

Litman, J., 'The exclusive right to read' (1994) 13 *Cardozo Arts & Entertainment Law Journal* 29.

'Lawful personal use' (2007) 85 *Texas Law Review* 1871.

'The public domain' (1990) 39(4) *Emory Law Journal* 965.

Liu, D., '*Meltwater* melts not water but principle! The danger of the court adjudicating an issue without the ambit of referral' (2013) 35(6) *European Intellectual Property Review* 327.

Lopez, M., 'CJEU ruling in Doke & Soulier case emphasizes the need for a real solution to the out-of-commerce problem', COMMUNIA, 23 November 2016 www.communia-association.org/2016/11/23/cjeu-ruling-doke-soulier-case-emphasizes-need-real-solution-commerce-problem/.

Loren, L., 'Building a reliable semicommons of creative works: enforcement of creative commons licenses and limited abandonment of copyright' (2007) 14 *George Mason Law Review* 271.

'Fair use: an affirmative defense?' (2015) 90 *Washington Law Review* 685.

'Fixation as notice in copyright' (2016) 96 *Boston University Law Review* 939.

Lucas-Schloetter, A., 'Is there a concept of European copyright law? History, evolution, policies and politics and the *Acquis Communautaire*', in I. Stamatoudi and P. Torremans (eds.), *EU Copyright Law: A Commentary* (Edward Elgar, 2016).

Lui, J., 'Regulatory copyright' (2004) 83 *North Carolina Law Review* 87.

McCutcheon, J., 'Digital access to culture: copyright in photographs of two-dimensional art under Australian copyright law' (2017) 7 (4) *Queen Mary Intellectual Property Journal* 416.

'The new defence of parody or satire under Australian copyright law' [2008] *Intellectual Property Quarterly* 163.

'The vanishing author in computer-generated works: a critical analysis of recent Australian case law' (2013) 36 *Melbourne University Law Review* 915.

McCutcheon, J. and Holloway, S., 'Whose fair dealing? Third party reliance on the fair dealing exception for parody or satire' (2016) 27(2) *Australian Intellectual Property Journal* 53.

McDonagh, L., 'Copyright, contract and FOSS', in N. Shemtov and I. Walden (eds.), *Free and Open Source Software: Policy Law and Practice* (Oxford University Press, 2013).

McQueen, H., Waelde, C., Laurie G. and Brown, A., *Contemporary Intellectual Property: Law and Policy* (2nd edn, Oxford University Press, 2011).

Madison, M., 'Rewriting fair use and the future of copyright reform' (2005) 23 *Cardozo Arts & Entertainment Law Journal* 391.

Maeir, H., 'German Federal Court of Justice rules on parody and free use' (2017) 12(1) *Journal of Intellectual Property Law & Practice* 16.

Mahoney, J., 'Lawrence Lessig's dystopian vision' (2004) 90 *Villanova Law Review* 2305.

Margoni, T., 'The digitization of cultural heritage: originality, derivative works and (non) original photographs', University of Glasgow, CREATe, 3 December 2014 https://papers.ssrn.com/sol3/papers.cfm?abstract_id= 2573104.

Martin, S., 'The mythology of the public domain: exploring the myths behind attacks on the duration of copyright protection' 36 *Loyola of Los Angeles Law Review* 253 (2002).

Meeker, H., *The Open Source Alternative: Understanding and Leveraging Opportunities* (John Wiley & Sons, 2008).

Mehra, S., 'Copyright and comics in Japan: does law explain why all the cartoons my kid watches are Japanese imports?' (2002) 55 *Rutgers Law Review*.

Mendis, D. and Stobo, V., 'UK: extended collective licensing', Kluwer copyright blog, 3 December 2014 http://copyrightblog.kluweriplaw.com/2014/12/03/uk-extended-collective-licensing/.

Mendis D. and Kretschmer, M., *The Treatment of Parodies under Copyright Law in Seven Jurisdictions: A Comparative Review of the Underlying Principles* (Intellectual Property Office (UK), 2013).

Menell, P., 'In search of copyright's lost ark: interpreting the right to distribute in the Internet age' (2011) 59 *Journal of the Copyright Society of the USA* 1.

Merges, R. P., 'Contracting into liability rules: intellectual property rights and collective rights organizations' (1996) 84(5) *California Law Review* 1293.

'The end of friction? Property rights and contract in the "Newtonian" world of online commerce' (1997) 12 *Berkeley Technology Law Journal* 115.
*Justifying Intellectual Property* (Harvard University Press, 2011).
'A new dynamism in the public domain' (2004) 71 *University of Chicago Law Review* 183.
'One hundred years of solicitude: intellectual property law, 1900–2000' (2000) 88 *California Law Review* 2187.
Mewhort, K., 'Creative Commons Licenses: options for Canadian open data providers', Canadian Internet Policy and Public Interest Clinic (CIPPIC), 1 June 2012 https://cippic.ca.
Ministry of Communication & Information Technology (India), 'Policy on adoption of open source software for Government of India', 2014 http://meity.gov.in/writereaddata/files/policy_on_adoption_of_oss.pdf.
Mitchell, I., 'Public sector and open source', in N. Shemtov and I. Walden (eds.), *Free and Open Source Software: Policy Law and Practice* (Oxford University Press, 2013).
Moglen, E., 'Enforcing the GNU GPL', GNU Operating System, 10 September 2001 www.gnu.org/philosophy/enforcing-gpl.html.
Monotti, A., 'Nature and basis of Crown Copyright in official publications' (1992) 9 *European Intellectual Property Review* 305.
Morley, J., 'The unfettered expansion of appropriation art protection by the fair use doctrine: searching for transformativeness in *Cariou* v. *Prince* and beyond' (2015) 55 *IDEA* 385.
The National Archives (UK), 'UK Government Licensing Framework' (UKGLF) www.nationalarchives.gov.uk/information-management/reusing-public-sector-information/uk-government-licensing-framework/.
National Copyright Administration China, 'Reply of the NCAC to the Inquiry from Hainan Provincial Copyright Administration Regarding the Issues of Copyright Licenses China', No. 22, 4 June 2003 www.ncac.gov.cn/.
National Library of Australia, 'Deposit of electronic publications with the National Library of Australia: Guide to requirements for publishers' (June 2016).
Netanel, N., 'Locating copyright within the First Amendment skein' (2001) 54 *Stanford Law Review* 1.
'Making sense of fair use' (2011) 15(3) *Lewis & Clark Law Review* 715.
Nimmer, D., '"Fairest of them all" and other fairy tales of fair use' (2003) 66 *Law & Contemporary Problems* 263.
Nimmer, D., Brown, E., and Frischling, G. N., 'The metamorphosis of contract into expand' (1999) 87 *California Law Review* 17.
Nimmer, M., 'Does copyright abridge the First Amendment guarantees of free speech and press?' (1970) 17 *UCLA Law Review* 1180.
O'Rourke, M., 'Copyright preemption after the ProCD case: a market-based approach' (1997) 12 *Berkeley Technology Law Journal* 53.
Ocasio, S., 'Pruning paracopyright protection: why courts should apply the merger and *scène à faire* doctrines at the copyrightability stage of the copyright infringement analysis' (2006) 3 *Seton Hall Circuit Review* 303.

Ochoa, T., 'Origins and meanings of the public domain' (2003) 28(2) *University of Dayton Law Review* 215.
'Protection of works of foreign origin under the 1909 Copyright Act' (2010) 26 *Santa Clara Computer & High Technology Law Journal* 285.
Ohly, A., 'Economic rights', in A. Ohly and E. Derclaye (eds.), *Research Handbook on the Future of EU Copyright* (Edward Elgar, 2009).
'European fundamental rights and intellectual property', in A. Ohly and J. Pila (eds.), *The Europeanization of Intellectual Property Law* (Oxford University Press, 2013).
Oliver, J., 'Copyright in the WTO: the panel decision on the three-step test' (2002) 25 *Columbia Journal of Law & the Arts* 119.
Open Source Initiative, 'The Open Source Definition' (2007) https://opensource.org/osd.
Ostrom, E., *Governing the Commons: The Evolution of Institutions for Collective Action* (Cambridge University Press, 1990).
Pallente, M., 'The curious case of copyright formalities' (2013) 28 *Berkeley Technology Law Journal* 1415.
Parliament of Australia, Joint Standing Committee on Treaties (JSCOT), 'The Australia–United States Free Trade Agreement' (June 2004).
Patry, W., 'Choice of law and international copyright' (2000) 48 *American Journal of Comparative Law* 383.
*The Fair Use Privilege in Copyright Law* (2nd edn, Bureau of National Affairs, 1995).
Patterson, L. Ray, '*Folsom* v. *Marsh* and its legacy' (1998) 5 *Journal of Intellectual Property Law* 431.
Patterson, L. Ray and Joyce, C., 'Monopolizing the law: the scope of copyright protection for law reports and statutory compilations' (1989) 36 *UCLA Law Review* 719.
Patterson, L. Ray and Lindberg, S., *The Nature of Copyright: A Law of Users' Rights* (University of Georgia Press, 1991).
Pearce, D. and Geddes, R., *Statutory Interpretation in Australia* (4th edn, Butterworths, 1996).
Perzanowski, A. and Schultz, J., 'Digital exhaustion' (2011) 58 *UCLA Law Review* 839.
'Legislating digital exhaustion' (2014) 29 *Berkeley Technology Law Journal* 1535.
Pessach, G., 'The new Israeli Copyright Act: a case-study in reverse comparative law' (2010) 41 *International Review of Intellectual Property and Competition Law (IIC)* 187.
Phillips, J., 'Copyright in obscene works: some British and American problems' (1977) 6 *Anglo-American Law Review* 138.
Phillips, J. and Bently, L., 'Copyright issues: the mysteries of section 18' (1999) 21(3) *European Intellectual Property Review* 133.
Pila, J., 'Copyright and its categories of original works' (2010) 30(2) *Oxford Journal of Legal Studies* 229.
Pilch, J., 'Fair use and beyond: the status of copyright limitations and exceptions in the Commonwealth of Independent States' (2004) 65(6) *College & Research Libraries* 468.

Poitraut, J.-L., 'An authors' rights-based copyright law: the fairness and morality of French and American law compared' (2006) 24 *Cardozo Arts & Entertainment Law Journal* 549.

Posner, R., 'The constitutionality of the Copyright Term Extension Act: economics, politics, law, and judicial technique in *Eldred* v. *Ashcroft*' (2003) 4 *Supreme Court Review* 143.

Productivity Commission (Aus.), 'Intellectual property arrangements', Report 78 (23 September 2016).

Qingjiang, K., 'The doctrine of Ordre public and the Sino–US copyright dispute', Society of International Economic Law, Online Proceedings Working Paper No. 07/08 (on SSRN) (17 June 2008).

Radin, M., 'Humans, computers and binding commitment' (2000) 75 *Indiana Law Journal* 1125.

Rahmatian, A., *Copyright and Creativity. The Making of Property Rights in Creative Works* (Edward Elgar, 2011).

'Originality in UK copyright law: the old "skill and labour" doctrine under pressure' (2013) 44 *International Review of Intellectual Property and Competition Law (IIC)* 4.

Reece, R., 'The first sale doctrine in the era of digital networks' (2003) 44 *Boston College Law Review* 577.

Reichman, J. and Uhler, P., 'A contractually reconstructed research commons for scientific data in a highly protectionist intellectual property environment' (2003) 66 *Law & Contemporary Problems* 315.

Reid, A., 'Claiming the copyright' (2016) 34 *Yale Law and Policy Review* 425.

Reinbothe, J. and von Lewinski, S., *The WIPO Treaties 1996* (Butterworths/LexisNexis, 2002).

Resnik, D., 'A pluralistic account of intellectual property' (2003) 46 *Journal of Business Ethics* 319.

Reynolds, G., 'The limits of statutory interpretation: towards explicit engagement, by the Supreme Court of Canada, with the Charter Right to freedom of expression in the context of copyright' (2016) 41 *Queen's Law Journal* 455.

Rice, D., 'Public goods, private contract, and public policy: federal preemption of software license prohibitions against reverse engineering' (1992) 53 *University of Pittsburgh Law Review* 543.

Richards, N., 'Intellectual privacy' (2008) 87 *Texas Law Review* 387.

Richardson, M., 'Freedom of political discussion and intellectual property law in Australia' (1997) 11 *European Intellectual Property Review* 631.

Ricketson, S., 'The birth of the Berne Union' (1986) 9 *Columbia-VLA Journal of Law & the Arts* 11.

'The copyright term' (1992) 23 *International Review of Intellectual Property and Competition Law (IIC)* 753.

*The Law of Intellectual Property* (The Law Book Company Limited, 1984).

'Reaping without sowing: unfair competition and intellectual property rights in Anglo-Australian law' (1984) 7 *UNSW Law Journal* 1.

'WIPO study on limitations and exceptions of copyright and related rights in the digital environment', WIPO SCCR, Ninth Session, Geneva, 23–27 June 2003.

Ricketson, S. and Creswell, C., *The Law of Intellectual Property: Copyright, Designs and Confidential Information* (2nd rev. edn, Thomson Legal & Regulatory, 1999, ongoing electronic resource).

Ricketson, S. and Ginsburg, J. C., *International Copyright and Neighbouring Rights: The Berne Convention and Beyond* (2nd edn, Oxford University Press, 2005).

Ricoli, M., Morando, F., Rubiano, C., Hsu, S., Ouma, M. and de Martin, J. C., 'Survey of private copyright documentation systems and practices', WIPO, 2011 www.wipo.int/export/sites/www/meetings/en/2011/wipo_cr_doc_ge_11/pdf/survey_private_crdocystems.pdf.

Riis, T. and Schovsbo, J., 'Extended collective licenses and the Nordic experience: it's a hybrid but is it a Volvo or a lemon?' (2010) 33(4) *Columbia Journal of Law & the Arts* 471.

Rosati, E., 'The CJEU decision in Soulier: what does it mean for laws other than the French one on out-of-print books?', The IPKat, 17 November 2016 http://ipkitten.blogspot.co.uk/2016/11/the-cjeu-decision-in-soulier-what-does.html.

'Copyright in the EU: in search of (in)flexibilities' (2014) 9(7) *Journal of Intellectual Property Law & Practice* 585.

'Just a laughing matter? Why the decision in *Deckmyn* is broader than parody' (2015) 52 *Common Market Law Review* 511.

'Originality in a work, or a work of originality: the effects of the *Infopaq* decision' (2011) 33(12) *European Intellectual Property Review* 746.

Rose, C., 'The comedy of the commons: custom, commerce, and inherently public property' (1986) 53 *University of Chicago Law Review* 711.

Rose, M., 'Nine-tenths of the law: the English copyright debates and the rhetoric of the public domain' (2003) 66 *Law and Contemporary Problems* 75.

Rosen, A., 'Reconsidering the idea/expression dichotomy' (1992) *UBC Law Review* 263.

Rosen, L., *Open Source Licensing: Software Freedom and Intellectual Property Law* (Prentice Hall, 2004).

'Why the public domain is not a license', Rosenlaw & Einschlag website, 2004 www.rosenlaw.com/lj16.htm.

Rothman, J., 'Best intentions: reconsidering best practices statements in the context of fair use and copyright law' (2010) 57 *Journal of the Copyright Society of the USA* 371.

Rothnie, W., 'Moral rights: consents *and* waivers?' (2002) 20 *Copyright Reporter* 145.

Saez, C., 'Copyright exceptions for libraries: WIPO should step up before someone else does', Intellectual Property Watch, 12 December 2014.

Sag, M., 'Predicting fair use' (2012) 73 *Ohio State Law Journal* 47.

'The prehistory of fair use' (2011) 76(4) *Brooklyn Law Review* 1371.

Sainsbury, M., 'Parody, satire and copyright infringement: the latest addition to Australian fair dealing law' (2007) 12 *Media and Arts Law Review* 292.

Samuels, E., 'The idea–expression dichotomy in copyright law' (1989) 56 *Tennessee Law Review* 321.

'The public domain in copyright law' (1993) 41 *Journal of the Copyright Society of the USA* 137.

'The public domain revisited' (2002) 36 *Loyola of Los Angeles Law Review* 389.
Samuelson, P., 'Challenges in mapping the public domain', in L. Guibault and P. B. Hugenholtz (eds.), *The Future of the Public Domain: Identifying the Commons in Information Law* (Kluwer Law International, 2006).
'Copyright and freedom of expression in historical perspective' (2002) 10 *Journal of Intellectual Property Law* 319.
'The Copyright Principles Project: directions for reform' (2010) 25 *Berkeley Technology Law Journal* 1175.
'Enriching discourse on public domains' (2006) 55 *Duke Law Journal* 783.
'Intellectual property and the digital economy: why the anti-circumvention regulations need to be revised' (1999) 14 *Berkeley Technology Law Journal* 519.
'Mapping the digital public domain: threats and opportunities' (2003) 66 *Law and Contemporary Problems* 147.
'Possible futures of fair use' (2015) 90 *Washington Law Review* 815.
'Preliminary thoughts on copyright reform' (2007) *Utah Law Review* 551.
'The quest for a sound conception of copyright's derivative work right' (2013) 101 *Georgetown Law Journal* 1505.
'The US Digital Agenda at WIPO' (1997) 37 *Virginia Journal of International Law* 369.
'Unbundling fair uses' (2009) 77 *Fordham Law Review* 2537.
Schellekens, M., 'Free and open source software: an answer to commodification', in L. Guibault and P. B. Hugenholtz (eds.), *The Future of the Public Domain: Identifying the Commons in Information Law* (Kluwer Law International, 2006).
Senftleben, M., *Copyright, Limitations and the Three-Step Test: An Analysis of the Three-Step Test in International and EC Copyright Law* (Kluwer Law International, 2004).
Seng, D., 'Comparative analysis of the national approaches to the liability of internet intermediaries' (preliminary version) (WIPO, 2010).
'Study on copyright limitations and exceptions for educational activities', WIPO SCCR, SCCR/33/6, 9 November 2016.
Seville, C., 'Copyright in perfumes: smelling a rat' [2007] *Cambridge Law Journal* 49.
*EU Intellectual Property Law and Policy* (Edward Elgar, 2009).
Shaffer, G., 'The new realist approach to international law' (2015) 28(2) *Leiden Journal of International Law* 189.
Shemtov, N., 'FOSS license: bare license or contract', Centre for Commercial Law Studies Queen Mary University of London presentation https://web.ua.es/es/contratos-id/documentos/itipupdate2011/shemtov.pdf.
Shemtov, N. and Walden, I. (eds.), *Free and Open Source Software: Policy Law and Practice* (Oxford University Press, 2013).
Singh, R. et al., *Iyengar's Commentary on The Copyright Act* (7th edn, Universal Law Publishing Company, 2010).
Sites, B., 'Fair use and the new transformative' (2016) 39(4) *Columbia Journal of Law & the Arts* 514.
Snow, N., 'The forgotten right of fair use' (2011) 62(1) *Case Western Law Review* 135.

Solove, D., 'Conceptualizing privacy' (2002) 90 *California Law Review* 1088.

Song, S., 'Reevaluating fair use in China – a comparative copyright analysis of Chinese fair use legislation, the US fair use doctrine, and the European fair dealing model' (2011) 51 *IDEA* 453.

Spies, A., 'Revering irreverance: a fair dealing exception for both weapon and target parodies' (2011) 34(3) *UNSW Law Journal* 1122.

Sprigman, C., 'Reform(alizing) copyright' (2004) 57 *Stanford Law Review* 485.

Stallman, R., 'Why open source misses the point of free software', GNU Operating System, undated www.gnu.org/philosophy/open-source-misses-the-point.en.html.

Stanfield, B., 'Finding the fact of familiarity: assessing judicial similarity tests in copyright infringement actions' (2001) 49 *Drake Law Review* 489.

Stanganelli, M., 'Spreading the news online: a fine balance of copyright and freedom of expression in news aggregation' (2012) 34(11) *European Intellectual Property Review* 745.

State Council (China), 'Explanation of the "Copyright Law of the People's Republic of China" (submission version of the revised draft)', 6 June 2014 (unofficial translation by Rogier Creemers, 18 June 2014).

Sterling, J. A. L. and Cook, T., *Sterling on World Copyright* (4th edn, Sweet & Maxwell, 2015).

Stewart, A., Griffith, P., Bannister, J. and Liberman, A., *Intellectual Property in Australia* (5th edn, LexisNexis Butterworths, 2014).

Strong, W., *The Copyright Book: A Practical Guide* (6th edn, MIT Press, 2014).

Strowel, A., '*Droit d'auteur* and copyright: between history and nature', in B. Sherman and A. Strowel (eds.), *Of Authors and Origins: Essays on Copyright Law* (Clarendon Press, 1994).

'Towards a European copyright law: four issues to consider', in I. Stamatoudi and P. Torremans (eds.), *EU Copyright Law: A Commentary* (Edward Elgar, 2016).

Strowel, A. and Kim, H., 'The balancing impact of general EU law on European intellectual property jurisprudence', in A. Ohly and J. Pila (eds.), *The Europeanization of Intellectual Property Law* (Oxford University Press, 2013).

Suber, P., 'Open access overview' (2013, updated periodically) https://legacy.earlham.edu/~peters/fos/overview.htm.

Suthersanen, U., 'The first global Copyright Act', in U. Suthersanen and Y. Gendreau (eds.), *A Shifting Empire: 100 Years of the Copyright Act 1911* (Edward Elgar, 2013).

Tang, G., *Copyright and the Public Interest in China* (Edward Elgar, 2011).

Taubman, A., 'The public domain and international intellectual property treaties', in C. Waelde and H. McQueen (eds.), *Intellectual Property: The Many Faces of the Public Domain* (Edward Elgar, 2007).

Tawfik, M., 'History in the balance: copyright and access to knowledge', in M. Geist (ed.), *In the Public Interest: The Future of Canadian Copyright Law* (Irwin Law, 2005).

Townsend-Gard, E., 'In the trenches with §104A: an evaluation of the parties' arguments in *Golan* v. *Holder* as it heads to the Supreme Court' (2011) 64 *Vanderbilt Law Review En Banc* 199.

'January 1, 2003: the birth of the unpublished public domain and its international implications' (2006) 24 *Cardozo Arts & Entertainment Law Journal* 687.

Trosow, S., 'Fair dealing practices in the post-secondary education sector after the pentalogy', in M. Geist (ed.), *The Copyright Pentalogy: How the Supreme Court of Canada Shook the Foundations of Canadian Copyright Law* (University of Ottawa Press, 2013).

Turetsky, M. W., 'Applying copyright abandonment to the digital age' (2010) 19 *Duke Law & Technology Review* 22.

Urban, J. M., Karaganis, J. and Schofield, B. L., *Notice and Takedown in Everyday Practice*, version 2 (American Assembly, 2017).

US Copyright Office, Library of Congress, 'Copyright protection not available for names, titles or short phrases', Circular No. 34 (United States Copyright Office, 2006).

'International Copyright Relations of the United States' Circular 38A (United States Copyright Office, 2017) www.copyright.gov/circs/circ38a.pdf.

'Legal issues in mass digitization: a preliminary analysis and discussion document' (United States Copyright Office, 2011) www.copyright.gov/docs/massdigitization/USCOMassDigitization_October2011.pdf.

'Orphan works and mass digitization: a report of the Register of Copyrights' (United States Copyright Office, 2015).

'Report on orphan works: a report of the Register of Copyrights' (United States Copyright Office, 2006).

'Reproduction of Copyrighted Works by Educators and Librarians' Circular 21 (United States Copyright Office, undated) www.copyright.gov/circs/circ21.pdf.

van Gompel, S., 'Formalities in the digital era: an obstacle or opportunity?', in L. Bently et al. (eds.), *Global Copyright: Three Hundred Years Since the Statute of Anne, From 1709 to Cyberspace* (Edward Elgar, 2010).

van Gompel, S. and Hugenholtz, P. B., 'The orphan works problem: the copyright conundrum of digitizing large-scale audiovisual archives, and how to solve it' (2010) 8(1) *Popular Communication: The International Journal of Media and Culture* 61–71.

Varian, H., 'Copyright term extension and orphan works' (2006) 15(6) *Industrial and Corporate Change* 965.

Vaughan-Nichols, S., 'It's an open-source world: 78 percent of companies run open-source software', ZDNet, 16 April 2016 www.zdnet.com/article/its-an-open-source-world-78-percent-of-companies-run-open-source-software/.

Vaver, D., 'Copyright defenses as user rights' (2013) 60 *Journal of the Copyright Society of the USA* 661.

*Copyright Law* (Irwin, 2000).

Vinelli, R., 'Bringing down the walls: how technology is being used to thwart parallel importers amid the international confusion concerning exhaustion of rights' (2009) 17(1) *Cardozo Journal of International & Comparative Law* 101.

Vise, D., *The Google Story* (Macmillan, 2005).

von Haller, M., 'Enforcement of open source licenses?' *Digital Business Law* (Bird & Bird, 24 January 2017).

von Lewinski, S., 'Introduction', in M. M. Walter and S. von Lewinski (eds.), *European Copyright Law: A Commentary* (Oxford University Press, 2010).
  'Rental and lending rights directive', in M. M. Walter and S. von Lewinski (eds.), *European Copyright Law: A Commentary* (Oxford University Press, 2010).
  'Status of harmonization: limitations of rights', in M. M. Walter and S. von Lewinski (eds.), *European Copyright Law: A Commentary* (Oxford University Press, 2010).
von Lewinski, S. and Walter, M. M., 'Information society directive', in M. M. Walter and S. von Lewinski (eds.), *European Copyright Law: A Commentary* (Oxford University Press, 2010).
Vousden, S., *Infopaq* and the Europeanisation of copyright law' (2010) 1(2) *WIPO Journal* 197.
Walden, I., 'Open Source as philosophy, methodology and commerce: using law with attitude', in N. Shemtov and I. Walden (eds.), *Free and Open Source Software: Policy Law and Practice* (Oxford University Press, 2013).
Walker, R. and Depoorter, B., 'Unavoidable aesthetic judgments in copyright law: a community of practice standard' (2015) 109(2) *Northwestern University Law Review* 343.
Walter, M. M., 'Fundamental rights', in M. M. Walter and S. von Lewinski (eds.), *European Copyright Law: A Commentary* (Oxford University Press, 2010).
  'Term directive', in M. M. Walter and S. von Lewinski (eds.), *European Copyright Law: A Commentary* (Oxford University Press, 2010).
Walter, M. M. and von Lewinski, S. (eds.), *European Copyright Law: A Commentary* (Oxford University Press, 2010).
Weatherall, K., 'Internet intermediaries and copyright: an Australian agenda for reform', Policy paper prepared for Australian Digital Alliance, April 2011 www.digital.org.au/our-work/publication/internet-intermediaries-and-copyright-australian-agenda-reform.
White, A., 'The copyright tree: using German moral rights as the roots for enhanced authorship protection in the United States' (2010) 9(1) *Loyola Law and Technology Annual* 30.
White, E., 'The Berne Convention's flexible fixation requirement: a problematic provision for user-generated content' (2013) 13(2) *Chicago Journal of International Law* 685.
WIPO, 'Limitations and exceptions' (WIPO, various dates) www.wipo.int/copyright/en/limitations/.
  'Summary of the responses to the questionnaire for survey on copyright registration and deposit systems' (WIPO, 2010) www.wipo.int/export/sites/www/copyright/en/registration/pdf/legal_deposit_summary_responses.pdf and www.wipo.int/export/sites/www/copyright/en/registration/pdf/registration_summary_responses.pdf
WIPO SCCR, 'The case for a treaty on exceptions and limitations for libraries and archives: background paper by IFLA, ICA, EIFL and INNOVARTE', Document presented by Brazil, WIPO Doc. SCCR/23/3 (18 November 2011).

'Draft WIPO Treaty on exceptions and limitations for the disabled, educational and research institutions, libraries and archive centers', Proposal by the African Group, SCCR/20/11 (15 June 2010).

'Objectives and principles for exceptions and limitations for educational, teaching, and research institutions', Submitted by the United States of America, SCCR/27/8 (26 May 2014).

'Objectives and principles for exceptions and limitations for libraries and archives', Document presented by the United States of America, WIPO Doc SCCR/26/8 (10 January 2014).

Wittgenstein, L., *Philosophical Investigations*, tr. G. Anscomb (3rd edn, Blackwell, 1973).

WTO Panel Report, 'China: measures affecting the protection and enforcement of intellectual property rights', WT/DS-362/R (26 January 2009).

Wu, T., 'Tolerated use' (2007–8) *Columbia Journal of Law & the Arts* 617.

Xalabarder, R., 'Study on copyright limitations and exceptions for educational activities in North America, Europe, Caucasus, Central Asia and Israel', WIPO SCCR, Nineteenth Session, SCCR/19/8 (Geneva, 14–18 December 2009).

Yen, A., '*Eldred*, the First Amendment, and aggressive copyright claims' (2003) 40(3) *Houston Law Review* 673.

Yong, W., 'Copyright limitation for the benefit of poverty alleviation: is Chinese copyright provision to be a model for developing countries?' (2015) 3 *China Legal Science* 129.

Yu, P., 'The US–China dispute over TRIPS enforcement', in C. Antons (ed.), *The Enforcement of Intellectual Property Rights: Comparative Perspectives from the Asia-Pacific Region* (Kluwer Law International, 2011).

Zeinstra, M., 'Research: Orphan Works Directive does not work for mass digitisation', COMMUNIA, 16 February 2016 www.communia-association.org/2016/02/16/orphan-works-directive-does-not-work/.

Zimmerman, D., 'Is there a right to have something to say? One view of the public domain' (2004) 73 *Fordham Law Review* 297.

'It's an original! (?) In pursuit of copyright's elusive essence' (2005) 28 *Columbia Journal of Law & the Arts* 187.

# Index

abandonment of copyright. *see* works dedicated to the public
ability to use works
　non-importance of origin of, 42
　as public rights, 49
access to information
　copyright public domain and, 19
　disabled persons. *see* disabled persons; visually impaired persons
　permission-free. *see* permission-free use and access
　requirements to provide free access, 166
　works unavailable to the public, 471
adaptations. *see* derivative works
addresses and lectures, permissible exception for press and media uses, 136
administrative documents. *see* government documents
Agitha, T. G., 464, 466, 472
aid and assistance
　developing countries. *see* developing countries; Paris Appendix
　disabled persons. *see* disabled persons; visually impaired persons
　poverty-stricken areas, 468
altered works. *see* derivative works
anonymous works, term of copyright protection, 103
applied art, works of
　as protectible subject matter, 110
　term of copyright protection, 103, 271
archives. *see* libraries, museums and archives
arrangements. *see* derivative works
artistic works
　impliedly excluded from copyright, 209
　as protectible subject matter, 107
Australia
　adaptation right, 287
　archives, exceptions for, 382
　artistic works, 209

broadcasts
　compulsory licences, 471
　term of copyright protection, 268
cinematographic works, term of copyright protection, 268
'closed list' of protected categories, 208
communication right, 292
compulsory licences
　'blanket' licences, 408, 413
　broadcasts, 471
　collecting societies rules, 411
　for education and research, 459
　government use, 471
　and public domain, 415
　reforms as to, 415
　sound recordings, 471
　statutory licences, 69, 409
constitutional exclusions from copyright, 234
contractual exclusions to public rights, 172
Crown copyright, term of copyright protection, 269
distribution right, 297
education and research, exceptions for, 373
exclusive rights, 282
extension of copyright term, 106
fair dealing exception, 219, 339, 341
fixation principle, 201
foreign works, term of copyright protection, 269
free use exceptions to copyright, 67
government documents, 224
idea/expression dichotomy, 317
instrumentalist approach to copyright, 15
insubstantial parts of works, 64, 307
insubstantial works, 197, 199
Internet-enabled (de facto) public rights, 532, 539
libraries, exceptions for, 382

589

Australia (cont.)
  moral rights
    term of protection, 274
    waiver of, 511
  'news of the day', 219
  Open Access Policy, 167
  Open Government Data (OGD) licences, 508
  orphan works, 450
  parody or satire, exception for, 366
  performance right, 292
  plain English summary of copyright public domain, 74
  public interest exceptions, 56, 242
  public policy exclusions, 56, 237
  quotation exception, 361
  reproduction in different forms, 284
  reproduction right, 283
  reproductions 'in part', 307
  'safe harbour' immunities, 164
  search engines, legal issues, 528
  sound recordings
    compulsory licences, 470
    term of copyright protection, 268
  statutory deposit system, 156
  technological protection measures, 178
  temporary reproductions, 286, 353
  term of copyright protection, 62, 107
    broadcasts, 268
    cinematographic works, 268
    Crown copyright, 269
    extension of, 267
    foreign works, 269
    lack of harmonisation with US and EU terms, 269
    moral rights, 274
    seventy years term after author's death (*pma*), 267
    sound recordings, 268
    unpublished works, abolition of perpetual protection, 267
  works dedicated to the public, 56, 62
authorial works as protectible subject matter, 107
authors. *see* creators of works
autonomy and public domain, 13, 16
availability of works, non-determinativeness of, 42

Bannerman, Sara, 458
bare licences
  Creative Commons (CC) licences as, 503
  FOSS licences as, 488, 489
Beijing Treaty, overview of, 91

Benabou, Valérie-Laure, 19, 36
'benign' parties, statutory immunities for, 160
benign uses of works, de facto public right
  category of public domain, 9, 55, 70
  conditions for creating rights, 521
  definition of, 71
  global examples, 72
  implied licences distinguished, 523
  innovations in, 547
  international copyright law, 72
  national laws, 72
  reform of public domain, 560
Benkler, Yochai, 16, 32, 34, 35, 51
Berne Convention
  overview of, 90
  Paris Appendix. *see* Paris Appendix
  three-step test for copyright exceptions and compulsory licences, 133
    disability exceptions, 133
    and neighbouring rights, 133
    operation of, 129
    other exceptions in relation, 131
    and TRIPs 'homestyle' decision, 129
Birnhack, Michael, 18
blind persons. *see* visually impaired persons
books
  comic books (dōjinshi, manga), de facto public rights, 534
  still in copyright, de facto public rights as to mass digitisation, 536
Boyle, James, 6, 29, 36, 37, 43, 48
Brexit (UK withdrawal from EU), 25
broadcasts
  compulsory licences, 470
  ephemeral recordings, permissible exception for, 137
  neighbouring and related rights, 113
  rebroadcasts and retransmissions, remunerated use exceptions, 142
  remunerated use exceptions, 142
  term of copyright protection, 268
browsable commons of the web, 525
browsing (Internet), de facto public rights, 524
Burrell, Robert, 172, 509, 512, 513
business ('homestyle') exemptions for public performances of musical works, 129, 138

cable retransmissions, remunerated use exceptions, 142
Canada
  archives, exceptions for, 384
  communication right, 289

# Index

education and research, exceptions for, 374
exceptions, exclusions and limitations to copyright, 327
fair dealing exception, 50, 339, 342
formalities, 100
free use exceptions to copyright, 67
government documents, 225
human rights exclusions from copyright, 234
libraries, exceptions for, 384
Open Government Data (OGD) licences, 506, 507
orphan works, 442
parody or satire, exception for, 367
public policy exclusions, 238
public rights, 50, 52
reproduction in material form, 285
search engines, legal issues, 529
sound recordings, compulsory licences, 471
temporary reproductions, 356
term of copyright protection, 62, 272
case law. *see* law reports
categories of public rights
  comparison with theoretical conceptualisations, 80
  Deazley's conceptualisation, 78
  definitions and examples of, 54, 57
  Dusollier's conceptualisation, 77
  hierarchy of, 45
  hypothesis of, 82
  national (territorial) basis of, 55
  overview of, 9, 55
  reform of public domain, 551
  Samuelson's conceptualisation, 76
category of public domain, 55
CC licences. *see* Creative Commons (CC) licences
Cerda Silva, Alberto, 464
Chander, Anupam, 17, 35
China
  compulsory licences
    aid for poverty-stricken areas, 468
    broadcasts, 471
    for education and research, 461
    government use, 471
    sound recordings, 470
    statutory licences, 69, 418
  constitutional exclusions from copyright, 234
  exceptions, exclusions and limitations to copyright, 345
  fixation principle, 204
  government documents, 222

'news of the day', 220
orphan works schemes, 448
public interest defence to enforcement, 64
public interest exceptions, 242
public policy exclusions, 53, 239
term of copyright protection, 62
  applied art works, 271
  cinematographic works, 271
  fifty years term after author's death (*pma*), 270
  foreign works, 271
  neighbouring and related rights, 271
  photographic works, 271
  translation licences, 466
CHIs. *see* cultural heritage institutions
cinematographic works
  newsreels, permissible exception for, 136
  term of copyright protection, 103, 260, 268, 271
civil law and common law contrasted, 20
CJEU. *see* Court of Justice of the EU
Cohen, Julie, 18
Coleman, Allison, 172
collections of works as protectible subject matter, 109
comic books (dōjinshi, manga), de facto public rights, 534
common law and civil law contrasted, 20
commons
  as alternative term to 'public domain', 47
  browsable commons of the web, 525
  creation of Internet global commons, 529
  Creative Commons licences, 37, 39
  definition of, 36
  searchable commons of the web, 526
  'tragedy of the commons', 38, 47
communication of information and opinion, copyright public domain and, 19
communication rights, 116, 288
comparative law, common law and civil law contrasted, 20
comparison of terms, rule of, 105
compilations of works as protectible subject matter, 109
compulsory licences
  to aid poverty-stricken areas, 468
  broadcasts, 470
  category of public domain, 9, 55, 68
  definition of, 68, 392
  for education and research
    developing countries. *see* Paris Appendix
    national laws, 459

compulsory licences (cont.)
    reform of public domain, 557
    summary overview, 462
    extended collective licences (ECLs)
        and compulsory licensing, 424
        harmonisation of laws (EU), 426
        inclusion in copyright public
            domain, 397
        international copyright law, 425
        libraries, museums and archives, 467
        mass digitisation. *see* mass digitisation
        national laws, 427
        operation of, 421
    further potential for, 473
    government use, 471
    harmonisation of laws (EU), 405
    innovations in, 546
    international copyright law, 68
        'equitable remuneration' and 'fair
            compensation', 400
        introduction to, 399
        practice, 405
        specific provisions, 400
        three-step test, 403
    introduction to, 392
    mass digitisation, 454
    national laws, 68, 408
    orphan works, 434, 436, 437
    performances, 470
    and public domain, 395, 429, 430
    reform of public domain, 558
    sound recordings, 470
    subject areas of, 433
    and three-step test for copyright
        exceptions, 133
    translations, 465
    translations and reproductions in
        developing countries. *see* Paris
        Appendix
    types of, 398
    visually impaired persons, assistance
        for, 469
    works unavailable to the public, 471
computer software. *see* software
computer-generated works, term of
    copyright protection, 260
constitutional and human rights exclusions
    from copyright
    category of public domain, 9, 55, 60
    definition of, 60
    international copyright law, 60, 227
    national laws, 61, 228, 233
    permission-free use and access, 61
    and public domain, 235
    reform of public domain, 552

summary overview, 245
contractual exclusions to public rights,
    168, 173
contractual licences
    Creative Commons (CC) licences as, 503
    FOSS licences as, 488, 489
contractual public domain, 37
'copyleft' (viral) licences, 487
copyright
    affirmation of role of, 20
    common law and civil law contrasted, 20
    critical perspective on, 13
    current study reconceptualisation of, 7
    definition of, 20
    enforcement of, 147
    essential prerequisites for, 182
    exceptions and limitations. *see*
        exceptions, exclusions and
        limitations to copyright
    infringement. *see* infringement of
        copyright
    international law. *see* international
        copyright law
    jurisdictional perspectives, 20
    maximalism. *see* proprietarianism
    minimum levels of protection, obligation
        to confer, 96
    national laws. *see* national laws
    and negative liberty, 7
    as negative rights, 15
    and neighbouring rights. *see* neighbouring
        and related rights
    owners. *see* owners of copyright
    perpetual, 263
    proprietarianism. *see* proprietarianism
    public domain. *see* copyright public
        domain
    retroactive protection, national treatment
        and, 97
    revived, 262
    term. *see* term of copyright protection
    territorial basis of, 55
    user/public-oriented perspective, 3, 16
copyright misuse doctrine (US), 171
copyright public domain
    commons. *see* commons
    comparison of conceptualisations of, 76
    constraints on, 152
    content of current study, 8
    contractual, 37
    creativity and, 17
    culture and, 18
    current study approach to, 6, 25
    current study assumptions about, 11
    current study methodology, 12

## Index

de facto. *see* Internet-enabled (de facto) public rights
definition of. *see* definition of copyright public domain
democracy and, 19
exclusive rights in relation, 544
hierarchy of public domain categories, 45
inclusion of exceptions in, 33
innovations in public domain categories, 546
international law. *see* international copyright law
licensing and. *see* licensing
national laws. *see* national laws
new perspective on, 543
as permission-free use and access, 78, 80
plain English positive statement of, 74
previous conceptualisations of, 4
public and private domains in relation, 43
'public domain', origin of term, 248
public domain theory, 153
public rights. *see* public rights
'realist' perspective of, 10
reform of. *see* reform of public domain
'scale' of private to public, 44
as sum of public rights, 72
supports for, 152
territorial basis of, 55
theoretical perspectives on, 12
values of, 17
copyright-expired works. *see* works where copyright has expired
copyright term. *see* term of copyright protection
copyright works. *see* works
Corbett, Susan, 497
Court of Justice of the EU (CJEU), judicial harmonisation by, 24
Creative Commons (CC) licences
attributes of, 495
estoppel, 504
extent and importance, 494
global standards for, 480
if contract or bare licence, 503
internationalisation in Version 4, 497
introduction to, 493
as neutral licence, 39
as part of public domain, 37, 70
potential legal issues, 503
privity, 504
and public domain, 498
public domain dedications (CC0), 514
Public Domain Mark, 515
revocation of, 504
suite of licences, 495

'creative spark' doctrine, 138
creators of works
authors' rights in civil law jurisdictions, 20
authorship threshold. *see* thresholds for authorship and originality
benefit from permission-free use and access, 47
copyright public domain as essential resource for, 17
fifty years copyright term after author's death (*pma*), 270
permission-free use and access to works, 40
seventy years copyright term after author's death (*pma*), 62, 256, 267
as users, 8, 18
Crews, Kenneth, 428
critical perspective on copyright law, 13
Crown copyright. *see* government documents
cultural heritage institutions (CHIs)
compulsory licences overview of, 467
reform of public domain, 559
Creative Commons (CC) public domain dedications (CC0), 514
digitisation of works. *see* mass digitisation
permitted use exception for orphan works, 445
and public domain, 469
reform of public domain, 557
*see also* libraries, museums and archives
culture and copyright public domain, 18

data streaming. *see* Internet streaming
databases, originality threshold, 192, 194, 196
de facto public domain. *see* benign uses of works; Internet-enabled (de facto) public rights
Deazley, Ronan, 16, 32, 34, 39, 42, 44, 46, 48, 78, 80, 153, 511
dedication of works to public. *see* works dedicated to the public
defences for infringement. *see* infringement of copyright
definition of copyright public domain
boundary of public and private domains, 46
'commons' as alternative term, 47
current study approach to, 27
dichotomy at level of exceptions, 45
early approaches to, 27
hierarchy of public domain categories, 45

definition of public domain (cont.)
  one definition or many, 28
  origin of ability to use, non-importance of, 42
  as permission-free use and access, 4, 8, 19, 31, 48, 51
  permission-free use and access, concept of, 31, 48
  positive definition, 30
  proposed definition, 40, 53
  public and private domains in relation, 43
  public rights, 49, 52
  'scale' of private to public, 44
  scope of, 33
  terminological issues, 47
  user-centred and use-centred definition, 42
democracy and copyright public domain, 19
deposit systems. *see* statutory deposit systems
derivative works
  adaptation rights, 116, 282, 287
  protectible subject matter, 109
  translations and reproductions
    compulsory licences by developing countries. *see* Paris Appendix licences, 465
    machine translations for private use, de facto public rights, 530
    and public domain, 466
    reform of public domain, 559
developing countries, compulsory licences. *see* Paris Appendix
Digital Single Market Strategy (EU), 23
digitisation. *see* mass digitisation
directives (EU), 22
disabled persons
  three-step test for copyright exceptions, 133
  *see also* visually impaired persons
distribution right, 118, 294
dōjinshi (Japanese self-published graphic stories), de facto public rights, 534
Drahos, Peter, 14, 16, 48
Drassinower, Abraham, 20, 279
Droz, Numa, 123
duration of copyright. *see* term of copyright protection
Dusollier, Severine, 19, 30, 33, 36, 77, 80

e-commerce, 'safe harbour' immunities for, 163
ECLs (extended collective licences). *see* compulsory licences
EEA. *see* European Economic Area

education and research
  compulsory licensing
    by developing countries. *see* Paris Appendix
    reform of public domain, 559
  exceptions for
    international copyright law, 369
    and public domain, 377
  permissible exception for, 134
  reform of public domain, 557
  teaching, permissible exception for, 134
Elkin-Koren, Niva, 497
enforcement
  international copyright law, 147
  public interest defence. *see* public interest defence to enforcement
  public policy refusals against. *see* public policy exclusions
ephemeral recordings by broadcasting organisations, permissible exception for, 137
estoppel, Creative Commons (CC) licences, 504
European Economic Area (EEA), relevance of EU directives to, 23
European law, constitutional and human rights exclusions from copyright, 60
European Union (EU)
  adaptation right, 287
  archives, exceptions for, 380
  compulsory licences
    broadcasts, 471
    for education and research, 461
    extended collective licences (ECLs), 426
    judicial harmonisation by CJEU, 407
    sound recordings, 471
    statutory harmonisation, 405
  constitutional exclusions from copyright, 60, 61, 230, 235
  contractual exclusions to public rights, 171
  databases, originality threshold applied to, 192, 194, 196
  Digital Single Market Strategy, 23
  directives, 22
  distribution right, 294
  education and research, exceptions for, 370
  EEA relevance of directives, 23
  exceptions, exclusions and limitations to copyright
    closed list of, 328
    constitutional and human rights exclusions, 60, 61, 230, 235
    parody or satire, 364

Index 595

partial harmonisation, 330
reform proposals, 332
regulatory framework, 329
terminology, 326
extended collective licences (ECLs), 426
extension of copyright term, 106
free of charge or open source software (FOSS) licences, 493
free use exceptions to copyright, 67
harmonisation
  judicial harmonisation by CJEU, 24
  originality threshold, 194, 196
  progress of, 22
  protection of computer programs and databases, 213
human rights exclusions from copyright, 60, 61, 230, 235
idea/expression dichotomy, 313
insubstantial parts of works, 64, 306
insubstantial works, 197
Internet-enabled public rights, 528
lending right, 300
libraries, exceptions for, 380
mass digitisation, 454, 455
'news of the day', 216
originality threshold, harmonisation of laws, 194, 196
Orphan Works Directive
  effectiveness, 439
  provisions, 437
orphan works schemes, 440
parody, exception for, 364
parody or satire, exception for, 364
quotation exception, 358
rental right, 300
reproduction right, 282
reproductions 'in part', 306
'safe harbour' immunities, 161, 163
satire, exception for, 364
search engines, legal issues, 528
sound recordings, compulsory licences, 471
technological protection measures, 177
temporary reproductions, 286
term of copyright protection, 62
  extension for sound recordings, 257
  'foreign' works, 258
  harmonisation, 255
  moral rights, 259
  other changes, 257
  seventy years after author's death (*pma*), 256
  transitional provisions, 259
term of copyright protection extension, 5
UK withdrawal (Brexit), 25

voluntary licences, 70
exceptions, exclusions and limitations to copyright
  categories of, 125, 350
  civil law (*droit d'auteur*) closed list systems, 328, 345
  comparative approaches to, 325, 347
  constitutional and related exclusions. *see* constitutional and human rights exclusions from copyright
  dichotomy at level of, 45
  'exceptions' and 'limitations' distinguished, 124, 326
  'exclusions', definition of, 125
  express exceptions. *see* free use exceptions to copyright
  express exclusions. *see* works expressly excluded from copyright
  facts and ideas, 4, 110
  fair dealing. *see* fair dealing exceptions
  fair use. *see* fair use exception
  free use exceptions. *see* free use exceptions to copyright
  and global public domain, 114
  harmonisation of laws (EU), 329
  implied exclusions. *see* works impliedly excluded from copyright
  importance of public interest limitations, 123
  inclusion in copyright public domain, 33
  international copyright law, 150, 328
  introduction to, 123
  national laws, 328
  open-ended exceptions. *see* fair dealing exceptions; fair use exception
  and public domain, 145, 389
  reform of public domain, 555
  remunerated use exceptions. *see* remunerated use exceptions
  scope of, 124
  three-step test. *see* three-step test for copyright exceptions
exclusions. *see* exceptions, exclusions and limitations to copyright
exclusive rights
  adaptation (derivative) right, 116, 282, 287
  communication right, 116, 288
  comparative approaches to definition of, 281
  copyright as consisting of, 7, 34
  dichotomy between public and private domains, 45
  distribution right, 116, 294
  'free use' exceptions to, 66

## 596  Index

exclusive rights (cont.)
  and global public domain, 114, 119
  lending right, 118, 300
  performance right, 116, 288
  public communication right (EU), 289
  public domains in relation, 544
  rental right, 118, 300
  reproduction in different forms, 284
  reproduction in 'material form', 284
  reproduction right, 282, 283
  temporary reproductions, 286
  uses clearly outside, 280
  uses of works outside, 280
    category of public domain, 9, 55, 65
    definition of, 66
    international copyright law, 66
    national laws, 66
    and public domain, 302
expired-copyright works. *see* works where copyright has expired
express exceptions. *see* free use exceptions to copyright
express exclusions. *see* works expressly excluded from copyright
expression
  fact/expression dichotomy, 320
  idea/expression dichotomy, 65, 110, 186, 229, 312, 322
  and public domain, 322
extended collective licences (ECLs). *see* compulsory licences
extension of copyright. *see* term of copyright protection

facts
  category of public domain, 9, 55, 65
  copyright not extending to, 4, 110
  definition of, 65
  fact/expression dichotomy, 320, 554
  international copyright law, 65
  national laws, 65
  non-infringing uses of, 312
  reform of public domain, 554
fair dealing exceptions
  common law, 67, 329
  and contractual exclusions to public rights, 171
  national laws, 339
  'news of the day', 218, 219
  as public rights, 50
  reform of public domain, 556
fair use exception
  amount and substantiality of part used, 337
  for education and research, 375

  effect of use on potential market, 337
  factors for, 335
  if 'right' or 'privilege'?, 327
  influence of, 333
  mass digitisation, 457
  nature of work, 336
  operation of, 334
  parody or satire, 367
  and permission-free use and access, 32
  as public right, 50
  purpose and character of use, 335
  quotations, 362
  reform of public domain, 556
fan fiction, de facto public rights, 534
Favale, Marcella, 434, 458
Ficsor, Mihály, 123
fifty years term after author's death (*pma*), 270
films. *see* cinematographic works
fixation principle
  introduction to, 200
  and public domain, 204, 206
  requirement for, 111
FOI. *see* freedom of information
foreign works
  national treatment, 266
  restoration of copyright, 266
  term of copyright protection, 258, 271
formalities
  definition of, 100
  prohibition of, 99
  and public domain, 101
FOSS licences. *see* free or open source software (FOSS) licences
France
  adaptation right, 288
  authors' rights (*droit d'auteur*), 20, 193
  compulsory licences, 407
  fixation principle, 203
  mass digitisation, 454
  moral rights, term of protection, 274
  'news of the day', 217
  Open Government Data (OGD) licences, 506
  'open list' of protected categories, 211
  orphan works schemes, 440
  parody or satire, exception for, 365
  quotation exception, 358
  reproduction right, 282
free access distribution
  open content distinguished, 166
  requirements to provide, 166
'free of known copyright restrictions', works that are, 515

Index    597

free or open source software (FOSS)
        licences
    classification of, 487
    conditions for, 483
    'copyleft' (viral) licences, 487
    emergence of, 37
    enforcement of
        civil law, 492
        common law, 490
    Free Software Definition, 484
    governance of, 486
    government supports for, 493
    if contract or bare licence, 489
    introduction to, 482
    legal status of, 488
    'no copyleft' licences, 487
    Open Source Definition, 483
    as part of public domain, 38, 70
    use of, 485
Free Software Definition, 484
free trade agreements (FTAs), intellectual
    property obligations in, 92
free use exceptions to copyright
    addresses and lectures, press and media
        uses of, 136
    business ('homestyle') exemptions for
        public performances of musical
        works, 129
    category of public domain, 9, 55, 66
    definition of, 67
    education and teaching, 134
    ephemeral recordings by broadcasting
        organisations, 137
    international copyright law, 67, 128
    minor exceptions or reservations, 138
    national laws, 67
    neighbouring rights, 138
    press and media, 135, 136
    and public domain, 140
    quotations, 134
    three-step test
        and, 133
        disability exceptions, 133
        'homestyle' decision, 129
        and neighbouring rights, 133
        operation of, 129
        other exceptions in relation, 131
    visually impaired persons, 140
freedom and copyright public domain,
    13, 16
freedom of expression
    copyright public domain and, 16, 19, 226
    human rights exclusions from
        copyright, 235
    'news of the day', 218

    and permission-free use and access, 245
    public policy exclusions from
        copyright, 240
freedom of information (FOI), 167

Geiger, Christophe, 395
Geist, Michael, 176
General Public Licence (GPL). *see* free or
    open source software (FOSS)
    licences
Germany
    adaptation right, 288
    authors' rights (*Urheberrecht*), 20, 193
    communication right, 288
    constitutional and human rights
        exclusions from copyright, 61
    exceptions, exclusions and limitations to
        copyright, 326
    fixation principle, 203
    free or open source software, 492
    government documents, 222
    human rights exclusions from
        copyright, 233
    mass digitisation, 454
    moral rights, term of protection, 274
    'news of the day', 217
    open content licences, 501
    Open Government Data (OGD)
        licences, 506
    parody or satire, exception for, 365
    quotation exception, 359
    reproduction right, 282
    technological protection measures, 179
    works dedicated to the public, 512
GFDL. *see* GNU Free Documentation
    License
Ginsburg, Jane, 129, 175, 176, 177, 403,
    437, 464
global public domain
    definition of, 88
    exclusive rights, 114, 119
    and international copyright law, 89,
        120
    introduction to, 87
    main multilateral agreements, 90
    minimum levels of copyright protection,
        obligation to confer, 96
    most-favoured-nation (MFN) principle,
        92, 96, 255
    national treatment and, 98
    national treatment principle, 95
    prohibition of formalities, 99
    protectible subject matter, 107
    structural effects of international
        agreements, 93

global public domain (cont.)
  term of copyright protection, 102
GNU Free Documentation License
    (GFDL), 500
Goldstein, Paul, 200
Gompel, Stef van, 453
good faith infringement defence, 165
Gorman, Robert, 289
government documents
  archives laws, 168
  Crown copyright, 60, 127, 167, 222,
    224, 269
  exemption from copyright, 505
  express exclusion from copyright, 59,
    127, 221
  free access to, 167
  law reports, de facto public rights of
    reproduction, 532, 536
  legislation, de facto public rights of
    reproduction, 532
  Open Government Data (OGD)
    licences, 505
  Parliamentary copyright, 127, 222, 224
  provision of reproductions, laws
    requiring, 168
government use of documents, compulsory
    licences, 471
GPL (General Public Licence). *see* free or
    open source software (FOSS)
    licences
graphic stories (dōjinshi, manga), de facto
    public rights, 534
Guadamuz, Andrés, 490, 492, 513, 514

Hardin, Garrett, 47
harmonisation of copyright laws. *see*
    European Union
headlines, denial of protection for, 196
Hess, Charlotte, 38, 49
Hudson, Emily, 509, 510, 512, 513
Hugenholtz, P. Bernt, 22, 200, 326, 453
Hughes, Justin, 199
human rights. *see* constitutional and human
    rights exclusions from copyright
Hungary, orphan works schemes, 447

ideas
  category of public domain, 9, 55, 65
  copyright not extending to, 4, 110
  definition of, 65
  idea/expression dichotomy, 65, 110, 186,
    229, 312, 322, 554
  international copyright law, 65
  national laws, 65
  non-infringing uses of, 312

  and public domain, 322
  reform of public domain, 554
implied licences, de facto public rights
    distinguished, 523
incidental copies, exception for, 351
India
  archives, exceptions for, 387
  compulsory licences
    assistance for disabled, 470
    broadcasts, 471
    for education and research, 462
    statutory licences, 69, 420
    works unavailable to the public, 472
  education and research, exceptions
    for, 376
  free or open source software (FOSS)
    licences, 493
  government documents, 225
  libraries, exceptions for, 387
  orphan works schemes, 447
  'safe harbour' immunities, 165
  search engines, legal issues, 529
  technological protection measures, 179
  temporary reproductions, 356
  translation licences, 466
  works dedicated to the public, 62, 512, 513
  works unavailable to the public, 471
industrial designs and models as protectible
    subject matter, 110
'industrious collection' doctrine, 190
information
  access to, 19
  communication of, 19
  public, permissible exception for,
    135, 136
infringement of copyright
  good faith defence, 165
  public interest defence. *see* public
    interest defence to enforcement
  *see also* non-infringing uses of protected
    works
innocent infringement defence, 165
instrumentalism
  application by current study, 13, 15
  in official policy documents, 15
  qualified, 14
insubstantial parts of works
  category of public domain, 9, 55, 64
  definition of, 64
  international copyright law, 64
  national laws, 64, 306
  non-infringing uses of, 305
  and public domain, 310
  reform of public domain, 554
  reproductions 'in part' (EU), 306

# Index

insubstantial works
  de minimis threshold, 196
  denial of protection for, 196
  labour, skill or judgement threshold, 197
  and public domain, 199, 206
intellectual commons. *see* commons
intellectual property rights (IPRs)
  as natural property right, 15
  public rights balanced with, 5
international copyright law
  benign uses of works, de facto public right, 72
  compulsory licences, 68
  constitutional and human rights exclusions from copyright, 60
  enforcement, 147
  facts and ideas, 65
  free use exceptions to copyright, 67
  global public domain. *see* global public domain
  insubstantial parts of works, 64
  public interest defence to enforcement, 64
  public policy exclusions, 63
  uses of works outside exclusive rights, 66
  voluntary licences, 70
  works dedicated to the public, 62
  works failing copyright minimum requirements, 57
  works where copyright has expired, 51
Internet browsing and searching, de facto public rights, 524
Internet commons (of the web)
  browsable, 525
  searchable, 526
Internet-enabled (de facto) public rights
  borderline cases, 530
  browsable commons of the web, 525
  browsing and searching, 524
  conditions for, 521
  creation of global commons, 529
  definition and indicia, 520
  fan fiction, 534
  global public rights, 518
  implied licences distinguished, 523
  importance of, 540
  in Internet-published content, 519
  mass digitisation
    books still in copyright, 536
    commercially published law reports, 536
    newspapers, 536

non-commercial digitisation of sets of works, 533
  non-profit journals, 534
  private use machine translations, 530
  and public domain, 536
  reproductions of legislation and case law, 532
  'rights cushion' distinguished, 522
  rights that are not, 522
  search engines, legal issues, 527
  searchable commons of the web versus exclusive rights, 525
  self-published graphic stories (dōjinshi, manga), 534
  'spillover' effects of national domains on other countries, 537, 539
  tolerated uses distinguished, 522, 536
Internet-published content, de facto public rights in, 519
Internet search engines
  finding works by using, 159
  legal issues, 527
Internet service providers (ISPs), 'safe harbour' immunities for, 160
Internet streaming
  remunerated use exceptions, 142
  streamed retransmissions, remunerated use exceptions, 142
IPRs. *see* intellectual property rights
ISPs. *see* Internet service providers

Japan
  government documents, 222
  orphan works, 442
  self-published graphic stories (dōjinshi, manga), de facto public rights, 534
  technological protection measures (TPMs), 179
Johnson, Phillip, 509, 510
journalism. *see* press
journals (non-profit), de facto public rights as to mass digitisation, 534
judicial harmonisation by CJEU, 24
jurisdictions. *see* national laws

known copyright restrictions, works free of, 515
Korea
  exceptions, exclusions and limitations to copyright, 346
  orphan works, 442
  quotation exception, 361
  search engines, legal issues, 529
  temporary reproductions, 355
Krasilovsky, M. William, 5

600  Index

Lange, David, 5, 6, 27
law reports, de facto public rights as to reproduction, 532, 536
laws. *see* government documents
lectures, permissible exception for press and media uses, 136
legal deposit. *see* statutory deposit systems
legal documents, published. *see* government documents
legal proceedings, express exclusion for speeches from, 127
legislation. *see* government documents
Lemley, Mark, 15
lending rights, 118, 300, 468
Lessig, Lawrence, 31, 36, 38, 153
liberty, copyright and negative liberty, 16
libraries, museums and archives
    archiving of government documents, laws for, 168
    compulsory licences
        extended collective licences (ECLs), 467
        international law, 467
    Creative Commons (CC) public domain dedications (CC0), 514
    exceptions for, 379
    harmonisation of laws (EU), 380
    and public domain, 387
    reform of public domain, 557
licensing
    compulsory licences. *see* compulsory licences
    voluntary licences. *see* voluntary licences
Liebowitz, Stan, 254
limitations. *see* exceptions, exclusions and limitations to copyright
limited liability schemes for orphan works, 448, 452
Lindberg, Stanley W., 5, 50
literary works
    authorial works as protectible subject matter, 107
    dōjinshi (Japanese self-published graphic stories), de facto public rights, 534
    insubstantial works, 196
    as protectible subject matter, 107
    pseudonymous works, term of copyright protection, 103
    sets of works, de facto public rights as to digitisation, 533
    unpublished works. *see* unpublished works
Litman, Jessica, 5, 17, 32
location systems. *see* registration, recordation and location systems

Locke, John, 247
Loren, Lydia Pallas, 503, 504

machine translations for private use, de facto public rights, 530
MacQueen, Hector, 171
mandatory exceptions. *see* free use exceptions to copyright
manga, Internet-enabled de facto public rights, 534
Margolis, Stephen, 254
Marrakesh Treaty
    overview of, 92
    *see also* visually impaired persons
mass digitisation
    harmonisation of laws (EU), 455
    Internet-enabled (de facto) public rights
        books still in copyright, 536
        commercially published law reports, 536
        newspapers, 536
        non-commercial digitisation of sets of works, 533
        non-profit journals, 534
    introduction to, 454
    national laws, 454
    reform of public domain, 559
maximalism. *see* proprietarianism
McDonagh, Luke, 488
mechanical recordings, remunerated use exception for, 142
media
    'news of the day'
        express exclusion from copyright, 59, 126, 216
        fair dealing exceptions, 218, 219
    newspapers, de facto public rights as to mass digitisation, 536
    newsreels, permissible exception for, 136
    permissible exceptions for, 135, 136
Mehra, Salil, 535
merger (of idea with expression) doctrine, 319
Merges, Robert, 15, 504, 523
MFN. *see* most-favoured-nation (MFN) principle
microworks, 196
Mill, John Stuart, 19
minimum human authorship doctrine, 189
minimum levels of copyright protection, obligation to confer, 96
minimum term. *see* term of copyright protection
minor exceptions or reservations to copyright, 138

# Index

Moglen, Eben, 490
moral rights
  international law, 273
  permission-free use and access, 104
  term of copyright protection, 104, 259, 273
  waiver of, 511
most-favoured-nation (MFN) principle
  exemption from, 105
  free trade agreements, 92
  national treatment and, 96
movies. *see* cinematographic works
museums. *see* libraries, museums and archives
musical works
  business ('homestyle') exemptions for public performances of, 129, 138
  mechanical recordings, remunerated use exception for, 142
  public performances of
    business ('homestyle') exemptions for, 129, 138
    minor exceptions or reservations to copyright, 138

names, denial of protection for, 198
national laws
  Australia. *see* Australia
  benign uses of works, de facto public right, 72
  Canada. *see* Canada
  China. *see* China
  compulsory licences, 68
  constitutional and human rights exclusions from copyright, 61
  copyright public domain
    essential prerequisites for, 182
    supports and constraints, 152
  facts and ideas, 65
  France. *see* France
  free use exceptions. *see* free use exceptions to copyright
  Germany. *see* Germany
  Hungary. *see* Hungary
  insubstantial parts of works, 64
  Japan. *see* Japan
  jurisdictional perspectives, 20
  Korea. *see* Korea
  New Zealand. *see* New Zealand
  public interest defence to enforcement, 64
  public policy exclusions, 63
  public rights
    constraints on, 168
    supports for, 153
  territorial basis of public rights, 55
  UK. *see* United Kingdom
  USA. *see* United States
  uses of works outside exclusive rights, 66
  voluntary licences, 70
  works dedicated to the public, 62
  works expressly excluded from copyright, 56, 215
  works failing copyright minimum requirements, 57, 185
  works impliedly excluded from copyright (statutory 'gaps'), 58, 207
  works where copyright has expired, 62
national public domains. *see* national laws
national treatment
  and global public domain, 98
  principle of, 95
  retroactive protection and, 97
natural property right, intellectual property as, 15
negative liberty, copyright and, 16
neighbouring and related rights
  free use exceptions to, 138
  protectible subject matter, 112
  and remunerated use exceptions, 143
  term of copyright protection, 271
  and three-step test for copyright exceptions, 133
  works and, 3
Netanel, Neil, 335
neutral licensing
  compulsory. *see* compulsory licences
  voluntary. *see* voluntary licences
New Zealand
  artistic works, 210
  government documents, 225
  originality threshold, 190
  technological protection measures (TPMs), 180
'news of the day'
  express exclusion from copyright, 59, 126, 216
  fair dealing exceptions, 218, 219
newspapers, de facto public rights as to mass digitisation, 536
newsreels, permissible exception for, 136
Nimmer, David, 335
'no copyleft' licences, 487
non-infringing uses of protected works
  introduction to, 279
  uses of ideas and facts, 312
  uses of 'insubstantial' parts, 305
  uses outside exclusive rights, 280

## 602　Index

non-original photographs, term of copyright protection, 260
non-profit journals, de facto public rights as to mass digitisation, 534

obscene publications. *see* public policy exclusions
official documents. *see* government documents
Okediji, Ruth, 464
open content licences
　definition of, 494
　enforcement actions, 501
　extent and importance, 500
　free access distribution distinguished, 166
　GNU Free Documentation License (GFDL), 500
　government supports for, 505
　introduction to, 493
　Open Data Commons (ODC) licences, 500
　Open Government Data (OGD) licences, 505
Open Data Commons (ODC) licences, 500
Open Government Data (OGD) licences, 505
Open Source Definition, 483
open source licences. *see* free or open source software
open-ended exceptions. *see* fair dealing exceptions; fair use exception
opinions, communication of, 19
*ordre public* exclusions. *see* public policy exclusions
originality
　civil law, 193
　databases, application to, 192, 194, 196
　harmonisation of laws (EU), 194
　and public domain, 191, 196
　standard of, 57
　threshold. *see* thresholds for authorship and originality
orphan works
　compulsory licences and ECL schemes in relation, 436, 437, 453
　definition of, 434
　harmonisation of laws (EU), 437
　hybrid approaches to, 453
　international copyright law, 436
　national laws
　　limited liability schemes, 452
　　official licensing schemes, 441, 451
　　overview of, 441
　　problems of, 434

　and public domain, 450
　reform of public domain, 558
　schemes, 435
　unpublished works, 437
Ostrom, Elinor, 37, 48, 49
owners of copyright, benefit from permission-free use and access, 47

Paris Appendix
　conditions for compulsory licences, 463
　effectiveness, 69, 144, 464, 465
　overview of, 143, 462
　and public domain, 465
Parliamentary copyright. *see* government documents
parody or satire
　exception for, 363
　and public domain, 368
　reform of public domain, 556
partially-sighted persons. *see* visually impaired persons
Patry, William, 249
Patterson, L. Ray, 5, 50
performance rights, 116, 288
performances
　compulsory licences, 470
　musical works, business ('homestyle') exemptions for public performances, 112, 138
　neighbouring and related rights, 112
　'performers', definition of, 112
permissible exceptions. *see* free use exceptions to copyright
permission-free use and access
　access and use distinguished, 34
　and, 35
　availability of, 40
　benefit from, 47
　copyright public domain as, 4, 8, 19, 31, 48, 51, 78, 80
　creativity and, 40
　and fair use exception, 32
　and freedom of expression, 245
　moral rights, 104
　protection by public domain, 52
　as public rights, 49, 76
　rights-based limitations on copyright, 61
　universal availability of works, 42
　uses that require payment, 35
　works expressly excluded from copyright, 226
　works failing copyright minimum requirements, 206
perpetual copyright, 263
phonograms. *see* sound recordings

# Index

Phonograms Convention, overview of, 91
photographs
  non-original photographs, term of copyright protection, 260
  originality threshold, 194
  term of copyright protection, 103, 271
phrases, denial of protection for, 198
pluralism, application by current study, 13
political speeches, express exclusion from copyright, 127
*post mortem auctoris, pma*, 62
poverty-stricken areas, compulsory licensing to aid, 468
pre-emption doctrine, 169
press. *see* media
print disabilities *see* visually impaired persons
privity, Creative Commons (CC) licences, 504
prohibition of formalities, 99
proprietarianism
  negative impact of, 16, 544
  reinforcement of, 11, 15, 26, 543
  rejection of, 11, 13, 20
protectible subject matter
  applied art, works of, 110
  authorial works, 107
  compilations and collections of works, 109
  derivative works, 109
  exceptions. *see* exceptions, exclusions and limitations to copyright
  fixation, requirement for, 111
  industrial designs and models, 110
  literary and artistic works, 107
  neighbouring rights, 112
  and public domain, 113
  scope of, 107
  software, 109
pseudonymous works, term of copyright protection, 103
public addresses, permissible exception for press and media uses, 136
public domain. *see* copyright public domain
public domain dedications. *see* works dedicated to the public
Public Domain Mark, 515
public information, permissible exception for, 135, 136
public interest defence to enforcement
  category of public domain, 9, 55, 63
  definition of, 63
  international copyright law, 64
  national laws, 64

public interest exceptions
  introduction to, 241
  national laws, 242
  and public domain, 244
  public policy exclusions distinguished, 241
  reform of public domain, 553
  summary overview, 245
public performances of musical works
  business ('homestyle') exemptions for, 129, 138
  minor exceptions or reservations to copyright, 138
public policy exclusions
  category of public domain, 9, 55, 63
  civil law, 239
  definition of, 63
  and freedom of expression, 240
  international copyright law, 63
  international law, 236
  introduction to, 236
  national laws, 63, 236
  and public domain, 240
  public interest exceptions distinguished, 241
  summary overview, 245
public policy refusals against enforcement, reform of public domain, 553
public rights
  ability to use works as, 49
  categories of. *see* categories of public rights
  concept of, 4, 7
  constraints on, 168, 181
  contractual exclusions, 168, 173
  and copyright public domain, 18
  copyright public domain as, 52
  creation by voluntary licences, 476
  intellectual property rights balanced with, 5
  Internet-enabled. *see* Internet-enabled (de facto) public rights
  permission-free use and access as, 49, 76
  plain English positive statement of, 74
  public domain as sum of, 72
  statutory 'safe harbour' immunities for 'benign' parties, 160
  supports for, 153

quotations
  exception for, 133, 357
  and public domain, 362
  reform of public domain, 556

# Index

Radin, Margaret, 504
Rahmatian, Andreas, 193
'realist' perspective of copyright public domain, 10
rebroadcasts and retransmissions, remunerated use exceptions, 142
recordings. *see* sound recordings
reform of public domain
  achievable reforms, 543
  constraints on public domains, 548
  contemporary values and future of public rights, 560
  exclusive rights and public domains in relation, 544
  future goals, 543
  future reforms, 562
  innovations in public domain categories, 546
  new perspective on public domains, 543
  strengthening of public domains, 551
  supports for public domains, 548
registration, recordation and location systems
  benefits of, 159
  locating works under public domain licences, 159
  official voluntary registration systems, 157
  public domain functions of, 157, 159
  recordation systems, 158
relinquishment of copyright. *see* works dedicated to the public
remunerated use exceptions
  broadcasts, 142
  compulsory licences in developing countries: translations and reproductions, 143
  international law, 141
  mechanical recording of musical works, 142
  and neighbouring rights, 143
  and public domain, 144
rental rights, 118, 300
reporting, permissible exception for, 135, 136
reproductions of documents
  compulsory licences by developing countries. *see* Paris Appendix
  in different forms, 284
  international copyright law, 115
  laws requiring provision of, 168
  legislation and case law, de facto public rights, 532
  in 'material form', 284
  rights of, 282, 283
  temporary. *see* temporary reproductions
research. *see* education and research, exceptions for
retroactive copyright protection, national treatment and, 97
revived copyright, 262
Richards, Neal, 180
Ricketson, Sam, 129, 175, 176, 177, 403, 437, 464
right to information (RTI), 167
'rights cushion' concept, 522
Riis, Thomas, 425
Rome Convention, overview of, 90
Rothnie, Warwick, 511
rule of comparison of terms, 105

safe harbour immunities
  examples of, 161, 162, 163, 164
  operation of, 160
  public domain functions of, 161, 165
Samuels, Edward, 33
Samuelson, Pamela, 6, 28, 31, 44, 76, 80, 335
Satellite Convention, overview of, 91
satire. *see* parody or satire
Schovsbo, Jens, 425
*scènes à faire* doctrine, 320
search engines. *see* Internet search engines
searchable commons of the web, exclusive rights versus, 526
searching (Internet), de facto public rights, 524
self-published graphic stories (dōjinshi, manga), de facto public rights, 534
Senftleben, Martin, 326
Seng, Daniel, 165, 428, 459, 464
sets of works, de facto public rights as to digitisation, 533
seventy years term after author's death (*pma*), 62, 256, 267
'shareware' licences, 479
'short phrases', denial of protection for, 198
short works, 196
'skill and judgment' doctrine, 189
slogans, denial of protection for, 196
Snow, Ned, 327
software
  FOSS. *see* free or open source software (FOSS) licences
  originality threshold, 194
  as protectible subject matter, 109
  'shareware' licences, 479
  voluntary neutral licences, 39

# Index

sound recordings
  compulsory licences, 470
  ephemeral recordings for broadcasts, permissible exception for, 137
  mechanical recordings, remunerated use exception for, 142
  neighbouring and related rights, 112
  Phonograms Convention, overview of, 91
  term of copyright protection, 257, 261, 268
South Korea. *see* Korea
speeches, express exclusion from copyright, 127
statutory deposit systems
  examples of, 155
  overview of, 153
  public domain functions of, 157
statutory exceptions. *see* exceptions, exclusions and limitations to copyright
statutory 'free use' exceptions. *see* free use exceptions to copyright
statutory 'gaps'. *see* works impliedly excluded from copyright
statutory immunities for 'benign' parties, 160
Sterling, Adrian, 511
streaming. *see* Internet streaming
subject matter. *see* protectable subject matter
Sunder, Madhavi, 17, 35
surveillance of uses and uses of works, 180
'sweat' doctrine, 188

Taubman, Antony, 88
teaching. *see* education and research
technological protection measures (TPMs), 173
  international law, 175
  national laws, 176, 178, 179
  and public domain, 174, 180
  works subject to, 44
temporary reproductions
  exception for, 351
  exclusive rights, 286
  and public domain, 356
  reform of public domain, 556
term of copyright protection
  anonymous and pseudonymous works, 103
  applied art, works of, 103
  cinematographic works, 103
  exemption from MFN principle, 105
  extension of, 5, 61, 106, 249
  fifty years after author's death (*pma*), 270

'foreign' works, 258
general minimum duration rule, 103
global public domain, 102
harmonisation of laws (EU), 62, 255
international copyright law, 61, 248, 254
introduction to, 247
limits on, 247
minimum requirements for, 104
moral rights, 104, 259, 273
national laws, 62, 248, 260, 272
neighbouring rights, 106
photographs, 103
and public domain, 251
public domain and, 106
realist perspective on, 275
rule of comparison of terms, 105
seventy years after author's death (*pma*), 62, 256, 267
sound recordings, 257
special duration rules, 103
term-expired works. *see* works where copyright has expired
territorial basis of public rights, 55
three-step test for copyright exceptions and, 133
  disability exceptions, 133
  and neighbouring rights, 133
  operation of, 129
  other exceptions in relation, 131
  and TRIPs 'homestyle' decision, 129
thresholds for authorship and originality
  civil law, 193
  common law, 187
  databases, application to, 192
  harmonisation of laws (EU), 194
  'industrious collection' doctrine, 190
  international law, 186
  minimum 'creative spark', 188
  minimum human authorship doctrine, 189
  originality and public domain, 191
  originality standard, 57
  and public domain, 205
  'skill and judgment' doctrine, 189
titles, denial of protection for, 196
TPMs. *see* technological protection measures
'tragedy of the commons'. *see* commons
transient copies, exception for, 351
translations. *see* derivative works
TRIPs Agreement, overview of, 91
typographical arrangements, term of copyright protection, 260

# Index

UCC. *see* Universal Copyright Convention
United Kingdom (UK)
  abandonment of copyright, 510
  adaptation right, 287
  archives, exceptions for, 382
  artistic works, 209
  cinematographic works, 260
  'closed list' of protected categories, 208
  communication right, 291
  compulsory licences
    cultural heritage institutions (CHIs), 467
    extended collective licences (ECLs), 427, 467
    overview of, 416
    sound recordings, 471
  computer-generated works, 260
  contractual exclusions to public rights, 171
  copyright term extension, 249
  cultural heritage institutions (CHIs), 445
  Deazley's conceptualisation of public domain, 78
  distribution right, 297
  education and research
    compulsory licences, 461
    exceptions for, 372
  exclusive rights, 281
  extended collective licences (ECLs)
    lending right, 468
    libraries, museums and archives, 467
    overview of provisions, 427
  fair dealing exception, 171, 218, 339, 340
  fixation principle, 201
  free or open source software, 492
  government documents, 224
  human rights exclusions from copyright, 234
  idea/expression dichotomy, 312, 314
  insubstantial parts of works, 64, 306
  insubstantial works, 197, 199
  lending right, 302, 468
  libraries, museums and archives
    exceptions for, 382
    extended collective licences (ECLs), 382
  moral rights, term of protection, 260, 274
  'news of the day', 218
  non-original photographs, 260
  Open Government Data (OGD) licences, 506
  originality threshold, 187, 195, 196
  orphan works
    compulsory licence regulations, 443
    permitted use exception for CHIs, 445
    regulations, 443
  parody or satire, exception for, 365
  performance right, 292
  perpetual copyright, 263
  public interest defence to enforcement, 64
  public interest exceptions, 242, 244
  public interest exceptions to enforcement, 56
  public policy exclusions, 236
  public-dedicated works, 512
  quotation exception, 359
  rental right, 302
  reproduction in different forms, 284
  reproduction right, 283
  reproductions 'in part', 306
  revived copyright, 262
  'safe harbour' immunities, 161, 164
  sound recordings, 261
  sound recordings, compulsory licences, 471
  technological protection measures, 178
  temporary reproductions, 286, 353
  typographical arrangements, 260
  unpublished works
    abolition of perpetual protection ('2039 rule'), 261
    publication right in, 262
  withdrawal from EU (Brexit), 25
  works dedicated to the public, 512
  works falling outside protected categories, 209
United States (US)
  adaptation right, 287
  archives, exceptions for, 385
  business ('homestyle') exemptions for public performances of musical works, 129, 138
  communication right, 293
  compulsory licences, 417, 471
  constitutional and human rights exclusions from copyright, 61
  constitutional exclusions from copyright, 228, 235
  contractual exclusions to public rights, 169
  copyright misuse doctrine, 171
  copyright term extension, 250
  Creative Commons (CC) licences, 480, 494, 503
  'creative spark' doctrine, 188
  distribution right (first sale doctrine), 298
  education and research, exceptions for, 375

# Index

enforcement of copyright, 147
extension of copyright term, 106
fact/expression dichotomy, 320
facts and ideas, 65
fair use. *see* fair use exception
first sale doctrine, 238
fixation principle, 202
foreign works
  national treatment, 266
  restoration of copyright, 266
formalities, 100
free or open source software, 490
free use exceptions to copyright, 67
government documents, 223
idea/expression dichotomy, 229, 318
insubstantial parts of works, 64, 308
insubstantial works, 198, 199
Internet-enabled (de facto) public rights, 527, 536
libraries, exceptions for, 385
mass digitisation
  benign uses of books still in copyright, 536
  fair use, 457
  proposed ECL, 456
merger (of idea with expression) doctrine, 319
moral rights, term of protection, 274
national treatment, 98
'news of the day', 221
open content licences, 502
'open list' of protected categories, 212
orphan works, limited liability scheme, 448
parody or satire, exception for, 367
performance right, 293
preemption doctrine, 169
public policy exclusions, 238
public rights, 50
quotation exception, 362
registration and recordation system, 159
reproduction in different forms, 284
reproduction in material form, 285
reproduction right, 283
reproductions 'in part', 308
rule of comparison of terms, 105
'safe harbour' immunities, 161, 162
Samuelson's 'map' of public domain, 76
*scènes à faire* doctrine, 320
search engines, legal issues, 527
sound recordings, compulsory licences, 471
statutory deposit system, 155
'sweat' doctrine, 188
technological protection measures, 176

temporary reproductions, 354
term of copyright protection
  extension of, 5, 263, 264
  extent of, 62
  moral rights, 274
  statutory provision, 263
  unpublished works in existence in 1978, 265
  works created on or after 1978, term of protection, 265
  uses clearly outside exclusive rights, 280
  voluntary licences, 70, 480
  works dedicated to the public, 62, 511
universal availability of works, non-determinativeness of, 42
Universal Copyright Convention (UCC), overview of, 90
unpublished works
  abolition of perpetual protection, 267
  abolition of perpetual protection ('2039 rule'), 261
  orphan works, 437
  publication right in, 262
  term of copyright protection, 265
users of works
  creators of works as, 8, 18
  perspective on copyright, 3, 16
  surveillance of, 180
  user-centred definition of copyright public domain, 42
  works in relation, 18
uses of works
  benign uses. *see* benign uses of works
  government use, statutory licence for, 471
  origin of ability to use, non-importance of, 42
  outside exclusive rights
    category of public domain, 9, 55, 65
    definition of, 66
    international copyright law, 66
    national laws, 66
    reform of public domain, 554
  permission-free. *see* permission-free use and access
  surveillance of, 180
  universal availability is not determinative, 42
  use-centred definition of copyright public domain, 42

Vaver, David, 50
viral ('copyleft') licences, 487

608    Index

visually impaired persons
  compulsory licensing, 469
  free use exceptions to copyright, 140, 146
  three-step test for copyright exceptions, 133
voluntary licences
  borderline cases, 479
  category of public domain, 9, 55, 69
  causes of global consistency, 480
  conditions for neutral licence schemes, 477
  creation of public rights by, 476
  Creative Commons. *see* Creative Commons (CC) licences
  definition of, 69
  definition of public domain, 37
  finding works under, 159
  FOSS. *see* free or open source (FOSS) licences
  global standards for, 480
  innovations in, 547
  international copyright law, 70, 476
  legal certainty for, 517
  licences not included, 479
  national laws, 70, 476
  'neutral' licences, 39, 475, 547
  open content licences, 493, 500
  and public domain, 475, 516
  reform of public domain, 559
  viral character of, 481

waiver of copyright. *see* works dedicated to the public
Walden, Ian, 511, 517
WIPO Performances and sound recordings Treaty (WPPT), overview of, 91
wired retransmissions, remunerated use exceptions, 142
Wittgenstein, Ludwig, 30
works
  definition of, 3
  digitisation. *see* mass digitisation
  fixation principle, 111, 200
  'free of known copyright restrictions', 515
  insubstantial. *see* insubstantial works
  originality. *see* thresholds for authorship and originality
  orphan. *see* orphan works
  protectible. *see* protectable subject matter
  on 'scale' of private to public, 44
  sets of works, de facto public rights as to digitisation, 533
  statutory deposit. *see* statutory deposit systems
  territorial basis of, 55
  unavailable to the public, 471
  universal availability of works, non-determinativeness of, 42
  users of works in relation, 3
works dedicated to the public
  accidental abandonment of copyright, 510
  category of public domain, 9, 55, 62
  Creative Commons (CC)
    public domain dedications (CC0), 514
    Public Domain Mark, 515
  definition of, 62
  international copyright law, 62, 509
  introduction to, 509
  national laws, 62, 510, 512
  need for statutory provision, 517
  reform of public domain, 560
works expressly excluded from copyright
  category of public domain, 9, 55, 59
  definition of, 59, 60
  government documents, 127
  international copyright law, 59, 215
  national laws, 56, 59
  permission-free use and access, 226
  and public domain, 128, 226
  reform of public domain, 552
  types of works, 215
works failing copyright minimum requirements
  category of public domain, 9, 55, 57
  definition of, 57
  fixation principle, 200
  international copyright law, 57
  introduction to, 185
  national laws, 57
  permission-free use and access, 206
  public domain perspective, 205
  reform of public domain, 551
  thresholds. *see* thresholds for authorship and originality
  types of works, 186
works impliedly excluded from copyright (statutory 'gaps')
  category of public domain, 55, 58
  'closed list' of protected categories, 208
  definition of, 58
  international copyright law, 58, 207
  national laws, 58
  'open list' of protected categories, 211
  and public domain, 213
  reform of public domain, 552
  summary overview, 214
  works falling outside protected categories, 209

works of applied art. *see* applied art, works of
works outside copyright protection. *see* constitutional and human rights exclusions from copyright; exceptions, exclusions and limitations to copyright; public interest defence to enforcement; public policy exclusions; works expressly excluded from copyright; works failing copyright minimum requirements; works impliedly excluded from copyright protection

works where copyright has expired
   category of public domain, 9, 55, 61
   copyright term. *see* term of copyright protection
   definition of, 61
   international copyright law, 61
   introduction to, 247
   national laws, 62
   reform of public domain, 553
Wu, Tim, 522, 537

Xalabarder, Raquel, 459

*Cambridge Intellectual Property and Information Law*

**Titles in the series (formerly known as *Cambridge Studies in Intellectual Property Rights*)**

Brad Sherman and Lionel Bently *The Making of Modern Intellectual Property Law*
Irini A. Stamatoudi *Copyright and Multimedia Products: A Comparative Analysis*
Pascal Kamina *Film Copyright in the European Union*
Huw Beverley-Smith *The Commercial Appropriation of Personality*
Mark J. Davison *The Legal Protection of Databases*
Robert Burrell and Allison Coleman *Copyright Exceptions: The Digital Impact*
Huw Beverley-Smith, Ansgar Ohly and Agnès Lucas-Schloetter *Privacy, Property and Personality: Civil Law Perspectives on Commercial Appropriation*
Catherine Seville *The Internationalisation of Copyright Law: Books, Buccaneers and the Black Flag in the Nineteenth Century*
Philip Leith *Software and Patents in Europe*
Geertrui Van Overwalle *Gene Patents and Clearing Models*
Lionel Bently, Jennifer Davis and Jane C. Ginsburg *Trade Marks and Brands: An Interdisciplinary Critique*
Jonathan Curci *The Protection of Biodiversity and Traditional Knowledge in International Law of Intellectual Property*
Lionel Bently, Jennifer Davis and Jane C. Ginsburg *Copyright and Piracy: An Interdisciplinary Critique*
Megan Richardson and Julian Thomas *Framing Intellectual Property: Legal Constructions of Creativity and Appropriation 1840–1940*
Dev Gangjee *Relocating the Law of Geographical Indications*
Andrew Kenyon, Megan Richardson and Ng-Loy Wee Loon *The Law of Reputation and Brands in the Asia Pacific*
Annabelle Lever *New Frontiers in the Philosophy of Intellectual Property*
Sigrid Sterckx and Julian Cockbain *Exclusions from Patentability: How the European Patent Office is Eroding Boundaries*
Sebastian Haunss *Conflicts in the Knowledge Society: The Contentious Politics of Intellectual Property*
Helena R. Howe and Jonathan Griffiths *Concepts of Property in Intellectual Property Law*
Rochelle Cooper Dreyfuss and Jane C. Ginsburg *Intellectual Property at the Edge: The Contested Contours of IP*
Normann Witzleb, David Lindsay, Moira Paterson and Sharon Rodrick *Emerging Challenges in Privacy Law: Comparative Perspectives*
Paul Bernal *Internet Privacy Rights: Rights to Protect Autonomy*
Peter Drahos *Intellectual Property, Indigenous People and their Knowledge*
Susy Frankel and Daniel Gervais *The Evolution and Equilibrium of Copyright in the Digital Age*
Kathy Bowrey and Michael Handler *Law and Creativity in the Age of the Entertainment Franchise*

Sean Bottomley *The British Patent System and the Industrial Revolution 1700–1852: From Privilege to Property*
Susy Frankel *Test Tubes for Global Intellectual Property Issues: Small Market Economies*
Jan Oster *Media Freedom as a Fundamental Right*
Sara Bannerman *International Copyright and Access to Knowledge*
Andrew T. Kenyon *Comparative Defamation and Privacy Law*
Pascal Kamina *Film Copyright in the European Union*, 2nd edition
Tim W. Dornis *Trademark and Unfair Competition Conflicts*
Ge Chen *Copyright and International Negotiations: An Engine of Free Expression in China?*
David Tan *The Commercial Appropriation of Fame: A Cultural Critique of the Right of Publicity and Passing Off*
Jay Sanderson *Plants, People and Practices: The Nature and History of the UPOV Convention*
Daniel Benoliel *Patent Intensity and Economic Growth*
Jeffrey A. Maine and Xuan-Thao Nguyen *The Intellectual Property Holding Company: Tax Use and Abuse from Victoria's Secret to Apple*
Megan Richardson *The Right to Privacy: Origins and Influence of a Nineteenth-Century Idea*
Martin Huscvec *Injunctions Against Intermediaries in the European Union: Accountable But Not Liable?*
Estelle Derclaye *The Copyright/Design Interface: Past, Present and Future*
Magdalena Kolasa *Trade Secrets and Employee Mobility: In Search of an Equilibrium*
Péter Mezei *Copyright Exhaustion: Law and Policy in the United States and the European Union*
Graham Greenleaf and David Lindsay *Public Rights: Copyright's Public Domains*